Classics

From the Renaissance to the nineteenth century, Latin and Greek were compulsory subjects in almost all European universities, and most early modern scholars published their research and conducted international correspondence in Latin. Latin had continued in use in Western Europe long after the fall of the Roman empire as the lingua franca of the educated classes and of law, diplomacy, religion and university teaching. The flight of Greek scholars to the West after the fall of Constantinople in 1453 gave impetus to the study of ancient Greek literature and the Greek New Testament. Eventually, just as nineteenth-century reforms of university curricula were beginning to erode this ascendancy, developments in textual criticism and linguistic analysis, and new ways of studying ancient societies, especially archaeology, led to renewed enthusiasm for the Classics. This collection offers works of criticism, interpretation and synthesis by the outstanding scholars of the nineteenth century.

The Golden Bough: The Third Edition

This work by Sir James Frazer (1854–1941) is widely considered to be one of the most important early texts in the fields of psychology and anthropology. At the same time, by applying modern methods of comparative ethnography to the classical world, and revealing the superstition and irrationality beneath the surface of the classical culture which had for so long been a model for Western civilisation, it was extremely controversial. Frazer was greatly influenced by E.B. Tylor's *Primitive Culture* (also reissued in this series), and by the work of the biblical scholar William Robertson Smith, to whom the first edition is dedicated. The twelve-volume third edition, reissued here, was greatly revised and enlarged, and published between 1911 and 1915; the two-volume first edition (1890) is also available in this series. Volume 6 (1914) examines the Egyptian myth of Osiris.

Cambridge University Press has long been a pioneer in the reissuing of out-of-print titles from its own backlist, producing digital reprints of books that are still sought after by scholars and students but could not be reprinted economically using traditional technology. The Cambridge Library Collection extends this activity to a wider range of books which are still of importance to researchers and professionals, either for the source material they contain, or as landmarks in the history of their academic discipline.

Drawing from the world-renowned collections in the Cambridge University Library and other partner libraries, and guided by the advice of experts in each subject area, Cambridge University Press is using state-of-the-art scanning machines in its own Printing House to capture the content of each book selected for inclusion. The files are processed to give a consistently clear, crisp image, and the books finished to the high quality standard for which the Press is recognised around the world. The latest print-on-demand technology ensures that the books will remain available indefinitely, and that orders for single or multiple copies can quickly be supplied.

The Cambridge Library Collection brings back to life books of enduring scholarly value (including out-of-copyright works originally issued by other publishers) across a wide range of disciplines in the humanities and social sciences and in science and technology.

The Golden Bough
The Third Edition

VOLUME 6: ADONIS ATTIS OSIRIS:
STUDIES IN THE HISTORY
OF ORIENTAL RELIGION 2

J.G. FRAZER

CAMBRIDGE
UNIVERSITY PRESS

CAMBRIDGE UNIVERSITY PRESS

Cambridge, New York, Melbourne, Madrid, Cape Town,
Singapore, São Paolo, Delhi, Mexico City

Published in the United States of America by Cambridge University Press, New York

www.cambridge.org
Information on this title: www.cambridge.org/9781108047357

© in this compilation Cambridge University Press 2012

This edition first published 1914
This digitally printed version 2012

ISBN 978-1-108-04735-7 Paperback

THE GOLDEN BOUGH

A STUDY IN MAGIC AND RELIGION

THIRD EDITION

PART IV

ADONIS ATTIS OSIRIS

VOL. II

MACMILLAN AND CO., Limited
LONDON · BOMBAY · CALCUTTA
MELBOURNE

THE MACMILLAN COMPANY
NEW YORK · BOSTON · CHICAGO
DALLAS · SAN FRANCISCO

THE MACMILLAN CO. OF CANADA, Ltd.
TORONTO

ADONIS
ATTIS OSIRIS

STUDIES IN THE HISTORY OF
ORIENTAL RELIGION

BY

J. G. FRAZER, D.C.L., LL.D., Litt.D.

FELLOW OF TRINITY COLLEGE, CAMBRIDGE
PROFESSOR OF SOCIAL ANTHROPOLOGY IN THE UNIVERSITY OF LIVERPOOL

THIRD EDITION, REVISED AND ENLARGED

IN TWO VOLUMES
VOL. II

MACMILLAN AND CO., LIMITED
ST. MARTIN'S STREET, LONDON
1914

CONTENTS

BOOK THIRD

OSIRIS . . . Pp. 1-218

CHAPTER I.—THE MYTH OF OSIRIS . . Pp. 3-23

Osiris the Egyptian counterpart of Adonis and Attis, 3 ; his myth, 3 *sqq.* ; the Pyramid Texts, 4-6 ; Osiris a son of the earth-god and the sky-goddess, 6 ; marries his sister Isis, 7 ; introduces the cultivation of corn and of the vine, 7 ; his violent death, 7 *sq.* ; Isis searches for his body and takes refuge in the swamps, 8 ; she conceives Horus the younger by the dead Osiris, 8 ; the body of Osiris floats to Byblus and is there found by Isis, 9 *sq.* ; the body rent in pieces by Set òr Typhon but recovered and buried by Isis, 10 *sq.* ; the members of Osiris treasured as relics in different places, 11 *sq.* ; laments of the sisters Isis and Nephthys for Osiris, 12 ; being brought to life Osiris reigns as king and judge of the dead in the other world, 12 *sq.* ; the confession of the dead, 13 *sq.* ; the fate of the wicked, 14 ; the resurrection of Osiris regarded by the Egyptians as a pledge of their own immortality, 15 *sq.* ; contests between Set and Horus, the brother and son of Osiris, for the crown of Egypt, 16-18 ; Busiris and Abydos the chief seats of the worship of Osiris, 18 ; the tomb of Osiris at Abydos, 18 *sq.* ; identified with the tomb of King Khent, 19 *sq.* ; the sculptured effigy of Osiris, 20 *sq.* ; the hawk crest, 21 *sq.* ; the association of Osiris with Byblus, 22 *sq.*

CHAPTER II.—THE OFFICIAL EGYPTIAN
CALENDAR . . . . . . Pp. 24-29

The date of a festival sometimes a clue to the nature of the god, 24 ; the year of the Egyptian calendar a vague or movable one, 24 *sq.* ; divorce of the official calendar from the natural calendar of the seasons, 25 *sq.* ; attempt of Ptolemy III. to reform the calendar by intercalation, 26 *sq.* ; the fixed Alexandrian year instituted by the Romans, 27-29.

v

CHAPTER III.—THE CALENDAR OF THE
EGYPTIAN FARMER . . . . Pp. 30-48

§ 1. *The Rise and Fall of the Nile*, pp. 30-32.—In Egypt the operations of
husbandry dependent on the annual rise and fall of the Nile, 30 *sq.* ;
irrigation, sowing, and harvest in Egypt, 30 *sq.* ; events of the agricultural
year probably celebrated with religious rites, 32.

§ 2. *Rites of Irrigation*, pp. 33-40.—Mourning for Osiris at midsummer when
the Nile begins to rise, 33 *sq.* ; simultaneous rise of Sirius, 34 ; Sirius
regarded as the star of Isis, 34 *sq.* ; its rising marked the beginning of
the sacred Egyptian year, 35 *sq.* ; importance of the observation of its
gradual displacement in the civil calendar, 36 *sq.* ; ceremonies observed
in Egypt and other parts of Africa at the cutting of the dams, 37-40.

§ 3. *Rites of Sowing*, pp. 40-45.—The sowing of the seed in November, 40 ;
Plutarch on the mournful character of the rites of sowing, 40-42 ; his
view that the worship of the fruits of the earth sprang from a verbal
misunderstanding, 42 *sq.* ; his theory an inversion of the truth, 43 ;
respect shown by savages for the fruits and animals which they eat,
43 *sq.* ; lamentations at sowing, 45.

§ 4. *Rites of Harvest*, pp. 45-48.—Lamentations of the Egyptian corn-reapers,
45 *sq.* ; similar ceremonies observed by the Cherokee Indians in the
cultivation of the corn, 46 *sq.* ; lamentations of Californian Indians at
cutting sacred wood, 47 *sq.* ; Arab ceremony of burying "the old man"
at harvest, 48.

CHAPTER IV.—THE OFFICIAL FESTIVALS OF
OSIRIS . . . . Pp. 49-95

§ 1. *The Festival at Sais*, pp. 49-51.—The Egyptian festivals stationary in the
solar year after the adoption of the Alexandrian calendar in 30 B.C.,
49 *sq.* ; the sufferings of Osiris displayed as a mystery at Sais, 50 ; the
illumination of the houses on that night suggestive of a Feast of All
Souls, 50 *sq.*

§ 2. *Feasts of All Souls*, pp. 51-83.—Annual festivals of the dead among the
natives of America, the East Indies, India, Eastern and Western Asia,
and Africa, 51-66 ; annual festivals of the dead among peoples of the
Aryan family, 67 *sqq.* ; annual festival of the dead among the old
Iranians, 67 *sq.* ; annual festivals of the dead in Europe, 69-80 ; transported to the New World, 80 *sq.* ; the Feast of All Souls on 2nd
November apparently an old Celtic festival of the dead, 81 *sq.* ; similar
origin suggested for the Feast of All Saints on 1st November, 82 *sq.*

§ 3. *The Festival in the Month of Athyr*, pp. 84-86.—Festival of the death and resurrection of Osiris in the month of Athyr, 84 *sq.* ; the finding of Osiris, 85 *sq.*

§ 4. *The Festival in the Month of Khoiak*, pp. 86-88.—The great Osirian inscription at Denderah, 86 ; the death, dismemberment, and reconstitution of Osiris represented at the festival of Khoiak, 87 *sq.*

§ 5. *The Resurrection of Osiris*, pp. 89-91.—The resurrection of Osiris represented on the monuments, 89 *sq.*; corn-stuffed effigies of Osiris buried with the dead to ensure their resurrection, 90 *sq.*

§ 6. *Readjustment of Egyptian Festivals*, pp. 91-95.—The festivals of Osiris in the months of Athyr and Khoiak apparently the same in substance, 91 *sq.* ; the festival of Khoiak perhaps transferred to Athyr when the Egyptians adopted the fixed Alexandrian year, 92 *sq.* ; at the same time the dates of all the official Egyptian festivals perhaps shifted by about a month in order to restore them to their natural places in the solar year, 93-95.

CHAPTER V.—THE NATURE OF OSIRIS . Pp. 96-114

§ 1. *Osiris a Corn-God*, pp. 96-107.—Osiris in one of his aspects a personification of the corn, 97 *sq.* ; the legend of his dismemberment perhaps a reminiscence of a custom of dismembering human victims, especially kings, in the character of the corn-spirit, 97 *sq.* ; Roman and Greek traditions of the dismemberment of kings and others, 98 *sq.* ; modern Thracian custom, 99 *sq.* ; dismemberment of the Norse King Halfdan the Black, 100; dismemberment of Segera, a magician of Kiwai, 101 ; custom of dismembering a king and burying the pieces in different places, 101 *sq.* ; fertilizing virtue of genital member, 102 *sq.* ; precautions afterwards taken to preserve the bodies of kings from mutilation, 103 ; graves of kings and chiefs kept secret to prevent the mutilation of their bodies, 104 *sq.* ; Koniag custom of dismembering whalers, 106 ; red-haired Egyptian victims perhaps representatives of the corn-spirit, 106 *sq.*

§ 2. *Osiris a Tree-Spirit*, pp. 107-112.—Osiris as a tree-spirit, 107 *sq.* ; his image enclosed in a pine-tree, 108 ; the setting up of the *ded* pillar at the festival of Osiris, 108 *sq.* ; Osiris associated with the pine, the sycamore, the tamarisk, and the acacia, 110 *sq.* ; his relation to fruit-trees, the vine, and ivy, 111 *sq.*

§ 3. *Osiris a God of Fertility*, pp. 112-113.—Osiris perhaps conceived as a god of fertility in general, 112 ; coarse symbolism to express this idea, 112 *sq.*

§ 4. *Osiris a God of the Dead*, pp. 113-114.—Osiris a god of the resurrection as well as of the corn, 113 *sq.* ; great popularity of his worship, 114.

CHAPTER VI.—ISIS . . . . Pp. 115-119

Multifarious attributes of Isis, 115 *sq.* ; Isis compared and contrasted with the
mother goddesses of Asia, 116 ; Isis perhaps originally a corn-goddess,
116 *sq.* ; refinement and spiritualization of Isis in later times, the popularity of her worship in the Roman Empire, 117 *sq.* ; resemblance of
Isis to the Madonna, 118 *sq.*

CHAPTER VII.—OSIRIS AND THE SUN Pp. 120-128

Osiris interpreted as the sun by many modern writers, 120 *sqq.* ; the later
identification of Osiris with Ra, the sun-god, no evidence that Osiris
was originally the sun, 120 *sq.* ; most Egyptian gods at some time
identified with the sun, 123 ; attempt of Amenophis IV. to abolish
all gods except the sun-god, 123-125 ; the death and resurrection of
Osiris more naturally explained by the decay and growth of vegetation
than by sunset and sunrise, 125-128.

CHAPTER VIII.—OSIRIS AND THE MOON Pp. 129-139

Osiris sometimes interpreted by the ancients as the moon, 129 ; evidence of the
association of Osiris with the moon, 129-131 ; identification of Osiris
with the moon apparently based on a comparatively late theory of the
moon as the cause of growth and decay, 131 *sq.* ; practical rules founded
on this theory, 132-137 ; the moon regarded as the source of moisture,
137 *sq.* ; the moon naturally worshipped by agricultural peoples, 138 *sq.* ;
later identification of the corn-god Osiris with the moon, 139.

CHAPTER IX.—THE DOCTRINE OF LUNAR
SYMPATHY . . . . . Pp. 140-150

The doctrine of lunar sympathy, 140 *sq.* ; ceremonies at new moon often magical
rather than religious, being intended not so much to propitiate the planet
as to renew sympathetically the life of man, 140 *sq.* ; the moon supposed
to exercise special influence on children, 144 *sqq.* ; Baganda ceremonies
at the new moon, 147 *sq.* ; use of the moon to increase money or decrease
sickness, 148-150.

CHAPTER X.—THE KING AS OSIRIS Pp. 151-157

Osiris personated by the King of Egypt, 151 ; the Sed festival intended to
renew the king's life, 151 *sqq.* ; identification of the king with the dead
Osiris at the festival, 153 *sq.* ; Professor Flinders Petrie's explanation of
the Sed festival, 154 *sq.* ; similar explanation suggested by M. Alexandre
Moret, 155 *sqq.*

CHAPTER XI.—THE ORIGIN OF OSIRIS . Pp. 158-200

Origin of the conception of Osiris as a god of vegetation and the dead, 158 ;
Osiris distinguished from the kindred deities Adonis and Attis by the
dominant position he occupied in Egyptian religion, 158 ; all great and
lasting religions founded by great men, 159 *sq.* ; the historical reality of
Osiris as an old king of Egypt supported by African analogies, 160 *sq.* ;
dead kings worshipped by the Shilluks of the White Nile, 161-167 ; dead
kings worshipped by the Baganda of Central Africa, 167-173 ; dead kings
worshipped in Kiziba, 173 *sq.* ; ancestral spirits worshipped by the Bantu
tribes of Northern Rhodesia, 174-176 ; the worship of ancestral spirits
apparently the main practical religion of all the Bantu tribes of Africa,
176-191 ; dead chiefs or kings worshipped by the Bantu tribes of Northern
Rhodesia, 191-193 ; dead kings worshipped by the Barotse of the Zambesi,
193-195 ; the worship of dead kings an important element in the religion
of many African tribes, 195 *sq.* ; some African gods, who are now distinguished from ghosts, may have been originally dead men, 196 *sq.* ;
possibility that Osiris and Isis may have been a real king and queen of
Egypt, perhaps identical with King Khent of the first dynasty and his
queen, 197-199 ; suggested parallel between Osiris and Charlemagne,
199 ; the question of the historical reality of Osiris left open, 199 *sq.*

CHAPTER XII.—MOTHER-KIN AND MOTHER
GODDESSES . . . . . Pp. 201-218

§ 1. *Dying Gods and Mourning Goddesses*, pp. 201-202.—Substantial similarity
of Adonis, Attis, and Osiris, 200 ; superiority of the goddesses associated
with Adonis, Attis, and Osiris a mark of the system of mother-kin, 201 *sq.*

§ 2. *Influence of Mother-Kin on Religion*, pp. 202-212.—Mother-kin and father-
kin, 202 ; mother-kin and goddesses predominant among the Khasis,
202-204 ; mother-kin and clan goddesses predominant among the Pelew
Islanders, 204 *sqq.* ; in the Pelew Islands the importance of women based
partly on mother-kin, partly on economic and religious grounds, 205-208 ;
parallel between the Pelew Islands and the ancient East, 208 ; mother-
kin not mother-rule, 208 *sq.* ; even with mother-kin the government in
the hands of men, not of women, 209-211 ; gynaecocracy a dream but
mother-kin a fact, 211 *sq.* ; influence of this fact on religion, 212.

§ 3. *Mother-Kin and Mother Goddesses in the Ancient East*, pp. 212-218.—
Mother-kin in Western Asia, 212 *sq.* ; mother-kin in Egypt, 213 *sq.* ;
Egyptian marriages of brothers and sisters based on the system of mother-
kin, 214 *sqq.* ; the traditional marriage of Osiris with his sister Isis a
reflection of a real social custom, 216 ; the end of Osiris, 216 *sq.* ; conservatism of the Egyptians, 217 *sq.* ; original type of Osiris better preserved
than those of Adonis and Attis, 218.

NOTES . . . . Pp. 219-268

  I. MOLOCH THE KING . . . Pp. 219-226

 II. THE WIDOWED FLAMEN . . Pp. 227-248

   § 1. *The Pollution of Death* . . . Pp. 227-230
   § 2. *The Marriage of the Roman Gods* . . Pp. 230-236
   § 3. *Children of Living Parents in Ritual* . Pp. 236-248

III. A CHARM TO PROTECT A TOWN . Pp. 249-252

IV. SOME CUSTOMS OF THE PELEW
     ISLANDERS . . . . . Pp. 253-268

   § 1. *Priests dressed as Women* . . . Pp. 253-264
   § 2. *Prostitution of Unmarried Girls* . . Pp. 264-266
   § 3. *Custom of slaying Chiefs* . . . Pp. 266-268

INDEX . . . . Pp. 269-321

BOOK THIRD

OSIRIS

CHAPTER I

THE MYTH OF OSIRIS

IN ancient Egypt the god whose death and resurrection were Osiris the Egyptian counter-part of Adonis and Attis. annually celebrated with alternate sorrow and joy was Osiris, the most popular of all Egyptian deities ; and there are good grounds for classing him in one of his aspects with Adonis and Attis as a personification of the great yearly vicissitudes of nature, especially of the corn. But the immense vogue which he enjoyed for many ages induced his devoted worshippers to heap upon him the attributes and powers of many other gods ; so that it is not always easy to strip him, so to say, of his borrowed plumes and to restore them to their proper owners. In the following pages I do not pretend to enumerate and analyse all the alien elements which thus gathered round the popular deity. All that I shall attempt to do is to peel off these accretions and to exhibit the god, as far as possible, in his primitive simplicity. The discoveries of recent years in Egypt enable us to do so with more confidence now than when I first addressed myself to the problem many years ago.

The story of Osiris is told in a connected form only The myth of Osiris. by Plutarch, whose narrative has been confirmed and to some extent amplified in modern times by the evidence of the monuments.[1]   Of the monuments which illustrate

---

[1] See Plutarch, *Isis et Osiris,* 12-20 ; R. V. Lanzone, *Dizionario di Mitologia Egizia* (Turin, 1881–1884), vol. ii. pp. 692 *sqq.* ; A. Erman, *Aegypten und aegyptisches Leben im Altertum* (Tübingen, N.D.), pp. 365-369 ; *id., Die ägyptische Religion*[2] (Berlin, 1909), pp. 38 *sqq.* ; A. Wiedemann, *Die Religion der alten Ägypter* (Münster i. w. 1890), pp. 109 *sqq.*; *id., Religion of the Ancient Egyptians* (London, 1897), pp. 207 *sqq.*; G. Maspero, *Histoire ancienne des Peuples de l'Orient Classique*, i. 172

the myth or legend of Osiris the oldest are a long series of hymns, prayers, incantations, and liturgies, which have been found engraved in hieroglyphics on the walls, passages, and galleries of five pyramids at Sakkara. From the place where they were discovered these ancient religious records are known as the Pyramid Texts. They date from the fifth and sixth dynasties, and the period of time during which they were carved on the pyramids is believed to have been roughly a hundred and fifty years from about the year 2625 B.C. onward. But from their contents it appears that many of these documents were drawn up much earlier; for in some of them there are references to works which have perished, and in others there are political allusions which seem to show that the passages containing them must have been composed at a time when the Northern and Southern Kingdoms were still independent and hostile states and had not yet coalesced into a single realm under the sway of one powerful monarch. As the union of the kingdoms appears to have taken place about three thousand four hundred years before our era, the whole period covered by the composition of the Pyramid Texts probably did not fall short of a thousand years. Thus the documents form the oldest body of religious literature surviving to us from the ancient world, and occupy a place in the history of Egyptian language and civilization like that which the Vedic hymns and incantations occupy in the history of Aryan speech and culture.[1]

The special purpose for which these texts were engraved on the pyramids was to ensure the eternal life and felicity of the dead kings who slept beneath these colossal monu-

---

sqq.; E. A. Wallis Budge, *The Gods of the Egyptians* (London, 1904), ii. 123 *sqq.*; *id.*, *Osiris and the Egyptian Resurrection* (London, 1911), i. 1 *sqq.*

[1] J. H. Breasted, *Development of Religion and Thought in Ancient Egypt* (London, 1912), pp. vii. *sq.*, 77 *sqq.*, 84 *sqq.*, 91 *sqq.* Compare *id.*, *History of the Ancient Egyptians* (London, 1908), p. 68 ; Ed. Meyer, *Geschichte des Altertums*,[2] i. 2. pp. 116 *sq.*; E. A.

Wallis Budge, *Osiris and the Egyptian Resurrection* (London, 1911), i. 100 *sqq.* The first series of the texts was discovered in 1880 when Mariette's workmen penetrated into the pyramid of King Pepi the First. Till then it had been thought by modern scholars that the pyramids were destitute of inscriptions. The first to edit the Pyramid Texts was Sir Gaston Maspero.

ments.   Hence the dominant note that sounds through the blissful
them all is an insistent, a passionate protest against the immor-
tality of
reality of death : indeed the word death never occurs in the Egyptian
Pyramid Texts except to be scornfully denied or to be kings.
applied to an enemy.   Again and again the indomitable
assurance is repeated that the dead man did not die but
lives.   " King Teti has not died the death, he has become
a glorious one in the horizon."   " Ho !   King Unis !   Thou
didst not depart dead, thou didst depart living."   " Thou
hast departed that thou mightest live, thou hast not departed that thou mightest die."   " Thou diest not."   " This
King Pepi dies not."   " Have ye said that he would die ?
He dies not ; this King Pepi lives for ever."   " Live ! Thou
shalt not die."   " Thou livest, thou livest, raise thee up."
" Thou diest not, stand up, raise thee up."   " O lofty one
among the Imperishable Stars, thou perishest not eternally." [1]   Thus for Egyptian kings death was swallowed up
in victory ; and through their tears Egyptian mourners
might ask, like Christian mourners thousands of years afterwards, " O death, where is thy sting ?   O grave, where is
thy victory ? "

Now it is significant that in these ancient documents, The
though the myth or legend of Osiris is not set forth at story of
Osiris
length, it is often alluded to as if it were a matter of com- in the
mon knowledge.   Hence we may legitimately infer the Pyramid
Texts.
great antiquity of the Osirian tradition in Egypt.   Indeed
so numerous are the allusions to it in the Pyramid Texts
that by their help we could reconstruct the story in its main
outlines even without the narrative of Plutarch. [2]   Thus the
discovery of these texts has confirmed our belief in the
accuracy and fidelity of the Greek writer, and we may
accept his account with confidence even when it records
incidents or details which have not yet been verified by a

[1] J. H. Breasted, *Development of Religion and Thought in Ancient Egypt*, pp. 91 *sq.* Among the earlier works referred to in the Pyramid Texts are "the chapter of those who ascend " and " the chapter of those who raise themselves up " (J. H. Breasted, *op. cit.* p. 85).   From their titles these works would seem to have recorded a belief in the resurrection and ascension of the dead.

[2] This has been done by Professor J. H. Breasted in his *Development of Religion and Thought in Ancient Egypt*, pp. 18 *sqq.*

comparison with original Egyptian sources. The tragic
tale runs thus :

Osiris a
son of the
earth-god
and the
sky-
goddess.
Osiris was the offspring of an intrigue between the
earth-god Seb (Keb or Geb, as the name is sometimes trans-
literated) and the sky-goddess Nut. The Greeks identified
his parents with their own deities Cronus and Rhea. When
the sun-god Ra perceived that his wife Nut had been un-
faithful to him, he declared with a curse that she should be
delivered of the child in no month and no year. But the
goddess had another lover, the god Thoth or Hermes, as the
Greeks called him, and he playing at draughts with the
moon won from her a seventy-second part [1] of every day,
and having compounded five whole days out of these parts
he added them to the Egyptian year of three hundred and
sixty days. This was the mythical origin of the five supplementary days which the Egyptians annually inserted at the
end of every year in order to establish a harmony between
lunar and solar time. [2] On these five days, regarded as
outside the year of twelve months, the curse of the sun-god
did not rest, and accordingly Osiris was born on the first of
them. At his nativity a voice rang out proclaiming that the
Lord of All had come into the world. Some say that a
certain Pamyles heard a voice from the temple at Thebes
bidding him announce with a shout that a great king, the
beneficent Osiris, was born. But Osiris was not the only
child of his mother. On the second of the supplementary
days she gave birth to the elder Horus, on the third to the
god Set, whom the Greeks called Typhon, on the fourth to
the goddess Isis, and on the fifth to the goddess Nephthys. [3]

---

[1] In Plutarch, *Isis et Osiris*, 12, we
must clearly read ἑβδομηκοστὸν δεύτερον
with Scaliger and Wyttenbach for the
ἑβδομηκοστόν of the MSS.

[2] Herodotus, ii. 4, with A. Wiedemann's note ; L. Ideler, *Handbuch der
mathematischen und technischen Chronologie* (Berlin, 1825–1826), i. 94 *sqq.* ;
A. Erman, *Aegypten und aegyptisches
Leben im Altertum*, pp. 468 *sq.* ; G.
Maspero, *Histoire ancienne des Peuples
de l'Orient Classique*, i. 208 *sq.*

[3] The birth of the five deities on the
five supplementary days is mentioned

by Diodorus Siculus (i. 13. 4) as well
as by Plutarch (*Isis et Osiris*, 12).
The memory of the five supplementary
days seems to survive in the modern
Coptic calendar of Egypt. The days
from the first to the sixth of Amshir
(February) are called "the days outside
the year" and they are deemed unlucky. "Any child begotten during
these days will infallibly be misshapen
or abnormally tall or short. This also
applies to animals so that cattle and
mares are not covered during these
days ; moreover, some say (though

Afterwards Set married his sister Nephthys, and Osiris married his sister Isis.

Reigning as a king on earth, Osiris reclaimed the Egyptians from savagery, gave them laws, and taught them to worship the gods. Before his time the Egyptians had been cannibals. But Isis, the sister and wife of Osiris, discovered wheat and barley growing wild, and Osiris introduced the cultivation of these grains amongst his people, who forthwith abandoned cannibalism and took kindly to a corn diet. Moreover, Osiris is said to have been the first to gather fruit from trees, to train the vine to poles, and to tread the grapes. Eager to communicate these beneficent discoveries to all mankind, he committed the whole government of Egypt to his wife Isis, and travelled over the world, diffusing the blessings of civilization and agriculture wherever he went. In countries where a harsh climate or niggardly soil forbade the cultivation of the vine, he taught the inhabitants to console themselves for the want of wine by brewing beer from barley. Loaded with the wealth that had been showered upon him by grateful nations, he returned to Egypt, and on account of the benefits he had conferred on mankind he was unanimously hailed and worshipped as a deity.[1] But his brother Set (whom the Greeks called Typhon) with seventy-two others plotted against him. Having taken the measure of his good brother's body by stealth, the bad brother Typhon fashioned and highly decorated a coffer of the same size, and once when they were all drinking and making merry he brought in the coffer and jestingly promised to give it to the one whom it should fit exactly. Well, they all tried one after the other, but it fitted none of them. Last of all Osiris stepped into it and lay down. On that the conspirators ran and slammed the lid down on him, nailed it fast, soldered it with molten lead, and flung the

Osiris introduces the cultivation of corn and of the vine.

His violent death.

---

others deny) that neither sowing nor planting should be undertaken." However, these unlucky days are not the true intercalary days of the Coptic calendar, which occur in the second week of September at the end of the Coptic year. See C. G. Seligmann, "Ancient Egyptian Beliefs in Modern

Egypt," *Essays and Studies presented to William Ridgeway* (Cambridge, 1913), p. 456. As to the unluckiness of intercalary days in general, see *The Scapegoat*, pp. 339 *sqq.*

[1] Plutarch, *Isis et Osiris*, 13; Diodorus Siculus, i. 14, 17, 20; Tibullus, i. 7. 29 *sqq.*

coffer into the Nile. This happened on the seventeenth day of the month Athyr, when the sun is in the sign of the Scorpion, and in the eight-and-twentieth year of the reign or the life of Osiris. When Isis heard of it she sheared off a lock of her hair, put on mourning attire, and wandered disconsolately up and down, seeking the body.[1]

Isis searches for his body.

By the advice of the god of wisdom she took refuge in the papyrus swamps of the Delta. Seven scorpions accompanied her in her flight. One evening when she was weary she came to the house of a woman, who, alarmed at the sight of the scorpions, shut the door in her face. Then one of the scorpions crept under the door and stung the child of the woman that he died. But when Isis heard the mother's lamentation, her heart was touched, and she laid her hands on the child and uttered her powerful spells; so the poison was driven out of the child and he lived. Afterwards Isis herself gave birth to a son in the swamps. She had conceived him while she fluttered in the form of a hawk over the corpse of her dead husband. The infant was the younger Horus, who in his youth bore the name of Harpocrates, that is, the child Horus. Him Buto, the goddess of the north, hid from the wrath of his wicked uncle Set. Yet she could not guard him from all mishap; for one day when Isis came to her little son's hiding-place she found him stretched lifeless and rigid on the ground : a scorpion had stung him. Then Isis prayed to the sun-god Ra for help. The god hearkened to her and staid his bark in the sky, and sent down Thoth to teach her the spell by which she might restore her son to life. She uttered the words of power, and straightway the poison flowed from the body of Horus, air passed into him, and he lived. Then Thoth ascended up into the sky and took his place once more in the bark of the sun, and the bright pomp passed onward jubilant.[2]

She takes refuge in the papyrus swamps.

Isis and her infant son Horus.

[1] Plutarch, *Isis et Osiris*, 13 *sq.*

[2] A. Erman, *Aegypten und aegyptisches Leben im Altertum*, p. 366; *id.*, *Die ägyptische Religion*[2] (Berlin, 1909), p. 40; A. Wiedemann, *Religion of the Ancient Egyptians* (London, 1897), pp. 213 *sq.*; E. A. Wallis Budge, *The Gods of the Egyptians*, i. 487 *sq.*,

ii. 206-211; *id.*, *Osiris and the Egyptian Resurrection* (London, 1911), i. 92-96, ii. 84, 274-276. These incidents of the scorpions are not related by Plutarch but are known to us from Egyptian sources. The barbarous legend of the begetting of Horus by the dead Osiris is told in unambiguous language in the

Meantime the coffer containing the body of Osiris had the tree, had it cut down and made into a pillar of his house ; but he did not know that the coffer with the dead Osiris was in it. Word of this came to Isis and she journeyed to Byblus, and sat down by the well, in humble guise, her face wet with tears. To none would she speak till the king's handmaidens came, and them she greeted kindly, and braided their hair, and breathed on them from her own divine body a wondrous perfume. But when the queen beheld the braids of her handmaidens' hair and smelt the sweet smell that emanated from them, she sent for the stranger woman and took her into her house and made her the nurse of her child. But Isis gave the babe her finger instead of her breast to suck, and at night she began to burn all that was mortal of him away, while she herself in the likeness of a swallow fluttered round the pillar that contained her dead brother, twittering mournfully. But the queen spied what she was doing and shrieked out when she saw her child in flames, and thereby she hindered him from becoming immortal. Then the goddess revealed herself and begged for the pillar of the roof, and they gave it her, and she cut the coffer out of it, and fell upon it and embraced it and lamented so loud that the younger of the king's children died of fright on the spot. But the trunk of the tree she wrapped in fine linen, and poured ointment on it, and gave it to the king and queen, and the wood stands in a temple of

Pyramid Texts, and it is illustrated by a monument which represents the two sister goddesses hovering in the likeness of hawks over the god, while Hathor sits at his head and the Frog-goddess Heqet squats in the form of a huge frog at his feet. See J. H. Breasted, *Development of Religion and Thought in Ancient Egypt*, p. 28, with note [2] ; E. A. Wallis Budge, *Osiris and the Egyptian Resurrection*, i. 280. Harpocrates is in Egyptian *Her-pe-khred*, "Horus the child" (A. Wiede-mann, *Religion of the Ancient Egyptians*, p. 223). Plutarch, who appears to distinguish him from Horus, says that Harpocrates was begotten by the dead Osiris on Isis, and that he was born untimely and was weak in his lower limbs (*Isis et Osiris*, 19). Elsewhere he tells us that Harpocrates "was born, incomplete and youthful, about the winter solstice along with the early flowers and blossoms" (*Isis et Osiris*, 65).

Isis and is worshipped by the people of Byblus to this day. And Isis put the coffer in a boat and took the eldest of the king's children with her and sailed away. As soon as they were alone, she opened the chest, and laying her face on the face of her brother she kissed him and wept. But the child came behind her softly and saw what she was about, and she turned and looked at him in anger, and the child could not bear her look and died ; but some say that it was not so, but that he fell into the sea and was drowned. It is he whom the Egyptians sing of at their banquets under the name of Maneros. But Isis put the coffer by and went to see her son Horus at the city of Buto, and Typhon found the coffer as he was hunting a boar one night by the light of a full moon.[1] And he knew the body, and rent it into fourteen pieces, and scattered them abroad. But Isis sailed up and down the marshes in a shallop made of papyrus, looking for the pieces ; and that is why when people sail in shallops made of papyrus, the crocodiles do not hurt them, for they fear or respect the goddess. And that is the reason, too, why there are many graves of Osiris in Egypt, for she buried each limb as she found it. But others will have it that she buried an image of him in every city, pretending it was his body, in order that Osiris might be worshipped in many places, and that if Typhon searched for the real grave he might not be able to find it.[2] However, the genital member of Osiris had been eaten by the fishes, so Isis made an image of it instead, and the image is used by the Egyptians at their festivals to this day.[3] " Isis," writes the historian Diodorus Siculus, " recovered all the parts of the body except the genitals ; and because she wished that her husband's grave should be unknown and honoured by all who dwell in the land of Egypt, she resorted to the following device. She moulded human images out of wax and spices, corresponding to the stature of Osiris, round each one of the parts of his body. Then she called in the priests according to their families and took an oath of them all that

The body of Osiris dismembered by Typhon, and the pieces recovered by Isis.

Diodorus Siculus on the burial of Osiris.

[1] Plutarch, *Isis et Osiris*, 8, 18.

[2] Plutarch, *Isis et Osiris*, 18.

[3] Plutarch, *Isis et Osiris*, 18. Com-   pare Hippolytus, *Refutatio omnium haeresium*, v. 7, p. 142, ed. L. Duncker and F. G. Schneidewin (Göttingen, 1859).

they would reveal to no man the trust she was about to repose in them.   So to each of them privately she said that
to them alone she entrusted the burial of the body, and reminding them of the benefits they had received she exhorted
them to bury the body in their own land and to honour
Osiris as a god.   She also besought them to dedicate one of
the animals of their country, whichever they chose, and to
honour it in life as they had formerly honoured Osiris, and
when it died to grant it obsequies like his.   And because she
would encourage the priests in their own interest to bestow
the aforesaid honours, she gave them a third part of the land
to be used by them in the service and worship of the gods.
Accordingly it is said that the priests, mindful of the benefits
of Osiris, desirous of gratifying the queen, and moved by the
prospect of gain, carried out all the injunctions of Isis.
Wherefore to this day each of the priests imagines that
Osiris is buried in his country, and they honour the beasts
that were consecrated in the beginning, and when the
animals die the priests renew at their burial the mourning
for Osiris.   But the sacred bulls, the one called Apis and
the other Mnevis, were dedicated to Osiris, and it was
ordained that they should be worshipped as gods in common
by all the Egyptians ; since these animals above all others
had helped the discoverers of corn in sowing the seed
and procuring the universal benefits of agriculture." [1]

Such is the myth or legend of Osiris, as told by Greek *The various members of Osiris treasured as relics in various parts of Egypt.* writers and eked out by more or less fragmentary notices or allusions in native Egyptian literature.   A long inscription in the temple at Denderah has preserved a list of the god's graves, and other texts mention the parts of his body which were treasured as holy relics in each of the sanctuaries. Thus his heart was at Athribis, his backbone at Busiris, his neck at Letopolis, and his head at Memphis.   As often happens in such cases, some of his divine limbs were miracu-
lously multiplied.   His head, for example, was at Abydos as
well as at Memphis, and his legs, which were remarkably
numerous, would have sufficed for several ordinary mortals.[2]

---

[1] Diodorus Siculus, i. 21. 5 - 11 ;
compare *id.*, iv. 6. 3 ; Strabo, xvii. 1.
23, p. 803.

[2] H. Brugsch, "Das Osiris-Mysterium von Tentyra," *Zeitschrift für
ägyptische Sprache und Alterthums-*

In this respect, however, Osiris was nothing to St. Denys, of whom no less than seven heads, all equally genuine, are extant.[1]

Osiris mourned by Isis and Nephthys.

According to native Egyptian accounts, which supplement that of Plutarch, when Isis had found the corpse of her husband Osiris, she and her sister Nephthys sat down beside it and uttered a lament which in after ages became the type of all Egyptian lamentations for the dead. " Come to thy house," they wailed, " Come to thy house. O god On! come to thy house, thou who hast no foes. O fair youth, come to thy house, that thou mayest see me. I am thy sister, whom thou lovest ; thou shalt not part from me. O fair boy, come to thy house. . . . I see thee not, yet doth my heart yearn after thee and mine eyes desire thee. Come to her who loves thee, who loves thee, Unnefer, thou blessed one ! Come to thy sister, come to thy wife, to thy wife, thou whose heart stands still. Come to thy housewife. I am thy sister by the same mother, thou shalt not be far from me. Gods and men have turned their faces towards thee and weep for thee together. . . . I call after thee and weep, so that my cry is heard to heaven, but thou hearest not my voice ; yet am I thy sister, whom thou didst love on earth ; thou didst love none but me, my brother ! my brother !"[2] This lament for the fair youth cut off in his prime reminds us of the laments for Adonis. The title of Unnefer or " the Good Being" bestowed on him marks the beneficence which tradition universally ascribed to Osiris ; it was at once his commonest title and one of his names as king.[3]

Being brought to life again, Osiris

The lamentations of the two sad sisters were not in vain. In pity for her sorrow the sun-god Ra sent down from heaven the jackal-headed god Anubis, who, with the

kunde, xix. (1881) pp. 77 sqq. ; V. Loret, " Les fêtes d'Osiris au mois de Khoiak," Recueil de Travaux relatifs à la Philologie et à l'Archéologie Égyptiennes et Assyriennes, iii. (1882) pp. 43 sqq. ; R. V. Lanzone, Dizionario di Mitologia Egizia, pp. 697 sqq. ; A. Wiedemann, Herodots zweites Buch (Leipsic, 1890), pp. 584 sqq. ; id., Die Religion der alten Ägypter, p. 115 ; id., Religion of the Ancient Egyptians, pp. 215 sqq. ; A. Erman,

Aegypten und aegyptisches Leben im Altertum, pp. 367 sq.

[1] J. Rendel Harris, The Annotators of the Codex Bezae (London, 1901), p. 104, note [2], referring to Dulaure.

[2] A. Erman, Die ägyptische Religion[2] (Berlin, 1909), pp. 39 sq. ; E. A. Wallis Budge, Osiris and the Egyptian Resurrection, ii. 59 sqq.

[3] A. Wiedemann, Religion of the Ancient Egyptians, p. 211.

aid of Isis and Nephthys, of Thoth and Horus, pieced
together the broken body of the murdered god, swathed it
in linen bandages, and observed all the other rites which
the Egyptians were wont to perform over the bodies of the
departed. Then Isis fanned the cold clay with her wings :
Osiris revived, and thenceforth reigned as king over the
dead in the other world.[1] There he bore the titles of Lord
of the Underworld, Lord of Eternity, Ruler of the Dead.[2]
There, too, in the great Hall of the Two Truths, assisted by
forty-two assessors, one from each of the principal districts of
Egypt, he presided as judge at the trial of the souls of the
departed, who made their solemn confession before him, and,
their heart having been weighed in the balance of justice, received the reward of virtue in a life eternal or the appropriate
punishment of their sins.[3] The confession or rather profession
which the *Book of the Dead* puts in the mouth of the deceased
at the judgment-bar of Osiris[4] sets the morality of the
ancient Egyptians in a very favourable light. In rendering
an account of his life the deceased solemnly protested that he
had not oppressed his fellow-men, that he had made none
to weep, that he had done no murder, neither committed
fornication nor borne false witness, that he had not falsified
the balance, that he had not taken the milk from the mouths
of babes, that he had given bread to the hungry and water
to the thirsty, and had clothed the naked. In harmony

reigns as king and judge of the dead in the other world.

The confession of the dead.

[1] A. Erman, *Die ägyptische Religion*,[2]
pp. 39 *sq.* ; G. Maspero, *Histoire
ancienne des Peuples de l'Orient
Classique*, i. 176; E. A. Wallis
Budge, *The Gods of the Egyptians*, ii.
140, 262 ; *id., Osiris and the Egyptian
Resurrection*, i. 70-75, 80-82. On
Osiris as king of the dead see Plutarch,
Isis et Osiris, 79.

[2] Miss Margaret A. Murray, *The
Osireion at Abydos* (London, 1904),
pp. 8, 17, 18.

[3] On Osiris as judge of the dead
see A. Wiedemann, *Die Religion der
alten Ägypter*, pp. 131 *sqq.* ; *id.,
Religion of the Ancient Egyptians*,
pp. 248 *sqq.* ; G. Maspero, *Histoire
ancienne des Peuples de l'Orient
Classique*, i. 187 *sqq.* ; E. A. Wallis
Budge, *The Book of the Dead*[2] (London,
1909), i. pp. liii. *sqq.* ; *id., The Gods of*

the Egyptians, ii. 141 *sqq.* ; *id., Osiris
and the Egyptian Resurrection*, i. 305
sqq. ; A. Erman, *Die ägyptische Religion*,[2] pp. 116 *sqq.*

[4] *The Book of the Dead*, ch. cxxv.
(vol. ii. pp. 355 *sqq.* of Budge's
translation; P. Pierret, *Le Livre des
Morts*, Paris, 1882, pp. 369 *sqq.*) ;
R. V. Lanzone, *Dizionario di Mitologia
Egizia*, pp. 788 *sqq.* ; A. Wiedemann,
Die Religion der alten Ägypter, pp.
132-134 ; *id., Religion of the Ancient
Egyptians*, pp. 249 *sqq.* ; G. Maspero,
*Histoire ancienne des Peuples de l'Orient
Classique*, i. 188-191 ; A. Erman,
Die ägyptische Religion,[2] pp. 117-121 ;
E. A. Wallis Budge, *Osiris and the
Egyptian Resurrection*, i. 337 *sqq.*; J.
H. Breasted, *Development of Religion
and Thought in Ancient Egypt*, pp.
297 *sqq.*

with these professions are the epitaphs on Egyptian graves, which reveal, if not the moral practice, at least the moral ideals of those who slept beneath them. Thus, for example, a man says in his epitaph: " I gave bread to the hungry and clothes to the naked, and ferried across in my own boat him who could not pass the water. I was a father to the orphan, a husband to the widow, a shelter from the wind to them that were cold. I am one that spake good and told good. I earned my substance in righteousness." [1] Those who had done thus in their mortal life and had been acquitted at the Great Assize, were believed to dwell thenceforth at ease in a land where the corn grew higher than on earth, where harvests never failed, where trees were always green, and wives for ever young and fair. [2]

The fate of the wicked. We are not clearly informed as to the fate which the Egyptians supposed to befall the wicked after death. In the scenes which represent the Last Judgment there is seen crouching beside the scales, in which the heart of the dead is being weighed, a monstrous animal known as the " Eater of the Dead." It has the head of a crocodile, the trunk of a lion, and the hinder parts of a hippopotamus. Some think that the souls of those whose hearts had been weighed in the balance and found wanting were delivered over to this grim monster to be devoured ; but this view appears to be conjectural. "Generally the animal seems to have been placed there simply as guardian of the entrance to the Fields of the Blessed, but sometimes it is likened to Set. Elsewhere it is said that the judges of the dead slay the wicked and drink their blood. In brief, here also we have conflicting statements, and can only gather that there seems to have been no general agreement among the dwellers in the Valley of the Nile as to the ultimate lot of the wicked." [3]

[1] A. Erman, *Die ägyptische Religion*,[2] p. 121. Compare A. Wiedemann, *Die Religion der alten Ägypter*, pp. 134 sq. ; *id.*, *Religion of the Ancient Egyptians*, p. 253.

[2] A. Wiedemann, *Religion of the Ancient Egyptians*, p. 254 ; E. A. Wallis Budge, *Osiris and the Egyptian Resurrection*, i. 305 sqq. ; G. Maspero, *op. cit.* i. 194 sq. ; A. Erman, *Die ägyptische Religion*,[2] pp. 121 sqq. ; E.

A. Wallis Budge, *Osiris and the Egyptian Resurrection*, i. 97 sq., 100 sqq. ; E. Lefébure, " Le Paradis Égyptien," *Sphinx*, iii. (Upsala, 1900) pp. 191 sqq.

[3] A. Wiedemann, *Religion of the Ancient Egyptians*, p. 249. Compare A. Erman, *Die ägyptische Religion*,[2] pp. 117, 121 ; E. A. Wallis Budge, *Osiris and the Egyptian Resurrection*, i. 317, 328.

In the resurrection of Osiris the Egyptians saw the pledge of a life everlasting for themselves beyond the grave. They believed that every man would live eternally in the other world if only his surviving friends did for his body what the gods had done for the body of Osiris. Hence the ceremonies observed by the Egyptians over the human dead were an exact copy of those which Anubis, Horus, and the rest had performed over the dead god. "At every burial there was enacted a representation of the divine mystery which had been performed of old over Osiris, when his son, his sisters, his friends were gathered round his mangled remains and succeeded by their spells and manipulations in converting his broken body into the first mummy, which they afterwards reanimated and furnished with the means of entering on a new individual life beyond the grave. The mummy of the deceased was Osiris ; the professional female mourners were his two sisters Isis and Nephthys ; Anubis, Horus, all the gods of the Osirian legend gathered about the corpse." In this solemn drama of death and resurrection the principal part was played by the celebrant, who represented Horus the son of the dead and resuscitated Osiris.[1] He formally opened the eyes and mouth of the dead man by rubbing or pretending to rub them four times with the bleeding heart and thigh of a sacrificed bull ; after which a pretence was made of actually opening the mouth of the mummy or of the statue with certain instruments specially reserved for the purpose. Geese and gazelles were also sacrificed by being decapitated ; they were supposed to represent the enemies of Osiris, who after the murder of the divine man had sought to evade the righteous punishment of their crime but had been detected and beheaded.[2]

[1] G. Maspero, "Le rituel du sacri- fice funéraire," Études de Mythologie et d'Archéologie Égyptiennes (Paris, 1893–1912), i. 291 sq.

[2] G. Maspero, op. cit. pp. 300-316. Compare A. Wiedemann, Die Religion der alten Ägypter, pp. 123 sqq. ; id., Religion of the Ancient Egyptians, pp. 234 sqq. ; E. A. Wallis Budge, The Book of the Dead [2] (London, 1909), i. pp. liii. sqq. ; id., The Gods of the

Egyptians, ii. 126, 140 sq. ; id., Osiris and the Egyptian Resurrection, i. 66 sqq., 101 sq., 176, 305, 399 sq. ; A. Moret, Du Caractère religieux de la Royauté Pharaonique (Paris, 1902), p. 312 ; id., Kings and Gods of Egypt (New York and London, 1912), pp. 91 sqq. ; id., Mystères Égyptiens (Paris, 1913), pp. 37 sqq. "In one of the ceremonies of the 'Opening of the Mouth' the deceased was temporarily

Every dead
Egyptian
identified
with Osiris.

Thus every dead Egyptian was identified with Osiris and bore his name. From the Middle Kingdom onwards it was the regular practice to address the deceased as "Osiris So-and-So," as if he were the god himself, and to add the standing epithet "true of speech," because true speech was characteristic of Osiris.[1] The thousands of inscribed and pictured tombs that have been opened in the valley of the Nile prove that the mystery of the resurrection was performed for the benefit of every dead Egyptian ;[2] as Osiris died and rose again from the dead, so all men hoped to arise like him from death to life eternal. In an Egyptian text it is said of the departed that "as surely as Osiris lives, so shall he live also; as surely as Osiris did not die, so shall he not die; as surely as Osiris is not annihilated, so shall he too not be annihilated." The dead man, conceived to be lying, like Osiris, with mangled body, was comforted by being told that the heavenly goddess Nut, the mother of Osiris, was coming to gather up his poor scattered limbs and mould them with her own hands into a form immortal and divine. "She gives thee thy head, she brings thee thy bones, she sets thy limbs together and puts thy heart in thy body." Thus the resurrection of the dead was conceived, like that of Osiris, not merely as spiritual but also as bodily. "They possess their heart, they possess their senses, they possess their mouth, they possess their feet, they possess their arms, they possess all their limbs."[3]

Combat
between
Set and

If we may trust Egyptian legend, the trials and contests of the royal house did not cease with the restoration of Osiris

---

placed in a bull's skin, which was probably that of one of the bulls which were offered up during the celebration of the service. From this skin the deceased obtained further power, and his emergence from it was the visible symbol of his resurrection and of his entrance into everlasting life with all the strength of Osiris and Horus" (E. A. Wallis Budge, *Osiris and the Egyptian Resurrection*, i. 400).

[1] A. Erman, *Aegypten und aegyptisches Leben im Altertum*, p. 416 ; J. H. Breasted, *History of the Ancient Egyptians*, pp. 149 *sq.*; Margaret A.

Murray, *The Osireion at Abydos* (London, 1904), p. 31. Under the earlier dynasties only kings appear to have been identified with Osiris.

[2] A. Moret, *Mystères Égyptiens* (Paris, 1913), p. 40.

[3] A. Erman, *Die ägyptische Religion*,[2] pp. 111-113. However, in later times the body with which the dead came to life was believed to be a spiritual, not a material body ; it was called *sāhu*. See E. A. Wallis Budge, *The Book of the Dead*,[2] i. pp. lvii. *sqq.*; *id.*, *Osiris and the Egyptian Resurrection*, ii. 123 *sq.*

to life and his elevation to the rank of presiding deity in the Horus, the world of the dead. When Horus the younger, the son of brother Osiris and Isis, was grown to man's estate, the ghost of his of Osiris, royal and murdered father appeared to him and urged him, crown of like another Hamlet, to avenge the foul unnatural murder Egypt. upon his wicked uncle. Thus encouraged, the youth attacked the miscreant. The combat was terrific and lasted many days. Horus lost an eye in the conflict and Set suffered a still more serious mutilation. At last Thoth parted the combatants and healed their wounds; the eye of Horus he restored by spitting on it. According to one account the great battle was fought on the twenty-sixth day of the month of Thoth. Foiled in open war, the artful uncle now took the law of his virtuous nephew. He brought a suit of bastardy against Horus, hoping thus to rob him of his inheritance and to get possession of it himself; nay, not content with having murdered his good brother, the unnatural Set carried his rancour even beyond the grave by accusing the dead Osiris of certain high crimes and misdemeanours. The case was tried before the supreme court of the gods in the great hall at Heliopolis. Thoth, the god of wisdom, pleaded the cause of Osiris, and the august judges decided that "the word of Osiris was true." Moreover, they pronounced Horus to be the true-begotten son of his father. So that prince assumed the crown and mounted the throne of the lamented Osiris. However, according to another and perhaps later version of the story, the victory of Horus over his uncle was by no means so decisive, and their struggles ended in a compromise, by which Horus reigned over the Delta, while Set became king of the upper valley of the Nile from near Memphis to the first cataract. Be that as it may, with the accession of Horus began for the Egyptians the modern period of the world, for on his throne all the kings of Egypt sat as his successors.[1]

These legends of a contest for the throne of Egypt

[1] Plutarch, *Isis et Osiris*, 19 and 55; A. Erman, *Aegypten und aegyptisches Leben im Altertum*, p. 368; *id.*, *Die ägyptische Religion*,[2] pp. 41 *sq.*; A. Wiedemann, *Die Religion der alten Ägypter*, p. 114; *id.*, *Religion of the Ancient Egyptians*, pp. 214 *sq.*; G. Maspero, *Histoire ancienne des Peuples de l'Orient Classique*, i. 176-178; E. A. Wallis Budge, *Osiris and the Egyptian Resurrection*, i. 62 *sq.*, 64, 89 *sqq.*, 309 *sqq.*

may perhaps contain a reminiscence of real dynastical struggles which attended an attempt to change the right of succession from the female to the male line. For under a rule of female kinship the heir to the throne is either the late king's brother, or the son of the late king's sister, while under a rule of male kinship the heir to the throne is the late king's son. In the legend of Osiris the rival heirs are Set and Horus, Set being the late king's brother, and Horus the late king's son ; though Horus indeed united both claims to the crown, being the son of the king's sister as well as of the king. A similar attempt to shift the line of succession seems to have given rise to similar contests at Rome.[1]

Thus according to what seems to have been the general native tradition Osiris was a good and beloved king of Egypt, who suffered a violent death but rose from the dead and was henceforth worshipped as a deity. In harmony with this tradition he was regularly represented by sculptors and painters in human and regal form as a dead king, swathed in the wrappings of a mummy, but wearing on his head a kingly crown and grasping in one of his hands, which were left free from the bandages, a kingly sceptre.[2] Two cities above all others were associated with his myth or memory. One of them was Busiris in Lower Egypt, which claimed to possess his backbone ; the other was Abydos in Upper Egypt, which gloried in the possession of his head.[3] Encircled by the nimbus of the dead yet living god, Abydos, originally an obscure place, became from the end of the Old Kingdom the holiest spot in Egypt ; his tomb there would seem to have been to the Egyptians what the Church of the Holy

[1] *The Magic Art and the Evolution of Kings*, ii. 290 *sqq.*

[2] A. Wiedemann, *Religion of the Ancient Egyptians*, p. 217. For details see E. A. Wallis Budge, *Osiris and the Egyptian Resurrection*, i. 30 *sqq.*

[3] J. H. Breasted, *History of the Ancient Egyptians* (London, 1908), p. 61 ; id., *Development of Religion and Thought in Ancient Egypt*, p. 38 ; E. A. Wallis Budge, *Osiris and the Egyptian Resurrection*, i. 37, 67, 81, 210, 212, 214, 290, ii. 1, 2, 8-13, 82-85 ; A. Erman, *Die ägyptische Religion*,[2] pp. 21, 23, 110 ; A. Wiedemann, *Religion of the Ancient Egyptians*, p. 289 ; Ed. Meyer, *Geschichte des Altertums*,[2] i. 2. pp. 70, 96, 97. It appears to be now generally held that the original seat of the worship of Osiris was at Busiris, but that at Abydos the god found a second home, which in time eclipsed the old one in glory. According to Professors Ed. Meyer and A. Erman, the god whom Osiris displaced at Abydos was Anubis.

Sepulchre at Jerusalem is to Christians. It was the wish of every pious man that his dead body should rest in hallowed earth near the grave of the glorified Osiris. Few indeed were rich enough to enjoy this inestimable privilege ; for, apart from the cost of a tomb in the sacred city, the mere transport of mummies from great distances was both difficult and expensive. Yet so eager were many to absorb in death the blessed influence which radiated from the holy sepulchre that they caused their surviving friends to convey their mortal remains to Abydos, there to tarry for a short time, and then to be brought back by river and interred in the tombs which had been made ready for them in their native land. Others had cenotaphs built or memorial tablets erected for themselves near the tomb of their dead and risen Lord, that they might share with him the bliss of a joyful resurrection.[1]

Hence from the earliest ages of Egyptian history Abydos would seem to have been a city of the dead rather than of the living ; certainly there is no evidence that the place was ever of any political importance.[2] No less than nine of the most ancient kings of Egypt known to us were buried here, for their tombs have been discovered and explored within recent years.[3] The royal necropolis lies on the edge of the desert about a mile and a half from the temple of Osiris.[4] Of the graves the oldest is that of King Khent, the second or third king of the first dynasty. His reign, which fell somewhere between three thousand four hundred

The tombs of the old kings at Abydos.

The tomb of King Khent identified

---

[1] Plutarch, *Isis et Osiris*, 20 ; A. Erman, *Aegypten und aegyptisches Leben im Altertum*, p. 417 ; J. H. Breasted, *History of the Ancient Egyptians* (London, 1908), pp. 148 *sq.*; Ed. Meyer, *Geschichte des Altertums*,[2] i. 2. p. 209 ; E. A. Wallis Budge, *Osiris and the Egyptian Resurrection*, i. 68 *sq.*, ii. 3.

[2] Ed. Meyer, *Geschichte des Altertums*,[2] i. 2. p. 125.

[3] J. H. Breasted, *History of the Ancient Egyptians*, pp. 43, 50 *sq.* The excavations were begun by E. Amélineau and continued by W. M. Flinders Petrie (Ed. Meyer, *Geschichte des Altertums*,[2] i. 2. p. 119). See

E. Amélineau, *Le Tombeau d'Osiris* (Paris, 1899) ; W. M. Flinders Petrie, *The Royal Tombs of the Earliest Dynasties*, Part ii. (London, 1901). The excavations of the former have been criticized by Sir Gaston Maspero (*Études de Mythologie et d'Archéologie Égyptiennes*, vi. (Paris, 1912) pp. 153-182).

[4] Ed. Meyer, *Geschichte des Altertums*,[2] i. 2. pp. 119, 124 ; E. A. Wallis Budge, *Osiris and the Egyptian Resurrection*, ii. 8. The place is now known by the Arabic name of Umm al-Ka'âb or "Mother of Pots" on account of the large quantity of pottery that has been found there.

with the
tomb of
Osiris.

and three thousand two hundred years before our era, seems to have marked an epoch in the history of Egypt, for under him the costume, the figure drawing, and the hieroglyphics all assumed the character which they thenceforth preserved to the very end of Egyptian nationality.[1] Later ages identified him with Osiris in a more intimate sense than that in which the divine title was lavished on every dead king and indeed on every dead man; for his tomb was actually converted into the tomb of Osiris and as such received in great profusion the offerings of the faithful. Somewhere between the twenty-second and the twenty-sixth dynasty a massive bier of grey granite was placed in the sepulchral chamber. On it, cut in high relief,

The sculp-
tured effigy
of Osiris.

reposes a shrouded figure of the dead Osiris. He lies at full length, with bare and upturned face. On his head is the White Crown of Upper Egypt; in his hands, which issue from the shroud, he holds the characteristic emblems of the god, the sceptre and the scourge. At the four corners of the bier are perched four hawks, representing the four children of Horus, each with their father's banner, keeping watch over the dead god, as they kept watch over the four quarters of the world. A fifth hawk seems to have been perched on the middle of the body of Osiris, but it had been broken off before the tomb was discovered in recent years, for only the bird's claws remain in position. Finely carved heads of lions, one at each corner of the bier, with the claws to match below, complete the impressive monument. The scene represented is unquestionably the impregnation of Isis in the form of a hawk by the dead Osiris; the Copts who dismantled the shrine appear to have vented their pious rage on the figure of the hawk Isis by carrying it off or smashing it. If any doubt could exist as to the meaning of these sculptured figures, it would be set at rest by the ancient inscriptions attached to them. Over against the right shoulder of the shrouded figure, who lies stretched on the bier, are carved in hieroglyphics the words, " Osiris, the

---

[1] Ed. Meyer, *Geschichte des Altertums*,[2] i. 2. pp. 119, 125, 127, 128, 129, 209. The king's Horus name has sometimes been read Zer, but according to Professor Meyer (*op. cit.* p. 128) and

Dr. Budge (*Osiris and the Egyptian Resurrection*, ii. 83) the true reading is Khent (Chent). The king's personal name was perhaps Ka (Ed. Meyer, *op. cit.* p. 128).

Good Being, true of speech"; and over against the place where the missing hawk perched on the body of the dead god is carved the symbol of Isis. Two relics of the ancient human occupants of the tomb escaped alike the fury of the fanatics and the avarice of the plunderers who pillaged and destroyed it. One of the relics is a human skull, from which the lower jawbone is missing; the other is an arm encircled by gorgeous jewelled bracelets of gold, turquoises, amethysts, and dark purple lapis lazuli. The former may be the head of King Khent himself; the latter is almost certainly the arm of his queen. One of the bracelets is composed of alternate plaques of gold and turquoise, each ornamented with the figure of a hawk perched on the top of it.[1] The hawk was the sacred bird or crest of the earliest dynasties of Egyptian kings. The figure of a hawk was borne before the king as a standard on solemn occasions: the oldest capital of the country known to us was called Hawk-town: there the kings of the first dynasty built a temple to the hawk: there in modern times has been found a splendid golden head of a hawk dating from the Ancient Empire; and on the life-like statue of King Chephren of the third dynasty we see a hawk with outspread wings protecting the back of the monarch's head.

The hawk the crest of the earliest dynasties.

[1] E. Amélineau, *Le Tombeau d'Osiris* (Paris, 1899), pp. 107-115; W. M. Flinders Petrie, *The Royal Tombs of the Earliest Dynasties*, Part ii. (London, 1901) pp. 8 *sq.*, 16-19, with the frontispiece and plates lx. lxi.; G. Maspero, *Études de Mythologie et d'Archéologie Égyptiennes* (Paris, 1893-1912), vi. 167-173; J. H. Breasted, *History of the Ancient Egyptians* (London, 1908), pp. 50 *sq.*, 148; E. A. Wallis Budge, *Osiris and the Egyptian Resurrection*, ii. 8-10, 13, 83-85. The tomb, with its interesting contents, was discovered and excavated by Monsieur E. Amélineau. The masses, almost the mountains, of broken pottery, under which the tomb was found to be buried, are probably remains of the vessels in which pious pilgrims presented their offerings at the shrine. See E. Amélineau, *op. cit.* pp. 85 *sq.*; J. H. Breasted, *op. cit.* pp. 51, 148. The high White Crown, worn by Osiris, was the symbol of the king's dominion over Upper Egypt; the flat Red Crown, with a high backpiece and a projecting spiral, was the symbol of his dominion over Lower Egypt. On the monuments the king is sometimes represented wearing a combination of the White and the Red Crown to symbolize his sovereignty over both the South and the North. White was the distinctive colour of Upper, as red was of Lower, Egypt. The treasury of Upper Egypt was called "the White House"; the treasury of Lower Egypt was called "the Red House." See Ed. Meyer, *Geschichte des Altertums*,[2] i. 2. pp. 103 *sq.*; J. H. Breasted, *History of the Ancient Egyptians* (London, 1908), pp. 34 *sq.*, 36, 41.

From the earliest to the latest times of Egyptian civilization "the Hawk" was the epithet of the king of Egypt
and of the king alone; it took the first place in the list of
his titles.[1] The sanctity of the bird may help us to understand why Isis took the form of a hawk in order to mate
with her dead husband; why the queen of Egypt wore on
her arm a bracelet adorned with golden hawks; and why in
the holy sepulchre the four sons of Horus were represented
in the likeness of hawks keeping watch over the effigy of
their divine grandfather.[2]

The asso-
ciation of
Osiris with
Byblus.

The legend recorded by Plutarch which associated the
dead Osiris with Byblus in Phoenicia[3] is doubtless late and
probably untrustworthy. It may have been suggested by
the resemblance which the worship of the Egyptian Osiris
bore to the worship of the Phoenician Adonis in that city.
But it is possible that the story has no deeper foundation
than a verbal misunderstanding. For Byblus is not only
the name of a city, it is the Greek word for papyrus; and
as Isis is said after the death of Osiris to have taken refuge
in the papyrus swamps of the Delta, where she gave birth to
and reared her son Horus, a Greek writer may perhaps have
confused the plant with the city of the same name.[4] How-

---

[1] A. Moret, *Mystères Égyptiens*
(Paris, 1913), pp. 159-162, with
plate iii. Compare Victor Loret,
"L'Égypte au temps du totémisme,"
*Conférences faites au Musée Guimet,
Bibliothèque de Vulgarisation*, xix.
(Paris, 1906) pp. 179-186. Both
these writers regard the hawk as the
totem of the royal clan. This view is
rejected by Prof. Ed. Meyer, who,
however, holds that Horus, whose
emblem was the hawk, was the oldest
national god of Egypt (*Geschichte des
Altertums*,[2] i. 2. pp. 102-106). He
prefers to suppose that the hawk, or
rather the falcon, was the emblem of a
god of light because the bird flies high
in the sky (*op. cit.* p. 73; according
to him the bird is not the sparrow-
hawk but the falcon, *ib.* p. 75). A
similar view is adopted by Professor
A. Wiedemann (*Religion of the
Ancient Egyptians*, p. 26). Compare
A. Erman, *Die ägyptische Religion*,[2]

pp. 10, 11. The native Egyptian
name of Hawk-town was Nechen, in
Greek it was Hieraconpolis (Ed. Meyer,
op. cit. p. 103). Hawks were worshipped by the inhabitants (Strabo,
xvii. I. 47, p. 817).

[2] According to the legend the four
sons of Horus were set by Anubis to
protect the burial of Osiris. They
washed his dead body, they mourned
over him, and they opened his cold
lips with their fingers. But they disappeared, for Isis had caused them to
grow out of a lotus flower in a pool of
water. In that position they are sometimes represented in Egyptian art
before the seated effigy of Osiris. See
A. Erman, *Die ägyptische Religion*,[2]
p. 43; E. A. Wallis Budge, *Osiris
and the Egyptian Resurrection*, i. 40,
41, 327.

[3] See above, pp. 9 *sq.*

[4] E. A. Wallis Budge, *Osiris and
the Egyptian Resurrection*, i. 16 *sq.*

ever that may have been, the association of Osiris with Adonis at Byblus gave rise to a curious tale. It is said that every year the people beyond the rivers of Ethiopia used to write a letter to the women of Byblus informing them that the lost and lamented Adonis was found. This letter they enclosed in an earthen pot, which they sealed and sent floating down the river to the sea. The waves carried the pot to Byblus, where every year it arrived at the time when the Syrian women were weeping for their dead Lord. The pot was taken up from the water and opened : the letter was read ; and the weeping women dried their tears, because the lost Adonis was found.[1]

[1] Cyril of Alexandria, *In Isaiam*, lib. ii. Tomus iii. (Migne's *Patrologia Graeca*, lxx. 441).

CHAPTER II

THE OFFICIAL EGYPTIAN CALENDAR

The date of a festival sometimes furnishes a clue to the nature of the god. A USEFUL clue to the original nature of a god or goddess is often furnished by the season at which his or her festival is celebrated. Thus, if the festival falls at the new or the full moon, there is a certain presumption that the deity thus honoured either is the moon or at least has lunar affinities. If the festival is held at the winter or summer solstice, we naturally surmise that the god is the sun, or at all events that he stands in some close relation to that luminary. Again, if the festival coincides with the time of sowing or harvest, we are inclined to infer that the divinity is an embodiment of the earth or of the corn. These presumptions or inferences, taken by themselves, are by no means conclusive ; but if they happen to be confirmed by other indications, the evidence may be regarded as fairly strong.

The year of the Egyptian calendar a vague or movable one. Unfortunately, in dealing with the Egyptian gods we are in a great measure precluded from making use of this clue. The reason is not that the dates of the festivals are always unknown, but that they shifted from year to year, until after a long interval they had revolved through the whole course of the seasons. This gradual revolution of the festal Egyptian cycle resulted from the employment of a calendar year which neither corresponded exactly to the solar year nor was periodically corrected by intercalation.[1]

---

[1] As to the Egyptian calendar see L. Ideler, *Handbuch der mathematischen und technischen Chronologie* (Berlin, 1825–1826), i. 93 *sqq.* ; Sir J. G. Wilkinson, *Manners and Customs of the Ancient Egyptians* (London, 1878), ii. 368 *sqq.* ; R. Lepsius, *Die Chronologie der Aegypter*, i. (Berlin, 1849) pp. 125 *sqq.* ; H. Brugsch, *Die Ägyptologie* (Leipsic, 1891), pp. 347-366 ; A. Erman, *Aegypten und aegyptisches Leben im Altertum*, pp. 468 *sq.* ; G. Maspero, *Histoire ancienne des Peuples de l'Orient Clas-*

The solar year is equivalent to about three hundred and sixty-five and a quarter days ; but the ancient Egyptians, ignoring the quarter of a day, reckoned the year at three hundred and sixty-five days only.[1]   Thus each of their calendar years was shorter than the true solar year by about a quarter of a day.   In four years the deficiency amounted to one whole day ; in forty years it amounted to ten days ; in four hundred years it amounted to a hundred days ; and so it went on increasing until after a lapse of four times three hundred and sixty-five, or one thousand four hundred and sixty solar years, the deficiency amounted to three hundred and sixty-five days, or a whole Egyptian year.   Hence one thousand four hundred and sixty solar years, or their equivalent, one thousand four hundred and sixty-one Egyptian years, formed a period or cycle at the end of which the Egyptian festivals returned to those points of the solar year at which they had been celebrated in the beginning.[2]   In the meantime they had been held successively on every day of the solar year, though always on the same day of the calendar.

Thus the official calendar was completely divorced, except at rare and long intervals, from what may be called the natural calendar of the shepherd, the husbandman, and the sailor—that is, from the course of the seasons in which the times for the various labours of cattle-breeding, tillage, and navigation are marked by the position of the sun in the sky, the rising or setting of the stars, the fall of rain, the growth of pasture, the ripening of the corn, the blowing of certain winds, and so forth.   Nowhere, perhaps, are the events of this natural calendar better marked or more regular in their recurrence than in Egypt ; nowhere accordingly could their divergence from the corresponding dates of the official calendar be more readily observed.   The

Thus the official calendar was divorced from the natural calendar, which is marked by the course of the seasons.

sique, i. 207 - 210 ; Ed. Meyer, "Aegyptische Chronologie," *Abhandlungen der königl. Preuss. Akademie der Wissenschaften*, 1904, pp. 2 *sqq.* ; *id.*, "Nachträge zur ägyptischen Chronologie," *Abhandlungen der königl. Preuss. Akademie der Wissenschaften*, 1907, pp. 3 *sqq.* ; *id.*, *Geschichte des Altertums*,[2] i. 2. pp. 28 *sqq.*, 98 *sqq.* ; F. K. Ginzel,

Handbuch der mathematischen und technischen Chronologie, i. (Leipsic, 1906) pp. 150 *sqq.*
[1] Herodotus, ii. 4, with A. Wiedemann's note ; Geminus, *Elementa Astronomiae*, 8, p. 106, ed. C. Manitius (Leipsic, 1898) ; Censorinus, *De die natali*, xviii. 10.
[2] Geminus, *Elementa Astronomiae*, 8, pp. 106 *sqq.*, ed. C. Manitius.

divergence certainly did not escape the notice of the Egyptians themselves, and some of them apparently attempted successfully to correct it. Thus we are told that the Theban priests, who particularly excelled in astronomy, were acquainted with the true length of the solar year, and harmonized the calendar with it by intercalating a day every few, probably every four, years.[1] But this scientific improvement was too deeply opposed to the religious conservatism of the Egyptian nature to win general acceptance. " The Egyptians," said Geminus, a Greek astronomer writing about 77 B.C., " are of an opposite opinion and purpose from the Greeks. For they neither reckon the years by the sun nor the months and days by the moon, but they observe a peculiar system of their own. They wish, in fact, that the sacrifices should not always be offered to the gods at the same time of the year, but that they should pass through all the seasons of the year, so that the summer festival should in time be celebrated in winter, in autumn, and in spring. For that purpose they employ a year of three hundred and sixty-five days, composed of twelve months of thirty days each, with five supplementary days added. But they do not add the quarter of a day for the reason I have given— namely, in order that their festivals may revolve." [2] So attached, indeed, were the Egyptians to their old calendar, that the kings at their consecration were led by the priest of Isis at Memphis into the holy of holies, and there made to swear that they would maintain the year of three hundred and sixty-five days without intercalation.[3]

The practical inconvenience of a calendar which marked true time only once in about fifteen hundred years might be

---

[1] Diodorus Siculus, i. 50. 2 ; Strabo, xvii. i. 46, p. 816. According to H. Brugsch (*Die Ägyptologie*, pp. 349 *sq.*), the Egyptians would seem to have denoted the movable year of the calendar and the fixed year of the sun by different written symbols. For more evidence that they were acquainted with a four years' period, corrected by intercalation, see R. Lepsius, *Chronologie der Aegypter*, i. 149 *sqq.*

[2] Geminus, *Elementa Astronomiae*, 8, p. 106, ed. C. Manitius. The same writer further (p. 108) describes as a popular Greek error the opinion that the Egyptian festival of Isis coincided with the winter solstice. In his day, he tells us, the two events were separated by an interval of a full month, though they had coincided a hundred and twenty years before the time he was writing.

[3] *Scholia in Caesaris Germanici Aratea*, p. 409, ed. Fr. Eyssenhardt, in his edition of Martianus Capella (Leipsic, 1866).

calmly borne by a submissive Oriental race like the ancient Egyptians, but it naturally proved a stumbling-block to the less patient temperament of their European conquerors. Accordingly in the reign of King Ptolemy III. Euergetes a decree was passed that henceforth the movable Egyptian year should be converted into a fixed solar year by the intercalation of one day at the end of every four years, " in order that the seasons may do their duty perpetually according to the present constitution of the world, and that it may not happen, through the shifting of the star by one day in four years, that some of the public festivals which are now held in the winter should ever be celebrated in the summer, and that other festivals now held in the summer should hereafter be celebrated in the winter, as has happened before, and must happen again if the year of three hundred and sixty-five days be retained." The decree was passed in the year 239 or 238 B.C. by the high priests, scribes, and other dignitaries of the Egyptian church assembled in convocation at Canopus ; but we cannot doubt that the measure, though it embodied native Egyptian science, was prompted by the king or his Macedonian advisers.[1] This sage attempt to reform the erratic calendar was not permanently successful. The change may indeed have been carried out during the reign of the king who instituted it, but it was abandoned by the year 196 B.C. at latest, as we learn from the celebrated inscription known as the Rosetta stone, in which a month of the Macedonian calendar is equated to the corresponding month of the movable Egyptian year.[2]   And the testimony of Geminus, which I have cited, proves that in the following century the festivals were still revolving in the old style.

The reform which the Macedonian king had vainly attempted to impose upon his people was accomplished by the practical Romans when they took over the administra-

Attempt of Ptolemy III. to reform the Egyptian calendar by intercalation.

Institution of the fixed Alexandrian year by the Romans.

---

[1] Copies of the decree in hieroglyphic, demotic, and Greek have been found inscribed on stones in Egypt. See Ch. Michel, *Recueil d'Inscriptions Grecques* (Brussels, 1900), pp. 415 *sqq.*, No. 551 ; W. Dittenberger, *Orientis Graeci Inscriptiones Selectae* (Leipsic, 1903–1905), vol. i. pp. 91 *sqq.*, No. 56 ; J. P. Mahaffy, *The Empire of the Ptolemies* (London, 1895), pp. 205 *sqq.*, 226 *sqq.* The star mentioned in the decree is the Dog-star (Sirius). See below, pp. 34 *sqq.*

[2] W. Dittenberger, *Orientis Graeci Inscriptiones Selectae*, vol. i. pp. 140 *sqq.*, No. 90, with note 25 of the editor.

tion of the country.   The expedient by which they effected the change was a simple one ; indeed it was no other than that to which Ptolemy Euergetes had resorted for the same purpose.   They merely intercalated one day at the end of every four years, thus equalizing within a small fraction four calendar years to four solar years.   Henceforth the official and the natural calendars were in practical agreement.   The movable Egyptian year had been converted into the fixed Alexandrian year, as it was called, which agreed with the Julian year in length and in its system of intercalation, though it differed from that year in retaining the twelve equal Egyptian months and five supplementary days.[1]   But while the new calendar received the sanction of law and regulated the business of government, the ancient calendar was too firmly established in popular usage to be at once displaced.   Accordingly it survived for ages side by side with its modern rival.[2]   The spread of Christianity, which required a fixed year for the due observance of its festivals, did much to promote the adoption of the new Alexandrian style, and by the beginning of the fifth century the ancient movable year of Egypt appears to have been not only dead but forgotten.[3]

---

[1] On the Alexandrian year see L. Ideler, *Handbuch der mathematischen und technischen Chronologie*, i. 140 *sqq.*   That admirable chronologer argued (pp. 153-161) that the innovation was introduced not, as had been commonly supposed, in 25 B.C., but in 30 B.C., the year in which Augustus defeated Mark Antony under the walls of Alexandria and captured the city.   However, the question seems to be still unsettled.   See F. K. Ginzel, *Handbuch der mathematischen und technischen Chronologie*, i. 226 *sqq.*, who thinks it probable that the change was made in 26 B.C.   For the purposes of this study the precise date of the introduction of the Alexandrian year is not material.

[2] In demotic the fixed Alexandrian year is called "the year of the Ionians," while the old movable year is styled "the year of the Egyptians." Documents have been found which are dated by the day and the month of both years.   See H. Brugsch, *Die Ägyptologie*, pp. 354 *sq.*

[3] L. Ideler, *op. cit.* i. 149-152. Macrobius thought that the Egyptians had always employed a solar year of $365\frac{1}{4}$ days (*Saturn.* i. 12. 2, i. 14. 3). The ancient calendar of the Mexicans resembled that of the Egyptians except that it was divided into eighteen months of twenty days each (instead of twelve months of thirty days each), with five supplementary days added at the end of the year.   These supplementary days (*nemontemi*) were deemed unlucky : nothing was done on them : they were dedicated to no deity ; and persons born on them were considered unfortunate.   See B. de Sahagun, *Histoire générale des choses de la Nouvelle - Espagne*, traduite par D. Jourdanet et R. Simeon (Paris, 1880), pp. 50, 164 ; F. S. Clavigero, *History of Mexico* (London, 1807), i. 290. Unlike the Egyptian calendar, however, the Mexican appears to have

been regularly corrected by intercalation so as to bring it into harmony with the solar year. But as to the mode of intercalation our authorities differ. According to the positive statement of Sahagun, one of the earliest and best authorities, the Mexicans corrected the deficiency of their year by intercalating one day in every fourth year, which is precisely the correction adopted in the Alexandrian and the Julian calendar. See B. de Sahagun, *op. cit.* pp. 286 *sq.*, where he expressly asserts the falsehood of the view that the bissextile year was unknown to the Mexicans. This weighty statement is confirmed by the practice of the Indians of Yucatan. Like the Aztecs, they reckoned a year to consist of 360 days divided into 18 months of 20 days each, with 5 days added so as to make a total of 365 days, but every fourth year they intercalated a day so as to make a total of 366 days. See Diego de Landa, *Relation des choses de Yucatan* (Paris, 1864), pp. 202 *sqq.* On the other hand the historian Clavigero, who lived in the eighteenth century, but used earlier authorities, tells us that the Mexicans " did not interpose a day every four years, but thirteen days (making use here even of this favourite number) every fifty-two years ; which produces the same regulation of time " (*History of Mexico*, Second Edition, London, 1807, vol. i. p. 293). However, the view that the Mexicans corrected their year by intercalation is rejected by Professor E. Seler. See his " Mexican Chronology," in *Bulletin 28* of the Bureau of American Ethnology (Washington, 1904), pp. 13 *sqq.* ; and on the other side Miss Zelia Nuttall, " The Periodical Adjustments of the Ancient Mexican Calendar," *American Anthropologist*, N.S. vi. (1904) pp 486-500.

CHAPTER III

THE CALENDAR OF THE EGYPTIAN FARMER

§ 1. *The Rise and Fall of the Nile*

In Egypt the operations of husbandry are dependent on the annual rise and fall of the Nile.

IF the Egyptian farmer of the olden time could thus get no help, except at the rarest intervals, from the official or sacerdotal calendar, he must have been compelled to observe for himself those natural signals which marked the times for the various operations of husbandry. In all ages of which we possess any records the Egyptians have been an agricultural people, dependent for their subsistence on the growth of the corn. The cereals which they cultivated were wheat, barley, and apparently sorghum (*Holcus sorghum*, Linnaeus), the *doora* of the modern fellaheen.[1] Then as now the whole country, with the exception of a fringe on the coast of the Mediterranean, was almost rainless, and owed its immense fertility entirely to the annual inundation of the Nile, which, regulated by an elaborate system of dams and canals, was distributed over the fields, renewing the soil year by year with a fresh deposit of mud washed down from the great equatorial lakes and the mountains of Abyssinia. Hence the rise of the river has always been watched by the inhabitants with the utmost anxiety ; for if it either falls short of or exceeds a certain height, dearth and famine are the inevitable consequences.[2] The water begins to rise early in

---

[1] Herodotus, ii. 36, with A. Wiedemann's note ; Diodorus Siculus, i. 14. 1, i. 17. 1 ; Pliny, *Nat. Hist.* v. 57 *sq.*, xviii. 60 ; Sir J. Gardiner Wilkinson, *Manners and Customs of the Ancient Egyptians* (London, 1878), ii. 398, 399, 418, 426 *sq.*; A. Erman, *Aegypten und aegyptisches Leben im*

Altertum, pp. 577 *sqq.* ; A. de Candolle, *Origin of Cultivated Plants* (London, 1884), pp. 354 *sq.*, 369, 381 ; G. Maspero, *Histoire ancienne des Peuples de l'Orient Classique*, i. 66.

[2] Herodotus, ii. 14 ; Diodorus Siculus, i. 36 ; Strabo, xvii. 1. 3, pp. 786-788 ; Pliny, *Nat. Hist.* xviii. 167-

June, but it is not until the latter half of July that it swells to a mighty tide. By the end of September the inundation is at its greatest height. The country is now submerged, and presents the appearance of a sea of turbid water, from which the towns and villages, built on higher ground, rise like islands. For about a month the flood remains nearly stationary, then sinks more and more rapidly, till by December or January the river has returned to its ordinary bed. With the approach of summer the level of the water continues to fall. In the early days of June the Nile is reduced to half its ordinary breadth; and Egypt, scorched by the sun, blasted by the wind that has blown from the Sahara for many days, seems a mere continuation of the desert. The trees are choked with a thick layer of grey dust. A few meagre patches of vegetables, watered with difficulty, struggle painfully for existence in the immediate neighbourhood of the villages. Some appearance of verdure lingers beside the canals and in the hollows from which the moisture has not wholly evaporated. The plain appears to pant in the pitiless sunshine, bare, dusty, ash-coloured, cracked and seamed as far as the eye can see with a network of fissures. From the middle of April till the middle of June the land of Egypt is but half alive, waiting for the new Nile.[1]

For countless ages this cycle of natural events has determined the annual labours of the Egyptian husbandman. The first work of the agricultural year is the cutting

Irrigation, sowing, and harvest in Egypt.

170; Seneca, *Natur. Quaest.* iv. 2. 1-10; E. W. Lane, *Manners and Customs of the Modern Egyptians* (Paisley and London, 1895), pp. 17 *sq.*, 495 *sqq.*; A. Erman, *op. cit.* pp. 21-25; G. Maspero, *op. cit.* i. 22 *sqq.* However, since the Suez Canal was cut, rain has been commoner in Lower Egypt (A. H. Sayce on Herodotus, ii. 14).

[1] G. Maspero, *Histoire ancienne des Peuples de l'Orient Classique*, i. 22-26; A. Erman, *Aegypten und aegyptisches Leben im Altertum*, p. 23. According to Lane (*op. cit.* pp. 17 *sq.*) the Nile rises in Egypt about the summer solstice (June 21) and reaches its greatest height by the autumnal equinox (Sep-

tember 22). This agrees exactly with the statement of Diodorus Siculus (i. 36. 2). Herodotus says (ii. 19) that the rise of the river lasted for a hundred days from the summer solstice. Compare Pliny, *Nat. Hist.* v. 57, xviii. 167; Seneca, *Nat. Quaest.* 2. 1. According to Prof. Ginzel the Nile does not rise in Egypt till the last week of June (*Handbuch der mathematischen und technischen Chronologie*, i. 154). For ancient descriptions of Egypt in time of flood see Herodotus, ii. 97; Diodorus Siculus, i. 36. 8 *sq.*; Strabo, xvii. 1. 4, p. 788; Aelian, *De natura animalium*, x. 43; Achilles Tatius, iv. 12; Seneca, *Natur. Quaest.* iv. 2. 8 and 11.

of the dams which have hitherto prevented the swollen river from flooding the canals and the fields. This is done, and the pent-up waters released on their beneficent mission, in the first half of August.[1] In November, when the inundation has subsided, wheat, barley, and sorghum are sown. The time of harvest varies with the district, falling about a month later in the north than in the south. In Upper or Southern Egypt barley is reaped at the beginning of March, wheat at the beginning of April, and sorghum about the end of that month.[2]

The events of the agricultural year were probably celebrated with religious rites.

It is natural to suppose that these various events of the agricultural year were celebrated by the Egyptian farmer with some simple religious rites designed to secure the blessing of the gods upon his labours. These rustic ceremonies he would continue to perform year after year at the same season, while the solemn festivals of the priests continued to shift, with the shifting calendar, from summer through spring to winter, and so backward through autumn to summer. The rites of the husbandman were stable because they rested on direct observation of nature : the rites of the priest were unstable because they were based on a false calculation. Yet many of the priestly festivals may have been nothing but the old rural festivals disguised in the course of ages by the pomp of sacerdotalism and severed, by the error of the calendar, from their roots in the natural cycle of the seasons.

[1] Sir J. Gardiner Wilkinson, *Manners and Customs of the Ancient Egyptians* (London, 1878), ii. 365 *sq.* ; E. W. Lane, *Manners and Customs of the Modern Egyptians* (Paisley and London, 1895), pp. 498 *sqq.* ; G. Maspero, *Histoire ancienne des Peuples de l'Orient Classique*, i. 23 *sq.*, 69. The last-mentioned writer says (p. 24) that the dams are commonly cut between the first and sixteenth of July, but apparently he means August.

[2] Sir J. D. Wilkinson, *op. cit.* ii. 398 *sq.*; Prof. W. M. Flinders Petrie, cited above, vol. i. p. 231, note [3]. According

to Pliny (*Nat. Hist.* xviii. 60) barley was reaped in Egypt in the sixth month from sowing, and wheat in the seventh month. Diodorus Siculus, on the other hand, says (i. 36. 4) that the corn was reaped after four or five months. Perhaps Pliny refers to Lower, and Diodorus to Upper Egypt. Elsewhere Pliny affirms (*Nat. Hist.* xviii. 169) that the corn was sown at the beginning of November, and that the reaping began at the end of March and was completed in May. This certainly applies better to Lower than to Upper Egypt.

§ 2. *Rites of Irrigation*

These conjectures are confirmed by the little we know Mourning both of the popular and of the official Egyptian religion. for Osiris at mid- Thus we are told that the Egyptians held a festival of Isis summer at the time when the Nile began to rise. They believed when the Nile begins that the goddess was then mourning for the lost Osiris, and to rise. that the tears which dropped from her eyes swelled the impetuous tide of the river.[1] Hence in Egyptian inscriptions Isis is spoken of as she "who maketh the Nile to swell and overflow, who maketh the Nile to swell in his season."[2] Similarly the Toradjas of Central Celebes imagine that showers of rain are the tears shed by the compassionate gods in weeping for somebody who is about to die ; a shower in the morning is to them an infallible omen of death.[3] However, an uneasy suspicion would seem to have occurred to the Egyptians that perhaps after all the tears of the goddess might not suffice of themselves to raise the water to the proper level ; so in the time of Rameses II. the king used on the first day of the flood to throw into the Nile a written order commanding the river to do its duty, and the submissive stream never failed to obey the royal mandate.[4] Yet the ancient belief survives in a modified form to this day. For the Nile, as we saw, begins to rise in June about the time of the summer solstice, and the people still attribute its increased volume to a miraculous drop which falls into the river on the night of the seventeenth of the month. The charms and divinations which they practise on that mystic night in order to ascertain the length of their own life and to rid the houses of bugs may well date from a remote antiquity.[5] Now if Osiris was in one of his aspects

[1] Pausanias, x. 32. 18.
[2] E. A. Wallis Budge, *Osiris and the Egyptian Resurrection*, ii. 278.
[3] N. Adriani en Alb. C. Kruijt, *De Bare'e-sprekende Toradjas van Midden-Celebes* (Batavia, 1912), i. 273. The more civilized Indians of tropical America, who practised agriculture and had developed a barbaric art, appear to have commonly represented the rain-god in human form with tears streaming down from his eyes. See T. A. Joyce, "The Weeping God," *Essays and Studies presented to William Ridgeway* (Cambridge, 1913), pp. 365-374.
[4] This we learn from inscriptions at Silsilis. See A. Moret, *Mystères Égyptiens* (Paris, 1913), p. 180.
[5] E. W. Lane, *Manners and Customs of the Modern Egyptians* (Paisley and London, 1895), ch. xxvi. pp. 495 *sq.*

a god of the corn, nothing could be more natural than that he should be mourned at midsummer. For by that time the harvest was past, the fields were bare, the river ran low, life seemed to be suspended, the corn-god was dead. At such a moment people who saw the handiwork of divine beings in all the operations of nature might well trace the swelling of the sacred stream to the tears shed by the goddess at the death of the beneficent corn-god her husband.

Sirius regarded as the star of Isis.

And the sign of the rising waters on earth was accompanied by a sign in heaven. For in the early days of Egyptian history, some three or four thousand years before the beginning of our era, the splendid star of Sirius, the brightest of all the fixed stars, appeared at dawn in the east just before sunrise about the time of the summer solstice, when the Nile begins to rise.[1] The Egyptians called it Sothis, and regarded it as the star of Isis,[2] just as the

---

[1] L. Ideler, *Handbuch der mathematischen und technischen Chronologie*, i. 124 *sqq.* ; R. Lepsius, *Die Chronologie der Aegypter*, i. 168 *sq.* ; F. K. Ginzel, *Handbuch der mathematischen und technischen Chronologie*, i. 190 *sq.* ; Ed. Meyer, "Nachträge zur ägyptischen Chronologie," *Abhandlungen der königl. Preuss. Akademie der Wissenschaften*, 1907 (Berlin, 1908), pp. 11 *sq.* ; *id.*, *Geschichte des Altertums*,[2] i. 28 *sq.*, 99 *sqq.* The coincidence of the rising of Sirius with the swelling of the Nile is mentioned by Tibullus (i. 7. 21 *sq.*) and Aelian (*De natura animalium*, x. 45). In later times, as a consequence of the precession of the equinoxes, the rising of Sirius gradually diverged from the summer solstice, falling later and later in the solar year. In the sixteenth and fifteenth century B.C. Sirius rose seventeen days after the summer solstice, and at the date of the Canopic decree (238 B.C.) it rose a whole month after the first swelling of the Nile. See L. Ideler, *op. cit.* i. 130 ; F. K. Ginzel, *op. cit.* i. 190 ; Ed. Meyer, "Nachträge zur ägyptischen Chronologie," pp. 11 *sq.* According to Censorinus (*De die natali*, xxi. 10), Sirius regularly rose in Egypt on the twentieth of July (Julian calendar) ;

and this was true of latitude 30° in Egypt (the latitude nearly of Heliopolis and Memphis) for about three thousand years of Egyptian history. See L. Ideler, *op. cit.* i. 128-130. But the date of the rising of the star is not the same throughout Egypt ; it varies with the latitude, and the variation within the limits of Egypt amounts to seven days or more. Roughly speaking, Sirius rises nearly a whole day earlier for each degree of latitude you go south. Thus, whereas near Alexandria in the north Sirius does not rise till the twenty-second of July, at Syene in the south it rises on the sixteenth of July. See R. Lepsius, *op. cit.* i. 168 *sq.* ; F. K. Ginzel, *op. cit.* i. 182 *sq.* Now it is to be remembered that the rising of the Nile, as well as the rising of Sirius, is observed earlier and earlier the further south you go. The coincident variation of the two phenomena could hardly fail to confirm the Egyptians in their belief of a natural or supernatural connexion between them.

[2] Diodorus Siculus, i. 27. 4 ; Plutarch, *Isis et Osiris*, 21, 22, 38, 61 ; Porphyry, *De antro nympharum*, 24 ; Scholiast on Apollonius Rhodius, ii. 517 ; Canopic decree, lines 36 *sq.*, in W. Dittenberger's *Orientis Graeci In-*

Babylonians deemed the planet Venus the star of Astarte. To both peoples apparently the brilliant luminary in the morning sky seemed the goddess of life and love come to mourn her departed lover or spouse and to wake him from the dead. Hence the rising of Sirius marked the beginning of the sacred Egyptian year,[1] and was regularly celebrated by a festival which did not shift with the shifting official year.[2]   The

The rising of Sirius marked the beginning of the sacred Egyptian year.

scriptiones Selectae, vol. i. p. 102, No. 56 (lines 28 *sq.* in Ch. Michel's *Recueil d'Inscriptions Grecques*, p. 417, No. 551); R. V. Lanzone, *Dizionario di Mitologia Egizia*, pp. 825 *sq.* On the ceiling of the Memnonium at Thebes the heliacal rising of Sirius is represented under the form and name of Isis (Sir J. G. Wilkinson, *Manners and Customs of the Ancient Egyptians*, London, 1878, iii. 102).

[1] Porphyry and the Canopic decree, *ll.cc.* ; Censorinus, *De die natali*, xviii. 10, xxi. 10. In inscriptions on the temple at Syene, the modern Assuan, Isis is called "the mistress of the beginning of the year," the goddess "who revolves about the world, near to the constellation of Orion, who rises in the eastern sky and passes to the west perpetually" (R. V. Lanzone, *op. cit.* p. 826). According to some, the festival of the rising of Sirius and the beginning of the sacred year was held on the nineteenth, not the twentieth of July. See Ed. Meyer, "Ägyptische Chronologie," *Abhandlungen der königl. Preuss. Akademie der Wissenschaften*, 1904, pp. 22 *sqq.* ; *id.*, "Nachträge zur ägyptischen Chronologie," *Abhandlungen der königl. Preuss. Akademie der Wissenschaften*, 1907, pp. 7 *sqq.* ; *id.*, *Geschichte des Altertums*,[2] i. 2. pp. 28 *sqq.*, 98 *sqq.*

[2] *Eudoxi ars astronomica, qualis in charta Aegyptiaca superest*, ed. F. Blass (Kiliae, 1887), p. 14, οἱ δὲ ἀσ[τρο]λ[ό]γοι καὶ οἱ ἱερογραμμ[ατεῖς] χ[ρῶν]ται ταῖς κατὰ σελή[ν]η[ν] ἡμ[έ]-ραις καὶ ἄγουσι πανδημ[ι]κὰς ἑ[op]τας τινὰς μὲν ὡς ἐνομί[σθ]η τὰ δὲ κατα-χυτήρια καὶ κυνὸς ἀνατολὴν καὶ σεληναῖα κατὰ θεό[ν], ἀναλεγόμενοι τὰς ἡμέρας ἐκ τῶν Αἰγυπτίων. This statement of Eudoxus or of one of his pupils is

important, since it definitely proves that, besides the shifting festivals of the shifting official year, the Egyptians celebrated other festivals, which were dated by direct observation of natural phenomena, namely, the annual inundation, the rise of Sirius, and the phases of the moon. The same distinction of the fixed from the movable festivals is indicated in one of the Hibeh papyri, but the passage is unfortunately mutilated. See *The Hibeh Papyri*, part i., edited by B. P. Grenfell and A. S. Hunt (London, 1906), pp. 145, 151 (pointed out to me by my friend Mr. W. Wyse). The annual festival in honour of Ptolemy and Berenice was fixed on the day of the rising of Sirius. See the Canopic decree, in W. Dittenberger's *Orientis Graeci Inscriptiones Selectae*, No. 56 (vol. i. pp. 102 *sq.*).

The rise of Sirius was carefully observed by the islanders of Ceos, in the Aegean. They watched for it with arms in their hands and sacrificed on the mountains to the star, drawing from its aspect omens of the salubrity or unhealthiness of the coming year. The sacrifice was believed to secure the advent of the cool North winds (the Etesian winds as the Greeks call them), which regularly begin to blow about this time of the year, and mitigate the oppressive heat of summer in the Aegean. See Apollonius Rhodius, *Argon.* ii. 516-527, with the notes of the Scholiast on vv. 498, 526 ; Theophrastus, *De ventis*, ii. 14 ; Clement of Alexandria, *Strom.* vi. 3. 29, p. 753, ed. Potter ; Nonnus, *Dionys.* v. 269-279 ; Hyginus, *Astronomica*, ii. 4 ; Cicero, *De divinatione*, i. 57. 130 ; M. P. Nilsson, *Griechische Feste* (Leipsic, 1906), pp. 6-8 ; C. Neu-

first day of the first month Thoth was theoretically supposed to date from the heliacal rising of the bright star, and in all probability it really did so when the official or civil year of three hundred and sixty-five days was first instituted. But the miscalculation which has been already explained[1] had the effect of making the star to shift its place in the calendar by one day in four years. Thus if Sirius rose on the first of Thoth in one year, it would rise on the second of Thoth four years afterwards, on the third of Thoth eight years afterwards, and so on until after the lapse of a Siriac or Sothic period of fourteen hundred and sixty solar years the first of Thoth again coincided with the heliacal rising of Sirius.[2] This observation of the gradual displacement of

---

mann und J. Partsch, *Physikalische Geographie von Griechenland* (Breslau, 1885), pp. 96 *sqq.* On the top of Mount Pelion in Thessaly there was a sanctuary of Zeus, where sacrifices were offered at the rising of Sirius, in the height of the summer, by men of rank, who were chosen by the priest and wore fresh sheep-skins. See [Dicaearchus,] "Descriptio Graeciae," *Geographi Graeci Minores*, ed. C. Müller, i. 107; *Historicorum Graecorum Fragmenta*, ed. C. Müller, ii. 262.

[1] Above, pp. 24 *sq.*

[2] We know from Censorinus (*De die natali*, xxi. 10) that the first of Thoth coincided with the heliacal rising of Sirius on July 20 (Julian calendar) in the year 139 A.D. Hence reckoning backwards by Sothic periods of 1460 solar years we may infer that Sirius rose on July 20th (Julian calendar) in the years 1321 B.C., 2781 B.C., and 4241 B.C.; and accordingly that the civil or vague Egyptian year of 365 days was instituted in one of these years. In favour of supposing that it was instituted either in 2781 B.C. or 4241 B.C., it may be said that in both these years the rising of Sirius nearly coincided with the summer solstice and the rising of the Nile; whereas in the year 1321 B.C. the summer solstice, and with it the rising of the Nile, fell nineteen days before the rising of Sirius and the first of Thoth. Now when we consider the close causal connexion

which the Egyptians traced between the rising of Sirius and the rising of the Nile, it seems probable that they started the new calendar on the first of Thoth in a year in which the two natural phenomena coincided rather than in one in which they diverged from each other by nineteen days. Prof. Ed. Meyer decides in favour of the year 4241 B.C. as the date of the introduction of the Egyptian calendar on the ground that the calendar was already well known in the Old Kingdom. See L. Ideler, *op. cit.* i. 125 *sqq.*; F. K. Ginzel, *op. cit.* i. 192 *sqq.*; Ed. Meyer, "Nachträge zur ägyptischen Chronologie," *Abhandlungen der königl. Preuss. Akademie der Wissenschaften*, 1907 (Berlin, 1908), pp. 11 *sq.*; *id.*, *Geschichte des Altertums*,[2] i. 2. pp. 28 *sqq.*, 98 *sqq.* When the fixed Alexandrian year was introduced in 30 B.C. (see above, pp. 27 *sq.*) the first of Thoth fell on August 29, which accordingly was thenceforth reckoned the first day of the year in the Alexandrian calendar. See L. Ideler, *op. cit.* i. 153 *sqq.* The period of 1460 solar or 1461 movable Egyptian years was variously called a Sothic period (Clement of Alexandria, *Strom.* i. 21. 136, p. 401 ed. Potter), a Canicular year (from *Canicula*, "the Dog-star," that is, Sirius), a heliacal year, and a year of God (Censorinus, *De die natali*, xviii. 10). But there is no evidence or probability that the

the star in the calendar has been of the utmost importance The observation of the gradual displacement of Sirius in the calendar led to the determination of the true length of the solar year. for the progress of astronomy, since it led the Egyptians directly to the determination of the approximately true length of the solar year and thus laid the basis of our modern calendar ; for the Julian calendar, which we owe to Caesar, was founded on the Egyptian theory, though not on the Egyptian practice.[1] It was therefore a fortunate moment for the world when some pious Egyptian, thousands of years ago, identified for the first time the bright star of Sirius with his goddess ; for the identification induced his countrymen to regard the heavenly body with an attention which they would never have paid to it if they had known it to be nothing but a world vastly greater than our own and separated from it by an inconceivable, if not immeasurable, abyss of space.

The cutting of the dams and the admission of the water

period was recognized by the Egyptian astronomers who instituted the movable year of 365 days. Rather, as Ideler pointed out (*op. cit.* i. 132), it must have been a later discovery based on continued observations of the heliacal rising of Sirius and of its gradual displacement through the whole length of the official calendar. Brugsch, indeed, went so far as to suppose that the period was a discovery of astronomers of the second century A.D., to which they were led by the coincidence of the first of Thoth with the heliacal rising of Sirius in 139 A.D. (*Die Ägyptologie*, p. 357). But the discovery, based as it is on a very simple calculation (365 × 4 = 1460), could hardly fail to be made as soon as astronomers estimated the length of the solar year at 365¼ days, and that they did so at least as early as 238 B.C. is proved conclusively by the Canopic decree. See above, pp. 25 *sq.*, 27. As to the Sothic period see further R. Lepsius, *Die Chronologie der Aegypter*, i. 165 *sqq.* ; F. K. Ginzel, *op. cit.* i. 187 *sqq.*

For the convenience of the reader I subjoin a table of the Egyptian months, with their dates, as these fell, (1) in a year when the first of Thoth coincided with July 20 of the Julian calendar, and (2) in the fixed Alexandrian year.

Egyptian Months.	Sothic Year beginning July 20	Alexandrian Year.
1 Thoth .	20 July .	29 August
1 Phaophi .	19 August .	28 September
1 Athyr .	18 September	28 October
1 Khoiak .	18 October .	27 November
1 Tybi .	17 November	27 December
1 Mechir .	17 December .	26 January
1 Phamenoth	16 January .	25 February
1 Pharmuthi .	15 February .	27 March
1 Pachon .	17 March .	26 April
1 Payni .	16 April .	26 May
1 Epiphi .	16 May .	25 June
1 Mesori .	15 June .	25 July
1 Supplementary day	15 July .	24 August

See L. Ideler, *op. cit.* i. 143 *sq.* ; F. K. Ginzel, *op. cit.* i. 200.

[1] The Canopic decree (above, p. 27) suffices to prove that the Egyptian astronomers, long before Caesar's time, were well acquainted with the approximately exact length of the solar year, although they did not use their knowledge to correct the calendar except for a short time in the reign of Ptolemy Euergetes. With regard to Caesar's debt to the Egyptian astronomers see Dio Cassius, xliii. 26 ; Macrobius, *Saturn.* i. 14. 3, i. 16. 39 ; L. Ideler, *Handbuch der mathematischen und technischen Chronologie*, i. 166 *sqq.*

Cere-
monies
observed in
Egypt at
the cutting
of the
dams early
in August.
into the canals and fields is a great event in the Egyptian year. At Cairo the operation generally takes place between the sixth and the sixteenth of August, and till lately was attended by ceremonies which deserve to be noticed, because they were probably handed down from antiquity. An ancient canal, known by the name of the Khalíj, formerly passed through the native town of Cairo. Near its entrance the canal was crossed by a dam of earth, very broad at the bottom and diminishing in breadth upwards, which used to be constructed before or soon after the Nile began to rise. In front of the dam, on the side of the river, was reared a truncated cone of earth called the 'arooseh or
" bride," on the top of which a little maize or millet was generally sown. This " bride " was commonly washed down by the rising tide a week or a fortnight before the cutting of the dam. Tradition runs that the old custom was to deck a young virgin in gay apparel and throw her into the river as a sacrifice to obtain a plentiful inundation.[1]
Certainly human sacrifices were offered for a similar purpose by the Wajagga of German East Africa down to recent years. These people irrigate their fields by means of skilfully constructed channels, through which they conduct the water of the mountain brooks and rivers to the thirsty land. They imagine that the spirits of their forefathers dwell in the rocky basins of these rushing streams, and that they would resent the withdrawal of the water to irrigate the fields if compensation were not offered to them. The water-rate paid to them consisted of a child, uncircumcised and of unblemished body, who was decked with ornaments and bells and thrown into the river to drown, before they ventured to draw off the water into the irrigation channel. Having thrown him in, his executioners shewed a clean pair of heels, because they expected the river to rise in flood at once on receipt of the water-rate.[2] In similar circumstances the Njamus of British East Africa sacrifice a sheep before they let the water of the stream flow into the ditch

---

[1] E. W. Lane, *Manners and Customs of the Modern Egyptians* (Paisley and London, 1895), ch. xxvi. pp. 499 *sq.*

[2] Bruno Gutmann, " Feldbausitten und Wachstumsbräuche der Wadschagga," *Zeitschrift für Ethnologie*, xlv. (1913) pp. 484 *sq.*

or artificial channel. The fat, dung, and blood of the animal are sprinkled at the mouth of the ditch and in the water ; thereupon the dam is broken down and the stream pours into the ditch. The sacrifice may only be offered by a man of the Il Mayek clan, and for two days afterwards he wears the skin of the beast tied round his head. No one may quarrel with this man while the water is irrigating the crops, else the people believe that the water would cease to flow in the ditch ; more than that, if the men of the Il Mayek clan were angry and sulked for ten days, the water would dry up permanently for that season. Hence the Il Mayek clan enjoys great consideration in the tribe, since the crops are thought to depend on their good will and good offices. Ten elders assist at the sacrifice of the sheep, though they may take no part in it. They must all be of a particular age ; and after the ceremony they may not cohabit with their wives until harvest, and they are obliged to sleep at night in their granaries. Curiously enough, too, while the water is irrigating the fields, nobody may kill waterbuck, eland, oryx, zebra, rhinoceros, or hippopotamus. Anybody caught red-handed in the act of breaking this game-law would at once be cast out of the village.[1]

Whether the " bride " who used to figure at the ceremony of cutting the dam in Cairo was ever a live woman or not, the intention of the practice appears to have been to marry the river, conceived as a male power, to his bride the corn-land, which was soon to be fertilized by his water. The ceremony was therefore a charm to ensure the growth of the crops. As such it probably dated, in one form or another, from ancient times. Dense crowds assembled to witness the cutting of the dam. The operation was performed before sunrise, and many people spent the preceding night on the banks of the canal or in boats lit with lamps on the river, while fireworks were displayed and guns discharged at frequent intervals. Before sunrise a great number of workmen began to cut the dam, and the task was accomplished about an hour before the sun appeared on the

Modern Egyptian ceremony at the cutting of the dams.

---

[1] Hon. K. R. Dundas, " Notes on the tribes inhabiting the Baringo District, East Africa Protectorate," *Journal of the Royal Anthropological Institute*, xl. (1910) p. 54.

horizon. When only a thin ridge of earth remained, a boat with an officer on board was propelled against it, and breaking through the slight barrier descended with the rush of water into the canal. The Governor of Cairo flung a purse of gold into the boat as it passed. Formerly the custom was to throw money into the canal. The populace used to dive after it, and several lives were generally lost in the scramble.[1] This practice also would seem to have been ancient, for Seneca tells us that at a place called the Veins of the Nile, not far from Philae, the priests used to cast money and offerings of gold into the river at a festival which apparently took place at the rising of the water.[2] At Cairo the time-honoured ceremony came to an end in 1897, when the old canal was filled up. An electric tramway now runs over the spot where for countless ages crowds of worshippers or holiday-makers had annually assembled to witness the marriage of the Nile.[3]

§ 3. *Rites of Sowing*

The sowing of the seed in November.

Plutarch on the mournful character of the rites of sowing.

The next great operation of the agricultural year in Egypt is the sowing of the seed in November, when the water of the inundation has retreated from the fields. With the Egyptians, as with many peoples of antiquity, the committing of the seed to the earth assumed the character of a solemn and mournful rite. On this subject I will let Plutarch speak for himself. "What," he asks, "are we to make of the gloomy, joyless, and mournful sacrifices, if it is wrong either to omit the established rites or to confuse and disturb our conceptions of the gods by absurd suspicions? For the Greeks also perform many rites which resemble those of the Egyptians and are observed about the same time. Thus at the festival of the Thesmophoria in Athens

---

[1] E. W. Lane, *op. cit.* pp. 500-504 ; Sir Auckland Colvin, *The Making of Modern Egypt* (London, 1906), pp. 278 *sq.* According to the latter writer, a dressed dummy was thrown into the river at each cutting of the dam.

[2] Seneca, *Naturales Quaestiones*, iv. 2. 7. The cutting of the dams

is mentioned by Diodorus Siculus (i. 36. 3), and the festival on that occasion (τὰ καταχυτήρια) is noticed by Eudoxus (or one of his pupils) in a passage which has already been quoted. See above, p. 35, note [2].

[3] Sir Auckland Colvin, *l.c.*

women sit on the ground and fast. And the Boeotians open the vaults of the Sorrowful One,[1] naming that festival sorrowful because Demeter is sorrowing for the descent of the Maiden. The month is the month of sowing about the setting of the Pleiades.[2] The Egyptians call it Athyr, the Athenians Pyanepsion, the Boeotians the month of Demeter. Theopompus informs us that the western peoples consider and call the winter Cronus, the summer Aphrodite, and the spring Persephone, and they believe that all things are brought into being by Cronus and Aphrodite. The Phrygians imagine that the god sleeps in winter and wakes in summer, and accordingly they celebrate with Bacchic rites the putting him to bed in winter and his awakening in summer. The Paphlagonians allege that he is bound fast and shut up in winter, but that he stirs and is set free in spring. And the season furnishes a hint that the sadness is for the hiding of those fruits of the earth which the ancients esteemed, not indeed gods, but great and necessary gifts bestowed by the gods in order that men might not lead the life of savages and of wild beasts. For it was that time of year when they saw some of the fruits vanishing and failing from the trees, while they sowed others grudgingly and with difficulty, scraping the earth with their hands and huddling it up again, on the uncertain chance that what they deposited in the ground would ever ripen and come to maturity. Thus they did in many respects like those who bury and mourn their dead. And just as we say that a purchaser of Plato's books purchases Plato, or that an actor who plays the comedies of Menander plays Menander, so the men of old did not hesitate to call the gifts and products of the gods by the names of the gods themselves, thereby honouring and glorifying the things on account of their utility. But in

The sadness of autumn

---

[1] Τῆς 'Αχαίας. Plutarch derives the name from ἄχος, "pain," "grief." But the etymology is uncertain. It has lately been proposed to derive the epithet from ὀχή, "nourishment." See M. P. Nilsson, *Griechische Feste* (Leipsic, 1906), p. 326. As to the vaults (μέγαρα) of Demeter see Pausanias, ix. 8. 1 ; Scholiast on Lucian, *Dial. Meretr.* ii. pp. 275 *sq.*, ed. H. Rabe (Leipsic, 1906).

[2] In antiquity the Pleiades set at dawn about the end of October or early in November. See L. Ideler, *Handbuch der mathematischen und technischen Chronologie*, i. 242 ; Aug. Mommsen, *Chronologie* (Leipsic, 1883), pp. 16, 27; G. F. Unger, "Zeitrechnung der Griechen und Römer," in Iwan Müller's *Handbuch der klassischen Altertumswissenschaft*, i.[1] (Nördlingen, 1886) pp. 558, 585.

after ages simple folk in their ignorance applied to the gods statements which only held true of the fruits of the earth, and so they came not merely to say but actually to believe that the growth and decay of plants, on which they subsisted,[1] were the birth and the death of gods. Thus they fell into absurd, immoral, and confused ways of thinking, though all the while the absurdity of the fallacy was manifest. Hence Xenophanes of Colophon declared that if the Egyptians deemed their gods divine they should not weep for them, and that if they wept for them they should not deem them divine. 'For it is ridiculous,' said he, 'to lament and pray that the fruits would be good enough to grow and ripen again in order that they may again be eaten and lamented.' But he was wrong, for though the lamentations are for the fruits, the prayers are addressed to the gods, as the causes and givers of them, that they would be pleased to make fresh fruits to spring up instead of those that perish." [2]

Plutarch's view that the worship of the fruits of the earth sprang from a verbal misunderstanding.

In this interesting passage Plutarch expresses his belief that the worship of the fruits of the earth was the result of a verbal misapprehension or disease of language, as it has been called by a modern school of mythologists, who explain the origin of myths in general on the same easy principle of metaphors misunderstood. Primitive man, on Plutarch's theory, firmly believed that the fruits of the earth on which he subsisted were not themselves gods but merely the gifts of the gods, who were the real givers of all good things. Yet at the same time men were in the habit of bestowing on these divine products the names of their divine creators, either out of gratitude or merely for the sake of brevity, as when we say that a man has bought a Shakespeare or acted Molière, when we mean that he has bought the works of Shakespeare or acted the plays of Molière. This abbreviated mode of expression was misunderstood in later times, and so

---

[1] Τὰς παρουσίας τῶν ἀναγκαίων καὶ ἀποκρύψεις.

[2] Plutarch, *Isis et Osiris*, 69-71. With the sleep of the Phrygian gods we may compare the sleep of Vishnu. The toils and anxieties of the Indian farmer "are continuous, and his only period of comparative rest is in the heavy rain time, when, as he says, the god Vishnu goes to sleep, and does not wake till October is well advanced and the time has come to begin cutting and crushing the sugar-cane and boiling down the juice" (W. Crooke, *Natives of Northern India*, London, 1907, p. 159).

people came to look upon the fruits of the earth as themselves divine instead of as being the work of divinities : in short, they mistook the creature for the creator. In like manner Plutarch would explain the Egyptian worship of animals as reverence done not so much to the beasts themselves as to the great god who displays the divine handiwork in sentient organisms even more than in the most beautiful and wonderful works of inanimate nature.[1]

The comparative study of religion has proved that these theories of Plutarch are an inversion of the truth. Fetishism, or the view that the fruits of the earth and things in general are divine or animated by powerful spirits, is not, as Plutarch imagined, a late corruption of a pure and primitive theism, which regarded the gods as the creators and givers of all good things. On the contrary, fetishism is early and theism is late in the history of mankind. In this respect Xenophanes, whom Plutarch attempts to correct, displayed a much truer insight into the mind of the savage. To weep crocodile tears over the animals and plants which he kills and eats, and to pray them to come again in order that they may be again eaten and again lamented—this may seem absurd to us, but it is precisely what the savage does. And from his point of view the proceeding is not at all absurd but perfectly rational and well calculated to answer his ends. For he sincerely believes that animals and fruits are tenanted by spirits who can harm him if they please, and who cannot but be put to considerable inconvenience by that destruction of their bodies which is unfortunately inseparable from the processes of mastication and digestion. What more natural, therefore, than that the savage should offer excuses to the beasts and the fruits for the painful necessity he is under of consuming them, and that he should endeavour to alleviate their pangs by soft words and an air of respectful sympathy, in order that they may bear him no grudge, and may in due time come again to be again eaten and again lamented? Judged by the standard of primitive manners the attitude of the walrus to the oysters was strictly correct :—

His theory is an inversion of the truth : for fetishism is the antecedent, not the corruption, of theism.

Lamentations of the savage for the animals and plants which he kills and eats.

---

[1] Plutarch, *Isis et Osiris*, 77.

" ' *I weep for you,*' *the Walrus said :*
' *I deeply sympathize.*'
With sobs and tears he sorted out
Those of the largest size,
Holding his pocket-handkerchief
Before his streaming eyes."

Respect
shown by
savages
for the
fruits and
the animals
which
they eat.

Many examples of such hypocritical lamentations for animals, drawn not from the fancy of a playful writer but from the facts of savage life, could be cited.[1]   Here I shall quote the general statement of a writer on the Indians of British Columbia, because it covers the case of vegetable as well as of animal food.   After describing the respectful welcome accorded by the Stlatlum Indians to the first "sock-eye" salmon which they have caught in the season, he goes on : "The significance of these ceremonies is easy to perceive when we remember the attitude of the Indians towards nature generally, and recall their myths relating to the salmon, and their coming to their rivers and streams. Nothing that the Indian of this region eats is regarded by him as mere food and nothing more.   Not a single plant, animal, or fish, or other object upon which he feeds, is looked upon in this light, or as something he has secured for himself by his own wit and skill.   He regards it rather as something which has been voluntarily and compassionately placed in his hands by the goodwill and consent of the 'spirit' of the object itself, or by the intercession and magic of his culture-heroes ; to be retained and used by him only upon the fulfilment of certain conditions.   These conditions include respect and reverent care in the killing or plucking of the animal or plant and proper treatment of the parts he has no use for, such as the bones, blood, and offal ; and the depositing of the same in some stream or lake, so that the object may by that means renew its life and physical form. The practices in connection with the killing of animals and the gathering of plants and fruits all make this quite clear, and it is only when we bear this attitude of the savage towards nature in mind that we can hope to rightly understand the motives and purposes of many of his strange customs and beliefs."[2]

[1] *Spirits of the Corn and of the Wild,* ii. 204 *sqq.*

[2] C. Hill Tout, "Report on the Ethnology of the Stlatlum Indians of

We can now understand why among many peoples of antiquity, as Plutarch tells us, the time of sowing was a time of sorrow. The laying of the seed in the earth was a burial of the divine element, and it was fitting that like a human burial it should be performed with gravity and the semblance, if not the reality, of sorrow. Yet they sorrowed not without hope, perhaps a sure and certain hope, that the seed which they thus committed with sighs and tears to the ground would yet rise from the dust and yield fruit a hundredfold to the reaper. "They that sow in tears shall reap in joy. He that goeth forth and weepeth, bearing precious seed, shall doubtless come again with rejoicing, bringing his sheaves with him."[1]

§ 4. *Rites of Harvest*

The Egyptian harvest, as we have seen, falls not in autumn but in spring, in the months of March, April, and May. To the husbandman the time of harvest, at least in a good year, must necessarily be a season of joy : in bringing home his sheaves he is requited for his long and anxious labours. Yet if the old Egyptian farmer felt a secret joy at reaping and garnering the grain, it was essential that he should conceal the natural emotion under an air of profound dejection. For was he not severing the body of the corn-god with his sickle and trampling it to pieces under the hoofs of his cattle on the threshing-floor?[2] Accordingly we are told that it was an ancient custom of the Egyptian corn-reapers to beat their breasts and lament over the first sheaf cut, while at the same time they called upon Isis.[3] The invocation seems to have taken the form of a melancholy chant, to which the Greeks gave the name of Maneros. Similar plaintive strains were chanted by corn-reapers in

British Columbia," *Journal of the Anthropological Institute*, xxxv. (1905) pp. 140 *sq.*

[1] Psalm cxxvi. 5 *sq.* Firmicus Maternus asks the Egyptians (*De errore profanarum religionum*, ii. 7), "*Cur plangitis fruges terrae et crescentia lugetis semina?*"

[2] As to the Egyptian modes of reaping and threshing see Sir J. Gardiner Wilkinson, *Manners and Customs of the Ancient Egyptians* (London, 1878), ii. 419 *sqq*; A. Erman, *Aegypten und aegyptisches Leben im Altertum*, pp. 572 *sqq.*

[3] Diodorus Siculus, i. 14. 2.

Phoenicia and other parts of Western Asia.[1] Probably all these doleful ditties were lamentations for the corn-god killed by the sickles of the reapers. In Egypt the slain deity was Osiris, and the name *Maneros* applied to the dirge appears to be derived from certain words meaning "Come to thy house," which often occur in the lamentations for the dead god.[2]

Similar ceremonies observed by the Cherokee Indians in the cultivation of the corn.

Ceremonies of the same sort have been observed by other peoples, probably for the same purpose. Thus we are told that among all vegetables corn (*selu*), by which is apparently meant maize, holds the first place in the household economy and the ceremonial observance of the Cherokee Indians, who invoke it under the name of "the Old Woman" in allusion to a myth that it sprang from the blood of an old woman killed by her disobedient sons. " Much ceremony accompanied the planting and tending of the crop. Seven grains, the sacred number, were put into each hill, and these were not afterwards thinned out. After the last working of the crop, the priest and an assistant—generally the owner of the field—went into the field and built a small enclosure in the centre. Then entering it, they seated themselves upon the ground, with heads bent down, and while the assistant kept perfect silence the priest, with rattle in hand, sang songs of invocation to the spirit of the corn. Soon, according to the orthodox belief, a loud rustling would be heard outside, which they would know

The Old Woman of the corn and the laments for her death.

was caused by the 'Old Woman' bringing the corn into the field, but neither must look up until the song was finished. This ceremony. was repeated on four successive nights, after which no one entered the field for seven other nights, when the priest himself went in, and, if all the sacred regulations had been properly observed, was rewarded by finding young ears upon the stalks. The corn ceremonies could be performed by the owner of the field himself, provided he was willing to pay a sufficient fee to the priest in order to learn the songs and ritual. Care was always taken to keep a

[1] Herodotus, ii. 79; Julius Pollux, iv. 54; Pausanias, ix. 29. 7; Athenaeus, xiv. 11 *sq.*, pp. 618-620. As to these songs see *Spirits of the Corn and of the Wild*, i. 214 *sqq.*

[2] H. Brugsch, *Adonisklage und Linoslied* (Berlin, 1852), p. 24, corrected by A. Wiedemann, *Herodots zweites Buch*, p. 336. As to the lamentations for Osiris see above, p. 12.

clean trail from the field to the house, so that the corn might be encouraged to stay at home and not go wandering elsewhere. Most of these customs have now fallen into disuse excepting among the old people, by many of whom they are still religiously observed. Another curious ceremony, of which even the memory is now almost forgotten, was enacted after the first working of the corn, when the owner or priest stood in succession at each of the four corners of the field and wept and wailed loudly. Even the priests are now unable to give a reason for this performance, which may have been a lament for the bloody death of Selu," the Old Woman of the Corn.[1] In these Cherokee practices the lamentations and the invocations of the Old Woman of the Corn resemble the ancient Egyptian customs of lamenting over the first corn cut and calling upon Isis, herself probably in one of her aspects an Old Woman of the Corn. Further, the Cherokee precaution of leaving a clear path from the field to the house resembles the Egyptian invitation to Osiris, "Come to thy house." So in the East Indies to this day people observe elaborate ceremonies for the purpose of bringing back the Soul of the Rice from the fields to the barn.[2] The Nandi of British East Africa perform a ceremony in September when the eleusine grain is ripening. Every woman who owns a plantation goes out with her daughters into the cornfields and makes a bonfire of the branches and leaves of certain trees (the *Solanum campylanthum* and *Lantana salvifolia*). After that they pluck some of the eleusine, and each of them puts one grain in her necklace, chews another and rubs it on her forehead, throat, and breast. "No joy is shown by the womenfolk on this occasion, and they sorrowfully cut a basketful of the corn which they take home with them and place in the loft to dry." [3]

Just as the Egyptians lamented at cutting the corn, so the Karok Indians of California lament at hewing the

---

[1] J. Mooney, "Myths of the Cherokee," *Nineteenth Annual Report of the Bureau of American Ethnology* (Washington, 1900), pp. 423 *sq.* I do not know what precisely the writer means by "the last working of the crop" and "the first working of the corn."

[2] *Spirits of the Corn and of the Wild*, i. 180 *sqq.*

[3] A. C. Hollis, *The Nandi* (Oxford, 1909), p. 46.

Lamentations of Indians at cutting sacred wood.

sacred wood for the fire in the assembly-room. The wood must be cut from a tree on the top of the highest hill. In lopping off the boughs the Indian weeps and sobs piteously, shedding real tears, and at the top of the tree he leaves two branches and a top-knot, resembling a man's head and outstretched arms. Having descended from the tree, he binds the wood in a faggot and carries it back to the assembly-room, blubbering all the way. If he is asked why he thus weeps at cutting and fetching the sacred fuel, he will either give no answer or say simply that he does it for luck.[1] We may suspect that his real motive is to appease the wrath of the tree-spirit, many of whose limbs he has amputated, though he took care to leave him two arms and a head.

Arab ceremony of burying "the old man" at harvest.

The conception of the corn-spirit as old and dead at harvest is very clearly embodied in a custom observed by the Arabs of Moab. When the harvesters have nearly finished their task and only a small corner of the field remains to be reaped, the owner takes a handful of wheat tied up in a sheaf. A hole is dug in the form of a grave, and two stones are set upright, one at the head and the other at the foot, just as in an ordinary burial. Then the sheaf of wheat is laid at the bottom of the grave, and the sheikh pronounces these words, " The old man is dead." Earth is afterwards thrown in to cover the sheaf, with a prayer, " May Allah bring us back the wheat of the dead." [2]

---

[1] S. Powers, *Tribes of California* (Washington, 1877), p. 25.

[2] A. Jaussen, " Coutumes Arabes,"

Revue Biblique, 1er avril 1903, p. 258; *id.*, *Coutumes des Arabes au pays de Moab* (Paris 1908), pp. 252 *sq.*

CHAPTER IV

THE OFFICIAL FESTIVALS OF OSIRIS

§ 1. *The Festival at Sais*

SUCH, then, were the principal events of the farmer's calendar in ancient Egypt, and such the simple religious rites by which he celebrated them. But we have still to consider the Osirian festivals of the official calendar, so far as these are described by Greek writers or recorded on the monuments. In examining them it is necessary to bear in mind that on account of the movable year of the old Egyptian calendar the true or astronomical dates of the official festivals must have varied from year to year, at least until the adoption of the fixed Alexandrian year in 30 B.C. From that time onward, apparently, the dates of the festivals were determined by the new calendar, and so ceased to rotate throughout the length of the solar year. At all events Plutarch, writing about the end of the first century, implies that they were then fixed, not movable ; for though he does not mention the Alexandrian calendar, he clearly dates the festivals by it.[1] Moreover, the long festal calendar of

With the adoption of the Alexandrian year in 30 B.C. the Egyptian festivals ceased to rotate through the natural year.

---

[1] Thus with regard to the Egyptian month of Athyr he tells us that the sun was then in the sign of the Scorpion (*Isis et Osiris*, 13), that Athyr corresponded to the Athenian month Pyanepsion and the Boeotian month Damatrius (*op. cit.* 69), that it was the month of sowing (*ib.*), that in it the Nile sank, the earth was laid bare by the retreat of the inundation, the leaves fell, and the nights grew longer than the days (*op. cit.* 39). These indications agree on the whole with the date of Athyr in the Alexandrian calendar, namely October 28-November 26. Again, he says (*op. cit.* 43) that the festival of the beginning of spring was held at the new moon of the month Phamenoth, which, in the Alexandrian calendar, corresponded to February 24-March 26. Further, he tells us that a festival was celebrated on the 23rd of Phaophi after the autumn equinox (*op. cit.* 52), and in the Alexandrian calendar Phaophi began on September 28, a few days after the autumn equinox.

Esne, an important document of the Imperial age, is obviously based on the fixed Alexandrian year; for it assigns
the mark for New Year's Day to the day which corresponds
to the twenty-ninth of August, which was the first day of
the Alexandrian year, and its references to the rising of the
Nile, the position of the sun, and the operations of agriculture are all in harmony with this supposition.[1]   Thus we
may take it as fairly certain that from 30 B.C. onwards the
Egyptian festivals were stationary in the solar year.

The sufferings of Osiris displayed as a mystery at Sais.   Herodotus tells us that the grave of Osiris was at Sais in
Lower Egypt, and that there was a lake there upon which the
sufferings of the god were displayed as a mystery by night.[2]
This commemoration of the divine passion was held once a
year: the people mourned and beat their breasts at it to testify
their sorrow for the death of the god ; and an image of a cow,
made of gilt wood with a golden sun between its horns, was
carried out of the chamber in which it stood the rest of the
year.[3]   The cow no doubt represented Isis herself, for cows
were sacred to her, and she was regularly depicted with the
horns of a cow on her head,[4] or even as a woman with the
head of a cow.[5]   It is probable that the carrying out of her cow-
shaped image symbolized the goddess searching for the dead
body of Osiris ; for this was the native Egyptian interpretation
of a similar ceremony observed in Plutarch's time about the
winter solstice, when the gilt cow was carried seven times
round the temple.[6]   A great feature of the festival was the

Once more, he observes that another
festival was held after the spring
equinox (*op. cit.* 65), which implies
the use of a fixed solar year. See
G. Parthey in his edition of Plutarch's
Isis et Osiris (Berlin, 1850), pp. 165-
169.

[1] H. Brugsch, *Die Ägyptologie*, p.
355.

[2] Herodotus, ii. 170.

[3] Herodotus, ii. 129-132.

[4] Herodotus, ii. 41, with Prof. A.
Wiedemann's note (*Herodots zweites
Buch*, pp. 187 *sqq.*); Diodorus
Siculus, i. 11. 4 ; Aelian, *De natura
animalium*, x. 27 ; Plutarch, *Isis et
Osiris*, 19 and 39. According to
Prof. Wiedemann "the Egyptian
name of the cow of Isis was *hes-t*, and

this is one of the rare cases in which
the name of the sacred animal agrees
with that of the deity." *Hest* was the
usual Egyptian form of the name
which the Greeks and Romans represented as Isis. See R. V. Lanzone,
Dizionario di Mitologia Egizia, pp.
813 *sqq.*

[5] In this form she is represented on
a relief at Philae pouring a libation in
honour of the soul of Osiris.   See
E. A. Wallis Budge, *Osiris and the
Egyptian Resurrection*, i. 8.   She is
similarly portrayed in a bronze statu-
ette, which is now in the Louvre.
See G. Perrot et Ch. Chipiez, *Histoire
de l'Art dans l'Antiquité*, i. (Paris,
1882) p. 60, fig. 40.

[6] Plutarch, *Isis et Osiris*, 52.   The

nocturnal illumination. People fastened rows of oil-lamps The illumina-
to the outside of their houses, and the lamps burned all tion of
night long. The custom was not confined to Sais, but was houses
observed throughout the whole of Egypt.[1] throughout Egypt on
This universal illumination of the houses on one night the night
of the year suggests that the festival may have been a com- of the festival
memoration not merely of the dead Osiris but of the dead suggests
in general, in other words, that it may have been a night of that the rite was a
All Souls.[2] For it is a widespread belief that the souls of Feast of All Souls.
the dead revisit their old homes on one night of the year;
and on that solemn occasion people prepare for the reception of the ghosts by laying out food for them to eat, and
lighting lamps to guide them on their dark road from and to
the grave. The following instances will illustrate the custom.

§ 2. Feasts of All Souls

The Esquimaux of St. Michael and the lower Yukon Annual
River in Alaska hold a festival of the dead every year at festival of the dead
the end of November or the beginning of December, as among
well as a greater festival at intervals of several years. At the Esqui-maux.
these seasons, food, drink, and clothes are provided for the
returning ghosts in the *kashim* or clubhouse of the village,
which is illuminated with oil lamps. Every man or The light-
woman who wishes to honour a dead friend sets up a lamp ing of the lamps for
on a stand in front of the place which the deceased used to the dead.
occupy in the clubhouse. These lamps, filled with seal oil,
are kept burning day and night till the festival is over.
They are believed to light the shades on their return to

interpretation is accepted by Prof. A. Wiedemann (*Herodots zweites Buch*, p. 482).

[1] Herodotus, ii. 62. In one of the Hibeh papyri (No. 27, lines 165-167) mention is made of the festival and of the lights which were burned throughout the district. See *The Hibeh Papyri*, part i., ed. B. P. Grenfell and A. S. Hunt (London, 1906), p. 149 (pointed out to me by Mr. W. Wyse). In the papyrus the festival is said to have been held in honour of Athena (*i.e.* Neith), the great goddess of Sais, who

was there identified with Isis. See A. Wiedemann, *Die Religion der alten Ägypter*, pp. 77 *sq.*; *id.*, *Religion of the Ancient Egyptians*, pp. 140 *sq.*

[2] In the period of the Middle Kingdom the Egyptians of Siut used to light lamps for the dead on the last day and the first day of the year. See A. Erman, "Zehn Vorträge aus dem mittleren Reich," *Zeitschrift für ägyptische Sprache und Alterthumskunde*, xx. (1882) p. 164; *id.*, *Aegypten und aegyptisches Leben im Altertum*, pp. 434 *sq.*

their old home and back again to the land of the dead. If any one fails to put up a lamp in the clubhouse and to keep it burning, the shade whom he or she desires to honour could not find its way to the place and so would miss the feast. On the eve of the festival the nearest male relation goes to the grave and summons the ghost by planting there a small model of a seal spear or of a wooden dish, according as the deceased was a man or a woman. The badges of the dead are marked on these implements. When all is ready, the ghosts gather in the fire-pit under the clubhouse, and ascending through the floor at the proper moment take possession of the bodies of their namesakes, to whom the offerings of food, drink, and clothing are made for the benefit of the dead. Thus each shade obtains the supplies he needs in the other world. The dead who have none to make offerings to them are believed to suffer great destitution. Hence the Esquimaux fear to die without leaving behind them some one who will sacrifice to their spirits, and childless people generally adopt children lest their shades should be forgotten at the festivals. When a person has been much disliked, his ghost is sometimes purposely ignored, and that is deemed the severest punishment that could be inflicted upon him. After the songs of invitation to the dead have been sung, the givers of the feast take a small portion of food from every dish and cast it down as an offering to the shades ; then each pours a little water on the floor so that it runs through the cracks. In this way they believe that the spiritual essence of all the food and water is conveyed to the souls. The remainder of the food is afterwards distributed among the people present, who eat of it heartily. Then with songs and dances the feast comes to an end, and the ghosts are dismissed to their own place. Dances form a conspicuous feature of the great festival of the dead, which is held every few years. The dancers dance not only in the clubhouse but also at the graves and on the ice, if the deceased met their death by drowning.[1]

The Indians of California used to observe annual cere-

Esquimaux festival of the dead.

---

[1] E. W. Nelson, " The Eskimo about Bering Strait," *Eighteenth Annual Report of the Bureau of Ethnology,* Part i. (Washington, 1899) pp. 363 *sqq.*

monies of mourning for the dead,[1] at some of which the souls of the departed were represented by living persons. Ten or more men would prepare themselves to play the part of the ghosts by fasting for several days, especially by abstaining from flesh. Disguised with paint and soot, adorned with feathers and grasses, they danced and sang in the village or rushed about in the forest by night with burning torches in their hands. After a time they presented themselves to the relations of the deceased, who looked upon these maskers as in very truth their departed friends and received them accordingly with an outburst of lamentation, the old women scratching their own faces and smiting their breasts with stones in token of mourning. These masquerades were generally held in February. During their continuance a strict fast was observed in the village.[2] Among the Konkaus of California the dance of the dead is always held about the end of August and marks their New Year's Day. They collect a large quantity of food, clothing, baskets, ornaments, and whatever else the spirits are supposed to need in the other world. These they hang on a semicircle of boughs or small trees, cut and set in the ground leafless. In the centre burns a great fire, and hard by are the graves. The ceremony begins at evening and lasts till daybreak. As darkness falls, men and women sit on the graves and wail for the dead of the year. Then they dance round the fire with frenzied yells and whoops, casting from time to time the offerings into the flames. All must be consumed before the first faint streaks of dawn glimmer in the East.[3] The Choctaws used to have a great respect for their dead. They did not bury their bodies but laid them on biers made of bark and supported by forked sticks about fifteen feet high.

Annual festivals of the dead among the Indians of California.

Annual festivals of the dead among the Choctaws and Pueblo Indians.

---

[1] S. Powers, *Tribes of California* (Washington, 1877), pp. 328, 355, 356, 384.

[2] Kostromitonow, "Bemerkungen über die Indianer in Ober-Kalifornien," in K. F. v. Baer and Gr. v. Helmersen's *Beiträge zur Kenntniss des russischen Reiches*, i. (St. Petersburg, 1839) pp. 88 *sq.* The natives of the western islands of Torres Straits used to hold a great death-dance at which disguised men personated the ghosts of the lately deceased, mimicking their characteristic gait and gestures. Women and children were supposed to take these mummers for real ghosts. See A. C. Haddon, in *Reports of the Cambridge Anthropological Expedition to Torres Straits*, v. (Cambridge, 1904) pp. 252-256; *The Belief in Immortality and the Worship of the Dead*, i. 176 *sqq.*

[3] S. Powers, *Tribes of California*, pp. 437 *sq.*

When the worms had consumed the flesh, the skeleton was dismembered, any remains of muscles and sinews were buried, and the bones were deposited in a box, the skull being reddened with ochre. The box containing the bones was then carried to the common burial ground. In the early days of November the tribe celebrated a great festival which they called the Festival of the Dead or of the Souls; every family then gathered in the common burial ground, and there with weeping and lamentation visited the boxes which contained the mouldering relics of their dead. On returning from the graveyard they held a great banquet, which ended the festival.[1] Some of the Pueblo Indians of New Mexico " believe that on a certain day (in August, I think) the dead rise from their graves and flit about the neighbouring hills, and on that day all who have lost friends carry out quantities of corn, bread, meat, and such other good things of this life as they can obtain, and place them in the haunts frequented by the dead, in order that the departed spirits may once more enjoy the comforts of this nether world. They have been encouraged in this belief by the priests, who were in the habit of sending out and appropriating to themselves all these things, and then making the poor simple Indians believe that the dead had eaten them."[2]

Annual festival of the dead among the Miztecs of Mexico.

The Miztecs of Mexico believed that the souls of the dead came back in the twelfth month of every year, which corresponded to our November. On this day of All Souls the houses were decked out to welcome the spirits. Jars of food and drink were set on a table in the principal room, and the family went forth with torches to meet the ghosts and invite them to enter. Then returning themselves to the house they knelt around the table, and with eyes bent on the ground prayed the souls to accept of the offerings and to procure the blessings of the gods upon the family. Thus they remained on bended knees and with downcast eyes till the morning, not daring to look at the table lest they

[1] Bossu, *Nouveaux Voyages aux Indes Occidentales* (Paris, 1768), ii. 95 *sq.*
[2] T. G. S. Ten Broeck, in H. R. Schoolcraft's *Indian Tribes of the* *United States* (Philadelphia, 1853–1856), iv. 78. The Pueblo village to which the writer particularly refers is Laguna.

should offend the spirits by spying on them at their meal. With the first beams of the sun they rose, glad at heart. The jars of food which had been presented to the dead were given to the poor or deposited in a secret place.[1] The Indians of Santiago Tepehuacan believe that the souls of their dead return to them on the night of the eighteenth of October, the festival of St. Luke, and they sweep the roads in order that the ghosts may find them clean on their passage.[2]

Again, the natives of Sumba, an East Indian island, celebrate a New Year's festival, which is at the same time a festival of the dead. The graves are in the middle of the village, and at a given moment all the people repair to them and raise a loud weeping and wailing. Then after indulging for a short time in the national pastimes they disperse to their houses, and every family calls upon its dead to come back. The ghosts are believed to hear and accept the invitation. Accordingly betel and areca nuts are set out for them. Victims, too, are sacrificed in front of every house, and their hearts and livers are offered with rice to the dead. After a decent interval these portions are distributed amongst the living, who consume them and banquet gaily on flesh and rice, a rare event in their frugal lives. Then they play, dance, and sing to their heart's content, and the festival which began so lugubriously ends by being the merriest of the year. A little before daybreak the invisible guests take their departure. All the people turn out of their houses to escort them a little way. Holding in one hand the half of a coco-nut, which contains a small packet of provisions for the dead, and in the other hand a piece of smouldering wood, they march in procession, singing a drawling song to the accompaniment of a gong and waving the lighted brands in time to the music. So they move through the darkness till with the last words of the song

Annual festival of the dead in Sumba.

---

[1] Brasseur de Bourbourg, *Histoire des nations civilisées du Mexique et de l'Amérique - Centrale* (Paris, 1857–1859), iii. 23 *sq.* ; H. H. Bancroft, *Native Races of the Pacific States* (London, 1875–1876), ii. 623. Similar customs are still practised by the Indians of a great part of Mexico and Central America (Brasseur de Bourbourg, *op. cit.* iii. 24, note [1]).

[2] " Lettre du curé de Santiago Tepehuacan à son évêque," *Bulletin de la Société de Géographie* (Paris), IIme Série, ii. (1834) p. 179.

they throw away the coco-nuts and the brands in the direction of the spirit-land, leaving the ghosts to wend their way thither, while they themselves return to the village.[1]

Annual festival of the dead in Kiriwina.

In Kiriwina, one of the Trobriand Islands, to the east of New Guinea, the spirits of the ancestors are believed to revisit their native village in a body once a year after the harvest has been got in. At this time the men perform special dances, the people openly display their valuables, spread out on platforms, and great feasts are made for the spirits. On a certain night, when the moon is at the full, all the people raise a great shout and so drive away the spirits to the spirit land.[2]

Festival of the dead among the Sea Dyaks of Borneo.

The Sea Dyaks of Borneo celebrate a great festival in honour of the dead at irregular intervals, it may be one or more years after the death of a particular person. All who have died since the last feast was held, and have not yet been honoured by such a celebration, are remembered at this time ; hence the number of persons commemorated may be great, especially if many years have elapsed since the last commemoration service. The preparations last many weeks : food and drink and all other necessaries are stored in plenty, and the whole neighbourhood for miles round is invited to attend. On the eve of the feast the women take bamboo splints and fashion out of them little models of various useful articles, and these models are hung over the graves for the use of the dead in the other world. If the feast is held in honour of a man, the things manufactured in his behoof will take the form of a bamboo gun, a shield, a war-cap, and so on ; if it is a woman who is commemorated, little models of a loom, a fish-basket, a winnowing-fan and such like things will be provided for her spirit ; and if it is a child for whom the rite is performed, toys of various kinds will be made ready for the childish ghost. Finally, to stay the appetite of ghosts who may be too sharp-set to wait for the formal banquet in the house,

[1] S. Roos, " Bijdrage tot de kennis van taal, land en volk op het eiland Soemba," *Verhandelingen van het Bataviaasch Genootschap van Kunsten en Wetenschappen*, xxxvi. (1872) pp. 63-65.

[2] Rev. S. B. Fellows, quoted by George Brown, D.D., *Melanesians and Polynesians* (London, 1910), p. 237.

a supply of victuals is very considerately placed outside the house on which the hungry spirits may fall to without delay. The dead arrive in a boat from the other world ; for living Dyaks generally travel by river, from which it necessarily follows that Dyak ghosts do so likewise. The ship in which the ghostly visitors voyage to the land of the living is not much to look at, being in appearance nothing but a tiny boat made out of a bamboo which has been used to cook rice. Even this is not set floating on the river but is simply thrown away under the house. Yet through the incantations uttered by the professional wailing-woman the bark is wafted away to the spirit world and is there converted into a large war-canoe. Gladly the ghosts embark and sail away as soon as the final summons comes. It always comes in the evening, for it is then that the wailer begins to croon her mournful ditties ; but the way is so long that the spirits do not arrive in the house till the day is breaking. To refresh them after their weary journey a bamboo full of rice-spirit awaits them ; and this they partake of by deputy, for a brave old man, who does not fear the face of ghosts, quaffs the beverage in their stead amid the joyful shouts of the spectators. On the morning after the feast the living pay the last offices of respect to the dead. Monuments made of ironwood, the little bamboo articles, and food of all kinds are set upon the graves. In consideration of these gifts the ghosts now relinquish all claims on their surviving relatives, and henceforth earn their own living by the sweat of their brow. Before they take their final departure they come to eat and drink in the house for the last time.[1]

Thus the Dyak festival of the dead is not an annual welcome accorded to all the souls of ancestors ; it is a propitiatory ceremony designed to secure once for all the eternal welfare of the recently departed, or at least to prevent their ghosts from returning to infest and importune the living. The same is perhaps the intention of the " soul departure " (*Kathi Kasham*) festival which the Tangkul

Annual festival of the dead among the Nagas of Manipur.

---

[1] E. H. Gomes, *Seventeen Years among the Sea Dyaks of Borneo* (London, 1911), pp. 216-218. For another and briefer account of this festival see *The Scapegoat*, p. 154.

Nagas of Manipur, in Assam, celebrate every year about the end of January. At this great feast the dead are represented by living men, chosen on the ground of their likeness to the departed, who are decked with ornaments and treated as if they were in truth the deceased persons come to life again. In that character they dance together in· the large open space of the village, they are fed by the female relations, and they go from house to house, receiving presents of cloth. The festival lasts ten days, but the great day is the ninth. Huge torches of pinewood are made ready to be used that evening when darkness has fallen. The time of departure of the dead is at hand. Their living representatives are treated to a last meal in the houses, and they distribute farewell presents to the sorrowing kinsfolk, who have come to bid them good-bye. When the sun has set, a procession is formed. At the head of it march men holding aloft the flaring, sputtering torches. Then follow the elders armed and in martial array, and behind them stalk the representatives of the dead, with the relations of the departed crowding and trooping about them. Slowly and mournfully the sad procession moves, with loud lamentations, through the darkness to a spot at the north end of the village which is overshadowed by a great tree. The light of the torches is to guide the souls of the dead to their place of rest; the warlike array of the elders is to guard them from the perils and dangers of the way. At the village boundary the procession stops and the torch-bearers throw down their torches. At the same moment the spirits of the dead are believed to pass into the dying flambeaux and in that guise to depart to the far country. There is therefore no further need for their living representatives, who are accordingly stripped of all their finery on the spot. When the people return home, each family is careful to light a pine torch and set it burning on a stone in the house just inside the front door ; this they do as a precaution to prevent their own souls from following the spirits of the dead to the other world. The expense of thus despatching the dead to their long home is very great ; when the head of a family dies, debts may be incurred and rice-fields and houses sold to defray the cost of carriage. Thus the living impoverish themselves in order to enrich the dead.[1]

The Oraons or Uraons of Bengal feast their dead every year on a day in January. This ceremony is called the Great Marriage, because by it the bones of the deceased are believed to be mysteriously reunited to each other. The Oraons treat the bones of the dead differently according to the dates of their death in the agricultural year. The bones of those who died before the seeds have sprouted in the fields are burnt, and the few charred bones which have not been reduced to ashes are gathered in an earthen pot. With the bones in the pot are placed offerings of rice, native gin, and money, and then they carry the urn to the river, where the bones of their forefathers repose. But the bones of all who die after the seeds have sprung up and before the end of harvest may not be taken to the river, because the people believe that were that to be done the crops would suffer. These bones are therefore put away in a pot under a stone near the house till the harvest is over. Then on the appointed day in January they are all collected. A banquet is given in honour of the dead, and then both men and women form a procession to accompany the bones to their last resting-place in the sands of the river. But first the relics of mortality are carried from house to house in the village, and each family pours rice and gin into the urn which contains the bones of its dead. Then the procession sets out for the river, men and women dancing, singing, beating drums, and weeping, while the earthen pots containing the bones are passed from hand to hand and dance with the jigging steps of the dancers. When they are yet some way from the spot, the bearers of the urns run forward and bury them in the sand of the river. When the rest come up, they all bathe and the Great Marriage is over.[2]

Annual festival of the dead among the Oraons of Bengal.

[1] Rev. Wm. Pettigrew, "Kathi Kasham, the 'Soul Departure' feast as practised by the Tangkkul Nagas, Manipur, Assam," *Journal and Proceedings of the Asiatic Society of Bengal*, N.S. vol. v. 1909 (Calcutta, 1910), pp. 37-46; T. C. Hodson, *The Naga Tribes of Manipur* (London, 1911), pp. 153-158.

[2] Rev. P. Dehon, S.J., "Religion and Customs of the Uraons," *Memoirs of the Asiatic Society of Bengal*, vol. i. No. 9 (Calcutta, 1906), p. 136. Compare Rev. F. Hahn, "Some Notes on the Religion and Superstition of the Orāõs," *Journal of the Asiatic Society of Bengal*, lxxii. Part iii. (Calcutta, 1904) pp. 12 *sq.* According to the latter

Annual festival of the dead in Bilaspore.

In the Bilaspore district of the Central Provinces, India, " the festival known as the Fortnight of the Manes—*Pitr Pāk*—occurs about September. It is believed that during this fortnight it is the practice of all the departed to come and visit their relatives. The homes are therefore cleaned, and the spaces in front of the house are plastered and painted in order to be pleasing to those who are expected. It is believed that the departed will return on the very date on which they went away. A father who left on the fourth, be it the fourth of the dark half or the light half of the moon, will return to visit his family on the fourth of the Fortnight of the Manes. On that day cakes are prepared, and with certain ceremony these are offered to the unseen hovering spirit. Their implicit belief is that the spirit will partake of the essence of the food, and that which remains— the material portion—may be eaten by members of the family. The souls of women, it is said, will all come on the ninth of the fortnight. On the thirteenth come those who have met with a violent death and who lost their lives by a fall, by snake-bite, or any other unusual cause. During the Fortnight of the Manes a woman is not supposed to put on new bangles and a man is not permitted to shave. In short, this is a season of sad remembrances, an annual festival for the departed." [1]

Annual festival of the dead among the Bghais and Hkamies.

The Bghais, a Karen tribe of Burma, hold an annual feast for the dead at the new moon which falls near the end of August or the beginning of September. All the villagers who have lost relatives within the last three years take part in it. Food and drink are set out on tables for the ghosts, and new clothes for them are hung up in the room. All being ready, the people beat gongs and begin to weep. Each one calls upon the relation whom he has lost to come and eat. When the dead are thought to have arrived, the

---

writer the pots containing the relics of the dead are buried, not in the sand of the river, but in a pit, generally covered with huge stones, which is dug for the purpose in some field or grove.

[1] E. M. Gordon, *Indian Folk Tales* (London, 1908), p. 18. According to Mr. W. Crooke, the Hindoo Feast of Lamps (*Diwâlî*) seems to have been based on "the idea that on this night the spirits of the dead revisit their homes, which are cleaned and lighted for their reception." See W. Crooke, *The Popular Religion and Folk-lore of Northern India* (Westminster, 1896), ii. 295 *sq.*

living address them, saying, " You have come to me, you have returned to me. It has been raining hard, and you must be wet. Dress yourselves, clothe yourselves with these new garments, and all the companions that are with you. Eat betel together with all that accompany you, all your friends and associates, and the long dead. Call them all to eat and drink." The ghosts having finished their repast, the people dry their tears and sit down to eat what is left. More food is then prepared and put into a basket, and at cock-crow next morning the contents of the basket are thrown out of the house, while the living weep and call upon their dead as before.[1] The Hkamies, a hill tribe of North Aracan, hold an important festival every year in honour of departed spirits. It falls after harvest and is called "the opening of the house of the dead." When a person dies and has been burnt, the ashes are collected and placed in a small house in the forest together with his spear or gun, which has first been broken. These little huts are generally arranged in groups near a village, and are sometimes large enough to be mistaken for one. After harvest all the relations of the deceased cook various kinds of food and take them with pots of liquor distilled from rice to the village of the dead. There they open the doors of the houses, and having placed the food and drink inside they shut them again. After that they weep, eat, drink, and return home.[2]

The great festival of the dead in Cambodia takes place on the last day of the month Phatrabot (September-October), but ever since the moon began to wane everybody has been busy preparing for it. In every house cakes and sweetmeats are set out, candles burn, incense sticks smoke, and the whole is offered to the ancestral shades with an invocation which is thrice repeated : " O all you our ancestors who are departed, deign to come and eat what we have prepared

Annual festival of the dead in Cambodia.

[1] Rev. F. Mason, D.D., "Physical Character of the Karens," *Journal of the Asiatic Society of Bengal*, 1866, Part ii. pp. 29 *sq.* Lights are not mentioned by the writer, but the festival being nocturnal we may assume that they are used for the convenience of the living as well as of the dead. In other respects the ceremonies are typical.

[2] R. F. St. Andrew St. John, "A Short Account of the Hill Tribes of North Aracan," *Journal of the Anthropological Institute*, ii. (1873) p. 238. At this festival the dead are apparently not supposed to return to the houses.

for you, and to bless your posterity and make it happy."
Fifteen days afterwards many little boats are made of bark
and filled with rice, cakes, small coins, smoking incense
sticks, and lighted candles. At evening these are set floating on the river, and the souls of the dead embark in them
to return to their own place. The living now bid them
farewell. "Go to the lands," they say, "go to the fields
you inhabit, to the mountains, under the stones which are
your abodes. Go away! return! In due time your sons
and your grandsons will think of you. Then you will
return, you will return, you will return." The river is now
covered with twinkling points of fire. But the current soon
bears them away, and as they vanish one by one in the
darkness the souls depart with them to the far country.[1]

Annual festival of the dead in Tonquin.

In Tonquin, as in Sumba, the dead revisit their kinsfolk
and their old homes at the New Year. From the hour of
midnight, when the New Year begins, no one dares to shut
the door of his house for fear of excluding the ghosts, who
begin to arrive at that time. Preparations have been made
to welcome and refresh them after their long journey. Beds
and mats are ready for their weary bodies to repose upon,
water to wash their dusty feet, slippers to comfort them, and
canes to support their feeble steps. Candles burn on the
domestic altar, and pastilles diffuse a fragrant odour. The
people bow before the unseen visitors and beseech them to
remember and bless their descendants in the coming year.
Having discharged this pious duty they abstain from sweeping the houses for three days lest the dust should incom-
mode the ghosts.[2]

Annual festival of the dead in Annam.

In Annam one of the most important festivals of the
year is the festival of Têt, which falls on the first three days
of the New Year. It is devoted to the worship of ancestors.
Everybody, even the poorest, must provide a good meal for
the souls of his dead at this time and must himself eat and

[1] E. Aymonier, *Notice sur le Cambodge* (Paris, 1875), p. 59 ; A. Leclère, *Le Buddhisme au Cambodge* (Paris, 1899), pp. 374-376. The departure of the souls is described only by the latter writer. Compare E. Aymonier, "Notes sur les coutumes et croyances superstitieuses des Cambodgiens," *Cochinchine Française, Excursions et Reconnaissances*, No. 16 (Saigon, 1883), pp. 205 *sq.*

[2] Mariny, *Relation nouvelle et curieuse des royaumes de Tunquin et de Lao* (Paris, 1666), pp. 251-253.

drink heartily. Some families, in order to discharge this pious duty, run into debt for the whole year. In the houses everything is put in order, washed, and scoured for the reception of the dear and distinguished guests. A tall bamboo pole is set up in the front of every house and allowed to stand there for seven days. A small basket containing areca, betel, and leaves of gilt paper is fastened to the pole. The erection of the pole is a sacred rite which no family omits to perform, though why they do so few people can say. Some, however, allege that the posts are intended to guide the ancestral spirits to their old homes. The ceremony of the reception of the shades takes place at nightfall on the last day of the year. The house of the head of the family is then decked with flowers, and in the room which serves as a domestic chapel the altar of the ancestors is surrounded with flowers, among which the lotus, the emblem of immortality, is most conspicuous. On a table are set red candles, perfumes, incense, sandal-wood, and plates full of bananas, oranges, and other fruits. The relations crouch before the altar, and kneeling at the foot of it the head of the house invokes the name of the family which he represents. Then in solemn tones he recites an incantation, mentioning the names of his most illustrious ancestors and marking time with the strokes of a hammer upon a gong, while crackers are exploded outside the room. After that, he implores the ancestral shades to protect their descendants and invites them to a repast, which is spread for them on a table. Round this table he walks, serving the invisible guests with his own hands. He distributes to them smoking balls of rice in little china saucers, and pours tea or spirits into each little cup, while he murmurs words of invitation and compliment. When the ghosts have eaten and drunk their fill, the head of the family returns to the altar and salutes them for the last time. Finally, he takes leaves of yellow paper, covered with gold and silver spangles, and throws them into a brazier placed at the foot of the ancestral tablets. These papers represent imaginary bars of gold and silver which the living send to the dead. Cardboard models of houses, furniture, jewels, clothes, of everything in short that the ghosts can need in the other world, are despatched to them in like manner in the flames. Then the family sits down to table and feasts on the remains of the ghostly banquet.[1]

Annual festival of friendless ghosts in Annam.

But in Annam it is not merely the spirits of ancestors who are thus feasted and supplied with all the necessaries of life. The poor ghosts of those who died without leaving descendants or whose bodies were left unburied are not forgotten by the pious Annamites. But these spirits come round at a different time of year from the others. The seventh month of the year is set apart for expiatory sacrifices destined to benefit these unhappy beings, and that is why in Annam nobody should marry or be betrothed in that month. The great day of the month is the fifteenth, which is called the Festival of the Souls. On that day the ghosts in question are set free by the lord of the underworld, and they come prowling about among the living. They are exceedingly dangerous, especially to children. Hence in order to appease their wrath and prevent them from entering the houses every family takes care to put out offerings for them in the street. Before every house on that night you may see candles lighted, paper garments of many colours, paper hats, paper boots, paper furniture, ingots of gold and silver paper, all hanging in tempting array from a string, while plates of food and cups of tea and rice-spirit stand ready for the use of hungry and thirsty souls. The theory is that the ghosts will be so busy consuming the victuals, appropriating the deceitful riches, and trying on the paper coats, hats, and boots that they will have neither the leisure nor the inclination to intrude upon the domestic circle indoors. At seven o'clock in the evening fire is put to the offerings, and the paper wardrobe, furniture, and money soon vanish crackling in the flames. At the same moment, peeping in at a door or window, you may see the domestic ancestral altar brilliantly illuminated. As for the food, it is supposed to be thrown on the fire or on the ground for the

---

[1] Le R. P. Cadière, "Coutumes populaires de la vallée du Nguôn-So'n," Bulletin de l'École Française d'Extrême-Orient, ii. (Hanoi, 1902) pp. 376-379 ; P. d'Enjoy, "Du droit successoral en Annam," etc., Bulletins de la Société d'Anthropologie de Paris, Ve Série, iv. (1903) pp. 500-502 ; E. Diguet, Les Annamites (Paris, 1906), pp. 372-375.

use of the ghosts, but practically it is eaten by vagabonds and beggars, who scuffle for the booty.[1]

In Cochinchina the ancestral spirits are similarly pro- Annual pitiated and fed on the first day of the New Year. The festivals of the dead in tablets which represent them are placed on the domestic Cochin- altar, and the family prostrate themselves before these china, Siam and emblems of the departed. The head of the family lights Japan. sticks of incense on the altar and prays the shades of his forefathers to accept the offerings and be favourable to their descendants. With great gravity he waits upon the ghosts, passing dishes of food before the ancestral tablets and pouring out wine and tea to slake the thirst of the spirits. When the dead are supposed to be satisfied with the shadowy essence of the food, the living partake of its gross material substance.[2] In Siam and Japan also the souls of the dead revisit their families for three days in every year, and the lamps which the Japanese kindle in multitudes on that occasion to light the spirits on their way have procured for the festival the name of the Feast of Lanterns. It is to be observed that in Siam, as in Tonquin and Sumba, the return of the ghosts takes place at the New Year.[3]

The Chewsurs of the Caucasus believe that the souls of Annual the departed revisit their old homes on the Saturday night festivals of the dead of the second week in Lent. This gathering of the dead among the is called the "Assembly of Souls." The people spare no Chewsurs and expense to treat the unseen guests handsomely. Beer is Armenians. brewed and loaves of various shapes baked specially for the occasion.[4] The Armenians celebrate the memory of the dead on many days of the year, burning incense and lighting tapers in their honour. One of their customs is to keep a "light of the dead" burning all night in the house in order that the ghosts may be able to enter. For if the

[1] E. Diguet, *Les Annamites* (Paris, 1906), pp. 254 *sq.* ; Paul Giran, *Magie et Religion Annamites* (Paris, 1912), pp. 258 *sq.* According to the latter writer the offerings to the vagrant souls are made on the first and last days of the month, while sacrifices of a more domestic character are performed on the fifteenth.

[2] L. E. Louvet, *La Cochinchine religieuse* (Paris, 1885), pp. 149-151.

[3] *The Scapegoat*, pp. 149 *sqq.*

[4] C. v. Hahn, " Religiöse Anschauungen und Totengedächtnisfeier der Chewsuren," *Globus*, lxxvi. (1899) pp. 211 *sq.*

spirits find the house dark, they spit down the chimney and depart, cursing the churlish inmates.[1]

Early in April every year the Dahomans of West Africa " set a table, as they term it, and invite friends to eat with the deceased relatives, whose spirits are supposed to move round and partake of the good things of this life. Even my interpreter, Madi-Ki Lemon, who pretends to despise the belief in fetish, sets a table to his ancestors, and will tell you that his grand- or great-grandfather, Corporal Lemon, makes a meal on this occasion which will last him till the next annual feast." [2] The Barea and apparently the Kunama, two heathen tribes who lead a settled agricultural life to the north of Abyssinia, celebrate every year a festival in the month of November. It is a festival of thanksgiving for the completion of the harvest, and at the same time a commemoration and propitiation of the dead. Every house prepares much beer for the occasion, and a small pot of beer is set out for each deceased member of the household. After standing for two days in the house the beer which was devoted to the dead is drunk by the living. At these festivals all the people of a district meet in a special place, and there pass the time in games and dances. Among the Barea the festive gatherings are held in a sacred grove. We are told that " he who owes another a drubbing on this day can pay his debt with impunity ; for it is a day of peace when all feuds are in abeyance." Wild honey may not be gathered till the festival has been held.[3] Apparently the festival is a sort of Saturnalia, such as is celebrated elsewhere at the end of harvest.[4] At that season there is food and to spare for the dead as well as the living.

[1] M. Abeghian, *Der armenische Volksglaube* (Leipsic, 1899), pp. 23 *sq.*

[2] Fred. E. Forbes, *Dahomey and the Dahomans* (London, 1851), ii. 73. Compare John Duncan, *Travels in Western Africa* (London, 1847), i. 125 *sq.*; A. B. Ellis, *The Ewe-speaking Peoples of the Slave Coast* (London, 1890), p. 108. The Tshi-speaking peoples of the Gold Coast and Ashantee celebrate an annual festival of eight days in honour of the dead. It falls towards the end of August. The offerings are presented to the departed at their graves. See A. B. Ellis, *The Tshi-speaking Peoples of the Gold Coast* (London, 1887), pp. 227 *sq.*; E. Perregaux, *Chez les Achanti* (Neuchâtel, 1908), pp. 136, 138. According to the latter writer the festival is celebrated at the time of the yam harvest.

[3] W. Munzinger, *Ostafrikanische Studien* (Schaffhausen, 1864), p. 473.

[4] *The Scapegoat*, pp. 136 *sq.*

Among peoples of the Aryan stock, so far back as we Annual can trace their history, the worship and propitiation of the festivals of the dead dead seem to have formed a principal element of the popular among religion ;[1] and like so many other races they appear to have peoples of the Aryan believed that once a year the souls of their departed kinsfolk stock. revisited their old homes and expected to be refreshed with abundance of good cheer by their surviving relations. This belief gave rise to the custom of celebrating an annual Feast of All Souls, which has come down to us from a dateless antiquity and is still observed year by year, with rites of primitive simplicity, in some parts of Europe. Such a Annual festival was held every year in spring by the old Iranians. festival of the dead The celebration fell at the end of the year and lasted ten (the Fra- days, namely the last five days of the last month and the five vashis) following supplementary days, which were regularly inserted among to make up a year of three hundred and sixty-five days ; for Iranians. the old Iranian, like the old Egyptian, year was a vague year of twelve months of thirty days each, with five supplementary days added at the end for the sake of bringing it into apparent, though not real, harmony with the sun's annual course in the sky. According to one calculation the ten days of the festival corresponded to the last days of February, but according to another they fell in March ; in later ages the Parsees assigned them to the time of the spring equinox. The name of the festival was Hamaspathmaedaya.[2] From a passage in the *Zend-Avesta*, the

[1] On the worship of the dead, and especially of ancestors, among Aryan peoples, see W. Caland, *Über Totenverehrung bei einigen der indo-germanischen Völker* (Amsterdam, 1888) ; O. Schrader, *Reallexikon der indogermanischen Altertumskunde* (Strasburg, 1901), pp. 21 *sqq.* ; *id., s.v.* " Aryan Religion," in Dr. J. Hastings's *Encyclopaedia of Religion and Ethics*, ii. (Edinburgh, 1909) pp. 16 *sqq.*

[2] As to the Iranian calendar see W. Geiger, *Altiranische Kultur im Altertum* (Erlangen, 1882), pp. 314 *sqq.* ; as to the Iranian worship of the sainted dead (the Fravashis) see *id.* pp. 286 *sqq.* As to the annual festival of the dead (Hamaspathmaedaya) see W. Caland, *Über Totenverehrung bei*

einigen der indo-germanischen Völker (Amsterdam, 1888), pp. 64 *sq.* ; N. Söderblom, *Les Fravashis* (Paris, 1899), pp. 4 *sqq.* ; J. H. Moulton, *Early Zoroastrianism* (London, 1913), pp. 256 *sqq.* All these writers agree that the Fravashis of the *Zend-Avesta* were originally the souls of the dead. See also James Darmesteter, *Zend-Avesta*, Part ii. (Oxford, 1883) p. 179 : " The Fravashi is the inner power in every being that maintains it and makes it grow and subsist. Originally the Fravashis were the same as the *Pitris* of the Hindus or the *Manes* of the Latins, that is to say, the everlasting and deified souls of the dead ; but in course of time they gained a wider domain, and not only men, but gods

ancient sacred book of the Iranians, we learn that on the ten nights of the festival the souls of the dead (the Fravashis) were believed to go about the village asking the people to do them reverence, to pray to them, to meditate on them, and to furnish them with meat and clothes, while at the same time they promised that blessings should rest on the pious householder who complied with their request.[1] The Arab geographer Albiruni, who flourished about the year one thousand of our era, tells us that among the Persians of his time the last five days of the month Aban were called Farwardajan. " During this time," he says, " people put food in the halls of the dead and drink on the roofs of the houses, believing that the spirits of their dead during these days come out from the places of their reward or their punishment, that they go to the dishes laid out for them, imbibe their strength and suck their taste. They fumigate their houses with juniper, that the dead may enjoy its smell. The spirits of the pious men dwell among their families, children, and relations, and occupy themselves with their affairs, although invisible to them." He adds that there was a controversy among the Persians as to the date of this festival of the dead, some maintaining that the five days during which it lasted were the last five days of the month Aban, whereas others held that they were the five supplementary days which were inserted between the months Aban and Adhar. The dispute, he continues, was settled by the adoption of all ten days for the celebration of the feast.[2]

Annual festival of the dead among the Persians.

---

and even physical objects, like the sky and the earth, etc., had each a Fravashi." Compare *id.*, *Ormazd et Ahriman* (Paris, 1877), pp. 130 *sqq.* ; N. Söderblom, *La Vie Future d'après Le Mazdéisme* (Paris, 1901), pp. 7 *sqq.* A different view of the original nature of the Fravashis was taken by C. P. Tiele, according to whom they were essentially guardian spirits. See C. P. Tiele, *Geschichte der Religion im Altertum* (Gotha, 1896–1903), ii. 256 *sqq.*

[1] *The Zend-Avesta*, translated by James Darmesteter, Part ii. (Oxford, 1883) pp. 192 *sq.* (*Sacred Books of the East*, vol. xxiii.).

[2] Albiruni, *The Chronology of Ancient Nations*, translated and edited by Dr. C. Edward Sachau (London, 1879), p. 210. In the *Dinkard*, a Pahlavi work which seems to have been composed in the first half of the ninth century A.D., the festival is spoken of as "those ten days which are the end of the winter and termination of the year, because the five Gathic days, among them, are for that purpose." By "the five Gathic days" the writer means the five supplementary days added at the end of the twelfth month to complete the year of 365 days. See *Pahlavi Texts* translated by E. W. West, Part iv. (Oxford, 1892) p. 17 (*The Sacred Books of the East*, vol. xxxvii.).

Similar beliefs as to the annual return of the dead sur- vive to this day in many parts of Europe and find expression in similar customs. The day of the dead or of All Souls, as we call it, is commonly the second of November. Thus in Lower Brittany the souls of the departed come to visit the living on the eve of that day. After vespers are over, the priests and choir walk in procession, "the procession of the charnel-house," chanting a weird dirge in the Breton tongue. Then the people go home, gather round the fire, and talk of the departed. The housewife covers the kitchen table with a white cloth, sets out cider, curds, and hot pancakes on it, and retires with the family to rest. The fire on the hearth is kept up by a huge log known as "the log of the dead" (*kef ann Anaon*). Soon doleful voices outside in the darkness break the stillness of night. It is the "singers of death" who go about the streets waking the sleepers by a wild and melancholy song, in which they remind the living in their comfortable beds to pray for the poor souls in pain. All that night the dead warm themselves at the hearth and feast on the viands prepared for them. Sometimes the awe-struck listeners hear the stools creaking in the kitchen, or the dead leaves outside rustling under the ghostly footsteps.[1] In the Vosges Mountains on All Souls' Eve the solemn sound of the church bells invites good Christians to pray for the repose of the dead. While the bells are ringing, it is customary in some families to uncover the beds and open the windows, doubtless in order to let the poor souls enter and rest. No one that evening would dare to remain deaf to the appeal of the bells. The prayers are prolonged to a late hour of the night. When the last *De profundis* has been uttered, the head of the family gently covers up the beds, sprinkles them with holy water, and shuts the windows. In some villages fire is kept up on the hearth and a basket of nuts is placed beside it for the use of the ghosts.[2] Again, in some parts of Saintonge and Aunis a Candlemas candle used to be lit before the domestic

---

[1] A. le Braz, *La Légende de la Morten Basse-Bretagne* (Paris, 1893), pp. 280-287. Compare J. Lecœur, *Esquisses du Bocage Normand* (Condé-sur-Noir-

eau, 1883–1887), ii. 283 *sqq.*
[2] L. F. Sauvé, *Le folk-lore des Hautes-Vosges* (Paris, 1889), pp. 295 *sq.*

crucifix on All Souls' Day at the very hour when the last
member of the family departed this life ; and some people,
just as in Tonquin, refrained from sweeping the house that
day lest they should thereby disturb the ghostly visitors.[1]

Feast of
All Souls
in Belgium.
In Bruges, Dinant, and other towns of Belgium holy
candles burn all night in the houses on the Eve of All
Souls, and the bells toll till midnight, or even till morning.
People, too, often set lighted candles on the graves. At
Scherpenheuvel the houses are illuminated, and the people
walk in procession carrying lighted candles in their hands.
A very common custom in Belgium is to eat " soul-cakes "
or " soul-bread " on the eve or the day of All Souls. The
eating of them is believed to benefit the dead in some way.
Perhaps originally, as among the Esquimaux of Alaska to
this day,[2] the ghosts were thought to enter into the bodies
of their relatives and so to share the victuals which the
survivors consumed. Similarly at festivals in honour of the
dead in Northern India it is customary to feed Brahmans,
and the food which these holy men partake of is believed
to pass to the deceased and to refresh their languid spirits.[3]
The same idea of eating and drinking by proxy may perhaps
partly explain many other funeral feasts. Be that as it may,
at Dixmude and elsewhere in Belgium they say that you
deliver a soul from Purgatory for every cake you eat. At
Antwerp they give a local colour to the soul-cakes by baking
them with plenty of saffron, the deep yellow tinge being suggestive of the flames of Purgatory. People in Antwerp at
the same season are careful not to slam doors or windows
for fear of hurting the ghosts.[4]

Feast of
All Souls in
Lechrain.
In Lechrain, a district of Southern Bavaria which
extends along the valley of the Lech from its source to
near the point where the river flows into the Danube, the
two festivals of All Saints and All Souls, on the first

---

[1] J. L. M. Nogués, *Les mœurs
d'autrefois en Saintonge et en Aunis*
(Saintes, 1891), p. 76. As to the
observance of All Souls' Day in other
parts of France see A. Meyrac, *Traditions, coutumes, légendes et contes des
Ardennes* (Charleville, 1890), pp. 22-
24 ; Ch. Beauquier, *Les mois en
Franche-Comté* (Paris, 1900), pp. 123-
125.

[2] Above, p. 52.

[3] W. Crooke, *The Natives of Northern India* (London, 1907), p. 219.

[4] Reinsberg-Düringsfeld, *Calendrier
Belge* (Brussels, 1861-1862), ii. 236-
240 ; *id.*, *Das festliche Jahr* (Leipsic,
1863), pp. 229 *sq.*

and second of November, have significantly fused in popular usage into a single festival of the dead. In fact, the people pay little or no heed to the saints and give all their thoughts to the souls of their departed kinsfolk. The Feast of All Souls begins immediately after vespers on All Saints' Day. Even on the eve of All Saints' Day, that is, on the thirty-first of October, which we call Hallowe'en, the graveyard is cleaned and every grave adorned. The decoration consists in weeding the mounds, sprinkling a layer of charcoal on the bare earth, and marking out patterns on it in red service-berries. The marigold, too, is still in bloom at that season in cottage gardens, and garlands of its orange blooms, mingled with other late flowers left by the departing summer, are twined about the grey mossgrown tombstones. The basin of holy water is filled with fresh water and a branch of box-wood put into it; for box-wood in the popular mind is associated with death and the dead. On the eve of All Souls' Day the people begin to visit the graves and to offer the soul-cakes to the hungry souls. Next morning, before eight o'clock, commence the vigil, the requiem, and the solemn visitation of the graves. On that day every household offers a plate of meal, oats, and spelt on a side-altar in the church; while in the middle of the sacred edifice a bier is set, covered with a pall, and surrounded by lighted tapers and vessels of holy water. The tapers burnt on that day and indeed generally in services for the departed are red. In the evening people go, whenever they can do so, to their native village, where their dear ones lie in the churchyard; and there at the graves they pray for the poor souls, and leave an offering of soul-cakes also on a side-altar in the church. The soul-cakes are baked of dough in the shape of a coil of hair and are made of all sizes up to three feet long. They form a perquisite of the sexton.[1]

The custom of baking soul-cakes, sometimes called simply " souls," on All Souls' Day is widespread in Southern Germany and Austria;[2] everywhere, we may assume, the cakes were originally intended for the benefit of the hungry dead, though

Soul-cakes and All Souls' Day in Southern Germany.

[1] Karl Freiherr von Leoprechting, *Aus dem Lechrain* (Munich, 1855), pp. 198-200.

[2] O. Freiherr von Reinsberg-Düringsfeld, *Das festliche Jahr* (Leipsic, 1863), p. 330. As to these cakes

they are often eaten by the living.   In the Upper Palatinate people throw food into the fire on All Souls' Day for the poor souls, set lights on the table for them, and pray on bended knees for their repose.   On the graves, too, lights are kindled, vessels of holy water placed, and food deposited for the refreshment of the souls.   All over the Upper Palatinate on All Souls' Day it is also customary to bake special cakes of fine bread and distribute them to the poor,[1] who eat them perhaps as the deputies of the dead.

Feast of All Souls in Bohemia.   The Germans of Bohemia observe All Souls' Day with much solemnity.   Each family celebrates the memory of its dead.   On the eve of the day it is customary to eat cakes and to drink cold milk for the purpose of cooling the poor souls who are roasting in purgatory ; from which it appears that spirits feel the soothing effect of victuals consumed vicariously by their friends on earth.   The ringing of the church bells to prayer on that evening is believed to be the signal at which the ghosts, released from the infernal gaol, come trooping to the old familiar fire-side, there to rest from their pangs for a single night.   So in many places people fill a lamp with butter, light it, and set it on the hearth,, that with the butter the poor ghosts may anoint the burns they have received from the sulphureous and tormenting flames of purgatory.   Next morning the chime of the church bells, ringing to early mass, is the knell that bids the souls return to their place of pain ; but such as have completed their penance take flight to heaven.   So on the eve of All Saints' Day each family gathers in the parlour or the kitchen, speaks softly of those they have lost, recalls what they said and did in life, and prays for the repose of their souls.   While the prayer is being said, the children kindle little wax lights which have been specially bought for the purpose that day. Next morning the families go to church, where mass is celebrated for the dead ; then they wend their way to the

---

(called "souls") in Swabia see E. Meyer, *Deutsche Sagen, Sitten und Gebräuche aus Schwaben* (Stuttgart, 1852), p. 452, § 174 ; Anton Birlinger, *Volksthümliches aus Schwaben* (Freiburg im Breisgau, 1861-1862), ii. 167 *sq.* The cakes are baked of white

flour, and are of a longish rounded shape with two small tips at each end.

[1] Adalbert Kuhn, *Mythologische Studien*, ii. (Gütersloh, 1912) pp. 41 *sq.*, citing F. Schönwerth, *Aus der Oberpfalz*, i. 283.

churchyard, where they deck the graves of their kinsfolk with flowers and wreaths and set little lights upon them. This custom of illumining the graves and decking them with flowers on the Eve or Day of All Souls is common all over Bohemia ; it is observed in Prague as well as in the country, by Czechs as well as by Germans. In some Czech villages four-cornered cakes of a special sort, baked of white wheaten meal with milk, are eaten on All Souls' Day or given to beggars that they may pray for the dead.[1] Among the Germans of Western Bohemia poor children go from house to house on All Souls' Day, begging for soul-cakes, and when they receive them they pray God to bless all poor souls. In the southern districts every farmer used to grind a great quantity of corn against the day and to bake it into five or six hundred little black soul-cakes which he gave away to the poor who came begging for them.[2]

All Souls' Day is celebrated with similar rites by the Germans of Moravia. " The festival of the farewell to summer," says a German writer on this subject, " was held by our heathen forefathers in the beginning of November, and with the memory of the departed summer they united the memory of the departed souls, and this last has survived in the Feast of All Souls, which is everywhere observed with great piety. On the evening of All Souls the relations of the departed assemble in the churchyards and adorn the graves of their dear ones with flowers and lights, while the children kindle little wax tapers, which have been bought for them, to light the ' poor souls.' According to the popular belief, the dead go in procession to the church about mid-night, and any stout-hearted young man can there see all the living men who will die within the year." [3]

In the Tyrol the beliefs and customs are similar. There, too, " soul-lights," that is, lamps filled with lard or butter are lighted and placed on the hearth on All Souls' Eve in order that poor souls, escaped from the fires of purgatory, may smear the melted grease on their burns and so alleviate their pangs.

Feast of All Souls in Moravia.

Feast of All Souls in the Tyrol.

---

[1] O. Freiherr von Reinsberg-Düringsfeld, *Fest-Kalender aus Böhmen* (Prague, N.D.), pp. 493-495.

[2] Alois John, *Sitte, Brauch und Volksglaube im deutschen Westböhmen* (Prague, 1905), p. 97.

[3] Willibald Müller, *Beiträge zur Volkskunde der Deutschen in Mähren* (Vienna and Olmütz, 1893), p. 330.

Some people also leave milk and dough-nuts for them on the table all night. The graves also are illuminated with wax candles and decked with such a profusion of flowers that you might think it was springtime.[1]   In the Italian Tyrol it is customary to give bread or money to the poor on All Souls' Day ; in the Val di Ledro children threaten to dirty the doors of houses if they do not get the usual dole. Some rich people treat the poor to bean-soup on that day. Others put pitchers full of water in the kitchen on All Souls'

Feast of
All Souls
in Baden. night that the poor souls may slake their thirst.[2]   In Baden it is still customary to deck the graves with flowers and lights on All Saints' Day and All Souls' Day. The lights are sometimes kindled in hollow turnips, on the sides of which inscriptions are carved and shine out in the darkness. If any child steals a turnip-lantern or anything else from a grave, the indignant ghost who has been robbed appears to the thief the same night and reclaims his stolen property. A relic of the old custom of feeding the dead survives in the practice of giving soul-cakes to godchildren.[3]

Annual
festivals of
the dead
among the
Letts and
Samagi-
tians.   The Letts used to entertain and feed the souls of the dead for four weeks from Michaelmas (September 29) to the day of St. Simon and St. Jude (October 28). They called the season *Wellalaick* or *Semlicka*, and regarded it as so holy that while it lasted they would not willingly thresh the corn, alleging that grain threshed at that time would be useless for sowing, since the souls of the dead would not allow it to sprout. But we may suspect that the original motive of the abstinence was a fear lest the blows of the flails should fall upon the poor ghosts swarming in the air. At this season the people were wont to prepare food of all sorts for the spirits and set it on the floor of a room, which had been well heated and swept for the purpose. Late in the evening the master of the house went into the room, tended the fire, and called upon his dead kinsfolk by their names to come and eat and drink. If he saw the ghosts, he would die within the year ; but if

[1] Ignaz V. Zingerle, *Sitten, Bräuche und Meiningen des Tiroler Volkes*[2] (Innsbruck, 1871), pp. 176-178.

[2] Christian Schneller, *Märchen und Sagen aus Wälschtirol* (Innsbruck, 1867), p. 238.

[3] Elard Hugo Meyer, *Badisches Volksleben im neunzehnten Jahrhundert* (Strasburg, 1900), p. 601.

he did not see them he would outlive it. When he thought the souls had eaten and drunk enough, he took the staff which served as a poker and laying it on the threshold cut it in two with an axe. At the same time he bade the spirits go their way, charging them to keep to the roads and paths and not to tread upon the rye. If the crops turned out ill next year, the people laid the failure at the door of the ghosts, who fancied themselves scurvily treated and had taken their revenge by trampling down the corn.[1] The Samagitians annually invited the dead to come from their graves and enjoy a bath and a feast. For their entertainment they prepared a special hut, in which they set out food and drink, together with a seat and a napkin for every soul who had been invited. They left the souls to revel by themselves for three days in the hut; then they deposited the remains of the banquet on the graves and bade the ghosts farewell. The good things, however, were usually consumed by charcoal burners in the forest. This feast of the dead fell early in November.[2] The Esthonians prepare a meal for their dead on All Souls' Day, the second of November, and invite them by their names to come and partake of it. The ghosts arrive in the early morning at the first cock-crow, and depart at the second, being ceremoniously lighted out of the house by the head of the family, who waves a white cloth after them and bids them come again next year.[3]

In some parts of the Russian Government of Olonets the inhabitants of a village sometimes celebrate a joint festival in honour of all their dead. Having chosen a house for the purpose, they spread three tables, one outside the front door, one in the passage, and one in the room which is heated by a stove. Then they go out to meet their

Festival of the dead in Russia.

---

[1] P. Einhorn, " Historia Lettica," in *Scriptores Rerum Livonicarum*, ii. (Riga and Leipsic, 1848) pp. 587, 598, 630 *sq.*, 645 *sq.* See also the description of D. Fabricius in his " Livonicae Historiae compendiosa series," *ib.* p. 441. Fabricius assigns the custom to All Souls' Day.

[2] J. Lasicius, " De diis Samagitarum caeterorumque Sarmatarum," in

Magazin herausgegeben von der lettisch-literärischen Gesellschaft, xiv. 1. (Mitau, 1868), p. 92.

[3] F. J. Wiedemann, *Aus dem inneren und äussern Leben der Ehsten* (St. Petersburg, 1876), pp. 366 *sq.* ; Boecler-Kreutzwald, *Der Ehsten abergläubische Gebräuche, Weisen und Gewohnheiten* (St. Petersburg, 1854), p. 89.

unseen guests and usher them into the house with these words, " Ye are tired, our own ones ; take something to eat." The ghosts accordingly refresh themselves at each table in succession. Then the master of the house bids them warm themselves at the stove, remarking that they must have grown cold in the damp earth. After that the living guests sit down to eat at the tables. Towards the end of the meal the host opens the window and lets the ghosts gently out of it by means of the shroud in which they were lowered into the grave. As they slide down it from the warm room into the outer air, the people tell them, " Now it is time for you to go home, and your feet must be tired ; the way is not a little one for you to travel. Here it is softer for you. Now, in God's name, farewell ! " [1]

Annual festivals of the dead among the Votiaks of Russia.   Among the Votiaks of Russia every family sacrifices to its dead once a year in the week before Palm Sunday. The sacrifice is offered in the house about midnight. Flesh, bread, or cakes and beer are set on the table, and on the floor beside the table stands a trough of bark with a lighted wax candle stuck on the rim. The master of the house, having covered his head with his hat, takes a piece of meat in his hand and says, " Ye spirits of the long departed, guard and preserve us well. Make none of us cripples. Send no plagues upon us. Cause the corn, the wine, and the food to prosper with us." [2] The Votiaks of the Governments of Wjatka and Kasan celebrate two memorial festivals of the dead every year, one in autumn and the other in spring. On a certain day koumiss is distilled, beer brewed, and potato scones baked in every house. All the members of a clan, who trace their descent through women from one mythical ancestress, assemble in a single house, generally in one which lies at the boundary of the clan land. Here an old man moulds wax candles ; and when the requisite number is made he sticks them on the shelf of the stove, and begins to mention the dead relations of the master of the house by name. For each of them he crumbles a piece of bread,

[1] W. R. S. Ralston, *Songs of the Russian People* [2] (London, 1872), pp. 321 *sq.* The date of the festival is not mentioned. Apparently it is celebrated at irregular intervals.

[2] M. Buch, *Die Wotjäken* (Stuttgart, 1882), p. 145.

gives each of them a piece of pancake, pours koumiss and beer, and puts a spoonful of soup into a trough made for the purpose. All persons present whose parents are dead follow his example. The dogs are then allowed to eat out of the trough. If they eat quietly, it is a sign that the dead live at peace ; if they do not eat quietly, it argues the contrary. Then the company sit down to table and partake of the meal. Next morning both the dead and the living refresh themselves with a drink, and a fowl is boiled. The proceedings are the same as on the evening before. But now they treat the souls for the last time as a preparation for their journey, saying : " Eat, drink, and go home to your companions. Live at peace, be gracious to us, keep our children, guard our corn, our beasts and birds." Then the people banquet and indulge in all sorts of improprieties. The women refrain from feasting until the dead have taken their departure ; but when the souls are gone, there is no longer any motive for abstinence, the koumiss circulates freely among the women, and they grow wanton. Yet at this, as at every other festival, the men and women eat in different parts of the room.[1]

On All Saints' Day, the first of November, shops and streets in the Abruzzi are filled with candles, which people buy in order to kindle them in the evening on the graves of their relations. For all the dead come to visit their homes that night, the Eve of All Souls, and they need lights to show them the way. For their use, too, lights are kept burning in the houses all night. Before people go to sleep they place on the table a lighted lamp or candle and a frugal meal of bread and water. The dead issue from their graves and stalk in procession through every street of the village. You can see them if you stand at a cross-road with your chin resting on a forked stick. First pass the souls of the good, and then the souls of the murdered and the damned. Once, they say, a man was thus peeping at the ghastly procession. The good souls told him he had

Feast of All Souls in the Abruzzi.

---

[1] J. Wasiljev, *Übersicht über die heidnischen Gebräuche, Aberglauben und Religion der Wotjäken* (Helsingfors, 1902), pp. 34 *sq.* (*Mémoires de la Société Finno-Ougrienne*, xviii.). As to the Votiak clans see the same work, pp. 42-44.

better go home. He did not, and when he saw the tail of the procession he died of fright.[1]

In our own country the old belief in the annual return of the dead long lingered in the custom of baking " soul-cakes " and eating them or distributing them to the poor on All Souls' Day. Peasant girls used to go from farmhouse to farmhouse on that day, singing,

> " *Soul, soul, for a soul cake,*
> *Pray you, good mistress, a soul cake.*" [2]

In Shropshire down to the seventeenth century it was customary on All Souls' Day to set on the table a high heap of soul-cakes, and most visitors to the house took one of them. The antiquary John Aubrey, who records the custom, mentions also the appropriate verses :

> " *A soul-cake, a soul-cake,*
> *Have mercy on all Christen soules for a soule-cake.*" [3]

Indeed the custom of soul-cakes survived in Shropshire down to the latter part of the nineteenth century and may not be extinct even now. "With us, All Saints' Day is known as 'Souling Day,' and up to the present time in many places, poor children, and sometimes men, go out ' souling ' : which means that they go round to the houses of all the more well-to-do people within reach, reciting a ditty peculiar to the day, and looking for a dole of cakes, broken victuals, ale, apples, or money. The two latter are now the usual rewards, but there are few old North Salopians who cannot remember when ' soul-cakes ' were made at all the farms and ' bettermost' houses in readiness for the day, and were given to all who came for them. We are told of

---

[1] G. Finamore, *Credenze, Usi e Costumi Abruzzesi* (Palermo, 1890), pp. 180-182. Mr. W. R. Paton writes to me (12th December 1906) : " You do not mention the practice[s] on the modern Greek feast τῶν ψυχῶν (in May) which quite correspond. The κόλυβα is made in every house and put on a table laid with a white table-cloth. A glass of water and a taper are put on the table, and all is left so for the whole night. Our Greek maid-servant says that when she was a child she remembers seeing the souls come and partake. Almost the same rite is practised for the κόλυβα made on the commemoration of particular dead.''

[2] John Brand, *Popular Antiquities of Great Britain* (London, 1882–1883), i. 393.

[3] John Aubrey, *Remaines of Gentilisme and Judaisme* (London, 1881), p. 23.

liberal housewives who would provide as many as a clothes-basket full." [1]   The same custom of going out " a-souling " on All Saints' Day or All Souls' Day used to be observed in the neighbouring counties of Staffordshire, Cheshire, Lancashire, Herefordshire, and Monmouthshire.   In Herefordshire the soul-cakes were made of oatmeal, and he or she who received one of them was bound to say to the giver :

> " *God have your saul,*
> *Beens and all.*" [2]

Thus the practice of "souling" appears to have prevailed especially in the English counties which border on Wales. In many parts of Wales itself down to the first half of the nineteenth century poor peasants used to go about begging for bread on All Souls' Day.   The bread bestowed on them was called *bara ran* or dole-bread.   "This custom was a survival of the Middle Ages, when the poor begged bread for the souls of their departed relatives and friends." [3]   However, the custom was not confined to the west of England, for at Whitby in Yorkshire down to the early part of the nineteenth century it was usual to make "soul mass loaves" on or about All Souls' Day.   They were small round loaves, sold by bakers at a farthing apiece, chiefly for presents to children.   In former times people used to keep one or two of them for good luck. [4]   In Aberdeenshire, also, "on All Souls' Day, baked cakes of a particular sort are given away to those who may chance to visit the house, where they are

[1] Miss C. S. Burne and Miss G. F. Jackson, *Shropshire Folk-lore* (London, 1883), p. 381.   The writers record (pp. 382 *sqq.*) some of the ditties which were sung on this occasion by those who begged for soul-cakes.

[2] J. Brand, *Popular Antiquities of Great Britain*, i. 392, 393 ; W. Hone, *Year Book* (London, N.D.), col. 1288 ; T. F. Thiselton Dyer, *British Popular Customs* (London, 1876), pp. 405, 406, 407, 409 ; J. Harland and T. T. Wilkinson, *Lancashire Folk-lore* (London, 1882), p. 251 ; Elizabeth Mary Wright, *Rustic Speech and Folk-lore* (Oxford, 1913), p. 300.

[3] Marie Trevelyan, *Folk-lore and Folk-stories of Wales* (London, 1909), p. 255.   See also T. F. Thiselton Dyer, *British Popular Customs* (London, 1876), p. 410, who, quoting Pennant as his authority, says that the poor people who received soul-cakes prayed God to bless the next crop of wheat.

[4] *County Folk-lore*, vol. ii. *North Riding of Yorkshire, York, and the Ainsty* (London, 1901), quoting George Young, *A History of Whitby and Streoneshalth Abbey* (Whitby, 1817), ii. 882.

made. The cakes are called 'dirge-loaf.'"[1] Even in the remote island of St. Kilda it was customary on All Saints' Day to bake a large cake in the form of a triangle, furrowed round ; the cake must be all eaten that night.[2]

Feast of All Souls among the Indians of Ecuador..

The same mode of celebrating All Souls' Day has been transported by Catholicism to the New World and imparted to the aborigines of that continent. Thus in Carchi, a province of Ecuador, the Indians prepare foods of various sorts against All Souls' Day, and when the day has come they take some of the provisions to the church and there deposit them on tables set out for the purpose. These good things are the perquisite of the priest, who celebrates mass for the dead. After the service the Indians repair to the cemetery, where with burning candles and pots of holy water they prostrate themselves before the tombs of their relations, while the priest or the sacristan recites prayers for the souls of the departed. In the evening the Indians return to their houses. A table with four lights on it is spread with food and drink, especially with such things as the dead loved in their life. The door is left open all night, no doubt to let the spirits of the dead enter, and the family sits up, keeping the invisible guests company through the long hours of darkness. From seven o'clock and onwards troops of children traverse the village and its neighbourhood. They go from house to house ringing a bell and crying, " We are angels, we descend from the sky, we ask for bread." The people go to their doors and beg the children to recite a *Pater Noster* or an *Ave Maria* for the dead whom they name. When the prayer has been duly said, they give the children a little of the food from the table. All night long this goes on, band succeeding band of children. At five o'clock in the morning the family consumes the remainder of the food of the souls.[3] Here the children going from door to door during the night of All Souls appear to personate the souls of the dead who are also abroad at that time ; hence to give bread to the children is the same thing as to

[1] T. F. Thiselton Dyer, *British Popular Customs*, p. 410.
[2] M. Martin, "Description of the Western Islands of Scotland," in John Pinkerton's *Voyages and Travels* (London, 1808–1814), iii. 666.
[3] Dr. Rivet, "Le Christianisme et les Indiens de la République de l'Équateur," *L'Anthropologie*, xvii. (1906) pp. 93 *sq.*

FEASTS OF ALL SOULS 81

give bread to the poor hungry souls. Probably the same explanation applies to the giving of soul-cakes to children and the poor on All Souls' Day in Europe.

A comparison of these European customs with the similar heathen rites can leave no room for doubt that the nominally Christian feast of All Souls is nothing but an old pagan festival of the dead which the Church, unable or unwilling to suppress, resolved from motives of policy to connive at. But whence did it borrow the practice of solemnizing the festival on that particular day, the second of November? In order to answer this question we should observe, first, that celebrations of this sort are often held at the beginning of a New Year,[1] and, second, that the peoples of North - Western Europe, the Celts and the Teutons, appear to have dated the beginning of their year from the beginning of winter, the Celts reckoning it from the first of November[2] and the Teutons from the first of October.[3] The difference of reckoning may be due to a difference of climate, the home of the Teutons in Central and Northern Europe being a region where winter sets in earlier than on the more temperate and humid coasts of the Atlantic, the home of the Celts. These considerations suggest that the festival of All Souls on the second of November originated with the Celts, and spread from them to the rest of the European peoples, who, while they preserved their old feasts of the dead practically unchanged, may have transferred them to the second of November. This conjecture is supported by what we know of the ecclesiastical institution, or rather recognition, of the festival. For

The nominally Christian feast of All Souls on Nov. 2 appears to be an old Celtic festival of the dead adopted by the Church in 998 A.D.

[1] See above, pp. 53, 55, 62, 65.

[2] Sir John Rhys, *Celtic Heathendom* (London and Edinburgh, 1888), pp. 460, 514 *sq.* ; *id.*, "Celtae and Galli," *Proceedings of the British Academy, 1905-1906* (London, N.D.), p. 78; *Balder the Beautiful*, i. 224 *sq.*

[3] K. Müllenhoff, *Deutsche Alter- tumskunde*, iv. (Berlin, 1900) pp. 379 *sq.* The first of October seems to have been a great festival among the Saxons and also the Samagitians. See Widukind, *Res gestae Saxonicae*, i. 12 (Migne's *Patrologia Latina*,

cxxxvii. 135); M. A. Michov, "De Sarmatia Asiana atque Europea," in S. Grynaeus's *Novus Orbis Regionum ac Insularum veteribus incognitarum* (Bâle, 1532), p. 520. I have to thank Professor H. M. Chadwick for pointing out these two passages to me. Mr. A. Tille prefers to date the Teutonic winter from Martinmas, the eleventh of November. See A. Tille, *Die Geschichte der deutschen Weih- nacht* (Leipsic, N.D.), pp. 23 *sqq.*; O. Schrader, *Reallexikon der indoger- manischen Altertumskunde* (Strasburg, 1901), p. 395.

that recognition was first accorded at the end of the tenth century in France, a Celtic country, from which the Church festival gradually spread over Europe.   It was Odilo, abbot of the great Benedictine monastery of Clugny, who initiated the change in 998 A.D. by ordering that in all the monasteries over which he ruled, a solemn mass should be celebrated on the second of November for all the dead who sleep in Christ.   The example thus set was followed by other religious houses, and the bishops, one after another, introduced the new celebration into their dioceses.   Thus the festival of All Souls gradually established itself throughout Christendom, though in fact the Church has never formally sanctioned it by a general edict nor attached much weight to its observance.   Indeed, when objections were raised to the festival at the Reformation, the ecclesiastical authorities seemed ready to abandon it.[1]   These facts are explained very simply by the theory that an old Celtic commemoration of the dead lingered in France down to the end of the tenth century, and was then, as a measure of policy and a concession to ineradicable paganism, at last incorporated in the Catholic ritual.   The consciousness of the heathen origin of the practice would naturally prevent the supreme authorities from insisting strongly on its observance.   They appear rightly to have regarded it as an outpost which they could surrender to the forces of rationalism without endangering the citadel of the faith.

Perhaps we may go a step further and explain in like manner the origin of the feast of All Saints on the first of November.   For the analogy of similar customs elsewhere would lead us to suppose that the old Celtic festival of the dead was held on the Celtic New Year's Day, that is, on the first, not the second, of November.   May not then the institution of the feast of All Saints on that day have been the first attempt of the Church to give a colour of Christianity to the ancient heathen rite by substituting the saints for the souls of the dead as the true object of worship?

Institution of the Feast of All Souls by the Abbot of Clugny.

The feast of All Saints on Nov. 1 seems also to have displaced a heathen festival of the dead.

---

[1] A. J. Binterim, *Die vorzüglichsten Denkwürdigkeiten der Christ-Katholischen Kirche*, v. 1 (Mayence, 1829), pp. 493 *sq.* ; J. J. Herzog und G. F. Plitt, *Real-Encyclopädie für protestan-* *tische Theologie und Kirche*,[2] i. (Leipsic, 1877), pp. 303 *sq.* ; W. Smith and S. Cheetham, *Dictionary of Christian Antiquities* (London, 1875–1880), i. 57 *sq.*

The facts of history seem to countenance this hypothesis. For the feast of All Saints was instituted in France and Germany by order of the Emperor Lewis the Pious in 835 A.D., that is, about a hundred and sixty years before the introduction of the feast of All Souls. The innovation was made by the advice of the pope, Gregory IV., whose motive may well have been that of suppressing an old pagan custom which was still notoriously practised in France and Germany. The idea, however, was not a novel one, for the testimony of Bede proves that in Britain, another Celtic country, the feast of All Saints on the first of November was already celebrated in the eighth century.[1] We may conjecture that this attempt to divert the devotion of the faithful from the souls of the dead to the saints proved a failure, and that finally the Church reluctantly decided to sanction the popular superstition by frankly admitting a feast of All Souls into the calendar. But it could not assign the new, or rather the old, festival to the old day, the first of November, since that was already occupied by the feast of All Saints. Accordingly it placed the mass for the dead on the next day, the second of November. On this theory the feasts of All Saints and of All Souls mark two successive efforts of the Catholic Church to eradicate an old heathen festival of the dead. Both efforts failed. "In all Catholic countries the day of All Souls has preserved the serious character of a festival of the dead which no worldly gaieties are allowed to disturb. It is then the sacred duty of the survivors to visit the graves of their loved ones in the churchyard, to deck them with flowers and lights, and to utter a devout prayer—a pious custom with which in cities' like Paris and Vienna even the gay and frivolous comply for the sake of appearance, if not to satisfy an impulse of the heart." [2]

---

[1] A. J. Binterim, *op. cit.* v. 1, pp. 487 *sqq.*; J. J. Herzog und G. F. Plitt, *op. cit.* i. p. 303; W. Smith and S. Cheetham, *Dictionary of Christian Antiquities*, i. 57. In the last of these works a passage from the *Martyrologium Romanum Vetus* is quoted which states that a feast of Saints (*Festivitas Sanctorum*) on the first of November was celebrated at Rome. But the date of this particular Martyrology is disputed. See A. J. Binterim, *op. cit.* v. 1, pp. 52-54.

[2] J. J. Herzog und G. F. Plitt, *op. cit.* i. 304. A similar attempt to reform religion by diverting the devotion of the people from the spirits of their dead appears to have been made in

§ 3. *The Festival in the Month of Athyr*

Festival of the death and resurrection of Osiris in the month of Athyr.

The foregoing evidence lends some support to the conjecture—for it is only a conjecture—that the great festival of Osiris at Sais, with its accompanying illumination of the houses, was a night of All Souls, when the ghosts of the dead swarmed in the streets and revisited their old homes, which were lit up to welcome them back again. Herodotus, who briefly describes the festival, omits to mention its date, but we can determine it with some probability from other sources. Thus Plutarch tells us that Osiris was murdered on the seventeenth of the month Athyr, and that the Egyptians accordingly observed mournful rites for four days from the seventeenth of Athyr.[1] Now in the Alexandrian calendar, which Plutarch used, these four days corresponded to the thirteenth, fourteenth, fifteenth, and sixteenth of November, and this date answers exactly to the other indications given by Plutarch, who says that at the time of the festival the Nile was sinking, the north winds dying away, the nights lengthening, and the leaves falling from the trees. During these four days a gilt cow swathed in a black pall was exhibited as an image of Isis.

---

antiquity by the doctors of the Persian faith. For that faith "in its most finished and purest form, in the *Gathas*, does not recognize the dead as objects worthy of worship and sacrifice. But the popular beliefs were too firmly rooted, and the Mazdeans, like the sectaries of many other ideal and lofty forms of religion, were forced to give way. As they could not suppress the worship and get rid of the primitive and crude ideas involved in it, they set about the reform in another way : they interpreted the worship in a new manner, and thus the worship of the dead became a worship of the gods or of a god in favour of the loved and lost ones, a pious commemoration of their names and their virtues." See N. Söderblom, *Les Fravashis* (Paris, 1899), pp. 6 *sq.* The *Gathas* form the oldest part of the *Zend-Avesta*. James Darmesteter, indeed, in his later life startled the learned world by a theory that the *Gathas* were a comparatively late work based on the teaching of Philo of Alexandria. But this attempt of a Jew to claim for his race the inspiration of the Persian scriptures has been coldly received by Gentile scholars. · See J. H. Moulton, *Early Zoroastrianism* (London, 1913), pp. 8 *sqq.*

[1] Plutarch, *Isis et Osiris*, 39. As to the death of Osiris on the seventeenth of Athyr see *ib.* 13 and 42. Plutarch's statement on this subject is confirmed by the evidence of the papyrus Sallier IV., a document dating from the 19th dynasty, which places the lamentation for Osiris at Sais on the seventeenth day of Athyr. See A. Wiedemann, *Herodots zweites Buch*, p. 262 ; *id.*, *Die Religion der alten Ägypter*, p. 112 ; *id.*, *Religion of the Ancient Egyptians*, pp. 211 *sq.*

This, no doubt, was the image mentioned by Herodotus in his account of the festival.[1] On the nineteenth day of the month the people went down to the sea, the priests carrying a shrine which contained a golden casket. Into this casket they poured fresh water, and thereupon the spectators raised a shout that Osiris was found. After that they took some vegetable mould, moistened it with water, mixed it with precious spices and incense, and moulded the paste into a small moon - shaped image, which was then robed and ornamented.[2] Thus it appears that the purpose of the ceremonies described by Plutarch was to represent dramatically, first, the search for the dead body of Osiris, and, second, its joyful discovery, followed by the resurrection of the dead god who came to life again in the new image of vegetable mould and spices. Lactantius tells us how on these occasions the priests, with their shaven bodies, beat their breasts and lamented, imitating the sorrowful search of Isis for her lost son Osiris, and how afterwards their sorrow was turned to joy when the jackal - headed god Anubis, or rather a mummer in his stead, produced a small boy, the living representative of the god who was lost and was found.[3] Thus Lactantius regarded Osiris as the son instead of the husband of Isis, and he makes no mention of the image of vegetable mould. It is probable that the boy who figured in the sacred drama played the part, not of Osiris, but of his son Horus ;[4] but as the death and resurrection of the god were celebrated in many cities of Egypt, it is also possible that in some places the part of the god come to life was played by a living actor instead of by

The finding of Osiris.

---

[1] See above, p. 50.

[2] Plutarch, *Isis et Osiris*, 39. The words which I have translated " vegetable mould " are γῆν κάρπιμον, literally, "fruitful earth." The composition of the image was very important, as we shall see presently.

[3] Lactantius, *Divin. Institut.* i. 21 ; *id., Epitome Inst. Divin.* 23 (18, ed. Brandt and Laubmann). The description of the ceremony which Minucius Felix gives (*Octavius*, xxii. 1) agrees closely with, and is probably copied

from, that of Lactantius. We know from Appian (*Bell. Civ.* iv. 6. 47) that in the rites of Isis a priest personated Anubis, wearing a dog's, or perhaps rather a jackal's, mask on his head ; for the historian tells how in the great proscription a certain Volusius, who was on the condemned list, escaped in the disguise of a priest of Isis, wearing a long linen garment and the mask of a dog over his head.

[4] The suggestion is due to Prof. A. Wiedemann (*Herodots zweites Buch*, p. 261).

an image.   Another Christian writer describes how the Egyptians, with shorn heads, annually lamented over a buried idol of Osiris, smiting their breasts, slashing their shoulders, ripping open their old wounds, until, after several days of mourning, they professed to find the mangled remains of the god, at which they rejoiced.[1]   However the details of the ceremony may have varied in different places, the pretence of finding the god's body, and probably of restoring it to life, was a great event in the festal year of the Egyptians. The shouts of joy which greeted it are described or alluded to by many ancient writers.[2]

§ 4. The Festival in the Month of Khoiak

The great Osirian inscription at Denderah.   The funeral rites of Osiris, as they were observed at his great festival in the sixteen provinces of Egypt, are described in a long inscription of the Ptolemaic period, which is engraved on the walls of the god's temple at Denderah, the Tentyra of the Greeks, a town of Upper Egypt situated on the western bank of the Nile about forty miles north of Thebes.[3]   Unfortunately, while the information thus furnished is remarkably full and minute on many points, the arrangement adopted in the inscription is so confused and the expression often so obscure that a clear and consistent account of the ceremonies as a whole can hardly be extracted from it.   Moreover, we learn from the document that the ceremonies varied somewhat in the several cities, the ritual of Abydos, for example, differing from that of Busiris.   Without attempting to trace all the particularities of local usage I shall briefly indicate what seem to have been the leading features of the festival, so far as these can be ascertained with tolerable certainty.[4]

1 Firmicus Maternus, *De errore profanarum religionum*, 2.   Herodotus tells (ii. 61) how the Carians cut their foreheads with knives at the mourning for Osiris.

2 In addition to the writers who have been already cited see Juvenal, viii. 29 *sq.* ; Athenagoras, *Supplicatio pro Christianis*, 22, pp. 112, 114, ed. J. C. T. Otto (Jena, 1857) ; Tertullian,

Adversus Marcionem, i. 13; Augustine, *De civitate Dei*, vi. 10.

3 W. Smith, *Dictionary of Greek and Roman Geography*, ii. 1127.

4 For complete translations of the inscription see H. Brugsch, " Das Osiris-Mysterium von Tentyra," *Zeitschrift für ägyptische Sprache und Alterthumskunde*, 1881, pp. 77-111 ; V. Loret, " Les fêtes d'Osiris au mois

The rites lasted eighteen days, from the twelfth to the thirtieth of the month Khoiak, and set forth the nature of Osiris in his triple aspect as dead, dismembered, and finally reconstituted by the union of his scattered limbs. In the first of these aspects he was called Chent-Ament (Khenti-Amenti), in the second Osiris-Sep, and in the third Sokari (Seker).[1] Small images of the god were moulded of sand or vegetable earth ,and corn; to which incense was sometimes added ;[2] his face was painted yellow and his cheek-bones green.[3] These images were cast in a mould of pure gold, which represented the god in the form of a mummy, with the white crown of Egypt on his head.[4] The festival opened on the twelfth day of Khoiak with a ceremony of ploughing and sowing. Two black cows were yoked to the plough, which was made of tamarisk wood, while the share was of black copper. A boy scattered the seed. One end of the field was sown with barley, the other with spelt, and the middle with flax. During the operation the chief celebrant recited the ritual chapter of "the sowing of the fields."[5] At Busiris on the twentieth of Khoiak sand and barley were put in the god's

The rites of Osiris in the month of Khoiak represented the god as dead, dismembered, and then reconstituted by the union of his scattered limbs.

de Khoiak," *Recueil de Travaux relatifs à la Philologie et à l'Archéologie Égyptiennes et Assyriennes,* iii. (1882) pp. 43-57, iv. (1883) pp. 21-33, v. (1884) pp. 85-103. On the document and the festivals described in it see further A. Mariette-Pacha, *Dendérah* (Paris, 1880), pp. 334-347 ; J. Dümichen, "Die dem Osiris im Denderatempel geweihten Räume," *Zeitschrift für ägyptische Sprache und Alterthumskunde,* 1882, pp. 88-101 ; H. Brugsch, *Religion und Mythologie der alten Aegypter* (Leipsic, 1885–1888), pp. 616-618 ; R. V. Lanzone, *Dizionario di Mitologia Egizia,* pp. 725-744 ; A. Wiedemann, *Herodots zweites Buch,* p. 262 ; *id.,* "Osiris végétant," *Le Muséon,* N.S. iv. (1903) p. 113 ; E. A. Wallis Budge, *The Gods of the Egyptians,* ii. 128 sq. ; *id., Osiris and the Egyptian Resurrection,* ii. 21 sqq. ; Miss Margaret A. Murray, *The Osireion at Abydos* (London, 1904), pp. 27 sq.

1 R. V. Lanzone, *op. cit.* p. 727.

2 H. Brugsch, in *Zeitschrift für ägyptische Sprache und Alterthums-*

kunde, 1881, pp. 80-82 ; A. Wiedemann, in *Le Muséon,* N.S. iv. (1903) p. 113. The corn used in the making of the images is called barley by Brugsch and Miss M. A. Murray (*l.c.*), but wheat (*blé*) by Mr. V. Loret.

3 H. Brugsch, *op. cit.* pp. 99, 101.

4 H. Brugsch, *op. cit.* pp. 82 sq. ; R. V. Lanzone, *op. cit.* p. 728 ; Miss Margaret A. Murray, *op. cit.* p. 27.

5 H. Brugsch, *op. cit.* pp. 90 sq., 96 sq., 98 ; R. V. Lanzone, *op. cit.* pp. 743 sq. ; E. A. Wallis Budge, *The Gods of the Egyptians,* ii. 128. According to Lanzone, the ploughing took place, not on the first, but on the last day of the festival, namely, on the thirtieth of Khoiak ; and that certainly appears to have been the date of the ploughing at Busiris, for the inscription directs that there "the ploughing of the earth shall take place in the Serapeum of *Aa-n-beh* under the fine Persea-trees on the last day of the month Khoiak" (H. Brugsch, *op. cit.* p. 84).

"garden," which appears to have been a sort of large flower-pot. This was done in the presence of the cow-goddess Shenty, represented seemingly by the image of a cow made of gilt sycamore wood with a headless human image in its inside. "Then fresh inundation water was poured out of a golden vase over both the goddess and the 'garden,' and the barley was allowed to grow as the emblem of the resurrection of the god after his burial in the earth, 'for the growth of the garden is the growth of the divine substance.'"[1]   On the twenty-second of Khoiak, at the eighth hour, the images of Osiris, attended by thirty-four images of deities, performed a mysterious voyage in thirty-four tiny boats made of papyrus, which were illuminated by three hundred and sixty-five lights.[2]   On the twenty-fourth of Khoiak, after sunset, the effigy of Osiris in a coffin of mulberry wood was laid in the grave, and at the ninth hour of the night the effigy which had been made and deposited the year before was removed and placed upon boughs of sycamore.[3]   Lastly, on the thirtieth day of Khoiak they repaired to the holy sepulchre, a subterranean chamber over which appears to have grown a clump of Persea-trees.   Entering the vault by the western door, they laid the coffined effigy of the dead god reverently on a bed of sand in the chamber.   So they left him to his rest, and departed from the sepulchre by the eastern door.   Thus ended the ceremonies in the month of Khoiak.[4]

The burial of Osiris.

[1] Miss Margaret A. Murray, *The Osireion at Abydos*, p. 28 ; H. Brugsch, *op. cit.* pp. 83, 92.   The headless human image in the cow may have stood for Isis, who is said to have been decapitated by her son Horus, and to have received from Thoth a cow's head as a substitute.   See Plutarch, *Isis et Osiris*, 20 ; G. Maspero, *Histoire ancienne des Peuples de l'Orient Classique*, i. 177 ; Ed. Meyer, *s.v.* "Isis," in W. H. Roscher's *Lexikon der griech. und röm. Mythologie*, ii. 366.

[2] H. Brugsch, *op. cit.* pp. 92 *sq.* ; R. V. Lanzone, *op. cit.* pp. 738-740 ; A. Wiedemann, *Herodots zweites Buch*, p. 262 ; Miss M. A. Murray, *op. cit.* p. 35.   An Egyptian calendar, written at Sais about 300 B.C., has under the date 26 Khoiak the following entry : "Osiris goes about and the golden

boat is brought forth."   See *The Hibeh Papyri*, Part i., edited by B. P. Grenfell and A. S. Hunt (London, 1906), pp. 146, 153.   In the Canopic decree " the voyage of the sacred boat of Osiris " is said to take place on the 29th of Khoiak from "the sanctuary in the Heracleum " to the Canopic sanctuary.   See W. Dittenberger, *Orientis Graeci Inscriptiones Selectae*, No. 56 (vol. i. pp. 105, 108).   Hence it would seem that the date of this part of the festival varied somewhat in different places or at different times.

[3] H. Brugsch, *op. cit.* p. 99 ; E. A. Wallis Budge, *The Gods of the Egyptians*, ii. 129 ; compare Miss Margaret A. Murray, *op. cit.* p. 28, who refers the ceremony to the twenty-fifth of Khoiak.

[4] H. Brugsch, *op. cit.* pp. 94, 99 ;

§ 5. *The Resurrection of Osiris*

In the foregoing account of the festival, drawn from the great inscription of Denderah, the burial of Osiris figures prominently, while his resurrection is implied rather than expressed. This defect of the document, however, is amply compensated by a remarkable series of bas-reliefs which accompany and illustrate the inscription. These exhibit in a series of scenes the dead god lying swathed as a mummy on his bier, then gradually raising himself up higher and higher, until at last he has entirely quitted the bier and is seen erect between the guardian wings of the faithful Isis, who stands behind him, while a male figure holds up before his eyes the *crux ansata*, the Egyptian symbol of life.[1] The resurrection of the god could hardly be portrayed more graphically. Even more instructive, however, is another representation of the same event in a chamber dedicated to Osiris in the great temple of Isis at Philae. Here we see the dead body of Osiris with stalks of corn springing from it, while a priest waters the stalks from a pitcher which he holds in his hand. The accompanying inscription sets forth that "this is the form of him whom one may not name, Osiris of the mysteries, who springs from the returning waters."[2] Taken together, the picture and the words seem to leave no doubt that Osiris was here conceived and represented as a personification of the corn which springs from

The resurrection of Osiris represented on the monuments.

A. Mariette-Pacha, *Dendérah*, pp. 336 *sq.*; R. V. Lanzone, *op. cit.* p. 744. Mariette supposed that after depositing the new image in the sepulchre they carried out the old one of the preceding year, thus setting forth the resurrection as well as the death of the god. But this view is apparently not shared by Brugsch and Lanzone.

[1] A. Mariette - Bey, *Dendérah*, iv. (Paris, 1873) plates 65, 66, 68, 69, 70, 71, 72, 88, 89, 90; R. V. Lanzone, *Dizionario di Mitologia Egizia*, pp. 757 *sqq.*, with plates cclxviii.-ccxcii.; E. A. Wallis Budge, *The Gods of the Egyptians*, ii. 131-138; *id.*, *Osiris and the Egyptian Resurrection*, ii. 31 *sqq.*

[2] H. Brugsch, *Religion und Mythologie der alten Aegypter*, p. 621; R. V. Lanzone, *Dizionario di Mitologia Egizia*, plate cclxi.; A. Wiedemann, "L'Osiris végétant," *Le Muséon*, N.S. iv. (1903) p. 112; E. A. Wallis Budge, *Osiris and the Egyptian Resurrection*, i. 58. According to Prof. Wiedemann, the corn springing from the god's body is barley. Similarly in a papyrus of the Louvre (No. 3377) Osiris is represented swathed as a mummy and lying on his back, while stalks of corn sprout from his body. See R. V. Lanzone, *op. cit.* pp. 801 *sq.*, with plate ccciii. 2; A. Wiedemann, "L'Osiris végétant," *Le Muséon*, N.S. iv. (1903) p. 112.

the fields after they have been fertilized by the inundation. This, according to the inscription, was the kernel of the mysteries, the innermost secret revealed to the initiated. So in the rites of Demeter at Eleusis a reaped ear of corn was exhibited to the worshippers as the central mystery of their religion.[1] We can now fully understand why at the great festival of sowing in the month of Khoiak the priests used to bury effigies of Osiris made of earth and corn. When these effigies were taken up again at the end of a year or of a shorter interval, the corn would be found to have sprouted from the body of Osiris, and this sprouting of the grain would be hailed as an omen, or rather as the cause, of the growth of the crops.[2] The corn-god produced the corn from himself: he gave his own body to feed the people: he died that they might live.

Corn-stuffed effigies of Osiris buried with the dead to ensure their resurrection.

And from the death and resurrection of their great god the Egyptians drew not only their support and sustenance in this life, but also their hope of a life eternal beyond the grave. This hope is indicated in the clearest manner by the very remarkable effigies of Osiris which have come to light in Egyptian cemeteries. Thus in the Valley of the Kings at Thebes there was found the tomb of a royal fan-bearer who lived about 1500 B.C. Among the rich contents of the tomb there was a bier on which rested a mattress of reeds covered with three layers of linen. On the upper side of the linen was painted a life-size figure of Osiris; and the interior of the figure, which was waterproof, contained a mixture of vegetable mould, barley, and a sticky fluid. The barley had sprouted and sent out shoots two or three inches long.[3] Again, in the cemetery at Cynopolis "were numerous burials of Osiris figures. These were made of grain wrapped up in cloth and roughly shaped like an Osiris, and placed inside a bricked-up recess at the side of the tomb, sometimes

---

[1] Hippolytus, *Refutatio omnium haeresium*, v. 8, p. 162 ed. L. Duncker and F. G. Schneidewin (Göttingen, 1859). See *Spirits of the Corn and of the Wild*, i. 38 *sq.*

[2] Prof. A. Erman rightly assumes (*Die ägyptische Religion*,[2] p. 234) that the images made in the month of Khoiak were intended to germinate as a symbol of the divine resurrection.

[3] A. Wiedemann, "L'Osiris végé-tant," *Le Muséon*, N.S. iv. (1903) p. 111; *Egyptian Exploration Fund Archaeological Report*, 1898–1899, pp. 24 *sq.*; A. Moret, *Kings and Gods of Egypt* (New York and London, 1912), p. 94, with plate xi.; *id., Mystères Égyptiens* (Paris, 1913), p. 41.

in small pottery coffins, sometimes in wooden coffins in the form of a hawk-mummy, sometimes without any coffins at all."[1] These corn-stuffed figures were bandaged like mummies with patches of gilding here and there, as if in imitation of the golden mould in which the similar figures of Osiris were cast at the festival of sowing.[2] Again, effigies of Osiris, with faces of green wax and their interior full of grain, were found buried near the necropolis of Thebes.[3] Finally, we are told by Professor Erman that between the legs of mummies "there sometimes lies a figure of Osiris made of slime ; it is filled with grains of corn, the sprouting of which is intended to signify the resurrection of the god."[4] We cannot doubt that, just as the burial of corn-stuffed images of Osiris in the earth at the festival of sowing was designed to quicken the seed, so the burial of similar images in the grave was meant to quicken the dead, in other words, to ensure their spiritual immortality.

§ 6. *Readjustment of Egyptian Festivals*

The festival of Osiris which Plutarch assigns to the month of Athyr would seem to be identical in substance with the one which the inscription of Denderah assigns to the following month, namely, to Khoiak. Apparently the essence of both festivals was a dramatic representation of the death and resurrection of the god ; in both of them Isis was figured by a gilt cow, and Osiris by an image moulded of moist vegetable earth. But if the festivals were the same, why were they held in different months? It is easy to suggest that different towns in Egypt celebrated the festival at different dates. But when we remember that according to the great inscription of Denderah, the authority of which is indisputable, the festival fell in the month of Khoiak in

The festivals of Osiris in the months of Athyr and Khoiak seem to have been substantially the same.

---

[1] B. P. Grenfell and A. S. Hunt, in *Egyptian Exploration Fund Archaeological Report*, 1902–1903, p. 5.
[2] Miss Margaret A. Murray, *The Osireion at Abydos*, pp. 28 *sq.*
[3] Sir J. Gardiner Wilkinson, *A Second Series of the Manners and Customs of the Ancient Egyptians* (London, 1841), ii. 300, note §. The

writer seems to have doubted whether these effigies represented Osiris. But the doubt has been entirely removed by subsequent discoveries. Wilkinson's important note on the subject is omitted by his editor, S. Birch (vol. iii. p. 375, ed. 1878).
[4] A. Erman, *Die ägyptische Religion*,[2] pp. 209 *sq.*

every province of Egypt, we shall be reluctant to suppose that at some one place, or even at a few places, it was exceptionally held in the preceding month of Athyr, and that the usually well-informed Plutarch described the exception as if it had been the rule, of which on this supposition he must have been wholly ignorant. More probably the discrepancy is to be explained by the great change which came over the Egyptian calendar between the date of the inscription and the lifetime of Plutarch. For when the inscription was drawn up in the Ptolemaic age the festivals were dated by the old vague or movable year, and therefore rotated gradually through the whole circle of the seasons; whereas at the time when Plutarch wrote, about the end of the first century, they were seemingly dated by the fixed Alexandrian year, and accordingly had ceased to rotate.[1]

The old festival of Khoiak may have been transferred to Athyr when the Egyptians adopted the fixed Alexandrian year in 30 B.C.

But even if we grant that in Plutarch's day the festivals had become stationary, still this would not explain why the old festival of Khoiak had been transferred to Athyr. In order to understand that transference it seems necessary to suppose that when the Egyptians gave to their months fixed places in the solar year by accepting the Alexandrian system of intercalation, they at the same time transferred the festivals from what may be called their artificial to their natural dates. Under the old system a summer festival was sometimes held in winter and a winter festival in summer; a harvest celebration sometimes fell at the season of sowing, and a sowing celebration at the season of harvest. People might reconcile themselves to such anomalies so long as they knew that they were only temporary, and that in the course of time the festivals would necessarily return to their proper seasons. But it must have been otherwise when they adopted a fixed instead of a movable year, and so arrested the rotation of the festivals for ever. For they could not but be aware that every festival would thenceforth continue to occupy for all time that particular place in the solar year which it chanced to occupy in the year 30 B.C., when the calendar became fixed. If in that particular year it happened, as it might have happened, that the summer

---

[1] See above, pp. 24 *sq.*, 27 *sq.*, 49 *sq.*

festivals were held in winter and the winter festivals in summer, they would always be so held in future; the absurdity and anomaly would never again be rectified as it had been before. This consideration, which could not have escaped intelligent men, must have suggested the advisability of transferring the · festivals from the dates at which they chanced to be celebrated in 30 B.C. to the dates at which they ought properly to be celebrated in the course of nature.

Now what in the year 30 B.C. was the actual amount of discrepancy between the accidental and the natural dates of the festivals? It was a little more than a month. In that year Thoth, the first month of the Egyptian calendar, happened to begin on the twenty-ninth of August,[1] whereas according to theory it should have begun with the heliacal rising of Sirius on the twentieth of July, that is, forty days or, roughly speaking, a month earlier. From this it follows that in the year 30 B.C. all the Egyptian festivals fell about a month later than their natural dates, and they must have continued to fall a month late for ever if they were allowed to retain those places in the calendar which they chanced to occupy in that particular year. In these circumstances it would be a natural and sensible thing to restore the festivals to their proper places in the solar year by celebrating them one calendar month earlier than before.[2] If this measure were adopted the

The transference would be intelligible if we suppose that in 30 B.C. the dates of all the Egyptian festivals were shifted backward by about a month in order to restore them to their natural places in the calendar.

---

[1] So it was reckoned at the time. But, strictly speaking, Thoth in that year began on August 31. The miscalculation originated in a blunder of the ignorant Roman pontiffs who, being charged with the management of the new Julian calendar, at first intercalated a day every third, instead of every fourth, year. See Solinus, *Collectanea*, i. 45-47 (p. 15, ed. Th. Mommsen, Berlin, 1864); Macrobius, *Saturn.* i. 14. 13 *sq.*; L. Ideler, *Handbuch der mathematischen und technischen Chronologie*, i. 157-161.

[2] Theoretically the shift should have been 40, or rather 42 days, that being the interval between July 20 and August 29 or 31 (see the preceding note). If that shift was actually made, the calendar date of any festival in the old vague

Egyptian year could be found by adding 40 or 42 days to its date in the Alexandrian year. Thus if the death of Osiris fell on the 17th of Athyr in the Alexandrian year, it should have fallen on the 27th or 29th of Khoiak in the old vague year; and if his resurrection fell on the 19th of Athyr in the Alexandrian year, it should have fallen on the 29th of Khoiak or the 1st of Tybi in the old vague year. These calculations agree nearly, but not exactly, with the somewhat uncertain indications of the Denderah calendar (above, p. 88), and also with the independent evidence which we possess that the resurrection of Osiris was celebrated on the 30th of Khoiak (below, pp. 108 *sq.*). These approximate agreements to some extent con-

festivals which had hitherto been held, for example, in the third month Athyr would henceforth be held in the second month Phaophi ; the festivals which had hitherto fallen in the fourth month Khoiak would thenceforth fall in the third month Athyr ; and so on. Thus the festal calendar would be reduced to harmony with the seasons instead of being in more or less flagrant discord with them, as it had generally been before, and must always have been afterwards if the change which I have indicated had not been introduced. It is only to credit the native astronomers and the Roman rulers of Egypt with common sense to suppose that they actually adopted the measure. On that supposition we can perfectly understand why the festival of sowing, which had formerly belonged to the month of Khoiak, was transferred to Athyr. For in the Alexandrian calendar Khoiak corresponds very nearly to December, and Athyr to November. But in Egypt the month of November, not the month of December, is the season of sowing. There was therefore every reason why the great sowing festival of the corn-god Osiris should be held in Athyr and not Khoiak, in November and not in December. In like manner we may suppose that all the Egyptian festivals were restored to their true places in the solar year, and that when Plutarch dates a festival both by its calendar month and by its relation to

---

firm my theory that, with the adoption of the fixed Alexandrian year, the dates of the official Egyptian festivals were shifted from their accidental places in the calendar to their proper places in the natural year.

Since I published in the first edition of this book (1906) my theory that with the adoption of the fixed Alexandrian year in 30 B.C. the Egyptian festivals were shifted about a month backward in the year, Professor Ed. Meyer has shown independent grounds for holding "that the festivals which gave rise to the later names of the (Egyptian) months were demonstrably held a month later in earlier ages, under the twentieth, eighteenth, indeed partly under the twelfth dynasty ; in other words, that after the end of the New Kingdom the festivals and the

corresponding names of the months were displaced one month backwards. It is true that this displacement can as yet be proved for only five months ; but as the names of these months and the festivals keep their relative position towards each other, the assumption is inevitable that the displacement affected not merely particular festivals but the whole system equally." See Ed. Meyer, *Nachträge . zur ägyptischen Chronologie* (Berlin, 1908), pp. 3 *sqq.* (*Abhandlungen der königl. Preuss. Akademie der Wissenschaften vom Jahre 1907*). Thus it is possible that the displacement of the festivals by a month backward in the calendar took place a good deal earlier than I had supposed. In the uncertainty of the whole question I leave my theory as it stood.

the cycle of the seasons, he is perfectly right in doing so, and we may accept his evidence with confidence instead of having to accuse him of ignorantly confounding the movable Egyptian with the fixed Alexandrian year. Accusations of ignorance levelled at the best writers of antiquity are apt to recoil on those who make them.[1]

[1] If the results of the foregoing inquiry be accepted, the resurrection of Osiris was regularly celebrated in Egypt on the 15th of November from the year 30 B.C. onward, since the 15th of November corresponded to the 19th of Athyr (the resurrection day) in the fixed Alexandrian year. This agrees with the indications of the Roman Rustic Calendars, which place the resurrection (*heuresis*, that is, the discovery of Osiris) between the 14th and the 30th of November. Yet according to the calendar of Philocalus, the official Roman celebration of the resurrection seems to have been held on the 1st of November, not on the 15th. How is the discrepancy to be explained? Th. Mommsen supposed that the festival was officially adopted at Rome at a time when the 19th of Athyr of the vague Egyptian year corresponded to the 31st of October or the 1st of November of the Julian calendar, and that the Romans, overlooking the vague or shifting character of the Egyptian year, fixed the resurrection of Osiris permanently on the 1st of November. Now the 19th of Athyr of the vague year corresponded to the 1st of November in the years 32-35 A.D. and to the 31st of October in the years 36-39; and it appears that the festival was officially adopted at Rome some time before 65 A.D. (Lucan, *Pharsalia*, viii. 831 *sqq.*). It is unlikely that the adoption took place in the reign of Tiberius, who died in 37 A.D.; for he is known to have persecuted the Egyptian religion (Tacitus, *Annals*, ii. 85; Suetonius, *Tiberius*, 36; Josephus, *Antiquit. Jud.* xviii. 3. 4); hence Mommsen concluded that the great festival of Osiris was officially adopted at Rome in the early years of the reign of Caligula, that is, in 37, 38, or 39 A.D. See Th. Mommsen, *Corpus Inscriptionum Latinarum*, i.[2] Pars prior (Berlin, 1893), pp. 333 *sq.*; H. Dessau, *Inscriptiones Latinae Selectae*, vol. ii. p. 995, No. 8745. This theory of Mommsen's assumes that in Egypt the festivals were still regulated by the old vague year in the first century of our era. It cannot, therefore, be reconciled with the conclusion reached in the text that the Egyptian festivals ceased to be regulated by the old vague year from 30 B.C. onward. How the difference of date between the official Roman and the Egyptian festival of the resurrection is to be explained, I do not pretend to say.

CHAPTER V

THE NATURE OF OSIRIS

§ 1. *Osiris a Corn-God*

THE foregoing survey of the myth and ritual of Osiris may suffice to prove that in one of his aspects the god was a personification of the corn, which may be said to die and come to life again every year. Through all the pomp and glamour with which in later times the priests had invested his worship, the conception of him as the corn-god comes clearly out in the festival of his death and resurrection, which was celebrated in the month of Khoiak and at a later period in the month of Athyr. That festival appears to have been essentially a festival of sowing, which properly fell at the time when the husbandman actually committed the seed to the earth. On that occasion an effigy of the corn-god, moulded of earth and corn, was buried with funeral rites in the ground in order that, dying there, he might come to life again with the new crops. The ceremony was, in fact, a charm to ensure the growth of the corn by sympathetic magic, and we may conjecture that as such it was practised in a simple form by every Egyptian farmer on his fields long before it was adopted and transfigured by the priests in the stately ritual of the temple. In the modern, but doubtless ancient, Arab custom of burying "the Old Man," namely, a sheaf of wheat, in the harvest-field and praying that he may return from the dead,[1] we see the germ out of which the worship of the corn-god Osiris was probably developed.

The details of his myth fit in well with this interpretation of the god. He was said to be the offspring of Sky and

[1] See above, p. 48.

Earth.[1] What more appropriate parentage could be invented for the corn which springs from the ground that has been fertilized by the water of heaven? It is true that the land of Egypt owed its fertility directly to the Nile and not to showers; but the inhabitants must have known or guessed that the great river in its turn was fed by the rains which fell in the far interior. Again, the legend that Osiris was the first to teach men the use of corn[2] would be most naturally told of the corn-god himself. Further, the story that his mangled remains were scattered up and down the land and buried in different places may be a mythical way of expressing either the sowing or the winnowing of the grain. The latter interpretation is supported by the tale that Isis placed the severed limbs of Osiris on a corn-sieve.[3] Or more probably the legend may be a reminiscence of a custom of slaying a human victim, perhaps a representative of the corn-spirit and distributing his flesh or scattering his ashes over the fields to fertilize them. In modern Europe the figure of Death is sometimes torn in pieces, and the fragments are then buried in the ground to make the crops grow well,[4] and in other parts of the world human victims are treated in the same way.[5] With regard to the ancient Egyptians we have it on the authority of Manetho that they used to burn red-haired men and scatter their ashes with winnowing fans,[6] and it is highly significant that this barbarous sacrifice was offered by the kings at the grave of Osiris.[7] We may conjecture that the victims represented Osiris himself, who was annually slain, dismembered, and buried in their persons that he might quicken the seed in the earth.

Possibly in prehistoric times the kings themselves

Osiris a child of Sky and Earth.

The legend of the dismemberment of Osiris points to the dismemberment of human beings, perhaps of the kings, in the character of the corn-spirit.

[1] See above, p. 6.
[2] See above, p. 7.
[3] Servius on Virgil, *Georg.* i. 166.
[4] *The Dying God*, p. 250.
[5] *Spirits of the Corn and of the Wild*, i. 236 *sqq.*
[6] Plutarch, *Isis et Osiris*, 73, compare 33.
[7] Diodorus Siculus, i. 88. 5. The slaughter may have been performed by the king with his own hand. On Egyptian monuments the king is often represented in the act of slaying

prisoners before a god. See A. Moret, *Du caractère religieux de la royauté Pharaonique* (Paris, 1902), pp. 179, 224; E. A. Wallis Budge, *Osiris and the Egyptian Resurrection*, i. 197 *sqq.* Similarly the kings of Ashantee and Dahomey used often themselves to cut the throats of the human victims. See A. B. Ellis, *The Tshi-speaking Peoples of the Gold Coast* (London, 1887), p. 162; *id.*, *The Ewe-speaking Peoples of the Slave Coast* (London, 1890), pp. 125, 129.

Roman and Greek traditions of the dismemberment of kings.

played the part of the god and were slain and dismembered in that character. Set as well as Osiris is said to have been torn in pieces after a reign of eighteen days, which was commemorated by an annual festival of the same length.[1] According to one story Romulus, the first king of Rome, was cut in pieces by the senators, who buried the fragments of him in the ground;[2] and the traditional day of his death, the seventh of July, was celebrated with certain curious rites, which were apparently connected with the artificial fertilization of the fig.[3] Again, Greek legend told how Pentheus, king of Thebes, and Lycurgus, king of the Thracian Edonians, opposed the vine-god Dionysus, and how the impious monarchs were rent in pieces, the one by the frenzied Bacchanals, the other by horses.[4] These Greek traditions may well be distorted reminiscences of a custom of sacrificing human beings, and especially divine kings, in the character of Dionysus, a god who resembled Osiris in many points and was said like him to have been torn limb from limb.[5] We are told that in Chios men were rent in pieces

[1] *Scholia in Caesaris Germanici Aratea*, in F. Eyssenhardt's edition of Martianus Capella, p. 408 (Leipsic, 1866).
[2] Dionysius Halicarnasensis, *Antiquit. Rom.* ii. 56. 4. Compare Livy, i. 16. 4; Florus, i. 1. 16 *sq.*; Plutarch, *Romulus*, 27. Mr. A. B. Cook was, I believe, the first to interpret the story as a reminiscence of the sacrifice of a king. See his article "The European Sky-God," *Folk-lore*, xvi. (1905) pp. 324 *sq.* However, the acute historian A. Schwegler long ago maintained that the tradition rested on some very ancient religious rite, which was afterwards abolished or misunderstood, and he rightly compared the legendary deaths of Pentheus and Orpheus (*Römische Geschichte*, Tübingen, 1853–1858, vol. i. pp. 534 *sq.*). See further W. Otto, "Juno," *Philologus*, lxiv. (1905) pp. 187 *sqq.*
[3] *The Magic Art and the Evolution of Kings*, ii. 313 *sqq.*
[4] Euripides, *Bacchae*, 43 *sqq.*, 1043 *sqq.*; Theocritus, xxvi.; Pausanias, ii. 2. 7; Apollodorus, *Bibliotheca*, iii. 5.

1 *sq.*; Hyginus, *Fab.* 132 and 184. The destruction of Lycurgus by horses seems to be mentioned only by Apollodorus. As to Pentheus see especially A. G. Bather, "The Problem of the Bacchae," *Journal of Hellenic Studies*, xiv. (1904) pp. 244-263.
[5] Nonnus, *Dionys.* vi. 165-205; Clement of Alexandria, *Protrept.* ii. 17 *sq.*, p. 15 ed. Potter; Justin Martyr, *Apology*, i. 54; Firmicus Maternus, *De errore profanarum religionum*, 6; Arnobius, *Adversus Nationes*, v. 19. According to the Clementine *Recognitiones*, x. 24 (Migne's *Patrologia Graeca*, i. 1434) Dionysus was torn in pieces at Thebes, the very place of which Pentheus was king. The description of Euripides (*Bacchae*, 1058 *sqq.*) suggests that the human victim was tied or hung to a pine-tree before being rent to pieces. We are reminded of the effigy of Attis which hung on the sacred pine (above, vol. i. p. 267), and of the image of Osiris which was made out of a pine-tree and then buried in the hollow of the trunk (below, p. 108). The pine-tree on which Pentheus was

as a sacrifice to Dionysus ;[1] and since they died the same death as their god, it is reasonable to suppose that they personated him. The story that the Thracian Orpheus was similarly torn limb from limb by the Bacchanals seems to indicate that he too perished in the character of the god whose death he died.[2] It is significant that the Thracian Lycurgus, king of the Edonians, is said to have been put to death in order that the ground, which had ceased to be fruitful, might regain its fertility.[3] In some Thracian villages at Carnival time a custom is still annually observed, which may well be a mitigation of an ancient practice of putting a man, perhaps a king, to death in the character of Dionysus for the sake of the crops. A man disguised in goatskins and fawnskins, the livery of Dionysus, is shot at and falls down as dead. A pretence is made of flaying his body and of mourning over him, but afterwards he comes to life again. Further, a plough is dragged about the village and seed is scattered, while prayers are said that the wheat, rye, and barley may be plentiful. One town (Viza), where these customs are observed, was the capital of the old Thracian kings. In another town (Kosti, near the Black Sea) the principal masker is called the king. He wears goatskins or sheepskins, and is attended by a boy who dispenses wine to the people. The king himself carries seed, which he casts on the ground before the church, after being invited to throw it on two

Modern Thracian pretence of killing a man, who is sometimes called a king, for the good of the crops.

pelted by the Bacchanals before they tore him limb from limb is said to have been worshipped as if it were the god himself by the Corinthians, who made two images of Dionysus out of it (Pausanias, ii. 2. 7). The tradition points to an intimate connexion between the tree, the god, and the human victim.

[1] Porphyry, *De abstinentia*, ii. 55. At Potniae in Boeotia a priest of Dionysus is said to have been killed by the drunken worshippers (Pausanias, ix. 8. 2). He may have been sacrificed in the character of the god.

[2] Lucian, *De saltatione*, 51 ; Plato, *Symposium*, 7, p. 179 D, E ; Pausanias, ix. 30. 5 ; Ovid, *Metam.* xi. 1-43 ; O. Gruppe, *s.v.* "Orpheus," in W. H. Roscher's *Lexikon der griech. und röm.*

Mythologie, iii. 1165 *sq*. That Orpheus died the death of the god has been observed both in ancient and modern times. See E. Rohde, *Psyche* [3] (Tübingen and Leipsic, 1903) ii. 118, note [2], quoting Proclus on Plato ; S. Reinach, "La mort d'Orphée," *Cultes, Mythes et Religions*, ii. (1906) pp. 85 *sqq.* According to Ovid, the Bacchanals killed him with hoes, rakes, and mattocks. Similarly in West Africa human victims used to be killed with spades and hoes and then buried in a field which had just been tilled (J. B. Labat, *Relation historique de l'Ethiopie occidentale*, Paris, 1732, i. 380). Such a mode of sacrifice points to the identification of the human victim with the fruits of the earth.

[3] Apollodorus, *Bibliotheca*, iii. 5. 1.

bands of married and unmarried men respectively. Finally, he is stripped of the skins and thrown into the river.[1]

Norwegian tradition of the dismemberment of a king, Halfdan the Black. Further, we read of a Norwegian king, Halfdan the Black, whose body was cut up and buried in different parts of his kingdom for the sake of ensuring the fruitfulness of the earth. He is said to have been drowned at the age of forty through the breaking of the ice in spring. What followed his death is thus related by the old Norse historian Snorri Sturluson : " He had been the most prosperous (literally, blessed with abundance) of all kings. So greatly did men value him that when the news came that he was dead and his body removed to Hringariki and intended for burial there, the chief men from Raumariki and Westfold and Heithmörk came and all requested that they might take his body with them and bury it in their various provinces ; they thought that it would bring abundance to those who obtained it. Eventually it was settled that the body was distributed in four places. The head was laid in a barrow at Steinn in Hringariki, and each party took away their own share and buried it. All these barrows are called Halfdan's barrows." [2] It should be remembered that this Halfdan belonged to the family of the Ynglings, who traced their descent from Frey, the great Scandinavian god of fertility.[3] Frey himself is said to have reigned as king of Frey, the Scandinavian god of fertility, buried at Upsala. Sweden at Upsala. The years of his reign were plenteous, and the people laid the plenty to his account. So when he

[1] R. M. Dawkins, " The Modern Carnival in Thrace and the Cult of Dionysus," *Journal of Hellenic Studies*, xxvi. (1906) pp. 191-206. See further *Spirits of the Corn and of the Wild*, i. 25 *sqq.*

[2] Snorri Sturluson, *Heimskringla*, *Saga Halfdanar Svarta*, ch. 9. I have to thank Professor H. M. Chadwick for referring me to this passage and translating it for me. See also *The Stories of the Kings of Norway* (*Heimskringla*), done into English by W. Morris and E. Magnússon (London, 1893–1905), i. 86 *sq.* Halfdan the Black was the father of Harold the Fair-haired, king of Norway (860–933 A.D.). Professor Chadwick tells me that, though the tradition as to the

death and mutilation of Halfdan was not committed to writing for three hundred years, he sees no reason to doubt its truth. He also informs me that the word translated " abundance " means literally " the produce of the season." " Plenteous years " is the rendering of Morris and Magnússon.

[3] As to the descent of Halfdan and the Ynglings from Frey, see *Heimskringla*, done into English by W. Morris and E. Magnússon, i. 23-71 (*The Saga Library*, vol. iii.). With regard to Frey, the god of fertility, both animal and vegetable, see E. H. Meyer, *Mythologie der Germanen* (Strasburg, 1903), pp. 366 *sq.* ; P. Hermann, *Nordische Mythologie* (Leipsic, 1903), pp. 206 *sqq.*

died, they would not burn him, as it had been customary to do with the dead before his time; but they resolved to preserve his body, believing that, so long as it remained in Sweden, the land would have abundance and peace. Therefore they reared a great mound, and put him in it, and sacrificed to him for plenty and peace ever afterwards. And for three years after his death they poured the tribute to him into the mound, as if he were alive; the gold they poured in by one window, the silver by a second, and the copper by a third.[1]

The natives of Kiwai, an island lying off the mouth of the Fly River in British New Guinea, tell of a certain magician named Segera, who had sago for his totem. When his son died, the death was set down to the magic of an enemy, and the bereaved father was so angry that by his spells he caused the whole crop of sago in the country to fail; only in his own garden the sago grew as luxuriantly as ever. When many had died of famine, the people went to him and begged him to remove the spells which he had cast on the sago palms, so that they might eat food and live. The magician, touched with remorse and pity, went round planting a sago shoot in every garden, and the shoots flourished, sago was plentiful once more, and the famine came to an end. When Segera was old and ill, he told the people that he would soon die, but that, nevertheless, he would cause their gardens to thrive. Accordingly, he instructed them that when he was dead they should cut him up and place pieces of his flesh in their gardens, but his head was to be buried in his own garden. Of him it is said that he outlived the ordinary age, and that no man knew his father, but that he made the sago good and no one was hungry any more. Old men who were alive a few years ago affirmed that they had known Segera in their youth, and the general opinion of the Kiwai people seems to be that Segera died not more than two generations ago.[2]

Taken all together, these legends point to a widespread practice of dismembering the body of a king or magician

Segera, a magician of Kiwai, said to have been cut up after death and the pieces buried in gardens to fertilize them.

---

[1] *Heimskringla*, done into English by W. Morris and E. Magnússon, i. 4, 22-24 (*The Saga Library*, vol. iii.).

[2] *Totemism and Exogamy*, ii. 32 *sq.*, from information supplied by Dr. C. G. Seligmann.

Apparently
widespread
custom
of dis-
membering
a king or
magician
and bury-
ing the
pieces in
different
parts of the
kingdom. and burying the pieces in different parts of the country in order to ensure the fertility of the ground and probably also the fecundity of man and beast. Whether regarded as the descendant of a god, as himself divine, or simply as a mighty enchanter, the king was believed to radiate magical virtue for the good of his subjects, quickening the seed in the earth and in the womb. This radiation of reproductive energy did not cease with his life ; hence the people deemed it essential to preserve his body as a pledge of the continued prosperity of the country. It would be natural to imagine that the spot where the dead king was buried would enjoy a more than ordinary share of his blessed influence, and accordingly disputes would almost inevitably arise between different districts for the exclusive possession of so powerful a talisman. These disputes could be settled and local jealousies appeased by dividing the precious body between the rival claimants, in order that all should benefit in equal measure by its life-giving properties. This was certainly done in Norway with the body of Halfdan the Black, the descendant of the harvest-god Frey ; it appears to have been done with the body of Segera, the sago-magician of Kiwai ; and we may conjecture that in prehistoric times it was done with the bodies of Egyptian kings, who personated Osiris, the god of fertility in general and of the corn in particular. At least such a practice would account for the legend of the mangling of the god's body and the distribution of the pieces throughout Egypt.

In this
dismem-
berment
a special
virtue
seems to
have been
ascribed
to the
genital
organs.   In this connexion the story that the genital member of Osiris was missing when Isis pieced together his mutilated body,[1] may not be without significance. When a Zulu medicine-man wishes to make the crops grow well, he will take the body of a man who has died in full vigour and cut minute portions of tissue from the foot, the leg, the arm, the face, and the nail of a single finger in order to compound a fertilizing medicine out of them. But the most important part of the medicine consists of the dead man's generative organs, which are removed entire. All these pieces of the corpse are fried with herbs

[1] See above, p. 10.

on a slow fire, then ground to powder, and sown over the fields.[1] We have seen that similarly the Egyptians scattered the ashes of human victims by means of winnowing-fans ;[2] and if my explanation of the practice is correct, it may well have been that they, like the Zulus, attributed a special power of reproduction to the genital organs, and therefore carefully excised them from the body of the victim in order to impart their virtue to the fields. I have conjectured that a similar use was made of the severed portions of the priests of Attis.[3]

To an ancient Egyptian, with his firm belief in a personal immortality dependent on the integrity of the body, the prospect of mutilation after death must have been very repugnant ; and we may suppose that the kings offered a strenuous resistance to the custom and finally succeeded in abolishing it. They may have represented to the people that they would attain their object better by keeping the royal corpse intact than by frittering it away in small pieces. Their subjects apparently acquiesced in the argument, or at all events in the conclusion ; yet the mountains of masonry beneath which the old Egyptian kings lay buried may have been intended to guard them from the superstitious devotion of their friends quite as much as from the hostile designs of their enemies, since both alike must have been under a strong temptation to violate the sanctity of the grave in order to possess themselves of bodies which were believed to be endowed with magical virtue of the most tremendous potency. In antiquity the safety of the state was often believed to depend on the possession of a talisman, which sometimes consisted of the bones of a king or hero. Hence the graves of such persons were sometimes kept secret.[4] The violation of royal tombs by a conqueror was not a mere insult : it was a deadly blow struck at the prosperity of the kingdom. Hence Ashurbanipal carried off to Assyria the bones of the kings of Elam, believing that thus he gave their shades no repose and deprived them of food and

The Egyptian kings probably opposed the custom and succeeded in abolishing it.

Precautions taken to preserve the bodies of kings from mutilation.

[1] Dudley Kidd, *Savage Childhood* (London, 1906), p. 291.

[2] Above, p. 97.

[3] Above, pp. 268 *sq.*

[4] See my notes on Pausanias, i. 28. 7 and viii. 47. 5 (vol. ii. pp. 366 *sq.*, vol. iv. pp. 433 *sq.*).

drink.[1] The Moabites burned the bones of the king of Edom into lime.[2] Lysimachus is said to have opened the graves of the kings of Epirus and scattered the bones of the dead.[3]

With savage and barbarous tribes in like manner it is not unusual to violate the sanctity of the tomb either for the purpose of wreaking vengeance on the dead or more commonly perhaps for the sake of gaining possession of the bones and converting them to magical uses. Hence the Mpongwe kings of the Gaboon region in West Africa are buried secretly lest their heads should fall into the hands of men of another tribe, who would make a powerful fetish out of the brains.[4] Again, in Togoland, West Africa, the kings of the Ho tribe are buried with great secrecy in the forest, and a false grave is made ostentatiously in the king's house. None but his personal retainers and a single daughter know where the king's real grave is. The intention of this secret burial is to prevent enemies from digging up the corpse and cutting off the head.[5] "The heads of important chiefs in the Calabar districts are usually cut off from the body on burial and kept secretly for fear the head, and thereby the spirit, of the dead chief, should be stolen from the town. If it were stolen it would be not only a great advantage to its new possessor, but a great danger to the chief's old town, because he would know all the peculiar ju-ju relating to it. For each town has a peculiar one, kept exceedingly secret, in addition to the general ju-jus, and this secret one would then be in the hands of the new owners of the spirit."[6] The graves of Basuto chiefs are kept secret lest certain more or less imaginary witches and wizards called *Baloi*, who haunt tombs, should get possession of the bones and work evil magic with them.[7] In the Thonga tribe of South Africa,

[1] R. F. Harper, *Assyrian and Babylonian Literature* (New York, 1901), p. 116 ; C. Fossey, *La Magie Assyrienne* (Paris, 1902), pp. 34 *sq.*

[2] Amos ii. 1.

[3] Pausanias, i. 9. 7 *sq.*

[4] P. B. du Chaillu, *Explorations and Adventures in Equatorial Africa* (London, 1861), pp. 18 *sq.*

[5] J. Spieth, *Die Ewe-Stämme* (Berlin, 1906), p. 107.

[6] Mary H. Kingsley, *Travels in West Africa* (London, 1897), pp. 449 *sq.* In West African jargon the word ju-ju means fetish or magic.

[7] Father Porte, " Les reminiscences d'un missionnaire du Basutoland," *Missions Catholiques*, xxviii. (1896) pp. 311 *sq.* As to the *Baloi*, see A. Merensky, *Beiträge zur Kenntniss Süd-Afrikas* (Berlin, 1875), pp. 138 *sq.* ; E. Gottschling, "The Bawenda,"

when a chief dies, he is buried secretly by night in a sacred wood, and few people know the place of the grave. With some clans of the tribe it is customary to level the mound over the grave so that no sign whatever remains to show where the body has been buried. This is said to be done lest enemies should exhume the corpse and cut off the ears, the diaphragm, and other parts in order to make powerful war-charms out of them.[1] By many tribes in Fiji "the burial - place of their chief is kept a profound secret, lest those whom he injured during his lifetime should revenge themselves by digging up and insulting or even eating his body. In some places the dead chief is buried in his own house, and armed warriors of his mother's kin keep watch night and day over his grave. After a time his bones are taken up and carried by night to some far-away inaccessible cave in the mountains, whose position is known only to a few trustworthy men. Ladders are constructed to enable them to reach the cave, and are taken down when the bones have been deposited there. Many frightful stories are told in connection with this custom, and it is certain that not even decomposition itself avails to baulk the last revenge of cannibals if they can find the grave. The very bones of the dead chief are not secure from the revenge of those whose friends he killed during his lifetime, or whom he otherwise so exasperated by the tyrannous exercise of his power as to fill their hearts with a deadly hate. In one instance within my own knowledge, when the hiding-place was discovered, the bones were taken away, scraped, and stewed down into a horrible hell - broth."[2] When a Melanesian dies who enjoyed a reputation for magical powers in his lifetime, his friends will sometimes hold a sham burial and keep the real grave secret for fear that men might come and dig up the skull and bones to make charms with them.[3]

Marginal notes: Burial-place of chiefs in Fiji kept secret. / Graves of Melanesian magicians kept secret.

Journal of the Anthropological Institute, xxxv. (1905) p. 375. For these two references I have to thank Mr. E. S. Hartland.

[1] Henri A. Junod, *The Life of a South African Tribe* (Neuchâtel, 1912–1913), i. 387 *sq*

[2] Lorimer Fison, "Notes on Fijian Burial Customs," *Journal of the Anthropological Institute,* x. (1881) pp. 141 *sq.*

[3] R. H. Codrington, *The Melanesians* (Oxford, 1891), p. 269.

Beliefs and practices of this sort are by no means confined to agricultural peoples. Among the Koniags of Alaska "in ancient times the pursuit of the whale was accompanied by numerous superstitious observances kept a secret by the hunters. Lieutenant Davidof states that the whalers preserved the bodies of brave or distinguished men in secluded caves, and before proceeding upon a whale-hunt would carry these dead bodies into a stream and then drink of the water thus tainted. One famous whaler of Kadiak who desired to flatter Baranof, the first chief manager of the Russian colonies, said to him, 'When you die I shall try to steal your body,' intending thus to express his great respect for Baranof. On the occasion of the death of a whaler his fellows would cut the body into pieces, each man taking one of them for the purpose of rubbing his spear-heads therewith. These pieces were dried or otherwise preserved, and were frequently taken into the canoes as talismans."[1]

To return to the human victims whose ashes the Egyptians scattered with winnowing-fans,[2] the red hair of these unfortunates was probably significant. If I am right, the custom of sacrificing such persons was not a mere way of wreaking a national spite on fair-haired foreigners, whom the black-haired Egyptians of old, like the black-haired Chinese of modern times, may have regarded as red-haired devils. For in Egypt the oxen which were sacrificed had also to be red ; a single black or white hair found on the beast would have disqualified it for the sacrifice.[3] If, as I conjecture, these human sacrifices were intended to promote the growth of the crops — and the winnowing of their ashes seems to support this view—red-haired victims were perhaps selected as best fitted to personate the spirit of the ruddy grain. For when a god is represented by a living person, it is natural that the human representative should be chosen on the ground of his supposed resemblance to the divine original.

[1] Ivan Petroff, *Report on the Population, Industries, and Resources of Alaska*, p. 142. The account seems to be borrowed from H. J. Holmberg, who adds that pains were taken to preserve the flesh from decay, "because they believed that their own life depended on it." See H. J. Holmberg, "Über die Völker des russischen Amerika," *Acta Societatis Scientiarum Fennicae*, iv. (Helsingfors, 1856) p. 391.

[2] Above, p. 97.

[3] Plutarch, *Isis et Osiris*, 31 ; Herodotus, ii. 38.

Hence the ancient Mexicans, conceiving the maize as a personal being who went through the whole course of life between seed-time and harvest, sacrificed new-born babes when the maize was sown, older children when it had sprouted, and so on till it was fully ripe, when they sacrificed old men.[1] A name for Osiris was the "crop" or "harvest";[2] and the ancients sometimes explained him as a personification of the corn.[3]

§ 2. *Osiris a Tree-Spirit*

But Osiris was more than a spirit of the corn; he was also a tree-spirit, and this may perhaps have been his primitive character, since the worship of trees is naturally older in the history of religion than the worship of the cereals. However that may have been, to an agricultural people like the Egyptians, who depended almost wholly on their crops, the corn-god was naturally a far more important

Osiris as a tree-spirit.

[1] Herrera, quoted by A. Bastian, *Die Culturländer des alten Amerika* (Berlin, 1878), ii. 639; *id.*, *General History of the vast Continent and Islands of America*, translated by Capt. J. Stevens (London, 1725-26), ii. 379 *sq.* (whose version of the passage is inadequate). Compare Brasseur de Bourbourg, *Histoire des nations civilisées du Mexique et de l'Amérique Centrale* (Paris, 1857-59), i. 327, iii. 525.

[2] E. Lefébure, *Le mythe Osirien* (Paris, 1874-75), p. 188.

[3] Firmicus Maternus, *De errore profanarum religionum*, 2, " *Defensores eorum volunt addere physicam rationem, frugum semina Osirim dicentes esse, Isim terram, Tyfonem calorem : et quia maturatae fruges calore ad vitam hominum colliguntur et divisae a terrae consortio separantur et rursus adpropinquante hieme seminantur, hanc volunt esse mortem Osiridis, cum fruges recondunt, inventionem vero, cum fruges genitali terrae fomento conceptae annua rursus coeperint procreatione generari.*" Tertullian, *Adversus Marcionem*, i. 13, " *Sic et Osiris quod semper sepelitur*

et in vivido quaeritur et cum gaudio invenitur, reciprocarum frugum et vividorum elementorum et recidivi anni fidem argumentantur." Plutarch, *Isis et Osiris*, 65, οὕτω δὲ καὶ τοῖς πολλοῖς καὶ φορτικοῖς ἐπιχειρήσομεν, εἴτε ταῖς καθ' ὥραν μεταβολαῖς τοῦ περιέχοντος εἴτε ταῖς καρπῶν γενέσεσι καὶ σποραῖς καὶ ἀρότοις χαίρουσι τὰ περὶ τοὺς θεοὺς τούτους συνοικειοῦντες, καὶ λέγοντες θάπτεσθαι μὲν "Οσιριν ὅτε κρύπτεται τῇ γῇ σπειρόμενος ὁ καρπός, αὖθις δ' ἀναβιοῦσθαι καὶ ἀναφαίνεσθαι ὅτε βλαστήσεως ἀρχή. Eusebius, *Praeparatio Evangelii*, iii. 11. 31, ὁ δὲ 'Όσιρις παρ' Αἰγυπτίοις τὴν κάρπιμον παρίστησι δύναμιν, ἣν θρήνοις ἀπομειλίσσονται εἰς γὴν ἀφανιζομένην ἐν τῷ σπόρῳ καὶ ὑφ' ἡμῶν καταναλισκομένην εἰς τὰς τροφάς. Athenagoras, *Supplicatio pro Christianis*, 22, pp. 112, 114 ed. J. C. T. Otto, τὰ δὲ στοιχεῖα καὶ τὰ μόρια αὐτῶν θεοποιοῦσιν, ἄλλοτε ἄλλα ὀνόματα αὐτοῖς τιθέμενοι, τὴν μὲν τοῦ σίτου σποράν 'Όσιριν (ὅθεν φασὶ μυστικῶς ἐπὶ τῇ ἀνευρέσει τῶν μελῶν ἢ τῶν καρπῶν ἐπιλεχθῆναι τῇ 'Ίσιδι · Εὑρήκαμεν, συγχαίρομεν). See also the passage of Cornutus quoted above, vol. i. p. 229, note [2].

personage than the tree-god, and attracted a larger share of their devotion.   The character of Osiris as a tree-spirit was represented very graphically in a ceremony described by

His image enclosed in a pine-tree.

Firmicus Maternus.[1]   A pine-tree having been cut down, the centre was hollowed out, and with the wood thus excavated an image of Osiris was made, which was then buried like a corpse in the hollow of the tree.   It is hard to imagine how the conception of a tree as tenanted by a personal being could be more plainly expressed.   The image of Osiris thus made was kept for a year and then burned, exactly as was done with the image of Attis which was attached to the pine-tree.[2]   The ceremony of cutting the tree, as described by Firmicus Maternus, appears to be alluded to by Plutarch.[3] It was probably the ritual counterpart of the mythical discovery of the body of Osiris enclosed in the *erica*-tree.[4]

The setting up of the *ded* pillar at the great festival of Osiris in the month of Khoiak.

Now we know from the monuments that at Busiris, Memphis, and elsewhere the great festival of Osiris closed on the thirtieth of Khoiak with the setting up of a remarkable pillar known as the *tatu, tat, tet, dad,* or *ded.*   This was a column with four or five cross-bars, like superposed capitals, at the top.   The whole roughly resembled a telegraph-post with the cross-pieces which support the wires.   Sometimes on the monuments a human form is given to the pillar by carving a grotesque face on it, robing the lower part, crowning the top with the symbols of Osiris, and adding two arms which hold two other characteristic emblems of the god, the crook and the scourge or flail.   On a Theban tomb the king himself, assisted by his relations and a priest, is represented hauling at the ropes by which the pillar is being raised, while the queen looks on and her sixteen daughters accompany the ceremony with the music of rattles and sistrums. Again, in the hall of the Osirian mysteries at Abydos the King Sety I. and the goddess Isis are depicted raising the column between them.   In Egyptian theology the pillar was interpreted as the backbone of Osiris, and whatever its meaning

---

[1] *De errore profanarum religionum,* 27.

[2] See above, vol. i. pp. 267, 277.

[3] Plutarch, *Isis et Osiris,* 21, αἰνῶ δὲ τομὴν ξύλου καὶ σχίσιν λίνου καὶ χοὰς

χεομένας, διὰ τὸ πολλὰ τῶν μυστικῶν ἀναμεμῖχθαι τούτοις.   Again, *ibid.* 42, τὸ δὲ ξύλον ἐν ταῖς λεγομέναις Ὀσίριδος ταφαῖς τέμνοντες κατασκευάζουσι λάρνακα μηνοειδῆ.

[4] See above, p. 9.

may have been, it was one of the holiest symbols of the national religion.   It might very well be a conventional way of representing a tree stripped of its leaves ; and if Osiris was a tree-spirit, the bare trunk and branches might naturally be described as his backbone.   The setting up of the column would thus, as several modern scholars believe, shadow forth the resurrection of the god, and the importance of the occasion would explain and justify the prominent part which the king appears to have taken in the ceremony.[1]   It is to be noted that in the myth of Osiris the *erica*-tree which shot up and enclosed his dead body, was cut down by a king and turned by him into a pillar of his house.[2]   We can hardly doubt, therefore, that this incident of the legend was supposed to be dramatically set forth in the erection of the *ded* column by the king.   Like the similar custom of cutting a pine-tree and fastening an image to it in the rites of Attis, the ceremony may have belonged to that class of customs of which the bringing in of the May-pole is among the most familiar.   The association of the king and queen of Egypt with the *ded* pillar reminds us of the association of a King and Queen of May with the May-pole.[3]   The resemblance may be more than superficial.

The setting up of the pillar may have been an emblem of the god's resurrection.

---

[1] As to the *tet* or *ded* pillar and its erection at the festival see H. Brugsch in *Zeitschrift für ägyptische Sprache und Alterthumskunde*, 1881, pp. 84, 96 ; *id.*, *Religion und Mythologie der alten Aegypter*, p. 618 ; A. Erman, *Aegypten und aegyptisches Leben im Altertum*, pp. 377 *sq.* ; *id.*, *Die ägyptische Religion*,[2] pp. 22, 64 ; C. P. Tiele, *History of the Egyptian Religion* (London, 1882), pp. 46 *sq.* ; Sir J. Gardiner Wilkinson, *Manners and Customs of the Ancient Egyptians* (London, 1878), iii. pp. 67, note [3], and 82 ; A. Wiedemann, *Religion of the Ancient Egyptians*, pp. 289 *sq.* ; G. Maspero, *Histoire ancienne des Peuples de l' Orient Classique*, i. 130 *sq.* ; A. Moret, *Du caractère religieux de la royauté Pharaonique*, p. 153, note [1]; *id.*, *Mystères Égyptiens*, pp. 12-16 ; E. A. Wallis Budge, *The Gods of the Egyptians*, ii. 122, 124, *sq.* ; *id. Osiris and the Egyptian Resurrection*, i. 6, 37, 48,

51 *sqq.* ; Miss Margaret A. Murray, *The Osireion at Abydos*, pp. 27, 28 ; Ed. Meyer, *Geschichte des Altertums*,[2] i. 2, p. 70.   In a letter to 'me (dated 8th December, 1910) my colleague Professor P. E. Newberry tells me that he believes Osiris to have been originally a cedar-tree god imported into Egypt from the Lebanon, and he regards the *ded* pillar as a lopped cedar-tree.   The flail, as a symbol of Osiris, he believes to be the instrument used to collect incense. A similar flail is used by peasants in Crete to extract the ladanum gum from the shrubs.   See P. de Tournefort, *Relation d'un Voyage du Levant* (Amsterdam, 1718), i. 29, with the plate.   For this reference I am indebted to Professor Newberry.

[2] Plutarch, *Isis et Osiris*, 15.'   See above, p. 9.

[3] *The Magic Art and the Evolution of Kings*, ii. 88-90.

Osiris
associated
with the
pine, the
sycamore,
the
tamarisk,
and the
acacia.

In the hall of Osiris at Denderah the coffin containing the hawk-headed mummy of the god is clearly depicted as enclosed within a tree, apparently a conifer, the trunk and branches of which are seen above and below the coffin.[1] The scene thus corresponds closely both to the myth and to the ceremony described by Firmicus Maternus. In another scene at Denderah a tree of the same sort is represented growing between the dead and the reviving Osiris, as if on purpose to indicate that the tree was the symbol of the divine resurrection.[2] A pine-cone often appears on the monuments as an offering presented to Osiris, and a manuscript of the Louvre speaks of the cedar as sprung from him.[3] The sycamore and the tamarisk were also his trees. In inscriptions he is spoken of as residing in them;[4] and in tombs his mother Nut is often portrayed standing in the midst of a sycamore-tree and pouring a libation for the benefit of the dead.[5] In one of the Pyramid Texts we read, "Hail to thee, Sycamore, which enclosest the god";[6] and in certain temples the statue of Osiris used to be placed for seven days upon branches of sycamores. The explanation appended in the sacred texts declares that the placing of the image on the tree was intended to recall the seven months passed by Osiris in the womb of his mother Nut, the goddess of the sycamore.[7] The rite recalls the story that Adonis was born after ten months' gestation from a myrrh-tree.[8] Further, in a sepulchre at How (Diospolis Parva) a tamarisk is depicted overshadowing the tomb of Osiris, while a bird is perched among the branches with the significant legend "the soul of Osiris,"[9]

[1] A. Mariette-Bey, *Dendérah*, iv. pl. 66.

[2] A. Mariette-Bey, *Dendérah*, iv. pl. 72. Compare E. Lefébure, *Le mythe Osirien*, pp. 194, 196, who regards the tree as a conifer. But it is perhaps a tamarisk.

[3] E. Lefébure, *op. cit.* pp. 195, 197.

[4] S. Birch, in Sir J. G. Wilkinson's *Manners and Customs of the Ancient Egyptians* (London, 1878), iii. 84.

[5] Sir J. G. Wilkinson, *op. cit.* iii. 62-64; E. A. Wallis Budge, *The Gods of the Egyptians*, ii. 106 *sq.*; G.

Maspero, *Histoire ancienne des Peuples de l'Orient Classique*, i. 185.

[6] J. H. Breasted, *Development of Religion and Thought in Ancient Egypt* (London, 1912), p. 28.

[7] A. Moret, *Kings and Gods of Egypt* (New York and London, 1912), p. 83.

[8] Above, vol. i. pp. 227 *sq.*

[9] Sir J. G. Wilkinson, *op. cit.* iii. 349 *sq.*; A. Erman, *Aegypten und aegyptisches Leben im Altertum*, p. 368; H. Brugsch, *Religion und Mythologie der alten Aegypter*, p. 621.

showing that the spirit of the dead god was believed to haunt his sacred tree.[1] Again, in the series of sculptures which illustrate the mystic history of Osiris in the great temple of Isis at Philae, a tamarisk is figured with two men pouring water on it. The accompanying inscription leaves no doubt, says Brugsch, that the verdure of the earth was believed to be connected with the verdure of the tree, and that the sculpture refers to the grave of Osiris at Philae, of which Plutarch tells us that it was overshadowed by a *methide* plant, taller than any olive-tree. This sculpture, it may be observed, occurs in the same chamber in which the god is represented as a corpse with ears of corn springing from him.[2] In inscriptions he is referred to as "the one in the tree," "the solitary one in the acacia," and so forth.[3] On the monuments he sometimes appears as a mummy covered with a tree or with plants ;[4] and trees are represented growing from his grave.[5]

It accords with the character of Osiris as a tree-spirit that his worshippers were forbidden to injure fruit-trees, and with his character as a god of vegetation in general that they were not allowed to stop up wells of water, which are so important for the irrigation of hot southern lands.[6]

Osiris in relation to fruit-trees, wells, the vine, and ivy.

[1] We may compare a belief of some of the Californian Indians that the owl is the guardian spirit and deity of the "California big tree," and that it is equally unlucky to fell the tree or to shoot the bird. See S. Powers, *Tribes of California* (Washington, 1877), p. 398. When a Maori priest desires to protect the life or soul (*hau*) of a tree against the insidious arts of magicians, he sets a bird-snare in the tree, and the first bird caught in the snare, or its right wing, embodies the life or soul of the tree. Accordingly the priest recites appropriate spells over the bird or its wing and hides it away in the forest. After that no evil-disposed magician can hurt the tree, since its life or soul is not in it but hidden away in the forest. See Elsdon Best, "Spiritual Concepts of the Maori," *Journal of the Polynesian Society*, ix. (1900) p. 195. Thus the bird or its wing is the depository of the external

soul of the tree. Compare *Balder the Beautiful*, ii. 95 *sqq*.
[2] Sir J. G. Wilkinson, *op. cit.* iii. 349 *sq.* ; H. Brugsch, *Religion und Mythologie der alten Aegypter*, p. 621 ; R. V. Lanzone, *Dizionario di Mitologia Egizia*, tav. cclxiii. ; Plutarch, *Isis et Osiris*, 20. In this passage of Plutarch it has been proposed by G. Parthey to read μυρίκης (tamarisk) for μηθίδης (*methide*), and the conjecture appears to be accepted by Wilkinson, *loc. cit.*
[3] E. Lefébure, *Le mythe Osirien*, p. 191.
[4] E. Lefébure, *op. cit.* p. 188.
[5] R. V. Lanzone, *Dizionario di Mitologia Egizia*, tav. ccciv. ; G. Maspero, *Histoire ancienne des Peuples de l'Orient Classique*, ii. 570, fig.
[6] Plutarch, *Isis et Osiris*, 35. One of the points in which the myths of Isis and Demeter agree is that both goddesses in the search for the loved and lost one are said to have sat down,

According to one legend, he taught men to train the vine to poles, to prune its superfluous foliage, and to extract the juice of the grape.[1]   In the papyrus of Nebseni, written about 1550 B.C., Osiris is depicted sitting in a shrine, from the roof of which hang clusters of grapes;[2] and in the papyrus of the royal scribe Nekht we see the god enthroned in front of a pool, from the banks of which a luxuriant vine, with many bunches of grapes, grows towards the green face of the seated deity.[3]   The ivy was sacred to him, and was called his plant because it is always green.[4]

§ 3. Osiris a God of Fertility

Osiris perhaps conceived as a god of fertility in general.   As a god of vegetation Osiris was naturally conceived as a god of creative energy in general, since men at a certain stage of evolution fail to distinguish between the reproductive powers of animals and of plants.   Hence a striking feature in his worship was the coarse but expressive symbolism by which this aspect of his nature was presented to the eye not merely of the initiated but of the multitude.   At his festival women used to go about the villages singing songs in his praise and carrying obscene images of him which they set in motion by means of strings.[5]   The custom was probably a charm to ensure the growth of the crops.   A similar image of him, decked with all the fruits of the earth, is said to have stood in a temple before a figure of Isis,[6] and in the chambers dedicated to him at Philae the dead god is portrayed lying on his bier in an attitude which indicates in the plainest way that even in death his generative virtue was not extinct but only suspended, ready to prove a source of life and fertility to the world when the opportunity should offer.[7]   Hymns

sad at heart and weary, on the edge of a well. Hence those who had been initiated at Eleusis were forbidden to sit on a well. See Plutarch, *Isis et Osiris*, 15 ; Homer, *Hymn to Demeter*, 98 *sq.* ; Pausanias, i. 39. 1 ; Apollodorus, *Bibliotheca*, i. 5. 1 ; Nicander, *Theriaca*, 486 ; Clement of Alexandria, *Protrept.* ii. 20, p. 16 ed. Potter.

[1] Tibullus, i. 7. 33-36 ; Diodorus Siculus, i. 17. 1, i. 20. 4.

[2] E. A. Wallis Budge, *Osiris and*

the *Egyptian Resurrection*, i. 38, 39.

[3] E. A. Wallis Budge, *op. cit.* i. 19, 45, with frontispiece.

[4] Diodorus Siculus, i. 17. 4 *sq.*

[5] Herodotus, ii. 48 ; Plutarch, *Isis et Osiris*, 12, 18, 36, 51 ; Diodorus Siculus, i. 21. 5, i. 22. 6 *sq.*, iv. 6. 3.

[6] Hippolytus, *Refutatio omnium haeresium*, v. 7, p. 144 ed. Duncker and Schneidewin.

[7] A. Mariette-Bey, *Dendérah*, iv. plates 66, 68, 69, 70, 88, 89, 90. Com-

addressed to Osiris contain allusions to this important side
of his nature. In one of them it is said that the world
waxes green in triumph through him ; and another declares,
"Thou art the father and mother of mankind, they live on
thy breath, they subsist on the flesh of thy body."[1] We
may conjecture that in this paternal aspect he was supposed,
like other gods of fertility, to bless men and women with
offspring, and that the processions at his festival were
intended to promote this object as well as to quicken the
seed in the ground. It would be to misjudge ancient
religion to denounce as lewd and profligate the emblems
and the ceremonies which the Egyptians employed for the
purpose of giving effect to this conception of the divine
power. The ends which they proposed to themselves in
these rites were natural and laudable ; only the means they
adopted to compass them were mistaken. A similar fallacy
induced the Greeks to adopt a like symbolism in their
Dionysiac festivals, and the superficial but striking resemblance thus produced between the two religions has perhaps
more than anything else misled inquirers, both ancient and
modern, into identifying worships which, though certainly
akin in nature, are perfectly distinct and independent in
origin.[2]

§ 4. Osiris a God of the Dead

We have seen that in one of his aspects Osiris was the
ruler and judge of the dead.[3] To a people like the Egyptians,
who not only believed in a life beyond the grave but actually
spent much of their time, labour, and money in preparing
for it, this office of the god must have appeared hardly, if
at all, less important than his function of making the earth
to bring forth its fruits in due season. We may assume
that in the faith of his worshippers the two provinces of the

As god of
the corn
Osiris
came to be
viewed as
the god of
the resur-
rection.

---

pare R. V. Lanzone, *Dizionario di
Mitologia Egizia*, tavv. cclxxi., cclxxii.,
cclxxvi., cclxxxv., cclxxxvi., cclxxxvii.,
cclxxxix., ccxc. ; E. A. Wallis Budge,
The Gods of the Egyptians, ii. 132,
136, 137.

[1] Miss Margaret A. Murray, *The
Osireion at Abydos*, p. 27.

[2] That the Greek Dionysus was

nothing but a slightly disguised form
of the Egyptian Osiris has been held
by Herodotus in ancient and by Mr.
P. Foucart in modern times. See
Herodotus, ii. 49 ; P. Foucart, *Le
culte de Dionysos en Attique* (Paris,
1904) (*Mémoires de l'Académie des
Inscriptions et Belles-Lettres*, xxxvii.).

[3] Above, pp. 13 *sq.*

god were intimately connected. In laying their dead in the grave they committed them to his keeping who could raise them from the dust to life eternal, even as he caused the seed to spring from the ground. Of that faith the corn-stuffed effigies of Osiris found in Egyptian tombs furnish an eloquent and unequivocal testimony.[1] They were at once an emblem and an instrument of resurrection. Thus from the sprouting of the grain the ancient Egyptians drew an augury of human immortality. They are not the only people who have built the same far-reaching hopes on the same slender foundation. " Thou fool, that which thou sowest, thou sowest not that body that shall be, but bare grain, it may chance of wheat, or of some other grain : but God giveth it a body as it hath pleased him, and to every seed his own body. So also is the resurrection of the dead. It is sown in corruption ; it is raised in incorruption : it is sown in weakness ; it is raised in power : it is sown a natural body ; it is raised a spiritual body." [2]

Great popularity of the worship of Osiris.

A god who thus fed his people with his own broken body in this life, and who held out to them a promise of a blissful eternity in a better world hereafter, naturally reigned supreme in their affections. We need not wonder, therefore, that in Egypt the worship of the other gods was over-shadowed by that of Osiris, and that while they were revered each in his own district, he and his divine partner Isis were adored in all.[3]

---

[1] Above, pp. 90 sq.

[2] 1 Corinthians xv. 36-38, 42-44.

[3] Herodotus, ii. 42. Compare E.

A. Wallis Budge, The Gods of the Egyptians, ii. 115 sq., 203 sq. ; id., Osiris and the Egyptian Resurrection, i. 22 sq.

CHAPTER VI

ISIS

THE original meaning of the goddess Isis is still more Multi-
difficult to determine than that of her brother and husband farious
attributes
Osiris. Her attributes and epithets were so numerous that of Isis.
in the hieroglyphics she is called "the many-named," "the
thousand-named," and in Greek inscriptions "the myriad-
named."[1] The late eminent Dutch scholar C. P. Tiele
confessed candidly that "it is now impossible to tell precisely to what natural phenomena the character of Isis at
first referred." Yet he adds, "Originally she was a goddess
of fecundity."[2] Similarly Dr. Budge writes that "Isis was
the great and beneficent goddess and mother, whose influence
and love pervaded all heaven and earth and the abode of
the dead, and she was the personification of the great
feminine, creative power which conceived, and brought forth
every living creature and thing, from the gods in heaven to
man on the earth, and to the insect on the ground; what
she brought forth she protected, and cared for, and fed, and
nourished, and she employed her life in using her power
graciously and successfully, not only in creating new beings
but in restoring those that were dead. She was, besides
these things, the highest type of a faithful and loving wife

---

[1] H. Brugsch, *Religion und Mythologie der alten Aegypter*, p. 645; W.
Dittenberger, *Orientis Graeci Inscriptiones Selectae*, vol. ii. p. 433, No.
695; *Corpus Inscriptionum Graecarum*,
iii. p. 1232, No. 4941. Compare H.
Dessau, *Inscriptiones Latinae Selectae*,
vol. ii. Pars i. p. 179, No. 4376 A.

In Egyptian her name is *Hest* or *Ast*,
but the derivation and meaning of the
name are unknown. See A. Wiedemann, *The Religion of the Ancient
Egyptians*, pp. 218 *sq.*

[2] C. P. Tiele, *History of Egyptian
Religion* (London, 1882), p. 57.

and mother, and it was in this capacity that the Egyptians honoured and worshipped her most."[1]

Thus in her character of a goddess of fecundity Isis answered to the great mother goddesses of Asia, though she differed from them in the chastity and fidelity of her conjugal life ; for while they were unmarried and dissolute, she had a husband and was a true wife to him as well as an affectionate mother to their son. Hence her beautiful Madonna-like figure reflects a more refined state of society and of morals than the coarse, sensual, cruel figures of Astarte, Anaitis, Cybele, and the rest of that crew. A clear trace, indeed, of an ethical standard very different from our own lingers in her double relation of sister and wife to Osiris ; but in most other respects she is rather late than primitive, the full-blown flower rather than the seed of a long religious development. The attributes ascribed to her were too various to be all her own. They were graces borrowed from many lesser deities, sweets rifled from a thousand humbler plants to feed the honey of her superb efflorescence. Yet in her complex nature it is perhaps still possible to detect the original nucleus round which by a slow process of accretion the other elements gathered.

For if her brother and husband Osiris was in one of his aspects the corn-god, as we have seen reason to believe, she must surely have been the corn-goddess. There are at least some grounds for thinking so. For if we may trust Diodorus Siculus, whose authority appears to have been the Egyptian historian Manetho, the discovery of wheat and barley was attributed to Isis, and at her festivals stalks of these grains were carried in procession to commemorate the boon she had conferred on men.[2] A further detail is added by Augustine. He says that Isis made the discovery of barley at the moment when she was sacrificing to the common ancestors of her husband and herself, all of whom had been kings, and that she showed the newly discovered ears of barley to Osiris and his councillor Thoth or Mercury, as Roman writers called him. That is why,

[1] E. A. Wallis Budge, *The Gods of the Egyptians*, ii. 203 *sq.*

[2] Diodorus Siculus, i. 14. 1 *sq.* Eusebius (*Praeparatio Evangelii*, iii. 3) quotes from Diodorus a long passage on the early religion of Egypt, prefacing it with the remark that Diodorus's account of the subject was more concise than that of Manetho.

adds Augustine, they identify Isis with Ceres.[1] Further, at harvest-time, when the Egyptian reapers had cut the first stalks, they laid them down and beat their breasts, wailing and calling upon Isis.[2] The custom has been already explained as a lament for the corn-spirit slain under the sickle.[3] Amongst the epithets by which Isis is designated in the inscriptions are " Creatress of green things," " Green goddess, whose green colour is like unto the greenness of the earth," " Lady of Bread," " Lady of Beer," " Lady of Abundance." [4] According to Brugsch she is " not only the creatress of the fresh verdure of vegetation which covers the earth, but is actually the green corn-field itself, which is personified as a goddess." [5] This is confirmed by her epithet *Sochit* or *Sochet*, meaning " a corn-field," a sense which the word still retains in Coptic.[6] The Greeks conceived of Isis as a corn-goddess, for they identified her with Demeter.[7] In a Greek epigram she is described as " she who has given birth to the fruits of the earth," and " the mother of the ears of corn " ; [8] and in a hymn composed in her honour she speaks of herself as " queen of the wheat-field," and is described as " charged with the care of the fruitful furrow's wheat-rich path." [9] Accordingly, Greek or Roman artists often represented her with ears of corn on her head or in her hand.[10]

Such, we may suppose, was Isis in the olden time, a rustic Corn-Mother adored with uncouth rites by Egyptian swains. But the homely features of the clownish goddess could hardly be traced in the refined, the saintly form which, spiritualized by ages of religious evolution, she presented to her worshippers of after days as the true wife, the tender

Refinement and spiritualization of Isis in later times: the popularity of her worship in the Roman empire.

[1] Augustine, *De civitate Dei*, viii. 27. Tertullian says that Isis wore a wreath of the corn she had discovered (*De corona*, 7).

[2] Diodorus Siculus, i. 14. 2.

[3] See above, p. 45, and vol. i. p. 232.

[4] H. Brugsch, *Religion und Mythologie der alten Aegypter*, p. 647 ; E. A. Wallis Budge, *Osiris and the Egyptian Resurrection*, ii. 277.

[5] H. Brugsch, *op. cit.* p. 649. Compare E. A. Wallis Budge, *The Gods of the Egyptians*, ii. 216.

[6] H. Brugsch, *loc. cit.*

[7] Herodotus, ii. 59, 156 ; Diodorus Siculus, i. 13, 25, 96 ; Apollolorus, *Bibliotheca*, ii. 1. 3 ; J. Tzetzes, *Schol. on Lycophron*, 212. See further W. Drexler, *s.v.* " Isis," in W. H. Roscher's *Lexikon der griech. und röm. Mythologie*, ii. 443 *sq.*

[8] *Anthologia Planudea*, cclxiv. 1.

[9] *Epigrammata Graeca ex lapidibus conlecta*, ed. G. Kaibel (Berlin, 1878), No. 1028, pp. 437 *sq.* ; *Orphica*, ed. E. Abel (Leipsic and Prague, 1885), pp. 295 *sqq.*

[10] W. Drexler, *op. cit.* ii. 448 *sqq.*

mother, the beneficent queen of nature, encircled with the nimbus of moral purity, of immemorial and mysterious sanctity. Thus chastened and transfigured she won many hearts far beyond the boundaries of her native land. In that welter of religions which accompanied the decline of national life in antiquity her worship was one of the most popular at Rome and throughout the empire. Some of the Roman emperors themselves were openly addicted to it.[1] And however the religion of Isis may, like any other, have been often worn as a cloak by men and women of loose life, her rites appear on the whole to have been honourably distinguished by a dignity and composure, a solemnity and decorum well fitted to soothe the troubled mind, to ease the burdened heart. They appealed therefore to gentle spirits, and above all to women, whom the bloody and licentious rites of other Oriental goddesses only shocked and repelled. We need not wonder, then, that in a period of decadence, when traditional faiths were shaken, when systems clashed, when men's minds were disquieted, when the fabric of empire itself, once deemed eternal, began to show ominous rents and fissures, the serene figure of Isis with her spiritual calm, her gracious promise of immortality, should have appeared to many like a star in a stormy sky, and should have roused in their breasts a rapture of devotion not unlike that which was paid in the Middle Ages to the Virgin Mary. Indeed her stately ritual, with its shaven and tonsured priests, its matins and vespers, its tinkling music, its baptism and aspersions of holy water, its solemn processions, its jewelled images of the Mother of God, presented many points of similarity to the pomps and ceremonies of Catholicism.[2] The resemblance need not be purely acci-

Resemblance of Isis to the Madonna.

[1] Otho often celebrated, or at least attended, the rites of Isis, clad in a linen garment (Suetonius, *Otho*, 12). Commodus did the same, with shaven head, carrying the effigy of Anubis. See Lampridius, *Commodus*, 9 ; Spartianus, *Pescennius Niger*, 6 ; *id.*, *Caracallus*, 9.

[2] L. Preller, *Römische Mythologie*[3] (Berlin, 1881-1883), ii. 373-385 ; J. Marquardt, *Römische Staatsverwaltung* (Leipsic, 1885), iii.[2] 77-81 ; E. Renan,

Marc-Aurèle et la fin du Monde Antique (Paris, 1882), pp. 570 *sqq.* ; J. Reville, *La religion romaine à Rome sous les Sévères* (Paris, 1886), pp. 54-61 ; G. Lafaye, *Histoire du culte des divinités d'Alexandrie* (Paris, 1884) ; E. Meyer and W. Drexler, *s.v.* "Isis," in W. H. Roscher's *Lexikon der griech. und röm. Mythologie*, ii. 360 *sqq.* ; S. Dill, *Roman Society in the Last Century of the Western Empire*[2] (London, 1899), pp. 79 *sq.*, 85 *sqq.* ; *id.*, *Roman Society*

dental. Ancient Egypt may have contributed its share to the gorgeous symbolism of the Catholic Church as well as to the pale abstractions of her theology.[1] Certainly in art the figure of Isis suckling the infant Horus is so like that of the Madonna and child that it has sometimes received the adoration of ignorant Christians.[2] And to Isis in her later character of patroness of mariners the Virgin Mary perhaps owes her beautiful epithet of *Stella Maris*, " Star of the Sea," under which she is adored by tempest-tossed sailors.[3] The attributes of a marine deity may have been bestowed on Isis by the sea-faring Greeks of Alexandria. They are quite foreign to her original character and to the habits of the Egyptians, who had no love of the sea.[4] On this hypothesis Sirius, the bright star of Isis, which on July mornings rises from the glassy waves of the eastern Mediterranean, a harbinger of halcyon weather to mariners, was the true *Stella Maris*, " the Star of the Sea."

---

from Nero to Marcus Aurelius (London, 1904), pp. 560 *sqq.* The chief passage on the worship of Isis in the West is the eleventh book of Apuleius's *Metamorphoses*. On the reputation which the goddess enjoyed as a healer of the sick see Diodorus Siculus, i. 25 ; W. Drexler, *op. cit.* ii. 521 *sqq.* The divine partner of Isis in later times, especially outside of Egypt, was Serapis, that is Osiris-Apis (*Aśar-Ḥāpi*), the sacred Apis bull of Memphis, identified after death with Osiris. His oldest sanctuary was at Memphis (Pausanias, i. 18. 4), and there was one at Babylon in the time of Alexander the Great (Plutarch, *Alexander*, 76 ; Arrian, *Anabasis*, vii. 26). Ptolemy I. or II. built a great and famous temple in his honour at Alexandria, where he set up an image of the god which was commonly said to have been imported from Sinope in Pontus. See Tacitus, *Histor.* iv. 83 *sq.*; Plutarch, *Isis et Osiris*, 27-29 ; Clement of Alexandria, *Protrept.* iv. 48, p. 42 ed. Potter. In after ages the institution of the worship of Serapis

was attributed to this Ptolemy, but all that the politic Macedonian monarch appears to have done was to assimilate the Egyptian Osiris to the Greek Pluto, and so to set up a god whom Egyptians and Greeks could unite in worshipping. Serapis gradually assumed the attributes of Aesculapius, the Greek god of healing, in addition to those of Pluto, the Greek god of the dead. See G. Lafaye, *Histoire du culte des divinités d'Alexandrie*, pp. 16 *sqq.* ; A. Wiedemann, *Herodots zweites Buch*, p. 589 ; E. A. Wallis Budge, *The Gods of the Egyptians*, ii. 195 *sqq.* ; A. Erman, *Die ägyptische Religion*,[2] pp. 237 *sq.*

[1] The resemblance of Isis to the Virgin Mary has often been pointed out. See W. Drexler, *s.v.* " Isis," in W. H. Roscher's *Lexikon der griech. und röm. Mythologie*, ii. 428 *sqq.*

[2] W. Drexler, *op. cit.* ii. 430 *sq.*

[3] Th. Trede, *Das Heidentum in der römischen Kirche* (Gotha, 1889–1891), iii. 144 *sq.*

[4] On this later aspect of Isis see W. Drexler, *op. cit.* ii. 474 *sqq.*

CHAPTER VII

OSIRIS AND THE SUN

Osiris interpreted as the sun by many modern writers. OSIRIS has been sometimes interpreted as the sun-god; and in modern times this view has been held by so many distinguished writers that it deserves a brief examination. If we inquire on what evidence Osiris has been identified with the sun or the sun-god, it will be found on analysis to be minute in quantity and dubious, where it is not absolutely worthless, in quality. The diligent Jablonski, the first modern scholar to collect and sift the testimony of classical writers on Egyptian religion, says that it can be shown in many ways that Osiris is the sun, and that he could produce a cloud of witnesses to prove it, but that it is needless to do so, since no learned man is ignorant of the fact.[1] Of the writers whom he condescends to quote, the only two who expressly identify Osiris with the sun are Diodorus and Macrobius. The passage in Diodorus runs thus:[2] "It is said that the aboriginal inhabitants of Egypt, looking up to the sky, and smitten with awe and wonder at the nature of the universe, supposed that there were two gods, eternal and primaeval, the sun and the moon, of whom they named the sun Osiris and the moon Isis." Even if Diodorus's authority for this statement is Manetho, as there is some ground for believing,[3] little or no weight can be attached to it. For it is plainly a philosophical, and therefore a late, explanation of the first beginnings of Egyptian religion, reminding us of Kant's familiar saying about the starry heavens and the moral law rather than of the

[1] P. E. Jablonski, *Pantheon Aegyptiorum* (Frankfort, 1750–1752), i. 125 *sq.*

[2] Diodorus Siculus, i. 11. 1.

[3] See p. 116, note [2].

rude traditions of a primitive people. Jablonski's second authority, Macrobius, is no better, but rather worse. For Macrobius was the father of that large family of mythologists who resolve all or most gods into the sun. According to him Mercury was the sun, Mars was the sun, Janus was the sun, Saturn was the sun, so was Jupiter, also Nemesis, likewise Pan, and so on through a great part of the pantheon.[1] It was natural, therefore, that he should identify Osiris with the sun,[2] but his reasons for doing so are exceedingly slight. He refers to the ceremonies of alternate lamentation and joy as if they reflected the vicissitudes of the great luminary in his course through the sky. Further, he argues that Osiris must be the sun because an eye was one of his symbols. It is true that an eye was a symbol of Osiris,[3] and it is also true that the sun was often called 'the eye of Horus ";[4] yet the coincidence hardly suffices to establish the identity of the two deities. The opinion that Osiris was the sun is also mentioned, but not accepted, by Plutarch,[5] and it is referred to by Firmicus Maternus.[6]

Amongst modern scholars, Lepsius, in identifying Osiris with the sun, appears to rely mainly on the passage of Diodorus already quoted. But the monuments, he adds, also show " that down to a late time Osiris was sometimes conceived as *Ra*. In this quality he is named *Osiris-Ra*

The later identification of Osiris with Ra, the sun-god, does not

---

[1] See Macrobius, *Saturnalia*, bk. i.
[2] *Saturn.* i. 21. 11.
[3] Plutarch, *Isis et Osiris*, 10 and 51 ; Sir J. G. Wilkinson, *Manners and Customs of the Ancient Egyptians* (London, 1878), iii. 353; R. V. Lanzone, *Dizionario di Mitologia Egizia*, pp. 782 *sq.* ; E. A. Wallis Budge, *The Gods of the Egyptians*, ii. 113 *sq.* ; J. H. Breasted, *Development of Religion and Thought in Ancient Egypt*, pp. 11 *sq.* Strictly speaking, the eye was the eye of Horus, which the dutiful son sacrificed in behalf of his father Osiris. " 'This act of filial devotion, preserved to us in the Pyramid Texts, made the already sacred Horus-eye doubly revered in the tradition and feeling of the Egyptians. It became the symbol of all sacrifice ; every gift or offer-

ing might be called a ' Horus-eye,' especially if offered to the dead. Excepting the sacred beetle, or scarab, it became the commonest and the most revered symbol known to Egyptian religion, and the myriads of eyes, wrought in blue or green glaze, or even cut from costly stone, which fill our museum collections, and are brought home by thousands by the modern tourist, are survivals of this ancient story of Horus and his devotion to his father" (J. H. Breasted, *op. cit.* p. 31)

[4] E. A. Wallis Budge, *The Gods of the Egyptians*, i. 467 ; A. Erman, *Die ägyptische Religion*,[2] p. 8.

[5] *Isis et Osiris*, 52.

[6] *De errore profanarum religionum*, 8.

prove that
Osiris was
originally
the sun.

even in the 'Book of the Dead,' and Isis is often called 'the royal consort of Ra.'"[1] That Ra was both the physical sun and the sun-god is undisputed; but with every deference for the authority of so great a scholar as Lepsius, we may doubt whether the identification of Osiris with Ra can be accepted as proof that Osiris was originally the sun.

Such
identifica-
tions
sprang
from
attempts to
unify and
amalga-
mate the
many
local cults
of Egypt.

For the religion of ancient Egypt[2] may be described as a confederacy of local cults which, while maintaining against each other a certain measure of jealous and even hostile independence, were yet constantly subjected to the fusing and amalgamating influence of political centralization and philosophic thought. The history of the religion appears to have largely consisted of a struggle between these opposite forces or tendencies. On the one side there was the conservative tendency to preserve the local cults with all their distinctive features, fresh, sharp, and crisp as they had been handed down from an immemorial past. On the other side there was the progressive tendency, favoured by the gradual fusion of the people under a powerful central government, first to dull the edge of these provincial distinctions, and finally to break them down completely and merge them in a single national religion. The conservative party probably mustered in its ranks the great bulk of the people, their prejudices and affections being warmly enlisted in favour of the local deity, with whose temple and rites they had been familiar from childhood; and the popular dislike of change, based on the endearing effect of old association, must have been strongly reinforced by the less disinterested opposition of the local clergy, whose material interests would necessarily suffer with any decay of their shrines. On the other hand the kings, whose power and glory rose with the political and ecclesiastical consolidation of the realm, were the natural champions of religious unity; and their efforts would be seconded by the refined and

---

[1] Lepsius, "Über den ersten ägyptischen Götterkreis und seine geschichtlich-mythologische Entstehung," in *Abhandlungen der königlichen Akademie der Wissenschaften zu Berlin*, 1851, pp. 194 *sq.*

[2] The view here taken of the history of Egyptian religion is based on the sketch in Ad. Erman's *Aegypten und aegyptisches Leben im Altertum*, pp. 351 *sqq.* Compare C. P. Tiele, *Geschichte der Religion im Altertum* (Gotha, 1896-1903), i. 79 *sq.*

thoughtful minority, who could hardly fail to be shocked by the many barbarous and revolting elements in the local rites. As usually happens in such cases, the process of religious unification appears to have been largely effected by discovering points of similarity, real or imaginary, between the provincial deities, which were thereupon declared to be only different names or manifestations of the same god.

Of the deities who thus acted as centres of attraction, absorbing in themselves a multitude of minor divinities, by far the most important was the sun-god Ra. There appear to have been few gods in Egypt who were not at one time or other identified with him. Ammon of Thebes, Horus of the East, Horus of Edfu, Chnum of Elephantine, Tum of Heliopolis, all were regarded as one god, the sun. Even the water-god Sobk, in spite of his crocodile shape, did not escape the same fate. Indeed one king, Amenophis IV., undertook to sweep away all the old gods at a stroke and replace them by a single god, the "great living disc of the sun." [1] In the hymns composed in his honour, this deity is referred to as "the living disc of the sun, besides whom there is none other." He is said to have made "the far heaven" and "men, beasts, and birds; he strengtheneth the eyes with his beams, and when he showeth himself, all flowers

Most Egyptian gods were at some time identified with the sun.

Attempt of Amenophis IV. to abolish all gods except the sun-god.

[1] On this attempted revolution in religion see Lepsius, in *Verhandlungen der königl. Akad. der Wissenschaften zu Berlin*, 1851, pp. 196-201 ; A. Erman, *Aegypten und aegyptisches Leben im Altertum*, pp. 74 *sq.*, 355-357 ; *id.*, *Die ägyptische Religion*,[2] pp. 76-84 ; H. Brugsch, *History of Egypt* (London, 1879), i. 441 *sqq.* ; A. Wiedemann, *Aegyptische Geschichte* (Gotha, 1884), pp. 396 *sqq.*; *id.*, *Die Religion der alten Ägypter*, pp. 20-22 ; *id.*, *Religion of the Ancient Egyptians*, pp. 35-43 ; C. P. Tiele, *Geschichte der Religion im Altertum*, i. 84-92 ; G. Maspero, *Histoire ancienne des Peuples de l'Orient Classique*, i. 316 *sqq.*; E. A. Wallis Budge, *The Gods of the Egyptians*, ii. 68-84 ; J. H. Breasted, *History of the Ancient Egyptians* (London, 1908), pp. 264-279 ; A. Moret, *Kings and Gods of Egypt* (New York and London, 1912), pp. 41-68.

A very sympathetic account of this remarkable religious reformer is given by Professor J. H. Breasted (*Development of Religion and Thought in Ancient Egypt*, pp. 319-343). Amenophis IV. reigned from about 1375 to 1358 B.C. His new capital, Akhetaton, the modern Tell-el-Amarna, was on the right bank of the Nile, between Memphis and Thebes. The king has been described as "of all the Pharaohs the most curious and at the same time the most enigmatic figure." To explain his bodily and mental peculiarities some scholars conjectured that through his mother, Queen Tii, he might have had Semitic blood in his veins. But this theory appears to have been refuted by the discovery in 1905 of the tomb of Queen Tii's parents, the contents of which are of pure Egyptian style. See A. Moret, *op. cit.* pp. 46 *sq.*

live and grow, the meadows flourish at his upgoing and
are drunken at his sight, all cattle skip on their feet,
and the birds that are in the marsh flutter for joy." It is
he "who bringeth the years, createth the months, maketh
the days, calculateth the hours, the lord of time, by whom
men reckon." In his zeal for the unity of god, the king
commanded to erase the names of all other gods from the
monuments, and to destroy their images. His rage was
particularly directed against the god Ammon, whose name
and likeness were effaced wherever they were found ; even
the sanctity of the tomb was violated in order to destroy
the memorials of the hated deity. In some of the halls of
the great temples at Carnac, Luxor, and other places, all the
names of the gods, with a few chance exceptions, were
scratched out. The monarch even changed his own name,
Amenophis, because it was compounded of Ammon, and
took instead the name of Chu-en-aten, "gleam of the sun's
disc." Thebes itself, the ancient capital of his glorious
ancestors, full of the monuments of their piety and idolatry,
was no longer a fit home for the puritan king. He deserted
it, and built for himself a new capital in Middle Egypt
at the place now known as Tell-el-Amarna. Here in a
few years a city of palaces and gardens rose like an
exhalation at his command, and here the king, his dearly
loved wife and children, and his complaisant courtiers
led a merry life. The grave and sombre ritual of Thebes
was discarded. The sun-god was worshipped with songs
and hymns, with the music of harps and flutes, with
offerings of cakes and fruits and flowers. Blood seldom
stained his kindly altars. The king himself celebrated the
offices of religion. He preached with unction, and we may
be sure that his courtiers listened with at least an outward
semblance of devotion. From the too-faithful portraits of
himself which he has bequeathed to us we can still picture
to ourselves the heretic king in the pulpit, with his tall,
lanky figure, his bandy legs, his pot-belly, his long, lean,
haggard face aglow with the fever of religious fanaticism.
Yet "the doctrine," as he loved to call it, which he
proclaimed to his hearers was apparently no stern message
of renunciation in this world, of terrors in the world to

come. The thoughts of death, of judgment, and of a
life beyond the grave, which weighed like a nightmare
on the minds of the Egyptians, seem to have been
banished for a time. Even the name of Osiris, the
awful judge of the dead, is not once mentioned in the
graves at Tell-el-Amarna. All this lasted only during the
life of the reformer. His death was followed by a violent
reaction. The old gods were reinstated in their rank and
privileges : their names and images were restored, and new
temples were built. But all the shrines and palaces reared
by the late king were thrown down: even the sculptures
that referred to him and to his god in rock-tombs and on
the sides of hills were erased or filled up with stucco : his
name appears on no later monument, and was carefully
omitted from all official lists. The new capital was
abandoned, never to be inhabited again. Its plan can
still be traced in the sands of the desert.

Failure of the attempt.

This attempt of King Amenophis IV. is only an extreme example of a tendency which appears to have
affected the religion of Egypt as far back as we can
trace it. Therefore, to come back to our point, in attempting to discover the original character of any Egyptian god,
no weight can be given to the identification of him with
other gods, least of all with the sun-god Ra. Far from
helping to follow up the trail, these identifications only cross
and confuse it. The best evidence for the original character
of the Egyptian gods is to be found in their ritual and
myths, so far as these are known, and in the manner in
which they are portrayed on the monuments. It is mainly
on evidence drawn from these sources that I rest my
interpretation of Osiris.

Identification with the sun is no evidence of the original character of an Egyptian god.

The ground upon which some modern writers seem chiefly
to rely for the identification of Osiris with the sun is that
the story of his death fits better with the solar phenomena
than with any other in nature. It may readily be admitted
that the daily appearance and disappearance of the sun
might very naturally be expressed by a myth of his death
and resurrection ; and writers who regard Osiris as the sun
are careful to indicate that it is the diurnal, and not the
annual, course of the sun to which they understand the

The solar theory of Osiris does not explain his death and resur- rection.

myth to apply. Thus Renouf, who identified Osiris with the sun, admitted that the Egyptian sun could not with any show of reason be described as dead in winter.[1] But if his daily death was the theme of the legend, why was it celebrated by an annual ceremony? This fact alone seems fatal to the interpretation of the myth as descriptive of sunset and sunrise. Again, though the sun may be said to die daily, in what sense can he be said to be torn in pieces?[2]

The death and resurrection of Osiris are more naturally explained by the annual decay and growth of vegetation.

In the course of our inquiry it has, I trust, been made clear that there is another natural phenomenon to which the conception of death and resurrection is as applicable as to sunset and sunrise, and which, as a matter of fact, has been so conceived and represented in folk-custom. That phenomenon is the annual growth and decay of vegetation. A strong reason for interpreting the death of Osiris as the decay of vegetation rather than as the sunset is to be found in the general, though not unanimous, voice of antiquity, which classed together the worship and myths of Osiris, Adonis, Attis, Dionysus, and Demeter, as religions of essentially the same type.[3] The consensus of ancient

---

[1] P. Le Page Renouf, *Lectures on the Origin and Growth of Religion*[2] (London, 1884), p. 113.

[2] The late eminent scholar C. P. Tiele, who formerly interpreted Osiris as a sun-god (*History of Egyptian Religion*, pp. 43 *sqq.*), afterwards adopted a view of his nature which approaches more nearly to the one advocated in this book. See his *Geschichte der Religion im Altertum*, i. 35 *sq.*, 123. Professor Ed. Meyer also formerly regarded Osiris as a sun-god; he now interprets him as a great vegetation god, dwelling in the depths of the earth and causing the plants and trees to spring from it. The god's symbol, the *ded* pillar (see above, pp. 108 *sq.*), he takes to be a tree-trunk with cross-beams. See Ed. Meyer, *Geschichte des Altertums*, i. p. 67, § 57 (first edition, 1884); *id.*, i.[2] 2. pp. 70, 84, 87 (second edition, 1909). Sir Gaston Maspero has also abandoned the theory that Osiris was the sun; he now supposes that the deity originally personified the Nile. See his *Histoire*

ancienne[4] (Paris, 1886), p. 35; and his *Histoire ancienne des Peuples de l'Orient Classique*, i. (Paris, 1895), p. 130. Dr. E. A. Wallis Budge also formerly interpreted Osiris as the Nile (*The Gods of the Egyptians*, i. 122, 123), and this view was held by some ancient writers (Plutarch, *Isis et Osiris*, 32, 34, 36, 38, 39). Compare Miss M. A. Murray, *The Osireion at Abydos* (London, 1904), p. 29. Dr. Budge now explains Osiris as a deified king. See his *Osiris and the Egyptian Resurrection*, vol. i. pp. xviii, 30 *sq.*, 37, 66 *sq.*, 168, 254, 256, 290, 300, 312, 384. As to this view see below, pp. 158 *sqq.*

[3] For the identification of Osiris with Dionysus, and of Isis with Demeter, see Herodotus, ii. 42, 49, 59, 144, 156; Plutarch, *Isis et Osiris*, 13, 35; Diodorus Siculus, i. 13, 25, 96, iv. 1; *Orphica*, Hymn 42; Eusebius, *Praepar. Evang.* iii. 11. 31; Servius on Virgil, *Aen.* xi. 287; *id.*, on Virgil, *Georg.* i. 166; J Tzetzes, *Schol. on Lycophron*, 212; Διηγήματα, xxii. 2,

opinion on this subject seems too great to be rejected as a mere fancy. So closely did the rites of Osiris resemble those of Adonis at Byblus that some of the people of Byblus themselves maintained that it was Osiris and not Adonis whose death was mourned by them.[1] Such a view could certainly not have been held if the rituals of the two gods had not been so alike as to be almost indistinguishable. Herodotus found the similarity between the rites of Osiris and Dionysus so great, that he thought it impossible the latter could have arisen independently ; they must, he supposed, have been recently borrowed, with slight alterations, by the Greeks from the Egyptians.[2] Again, Plutarch, a very keen student of comparative religion, insists upon the detailed resemblance of the rites of Osiris to those of Dionysus.[3] We cannot reject the evidence of such intelligent and trustworthy witnesses on plain matters of fact which fell under their own cognizance. Their explanations of the worships it is indeed possible to reject, for the meaning of religious cults is often open to question ; but resemblances of ritual are matters of observation. Therefore, those who explain Osiris as the sun are driven to the alternative of either dismissing as mistaken the testimony of antiquity to the similarity of the rites of Osiris, Adonis, Attis, Dionysus, and Demeter, or of interpreting all these rites as sun-worship. No modern scholar has fairly faced and accepted either side of this alternative. To accept the former would be to affirm

---

in *Mythographi Graeci*, ed. A. Westermann (Brunswick, 1843), p. 368 ; Nonnus, *Dionys.* iv. 269 *sq.* ; Cornutus, *Theologiae Graecae Compendium*, 28 ; Ausonius, *Epigrammata*, 29 and 30. For the identification of Osiris with Adonis and Attis see Stephanus Byzantius, *s.v.* 'Αμαθοῦς ; Damascius, "Vita Isodori," in Photius, *Bibliotheca*, ed. Im. Bekker (Berlin, 1824), p. 343*a*, lines 21 *sq.* ; Hippolytus, *Refutatio omnium haeresium*, v. 9. p. 168 ed. Duncker and Schneidewin ; *Orphica*, Hymn 42. For the identification of Attis, Adonis, and Dionysus see Socrates, *Historia Ecclesiastica*, iii. 23 (Migne's *Patrologia Graeca*, lxvii. 448) ; Plutarch, *Quaestiones Conviviales*, iv. 5. 3 ; Clement of Alexandria, *Protrept.* ii. 19, p. 16 ed. Potter.

[1] Lucian, *De dea Syria*, 7. According to Professor Ed. Meyer, the relations of Egypt to Byblus were very ancient and close ; he even suggests that Byblus may have been from early times an Egyptian colony, or at all events an Egyptian military post, in the city. The commercial importance of Byblus arose from its possession of the fine cedar forests on the Lebanon ; the timber was exported to Egypt, where it was in great demand. See Ed. Meyer, *Geschichte des Altertums*,[2] i. 2. pp. xix, 391 *sqq.*

[2] Herodotus, ii. 49.

[3] Plutarch, *Isis et Osiris*, 35.

that we know the rites of these deities better than the men who practised, or at least who witnessed them. To accept the latter would involve a wrenching, clipping, mangling, and distorting of myth and ritual from which even Macrobius shrank.[1]   On the other hand, the view that the essence of all these rites was the mimic death and revival of vegetation, explains them separately and collectively in an easy and natural way, and harmonizes with the general testimony borne by the ancients to their substantial similarity.

---

[1] Osiris, Attis, Adonis, and Dionysus were all resolved by him into the sun ; but he spared Demeter (Ceres), whom, however, he interpreted as the moon. See the *Saturnalia*, bk. i.

CHAPTER VIII

OSIRIS AND THE MOON

BEFORE we conclude this study of Osiris it will be worth while to consider an ancient view of his nature, which deserves more attention than it has received in modern times. We are told by Plutarch that among the philosophers who saw in the gods of Egypt personifications of natural objects and forces, there were some who interpreted Osiris as the moon and his enemy Typhon as the sun, "because the moon, with her humid and generative light, is favourable to the propagation of animals and the growth of plants ; while the sun with his fierce fire scorches and burns up all growing things, renders the greater part of the earth uninhabitable by reason of his blaze, and often overpowers the moon herself." [1] Whatever may be thought of the physical qualities here attributed to the moon, the arguments adduced by the ancients to prove the identity of Osiris with that luminary carry with them a weight which has at least not been lightened by the results of modern research. An examination of them and of other evidence pointing in the same direction will, perhaps, help to set the original character of the Egyptian deity in a clearer light. [2]

1. Osiris was said to have lived or reigned twenty-eight years. This might fairly be taken as a mythical expression for a lunar month. [3]

2. His body was reported to have been rent into fourteen pieces. [4] This might be interpreted of the waning moon,

---

[1] Plutarch, *Isis et Osiris*, 41.
[2] On Osiris as a moon-god see E. A. Wallis Budge, *Osiris and the Egyptian Resurrection*, i. 19-22, 59, 384 *sqq.*
[3] Plutarch, *Isis et Osiris*, 13, 42.
[4] *Ibid.* 18, 42. The hieroglyphic texts sometimes speak of fourteen

Evidence
of the
association
of Osiris
with the
moon.
which appears to lose a portion of itself on each of the fourteen days that make up the second half of a lunar month.
It is expressly said that his enemy Typhon found the body
of Osiris at the full moon ;[1] thus the dismemberment of the
god would begin with the waning of the moon. To primitive
man it seems manifest that the waning moon is actually
dwindling, and he naturally enough explains its diminution
by supposing that the planet is being rent or broken in
pieces or eaten away. The Klamath Indians of Oregon
speak of the moon as "the one broken to pieces" with
reference to its changing aspect ; they never apply such a
term to the sun,[2] whose apparent change of bulk at different
seasons of the year is far too insignificant to attract the
attention of the savage, or at least to be described by him in
such forcible language. The Dacotas believe that when the
moon is full, a great many little mice begin to nibble at one
side of it and do not cease till they have eaten it all up,
after which a new moon is born and grows to maturity, only
to share the fate of its countless predecessors.[3] A similar
belief is held by the Huzuls of the Carpathians, except that
they ascribe the destruction of the old moon to wolves
instead of to mice.[4]

3. At the new moon of the month Phamenoth, which
was the beginning of spring, the Egyptians celebrated what
they called "the entry of Osiris into the moon."[5]

4. At the ceremony called "the burial of Osiris" the
Egyptians made a crescent-shaped chest "because the
moon, when it approaches the sun, assumes the form of a
crescent and vanishes."[6]

5. The bull Apis, held to be an image of the soul of
Osiris,[7] was born of a cow which was believed to have been

---

pieces, and sometimes of sixteen, or
even eighteen. But fourteen seems to
have been the true number, because
the inscriptions of Denderah, which
refer to the rites of Osiris, describe the
mystic image of the god as composed
of fourteen pieces. See E. A. Wallis
Budge, *The Gods of the Egyptians*, ii.
126 *sq.* ; *id., Osiris and the Egyptian
Resurrection*, i. 386 *sq.*
[1] Plutarch, *Isis et Osiris*, 8.

[2] A. S. Gatschet, *The Klamath
Indians of South-Western Oregon*
(Washington, 1890), p. lxxxix.
[3] S. R. Riggs, *Dakota Grammar,
Texts, and Ethnography* (Washington,
1893), p. 16.
[4] R. F. Kaindl, *Die Huzulen*
(Vienna, 1894), p. 97.
[5] Plutarch, *Isis et Osiris*, 43.
[6] *Ibid.* 43.
[7] *Ibid.* 20, 29.

impregnated, not in the vulgar way by a bull, but by a divine influence emanating from the moon.[1]

6. Once a year, at the full moon, pigs were sacrificed simultaneously to the moon and Osiris.[2]

7. In a hymn supposed to be addressed by Isis to Osiris, it is said that Thoth—

> "*Placeth thy soul in the bark Ma-at,*
> *In that name which is thine, of GOD MOON.*"

And again :—

> "*Thou who comest to us as a child each month,*
> *We do not cease to contemplate thee.*
> *Thine emanation heightens the brilliancy*
> *Of the stars of Orion in the firmament.*"[3]

Here then Osiris is identified with the moon in set terms. If in the same hymn he is said to "illuminate us like Ra" (the sun), that is obviously no reason for identifying him with the sun, but quite the contrary. For though the moon may reasonably be compared to the sun, neither the sun nor anything else can reasonably be compared to itself.

8. In art Osiris is sometimes represented as a human-headed mummy grasping in his hands his characteristic emblems and wearing on his head, instead of the usual crown, a full moon within a crescent.[4]

Now if in one of his aspects Osiris was originally a deity of vegetation, we can easily enough understand why in a later and more philosophic age he should come to be thus identified or confounded with the moon.[5] For as soon as he begins to meditate upon the causes of

The identification of Osiris with the moon appears to be based

---

[1] Plutarch, *Isis et Osiris*, 43 ; *id.*, *Quaest. Conviv.* viii. 1. 3. Compare Herodotus, iii. 28 ; Aelian, *Nat. Anim.* xi. 10 ; Mela, i. 9. 58.

[2] Herodotus, ii. 47 ; Plutarch, *Isis et Osiris*, 8. As to pigs in relation to Osiris, see *Spirits of the Corn and of the Wild*, ii. 24 *sqq.*

[3] P. J. de Horrack, "Lamentations of Isis and Nephthys," *Records of the Past*, ii. (London, N.D.) pp. 121 *sq.* ; H. Brugsch, *Religion und Mythologie der alten Aegypter*, pp. 629 *sq.* ; E. A. Wallis Budge, *Osiris and the Egyptian Resurrection*, i. 389. "Apart from the fact that Osiris is actually called

Âsâr Aâh, i.e. 'Osiris the Moon,' there are so many passages which prove beyond all doubt that at one period at least Osiris was the Moon-god, that it is difficult to understand why Diodorus stated that Osiris was the sun and Isis the moon" (E. A. Wallis Budge, *op. cit.* i. 21).

[4] E. A. Wallis Budge, *Osiris and the Egyptian Resurrection*, i. 59.

[5] According to C. P. Tiele (*Geschichte der Religion im Altertum*, i. 79) the conception of Osiris as the moon was late and never became popular. This entirely accords with the view adopted in the text.

on a comparatively late theory that all things grow and decay with the waxing and waning of the moon. things, the early philosopher is led by certain obvious, though fallacious, appearances to regard the moon as the ultimate cause of the growth of plants.   In the first place he associates its apparent growth and decay with the growth and decay of sublunary things, and imagines that in virtue of a secret sympathy the celestial phenomena really produce those terrestrial changes which in point of fact they merely resemble.   Thus Pliny says that the moon may fairly be considered the planet of breath, " because it saturates the earth and by its approach fills bodies, while by its departure it empties them.   Hence it is," he goes on, " that shell-fish increase with the increase of the moon and that bloodless creatures especially feel breath at that time ; even the blood of men grows and diminishes with the light of the moon, and leaves and herbage also feel the same influence, since the lunar energy penetrates all things." [1]   " There is no doubt," writes Macrobius, " that the moon is the author and framer of mortal bodies, so much so that some things expand or shrink as it waxes or wanes." [2]   Again, Aulus Gellius puts in the mouth of a friend the remark that " the same things which grow with the waxing, do dwindle with the waning moon," and he quotes from a commentary of Plutarch's on Hesiod a statement that the onion is the only vegetable which violates this great law of nature by sprouting in the wane and withering in the increase of the moon. [3]   Scottish Highlanders allege that in the increase of the moon everything has a tendency to grow or stick together ; [4] and they call the second moon of autumn " the ripening moon " (*Gealach an abachaidh*), because they imagine that crops ripen as much by its light as by day. [5]

Practical rules founded on this lunar theory.   From this supposed influence of the moon on the life of plants and animals, men in ancient and modern times have deduced a whole code of rules for the guidance of the husbandman, the shepherd, and others in the conduct of

---

[1] Pliny, *Nat. Hist.* ii. 221.

[2] Macrobius, *Comment. in somnium Scipionis*, i. 11. 7.

[3] Aulus Gellius, xx. 8.   For the opinions of the ancients on this subject see further W. H. Roscher, *Über Selene und Verwandtes* (Leipsic, 1890), pp. 61 *sqq.*

[4] John Ramsay of Ochtertyre, *Scotland and Scotsmen in the Eighteenth Century*, edited by A. Allardyce (Edinburgh and London, 1888), ii. 449.

[5] J. G. Campbell, *Witchcraft and Second Sight in the Highlands and Islands of Scotland* (Glasgow, 1902), pp. 306 *sq.*

their affairs. Thus an ancient writer on agriculture lays it down as a maxim, that whatever is to be sown should be sown while the moon is waxing, and that whatever is to be cut or gathered should be cut or gathered while it is waning.[1] A modern treatise on superstition describes how the superstitious man regulates all his conduct by the moon : " Whatever he would have to grow, he sets about it when she is in her increase ; but for what he would have made less he chooses her wane."[2]   In Germany the phases of the moon are observed by superstitious people at all the more or even less important actions of life, such as tilling the fields, building or changing houses, marriages, hair-cutting, bleeding, cupping, and so forth.   The particular rules vary in different places, but the principle generally followed is that whatever is done to increase anything should be done while the moon is waxing ; whatever is done to diminish anything should be done while the moon is waning.   For example, sowing, planting, and grafting should be done in the first half of the moon, but the felling of timber and mowing should be done in the second half.[3]   In various parts of Europe it is believed that plants, nails, hair, and corns, cut while the moon is on the increase, will grow again fast, but that if cut while it is on the decrease they will grow slowly or waste

Supposed influence of the phases of the moon on the operations of husbandry.

[1] Palladius, *De re rustica*, i. 34. 8. Compare *id.* i. 6. 12 ; Pliny, *Nat. Hist.* xviii. 321, "*omnia quae caeduntur, carpuntur, tondentur innocentius decrescente luna quam crescente fiunt*" ; *Geoponica*, i. 6. 8, τινὲς δοκιμάζουσι μηδὲν φθινούσης τῆς σελήνης ἀλλὰ αὐξανομένης φυτεύειν.

[2] J. Brand, *Popular Antiquities of Great Britain* (London, 1882–1883), iii. 144, quoting Werenfels, *Dissertation upon Superstition* (London, 1748), p. 6.

[3] A. Wuttke, *Der deutsche Volksaberglaube*[3] (Berlin, 1869), § 65, pp. 57 *sq.*   Compare J. Grimm, *Deutsche Mythologie*[4] (Berlin, 1875–1878), ii. 595 ; Montanus, *Die deutsche Volksfeste, Volksbräuche und deutscher Volksglaube* (Iserlohn, N.D.), p. 128 ; M. Prätorius, *Deliciae Prussicae* (Berlin, 1871), p. 18 ; O. Schell, " Einige

Bemerkungen über den Mond im heutigen Glauben des bergischen Volkes," *Am Ur-quell*, v. (1894) p. 173.   The rule that the grafting of trees should be done at the waxing of the moon is laid down by Pliny (*Nat. Hist.* xvii. 108). At Deutsch-Zepling in Transylvania, by an inversion of the usual custom, seed is generally sown at the waning of the moon (A. Heinrich, *Agrarische Sitten und Gebräuche unter den Sachsen Siebenbürgens*, Hermannstadt, 1880, p. 7).   Some French peasants also prefer to sow in the wane (F. Chapiseau, *Folk-lore de la Beauce et du Perche*, Paris, 1902, i. 291).   In the Abruzzi also sowing and grafting are commonly done when the moon is on the wane ; timber that is to be durable must be cut in January during the moon's decrease (G. Finamore, *Credenze, Usi e Costumi Abruzzesi*, Palermo, 1890, p. 43).

away.[1]   Hence persons who wish their hair to grow thick and long should cut it in the first half of the moon.[2]   On the same principle sheep are shorn when the moon is waxing, because it is supposed that the wool will then be longest and most enduring.[3]   Some negroes of the Gaboon think that taro and other vegetables never thrive if they are planted after full moon, but that they grow fast and strong if they are planted in the first quarter.[4]   The Highlanders of Scotland used to expect better crops of grain by sowing their seed in the moon's increase.[5]   On the other hand they thought that garden vegetables, such as onions and kail, run to seed if they are sown in the increase, but that they grow to pot-herbs if they are sown in the wane.[6]   So Thomas Tusser advised the peasant to sow peas and beans in the wane of the moon "that they with the planet may rest and arise."[7]   The Zulus welcome

---

[1] P. Sébillot, *Traditions et Superstitions de la Haute-Bretagne* (Paris, 1882), ii. 355 ; L. F. Sauvé, *Folk-lore des Hautes-Vosges* (Paris, 1889), p. 5 ; J. Brand, *Popular Antiquities of Great Britain*, iii. 150 ; Holzmayer, "Osiliana," *Verhandlungen der gelehrten Estnichen Gesellschaft zu Dorpat*, vii. (1872) p. 47.

[2] The rule is mentioned by Varro, *Rerum Rusticarum*, i. 37 (where we should probably read "*ne decrescente tondens calvos fiam*," and refer *istaec* to the former member of the preceding sentence) ; A. Wuttke, *l.c.* ; Montanus, *op. cit.* p. 128 ; P. Sébillot, *l.c.* ; E. Meier, *Deutsche Sagen, Sitten und Gebräuche aus Schwaben* (Stuttgart, 1852), p. 511, § 421 ; W. J. A. von Tettau und J. D. H. Temme, *Die Volkssagen Ostpreussens, Litthauens und Westpreussens* (Berlin, 1837), p. 283 ; A. Kuhn, *Märkische Sagen und Märchen* (Berlin, 1843), p. 386, § 92 ; L. Schandein, in *Bavaria, Landes- und Volkskunde des Königreichs Bayern* (Munich, 1860–1867), iv. 2, p. 402 ; F. S. Krauss, *Volksglaube und religiöser Brauch der Südslaven* (Münster, i. W. 1890), p. 15 ; E. Krause, "Abergläubische Kuren und sonstiger Aberglaube in Berlin," *Zeitschrift für Ethnologie*, xv. (1883) p. 91 ; R.

Wuttke, *Sächsische Volkskunde*[2] (Dresden, 1901), p. 369 ; C. S. Burne and G. F. Jackson, *Shropshire Folk-lore* (London, 1883), p. 259.   The reason assigned in the text was probably the original one in all cases, though it is not always the one alleged now.

[3] F. S. Krauss, *op. cit.* p. 16 ; Montanus, *l.c.* ; Varro, *Rerum Rusticarum*, i. 37 (see above, note [2]).   However, the opposite rule is observed in the Upper Vosges, where it is thought that if the sheep are shorn at the new moon the quantity of wool will be much less than if they were shorn in the waning of the moon (L. F. Sauvé, *Folk-lore des Hautes-Vosges*, p. 5).   In the Bocage of Normandy, also, wool is clipped during the waning of the moon ; otherwise moths would get into it (J. Lecœur, *Esquisses du Bocage Normand*, Condé-sur-Noireau, 1883–1887, ii. 12).

[4] Father Lejeune, "Dans la forêt," *Missions Catholiques*, xxvii. (1895) p. 272.

[5] S. Johnson, *Journey to the Western Islands of Scotland* (Baltimore, 1810), p. 183.

[6] J. G. Campbell, *Witchcraft and Second Sight in the Highlands and Islands of Scotland*, p. 306.

[7] Thomas Tusser, *Five Hundred Points of Good Husbandry*, New

the first appearance of the new moon with beating of drums and other demonstrations of joy ; but next day they abstain from all labour, " thinking that if anything is sown on those days they can never reap the benefit thereof." [1] But in this matter of sowing and planting a refined distinction is sometimes drawn by French, German, and Esthonian peasants ; plants which bear fruit above ground are sown by them when the moon is waxing, but plants which are cultivated for the sake of their roots, such as potatoes and turnips, are sown when the moon is waning.[2] The reason for this distinction seems to be a vague idea that the waxing moon is coming up and the waning moon going down, and that accordingly fruits which grow upwards should be sown in the former period, and fruits which grow downwards in the latter. Before beginning to plant their cacao the Pipiles of Central America exposed the finest seeds for four nights to the moonlight,[3] but whether they did so at the waxing or waning of the moon is not said. Even pots, it would seem, are not exempt from this great law of nature. In Uganda " potters waited for the new moon to appear before baking their pots ; when it was some days old, they prepared their fires and baked the vessels. No potter would bake pots when the moon was past the full, for he believed that they would be a failure, and would be sure to crack or break in the burning, if he did so, and that his labour accordingly would go for nothing." [4]

Again, the waning of the moon has been commonly recommended both in ancient and modern times as the proper time for felling trees,[5] apparently because it was

The phases of the moon in relation

Edition (London, 1812), p. 107 (under February).

[1] Fairweather, in W. F. Owen's *Narrative of Voyages to explore the Shores of Africa, Arabia, and Madagascar* (London, 1833), ii. 396 *sq.*

[2] A. Wuttke, *Der deutsche Volksaberglaube,*[3] § 65, p. 58; J. Lecœur, *loc. cit.*; E. Meier, *Deutsche Sagen, Sitten und Gebräuche aus Schwaben,* p. 511, § 422 ; Th. Siebs, "Das Saterland," *Zeitschrift für Volkskunde,* iii. (1893) p. 278 ; Holzmayer, *op. cit.* p. 47.

[3] H. H. Bancroft, *Native Races of*

the *Pacific States* (London, 1875–1876), ii. 719 *sq.*

[4] Rev. J. Roscoe, *The Baganda* (London, 1911), p. 402.

[5] Cato, *De agri cultura,* 37. 4 ; Varro, *Rerum Rusticarum,* i. 37 ; Pliny, *Nat. Hist.* xvi. 190 ; Palladius, *De re rustica,* ii. 22, xii. 15 ; Plutarch, *Quaest. Conviv.* iii. 10. 3 ; Macrobius, *Saturn.* vii. 16 ; A. Wuttke, *l.c.* : *Bavaria, Landes- und Volkskunde des Königreichs Bayern,* iv. 2, p. 402 ; W. Kolbe, *Hessische Volks-Sitten und Gebräuche* [2] (Marburg, 1888), p. 58 ;

thought fit and natural that the operation of cutting down should be performed on earth at the time when the lunar orb was, so to say, being cut down in the sky.   In France before the Revolution the forestry laws enjoined that trees should only be felled after the moon had passed the full; and in French bills announcing the sale of timber you may still read a notice that the wood was cut in the waning of the moon.[1]   So among the Shans of Burma, when a house is to be built, it is a rule that "a lucky day should be chosen to commence the cutting of the bamboos.   The day must not only be a fortunate one for the builder, but it must also be in the second half of the month, when the moon is waning.   Shans believe that if bamboos are cut during the first half of the month, when the moon is waxing, they do not last well, as boring insects attack them and they will soon become rotten.   This belief is prevalent all over the East."[2]   A like belief obtains in various parts of Mexico. No Mexican will cut timber while the moon is increasing; they say it must be cut while the moon is waning or the wood will certainly rot.[3]   In Colombia, South America, people think that corn should only be sown and timber felled when the moon is on the wane.   They say that the waxing moon draws the sap up through the trunk and branches, whereas the sap flows down and leaves the wood dry during the wane of the moon.[4]   But sometimes the opposite rule is

L. F. Sauvé, *Folk-lore des Hautes-Vosges*, p. 5; F. Chapiseau, *Folk-lore de la Beauce et du Perche*, i. 291 *sq.*; M. Martin, "Description of the Western Islands of Scotland," in J. Pinkerton's *Voyages and Travels*, iii. 630; J. G. Campbell, *Witchcraft and Second Sight in the Highlands and Islands of Scotland*, p. 306; G. Amalfi, *Tradizioni ed Usi nella penin-sola Sorrentina* (Palermo, 1890), p. 87; K. von den Steinen, *Unter den Naturvölkern Zentral-Brasiliens* (Berlin, 1894), p. 559.   Compare F. de Castelnau, *Expédition dans les parties centrales de l'Amérique du Sud* (Paris, 1851–1852), iii. 438.   Pliny, while he says that the period from the twentieth to the thirtieth day of the lunar month was the season generally

recommended, adds that the best time of all, according to universal opinion, was the interlunar day, between the old and the new moon, when the planet is invisible through being in conjunction with the sun.

[1] J. Lecœur, *Esquisses du Bocage Normand*, ii. 11 *sq.*

[2] Mrs. Leslie Milne, *Shans at Home* (London, 1910), p. 100.

[3] Letter of Mr. A. S. F. Marshall, dated Hacienda "La Maronna," Cd. Porfirio Diaz, Coah., Mexico, 2nd October 1908.   The writer gives instances confirmatory of this belief.   I have to thank Professor A. C. Seward of Cambridge for kindly showing me this letter.

[4] Letter of Mr. Francis S. Schloss to me, dated 58 New Cavendish

adopted, and equally forcible arguments are urged in its defence. Thus, when the Wabondei of Eastern Africa are about to build a house, they take care to cut the posts for it when the moon is on the increase ; for they say that posts cut when the moon is wasting away would soon rot, whereas posts cut while the moon is waxing are very durable.[1] The same rule is observed for the same reason in some parts of Germany.[2]

But the partisans of the ordinarily received opinion have sometimes supported it by another reason, which introduces us to the second of those fallacious appearances by which men have been led to regard the moon as the cause of growth in plants. From observing rightly that dew falls most thickly on cloudless nights, they inferred wrongly that it was caused by the moon, a theory which the poet Alcman expressed in mythical form by saying that dew was a daughter of Zeus and the moon.[3] Hence the ancients concluded that the moon is the great source of moisture, as the sun is the great source of heat.[4] And as the humid power of the moon was assumed to be greater when the planet was waxing than when it was waning, they thought that timber cut during the increase of the luminary would be saturated with moisture, whereas timber cut in the wane would be comparatively dry. Hence we are told that in antiquity carpenters would reject timber felled when the moon was growing or full, because they believed that such timber teemed with sap ;[5] and in the Vosges at the present day people allege that wood cut at the new moon does not dry.[6] We have seen that the same reason is assigned for the same practice in Colombia.[7] In the Hebrides peasants

The moon regarded as the source of moisture.

Street, W., 12th May 1912. Mr. Schloss adds that "as a matter of practical observation, timber, etc., should only be felled when the moon is waning. This has been stated to me not only by natives, but also by English mining engineers of high repute, who have done work in Colombia."

[1] O. Baumann, *Usambara und seine Nachbargebiete* (Berlin, 1891), p. 125.

[2] Montanus, *Die deutsche Volksfeste, Volksbräuche und deutscher Volksglaube,* p. 128.

[3] Plutarch, *Quaest. Conviv.* iii. 10. 3 ; Macrobius, *Saturn.* vii. 16. See further, W. H. Roscher, *Über Selene und Verwandtes* (Leipsic, 1890), pp. 49 *sqq.*

[4] Plutarch and Macrobius, *ll.cc.* ; Pliny, *Nat. Hist.* ii. 223, xx. 1 ; Aristotle, *Problemata*, xxiv. 14, p. 937 B, 3 *sq.* ed. I. Bekker (Berlin).

[5] Macrobius and Plutarch, *ll.cc.*

[6] L. F. Sauvé, *Folk-lore des Hautes-Vosges,* p. 5.

[7] Above, p. 136.

give the same reason for cutting their peats when the moon is on the wane; " for they observe that if they are cut in the increase, they continue still moist and never burn clear, nor are they without smoke, but the contrary is daily observed of peats cut in the decrease." [1]

The moon, being viewed as the cause of vegetable growth, is naturally worshipped by agricultural peoples.

Thus misled by a double fallacy primitive philosophy comes to view the moon as the great cause of vegetable growth, first, because the planet seems itself to grow, and second, because it is supposed to be the source of dew and moisture. It is no wonder, therefore, that agricultural peoples should adore the planet which they believe to influence so profoundly the crops on which they depend for subsistence. Accordingly we find that in the hotter regions of America, where maize is cultivated and manioc is the staple food, the moon was recognized as the principal object of worship, and plantations of manioc were assigned to it as a return for the service it rendered in the production of the crops. The worship of the moon in preference to the sun was general among the Caribs, and, perhaps, also among most of the other Indian tribes who cultivated maize in the tropical forests to the east of the Andes ; and the same thing has been observed, under the same physical conditions, among the aborigines of the hottest region of Peru, the northern valleys of Yuncapata. Here the Indians of Pacasmayu and the neighbouring valleys revered the moon as their principal divinity. The " house of the moon " at Pacasmayu was the chief temple of the district ; and the same sacrifices of maize-flour, of wine, and of children which were offered by the mountaineers of the Andes to the Sun-god, were offered by the lowlanders to the Moon-god in order that he might cause their crops to thrive.[2]   In ancient

---

[1] M. Martin, " Description of the Western Islands of Scotland," in J. Pinkerton's *Voyages and Travels*, iii. 630.

[2] E. J. Payne, *History of the New World called America*, i. (Oxford, 1892) p. 495.   In his remarks on the origin of moon-worship this learned and philosophical historian has indicated (*op. cit.* i. 493 *sqq.*) the true causes which lead primitive man to trace the growth of plants to the influence of

the moon. Compare Sir E. B. Tylor, *Primitive Culture* [2] (London, 1873), i. 130. Payne suggests that the custom of naming the months after the principal natural products that ripen in them may have contributed to the same result. The custom is certainly very common among savages, as I hope to show elsewhere, but whether it has contributed to foster the fallacy in question seems doubtful.

The Indians of Brazil are said to

Babylonia, where the population was essentially agricultural, the moon-god took precedence of the sun-god and was indeed reckoned his father.[1]

Hence it would be no matter for surprise if, after worshipping the crops which furnished them with the means of subsistence, the ancient Egyptians should in later times have identified the spirit of the corn with the moon, which a false philosophy had taught them to regard as the ultimate cause of the growth of vegetation. In this way we can understand why in their most recent forms the myth and ritual of Osiris, the old god of trees and corn, should bear many traces of efforts made to bring them into a superficial conformity with the new doctrine of his lunar affinity.

Thus Osiris, the old corn-god, was afterwards identified with the moon.

pay more attention to the moon than to the sun, regarding it as a source both of good and ill. See J. B. von Spix und C. F. von Martius, *Reise in Brasilien* (Munich, 1823-1831), i. 379. The natives of Mori, a district of Central Celebes, believe that the rice-spirit Omonga lives in the moon and eats up the rice in the granary if he is not treated with due respect. See A. C. Kruijt, "Eenige ethnografische aantee-keningen omtrent de Toboengkoe en de Tomori," *Mededeelingen van wege het Nederlandsche Zendelinggenootschap,* xliv. (1900) p. 231.

[1] E. A. Budge, *Nebuchadnezzar, King of Babylon, on recently-discovered inscriptions of this King,* pp. 5 *sq.*; A. H. Sayce, *Religion of the Ancient Babylonians,* p. 155; M. Jastrow, *Religion of Babylonia and Assyria,* pp. 68 *sq.,* 75 *sq.*; L. W. King, *Babylonian Religion and Mythology* (London, 1899), pp. 17 *sq.* The Ahts of Vancouver Island, a tribe of fishers and hunters, view the moon as the husband of the sun and as a more powerful deity than her (G. M. Sproat, *Scenes and Studies of Savage Life,* London, 1868, p. 206).

CHAPTER IX

THE DOCTRINE OF LUNAR SYMPATHY

IN the preceding chapter some evidence was adduced of the sympathetic influence which the waxing or waning moon is popularly supposed to exert on growth, especially on the growth of vegetation. But the doctrine of lunar sympathy does not stop there ; it is applied also to the affairs of man, and various customs and rules have been deduced from it which aim at the amelioration and even the indefinite extension of human life. To illustrate this application of the popular theory at length would be out of place here, but a few cases may be mentioned by way of specimen.

Theory
that all
things wax
or wane
with the
moon. The natural fact on which all the customs in question seem to rest is the apparent monthly increase and decrease of the moon. From this observation men have inferred that all things simultaneously wax or wane in sympathy with it.[1] Thus the Mentras or Mantras of the Malay Peninsula have a tradition that in the beginning men did not die but grew thin with the waning of the moon, and waxed fat as she neared the full.[2] Of the Scottish Highlanders we are told that "the moon in her increase, full growth, and in her wane are with them the emblems of a rising, flourishing, and declining fortune. At the last period of her revolution they carefully avoid to engage in any business of importance ; but the first and middle they seize with avidity, presaging the most auspicious issue to their undertakings."[3] Similarly

---

[1] This principle is clearly recognized and well illustrated by J. Grimm (*Deutsche Mythologie*,[4] ii. 594-596).

[2] D. F. A. Hervey, "The Mentra Traditions," *Journal of the Straits · Branch of the Royal Asiatic Society,* No. 10 (Singapore, 1883), p. 190 ; W. W. Skeat and C. O. Blagden, *Pagan Races of the Malay Peninsula* (London, 1906), ii. 337.

[3] Rev. J. Grant (parish minister of Kirkmichael), in Sir John Sinclair's

in some parts of Germany it is commonly believed that whatever is undertaken when the moon is on the increase succeeds well, and that the full moon brings everything to perfection ; whereas business undertaken in the wane of the moon is doomed to failure.[1]   This German belief has come down, as we might have anticipated, from barbaric times ; for Tacitus tells us that the Germans considered the new or the full moon the most auspicious time for business ;[2] and Caesar informs us that the Germans despaired of victory if they joined battle before the new moon.[3]   The Spartans seem to have been of the same opinion, for it was a rule with them never to march out to war except when the moon was full.   The rule prevented them from sending troops in time to fight the Persians at Marathon,[4] and but for Athenian valour this paltry superstition might have turned the scale of battle and decided the destiny of Greece, if not of Europe, for centuries.   The Athenians themselves paid dear for a similar scruple : an eclipse of the moon cost them the loss of a gallant fleet and army before Syracuse, and practically sealed the fate of Athens, for she never recovered from the blow.[5]   So heavy is the sacrifice which superstition demands of its votaries.   In this respect the Greeks were on a level with the negroes of the Sudan, among whom, if a march has been decided upon during the last quarter of the moon, the departure is always deferred until the first day of the new moon.   No chief would dare to undertake an expedition and lead out his warriors before the appearance of the crescent.   Merchants and private persons observe the same rule on their journeys.[6]   In like manner the Mandingoes of Senegambia pay great attention to the changes of the moon, and think it very unlucky to begin a journey or any other work of consequence in the last quarter.[7]

It is especially the appearance of the new moon, with

Statistical Account of Scotland (Edinburgh, 1791–1799), xii. 457.
[1] A. Kuhn und W. Schwartz, *Norddeutsche Sagen, Märchen und Gebräuche* (Leipsic, 1848), p. 457, § 419.
[2] Tacitus, *Germania*, 11.
[3] Caesar, *De bello Gallico*, i. 50.
[4] Herodotus, vi. 106 ; Lucian, *De astrologia*, 25 ; Pausanias, i. 28. 4.
[5] Thucydides, vii. 50.
[6] Le capitaine Binger, *Du Niger au Golfe de Guinée* (Paris, 1892), ii. 116.
[7] Mungo Park, *Travels in the Interior Districts of Africa*[5] (London, 1807), pp. 406 *sq.*

The ceremonies observed at new moon are often magical rather than religious, being intended to renew sympathetically the life of man.

its promise of growth and increase, which is greeted with ceremonies intended to renew and invigorate, by means of sympathetic magic, the life of man. Observers, ignorant of savage superstition, have commonly misinterpreted such customs as worship or adoration paid to the moon. In point of fact the ceremonies of new moon are probably in many cases rather magical than religious. The Indians of the Ucayali River in Peru hail the appearance of the new moon with great joy. They make long speeches to her, accompanied with vehement gesticulations, imploring her protection and begging that she will be so good as to invigorate their bodies.[1] On the day when the new moon first appeared, it was a custom with the Indians of San Juan Capistrano, in California, to call together all the young men for the purpose of its celebration. "*Correr la luna !*" shouted one of the old men, " Come, my boys, the moon ! the moon !" Immediately the young men began to run about in a disorderly fashion as if they were distracted, while the old men danced in a circle, saying, " As the moon dieth, and cometh to life again, so we also having to die will again live." [2] An old traveller tells us that at the appearance of every new moon the negroes of the Congo clapped their hands and cried out, sometimes falling on their knees, " So may I renew my life as thou art renewed." But if the sky happened to be clouded, they did nothing, alleging that the planet had lost its virtue.[3] A somewhat similar custom prevails among the Ovambo of South-Western Africa. On the first moonlight night of the new moon, young and old, their bodies smeared with white earth, perhaps in imitation of the planet's silvery light, dance to the moon and address to it wishes which they feel sure will be granted.[4] We may conjecture that among these wishes is a prayer for a renewal of life. When a Masai sees the new moon he throws a twig or stone at it with his left hand, and says, " Give me

---

[1] W. Smythe and F. Lowe, *Narrative of a Journey from Lima to Para* (London, 1836), p. 230.

[2] Father G. Boscana, "Chinig-chinich," in *Life in California, by an American* [A. Robinson] (New York, 1846), pp. 298 *sq,*

[3] Merolla, "Voyage to Congo," in J. Pinkerton's *Voyages and Travels,* xvi. 273.

[4] H. Schinz, *Deutsch - Südwest-Afrika* (Oldenburg and Leipsic, N.D.), p. 319.

long life," or "Give me strength"; and when a pregnant woman sees the new moon she milks some milk into a small gourd, which she covers with green grass. Then she pours the milk away in the direction of the moon and says, "Moon, give me my child safely."[1] Among the Wagogo of German East Africa, at sight of the new moon some people break a stick in pieces, spit on the pieces, and throw them towards the moon, saying, "Let all illness go to the west, where the sun sets."[2] Among the Boloki of the Upper Congo there is much shouting and gesticulation on the appearance of a new moon. Those who have enjoyed good health pray that it may be continued, and those who have been sick ascribe their illness to the coming of the luminary and beg her to take away bad health and give them good health instead.[3] The Esthonians think that all the misfortunes which might befall a man in the course of a month may be forestalled and shifted to the moon, if a man will only say to the new moon, "Good morrow, new moon. I must grow young, you must grow old. My eyes must grow bright, yours must grow dark. I must grow light as a bird, you must grow heavy as iron."[4] On the fifteenth day of the moon, that is, at the time when the luminary has begun to wane, the Coreans take round pieces of paper, either red or white, which represent the moon, and having fixed them perpendicularly on split sticks they place them on the tops of the houses. Then persons who have been forewarned by fortune-tellers of impending evil pray to the moon to remove it from them.[5]

[1] A. C. Hollis, *The Masai* (Oxford, 1905), p. 274.

[2] H. Cole, "Notes on the Wagogo of German East Africa," *Journal of the Anthropological Institute*, xxxii. (1902) p. 330.

[3] John H. Weeks, *Among Congo Cannibals* (London, 1913), p. 142.

[4] J. G. Kohl, *Die deutsch-russischen Ostseeprovinzen* (Dresden and Leipsic, 1841), ii. 279. Compare Boecler-Kreutzwald, *Der Ehsten abergläubische Gebräuche, Weisen und Gewohnheiten* (St. Petersburg, 1854), pp. 142 *sq.*; J. Grimm, *Deutsche Mythologie*,[4] ii. 595, note [1]. The power of regenera-

tion ascribed to the moon in these customs is sometimes attributed to the sun. Thus it is said that the Chiriguanos Indians of South - Eastern Bolivia often address the sun as follows: "Thou art born and disappearest every day, only to revive always young. Cause that it may be so with me." See A. Thouar, *Explorations dans l'Amérique du Sud* (Paris, 1891), p. 50.

[5] W. Woodville Rockhill, "Notes on some of the Laws, Customs, and Superstitions of Korea," *The American Anthropologist*, iv. (Washington, 1891), p. 185.

Attempts to eat or drink the moonlight.

In India people attempt to absorb the vital influence of the moon by drinking water in which the luminary is reflected. Thus the Mohammedans of Oude fill a silver basin with water and hold it so that the orb of the full moon is mirrored in it. The person to be benefited must look steadfastly at the moon in the basin, then shut his eyes and drink the water at one gulp. Doctors recommend the draught as a remedy for nervous disorders and palpitation of the heart. Somewhat similar customs prevail among the Hindoos of Northern India. At the full moon of the month of Kuar (September-October) people lay out food on the house-tops, and when it has absorbed the rays of the moon they distribute it among their relations, who are supposed to lengthen their life by eating of the food which has thus been saturated with moonshine. Patients are often made to look at the moon reflected in melted butter, oil, or milk as a cure for leprosy and the like diseases.[1]

The supposed influence of moonlight on children: presentation of infants to the new moon.

Naturally enough the genial influence of moonshine is often supposed to be particularly beneficial to children; for will not the waxing moon help them to wax in strength and stature? Hence in the island of Kiriwina, one of the Trobriands Group to the east of New Guinea, a mother always lifts up or presents her child to the first full moon after its birth in order that it may grow fast and talk soon.[2] So among the Baganda of Central Africa it was customary for each mother to take her child out at the first new moon after its birth, and to point out the moon to the infant; this was thought to make the child grow healthy and strong.[3] Among the Thonga of South Africa the presentation of the baby to the moon does not take place until the mother has resumed her monthly periods, which usually happens in the third month after the birth. When the new moon appears, the mother takes a torch or a burning brand from the fire and goes to the ash-heap behind the hut. She is followed by the grandmother carrying the child. At the ash-heap the mother throws the burning stick towards the moon, while the grandmother tosses the

[1] W. Crooke, *Popular Religion and Folk-lore of Northern India* (Westminster, 1896), i. 14 *sq.*

[2] George Brown, D.D., *Melanesians and Polynesians* (London, 1910), p. 37.

[3] Rev. J. Roscoe, *The Baganda* (London, 1911), p. 58.

baby into the air, saying, "This is your moon!" The child squalls and rolls over on the ash-heap. Then the mother snatches up the infant and nurses it; so they go home.[1]

The Guarayos Indians, who inhabit the gloomy tropical forests of Eastern Bolivia, lift up their children in the air at new moon in order that they may grow.[2] Among the Apinagos Indians, on the Tocantins River in Brazil, the French traveller Castelnau witnessed a remarkable dance by moonlight. The Indians danced in two long ranks which faced each other, the women on one side, the men on the other. Between the two ranks of dancers blazed a great fire. The men were painted in brilliant colours, and for the most part wore white or red skull-caps made of maize-flour and resin. Their dancing was very monotonous and consisted of a jerky movement of the body, while the dancer advanced first one leg and then the other. This dance they accompanied with a melancholy song, striking the ground with their weapons. Opposite them the women, naked and unpainted, stood in a single rank, their bodies bent slightly forward, their knees pressed together, their arms swinging in measured time, now forward, now backward, so as to join hands. A remarkable figure in the dance was a personage painted scarlet all over, who held in his hand a rattle composed of a gourd full of pebbles. From time to time he leaped across the great fire which burned between the men and the women. Then he would run rapidly in front of the women, stopping now and then before one or other and performing a series of strange gambols, while he shook his rattle violently. Sometimes he would sink with one knee to the ground, and then suddenly throw himself backward. Altogether the agility and endurance which he displayed were remarkable. This dance lasted for hours. When a woman was tired out she withdrew, and her place was taken by another; but the same men danced the monotonous dance all night. Towards midnight the moon attained the zenith and flooded the scene with her bright rays. A change

Infants presented to the moon by the Guarayos Indians of Bolivia and the Apinagos Indians of Brazil.

[1] Henri A. Junod, *The Life of a South African Tribe* (Neuchatel, 1912–1913), i. 51.

[2] A. d'Orbigny, *Voyage dans l'Amérique Méridionale*, iii. 1ʳᵉ Partie (Paris and Strasburg, 1844), p. 24.

now took place in the dance. A long line of men and women advanced to the fire between the ranks of the dancers. Each of them held one end of a hammock in which lay a new-born infant, whose squalls could be heard. These babes were now to be presented by their parents to the moon. On reaching the end of the line each couple swung the hammock, accompanying the movement by a chant, which all the Indians sang in chorus. The song seemed to consist of three words, repeated over and over again. Soon a shrill voice was heard, and a hideous old hag, like a skeleton, appeared with her arms raised above her head. She went round and round the assembly several times, then disappeared in silence. While she was present, the scarlet dancer with the rattle bounded about more furiously than ever, stopping only for a moment while he passed in front of the line of women. His body was contracted and bent towards them, and described an undulatory movement like that of a worm writhing. He shook his rattle violently, as if he would fain kindle in the women the fire which burned in himself. Then rising abruptly he would resume his wild career. During this time the loud voice of an orator was heard from the village repeating a curious name without cessation. Then the speaker approached slowly, carrying on his back some gorgeous bunches of brilliant feathers and under his arm a stone axe. Behind him walked a young woman bearing an infant in a loose girdle at her waist ; the child was wrapped in a mat, which protected it against the chill night air. The couple paced slowly for a minute or two, and then vanished without speaking a word. At the same moment the curious name which the orator had shouted was taken up by the whole assembly and repeated by them again and again. This scene in its turn lasted a long time, but ceased suddenly with the setting of the moon. The French traveller who witnessed it fell asleep, and when he awoke all was calm once more : there was nothing to recall the infernal dances of the night.[1]

In explanation of these dances Castelnau merely observes

---

[1] F. de Castelnau, *Expédition dans les parties centrales de l'Amérique du Sud* (Paris, 1850–1851), ii. 31-34.

that the Apinagos, like many other South American Indians, pay a superstitious respect to the moon. We may suppose that the ceremonious presentation of the infants to the moon was intended to ensure their life and growth. The names solemnly chanted by the whole assembly were probably those which the parents publicly bestowed on their children. As to the scarlet dancer who leaped across the fire, we may conjecture that he personated the moon, and that his strange antics in front of the women were designed to impart to them the fertilizing virtue of the luminary, and perhaps to facilitate their delivery.

Among the Baganda of Central Africa there is general rejoicing when the new moon appears, and no work is done for seven days. When the crescent is first visible at evening, mothers take out their babies and hold them at arms' length, saying, " I want my child to keep in health till the moon wanes." At the same time a ceremony is performed which may be intended to ensure the king's life and health throughout the ensuing month. It is a custom with the Baganda to preserve the king's navel-string with great care during his life. The precious object is called the " Twin " of the king, as if it were his double ; and the ghost of the royal afterbirth is believed to be attached to it. Enclosed in a pot, which is wrapt in bark cloths, the navel-string is kept in a temple specially built for it near the king's enclosure, and a great minister of state acts as its guardian and priest. Every new moon, at evening, he carries it in state, wrapped in bark cloths, to the king, who takes it into his hands, examines it, and returns it to the minister. The keeper of the navel-string then goes back with it to the house and sets it in the doorway, where it remains all night. Next morning it is taken from its wrappings and again placed in the doorway until the evening, when it is once more swathed in bark cloths and restored to its usual place.[1] Apparently the navel-string is conceived as a vital portion, a sort of external soul, of the

---

[1] J. Roscoe, " Further Notes on the Manners and Customs of the Baganda." *Journal of the Anthropological Institute,* xxxii. (1902) pp. 63, 76 ; *id.*, *The Baganda* (London, 1911) pp. 235 *sq.*

In the former passage the part of the king's person which is treated with this ceremony is said to be the placenta, not the navel-string.

king ; and the attentions bestowed on it at the new moon may be supposed to refresh and invigorate it, thereby refreshing and invigorating the king's life.

Baleful influence supposed to be exercised by the moon on children.

The Armenians appear to think that the moon exercises a baleful influence on little children. To avert that influence a mother will show the moon to her child and say, "Thine uncle, thine uncle." For the same purpose the father and mother will mount to the roof of the house at new moon on a Wednesday or Friday. The father then puts the child on a shovel and gives it to the mother, saying, "If it is thine, take it to thee. But if it is mine, rear it and give it to me back." The mother then takes the child and the shovel, and returns them to the father in like manner.[1] A similar opinion as to the noxious influence of moonshine on children was apparently held by the ancient Greeks ; for Greek nurses took great care never to show their infants to the moon.[2] Some Brazilian Indians in like manner guard babies against the moon, believing that it would make them ill. Immediately after delivery mothers will hide themselves and their infants in the thickest parts of the forest in order that the moonlight may not fall on them.[3] It would be easy to understand why the waning moon should be deemed injurious to children ; they might be supposed to peak and pine with its dwindling light. Thus in Angus it is thought that if a child be weaned during the waning of the moon, it will decay all the time that the moon continues to wane.[4] But it is less easy to see why the same deleterious influence on children should be ascribed to moonlight in general.

Use of the moon to increase money or decrease sickness.

There are many other ways in which people have sought to turn lunar sympathy to practical account. Clearly the increase of the moon is the time to increase your goods, and the decrease of the moon is the time to diminish your ills. Acting on this imaginary law of nature many persons in Europe show their money to the new moon or turn it in

[1] M. Abeghian, *Der armenische Volksglaube* (Leipsic, 1899), p. 49.

[2] Plutarch, *Quaestiones Conviviales*, iv. 10. 3. 7.

[3] J. B. von Spix und C. F. Ph. von Martius, *Reise in Brasilien* (Munich, 1823–1831), i. 381, iii. 1186.

[4] J. Jamieson, *Dictionary of the Scottish Language*, New Edition edited by J. Longmuir and D. Donaldson (Paisley, 1879–1882), iii. 300 (*s.v.* "Mone").

their pockets at that season, in the belief that the money will grow with the growth of the planet ; sometimes, by way of additional precaution, they spit on the coin at the same time.[1] "Both Christians and Moslems in Syria turn their silver money in their pockets at the new moon for luck ; and two persons meeting under the new moon will each take out a silver coin and embrace, saying, ' May you begin and end ; and may it be a good month to us.' "[2] Conversely the waning of the moon is the most natural time to get rid of bodily ailments. In Brittany they think that warts vary with the phases of the moon, growing as it waxes and vanishing away as it wanes.[3] Accordingly, they say in Germany that if you would rid yourself of warts you should treat them when the moon is on the decrease.[4] And a German cure for toothache, earache, headache, and so forth, is to look towards the waning moon and say, "As the moon decreases, so may my pains decrease also."[5] However, some Germans reverse the rule. They say, for example, that if you are afflicted with a wen, you should face the waxing moon, lay your finger on the wen, and say thrice, "What I see waxes ; what I touch, let it vanish away." After each of these two sentences you should cross yourself thrice. Then go home without speaking to any one, and repeat three paternosters behind the kitchen door.[6] The Huzuls of the Carpathians recommend a somewhat similar, and no doubt equally efficacious, cure for waterbrash. They say that at new moon the patient should run thrice round the house and then say to the moon, "Moon, moon, where wast thou?" "Behind the mountain." "What hast thou eaten there?" "Horse flesh." "Why hast thou brought me nothing?" "Because I forgot." "May the waterbrash

[1] F. Panzer, *Beitrag zur deutschen Mythologie* (Munich, 1848–1855), ii. 260 ; P. Drechsler, *Sitte, Brauch und Volksglaube in Schlesien*, ii. (Leipsic, 1906) p. 131 ; W. Henderson, *Folklore of the Northern Counties of England* (London, 1879), p. 114 ; C. S. Burne and G. F. Jackson, *Shropshire Folk-lore* (London, 1883), p. 257 ; W. Gregor, *Folk-lore of the North-East of Scotland* (London, 1881), p. 151.

[2] C. R. Conder, *Heth and Moab*

(London, 1883), p. 286.

[3] P. Sébillot, *Traditions et Superstitions de la Haute-Bretagne* (Paris, 1882), ii. 355.

[4] A. Kuhn, *Märkische Sagen und Märchen* (Berlin, 1843), p. 387, § 93.

[5] *Die gestriegelte Rockenphilosophie* (Chemnitz, 1759), p. 447.

[6] F. Panzer, *Beitrag zur deutschen Mythologie*, ii. 302. Compare J. Grimm, *Deutsche Mythologie*,[4] ii. 596.

forget to burn me!"[1]   Thus a curative virtue appears to be attributed by some people to the waning and by others to the waxing moon.   There is perhaps just as much, or as little, to be said for the one attribution as for the other.

[1] R. F. Kaindl, "Zauberglaube bei den Huzulen," *Globus*, lxxvi. (1899) p. 256.

CHAPTER X

THE KING AS OSIRIS

IN the foregoing discussion we found reason to believe that the Semitic Adonis and the Phrygian Attis were at one time personated in the flesh by kings, princes, or priests who played the part of the god for a time and then either died a violent death in the divine character or had to redeem their life in one way or another, whether by performing a make-believe sacrifice at some expense of pain and danger to themselves, or by delegating the duty to a substitute.[1] Further, we conjectured that in Egypt the part of Osiris may have been played by the king himself.[2] It remains to adduce some positive evidence of this personation. Osiris personated by the king of Egypt.

A great festival called the Sed was celebrated by the Egyptians with much solemnity at intervals of thirty years. Various portions of the ritual are represented on the ancient monuments of Hieraconpolis and Abydos and in the oldest decorated temple of Egypt known to us, that of Usirniri at Busiris, which dates from the fifth dynasty. It appears that the ceremonies were as old as the Egyptian civilization, and that they continued to be observed till the end of the Roman period.[3] The reason for holding them at intervals of thirty The Sed festival celebrated in Egypt at intervals of thirty years.

---

[1] See above, vol. i. pp. 16 *sq.*, 48 *sqq.*, 110, 114, 170 *sq.*, 172 *sqq.*, 176 *sqq.*, 179 *sqq.*, 285 *sqq.*, 288 *sqq.*

[2] See above, pp. 97 *sq.*, 101 *sq.*

[3] A. Moret, *Du caractère religieux de la royauté Pharaonique* (Paris, 1902), pp. 235-238. The festival is discussed at length by M. Moret (*op. cit.* pp. 235-273). See further R. Lepsius, *Die Chronologie der Aegypter*, i. 161-165; Miss M. A. Murray, *The Osireion* at *Abydos*, pp. 32-34; W. M. Flinders Petrie, *Researches in Sinai* (London, 1906), pp. 176-185. In interpreting the festival I follow Professor Flinders Petrie. That the festival occurred, theoretically at least, at intervals of thirty years, appears to be unquestionable; for in the Greek text of the Rosetta Stone Ptolemy V. is called "lord of periods of thirty years," and though the corresponding part of the hieroglyphic

years is uncertain, but we can hardly doubt that the period was determined by astronomical considerations. According to one view, it was based on the observation of Saturn's period of revolution round the sun, which is, roughly speaking, thirty years, or, more exactly, twenty-nine years and one hundred and seventy-four days.[1] According to another view, the thirty years' period had reference to Sirius, the star of Isis. We have seen that on account of the vague character of the old Egyptian year the heliacal rising of Sirius shifted its place gradually through every month of the calendar.[2] In one hundred and twenty years the star thus passed through one whole month of thirty days. To speak more precisely, it rose on the first of the month during the first four years of the period : it rose on the second of the month in the second four years, on the third of the month in the third four years ; and so on successively, till in the last four years of the hundred and twenty years it rose on the last day of the month. As the Egyptians watched the annual summer rising of the star with attention and associated it with the most popular of their goddesses, it would be natural that its passage from one month to another, at intervals of one hundred and twenty years, should be the occasion of a great festival, and that the long period of one hundred and twenty years should be divided into four minor periods of thirty years respectively, each celebrated by a minor festival.[3] If this theory of the Sed festivals is correct, we should expect to find that every fourth celebration was distinguished from the rest by a higher degree of solemnity, since it marked the completion of a twelfth part of the star's journey through the twelve

---

text is lost, the demotic version of the words is "master of the years of the Sed festival." See R. Lepsius, *op. cit.* pp. 161 *sq.* ; W. Dittenberger, *Orientis Graeci Inscriptiones Selectae*, No. 90, line 2 (vol. i. p. 142) ; A. Moret, *op. cit.* 260. However, the kings appear to have sometimes celebrated the festival at much shorter intervals, so that the dates of its recurrence cannot safely be used for chronological purposes. See Ed. Meyer, *Nachträge zur ägyptischen*

Chronologie (Berlin, 1908), pp. 43 *sq.* (*Abhandlungen der königl. Akademie der Wissenschaften vom Jahre 1907*) ; *id.*, *Geschichte des Altertums*,[2] i. 2. pp. xix. 130.

[1] This was Letronne's theory (R. Lepsius, *op. cit.* p. 163).

[2] See above, pp. 24 *sqq.*, 34 *sqq.*

[3] This was in substance the theory of Biot (R. Lepsius, *l.c.*), and it is the view of Professor W. M. Flinders Petrie (*Researches in Sinai*, pp. 176 *sqq.*).

months. Now it appears that in point of fact every fourth
Sed festival was marked off from its fellows by the adjective
tep or "chief," and that these "chief" celebrations fell as a
rule in the years when Sirius rose on the first of the month.[1]
These facts confirm the view that the Sed festival was closely
connected with the star Sirius, and through it with Isis.

However, we are here concerned rather with the meaning *Intention*
and the rites of the festival than with the reasons for holding *of the Sed festival to*
it once every thirty years. The intention of the festival *renew the king's life.*
seems to have been to procure for the king a new lease of
life, a renovation of his divine energies, a rejuvenescence.
In the inscriptions of Abydos we read, after an account of
the rites, the following address to the king : " Thou dost
recommence thy renewal, thou art granted to flourish again
like the infant god Moon, thou dost grow young again, and
that from season to season, like Nun at the beginning of
time, thou art born again in renewing the Sed festivals.
All life comes to thy nostril, and thou art king of the whole
earth for ever." [2]   In short, on these occasions it appears to
have been supposed that the king was in a manner born
again.

But how was the new birth effected ? Apparently the *The king identified with the dead Osiris at the Sed festival.*
essence of the rites consisted in identifying the king with
Osiris ; for just as Osiris had died and risen again from the
dead, so the king might be thought to die and to live again
with the god whom he personated. The ceremony would
thus be for the king a death as well as a rebirth. Accordingly in pictures of the Sed festival on the monuments we
see the king posing as the dead Osiris. He sits in a shrine
like a god, holding in his hands the crook and flail of
Osiris : he is wrapped in tight bandages like the mummified
Osiris ; indeed, there is nothing but his name to prove that
he is not Osiris himself. This enthronement of the king in
the attitude of the dead god seems to have been the principal
event of the festival.[3]   Further, the queen and the king's
daughters figured prominently in the ceremonies.[4]   A

[1] W. M. Flinders Petrie, *Researches in Sinai*, p. 180.
[2] A. Moret, *Du caractère religieux de la royauté Pharaonique*, pp. 255 *sq.*
[3] W. M. Flinders Petrie, *Researches*

in Sinai, p. 181.
[4] A. Moret, *op. cit.* p. 240 ; Miss M. A. Murray, *The Osireion at Abydos*, pp. 33 *sq.*, with the slip inserted at p. 33 ; W. Flinders Petrie, *op. cit.* p. 184.

discharge of arrows formed part of the rites ;[1] and in some sculptures at Carnac the queen is portrayed shooting arrows towards the four quarters of the world, while the king does the same with rings.[2] The oldest illustration of the festival is on the mace of Narmer, which is believed to date from 5500 B.C. Here we see the king seated as Osiris in a shrine at the top of nine steps. Beside the shrine stand fan-bearers, and in front of it is a figure in a palanquin, which, according to an inscription in another representation of the scene, appears to be the royal child. An enclosure of curtains hung on poles surrounds the dancing-ground, where three men are performing a sacred dance. A procession of standards is depicted beside the enclosure ; it is headed by the standard of the jackal-god Up-uat, the " opener of ways " for the dead.[3] Similarly on a seal of King Zer, or rather Khent, one of the early kings of the first dynasty, the monarch appears as Osiris with the standard of the jackal-god before him. In front of him, too, is the ostrich feather on which " the dead king was supposed to ascend into heaven. Here, then, the king, identified with Osiris, king of the dead, has before him the jackal-god, who leads the dead, and the ostrich feather, which symbolizes his reception into the sky." [4] There are even grounds for thinking that in order to complete the mimic death of the king at the Sed festival an effigy of him, clad in the costume of Osiris, was solemnly buried in a cenotaph.[5]

Professor Flinders Petrie's explanation of the Sed festival.

According to Professor Flinders Petrie, " the conclusion may be drawn thus. In the savage age of prehistoric times, the Egyptians, like many other African and Indian peoples, killed their priest-king at stated intervals, in order that the ruler should, with unimpaired life and health, be enabled to maintain the kingdom in its highest condition. The royal daughters were present in order that they might be married to his successor. The jackal-god went before

[1] A. Moret, *op. cit.* p. 242.

[2] Miss M. A. Murray, *op. cit.*, slip inserted at p. 33.

[3] W. M. Flinders Petrie, *Researches in Sinai*, p. 183.

[4] W. M. Flinders Petrie, *l.c.* As to the king's name (Khent instead of Zer)

see above, p. 20, note[1].

[5] J. Capart, " Bulletin critique des religions de l'Égypte," *Revue de l'Histoire des Religions*, liii. (1906) pp. 332-334. I have to thank Professor W. M. Flinders Petrie for calling my attention to this passage.

him, to open the way to the unseen world ; and the ostrich feather received and bore away the king's soul in the breeze that blew it out of sight. This was the celebration of the 'end,' the *sed* feast. The king thus became the dead king, patron of all those who had died in his reign, who were his subjects here and hereafter. He was thus one with Osiris, the king of the dead. This fierce custom became changed, as in other lands, by appointing a deputy king to die in his stead ; which idea survived in the Coptic Abu Nerūs, with his tall crown of Upper Egypt, false beard, and sceptre. After the death of the deputy, the real king renewed his life and reign. Henceforward this became the greatest of the royal festivals, the apotheosis of the king during his life, after which he became Osiris upon earth and the patron of the dead in the underworld." [1]

A similar theory of the Sed festival is maintained by another eminent Egyptologist, M. Alexandre Moret. He says: " In most of the temples of Egypt, of all periods, pictures set forth for us the principal scenes of a solemn festival called ' festival of the tail,' the Sed festival. It consisted essentially in a representation of the ritual death of the king followed by his rebirth. In this case the king is identified with Osiris, the god who in historical times is the hero of the sacred drama of humanity, he who guides us through the three stages of life, death, and rebirth in the other world. Hence, clad in the funeral costume of Osiris, with the tight-fitting garment clinging to him like a shroud, Pharaoh is conducted to the tomb ; and from it he returns rejuvenated and reborn like Osiris emerging from the dead. How was this fiction carried out? how was this miracle performed? By the sacrifice of human or animal victims. On behalf of the king a priest lay down in the skin of the animal victim : he assumed the posture characteristic of an embryo in its mother's womb : when he came forth from the skin he was deemed to be reborn ; and Pharaoh, for whom this rite was celebrated, was himself reborn, or to adopt the Egyptian ex-

Alexandre Moret's theory that at the Sed festivals the king was supposed to die and to be born again.

[1] W. M. Flinders Petrie, *Researches in Sinai*, p. 185. As to the Coptic mock-king see C. B. Klunzinger, *Bilder aus Oberägypten, der Wüste und dem Rothen Meere* (Stuttgart, 1877), pp. 180 *sq.* ; *The Dying God*, pp. 151 *sq.* For examples of human sacrifices offered to prolong the lives of kings see below, vol. ii. pp. 219 *sqq.*

pression, 'he renewed his births.' And in testimony of the due performance of the rites the king girt his loins with the tail, a compendious representative of the skin of the sacrificed beast, whence the name of 'the festival of the tail.'

"How are we to explain the rule that at a certain point of his reign every Pharaoh must undergo this ritual death followed by fictitious rebirth? Is it simply a renewal of the initiation into the Osirian mysteries? or does the festival present some more special features? The ill-defined part played by the royal children in these rites seems to me to indicate that the Sed festival represents other episodes which refer to the transmission of the regal office. At the dawn of civilization in Egypt the people were perhaps familiar with the alternative either of putting their king to death in his full vigour in order that his power should be transmitted intact to his successor, or of attempting to rejuvenate him and to 'renew his life.' The latter measure was an invention of the Pharaohs. How could it be carried out more effectively than by identifying themselves with Osiris, by applying to themselves the process of resurrection, the funeral rites by which Isis, according to the priests, had magically saved her husband from death? Perhaps the fictitious death of the king may be regarded as a mitigation of the primitive murder of the divine king, a transition from a barbarous reality to symbolism." [1]

---

[1] A. Moret, *Mystères Égyptiens* (Paris, 1913), pp. 187-190. For a detailed account of the Egyptian evidence, monumental and inscriptional, on which M. Moret bases his view of the king's rebirth by deputy from the hide of a sacrificed animal, see pp. 16 *sqq.*, 72 *sqq.* of the same work. Compare his article, "Du sacrifice en Égypte," *Revue de l'Histoire des Religions*, lvii. (1908) pp. 93 *sqq.* In support of the view that the king of Egypt was deemed to be born again at the Sed festival it has been pointed out that on these solemn occasions, as we learn from the monuments, there was carried before the king on a pole an object shaped like a placenta, a part of the human body which many savage or barbarous peoples regard as the twin

brother or sister of the new-born child. See C. G. Seligmann and Margaret A. Murray, "Note upon an early Egyptian standard," *Man*, xi. (1911) pp. 165-171. The object which these writers take to represent a human placenta is interpreted by M. Alexandre Moret as the likeness of a human embryo. As to the belief that the afterbirth is a twin brother or sister of the infant, see above, vol. i. p. 93, and below, pp. 169 *sq.*; *The Magic Art and the Evolution of Kings*, i. 82 *sqq.*

Professor J. H. Breasted thinks that the Sed festival is probably "the oldest religious feast of which any trace has been preserved in Egypt"; he admits that on these occasions "the king assumed the costume and insignia of

Whether this interpretation of the Sed festival be accepted in all its details or not, one thing seems quite certain : on these solemn occasions the god Osiris was personated by the king of Egypt himself. That is the point with which we are here chiefly concerned.

Osiris personated by the king of Egypt.

Osiris, and undoubtedly impersonated him," and further that "one of the ceremonies of this feast symbolized the resurrection of Osiris"; but he considers that the significance of the festival is as yet obscure. See J. H. Breasted, *Development of Religion and Thought in Ancient Egypt* (London, 1912), p. 39.

CHAPTER XI

THE ORIGIN OF OSIRIS

How did the conception of Osiris as a god of vegetation and of the dead originate?

THUS far we have discussed the character of Osiris as he is presented to us in the art and literature of Egypt and in the testimonies of Greek writers ; and we have found that judged by these indications he was in the main a god of vegetation and of the dead. But we have still to ask, how did the conception of such a composite deity originate? Did it arise simply through observation of the great annual fluctuations of the seasons and a desire to explain them? Was it a result of brooding over the mystery of external nature? Was it the attempt of a rude philosophy to lift the veil and explore the hidden springs that set the vast machine in motion? That man at a very early stage of his long history meditated on these things and evolved certain crude theories which partially satisfied his craving after knowledge is certain ; from such meditations of Babylonian and Phrygian sages appear to have sprung the pathetic figures of Adonis and Attis; and from such meditations of Egyptian sages may have sprung the tragic figure of Osiris.

While Adonis and Attis were subordinate figures in their respective pantheons, Osiris was the greatest and most popular god of Egypt.

Yet a broad distinction seems to sever the myth and worship of Osiris from the kindred myths and worships of Adonis and Attis. For while Adonis and Attis were minor divinities in the religion of Western Asia, completely overshadowed by the greater deities of their respective pantheons, the solemn figure of Osiris towered in solitary grandeur over all the welter of Egyptian gods, like a pyramid of his native land lit up by the last rays of the setting sun when all below it is in shadow. And whereas legend generally represented Adonis and Attis as simple swains, mere herdsmen

or hunters whom the fatal love of a goddess had elevated
above their homely sphere into a brief and melancholy pre-
eminence, Osiris uniformly appears in tradition as a great
and beneficent king.   In life he ruled over his people,
beloved and revered for the benefits he conferred on them
and on the world ; in death he reigned in their hearts and
memories as lord of the dead, the awful judge at whose bar
every man must one day stand to give an account of the
deeds done in the body and to receive the final award.   In
the faith of the Egyptians the cruel death and blessed
resurrection of Osiris occupied the same place as the death
and resurrection of Christ hold in the faith of Christians.
As Osiris died and rose again from the dead, so they hoped
through him and in his dear name to wake triumphant from
the sleep of death to a blissful eternity.   That was their
sheet-anchor in life's stormy sea ; that was the hope which
supported and consoled millions of Egyptian men and
women for a period of time far longer than that during
which Christianity has now existed on earth.   In the long
history of religion no two divine figures resemble each
other more closely in the fervour of personal devotion which
they have kindled and in the high hopes which they have
inspired than Osiris and Christ.   The sad figure of Buddha
indeed has been as deeply loved and revered by countless
millions ; but he had no glad tidings of immortality for men,
nothing but the promise of a final release from the burden
of mortality.

And if Osiris and Christ have been the centres of the *The*
like enthusiastic devotion, may not the secret of their in- *personal*
devotion
fluence have been similar?   If Christ lived the life and died *of the*
the death of a man on earth, may not Osiris have done so *Egyptians*
to Osiris
likewise?   The immense and enduring popularity of his *suggests*
worship speaks in favour of the supposition ; for all the *that he*
may have
other great religious or semi-religious systems which have *been a real*
won for themselves a permanent place in the affections of *man ; for*
all the per-
mankind, have been founded by individual great men, who *manent*
religious
by their personal life and example exerted a power of *or semi-*
attraction such as no cold abstractions, no pale products of *religious*
systems of
the collective wisdom or folly could ever exert on the minds *the world*
and hearts of humanity.   Thus it was with Buddhism, with *have been*
founded by

individual Confucianism, with Christianity, and with Mohammedanism ;
great men. and thus it may well have been with the religion of Osiris.
Certainly we shall do less violence to the evidence if we
accept the unanimous tradition of ancient Egypt on this
point than if we resolve the figure of Osiris into a myth pure
and simple. And when we consider that from the earliest
to the latest times Egyptian kings were worshipped as gods
both in life and in death, there appears to be nothing extravagant or improbable in the view that one of them by his
personal qualities excited a larger measure of devotion than
usual during his life and was remembered with fonder affec-
tion and deeper reverence after his death ; till in time his
beloved memory, dimmed, transfigured, and encircled with a
halo of glory by the mists of time, grew into the dominant
religion of his people. At least this theory is reasonable
enough to deserve a serious consideration. If we accept it,
we may suppose that the mythical elements, which legend
undoubtedly ascribed to Osiris, were later accretions which
gathered about his memory like ivy about a ruin. There is
no improbability in such a supposition ; on the contrary, all
analogy is in its favour, for nothing is more certain than
that myths grow like weeds round the great historical figures
of the past.

The   In recent years the historical reality of Osiris as a king
historical who once lived and reigned in Egypt has been maintained
reality of
Osiris as an by more than one learned scholar ;[1] and without venturing
old king of to pronounce a decided opinion on so obscure and difficult a
Egypt can
be sup-   question, I think it worth while, following the example of
ported by Dr. Wallis Budge, to indicate certain modern African analo-
modern
African   gies which tend to confirm the view that beneath the
analogies. mythical wrappings of Osiris there lay the mummy of a
dead man. At all events the analogies which I shall cite
suffice to prove that the custom of worshipping dead kings
has not been confined to Egypt, but has been apparently
widespread throughout Africa, though the evidence now at
our disposal only enables us to detect the observance of the

---

[1] It is maintained by the discoverer
of the tomb of Osiris at Abydos,
Monsieur E. Amélineau, in his work
Le Tombeau d'Osiris (Paris, 1899) and
by Dr. E. A. Wallis Budge in his
elaborate treatise *Osiris and the Egyptian Resurrection*, in which the author
pays much attention to analogies drawn
from the religion and customs of modern
African tribes.

custom at a few points of the great continent. But even if
the resemblance in this respect between ancient Egypt and
modern Africa should be regarded as established, it would
not justify us in inferring an ethnical affinity between the
fair or ruddy Egyptians and the black aboriginal races,
who occupy almost the whole of Africa except a comparatively narrow fringe on the northern sea-board. Scholars
are still divided on the question of the original home and
racial relationship of the ancient Egyptians. It has been
held on the one hand that they belong to an indigenous white race which has been always in possession of the
Mediterranean coasts of Africa ; and on the other hand
it has been supposed that they are akin to the Semites
in blood as well as in language, and that they entered
Africa from the East, whether by gradual infiltration or
on a sudden wave of conquest like the Arabs in the
decline of the Roman empire.[1]   On either view a great gulf
divided them from the swarthy natives of the Sudan, with
whom they were always in contact on their southern border ;
and though a certain admixture may have taken place
through marriage between the two races, it seems unsafe to
assume that the religious and political resemblances which
can be traced between them are based on any closer relationship than the general similarity in structure and functions
of the human mind.

In a former part of this work we saw that the Shilluks, The
a pastoral and partially agricultural people of the White spirits of
dead kings
Nile, worship the spirits of their dead kings.[2]   The graves worshipped
of the deceased monarchs form indeed the national or tribal by the
Shilluks

---

[1] G. Maspero, *Histoire ancienne
des Peuples de l'Orient Classique*, i. 43
sqq. ; J. H. Breasted, *History of the
Ancient Egyptians*, pp. 29 *sq.* ; Ed.
Meyer, *Geschichte des Altertums*,[2] i. 2.
pp. 41 *sqq.* The affinity of the Egyptian
language to the Semitic family of
speech seems now to be admitted even
by historians who maintain the African
origin of the Egyptians.

[2] *The Dying God*, pp. 17 *sqq.* The
information there given was kindly supplied by Dr. C. G. Seligmann, who has

since published it with fuller details.
See C. G. Seligmann, *The Cult of
Nyakang and the Divine Kings of the
Shilluk* (Khartoum, 1911), pp. 216-232
(reprint from *Fourth Report of the
Wellcome Tropical Research Labora-
tories, Gordon Memorial College, Khartoum*) ; W. Hofmayr, " Religion der
Schilluk," *Anthropos*, vi. (1911) pp.
120-131 ; Diedrich Westermann, *The
Shilluk People, their Language and Folk-
lore* (Berlin, preface dated 1912), pp.
xxxix. *sqq.* In what follows I have
drawn on all these authorities.

temples ; and as each king is interred at the village where
he was born and where his afterbirth is buried, these grave-
shrines are scattered over the country.   Each of them
usually comprises a small group of round huts, resembling
the common houses of the people, the whole being enclosed
by a fence ; one of the huts is built over the grave, the
others are occupied by the guardians of the shrine, who at
first are generally the widows or old men-servants of the
deceased king.   When these women or retainers die, they
are succeeded in office by their descendants, for the tombs
are maintained in perpetuity, so that the number of

temples and of gods is always on the increase.   Cattle are
dedicated to these royal shrines and animals sacrificed at
them.   For example, when the millet crop threatens to fail
or a murrain breaks out among the beasts, one of the dead
kings will appear to somebody in a dream and demand a
sacrifice.   The dream is reported to the king, and he
immediately orders a bullock and a cow to be sent to the
grave of the dead king who appeared in a vision of the
night to the sleeper.   This is done ; the bullock is killed and
the cow added to the sacred herd of the shrine.   It is
customary, also, though not necessary, at harvest to offer
some of the new millet at the temple-tombs of the kings ;
and sick people send animals to be sacrificed there on their
behalf.   Special regard is paid to trees that grow near
the graves of the kings ; and the spirits of the departed
monarchs are believed to appear from time to time in the
form of certain animals.   One of them, for example, always
takes the shape of a certain insect, which seems to be the
larva of the *Mantidae.*   When a Shilluk finds one of these
insects, he will take it up in his hands and deposit it reveren-
tially at the shrine.   Other kings manifest themselves as a
certain species of white birds ; others assume the form of
giraffes.   When one of these long-legged and long-necked
creatures comes stalking up fearlessly to a village where
there is a king's grave, the people know that the king's soul
is in the animal, and the attendants at the royal tomb testify
their joy at the appearance of their master by sacrificing a
sheep or even a bullock.

But of all the dead kings none is revered so deeply or

occupies so large a place in the minds of the people as Worship of
Nyakang, the traditional founder of the dynasty and the Nyakang,
the first
ancestor of all the kings who have reigned after him to the of the
present day.   Of these kings the Shilluks have preserved Shilluk
kings.
the memory and the genealogy ; twenty-six seem to have
sat on the throne since Nyakang, but the period of time
covered by their reigns is much shorter than it would have
been under conditions such as now prevail in Europe ; for
down to the time when their country came under British
rule it was the regular custom of the Shilluks to put their
kings to death as soon as they showed serious symptoms of
bodily or mental decay.   The custom was based on " the
conviction that the king must not be allowed to become ill
or senile, lest with his diminishing vigour the cattle should
sicken and fail to bear their increase, the crops should rot in
the fields, and man, stricken with disease, should die in ever-
increasing numbers." [1]   It is said that Nyakang, like Romulus,
disappeared in a great storm, which scattered all the people
about him ; in their absence the king took a cloth, tied it
tightly round his neck, and strangled himself.   According
to one account, that is the death which all his successors on
the throne have died ; [2] but while tradition appears to be
unanimous as to the custom of regicide, it varies as to the
precise mode in which the kings were relieved of their office
and of life.   But still the people are convinced that Nyakang
did not really die but only vanished mysteriously away like
the wind.   When a missionary asked the Shilluks as to the
manner of Nyakang's death, they were filled with amazement
at his ignorance and stoutly maintained that he never died, for
were he to die all the Shilluks would die also. [3]   The graves
of this deified king are shown in various parts of the country.

From time to time the spirit of Nyakang manifests itself The
to his people in the form of an animal.   Any creature of spirit of
Nyakang
regal port or surpassing beauty may serve as his temporary supposed
incarnation.   Such among wild animals are lions, crocodiles, to manifest
itself in
little yellow snakes that crawl about men's houses, the finest certain
sorts of antelopes, flamingoes with their rose-pink and scarlet animals.

[1] C. G. Seligmann, *The Cult of*   *People*, p. xlii.
Nyakang, p. 221.
[2] D. Westermann, *The   Shilluk*   [3] D. Westermann, *l.c.*

plumage, and butterflies of all sorts with their brilliant and varied hues. An unusually fine head of cattle is also recognized as the abode of the great king's soul ; for example he once appeared in the shape of a white bull, whereupon the living king commanded special sacrifices to be offered in honour of his deified predecessor. When a bird in which the royal spirit is known to be lodged lights on a tree, that tree becomes sacred to Nyakang ; beads and cloths are hung on its boughs, sacrifices and prayers are offered below it. Once when the Turks unknowingly felled such a tree, fear and horror fell on the Shilluks who beheld the sacrilege. They filled the air with lamentations and killed an ox to appease their insulted ancestor.[1] Particular regard is also paid to trees that grow near the graves of Nyakang, though they are not regularly worshipped.[2] In one place two gigantic baobab trees are pointed out as marking the spot where Nyakang once stood, and sacrifices are now offered under their spreading shade.[3]

The deified Nyakang seems to have been a real man.   There seems to be no doubt that in spite of the mythical elements which have gathered round his memory, Nyakang was a real man, who led the Shilluks to their present home on the Nile either from the west or from the south ; for on this point tradition varies. " The first and most important ancestor, who is everywhere revered, is Nyakang, the first Shilluk king. He always receives the honourable titles of Father (*uò*), Ancestor (*qua*), King (*red*) or Kings (*ror*), Ancestors, and Great Man Above (*čal duong mal*) to distinguish him from the other great men on earth. Nyakang, as we know, was an historical personage ; he led the Shilluks to the land which they now occupy ; he helped them to victory, made them great and warlike, regulated marriage and law, distributed the country among them, divided it into districts, and in order to increase the dependence of the people on him and to show them his power, became their greatest benefactor by giving himself out as the bestower of rain."[4] Yet Nyakang is now universally revered by the people as a demi-god ; indeed for all practical pur-

[1] W. Hofmayr, "Religion der Schilluk," *Anthropos*, vi. (1911) pp. 123 *sq.*; C. G. Seligmann, *op. cit.* p. 230 ; D. Westermann, *op. cit.* p. xliii.
[2] C. G. Seligmann, *op. cit.* pp. 229 *sq.*

[3] W. Hofmayr, *op. cit.* p. 125.
[4] W. Hofmayr, *op. cit.* p. 123. This writer spells the name of the deified king as Nykang. I have adopted Dr. Seligmann's spelling.

poses his worship quite eclipses that of the supreme god Juok, the creator, who, having ordered the world, committed it to the care of ancestral spirits and demons, and now, dwelling aloft, concerns himself no further with human affairs. Hence men pay little heed to their creator and seldom take his name into their lips except in a few conventional forms of salutation at meeting and parting like our "Good-bye." Far otherwise is it with Nyakang. He "is the ancestor of the Shilluk nation and the founder of the Shilluk dynasty. He is worshipped, sacrifices and prayers are offered to him ; he may be said to be lifted to the rank of a demi-god, though they never forget that he has been a real man. He is expressly designated as 'little' in comparison with God." Yet "in the political, religious and personal life Nyakang takes a far more important place than Juok. Nyakang is the national hero, of whom each Shilluk feels proud, who is praised in innumerable popular songs and sayings ; he is not only a superior being, but also a man. He is the sublime model for every true Shilluk ; everything they value most in their national and private life has its origin in him : their kingdom and their fighting as well as cattle-breeding and farming. While Nyakang is their good father, who only does them good, Juok is the great, uncontrollable power, which is to be propitiated, in order to avoid his inflictions of evil."[1] Indeed "the whole working religion of the Shilluk is a cult of Nyakang, the semi-divine ancestor of their kings, in each of whom his spirit is immanent."[2] The transmission of the divine or semi-divine spirit of Nyakang to the reigning monarch appears to take place at the king's installation and to be effected by means of a rude wooden effigy of Nyakang, in which the spirit of that deified man is perhaps supposed to be immanent. But however the spiritual transmission may be carried out, "the fundamental idea of the cult of the Shilluk divine kings is the immanence in each of the spirit of Nyakang."[3] Thus the Shilluk kings are encircled with a

[1] Diederich Westermann, *The Shilluk People, their Language and Folklore* (Berlin, preface dated 1912), pp. xlii, xliii. Mr. Westermann gives the names of the demi-god and the god as Nyikang and Jwok respectively. For the sake of uniformity I have altered them to Nyakang and Juok, the forms adopted by Dr. C. G. Seligmann.

[2] C. G. Seligmann, *The Cult of Nyakang and the Divine Kings of the Shilluk* (Khartoum, 1911), p. 220.

[3] C. G. Seligmann, *op. cit.* p. 231.

certain halo of divinity because they are thought to be animated by the divine spirit of their ancestor, the founder of the dynasty.

The belief in the former humanity of Nyakang is confirmed by the analogy of his worship to that of the dead Shilluk kings.

The universal belief of the Shilluks in the former humanity of Nyakang is strongly confirmed by the exact parallelism which prevails between his worship and that of the dead kings his successors. Like them he is worshipped at his tomb; but unlike them he has not one tomb only, but ten scattered over the country. Each of these tombs is called "the grave of Nyakang," though the people well know that nobody is buried there. Like the grave-shrines of the other kings, those of Nyakang consist of a small group of circular huts of the ordinary pattern enclosed by a fence. Only children under puberty and the few old people whose duty it is to take care of the shrines may enter these sacred enclosures. The rites performed at them resemble those observed at the shrines of the kings. Two great ceremonies are annually performed at the shrines of Nyakang : one is observed before the beginning of the rainy season in order to ensure a due supply of rain; the other is a thanksgiving at harvest, when porridge made from the new grain is poured out on the threshold of Nyakang's hut and smeared on the outer walls of the building. Even before the millet is reaped the people cut some of the ripening ears and thrust them into the thatch of the sacred hut. Thus it would seem that the Shilluks believe themselves to be dependent on the favour of Nyakang for the rain and the crops. " As the giver of rain, Nyakang is the first and greatest benefactor of the people. In that country rain is everything, without rain there is nothing. The Shilluk does not trouble his head about artificial irrigation, he waits for the rain. If the rain falls, then the millet grows, the cows thrive, man has food and can dance and marry ; for that is the ideal of the Shilluks." [1] Sick people also bring or send sheep as an offering to the nearest shrine of Nyakang in order that they may be healed of their sickness. The attendants of the

---

[1] W. Hofmayr, *op. cit.* p. 125. " It must be remembered that the due growth of the crops, *i.e.* of the most important part of the vegetable world, depends on the well-being of the divine king" (C. G. Seligmann, *op. cit.* p. 229).

sanctuary slaughter the animal, consume its flesh, and give the sufferer the benefit of their prayers.[1]

The example of Nyakang seems to show that under favourable circumstances the worship of a dead king may develop into the dominant religion of a people.   There is, therefore, no intrinsic improbability in the view that in ancient Egypt the religion of Osiris originated in that way.   Certainly some curious resemblances can be traced between the dead Nyakang and the dead Osiris.   Both died violent and mysterious deaths : the graves of both were pointed out in many parts of the country : both were deemed the great sources of fertility for the whole land : and both were associated with certain sacred trees and animals, particularly with bulls.   And just as Egyptian kings identified themselves both in life and in death with their deified predecessor Osiris, so Shilluk kings are still believed to be animated by the spirit of their deified predecessor Nyakang and to share his divinity. *Comparison of Nyakang with Osiris.*

Another African people who regularly worship, or rather used to worship, the spirits of their dead kings are the Baganda.   Their country Uganda lies at the very source of the Nile, where the great river issues from Lake Victoria Nyanza.   Among them the ghosts of dead kings were placed on an equality with the gods and received the same honour and worship ; they foretold events which concerned the State, and they advised the living king, warning him when war was likely to break out.   The king consulted them periodically, visiting first one and then another of the temples in which the mortal remains of his predecessors were preserved with religious care.   But the temple (*malolo*) of a king contained only his lower jawbone and his navel-string (*mulongo*) ; his body was buried elsewhere.[2]   For curiously enough the Baganda believed that the part of the body to which the ghost of a dead man adheres above all others is the lower jawbone ; wherever that portion of his person may be carried, the ghost, in the opinion of these people, will follow it, even to the ends of the earth, and will be perfectly content to remain with it so long as the jawbone is *The spirits of dead kings worshipped by the Baganda of Central Africa.*

[1] C. G. Seligmann, *op. cit.* p. 227.

[2] Rev. J. Roscoe, *The Baganda* (London, 1911), p. 283.

honoured.[1] Hence the jawbones of all the kings of Uganda from the earliest times to the present day have been preserved with the utmost care, each of them being deposited, along with the stump of the monarch's navel-string, in a temple specially dedicated to the worship of the king's ghost; for it is believed that the ghosts of the deceased monarchs would quarrel if they shared the same temple, the question of precedence being one which it would be very difficult for them to adjust to their mutual satisfaction.[2] All the temples of the dead kings stand in the district called Busiro, which means the place of the graves, because the tombs as well as the temples of the departed potentates are situated within its boundaries. The supervision of the temples and of the estates attached to them was a duty incumbent on the *Mugema* or earl of Busiro, one of the few hereditary chiefs in the country. His principal office was that of Prime Minister (*Katikiro*) to the dead kings.[3]

Tombs of the dead kings of Uganda.

When a king dies, his body is sent to Busiro and there embalmed. Then it is laid to rest in a large round house, which has been built for its reception on the top of a hill. This is the king's tomb. It is a conical structure supported by a central post, with a thatched roof reaching down to the ground. Round the hut a high strong fence of reeds is erected, and an outer fence encircles the whole at some distance lower down the hill. Here the body is placed on a bedstead; the sepulchral chamber is filled with bark cloths till it can hold no more, the mainpost is cut down, and the door of the tomb closed, so that no one can enter it again. When that was done, the wives of the late king used to be brought, with their arms pinioned, and placed at intervals round the outer wall of the tomb, where they were clubbed to death. Hundreds of men were also killed in the space between the two fences, that their ghosts might wait on the ghost of the dead king in the other world. None of their bodies were buried; they were left to rot where they fell. Then the gates in the fences were closed; and three chiefs

[1] Rev. J. Roscoe, *op. cit.* pp. 113, 282.

[2] Rev. J. Roscoe, *op. cit.* pp. 110, 282, 285.

[3] Rev. J. Roscoe, *op. cit.* pp. 104, 252 *sq.*; L. F. Cunningham, *Uganda and its People* (London, 1905), p. 226).

with their men guarded the dead bodies from the wild beasts and the vultures. But the hut in which the king's body reposed was never repaired ; it was allowed to moulder and fall into decay.[1]

Five months later the jawbone of the royal corpse was removed in order to be fashioned into an effigy or representative of the dead king. For this purpose three chiefs entered the tomb, not through the door, but by cutting a hole through the wall, and having severed the head from the body they brought it out, carefully filling up the hole in the wall behind them, replacing the thatch, and securing the gates in the fence. When the jawbone had been removed by a chief of the Civet clan, the skull was sent back to Busiro and buried with honour near the mouldering tomb. In contrast to the neglect of the tomb where the royal body lay, the place where the skull was buried was kept in good repair and guarded by some of the old princesses and widows. As for the jawbone, it was put in an ant-hill and left there till the ants had eaten away all the flesh. Then, after it had been washed in beer and milk, it was decorated with cowry-shells and placed in a wooden vessel ; this vessel was next wrapt in bark cloths till it assumed a conical shape, about two and a half feet high by a foot and a half broad at the base. This conical packet, decorated on the outside with beads, was treated as an image of the deceased king or rather as if it were the king himself in life, for it was called simply "The King." Beside it was placed the stump of the king's navel-string, similarly wrapt in bark cloths and decorated, though not made up into a conical shape.[2] The reason for preserving both the jawbone and the navel-string was that the ghost of the king was supposed to attach itself to his jawbone, and the ghost of his double to his navel-string. For in the belief of the Baganda every person has a double, namely, the afterbirth or placenta, which is born immediately after him and is regarded by the

Ghosts of the dead kings of Uganda supposed to adhere to their lower jaw-bones and their navel-strings, which are accordingly preserved in temples dedicated to the worship of the kings.

---

[1] Rev. J. Roscoe, *The Baganda*, pp. 104-107, *id.*, "Notes on the Manners and Customs of the Baganda," *Journal of the Anthropological Institute*, xxxi. (1901) p. 129 ; *id.*, "Further Notes on the Manners and Customs of the Baganda," *ibid.*, xxxii. (1902) pp. 44 *sq.* Compare L. F. Cunningham, *Uganda and its People* (London, 1905), pp. 224, 226.

[2] Rev. J. Roscoe, *The Baganda*, pp. 109 *sq.*

people as a second child. Now that double has a ghost of its own, which adheres to the navel-string; and if the person is to remain healthy, it is essential that the ghost of his double should be carefully preserved. Hence every Baganda man and woman keeps his or her navel-string wrapt up in bark cloth as a treasure of great price on which his health and prosperity are dependent; the precious little bundle is called his Twin (*mulongo*), because it contains the ghost of his double, the afterbirth. If that is deemed necessary for everybody, much more is it deemed essential for the welfare of the king; hence during his life the stump of his navel-string is kept, as we saw,[1] by one of the principal ministers of state and is inspected by the king himself every month. And when his majesty has departed this life, the unity of his spirit imperatively demands that his own ghost and the ghost of his double should be kept together in the same place; that is why the jawbone and the navel-string of every dead king are carefully preserved in the same temple, because the two ghosts adhere respectively to these two parts of his person, and it would be unreasonable and indeed cruel to divide them.[2]

The temples of the dead kings of Uganda. The two ghosts having been thus safely lodged in the two precious parcels, the next thing was to install them in the temple, where they were to enter on their career of beneficent activity. A site having been chosen, the whole country supplied the labour necessary for building the temple; and ministers were appointed to wait upon the dead king. The officers of state who had held important posts during his life retained their titles and continued to discharge their duties towards their old master in death. Accordingly houses were built for them near the temple. The dowager queen also took up her residence at the entrance to the temple enclosure, and became its principal guardian. Many also of the king's widows of lower rank were drafted off to live inside the enclosure and keep watch over it. When the queen or any of these widows died, her place was supplied by another princess or a

---

[1] Above, p. 147.

[2] Rev. J. Roscoe, "Kibuka, the War God of the Baganda," *Man*, vii. (1907) pp. 164 *sq.*; *id.*, *The Baganda*, pp. 235 *sq.*

woman of the same clan ; for the temple was maintained in perpetuity.   However, when the reigning king died, the temple of his predecessor lost much of its importance, though it was still kept up in a less magnificent style ; indeed no temple of a dead king was allowed to disappear altogether.[1]   Of all the attendants at the temple the most important probably was the prophet or medium (*mandwa*), whose business it was from time to time to be inspired by the ghost of the deceased monarch and to give oracles in his name.   To this holy office he dedicated himself by drinking a draught of beer and a draught of milk out of the dead king's skull.[2]

The temple consecrated to the worship of a king regularly stood on a hill.   The site was generally chosen by the king in his life, but sometimes his choice was set aside by his successor, who gave orders to build the temple in another place.[3]   The structure was a large conical or bee-hive-shaped hut of the ordinary pattern, divided internally into two chambers, an outer and an inner.   Any person might enter the outer chamber, but the inner was sacred and no profane person might set foot in it ; for there the holy relics of the dead king, his jawbone and his navel-string, were kept for safety in a cell dug in the floor, and there, in close attendance on them, the king's ghost was believed to dwell.   In front of the partition which screened this Holy of Holies from the gaze of the multitude there stood a throne, covered with lion and leopard skins and fenced off from the rest of the sacred edifice by a glittering rail of brass spears, shields, and knives. A forest of poles, supporting the roof, formed a series of aisles in perfect line, and at the end of the central nave appeared, like the altar of a Christian church, the throne in all its glory.   When the king's ghost held a reception, the holy relics, the jawbone and the navel-string, each in its decorated wrappings, were brought forth and set on the throne ; and every person who entered the temple bowed to the ground

Oracles given by the dead kings of Uganda by the mouth of an inspired prophet.

---

[1] Rev. J. Roscoe, *The Baganda*, pp. 110-112, 283 *sq*.

[2] Rev. J. Roscoe, " Notes on the Manners and Customs of the Baganda," *Journal of the Anthropological Institute*, xxxi. (1901) pp. 129 *sq*.; *id.*,

" Further Notes on the Manners and Customs of the Baganda," *ibid.*, xxxii. (1902) p. 45.

[3] Rev. J. Roscoe, *The Baganda*, p. 283.

and greeted the jawbone in an awestruck voice, for he regarded it as the king in person.   Solemn music played during the reception, the drums rolling and the women chanting, while they clapped their hands to the rhythm of the songs.   Sometimes the dead king spoke to the congregation by the voice of his prophet.   That was a great event. When the oracle was about to be given to the expectant throng, the prophet stepped up to the throne, and addressing the spirit informed him of the business in hand.   Then he smoked one or two pipes, and the fumes bringing on the prophetic fit, he began to rave and to speak in the very voice and with the characteristic turns of speech of the departed monarch, for the king's spirit was now in him. This message from the world beyond the grave was naturally received with rapt attention.   Gradually the fit of inspiration passed : the voice of the prophet resumed its natural tones : the spirit had departed from him and returned to its abode in the inner room.   Such a solemn audience used to be announced beforehand by the beating of the drums in the early morning, and the worshippers brought with them to the temple offerings of food for the dead king, as if he were still alive.[1]

Visit paid by the living king to the temple of his dead father.   But the greatest day of all was when the reigning king visited the temple of his father.   This he did as a rule only once during his reign.   Nor did the people approve of the visits being repeated, for each visit was the signal for the death of many.   Yet, attracted by a painful curiosity, crowds assembled, followed the monarch to the temple, and thronged to see the great ceremony of the meeting between the king and the ghost of his royal father.   The sacred relics were displayed : an old man explained them to the monarch and placed them in his hands : the prophet, inspired by the dead king's spirit, revealed to the living king his destiny.   The interview over, the king was carried back to his house.   It was on the return journey that he always gave, suddenly and without warning, the signal of death.   Obedient to his

[1] Rev. J. Roscoe, "Notes on the Manners and Customs of the Baganda," Journal of the Anthropological Institute, xxxi. (1901) p. 130 ; id., "Further Notes on the Manners and Customs of the Baganda," ibid., xxxii. (1902) p. 46 ; id., The Baganda, pp. 283-285.

orders the guards rushed upon the crowd, captured hundreds Human
of spectators, pinioned them, marched them back to the victims sacrificed
temple, and slaughtered them within the precincts, that their in order
ghosts might wait on the ghost of the dead king.[1] But that their ghosts
though the king rarely visited his father's ghost at the might serve
temple, he had a private chapel for the ghost within the vast the ghost of the dead
enclosure of the royal residence ; and here he often paid king.
his devotions to the august spirit, of whom he stood greatly
in awe.   He took his wives with him to sing the departed
monarch's praise, and he constantly made offerings at the
shrine.   Thither, too, would come the prophet to suck words
of wisdom from the venerable ghost and to impart them
to the king, who thus walked in the counsel of his glorified
father.[2]

In Kiziba, a district of Central Africa on the western The souls
side of Lake Victoria Nyanza, the souls of dead kings of dead kings
become ruling spirits ; temples are built in their honour and worshipped
priests appointed to serve them.   The people are composed in Kiziba.
of two different races, the Bairu, who are aboriginals, and
the Bahima, who are immigrants from the north.   The
royal family belongs to the Bahima stock.   In his lifetime
the king's person is sacred ; and all his actions, property,
and so forth are described by special terms appropriated to
that purpose.   The people are divided into totemic clans :
the totems (*muziro*) are mostly animals or parts of animals :
no man may kill or eat his totem animal, nor marry a
woman who has the same totem as himself.   The royal
family seems to have serpents for their totem ; after death
the king's soul lives in a serpent, while his body is buried in
the hut where he died.   The people revere a supreme god
named Rugaba, who is believed to have created man and
cattle ; but they know little about him, and though they

---

[1] Rev. J. Roscoe, *The Baganda*, pp. 112, 284.

[2] Rev. J. Roscoe, *The Baganda*, p. 112.   It may be worth while to quote an early notice of the worship of the Kings of Uganda.   See C. T. Wilson and R. W. Felkin, *Uganda and the Egyptian Soudan* (London, 1882), i. 208 : " The former kings of the country appear also to be regarded as demi-gods, and their graves are kept with religious care, and houses are erected over them, which are under the constant supervision of one of the principal chiefs of the country, and where human sacrifices are also occasionally offered."   The graves here spoken of are no doubt the temples in which the jawbones and navel-strings of the dead kings are kept and worshipped.

occasionally pray to him, particularly in the case of a difficult birth, he has no priests and receives no sacrifices. The business of the priests is to act as intermediaries, not between God and man, but between men and the spirits. The spirits are believed to have been formerly kings of the world. The highest of them is a certain Wamara, who rules over the souls of the dead, and who would seem to have been a great king in his life. Temples are built for him ; they are like the houses of men, but only half as large. A perpetual holy fire is kept up in each temple, and the priest passes the night in it. He receives white sheep or goats as victims, and generally acts also as a diviner or physician. When a man is very ill, he thinks that Wamara, the lord of the spirits of the dead, is summoning him to the far country ; so he sends a sacrifice to Wamara's priest, who prays to the spirit to let the sick man live yet a while.[1] This great spirit of an ancient king, who now rules over the dead, resembles the Egyptian Osiris.

The worship of ancestral spirits among the Bantu tribes of Northern Rhodesia.   The Bantu tribes who inhabit the great tableland of Northern Rhodesia revere a supreme being whom they call Leza, but their ideas about him are hazy. Thunder, lightning, earthquakes, rain, and other natural phenomena are grouped together under his name as manifestations of his power. Among the more progressive tribes, such as the Awemba and the Wabisa, the great god is thought to take some interest in human affairs ; and though they do not pray to him, they nevertheless invoke him by his names of praise, which set forth his attributes as the protector and judge of mankind. It is he, too, who receives the souls of the departed. "Yet, as far as the dominant Wemba tribe is concerned, the cult of Leza is outside their ordinary religion. There is no direct access to him by prayer or by sacrifices, which are made to Mulenga and the other great

<hr />

[1] Hermann Rehse, *Kiziba, Land und Leute* (Stuttgart, 1910), pp. 4-7, 106 *sqq.*, 121, 125 *sqq.*, 130. Among the totems of the people are the long-tailed monkey (*Cercopithecus*), a small species of antelope, the locust, the hippopotamus, the buffalo, the otter, dappled cows, and the hearts of all animals. The members of the clan which is charged with the duty of burying the king's body have for their totem the remains of a goat that has been killed by a leopard. See H. Rehse, *op. cit.* pp. 5 *sq.*

tribal and ancestral spirits instead.   For upon such animism is founded the whole fabric of Wemba religion."[1]   The ancestral spirits whom the Awemba and all other tribes of this region worship may be divided into two main classes. First come the spirits of departed chiefs, who are publicly worshipped by the whole tribe ; and second come the spirits of near relations who are worshipped privately by each head of a family.[2]   "Among the Awemba there is no special shrine for these purely family spirits, who are worshipped inside the hut, and to whom family sacrifice of a sheep, a goat, or a fowl is made, the spirit receiving the blood spilt on the ground, while all the members of the family partake of the flesh together.   For a religious Wemba man the cult of the spirit of his nearest relations (of his grandparents, or of his deceased father, mother, elder brother, or maternal uncle) is considered quite sufficient.   Out of these spirit relatives a man will worship one whom he considers as his special familiar, for various reasons.   For instance, the diviner may have told him that his last illness was caused because he had not respected the spirit of his uncle ; accordingly he will be careful in future to adopt his uncle as his tutelary spirit.   As a mark of such respect he may devote a cow or a goat to one of the spirits of his ancestors.   Holding the fowl, for instance, in his hands, he will dedicate it, asking the spirit to come and abide in it, upon which the fowl is let go, and is afterwards called by the name of the spirit.   If the necessities, however, of the larder demand that it should be killed, another animal is taken, and the spirit is asked to accept it as a substitute !   Before beginning any special task, such as hoeing a new garden, or going on a journey, Wemba men invoke their tutelary spirits to be with them and to assist their efforts, in short ejaculatory prayers usually couched in a set formula.   Among many of the tribes in the North Luangwa district longer formal prayers are still made to all the deceased ancestors of the clan at the time of harvest, asking them to protect the crops and to drive away illnesses and evil spirits from

---

[1] C. Gouldsbury and H. Sheane, *The Great Plateau of Northern Rhodesia* (London, 1911), pp. 80 *sq.*

[2] C. Gouldsbury and H. Sheane, *The Great Plateau of Northern Rhodesia,* pp. 82 *sq.*

the family, which honours them with libations of beer and offerings of the first-fruits." [1]

The worship of ancestral spirits is apparently the main practical religion of all the Bantu tribes.

Thus among these tribes, who all belong to the great Bantu family, the public worship which a whole tribe pays to the souls of its dead chiefs is probably nothing but an extension of the private worship which every family pays privately to the souls of its dead members. And just as the members of his family whom a man worships privately are not mythical beings conjured up by imagination out of a distant past, but were once real men like himself whom he knew in life, it may be his father, or uncle, or elder brother, so we may be sure that in like manner the dead chiefs revered by the whole tribe are not creations of the mythical fancy, but were once real men of flesh and blood, who ruled over the tribe, and whose memory has been more or less faithfully preserved by tradition. In this respect the tribes of Northern Rhodesia are typical of all the tribes of that great Bantu family which occupies nearly the whole southern half of Africa, from the great equatorial lakes to the Cape of Good Hope. The main practical religion of all these numerous and widespread peoples appears to be the worship of their ancestors.

The worship of ancestral spirits among the Bantu tribes of South Africa.

To adduce in full the evidence which points to this conclusion would lead us too far from our present subject; it must suffice to cite a few typical statements of competent authorities which refer to different tribes of the Bantu stock. Speaking with special reference to the tribes of South-Eastern Africa, the Rev. James Macdonald tells us that "the religion of the Bantu, which they not only profess but really regulate their conduct by, is based on the belief that the spirits of their ancestors interfere constantly in their affairs. Every man worships his own ancestors and offers sacrifices to avert their wrath. The clan worships the spirits of the ancestors of its chiefs, and the tribe worships the spirits of the ancestors of the paramount chief." [2] "The religion of the Bantu was based upon the supposition of the

---

[1] C. Gouldsbury and H. Sheane, *op. cit.* pp. 84 *sq.*

[2] Rev. James Macdonald, "Manners, Customs, Superstitions, and Religions of South African Tribes," *Journal of the Anthropological Institute*, xix. (1890) p. 286. Compare *id.*, *Light in Africa* (London, 1890), p. 191.

existence of spirits that could interfere with the affairs of this world. These spirits were those of their ancestors and their deceased chiefs, the greatest of whom had control over lightning. When the spirits became offended or hungry they sent a plague or disaster until sacrifices were offered and their wrath or hunger was appeased. The head of a family of commoners on such an occasion killed an animal, and all ate of the meat, as the hungry ghost was supposed to be satisfied with the smell." [1] For example, in the year 1891 the son of a chief of the Pondomisi tribe was arrested for an assault and sent for trial before a colonial court. It chanced to be a season of intense heat and severe drought, and the Pondomisi tribe attributed these calamities to the wrath of a dead chief named Gwanya, very famous in his lifetime, whose body, fastened to a log, had been buried under a heap of stones in a deep pool of the Lina river. This redoubtable chieftain was the seventh ancestor in the direct line of the man who had committed the assault ; and he warmly resented the indignity which the whites had done to a noble scion of his house by consigning him to durance vile. To appease the natural indignation of the ghost, the tribesmen killed cattle on the banks of the pool which contained his grave, and threw the flesh into the water along with new dishes full of beer. The prisoner, however, was convicted of the assault and sentenced by the ruthless magistrate, who was no respecter of ghosts, to pay a fine. But the tribe clubbed together and paid the fine for him ; and a few days later rain fell in plenty. The mollified ghost had opened the celestial sluices. [2]

Another writer, describing the religion of the South

[1] G. McCall Theal, *Records of South-Eastern Africa*, vii. (1901) pp. 399 *sq*. With regard to the ghost who controls lightning see Mr. Warner's notes in Col. Maclean's *Compendium of Kafir Laws and Customs* (Cape Town, 1866), pp. 82 *sq*. : " The Kafirs have strange notions respecting the lightning. They consider that it is governed by the *umshologu*, or ghost, of the greatest and most renowned of their departed chiefs ; and who is emphatically styled the *inkosi* ; but they are not at all clear as to which of their ancestors is intended by this designation. Hence they allow of no lamentation being made for a person killed by lightning ; as they say that it would be a sign of disloyalty to lament for one whom the *inkosi* had sent for, and whose services he consequently needed ; and it would cause him to punish them, by making the lightning again to descend and do them another injury."

[2] G. McCall Theal, *op. cit.* vii. 400.

African Bantus, tells us that "the ancestral spirits love the very things they loved before they passed through the flesh; they cherish the same desires and have the same antipathies. The living cannot add to the number of the wives of ancestral spirits; but they can kill cattle in their honour and keep their praise and memory alive on earth. Above all things, they can give them beef and beer. And if the living do not give them sufficient of these things the spirits are supposed to give the people a bad time : they send drought, and sickness, and famine, until people kill cattle in their honour. When men are alive they love to be praised and flattered, fed and attended to; after death they want the very same things, for death does not change personality. . . . In time of drought, or sickness, or great trouble, there would be great searchings of heart as to which ancestor had been neglected, for the trouble would be supposed to be caused by the neglected ancestor. Most of the people would get the subject on their nerves (at least, as far as a Kafir could get anything on the leather strings which do duty for nerves), and some one would be sure to have a vivid dream in which an ancestor would complain that the people had not praised him half enough of late. So an ox would be killed, either by the head-man of the kraal or by a diviner. Then the man would say over the ox as it was being killed, ' Cry out, ox of So-and-So ; listen to us, So-and-So ; this is your ox; we praise you by all your laud-giving names, and tell of all your deeds ; do not be angry with us any more ; do you not see that this is your ox ? Do not accuse us of neglecting you ; when, forsooth, have we ceased to praise you and offer you meat and beer ? Take note, then, that here is another ox we are offering to you.' When the ox is dead some of the meat is mixed with herbs and medicines and placed in a hut with a bowlful of blood. This meat is placed in the part of the hut where the man loved to sit while he was alive, and some one is told off to guard the sacrifice. The meat is left for a night, or longer, and the spirits are supposed to come and enjoy the smell, or drink the serum which oozes from the meat, and to inhale the smell of the beer. The priest or diviner will then sprinkle the people and the huts with medicine made from the contents of the

stomach of the ox.   He places a little on a sherd ; when
this is dry he burns it and calls on the spirits to smell the
incense.   After the meat has been left for a certain time it
is taken out and cooked, and eaten by the men near the
cattle kraal in public. . . . If the trouble does not vanish
after this ceremony the people get angry and say to the
spirits, 'When have we ceased to kill cattle for you, and
when have we ever refused to praise you by your praise-
names?   Why, then, do you treat us so shabbily ?   If you
do not behave better we shall utterly forget your names, and
then what will you do when there is no one to praise you ?
You will have to go and live on grasshoppers.   If you do
not mend your ways we shall forget you.   What use is it
that we kill oxen for you and praise you ?   You do not give
us rain or crops, or cause our cattle to bear well ; you show
no gratitude in return for all we do for you.   We shall
utterly disown you.   We shall tell the people that, as for us,
we have no ancestral spirits, and this will be to your shame.
We are disgusted with you.' "[1]   Thus the sweet savour of
beef and beer does not suffice to content Caffre ghosts ;
they share the love of praise and flattery with many gods
of higher rank.

Among the Basutos, an important Bantu people of ^{Worship} Worship
South Africa, " each family is supposed to be under the of the dead
among the
direct influence and protection of its ancestors ; but the Basutos.
tribe, taken as a whole, acknowledges for its national gods
the ancestors of the reigning sovereign.   Thus, the Basutos
address their prayers to Monaheng and Motlumi, from
whom their chiefs are descended.   The Baharutsis and the
Barolongs invoke Tobege and his wife Mampa.   Mampa
makes known the will of her husband, announcing each of
her revelations by these words, ' O re ! O re !' ' He has
said ! he has said ! '   They make a distinction between the
ancient and modern divinities.   The latter are considered
inferior in power, but more accessible ; hence this formula,
which is often used : ' New gods ! entreat the ancient gods
for us !'   In all countries spirits are more the objects of
fear than of love.   A deep feeling of terror generally accom-
panies the idea that the dead dispose of the lot of the living.

[1] Dudley Kidd, *The Essential Kafir* (London, 1904), pp. 88-91.

The ancients spoke much of incensed shades. If they sacrificed to the manes, it was generally in order to appease them. These ideas perfectly correspond to those of the Basutos. They conjure rather than pray; although they seek to gain favours, they think more of averting chastisement. Their predominating idea as to their ancestors is, that they are continually endeavouring to draw them to themselves. Every disease is attributed to them; thus medicine among these people is almost entirely a religious affair. The first thing is to discover, by means of the *litaola* (divining bones), under the influence of what *molimo* the patient is supposed to be. Is it an ancestor on the father's side or the mother's? According as fate decides, the paternal or maternal uncle will offer the purifying sacrifice, but rarely the father or brother. This sacrifice alone can render efficacious the medicines prescribed by the *ngaka* (doctor). . . . As soon as a person is dead he takes his place among the family gods. His remains are deposited in the cattle-pen. An ox is immolated over his grave: this is the first oblation made to the new divinity, and at the same time an act of intercession in his favour, serving to ensure his happy reception in the subterranean regions. All those present aid in sprinkling the grave, and repeat the following prayer: ' Repose in peace with the gods; give us tranquil nights.' "[1]

Worship of the dead among the Thonga.   Similarly among the Thonga, another Bantu tribe of South Africa, "any man, who has departed this earthly life, becomes a *shikwembu*, a god ";[2] "when an old decrepit man or woman dies, he at once becomes a god: he has entered the domain of infinity."[3] In this tribe " the spirits of the ancestors are the main objects of religious worship. They form the principal category of spirits."[4] " On the one hand, the ancestor-gods are truly gods, endowed with the attributes of divinity; whilst, on the other, they seem to be nothing but mere human beings, exactly on the same level as their worshippers."[5] There are two great classes

---

[1] Rev. E. Casalis, *The Basutos* (London, 1861), pp. 248-250.
[2] Henri A. Junod, *The Life of a South African Tribe* (Neuchâtel, 1912–

1913), ii. 347.
[3] H. A. Junod, *op. cit.* ii. 385.
[4] H. A. Junod, *op. cit.* ii. 344.
[5] H. A. Junod, *op. cit.* ii. 385.

of these ancestor-gods, to wit, "those of the family, and those of the country, the latter being those of the reigning family. They do not differ as regards their nature. In national calamities those of the country are invoked, whilst, for purely family matters, those of the family are called upon. Moreover, each family has two sets of gods, those on the father's side and those on the mother's, those of *kweru* and those of *bakokwana*. They are equal in dignity. Both can be invoked, and the divinatory bones are always asked to which the offering must be made. It seems, however, as if the gods on the mother's side were more tender-hearted and more popular than those on the father's. The reason for this is, perhaps, that relations are easier with the family of the mother than with that of the father. It is also just possible that it is a relic of the matriarchal period, when the ancestors of the mother only were known, and consequently invoked. At any rate, the part played by *batukulu* [uterine] nephews in the offerings shows that they are the true representatives of the gods, not of those of their father, but of their mother." [1] Among the Thonga "the belief in the continuation of life after death is universal, being at the base of the ancestrolatry, which is the religion of the tribe." [2] " How real is the ancestrolatry, the religion of the Thonga, of, in fact, all the South African Bantus ! How frequent and manifold are its manifestations ! This is the first, and the most perceptible set of their religious intuitions, and any European, who has stayed in their villages, learnt their language, and tried to understand their customs, has had the opportunity of familiarizing himself with this religion." [3]

Among the Basutos and Bechuanas, who also belong to the great Bantu family, the sacrificial ritual is not highly developed. " Only in great misfortunes which affect the whole people or the royal family, a black ox is slaughtered ; for in such cases they always think that the angry spirits of the departed are the cause of all the suffering. ' *Re amogioa kı badimo*,' say the people, ' the spirits are robbing us.' The ox is led to the chief's grave ; there they

Sacrifices to dead chiefs among the Basutos and Bechuanas.

[1] H. A. Junod, *op. cit.* ii. 348 *sq*.   [2] H. A. Junod, *op. cit.* ii. 341.
[3] H. A. Junod, *op. cit.* ii. 346.

pray, ' Lord, we are come to call upon thee, we who are thy children ; make not our hearts troubled ; take not, Lord, that which is ours.' The old chief is honoured and praised in songs, he is invoked by all his praise-names, the ox is killed and its flesh eaten, but the blood and the contents of the stomach are poured on the grave, and there the bones of the sacrificed animal are also deposited." [1]

Worship of the dead among the Zulus. The Zulus, another great Bantu tribe of South Africa, believe in the existence of a being whom they call Unkulunkulu, which means " the Old-Old-one, the most ancient man." They say that " it is he who was the first man ; he broke off in the beginning. We do not know his wife ; and the ancients do not tell us that he had a wife." [2] This Old-Old-one or Great-Great-one " is represented as having made all things—men, cattle, water, fire, the mountains, and whatever else is seen. He is also said to have appointed their names. Creation was effected by splitting a reed, when the first man and other things issued from the cleft." [3] Further, the Zulus and other Caffre tribes of Natal " believe that, when a person dies, his *i-hloze* or *isi-tute* survives. These words are translated ' spirit,' and there seems no objection to the rendering. They refer to something mani-festly distinguished from the body, and the nature of which the prophets endeavour to explain by saying that it is identical with the shadow. The residence of the *ama-hloze*, or spirits, seems to be beneath ; the practice of breaking a man's assagais, before they are buried with him, shows that he is believed to return to earth through the grave ; while it appears to be generally thought that, if the earth were removed from the grave, the ghost would return and frighten his descendants. When spirits have entered the future state, they are believed to possess great power ; prosperity is ascribed to their favour, and misfortune to their anger ; they are elevated in fact to the rank of deities, and (except where the Great-Great is worshipped concurrently with them) they are the only objects of a Kafir's adoration. Their attention

[1] A. Merensky, *Beiträge zur Kennt-nis Süd-Afrikas* (Berlin, 1875), p. 130.
[2] Rev. H. Callaway, *The Religious System of the Amazulu*, i. (Natal,

Springvale, etc., 1868) pp. 1 *sq.*
[3] Rev. Joseph Shooter, *The Kafirs of Natal and the Zulu Country* (London, 1857), p. 159.

(or providence) is limited to their own relatives—a father caring for the family, and a chief for the tribe, which they respectively left behind them.   They are believed to occupy the same relative position as they did in the body, the departed spirit of a chief being sometimes invoked to compel a man's ancestors to bless him." [1]

   " To these shades of the dead, especially to the ghosts of their great men, as Jama, Senzangakona, and Chaka, their former kings, they look for help, and offer sacrifices ; that is, slaughter cattle to them, and offer a sort of prayer, in time of danger and distress. . . . When they are sick, they slaughter cattle to the shades, and say, ' Father, look on me, that this disease may cease from me.   Let me have health on the earth, and live a long time.'   They carry the meat into the house, and shut it up there, saying, ' Let the paternal shades eat, so shall they know that the offering was made for them, and grant us great wealth, so that both we and our children may prosper.'   In the cattle-fold they talk a long time, praising the ghosts ; they take the contents of the stomach, and strew it upon all the fold.   Again they take it, and strew it within the houses, saying, ' Hail, friend ! Thou of such a place, grant us a blessing, beholding what we have done.   You see this distress ; may you remove it, since we have given you our animal.   We know not what more you want, whether you still require anything more or not.'   They say, ' May you grant us grain, that it may be abundant, that we may eat, of course, and not be in need of anything, since now we have given you what you want.'   They say, ' Yes, for a long time have you preserved me in all my going. Behold, you see, I have just come to have a kraal.   This kraal was built by yourself, father ; and now why do you consent to diminish your own kraal ?   Build on us as you have begun, let it be large, that your offspring, still here above, may increase, increasing in knowledge of you, whence cometh great power.'   Sometimes they make beer for the ghosts, and leave a little in the pot, saying, ' It will be eaten by the ghosts that they may grant an abundant harvest again, that we may not have a famine.'   If one is on the point of being injured by anything, he says, ' I was pre-

Sacrifices and prayers to the dead among the Zulus.

served by our divinity, which was still watching over me.'
Perhaps he slaughters a goat in honour of the same, and
puts the gall on his head ; and when the goat cries out for
pain of being killed, he says, ' Yes, then, there is your animal,
let it cry, that ye may hear, ye our gods who have preserved
me ; I myself am desirous of living on thus a long time here
on the earth ; why then do you call me to account, since I
think I am all right in respect to you ? And while I live, I
put my trust in you, our paternal and maternal gods.' " [1]

A native
Zulu
account
of the
worship of
the dead.

"Black people," say the Zulus, "do not worship all
Amatongo indifferently, that is, all the dead of their tribe.
Speaking generally, the head of each house is worshipped
by the children of that house ; for they do not know the
ancients who are dead, nor their laud-giving names, nor their
names. But their father whom they knew is the head by
whom they begin and end in their prayer, for they know
him best, and his love for his children ; they remember his
kindness to them whilst he was living ; they compare his
treatment of them whilst he was living, support themselves
by it, and say, ' He will still treat us in the same way now
he is dead. We do not know why he should regard others
besides us ; he will regard us only.' So it is then although
they worship the many Amatongo of their tribe, making a
great fence around them for their protection ; yet their father
is far before all others when they worship the Amatongo.
Their father is a great treasure to them even when he is
dead. And those of his children who are already grown up
know him thoroughly, his gentleness, and his bravery. And
if there is illness in the village, the eldest son lauds him
with the laud-giving names which he gained when fighting
with the enemy, and at the same time lauds all the other
Amatongo ; the son reproves the father, saying, ' We for our
parts may just die. Who are you looking after ? Let us
die all of us, that we may see into whose house you will
enter.[2] You will eat grasshoppers ; you will no longer be

[1] Rev. Lewis Grout, *Zulu-land, or
Life among the Zulu-Kafirs* (Philadelphia, N.D.), pp. 137, 143-145.

[2] "That is, they suggest to the
Itongo [ancestral spirit, singular of
Amatongo], by whose ill-will or want

of care they are afflicted, that if they
should all die in consequence, and thus
his worshippers come to an end, he
would have none to worship him ; and
therefore for his own sake, as well as
for theirs, he had better preserve his

invited to go anywhere, if you destroy your own village.'
After that, because they have worshipped him, they take
courage saying, ' He has heard ; he will come and treat our
diseases, and they will cease.' Such then is the faith which
children have in the Itongo [ancestral spirit] which is their
father. And if there is a chief wife of a village, who has
given birth to children, and if her husband is not dead, her
Itongo is much reverenced by her husband and all the
children. And that chief wife becomes an Itongo which
takes great care of the village. But it is the father especially
that is the head of the village."[1] Thus among the Zulus
it is the spirits of those who have just died, especially the
spirits of fathers and mothers, who are most revered and
worshipped. The spirits of the more remote dead are forgotten.

When the missionaries inquired into the religious ideas
of the Herero, a Bantu tribe of German South-West Africa,
they heard much of a certain Mukuru, whom at first they
took to be the great god of heaven and earth. Accordingly they adopted Mukuru as the native name for the
Christian God, and set out on their mission to preach the
glad tidings of Mukuru and his divine Son to the poor
benighted heathen. But their first experiences were dis-
concerting. Again and again when they arrived in
a village and announced their intention to the chief, they
were brought up very short by that great man, who told
them with an air of astonishment that he himself was
Mukuru. For example, Messrs. Büttner and Irle paid a visit
to an old chief named Tjenda and remonstrated with him on
the impropriety of which he had been guilty in giving a
baptized girl in marriage to a native gentleman whose
domestic arrangements were framed on the polygamous
patriarchal pattern. " Mukuru will punish you for that,"
said Mr. Büttner. " What ? " roared the chief. " Who's
Mukuru ? Why, I am Mukuru in my own tribe," and he

The
worship
of the dead
among the
Herero
of German
South-
West
Africa.

people, that there may be a village for
him to enter, and meat of the sacrifices
for him to eat."
[1] Rev. Henry Callaway, *The Religious System of the Amazulu*, Part ii.,

*Amatongo or Ancestor Worship as exist-
ing among the Amazulu, in their own
words, with a translation into English*
(Natal, Springvale, etc., 1869), pp.
144-146.

bundled the two missionaries out of the village.   A repetition of these painful incidents at last impressed on the minds of the missionaries the conviction that Mukuru was not God at all but merely the head of a family, an ancestor, whether alive or dead.[1]   They ascertained at the same time that the Herero recognize a good god who dwells in heaven and bears the name of Ndjambi Karunga.   But they do not worship him nor bring him offerings, because he is so kind that he hurts nobody, and therefore they need not fear him. " Rather they share the opinion of the other Bantu tribes that Ndjambi, the good Creator, has withdrawn to heaven and left the government on earth to the demons." [2]   " It is true that the Herero are acquainted with punishment for

Ancestral spirits (*Ovakuru*) worshipped by the Herero. what is bad.   But that punishment they ascribe to Mukuru or their ancestors.   It is their ancestors (*Ovakuru*[3]) whom they must fear ; it is they who are angry and can bring danger and misfortune on a man.   So it is intelligible that the whole of their worship turns, not on Ndjambi Karunga, but on their ancestors.   It is in order to win and keep their favour, to avert their displeasure and wrath, in short to propitiate them, that the Herero bring their many offerings ; they do so not out of gratitude, but out of fear, not out of love, but out of terror.   Their religion is a worship of ancestors with here and there touches of fetishism." [4]   " Thus among the Herero, as among all Bantu tribes, there exists a religious dualism : they know the highest, the true God, but they worship their ancestors." [5]   And among the worshipful

<hr/>

[1] Missionar J. Irle, *Die Herero, ein Beitrag zur Landes- Volks- und Missionskunde* (Gütersloh, 1906), pp. 72 sq.

[2] J. Irle, *op. cit.* p. 73.

[3] *Ovakuru*, the plural form of *Mukuru*.

[4] J. Irle, *op. cit.* p. 74.

[5] J. Irle, *op. cit.* p. 75.   The writer tells us (*l.c.*) that the Herero name for the good celestial God, whom they acknowledge but do not worship, is common, in different forms, to almost all the Bantu tribes.   Among the Ovambo it is Kalunga ; among tribes of Loango, the Congo, Angola and Benguela it is Zambi, Njambi, Ambi,

Njame, Onjame, Ngambe, Nsambi ; in the Cameroons it is Nzambi, etc. Compare John H. Weeks, *Among Congo Cannibals* (London, 1913), pp. 246 sq. : " We have found a vague knowledge of a Supreme Being, and a belief in Him, very general among those tribes on the Congo with which we have come into contact. . . . On the Lower Congo He is called *Nzambi*, or by His fuller title *Nzambi a mpungu* ; no satisfactory root word has yet been found for *Nzambi*, but for *mpungu* there are sayings and proverbs that clearly indicate its meaning as, most of all, supreme, highest, and *Nzambi a mpungu* as the Being most High,

ancestors "the old dead chiefs of every tribe take the first place. The son of a great dead chief and the whole tribe worship that old father as their god. But the remote ancestors of that chief they do not worship, indeed they hardly know them by name and can no longer point to their graves." [1] Thus with the Herero, as with the Zulus, it is the recent and well-remembered dead who are chiefly or exclusively worshipped; as the souls of the departed recede

---

or Supreme. On the Upper Congo among the Bobangi folk the word used for the Supreme Being is *Nyambe*; among the Lulanga people, *Nzakomba*; among the Boloki, *Njambe*; among the Bopoto people it is *Libanza*. . . . It is interesting to note that the most common name for the Supreme Being on the Congo is also known, in one form or another, over an extensive area of Africa reaching from 6° north of the Equator away to extreme South Africa; as, for example, among the Ashanti it is *Onyame*, at Gaboon it is *Anyambie*, and two thousand miles away among the Barotse folk it is *Niambe*. These are the names that stand for a Being who is endowed with strength, wealth, and wisdom by the natives; and He is also regarded and spoken of by them as the principal Creator of the world, and the Maker of all things. . . . But the Supreme Being is believed by the natives to have withdrawn Himself to a great distance after performing His creative works; that He has now little or no concern in mundane affairs; and apparently no power over spirits and no control over the lives of men, either to protect them from malignant spirits or to help them by averting danger. They also consider the Supreme Being (*Nzambi*) as being so good and kind that there is no need to appease Him by rites, ceremonies or sacrifices. Hence they never pray to this Supreme One, they never worship Him, or think of Him as being interested in the doings of the world and its peoples."

[1] J. Irle, *op. cit.* p. 77. Mr. Irle's account of the religion of the Herero or Ovaherero is fully borne out by

the testimony of earlier missionaries among the tribe. See Rev. G. Viehe, "Some Customs of the Ova-herero" (*South African*) *Folk-lore Journal*, i. (Cape Town, 1879) pp. 64 *sq.*: "The religious customs and ceremonies of the Ovaherero are all rooted in the presumption that the deceased continue to live, and that they have a great influence on earth, and exercise power over the life and death of man. This influence and power is ascribed especially to those who have been great men, and who become *Ovakuru* after death. The numerous religious customs and ceremonies are a worshipping of the ancestors." Further, Mr. Viehe reports that "the Ovaherero have a slight idea of another being (Supreme being?) which differs greatly from the *Ovakuru*, is superior to them, and is supposed never to have been a human being. It is called *Karunga*. . . . *Karunga* does only good; whilst the influence of the *Ovakuru* is more feared than wished for; and, therefore, it is not thought necessary to bring sacrifices to *Karunga* to guard against his influence." He is situated so high, and is so superior to men "that he takes little special notice of them; and so the Ovaherero, on their part, also trouble themselves little about this superior being" (*op. cit.* p. 67 note *). Similar evidence is given by another missionary as to the belief of the Herero in a superior god Karunga and their fear and worship of ancestral spirits. See the Rev. H. Beiderbecke, "Some Religious Ideas and Customs of the Ovaherero" (*South African*) *Folk-lore Journal*, ii. (Cape Town, 1880) pp. 88 *sqq.*

further and further into the past their memory perishes, and
the nimbus of supernatural glory which encircled it for a time
fades gradually away.

The worship of the dead among the Ovambo.

The religion of the Ovambo, another Bantu tribe of
German South-West Africa, is similar. They also recognize
a great being named Kalunga, who created the world and
man, but they neither fear nor worship him. A far greater
part is played in the religion of the Ovambo by their belief
in spirits, and amongst the worshipful spirits a conspicuous
place is assigned to the souls of the dead. Every man
leaves behind him at death a spirit, which continues to exist
on earth and can influence the living; for example, it may
enter into their bodies and thereby cause all sorts of sickness. However, the souls of ordinary dead men can exert
their influence only on members of their own families; the
souls of dead chiefs, on the other hand, have power over the
rain, which they can either give or withhold. To these
powerful spirits a portion of the new corn is offered at
harvest as a thank - offering for their forbearance in not
visiting the people with sickness, and above all for their
bounty in sending down the fertilizing showers on the crops.
The souls of dead magicians are particularly dreaded; and
to prevent the multiplication of these dangerous spirits it
is customary to dismember their bodies, severing the arms
and legs from the trunk and cutting the tongue out of
the mouth. If these precautions are taken immediately
after death, the soul of the dead man cannot become
a dangerous ghost; the mutilation of his body has practically disarmed his spirit.[1]

The worship of the dead among the Wahehe of German East Africa.

The Wahehe, a Bantu tribe of German East Africa,
believe in a great invisible spirit named Nguruhi, who created
the world and rules both human destiny and the elements.
He it is who makes the rain to fall, the sun to shine,
the wind to blow, the thunder to roll, and the crops to
grow. "This god is accordingly conceived as all-powerful,
yet with the limitation that he only exercises a general
power of direction over the world, especially human fate,
while the *masoka*, the spirits of the dead, wield a per-

[1] Hermann Tönjes, *Ovamboland, Land, Leute, Mission* (Berlin, 1911), pp.
193-197.

manent and very considerable influence on the course of particular events. Nguruhi is lord also of all the spirits of the dead (*masoka*), but his relation to them has not been further thought out. With this Supreme Being the people hold no intercourse by means of prayer, sacrifice, or in any other way. He stands remote from the religious life of the Wahehe and really serves only as an explanation of all those things and events which are otherwise inexplicable. All religious intercourse, all worship centres alone on the spirits of the dead. Hence if we speak of a religion of the Wahehe, it must be described as a pure worship of ancestors."[1] The human soul quits the body at death and at once becomes an ancestral spirit (*m'soka*), invisible and endowed with complete liberty of motion. Even the youngest children have souls which rank among the ancestral spirits at death. Hence the great multitude of the dead comprises spirits of all ages, from the infant one day old to the grey-haired patriarch. They are good or bad according as they were good or bad in life, and their social position also is unchanged. He who was powerful in life is powerful also in death ; he who was a nobody among men is a nobody also among the spirits. Hence the ghost of a great man can do more for the living than the ghost of a common man ; and the ghost of a man can do more than the ghost of a woman. Yet even the meanest ghost has power over the greatest living man, who can only defend himself by appealing for help to stronger ancestral spirits. Thus while the Supreme Being exercises a general superintendence over affairs, the real administration is in the hands of the ancestral spirits. While he, for example, regulates the weather as a whole, it is the ghosts who cause each particular shower to fall or the sun to break out in glory from the clouds. If he sends plagues on the whole people or stays the ravages of disease, it is the ghosts who make each individual sick or sound. These powerful spirits exert themselves especially to help their descendants, though they

[1] E. Nigmann, *Die Wahehe* (Berlin, 1908), pp. 22 *sq.* The writer does not describe the Wahehe as a Bantu tribe, but from the characteristic prefixes which they employ to designate the tribe, individual tribesmen, the country, and so forth (*op. cit.* p. 124) we may infer that the people belong to the Bantu stock.

do not hesitate to plague their own kith and kin if they think themselves neglected. They flit freely through the air and perch on trees, mountains, and so forth, but they lodge by preference at their graves, and you are always sure of finding them there, if you wish to consult them.[1] That is why in the country of the Wahehe the only places of sacrifice are the graves ; temples and altars are unknown.[2] However, it is only the bodies of considerable persons that are buried ; the corpses of common folk are simply thrown away in the bush ;[3] so that the number of graves and consequently of sacrificial places is strictly limited. The spirits of the dead appear to the living most commonly in dreams to give them information or warning, but oftener to chide and torment them. So the sleeper wakes in a fright and consults a diviner, who directs him what he must do in order to appease the angry ghost. Following the directions of his spiritual adviser the man sacrifices an ox, or it may be only a sheep or a fowl, at the tomb of one of his ancestors, prays to the ghost, and having scattered a few morsels of the victim's flesh on the grave, and spat a mouthful of beer upon it, retires with his family to feast on the remainder of the carcase. Such sacrifices to the dead are offered on occasion of sickness, the lack of male heirs, a threatened war, an intended journey, in short, before any important undertaking of which the issue is doubtful ; and they are accompanied by prayers for health, victory, good harvests, and so forth.[4]

The worship of the dead among the Bahima of Ankole, in Central Africa.   Once more, the Bahima, a Bantu people of Ankole, in Central Africa, believe in a supreme god Lugaba, who dwells in the sky and created man and beast ; but " this supreme being is not worshipped nor are offerings made to him ; he has no sacred place. Although they talk freely about him, and acknowledge him to be their great benefactor, they accept all his gifts as a matter of course, and make him no offering in return. . . . One must not, therefore, conclude that the Bahima are an irreligious people ; like most of the Bantu tribes their religion consists chiefly in dealing with ghosts of departed relatives, and in standing well with them ;

[1] E. Nigmann, *Die Wahehe*, pp. 23 *sq.*
[2] E. Nigmann, *op. cit.* p. 35.
[3] E. Nigmann, *op. cit.* p. 39.
[4] E. Nigmann, *op. cit.* pp. 24 *sqq.*, 35 *sqq.*

from the king to the humblest peasant the ghosts call for daily consideration and constant offerings, whilst the deities are only sought in case of great trials or national calamities." [1]

To return, now, to the worship of dead chiefs or kings among the Bantu tribes of Northern Rhodesia. The spirits of dead chiefs had priestesses to wait upon them, who were called the "wives of the departed." These were elderly women who led a celibate life and swept the huts dedicated to the ghosts of the chiefs. The aid of these dead potentates was invoked in time of war and in seasons of drought, and special offerings were brought to their shrines at harvest.[2] Among the Awemba, who form the aristocracy of the country,[3] when a diviner announced that a drought was caused by the spirits of dead chiefs or kings buried at Mwaruli, a bull would be sent to be sacrificed to the souls of the deceased rulers ; or if the drought was severe, a human victim would be despatched, and the high priest would keep him caged in a stoutly woven fish-basket, until the preparations for the sacrifice were complete.[4] Among the Yombe no one might eat of the first-fruits of the crops until the living chief had sacrificed a bull before the tomb of his grandfather, and had deposited pots of fresh beer and porridge, made from the first-fruits, in front of the shrine. The ground about the tomb was then carefully weeded, and the blood of the sacrificial victim sprinkled on the freshly turned up soil and on the rafters of the little hut. After thanking the ghost of his grandfather for the harvest, and begging him to partake of the first-fruits, the chief and his train withdrew to feast on the carcase and the fresh porridge and beer at the village.[5] When the head chief or king of the Awemba had resolved

The worship of dead chiefs or kings among the Bantu tribes of Northern Rhodesia.

[1] Rev. J. Roscoe, "The Bahima, a Cow Tribe of Enkole," *Journal of the Royal Anthropological Institute*, xxxvii. (1907) pp. 108 *sq.* The supreme god Lugaba is no doubt the same with the supreme god Rugaba worshipped by the Bahimas in Kiziba. See above, p. 173. With regard to the religion of the Baganda the same authority tells us that "the last, and possibly the most venerated, class of religious objects were the ghosts of departed relatives. The power of ghosts for good or evil was incalculable" (*The Baganda*, p. 273).

[2] C. Gouldsbury and H. Sheane, *The Great Plateau of Northern Rhodesia*, p. 83.

[3] C. Gouldsbury and H. Sheane, *op. cit.* p. 11.

[4] C. Gouldsbury and H. Sheane, *op. cit.* p. 292.

[5] C. Gouldsbury and H. Sheane, *op. cit.* pp. 294 *sq.*

to make war on a distant enemy, he and the older men of the tribe would pray daily for victory to the spirits of the dead kings, his predecessors. The day before the army was to set forth, the great war-drum boomed out and the warriors flocked together from the outlying districts under their respective captains. In the dusk of the evening the king and the elderly women, who passed for the wives of the dead kings and tended their shrines at the capital, went and prayed at these shrines that the souls of the departed monarchs would keep the war-path free from foes and lead the king in a straight course to the enemy's stockade. These solemn prayers the king led in person, and the women beat their bare breasts as they joined in the earnest appeal. Next morning the whole army was marshalled in front of the ghost-huts of the dead kings: the living king danced a war-dance before his ancestors, while his chief wife sprinkled him with holy flour; and all prostrated themselves in supplication before the shrines.[1]

Among these tribes the spirits of dead chiefs or kings are thought sometimes to take bodily possession of men and women or to be incarnate in animals. Among these tribes of Northern Rhodesia the spirits of dead chiefs or kings sometimes take possession of the bodies of live men or women and prophesy through their mouths. When the spirit of a dead chief comes over a man, he begins to roar like a lion, whereupon the women gather together and beat the drums, shouting that the chief has come to visit the village. The man thus temporarily inspired will prophesy of future wars or impending attacks by lions. While the inspiration lasts, he may eat nothing cooked by fire, but only unfermented dough. However, the spirit of a departed chief takes possession of women oftener than of men. "These women assert that they are possessed by the soul of some dead chief, and when they feel the divine afflatus, whiten their faces to attract attention, and anoint themselves with flour, which has a religious and sanctifying potency. One of their number beats a drum, and the others dance, singing at the same time a weird song, with curious intervals. Finally, when they have arrived at the requisite pitch of religious exaltation, the possessed woman falls to the ground, and bursts forth

---

[1] J. H. West Sheane, "Wemba Warpaths," *Journal of the African*   *Society*, No. xli. (October, 1911) pp. 25 *sq.*

into a low and almost inarticulate chant, which has a most uncanny effect. All are silent at once, and the *bashing'anga* (medicine-men) gather round to interpret the voice of the spirit." [1]   Sometimes the spirits of departed chiefs are reincarnated in animals, which are then revered as the abodes of the dead rulers. Thus the paramount chief of the Amambwe is incarnated after death in the form of a young lion, while Bisa and Wiwa chiefs come back in the shape of pythons. In one of the rest-houses near Fife a tame python waxed fat on the offerings of fowls and sour beer which the Winamwanga presented to it in the fond belief that it housed the spirit of one of their dead chiefs. One day unfortunately for himself the reptile deity ventured to dispute the possession of the rest-house with a German cattle-dealer who was passing by ; a discharge of shot settled the dispute in favour of the cattle-dealer, and the worshippers of the deity beheld him no more.[2]

Another Bantu people who worship the spirits of their dead kings are the Barotse or Marotse of the Upper Zambesi. The Barotse believe in a supreme god, the creator of all things, whom they call Niambe. He lives in the sun, and by his marriage with the moon begat the world, the animals, and last of all men. But the cunning and ferocity of his creature man terrified the beneficent creator, so that he fled from earth and escaped up the thread of a spider's web to heaven. There he still retains a certain power to interfere in human affairs, and that is why men sometimes pray and sacrifice to him. For example, the worshipper salutes the rising sun and offers him a vessel of water, no doubt to quench the thirst of the deity on his hot journey across the sky. Again, when a long drought has prevailed, a black ox is sacrificed to Niambe " as a symbol of the clouds big with the longed-for rain." And before they sow the fields, the women pile the seeds and their digging hoes in a heap, and pray to the god that he would render their labour fruitful.[3]

Belief of the Barotse in a supreme god Niambe.

---

[1] C. Gouldsbury and H. Sheane, *The Great Plateau of Northern Nigeria,* p. 83.
    [2] C. Gouldsbury and H. Sheane,

op. cit. p. 84.
    [3] Eugène Béguin, *Les Ma-rotsé* (Lausanne and Fontaines, 1903), pp. 118 *sq.*

Yet while they acknowledge the divine supremacy of Niambe, the Barotse address their prayers most frequently to the inferior deities, the *ditino*, who are the deified kings of the country. The tombs of the departed monarchs may be seen near the villages which they inhabited in life. Each tomb stands in a grove of beautiful trees and is encircled by a tall palisade of pointed stakes, covered with fine mats, like the palisade which surrounds the royal residence of a living king. Such an enclosure is sacred ; the people are forbidden to enter it lest they should disturb the ghost of him who sleeps below. But the inhabitants of the nearest village are charged with the duty of keeping the tomb and the enclosure in good order, repairing the palisade, and replacing the mats when they are worn out. Once a month, at the new moon, the women sweep not only the grave and the enclosure but the whole village. The guardian of the tomb is at the same time a priest ; he acts as intermediary between the god and the people who come to pray to the deity. He bears the title of Ngomboti ; he alone has the right to enter the sacred enclosure ; the profane multitude must stand at a respectful distance. Even the king himself, when he comes to consult one of his ancestors, is forbidden to set foot on the holy ground. In presence of the god, or, as they call him, the Master of the Tomb, the monarch must bear himself like a slave in the presence of his lord. He kneels down near the entrance, claps his hands, and gives the royal salute ; and from within the enclosure the priest solemnly returns the salute, just as the king himself, when he holds his court, returns the salute of his subjects. Then the suppliant, whether king or commoner, makes his petition to the deity and deposits his offering ; for no man may pray to the god with empty hands. Inside the enclosure, close to the entrance, is a hole which is supposed to serve as a channel of communication with the spirit of the deified king. In it the offerings are placed. Often they consist of milk which is poured into the hole ; and the faster it drains away, the more favourably inclined is the god thought to be to the petitioner. More solid offerings, such as flesh, clothes, and glass beads, become the property of the priest after they have been allowed to lie for a decent time beside the sacred

aperture of the tomb. The spirits of dead kings are thus consulted on matters of public concern as well as by private individuals touching their own affairs. If a war is to be waged, if a plague is raging among the people or a murrain among the cattle, if the land is parched with drought, in short, if any danger threatens or any calamity has afflicted the country, recourse is had to these local gods, dwelling each in his shady grove, not far from the abodes of the living. They are near, but the great god in heaven is far away. What wonder, therefore, that their help is often sought while he is neglected? They are national heroes as well as gods; their history is remembered; men tell of the doughty deeds they did in their lifetime; why should they not be able to succour their votaries now that they have put on immortality? All over the country these temple-tombs may be seen. They serve as historical monuments to recall to the people the names of their former kings and the annals of their country. One of the most popular of the royal shrines is near Senanga at the southern end of the great plain of the Barotse. Voyagers who go down the Zambesi do not fail to pay their devotions at the shrine, that the god of the place may make their voyage to prosper and may guard the frail canoe from shipwreck in the rush and roar of the rapids; and when they return in safety they repair again to the sacred spot to deposit a thank-offering for the protection of the deity.[1]

The foregoing examples suffice to prove that the worship of dead chiefs and kings has been an important, perhaps we may even say, the most important element in the religion of many African tribes. Regarded from the native point of view nothing could be more natural. The king rules over his people in life; and since all these tribes entertain a firm and unquestioning belief not only in the existence but in the power of the spirits of the dead, they necessarily conclude that of all the departed spirits none can be so potent for good or evil, none therefore need to be propitiated so earnestly by prayer and sacrifice, as the souls of dead kings. Thus while every family worships privately the

Thus the worship of dead kings has been an important element in the religion of many African tribes.

---

[1] Eugène Béguin, *Les Ba-rotsé*, pp. 120-123. Compare *Totemism and Exogamy*, iv. 306 *sq.*

spirits of its own ancestors, the whole tribe worships publicly the spirits of its departed monarchs, paying to each of these invisible potentates, whose reality they never dream of doubting, a homage of precisely the same sort as that which they render to his living successor on the throne. Such a religion of the dead is by no means incompatible with the recognition of higher spiritual powers who may have an origin quite independent of the worship of ancestors. We have seen in point of fact that many tribes, whose practical religion is concentrated chiefly on their dead, nevertheless acknowledge the existence of a supreme god, the creator of man and of all things, whom they do not regard as a glorified ghost. The Baganda, the most progressive and advanced of all the Bantu tribes, had a whole pantheon of gods whom they sharply distinguished from the worshipful spirits of their forefathers.

Perhaps some African gods, who are now distinguished from ghosts, were once dead men.

Yet in spite of this distinction we may suspect that in many cases the seeming line of division between gods and worshipful ghosts is deceptive ; and that the magic touch of time, which distorts and magnifies the past, especially among peoples who see it only through the haze of oral tradition, has glorified and transfigured many a dead man into a deity. This at all events seems to have been the history of some of the Baganda gods. On this subject our best authority says that " the principal gods appear to have been at one time human beings, noted for their skill and bravery, who were afterwards deified by the people and invested with supernatural powers." [1]   " Mukasa held the highest rank among the gods of Uganda. He was a benign god ; he never asked for the life of any human being, but animals were sacrificed to him at the yearly festivals, and also at other times when the king, or a leading chief, wished to consult him. He had nothing to do with war, but sought to heal the bodies and minds of men. He was the god of plenty ; he gave the people an increase of food, cattle, and children. From the legends still current it seems to be almost certain that he was a human being who, because of his benevolence, came to be regarded as a god. . . . The legends about Mukasa are of great interest ; they show how the human element

[1] Rev. J. Roscoe, *The Baganda* (London, 1911), p. 271.

has been lost in the divine, how the natural has been effaced by the supernatural, until, in the minds of the common people, only the supernatural remains."[1]

If we cannot prove that the great god Mukasa himself was once a man, we have very tangible evidence that his brother the war-god Kibuka was so. For like the dead kings of Uganda, Kibuka was worshipped in a great conical hut resembling the huts which living people inhabit : like them, his spirit was supposed to enter from time to time into the body of his priest and to give oracles through him ; and like them he was represented in his temple by his personal relics, his jawbone and his navel-string, which were rescued from the ruins of his temple and now rest in the Ethnological Museum at Cambridge. In face of this complete parallelism between the god and the kings whose personal existence is not open to question, it seems difficult to doubt that Kibuka was once like them a real man, and that he spoke with the jawbone and made bodily use of the other corporeal organs which were preserved in his temple.[2]

The human remains of Kibuka, the war-god of the Baganda.

These analogies lend some support to the theory that in ancient Egypt, where the kings were worshipped by their people both in life and death, Osiris may have been originally nothing but one of these deified monarchs whose worship gradually eclipsed that of all the rest and ended by rivalling or even surpassing that of the great sun-god himself. We have seen that at Abydos, one of the principal centres of his worship, the tomb of Osiris was identified with the tomb of King Khent, one of the earliest monarchs of the first Egyptian dynasty, and that in this tomb were found a woman's richly jewelled arm and a human skull lacking the lower jawbone, which may well be the head of the king himself and the arm of his queen. The carved monument of Osiris which was found in the sepulchral chamber appears indeed to be a

Thus it is possible that Osiris and Isis may have been a real king and queen of Egypt, perhaps identical with King Khent and his queen.

---

[1] Rev. J. Roscoe, *op. cit.* pp. 290, 291. In the worship of Mukasa "the principal ceremony was the annual festival, when the king sent his presents to the god, to secure a blessing on the crops and on the people for the year" (J. Roscoe, *op. cit.* p. 298).

[2] Rev. J. Roscoe, "Kibuka, the War God of the Baganda," *Man*, vii.

1907) pp. 161-166; *id.*, *The Baganda*, pp. 301-308. Among the personal relics of Kibuka kept in his temple were his genital organs ; these also were rescued when the Mohammedans burned down his temple in the civil wars of 1887-1890. They are now with the rest of the god's, or rather the man's, remains at Cambridge.

work of late Egyptian art, but it may have replaced an earlier sarcophagus.   Certainly we may reasonably suppose that the identification of the tomb of Osiris with the tomb of King Khent was very ancient; for though the priests may have renewed the sculptured effigy of the dead god, they would hardly dare to shift the site of the Holy Sepulchre.[1]   Now the sepulchre is distant about a mile and a half from the temple in which Osiris was worshipped as a god.   There is thus a curious coincidence, if there is nothing more, between the worship of Osiris and the worship of the dead kings of Uganda.   As a dead king of Uganda was worshipped in a temple, while his headless body reposed at some distance in a royal tomb, and his head, without the lower jawbone, was buried by itself near the grave, so Osiris was worshipped in a temple not far from the royal tomb which tradition identified with his grave.   Perhaps after all tradition was right.   It is possible, though it would be very rash to affirm, that Osiris was no other than the historical King Khent of the first dynasty;[2] that the skull found in the tomb is the skull of Osiris himself; and that while it reposed in the grave the missing jawbone was preserved, like the jawbone of a dead king of Uganda, as a holy and perhaps

[1] This consideration is rightly urged by H. Schäfer as a strong argument in favour of the antiquity of the tradition which associated the grave of Osiris with the grave of King Khent. See H. Schäfer, *Die Mysterien des Osiris in Abydos* (Leipsic, 1904), pp. 28 *sq.*

[2] One of the commonest and oldest titles of Osiris was Chent (Khent)-Ament or Chenti (Khenti)-Amenti, as the name is also written. It means "Chief of those who are in the West" and refers to the Egyptian belief that the souls of the dead go westward. See R. V. Lanzone, *Dizionario di Mitologia Egizia*, p. 727 ; H. Brugsch, *Religion und Mythologie der alten Aegypter*, p. 617; A. Erman, *Die ägyptische Religion*,[2] pp. 23, 103 *sq.* ; J. H. Breasted, *Development of Religion and Thought in Ancient Egypt*, pp. 38, 143 (who spells the name Khenti-Amentiu) ; E. A. Wallis Budge, *Osiris and the Egyptian Resurrection*,

i. 31 *sq.*, 67. "Khenti-Amenti was one of the oldest gods of Abydos, and was certainly connected with the dead, being probably the ancient local god of the dead of Abydos and its neigbourhood. Now, in the Pyramid Texts, which were written under the VIth dynasty, there are several mentions of Khenti-Amenti, and in a large number of instances the name is preceded by that of Osiris. It is quite clear, therefore, that the chief attributes of the one god must have resembled those of the other, and that Osiris Khenti-Amenti was assumed to have absorbed the powers of Khenti-Amenti. In the representations of the two gods which are found at Abydos there is usually no difference, at least not under the XVIIIth and XIXth dynasties" (E. A. Wallis Budge, *op. cit.* i. 31). However, it would be unsafe to infer that the resemblance between the name of the god and the name of the king is more than accidental.

oracular relic in the neighbouring temple. If that were so, we should be almost driven to conclude that the bejewelled woman's arm found in the tomb of Osiris is the arm of Isis.

In support of the conclusion that the myth and religion of Osiris grew up round the revered memory of a dead man we may quote the words in which the historian of European morals describes the necessity under which the popular imagination labours of embodying its cherished ideals in living persons. He is referring to the dawn of the age of chivalry, when in the morning twilight the heroic figure of Charlemagne rose like a bright star above the political horizon, to be thenceforth encircled by a halo of romance like the nimbus that shone round the head of Osiris. " In order that the tendencies I have described should acquire their full force, it was necessary that they should be represented or illustrated in some great personage, who, by the splendour and the beauty of his career, could fascinate the imaginations of men. It is much easier to govern great masses of men through their imagination than through their reason. Moral principles rarely act powerfully upon the world, except by way of example or ideals. When the course of events has been to glorify the ascetic or monarchical or military spirit, a great saint, or sovereign, or soldier will arise, who will concentrate in one dazzling focus the blind tendencies of his time, kindle the enthusiasm and fascinate the imagination of the people. But for the prevailing tendency, the great man would not have arisen, or would not have exercised his great influence. But for the great man, whose career appealed vividly to the imagination, the prevailing tendency would never have acquired its full intensity." [1]

Suggested parallel between Osiris and Charlemagne.

Whether the parallel thus suggested between Charlemagne, the mediaeval ideal of a Christian knight, and Osiris, the ancient Egyptian ideal of a just and beneficent monarch, holds good or not, it is now impossible to determine. For while Charlemagne stands near enough to allow us clearly to discern his historical reality, Osiris is so remote that we can no longer discriminate with any certitude between the

The question of the historical reality of Osiris left open.

[1] W. E. H. Lecky, *History of European Morals from Augustus to* *Charlemagne,* Third Edition (London, 1877), ii. 271.

elements of history and fable which appear to have blended in his traditional character. I am content to indicate bare possibilities : dogmatism on such points would be in the highest degree rash and unbecoming. Whether Osiris and Isis were from first to last purely imaginary beings, the ideal creations of a primitive philosophy, or whether they were originally a real man and woman about whom after death the myth-making fancy wove its gossamer rainbow-tinted web, is a question to which I am not bold enough to give a decided answer.

CHAPTER XII

MOTHER-KIN AND MOTHER GODDESSES

§ 1. *Dying Gods and Mourning Goddesses*

WE have now concluded our inquiry into the nature and worship of the three Oriental deities Adonis, Attis, and Osiris. The substantial similarity of their mythical character justifies us in treating of them together. All three apparently embodied the powers of fertility in general and of vegetation in particular. All three were believed to have died and risen again from the dead; and the divine death and resurrection of all three were dramatically represented at annual festivals, which their worshippers celebrated with alternate transports of sorrow and joy, of weeping and exultation. The natural phenomena thus mythically conceived and mythically represented were the great changes of the seasons, especially the most striking and impressive of all, the decay and revival of vegetation; and the intention of the sacred dramas was to refresh and strengthen, by sympathetic magic, the failing energies of nature, in order that the trees should bear fruit, that the corn should ripen, that men and animals should reproduce their kinds.

But the three gods did not stand by themselves. The mythical personification of nature, of which all three were in at least one aspect the products, required that each of them should be coupled with a goddess, and in each case it appears that originally the goddess was a more powerful and important personage than the god. At all events it is always the god rather than the goddess who comes to a sad end, and whose death is annually mourned. Thus, whereas Osiris was slain by Typhon, his divine spouse Isis survived

Essential similarity of Adonis, Attis, and Osiris.

The superiority of the goddesses associated with Adonis, Attis, and Osiris points to a system of mother-kin.

and brought him to life again.   This feature of the myth seems to indicate that in the beginning Isis was, what Astarte and Cybele always continued to be, the stronger divinity of the pair.   Now the superiority thus assigned to the goddess over the god is most naturally explained as the result of a social system in which maternity counted for more than paternity, descent being traced and property handed down through women rather than through men.   At all events this explanation cannot be deemed intrinsically improbable if we can show that the supposed cause has produced the very same effect among existing peoples, about whose institutions we possess accurate information.   This I will now endeavour to do.

§ 2. *Influence of Mother-Kin on Religion*

Mother-kin and father-kin.

The social system which traces descent and transmits property through the mother alone may be called mother-kin, while the converse system which traces descent and transmits property through the father alone may be called father-kin.[1]   A good example of the influence which mother-kin may exert on religion is furnished by the Khasis of Assam, whose customs and beliefs have lately been carefully recorded by a British officer specially charged with the study of the native races of the province.[2]   Like the ancient Egyptians and the Semites of Syria and Mesopotamia, the Khasis live in settled villages and maintain themselves chiefly by the cultivation of the ground ; yet "their social organization presents one of the most perfect examples still surviving of matriarchal institutions, carried out with a logic and thoroughness which, to those accustomed to regard the status and authority of the father as the foundation of society, are exceedingly remarkable.   Not only is the mother the head and source, and only bond of union, of the family : in the most primitive part of the hills, the Synteng country, she is the only owner of real property, and through her alone is

The Khasis of Assam have mother-kin, and among them goddesses predominate over gods and priestesses over priests.

---

[1] I have adopted the terms "mother-kin" and "father-kin" as less ambiguous than the terms "mother-right" and "father-right," which I formerly employed in the same sense.

[2] *The Khasis*, by Major P. R. T. Gurdon, I.A., Deputy Commissioner Eastern Bengal and Assam Commission, and Superintendent of Ethnography in Assam (London, 1907).

inheritance transmitted.[1] The father has no kinship with his children, who belong to their mother's clan ; what he earns goes to his own matriarchal stock, and at his death his bones are deposited in the cromlech of his mother's kin. In Jowai he neither lives nor eats in his wife's house, but visits it only after dark. In the veneration of ancestors, which is the foundation of the tribal piety, the primal ancestress (*Ka Iāwbei*) and her brother are the only persons regarded. The flat memorial stones set up to perpetuate the memory of the dead are called after the woman who represents the clan (*māw kynthei*), and the standing stones ranged behind them are dedicated to the male kinsmen on the mother's side. In harmony with this scheme of ancestor worship, the other spirits to whom propitiation is offered are mainly female, though here male personages also figure. The powers of sickness and death are all female, and these are those most frequently worshipped. The two protectors of the household are goddesses, though with them is also revered the first father of the clan, *U Thāwlang*. Priestesses assist at all sacrifices, and the male officiants are only their deputies ; in one important state, Khyrim, the High Priestess and actual head of the State is a woman, who combines in her person sacerdotal and regal functions." [2] Thus amongst the Khasis of the present day the

[1] "The Khasi saying is, '*long jaid na ka kynthei*' (from the woman sprang the clan). The Khasis, when reckoning descent, count from the mother only ; they speak of a family of brothers and sisters, who are the great grandchildren of one great grandmother, as *shi kpoh*, which, being literally translated, is one womb, *i.e.* the issue of one womb. The man is nobody" (P. R. T. Gurdon, *The Khasis*, p. 82). "All land acquired by inheritance must follow the Khasi law of entail, by which property descends from the mother to the youngest daughter, and again from the latter to her youngest daughter. Ancestral landed property must therefore be always owned by women. The male members of the family may cultivate such lands, but they must carry all the produce to the house of their mother, who will divide it amongst the members of the family" (*op. cit.* p. 88). "The rule amongst the Khasis is that the youngest daughter 'holds' the religion, '*ka bat ka niam.*' Her house is called, '*ka iing seng*,' and it is here that the members of the family assemble to witness her performance of the family ceremonies. Hers is, therefore, the largest share of the family property, because it is she whose duty it is to perform the family ceremonies, and propitiate the family ancestors" (*op. cit.* p. 83).

[2] Sir C. J. Lyall, in his Introduction to *The Khasis*, by Major P. R. T. Gurdon, pp. xxiii. *sq.* Sir C. J. Lyall himself lived for many years among the Khasis and studied their customs. For the details of the evidence on which his summary is based see especially pp. 63 *sqq.*, 68 *sq.*, 76, 82 *sqq.*, 88, 106 *sqq.*, 109 *sqq.*, 112 *sq.*, 121, 150, of

superiority of the goddess to the god, and especially of the revered ancestress to the revered ancestor, is based directly on the social system which traces descent and transmits property through women only.   It is not unreasonable therefore to suppose that in Western Asia the superiority of the Mother Goddess to the Father God originated in the same archaic system of mother-kin.

Again, the Pelew Islanders have mother-kin, and the deities of their clans are all goddesses.   Another instance of the same cause producing the same effect may be drawn from the institutions of the Pelew Islanders, which have been described by an accurate observer long resident in the islands.   These people, who form a branch of the Micronesian stock, are divided into a series of exogamous families or clans with descent in the female line,[1] so that, as usually happens under such a system, a man's heirs are not his own children but the children of his sister or of his maternal aunt.[2]   Every family or clan traces its descent from a woman, the common mother of the whole kin,[3] and accordingly the members of the clan worship a goddess, not a god.[4]   These families or clans, with female descent and a worship of goddesses rather than of gods, are grouped together in villages, each village comprising

Major Gurdon's book. As to the Khasi priestesses, see above, vol. i. p. 46.

[1] J. Kubary, *Die socialen Einrichtungen der Pelauer* (Berlin, 1885), pp. 35 *sq.*   The writer calls one of these kins indifferently a *Familie* or a *Stamm*.

[2] J. S. Kubary, "Die Todtenbestattung auf den Pelau-Inseln," *Original-Mittheilungen aus der ethnologischen Abtheilung der königlichen Museen zu Berlin*, i. (Berlin, 1885) p. 7.

[3] J. Kubary, *Die socialen Einrichtungen der Pelauer*, p. 40.

[4] J. Kubary, "Die Religion der Pelauer," in A. Bastian's *Allerlei aus Volks- und Menschenkunde* (Berlin, 1888), i. 20-22.   The writer says that the family or clan gods of the Pelew Islanders are too many to be enumerated, but he gives as a specimen a list of the family deities of one particular district (Ngarupesang).   Having done so he observes that they are all god-

desses, and he adds that "this is explained by the importance of the woman for the clan.   The deity of the mother is inherited, that of the father is not" (*op. cit.* p. 22).   As he says nothing to indicate that the family deities of this particular district are exceptional, we may infer, as I have done, that the deities of all the families or clans are goddesses.   Yet a few pages previously (pp. 16 *sq.*) he tells us that a village which contains twenty families will have at least forty deities, if not more, "for some houses may have two *kalids* [deities], and every house has also a goddess."   This seems to imply that the families or clans have gods as well as goddesses.   The seeming discrepancy is perhaps to be explained by another statement of the writer that "in the family only the *kalids* [deities] of the women count" ("*sich geltend machen*," J. Kubary, *Die socialen Einrichtungen der Pelauer*, p. 38).

about a score of clans and forming with its lands a petty independent state.[1] Every such village-state has its special deity or deities, generally a god and a goddess. But these political deities of the villages are said to be directly derived from the domestic deities of the families or clans,[2] from which it seems to follow that among these people gods are historically later than goddesses and have been developed out of them.[3] The late origin of the gods as compared with the goddesses is further indicated by the nature of their names.[4]

This preference for goddesses over gods in the clans of the Pelew Islanders has been explained, no doubt rightly, by the high importance of women in the social system of the people.[5] For the existence of the clan depends entirely on the life of the women, not at all upon the life of the men. If the women survive, it is no matter though every man of the clan should perish ; for the women will, as usual, marry men of another clan, and their offspring will inherit their mother's clan, thereby prolonging its existence. Whereas if the women of the clan all die out, the clan necessarily becomes extinct, even though every man of it should survive ; for the men must, as usual, marry women of another clan, and their offspring will inherit their mothers' clan, not the clan of their fathers, which accordingly, with the death of the fathers, is wiped out from the community. Hence in these islands women bear the titles of *Adhalál a pelú*, ' Mothers of the Land," and *Adhalál a blay*, " Mothers of the Clan," and they are said to enjoy complete equality with the men in every respect.[6] Indeed, in one passage our principal authority speaks of " the predominance of feminine influence in the social condition of the people," and asserts without qualification that the women are politically and

This preference for goddesses is to be explained by the importance of women in the social system of the Pelew Islanders.

---

[1] J. Kubary, *Die socialen Einrichtungen der Pelauer*, pp. 33 *sq.*, 63 ; *id.*, " Die Religion der Pelauer," in A. Bastian's *Allerlei aus Volks- und Menschenkunde*, i. 16.

[2] J. Kubary, " Die Religion der Pelauer," in A. Bastian's *Allerlei aus Volks- und Menschenkunde*, i. 15-17, 22, 25-27.

[3] From the passages cited in the preceding note it appears that this was Kubary's opinion, though he has not stated it explicitly.

[4] J. Kubary, " Die Religion der Pelauer," in A. Bastian's *Allerlei aus Volks- und Menschenkunde*, i. 28 *sq.*

[5] J. Kubary, *Die socialen Einrichtungen der Pelauer*, p. 38. See also above, p. 204, note [4].

[6] J. Kubary, *l.c.*

socially superior to the men.[1]   The eldest women of the clan exercise, he tells us, the most decisive influence on the conduct of its affairs, and the headman does nothing without full consultation with them, a consultation which in the great houses extends to affairs of state and foreign politics.[2]   Nay, these elder women are even esteemed and treated as equal to the deities in their lifetime.[3]

The high position of women in the Pelew Islands has also an industrial basis ; for they alone cultivate the taro, the staple food of the people.

But the high position which women thus take in Pelew society is not a result of mother-kin only.   It has an industrial as well as a kinship basis.   For the Pelew Islanders subsist mainly on the produce of their taro fields, and the cultivation of this, their staple food, is the business of the women alone.   " This cardinal branch of Pelew agriculture, which is of paramount importance for the subsistence of the people, is left entirely in the hands of the women.   This fact may have contributed materially to the predominance of female influence in the social condition of the people.   The women do not merely bestow life on the people, they also do that which is most essential for the preservation of life, and therefore they are called *Adhalál a pelú*, the 'Mothers of the Land,' and are politically and socially superior to men.   Only their offspring enjoy the privilege of membership of the state (the children of the men are, strictly speaking, strangers destitute of rights), and the oldest women of the families are esteemed and treated as equal to deities even in their lifetime, and they exercise a decisive influence on the conduct of affairs of state.   No chief would venture to come to a decision without first consulting with the *Adhalál a blay*, the 'Mothers of the Family.'   From this point of view it is impossible to regard the assignment of the taro cultivation to women as a consequence of their subordinate position in society : the women themselves do not so regard it.   The richest woman of the village looks with pride on her taro patch, and although she has female followers enough to allow her merely to superintend the work without taking part in it, she nevertheless prefers to lay aside her fine apron and to betake herself to the deep

---

[1] See the statement of Kubary quoted in the next paragraph.

[2] J. Kubary, *Die socialen Einrich-*

tungen der Pelauer, p. 39.

[3] See the statement of Kubary quoted in the next paragraph.

mire, clad in a small apron that hardly hides her nakedness, with a little mat on her back to protect her from the burning heat of the sun, and with a shade of banana leaves for her eyes. There, dripping with sweat in the burning sun and coated with mud to the hips and over the elbows, she toils to set the younger women a good example. Moreover, as in every other occupation, the *kaliths*, the gods, must also be invoked, and who could be better fitted for the discharge of so important a duty than the Mother of the House?"[1] It seems clear that in any agricultural people who, like the Pelew Islanders, retain mother-kin and depute the labours of husbandry to women, the conception of a great Mother Goddess, the divine source of all fertility, might easily originate. Perhaps the same social and industrial conditions may have combined to develop the great Mother Goddesses of Western Asia and Egypt.

But in the Pelew Islands women have yet another road to power. For some of them are reputed to be the wives of gods, and act as their oracular mouthpieces. Such prophetesses are called *Amlaheys*, and no surprise is felt when one of them is brought to bed. Her child passes for the offspring of the god, her divine husband, and goes about with his hair hanging loose in token of his superhuman parentage. It is thought that no mortal man would dare to intrigue with one of these human wives of a god, since the jealous deity would surely visit the rash culprit with deadly sickness and a lingering decline.[2] But in these islands men as well as women are often possessed by a deity and speak in his name. Under his inspiration they mimic, often with great histrionic skill, the particular appearance and manner which are believed to be characteristic of the indwelling divinity. These inspired men (*Korongs*) usually enjoy great consideration and exert a powerful influence over the whole community. They always acquire wealth in the exercise of their profession. When they are not themselves chiefs, they are treated as chiefs or even preferred to them. In not a few places the deity whom

Both men and women in the Pelew Islands attain to power by posing as the inspired mouthpieces of the gods.

---

[1] J. S. Kubary, *Ethnographische Beiträge zur Kenntniss des Karolinen Archipels* (Leyden, 1895), p. 159. On the importance of the taro or sweet potato as the staple food of the people, see *ib.* pp. 156 *sq.*

[2] J. Kubary, "Die Religion der Pelauer," in A. Bastian's *Allerlei aus Volks- und Menschenkunde*, i. 34.

they personate is also the political head of the land ; and in that case his inspired priest, however humble his origin, ranks as a spiritual king and rules over all the chiefs. Indeed we are told that, with the physical and intellectual decay of the race, the power of the priests is more and more in the ascendant and threatens, if unchecked, to develop before long into an absolute theocracy which will swallow up every other form of government.[1]

Parallel between the Pelew Islands of to-day and the religious and social state of Western Asia and Egypt in antiquity.

Thus the present, or at least the recent, state of society and religion in the Pelew Islands presents some interesting parallels to the social and religious condition of Western Asia and Egypt in early days, if the conclusions reached in this work are correct. In both regions we see a society based on mother-kin developing a religion in which goddesses of the clan originally occupied the foremost place, though in later times, as the clans coalesced into states, the old goddesses have been rivalled and to some extent supplanted by the new male gods of the enlarged pantheon. But in the religion of the Pelew Islanders, as in that of the Khasis and the ancient Egyptians, the balance of power has never wholly shifted from the female to the male line, because society has never passed from mother-kin to father-kin. And in the Pelew Islands as in the ancient East we see the tide of political power running strongly in the direction of theocracy, the people resigning the conduct of affairs into the hands of men who claimed to rule them in the name of the gods. In the Pelew Islands such men might have developed into divine kings like those of Babylon and Egypt, if the natural course of evolution had not been cut short by the intervention of Europe.[2]

The evidence of the Khasis and the Pelew Islanders, two peoples very remote and very different from each other, suffices to prove that the influence which mother-kin may exert on religion is real and deep. But in order

[1] J. Kubary, "Die Religion der Pelauer," in A. Bastian's *Allerlei aus Volks- und Menschenkunde*, i. 30-35. The author wrote thus in the year 1883, and his account of the Pelew religion was published in 1888. Compare his work *Die socialen Einrich-* *tungen der Pelauer*, p. 81. Great changes have probably taken place in the islands since Kubary wrote.

[2] For some other parallels between the state of society and religion in these two regions, see Note IV. at the end of the volume.

to dissipate misapprehensions, which appear to be rife on this subject, it may be well to remind or inform the reader that the ancient and widespread custom of tracing descent and inheriting property through the mother alone does not by any means imply that the government of the tribes which observe the custom is in the hands of women ; in short, it should always be borne in mind that mother-kin does not mean mother-rule. On the contrary, the practice of mother-kin prevails most extensively amongst the lowest savages, with whom woman, instead of being the ruler of man, is always his drudge and often little better than his slave. Indeed, so far is the system from implying any social superiority of women that it probably took its rise from what we should regard as their deepest degradation, to wit, from a state of society in which the relations of the sexes were so loose and vague that children could not be fathered on any particular man.[1]

When we pass from the purely savage state to that higher plane of culture in which the accumulation of property, and especially of landed property, has become a powerful instrument of social and political influence, we naturally find that wherever the ancient preference for the female line of descent has been retained, it tends to increase the importance and enhance the dignity of woman ; and her aggrandizement is most marked in princely families, where she either herself holds royal authority as well as private property, or at least transmits them both to her consort or her children. But this social advance of women has never been carried so far as to place men as a whole in a position of political subordination to them. Even where the system of mother-kin in regard to descent and property has prevailed most fully, the actual government has generally, if not invariably, remained in the hands of men. Exceptions have no doubt occurred ; women have occasionally arisen

---

[1] Compare E. Stephan und F. Graebner, *Neu-Mecklenburg* (Berlin, 1907), p. 107 note [1] : "It is necessary always to repeat emphatically that the terms father-right and mother-right indicate simply and solely the group-membership of the individual and the systems of relationship which that membership implies, but that they have nothing at all to do with the higher or lower position of women. Rather the opposite might be affirmed, namely, that woman is generally more highly esteemed in places where father-right prevails than in places where mother-right is the rule."

who by sheer force of character have swayed for a time the destinies of their people. But such exceptions are rare and their effects transitory ; they do not affect the truth of the general rule that human society has been governed in the past and, human nature remaining the same, is likely to be governed in the future, mainly by masculine force and masculine intelligence.

Thus while the Khasis and Pelew Islanders have mother-kin, they are governed by men, not by women.

To this rule the Khasis, with their elaborate system of mother-kin, form no exception. For among them, while landed property is both transmitted through women and held by women alone, political power is transmitted indeed through women, but is held by men ; in other words, the Khasi tribes are, with a single exception, governed by kings, not by queens. And even in the one tribe, which is nominally ruled by women, the real power is delegated by the reigning queen or High Priestess to her son, her nephew, or a more distant male relation. In all the other tribes the kingship may be held by a woman only on the failure of all male heirs in the female line.[1] So far is mother-kin from implying mother-rule. A Khasi king inherits power in right of his mother, but he exercises it in his own. Similarly the Pelew Islanders, in spite of their system of mother-kin, are governed by chiefs, not by chieftainesses. It is true that there are chieftainesses, and that they indirectly exercise much influence ; but their direct authority is limited to the affairs of women, especially to the administration of the women's clubs or associations, which

[1] Major P. R. T. Gurdon, *The Khasis*, pp. 66-71. The rule of succession is as follows. A *Siem*, or king, " is succeeded by the eldest of his uterine brothers ; failing such brothers, by the eldest of his sisters' sons ; failing such nephews, by the eldest of the sons of his sisters' daughters ; failing such grand-nephews, by the eldest of the sons of his mother's sisters ; and, failing such first cousins, by the eldest of his male cousins on the female side, other than first cousins, those nearest in degree of relationship having prior claim. If there were no heirs male, as above, he would be succeeded by the eldest of his uterine sisters ; in the absence of such sisters, by the eldest of his sisters' daughters ; failing such nieces, by the eldest of the daughters of his sisters' daughters ; failing such grand-nieces, by the eldest of the daughters of his mother's sisters ; and failing such first cousins, by the eldest of his female cousins on the female side, other than first cousins, those nearest in degree of relationship having prior claim. A female *Siem* would be succeeded by her eldest son, and so on " (*op. cit.* p. 71). The rule illustrates the logical precision with which the system of mother-kin is carried out by these people even when the intention is actually to exclude women from power.

answer to the clubs or associations of the men.[1] And to take another example, the Melanesians, like the Khasis and the Pelew Islanders, have the system of mother-kin, being similarly divided into exogamous clans with descent in the female line ; " but it must be understood that the mother is in no way the head of the family. The house of the family is the father's, the garden is his, the rule, and government are his." [2]

We may safely assume that the practice has been the same among all the many peoples who have retained the ancient system of mother-kin under a monarchical constitution. In Africa, for example, the chieftainship or kingship often descends in the female line, but it is men, not women, who inherit it.[3] The theory of a gynaecocracy is in truth a dream of visionaries and pedants. And equally chimerical is the idea that the predominance of goddesses under a system of mother-kin like that of the Khasis is a creation of the female mind. If women ever created gods, they would be more likely to give them masculine than feminine features. In point of fact the great religious ideals which have permanently impressed themselves on the world seem always to have been a product of the male imagination. Men make gods and women worship them. The combination of ancestor-worship with mother-kin furnishes a simple and sufficient explanation of the superiority of goddesses over gods in a state of society where these conditions prevail. Men naturally assign the first place in their devotions to the ancestress from whom they trace their descent. We need not resort to a fantastic hypothesis of the preponderance, of the feminine fancy in order to account for the facts.

The theory that under a system of mother-kin the women rule the men and set up goddesses for them to

The theory of a gynae-cocracy and of the predominance of the female imagination in religion is an idle dream.

J. Kubary, *Die socialen Einrichtungen der Pelauer*, pp. 35, 39 *sq.*, 73-83. See also above, pp. 204 *sq.*

[2] R. H. Codrington, *The Melanesians* (Oxford, 1891), p. 34.

[3] See A. H. Post, *Afrikanische Jurisprudenz* (Oldenburg and Leipsic, 1887), i. 140 *sq.* Captain W. Gill reports that the Su-Mu, a Man-Tzŭ tribe in Southern China numbering some three and a half millions, is always ruled by a queen (*The River of Golden Sand*, London, 1880, i. 365). But Capt. Gill was not nearer to the tribe than a six days' journey ; and even if his report is correct we may suppose that the real power is exercised by men, just as it is in the solitary Khasi tribe which is nominally governed by a woman.

But mother-kin is a solid fact, which can hardly have failed to modify the religion of the peoples who practise it.

worship is indeed so improbable in itself, and so contrary to experience, that it scarcely deserves the serious attention which it appears to have received.[1] But when we have brushed aside these cobwebs, as we must do, we are still left face to face with the solid fact of the wide prevalence of mother-kin, that is, of a social system which traces descent and transmits property through women and not through men. That a social system so widely spread and so deeply rooted should have affected the religion of the peoples who practise it, may reasonably be inferred, especially when we remember that in primitive communities the social relations of the gods commonly reflect the social relations of their worshippers. How the system of mother-kin may mould religious ideas and customs, creating goddesses and assigning at least a nominal superiority to priestesses over priests, is shown with perfect lucidity by the example of the Khasis, and hardly less clearly by the example of the Pelew Islanders. It cannot therefore be rash to hold that what the system has certainly done for these peoples, it may well have done for many more. But unfortunately through lack of documentary evidence we are seldom able to trace its influence so clearly.

§ 3. *Mother-Kin and Mother Goddesses in the Ancient East*

Mother-kin and mother-goddesses in Western Asia.

While the combination of mother-kin in society with a preference for goddesses in religion is to be found as a matter of fact among the Khasis and Pelew Islanders of to-day, the former prevalence of mother-kin in the lands where the great goddesses Astarte and Cybele were worshipped is a matter of inference only. In later times father-kin had certainly displaced mother-kin among the Semitic worshippers of Astarte, and probably the same change had taken place among the Phrygian worshippers of Cybele. Yet the older

[1] The theory, or at all events the latter part of it, has been carefully examined by Dr. L. R. Farnell; and if, as I apprehend, he rejects it, I agree with him. See his article "Sociological Hypotheses concerning the position of Women in Ancient Religion," *Archiv für Religionswissen-* *schaft*, vii. (1904) pp. 70-94; his *Cults of the Greek States* (Oxford, 1896–1909), iii. 109 *sqq.*; and *The Hibbert Journal*, April 1907, p. 690. But I differ from him, it seems, in thinking that mother-kin is favourable to the growth of mother goddesses.

custom lingered in Lycia down to the historical period ; [1] and we may conjecture that in former times it was widely spread through Asia Minor. The secluded situation and rugged mountains of Lycia favoured the survival of a native language and of native institutions long after these had disappeared from the wide plains and fertile valleys which lay on the highroads of war and commerce. Lycia was to Asia Minor what the highlands of Wales and of Scotland have been to Britain, the last entrenchments where the old race stood at bay. And even among the Semites of antiquity, though father-kin finally prevailed in matters of descent and property, traces of an older system of mother-kin, with its looser sexual relations, appear to have long survived in the sphere of religion. At all events one of the most learned and acute of Semitic scholars adduced what he regarded as evidence sufficient to prove " that in old Arabian religion gods and goddesses often occurred in pairs, the goddess being the greater, so that the god cannot be her Baal, that the goddess is often a mother without being a wife, and the god her son, and that the progress of things was towards changing goddesses into gods or lowering them beneath the male deity." [2]

In Egypt the archaic system of mother-kin, with its preference for women over men in matters of property and inheritance, lasted down to Roman times, and it was tradi-

Mother-kin in ancient Egypt.

[1] The Lycians traced their descent through women, not through men ; and among them it was the daughters, not the sons, who inherited the family property. See Herodotus, i. 174 ; Nicolaus Damascenus, in Stobaeus, *Florilegium*, xliv. 41 (*Fragmenta Historicorum Graecorum*, ed. C. Müller, iii. 461) ; Plutarch, *De mulierum virtutibus*, 9. An ancient historian even asserts that the Lycians were ruled by women (ἐκ παλαιοῦ γυναικοκρατοῦνται, Heraclides Ponticus, Frag. 15, in *Fragmenta Historicorum Graecorum*, ed. C. Müller, ii. 217). Inscriptions found at Dalisandos, in Isauria, seem to prove that it was not unusual there to trace descent through the mother even in the third or the fourth century after Christ. See Sir

W. M. Ramsay, "The Permanence of Religion at Holy Places in the East," *The Expositor*, November 1906, p. 475. Dr. L. Messerschmidt seems to think that the Lycians were Hittites (*The Hittites*, p. 20). Scholars are not agreed as to the family of speech to which the Lycian language belongs. Some think that it was an Indo-European tongue ; but this view is now abandoned by Professor Ed. Meyer (*Geschichte des Altertums*,[2] i. 2. p. 626).

[2] W. Robertson Smith, *Kinship and Marriage in Early Arabia*[2] (London, 1903), p. 306. The hypothesis of the former existence of mother-kin among the Semites is rejected by Professor Ed. Meyer (*Geschichte des Altertums*,[2] i. 2, p. 360) and W. W. Graf Baudissin (*Adonis und Esmun*, pp. 46 *sq.*).

tionally based on the example of Isis, who had avenged her husband's murder and had continued to reign after his decease, conferring benefits on mankind.   " For these reasons," says Diodorus Siculus, " it was appointed that the queen should enjoy greater power and honour than the king, and that among private people the wife should rule over her husband, in the marriage contract the husband agreeing to obey his wife in all things." [1]   A corollary of the superior position thus conceded to women in Egypt was that the obligation of maintaining parents in their old age rested on the daughters, not on the sons, of the family.[2]

Marriages of brothers with sisters in ancient Egypt.

The same legal superiority of women over men accounts for the most remarkable feature in the social system of the ancient Egyptians, to wit, the marriage of full brothers with full sisters.   That marriage, which to us seems strange and unnatural, was by no means a whim of the reigning Ptolemies ; on the contrary, these Macedonian conquerors appear, with characteristic prudence, to have borrowed the custom from their Egyptian predecessors for the express purpose of conciliating native prejudice.   In the eyes of the Egyptians " marriage between brother and sister was the best of marriages, and it acquired an ineffable degree of sanctity when the brother and sister who contracted it were themselves born of a brother and sister, who had in their turn also sprung from a union of the same sort." [3]   Nor did the principle apply only to gods and kings.   The common people acted on it in their daily life.   They regarded marriages between brothers and sisters as the most natural and reasonable of all.[4]   The evidence of legal documents,

---

[1] Diodorus Siculus, i. 27. 1 *sq.* In spite of this express testimony to the existence of a true gynaecocracy in ancient Egypt, I am of opinion that the alleged superiority of the queen to the king and of the wife to her husband must have been to a great extent only nominal.   Certainly we know that it was the king and not the queen who really governed the country ; and we can hardly doubt that in like manner it was for the most part the husband and not the wife who really ruled the house, though unquestionably in regard to property the law seems to have

granted important rights to women which it denied to men.   On the position of women in ancient Egypt see especially the able article of Miss Rachel Evelyn White (Mrs. Wedd), "Women in Ptolemaic Egypt," *Journal of Hellenic Studies,* xviii. (1898) pp. 238-256.

[2] Herodotus, ii. 35.

[3] Sir Gaston Maspero, quoted by Miss R. E. White, *op. cit.* p. 244.

[4] J. Nietzold, *Die Ehe in Ägypten zur ptolemäisch-römischen Zeit* (Leipzic, 1903), p. 12.

including marriage contracts, tends to prove that such unions were the rule, not the exception, in ancient Egypt, and that they continued to form the majority of marriages long after the Romans had obtained a firm footing in the country. As we cannot suppose that Roman influence was used to promote a custom which must have been abhorrent to Roman instincts, we may safely assume that the proportion of brother and sister marriages in Egypt had been still greater in the days when the country was free.[1]

It would doubtless be a mistake to treat these marriages as a relic of savagery, as a survival of a tribal communism which knew no bar to the intercourse of the sexes. For such a theory would not explain why union with a sister was not only allowed, but preferred to all others. The true motive of that preference was most probably the wish of brothers to obtain for their own use the family property, which belonged of right to their sisters, and which otherwise they would have seen in the enjoyment of strangers, the husbands of their sisters. This is the system which in Ceylon is known as *beena* marriage. Under it the daughter, not the son, is the heir. She stays at home, and her husband comes and lives with her in the house ; but her brother goes away and dwells in his wife's home, inheriting nothing from his parents.[2] Such a system could not fail in time to prove irksome. Men would be loth to quit the old home, resign the ancestral property to a stranger, and go out to seek their fortune empty-handed in the world. The remedy was obvious. A man had nothing to do but to marry his sister himself instead of handing her over to another. Having done so he stayed at home and enjoyed the family estate in virtue of his marriage with the heiress. This simple and perfectly effective expedient for keeping the property in the

Such marriages were based on a wish to keep the property in the family.

[1] A. Erman, *Ägyten und ägyptisches Leben im Altertum*, pp. 221 sq.; U. Wilcken, "Arsinoitische Steuerprofessionen aus dem Jahre 189 n. Chr.," *Sitzungsberichte der könig. Preuss. Akademie der Wissenschaften zu Berlin*, 1883, p. 903 ; J. Nietzold, *Die Ehe in Ägypten zur ptolemäisch-römischen Zeit*, pp. 12-14.

[2] J. F. McLennan, *Studies in Ancient History* (London, 1886), pp. 101 sqq. Among the Kocchs of North-Eastern India "the property of the husband is made over to the wife ; when she dies it goes to her daughters, and when he marries he lives with his wife's mother" (R. G. Latham, *Descriptive Ethnology*, London, 1859, i. 96).

family most probably explains the custom of brother and sister marriage in Egypt.[1]

Thus the traditional marriage of Osiris with his sister Isis reflected a real social custom

Thus the union of Osiris with his sister Isis was not a freak of the story-teller's fancy : it reflected a social custom which was itself based on practical considerations of the most solid kind. When we reflect that this practice of mother-kin as opposed to father-kin survived down to the latest times of antiquity, not in an obscure and barbarous tribe, but in a nation whose immemorial civilization was its glory and the wonder of the world, we may without being extravagant suppose that a similar practice formerly prevailed in Syria and Phrygia, and that it accounts for the superiority of the goddess over the god in the divine partnerships of Adonis and Astarte, of Attis and Cybele. But the ancient system both of society and of religion had undergone far more change in these countries than in Egypt, where to the last the main outlines of the old structure could be traced in the national institutions to which the Egyptians clung with a passionate, a fanatical devotion. Mother-kin, the divinity of kings and queens, a sense of the original connexion of the gods with nature— these things outlived the Persian, the Macedonian, the Roman conquest, and only perished under the more powerful solvent

The passing of the old world in Egypt.

of Christianity. But the old order did not vanish at once with the official establishment of the new religion. In the age of Constantine the Greeks of Egypt still attributed the rise of the Nile to Serapis, the later form of Osiris, alleging

---

[1] This is in substance the explanation which Miss Rachel Evelyn White (Mrs. Wedd) gives of the Egyptian custom. See her paper, " Women in Ptolemaic Egypt," *Journal of Hellenic Studies*, xviii. (1898) p. 265. Similarly Mr. J. Nietzold observes that " economical considerations, especially in the case of great landowners, may often have been the occasion of marriages with sisters, the intention being in this way to avoid a division of the property" (*Die Ehe in Ägypten*, p. 13). The same explanation of the custom has been given by Prof. W. Ridgeway. See his " Supplices of Aeschylus," in *Praelections delivered before the Senate* of the *University of Cambridge* (Cambridge, 1906), pp. 154 *sq.* I understand from Professor W. M. Flinders Petrie that the theory has been a commonplace with Egyptologists for many years. McLennan explained the marriage of brothers and sisters in royal families as an expedient for shifting the succession from the female to the male line ; but he did not extend the theory so as to explain similar marriages among common people in Egypt, perhaps because he was not aware of the facts. See J. F. McLennan, *The Patriarchal Theory*, edited and completed by D. McLennan (London, 1885), p. 95.

that the inundation could not take place if the standard cubit, which was used to measure it, were not deposited according to custom in the temple of the god. The emperor ordered the cubit to be transferred to a church ; and next year, to the general surprise, the river rose just as usual.[1] Even at a later time Athanasius himself had to confess with sorrow and indignation that under his own eyes the Egyptians still annually mourned the death of Osiris.[2] The end came with the destruction of the great Serapeum at Alexandria, the last stronghold of the heathen in Egypt. It perished in a furious and bloody sedition, in which Christians and pagans seem to have vied with each other in mutual atrocities. After its fall the temples were levelled with the ground or converted into churches, and the images of the old gods went to the melting-pot to be converted into base uses for the rabble of Alexandria.[3]

The singular tenacity with which the Egyptian people maintained their traditional beliefs and customs for thousands of years sprang no doubt from the stubborn conservatism of the national character. Yet that conservatism was itself in great measure an effect of geographical and climatic conditions and of the ways of life which they favoured. Surrounded on every side by deserts or almost harbourless seas, the Egyptians occupied a position of great natural strength which for long ages together protected them from invasion and allowed their native habits to set and harden, undisturbed by the subversive influence of foreign conquest. The wonderful regularity of nature in Egypt also conduced to a corresponding stability in the minds of the people. Year in, year out, the immutable succession of the seasons brought with it the same unvarying round of agricultural toil. What the fathers had done, the sons did in the same manner at the same season, and so it went on from

Egyptian conservatism partly an effect of natural conditions and habits of life.

[1] Socrates, *Historia Ecclesiastica*, i. 18 (Migne's *Patrologia Graeca*, lxvii. 121). The learned Valesius, in his note on this passage, informs us that the cubit was again transferred by the Emperor Julian to the Serapeum, where it was left in peace till the destruction of that temple.

[2] Athanasius, *Oratio contra Gentes*,

10 (Migne's *Patrologia Graeca*, xxv. 24).

[3] Socrates, *Historia Ecclesiastica*, v. 16 *sq.* (Migne's *Patrologia Graeca*, lxvii. 604 *sq.*) ; Sozomenus, *Historia Ecclesiastica*, vii. 15 (Migne's *Patrologia Graeca*, lxvii. 1152 *sq.*). These events took place under the Emperor Theodosius in the year 391 A.D.

generation to generation. This monotonous routine is common indeed to all purely agricultural communities, and everywhere tends to beget in the husbandman a settled phlegmatic habit of mind very different from the mobility, the alertness, the pliability of character which the hazards and uncertainties of commerce and the sea foster in the merchant and the sailor. The saturnine temperament of the farmer is as naturally averse to change as the more mercurial spirit of the trader and the seaman is predisposed to it. But the stereotyping of ideas and of customs was carried further in Egypt than in most lands devoted to husbandry by reason of the greater uniformity of the Egyptian seasons and the more complete isolation of the country.

The old type of Osiris better preserved than those of Adonis and Attis.

The general effect of these causes was to create a type of national character which presented many points of resemblance to that of the Chinese. In both we see the same inflexible strength of will, the same astonishing industry, the same strange blend of humanity and savagery, the same obstinate adherence to tradition, the same pride of race and of ancient civilization, the same contempt for foreigners as for upstarts and barbarians, the same patient outward submission to an alien rule combined with an unshakeable inward devotion to native ideals. It was this conservative temper of the people, bred in great measure of the physical nature of their land, which, so to say, embalmed the memory of Osiris long after the corresponding figures of Adonis and Attis had suffered decay. For while Egypt enjoyed profound repose, the tides of war and conquest, of traffic and commerce, had for centuries rolled over Western Asia, the native home of Adonis and Attis; and if the shock of nationalities in this great meeting-ground of East and West was favourable to the rise of new faiths and new moralities, it was in the same measure unfavourable to the preservation of the old.

NOTES

I

MOLOCH THE KING

I CANNOT leave the evidence for the sacred character of Jewish kings [1] without mentioning a suggestion which was made to me by my friend and teacher the Rev. Professor R. H. Kennett. He thinks that Moloch, to whom first-born children were burnt by their parents in the valley of Hinnom, outside the walls of Jerusalem, [2] may have been originally the human king regarded as an incarnate deity. Certainly the name of Moloch, or rather Molech (for so it is always written in the Massoretic text [3]), is merely a slightly dis- *Moloch perhaps the human king regarded as an incarnate deity.*

[1] See above, vol. i. pp. 17 *sqq.*

[2] *The Dying God*, pp. 168 *sqq.* ; G. F. Moore, in *Encyclopaedia Biblica*, *s.v.* "Molech." The phrase translated "make pass through the fire to Molech" (2 Kings xxiii. 10) means properly, Professor Kennett tells me, "make to pass over by means of fire to Molech," where the verb has the sense of "make over to," "dedicate," "devote," as appears from its use in Exodus xiii. 12 ("set apart," English Version) and Ezekiel xx. 26. That the children were not made simply to pass through the fire, but were burned in it, is shown by a comparison of 2 Kings xvi. 3, xxiii. 10, Jeremiah xxxii. 35, with 2 Chronicles xxviii. 3, Jeremiah vii. 31, xix. 5. As to the use of the verb הֶעֱבִיר in the sense of "dedicate," "devote," see G. F. Moore, *s.v.* "Molech," *Encyclopaedia Biblica*, iii. 3184 ; F. Brown, S. R. Driver, and C. A. Briggs, *Hebrew and English Lexicon of the Old Testament* (Oxford, 1906), p. 718. "The testimony of both the prophets and

the laws is abundant and unambiguous that the victims were slain and burnt as a holocaust" (G. F. Moore, in *Encyclopaedia Biblica*, iii. 3184). Similarly Principal J. Skinner translates the phrase in 2 Kings xvi. 3 by "dedicated his son by fire," and remarks that the expression, "whatever its primary sense may be, undoubtedly denoted actual burning" (commentary on Kings in *The Century Bible*). The practice would seem to have been very ancient at Jerusalem, for tradition placed the attempted burnt-sacrifice of Isaac by his father Abraham on Mount Moriah, which was no other than Mount Zion, the site of the king's palace and of the temple of Jehovah. See Genesis xxii. 1-18 ; 2 Chronicles iii. 1 ; J. Benzinger, *Hebräische Archäologie* (Freiburg i. Baden and Leipsic, 1894), pp. 45, 233 ; T. K. Cheyne, *s.v.* "Moriah," *Encyclopaedia Biblica*, iii. 3200 *sq.*

[3] Leviticus xviii. 21, xx. 2-5 ; 1 Kings xi. 7 ; 2 Kings xxiii. 10 : Jeremiah xxxii. 35.

guised form of *melech*, the ordinary Hebrew word for "king," the scribes having apparently given the dreadful word the vowels of bosheth, "shameful thing."[1]   But it seems clear that in historical times the Jews who offered these sacrifices identified Molech, not with the human king, but with Jehovah, though the prophets protested against the custom as an outrage on the divine majesty.[2]

The sacrifices to Moloch may have been intended to prolong the king's life. Vicarious sacrifices for a king or queen in Sweden, Persia, and Madagascar.

If, however, these sacrifices were originally offered to or in behalf of the human king, it is possible that they were intended to prolong his life and strengthen his hands for the performance of those magical functions which he was expected to discharge for the good of his people.   The old kings of Sweden answered with their heads for the fertility of the ground,[3] and we read that one of them, Aun or On by name, sacrificed nine of his sons to Odin at Upsala in order that his own life might be spared.   After the sacrifice of his second son he received from the god an oracle that he should live as long as he gave him one of his sons every tenth year.   When he had thus sacrificed seven sons, the ruthless father still lived, but was so feeble that he could no longer walk and had to be carried in a chair.   Then he offered up his eighth son and lived ten years more, bedridden.   After that he sacrificed his ninth son, and lived ten years more, drinking out of a horn like a weaned child.   He now wished to sacrifice his last remaining son to Odin, but the Swedes would not let him, so he died and was buried in a mound at Upsala.[4]   In this Swedish tradition the king's children seem to have been looked upon as substitutes offered to the god in place of their father, and apparently this was also the current explanation of the slaughter of the first-born in the later times of Israel.[5] On that view the sacrifices were vicarious, and therefore purely religious, being intended to propitiate a stern and exacting deity. Similarly we read that when Amestris, wife of Xerxes, was grown old, she sacrificed on her behalf twice seven noble children to the

[1] W. Robertson Smith, *The Religion of the Semites*,[2] p. 372, note [1].

[2] "It is plain, from various passages of the prophets, that the sacrifices of children among the Jews before the captivity, which are commonly known as sacrifices to Moloch, were regarded by the worshippers as oblations to Jehovah, under the title of king" (W. Robertson Smith, *Religion of the Semites*,[2] p. 372, referring to Jeremiah vii. 31, xix. 5, xxxii. 35; Ezekiel xxiii. 39; Micah vi. 7). The same view is taken by Prof. G. F. Moore, in *Encyclopaedia Biblica*, *s.v.* "Molech," vol. iii. 3187 *sq.*

[3] *The Magic Art and the Evolution of Kings*, i. 366 *sq.*

[4] "Ynglinga Saga," 29, in *The Heimskringla or Chronicle of the Kings of Norway*, translated by S. Laing (London, 1844), i. 239 *sq.*; H. M. Chadwick, *The Cult of Othin* (London, 1899), pp. 4, 27; *The Dying God*, pp. 160 *sq.*   Similarly in Peru, when a person of note was sick, he would sometimes sacrifice his son to the idol in order that his own life might be spared.   See A. de Herrera, *The General History of the Vast Continent and Islands of America*, translated by Capt. J. Stevens (London, 1725–1726), iv. 347 *sq.*

Micah vi. 6-8.

earth god by burying them alive.[1] If the story is true—and it rests
on the authority of Herodotus, a nearly contemporary witness—we
may surmise that the aged queen acted thus with an eye to the
future rather than to the past; she hoped that the grim god of
the nether-world would accept the young victims in her stead, and
let her live for many years. The same idea of vicarious suffering
comes out in a tradition told of a certain Hova king of Madagascar,
who bore the sonorous name of Andriamasinavalona. When he had
grown sickly and feeble, the oracle was consulted as to the best way
of restoring him to health. "The following result was the consequence of the directions of the oracle. A speech was first delivered
to the people, offering great honours and rewards to the family of
any individual who would freely offer himself to be sacrificed, in
order to the king's recovery. The people shuddered at the idea,
and ran away in different directions. One man, however, presented
himself for the purpose, and his offer was accepted. The sacrificer
girded up his loins, sharpened his knife, and bound the victim.
After which, he was laid down with his head towards the east, upon
a mat spread for the purpose, according to the custom with animals
on such occasions, when the priest appeared, to proceed with all
solemnity in slaughtering the victim by cutting his throat. A
quantity of red liquid, however, which had been prepared from a
native dye, was spilled in the ceremony; and, to the amazement
of those who looked on, blood seemed to be flowing all around. The
man, as might be supposed, was unhurt; but the king rewarded him
and his descendants with the perpetual privilege of exemption from
capital punishment for any violation of the laws. The descendants
of the man to this day form a particular class, called *Tay maty
manota*, which may be translated, 'Not dead, though transgressing.'
Instances frequently occur, of individuals of this class appropriating
bullocks, rice, and other things belonging to the sovereign, as if
they were their own, and escaping merely with a reprimand, while
a common person would have to suffer death, or be reduced to
slavery." [2]

Sometimes, however, the practices intended to prolong the king's
life seem to rest on a theory of nutrition rather than of substitution;
in other words, the life of the victims, instead of being offered
vicariously to a god, is apparently supposed to pass directly into the
body of the sacrificer, thus refreshing his failing strength and prolonging his existence. So regarded, the custom is magical rather
than religious in character, since the desired effect is thought to
follow directly without the intervention of a deity. At all events, it
can be shown that sacrifices of this sort have been offered to prolong
the life of kings in other parts of the world. Thus in regard to

Other sacrifices for prolonging the king's life appear to be magical rather than religious.

---

[1] Herodotus, vii. 114; Plutarch,   [2] W. Ellis, *History of Madagascar*
De superstitione, 13.   (London, N.D.), i. 344 *sq.*

some of the negroes who inhabit the delta of the Niger we read that : "A custom which formerly was practised by the Ibani, and is still prevalent among all the interior tribes, consists in prolonging the life of a king or ancestral representative by the daily, or possibly weekly, sacrifice of a chicken and egg. Every morning, as soon as the patriarch has risen from his bed, the sacrificial articles are procured either by his mother, head wife, or eldest daughter, and given to the priest, who receives them on the open space in front of the house. When this has been reported to the patriarch, he comes outside and, sitting down, joins in the ceremony. Taking the chicken in his hand, the priest first of all touches the patriarch's face with it, and afterwards passes it over the whole of his body. He then cuts its throat and allows the blood to drop on the ground. Mixing the blood and the earth into a paste, he rubs it on the old man's forehead and breast, and this is not to be washed off under any circumstances until the evening. The chicken and the egg, also a piece of white cloth, are now tied on to a stick, which, if a stream is in the near vicinity, is planted in the ground at the waterside. During the carriage of these articles to the place in question, all the wives and many members of the household accompany the priest, invoking the deity as they go to prolong their father's life. This is done in the firm conviction that through the sacrifice of each chicken his life will be accordingly prolonged." [1]

The ceremony thus described is, like so many other rites, a combination of magic and religion ; for whereas the prayers to the god are religious, the passing of the victim over the king's body and the smearing of him with its blood are magical, being plainly intended to convey to him directly, without the mediation of any deity, the life of the fowl. In the following instances the practices Customs
observed
by the
Zulus and
Caffres to
prolong the
king's life. for prolonging the king's life seem to be purely magical. Among the Zulus, at one of the annual feasts of first-fruits, a bull is killed by a particular regiment. In slaughtering the beast they may not use spears or sticks, but must break its neck or choke it with their bare hands. "It is then burned, and the strength of the bull is supposed to enter into the king, thereby prolonging his life." [2] Again, in an early Portuguese historian we read of a Caffre king of East Africa that "it is related of this Monomotapa that he has a house where he commands bodies of men who have died at the hands of the law to be hung up, and where thus hanging all the humidity

---

[1] Major A. G. Leonard, *The Lower Niger and its Tribes* (London, 1906), p. 457.

[2] D. Leslie, *Among the Zulus and Amatongas* [2] (Edinburgh, 1875), p. 91. This sacrifice may be the one described by J. Shooter, *The Kafirs of Natal*

(London, 1857), p. 26. The reason for not stabbing the animal is perhaps a wish not to lose any of the blood, but to convey its life intact to the king. The same reason would explain the same rule which the Baganda observed in killing a human victim for the same purpose (see below, p. 224).

of their bodies falls into vases placed underneath, and when all has dropped from them and they shrink and dry up he commands them to be taken down and buried, and with the fat and moisture in the vases they say he makes ointments with which he anoints himself in order to enjoy long life—which is his belief—and also to be proof against receiving harm from sorcerers." [1]

The Baganda of Central Africa used to kill men on various occasions for the purpose of prolonging the king's life; in all cases it would seem to be thought that the life of the murdered man was in some mysterious fashion transferred to the king, so that the monarch received thereby a fresh accession of vital energy. For example, whenever a particular royal drum had a new skin put on it, not only was a cow killed to furnish the skin and its blood run into the drum, but a man was beheaded and the spouting blood from the severed neck was allowed to gush into the drum, "so that, when the drum was beaten, it was supposed to add fresh life and vigour to the king from the life of the slain man." [2] Again, at the coronation of a new king, a royal chamberlain was chosen to take charge of the king's inner court and to guard his wives. From the royal presence the chamberlain was conducted, along with eight captives, to one of the human shambles; there he was blindfolded while seven of the men were clubbed to death, only the dull thud and crashing sound telling him of what was taking place. But when the seven had been thus despatched, the bandages were removed from the chamberlain's eyes and he witnessed the death of the eighth. As each man was killed, his belly was ripped open and his bowels pulled out and hung round the chamberlain's neck. These deaths were said to add to the King's vigour and to make the chamberlain strong and faithful. [3] Nor were these the only human sacrifices offered at a king's coronation for the purpose of strengthening the new monarch. When the king had reigned two or three months, he was expected to hunt first a leopard and then a bushbuck. On the night after the hunt of the bushbuck, one of the ministers of State caught a man and brought him before the king in the dark; the king speared him slightly, then the man was strangled and the body thrown into a papyrus swamp, that it might never be found again. Another ceremony performed about this time to confirm the king in his kingdom was to catch a man, bind him, and bring him before the king, who wounded him slightly with a spear. Then the man was put to death. These men were killed to invigorate the king. [4]

Customs observed by the Baganda to prolong the king's life.

Human victims killed in order to invigorate the king.

---

[1] J. Dos Santos, *Eastern Ethiopia*, bk. ii. chap. 16 (G. M'Call Theal's *Records of South-Eastern Africa*, vii. 289).

[2] Rev. J. Roscoe, *The Baganda*

(London, 1911), pp. 27 *sq.*

[3] Rev. J. Roscoe, *The Baganda*, p. 200.

[4] Rev. J. Roscoe, *The Baganda*, pp. 209 *sq.*

Chief's son killed to provide the king with anklets.

When a king of Uganda had reigned some time, apparently several years, a ceremony was performed for the sake of prolonging his life. For this purpose the king paid a visit—a fatal visit—to a chief of the Lung-fish clan, who bore the title of Nankere and resided in the district of Busiro, where the tombs and temples of the kings were situated. When the time for the ceremony had been appointed, the chief chose one of his own sons, who was to die that the king might live. If the chief had no son, a near relation was compelled to serve as a substitute. The hapless youth was fed and clothed and treated in all respects like a prince, and taken to live in a particular house near the place where the king was to lodge for the ceremony. When the destined victim had been feasted and guarded for a month, the king set out on his progress from the capital. On the way he stopped at the temple of the great god Mukasa; there he changed his garments, leaving behind him in the temple those which he had been wearing. Also he left behind him all his anklets, and did not put on any fresh ones, for he was shortly to receive new anklets of a remarkable kind. When the king arrived at his destination, the chief met him, and the two exchanged a gourd of beer. At this interview the king's mother was present to see her son for the last time; for from that moment the two were never allowed to look upon each other again. The chief addressed the king's mother informing her of this final separation; then turning to the king he said, "You are now of age; go and live longer than your forefathers." Then the chief's son was introduced. The chief took him by the hand and presented him to the king, who passed him on to the body-guard; they led him outside and killed him by beating him with their clenched fists. The muscles from the back of the body of the murdered youth were removed and made into two anklets for the king, and a strip of skin cut from the corpse was made into a whip, which was kept in the royal enclosure for special feasts. The dead body was thrown on waste land and guarded against wild beasts, but not buried.[1]

The king's game.

When that ceremony was over, the king departed to go to another chief in Busiro; but on the way thither he stopped at a place called Baka and sat down under a great tree to play a game of spinning fruit-stones. It is a children's game, but it was no child's play to the man who ran to fetch the fruit-stones for the king to play with; for he was caught and speared to death on the spot for the purpose of prolonging the king's life. After the game had been played the king with his train passed on and lodged with a certain princess till the anklets made from the muscles of the chief's murdered son were ready for him to wear;

---

[1] Rev. J. Roscoe, *The Baganda*, pp. 210 *sq.*

it was the princess who had to superintend the making of these royal ornaments.[1]

When all these ceremonies were over, the king made a great feast. At this feast a priest went about carrying under his mantle the whip that had been made from the skin of the murdered young man. As he passed through the crowd of merrymakers, he would flick a man here and there with the whip, and it was believed that the man on whom the lash lighted would be child-less and might die, unless he made an offering of either nine or ninety cowrie shells to the priest who had struck him. Naturally he hastened to procure the shells and take them to the striker, who, on receiving them, struck the man on the shoulder with his hand, thus restoring to him the generative powers of which the blow of the whip had deprived him. At the end of the feast the drummers removed all the drums but one, which they left as if they had forgotten it. Somebody in the crowd would notice the apparent oversight and run after the drummers with the drum, saying, " You have left one behind." The thanks he received was that he was caught and killed and the bones of his upper arm made into drumsticks for that particular drum. The drum was never afterwards brought out during the whole of the king's reign, but was kept covered up till the time came to bring it out on the corresponding feast of his successor. Yet from time to time the priest, who had flicked the revellers with the whip of human skin, would dress himself up in a mantle of cow-hide from neck to foot, and concealing the drumstick of human bones under his robe would go into the king's presence, and suddenly whipping out the bones from his bosom would brandish them in the king's face. Then he would as suddenly hide them again, but only to repeat the manoeuvre. After that he retired and restored the bones to their usual place. They were decorated with cowrie shells and little bells, which jingled as he shook them at the king.[2]

The precise meaning of these latter ceremonies is obscure ; but we may suppose that just as the human blood poured into a drum was thought to pass into the king's veins in the booming notes of the drum, so the clicking of the human bones and the jingling of their bells were supposed to infuse into the royal person the vigour of the murdered man. The purpose of flicking commoners with the whip made of human skin is even more obscure ; but we may conjecture that the life or virility of every man struck with the whip was supposed to be transmitted in some way to the king, who thus recruited his vital, and especially his reproductive, energies at this solemn feast. If I am right in my interpretation, all these Baganda

The whip of human skin.

Modes in which the strength of the human victims was thought to pass into the king.

---

[1] Rev. J. Roscoe, *The Baganda*, pp. 211 *sq.* I have abridged the

account of the ceremonies.
[2] Rev. J. Roscoe, *op. cit.* pp. 213 *sq.*

modes of strengthening the king and prolonging his life belonged to the nutritive rather than to the vicarious type of sacrifice, from which it will follow that they were magical rather than religious in character.

Massacres perpetrated when a king of Uganda was ill.

The same thing may perhaps be said of the wholesale massacres which used to be perpetrated when a king of Uganda was ill. At these times the priests informed the royal patient that persons marked by a certain physical peculiarity, such as a cast of the eye, a particular gait, or a distinctive colouring, must be put to death. Accordingly the king sent out his catchpoles, who waylaid such persons in the roads and dragged them to the royal enclosure, where they were kept until the tale of victims prescribed by the priest was complete. Before they were led away to one of the eight places of execution, which were regularly appointed for this purpose in different parts of the kingdom, the victims had to drink medicated beer with the king out of a special pot, in order that he might have power over their ghosts, lest they should afterwards come back to torment him. They were killed, sometimes by being speared to death, sometimes by being hacked to pieces, sometimes by being burned alive. Contrary to the usual custom of the Baganda, the bodies, or what remained of the bodies, of these unfortunates were always left unburied on the place of execution.[1] In what way precisely the sick king was supposed to benefit by these massacres of his subjects does not appear, but we may surmise that somehow the victims were believed to give their lives for him or to him.

Yet the sacrifices of children to Moloch may be otherwise explained.

Thus it is possible that in Israel also the sacrifices of children to Moloch were in like manner intended to prolong the life of the human king (*melech*) either by serving as substitutes for him or by recruiting his failing energies with their vigorous young life. But it is equally possible, and perhaps more probable, that the sacrifice of the first-born children was only a particular application of the ancient law which devoted to the deity the first-born of every womb, whether of cattle or of human beings.[2]

[1] From information furnished by my friend the Rev. J. Roscoe. Compare   his book, *The Baganda*, pp. 331 *sqq.*
[2] See *The Dying God*, pp. 166 *sqq.*

II

THE WIDOWED FLAMEN

§ 1. *The Pollution of Death*

A DIFFERENT explanation of the rule which obliged the Flamen Dialis to resign the priesthood on the death of his wife [1] has been suggested by my friend Dr. L. R. Farnell. He supposes that such a bereavement would render the Flamen ceremonially impure, and therefore unfit to hold office. [2] It is true that the ceremonial pollution caused by death commonly disqualifies a man for the discharge of sacred functions, but as a rule the disqualification is only temporary and can be removed by seclusion and the observance of purificatory rites, the length of the seclusion and the nature of the purification varying with the degree of relationship in which the living stand to the dead. Thus, for example, if one of the sacred eunuchs at Hierapolis-Bambyce saw the dead body of a stranger, he was unclean for that day and might not enter the sanctuary of the goddess ; but next day after purifying himself he was free to enter. But if the corpse happened to be that of a relation he was unclean for thirty days and had to shave his head before he might set foot within the holy precinct. [3] Again, in the Greek island of Ceos persons who had offered the annual sacrifices to their departed friends were unclean for two days afterwards and might not enter a sanctuary ; they had to purify themselves with water. [4] Similarly no one might go into the shrine of Men Tyrannus for ten days after being in contact with the dead. [5] Once more, at Stratonicea in Caria a chorus of thirty noble boys, clad in white and holding branches in their hands, used to sing a hymn daily in honour of Zeus and Hecate ; but if one of them were sick or had suffered a domestic bereavement, he was for the time being excused, not permanently excluded, from the

[marginal note:] Theory that the resignation of the widowed Flamen Dialis was caused by the pollution of death.

[1] See above, vol. i. p. 45.

[2] *The Hibbert Journal*, April 1907, p. 689.

[3] Lucian, *De dea Syria*, 53.

[4] G. Dittenberger, *Sylloge Inscriptionum Graecarum*,[2] vol. ii. pp. 725 *sqq.*, Nos. 877, 878.

[5] G. Dittenberger, *op. cit.* vol. ii. pp. 429 *sq.*, No. 633.

227

performance of his sacred duties.[1] On the analogy of these and similar cases we should expect to find the widowed Flamen temporarily debarred from the exercise of his office, not permanently relieved of it.

Apparent parallel among the Todas.   However, in support of Dr. Farnell's view I would cite an Indian parallel which was pointed out to me by Dr. W. H. R. Rivers. Among the Todas of the Neilgherry Hills in Southern India the priestly dairyman (*palol*) is a sacred personage, and his life, like that of the Flamen Dialis, is hedged in by many taboos. Now when a death occurs in his clan, the dairyman may not attend any of the funeral ceremonies unless he gives up office, but he may be re-elected after the second funeral ceremonies have been completed, In the interval his place must be taken by a man of another clan. Some eighteen or nineteen years ago a man named Karkievan resigned the office of dairyman when his wife died, but two years later he was re-elected and has held office ever since. There have meantime been many deaths in his clan, but he has not attended a funeral, and has not therefore had to resign his post again. Apparently in old times a more stringent rule prevailed, and the dairyman was obliged to vacate office whenever a death occurred in his clan. For, according to tradition, the clan of Keadrol was divided into its two existing divisions for the express purpose of ensuring that there might still be men to undertake the office of dairyman when a death occurred in the clan, the men of the one division taking office whenever there was a death in the other.[2]

At first sight this case may seem exactly parallel to the case of the Flamen Dialis and the Flaminica on Dr. Farnell's theory ; for here there can be no doubt whatever that it is the pollution of death which disqualifies the sacred dairyman from holding office, since, if he only avoids that pollution by not attending the funeral, he is allowed at the present day to retain his post. On this analogy we might suppose that it was not so much the death of his wife as the attendance at her funeral which compelled the Flamen Dialis to resign, especially as we know that he was expressly forbidden to touch a dead body or to enter the place where corpses were burned.[3]

But on inspection the analogy breaks down.   But a closer inspection of the facts proves that the analogy breaks down at some important points. For though the Flamen Dialis was forbidden to touch a dead body or to enter a place where corpses were burned, he was permitted to attend a funeral ;[4] so that there could hardly be any objection to his attending the funeral of

[1] *Corpus Inscriptionum Graecarum*, ed. Aug. Boeckh, etc. (Berlin, 1828–1877), vol. ii. pp. 481 *sqq.*, No. 2715, οὔσης ἐξουσίας το[ῖς παισίν, ἐά]ν τινες αὐτῶν μὴ ὦσιν ὑγιεῖς ἢ πένθει οἰκείῳ κατέχωνται, where I understand ἐξουσία to mean " leave of absence."

[2] W. H. R. Rivers, *The Todas* (London, 1906), pp. 99 *sq.*

[3] Aulus Gellius, x. 15. 24.

[4] Aulus Gellius, *l.c.* : "*funus tamen exequi non est religio.*"

his wife. This permission clearly tells against the view that it was the mere pollution of death which obliged him to resign office when his wife died. Further, and this is a point of fundamental difference between the two cases, whereas the Flamen Dialis was bound to be married, and married too by a rite of special solemnity,[1] there is no such obligation on the sacred dairyman of the Todas; indeed, if he is married, he is bound to live apart from his wife during his term of office.[2] Surely the obligation laid on the Flamen Dialis to be married of itself implies that with the death of his wife he necessarily ceased to hold office: there is no need to search for another reason in the pollution of death which, as I have just shown, does not seem to square with the permission granted to the Flamen to attend a funeral. That this is indeed the true explanation of the rule in question is strongly suggested by the further and apparently parallel rule which forbade the Flamen to divorce his wife; nothing but death might part them.[3] Now the rule which enjoined that a Flamen must be married, and the rule which forbade him to divorce his wife, have obviously nothing to do with the pollution of death, yet they can hardly be separated from the other rule that with the death of his wife he vacated office. All three rules are explained in the most natural way on the hypothesis which I have adopted, namely, that this married priest and priestess had to perform in common certain rites which the husband could not perform without his wife. The same obvious solution of the problem was suggested long ago by Plutarch, who, after asking why the Flamen Dialis had to lay down office on the death of his wife, says, amongst other things, that "perhaps it is because she performs sacred rites along with him (for many of the rites may not be performed without the presence of a married woman), and to marry another wife immedi-

[1] Gaius, *Instit.* i. 112, "*quod jus etiam nostris temporibus in usu est: nam flamines majores, id est Diales, Martiales, Quirinales, item reges sacrorum, nisi* (qui) *ex farreatis nati* sunt *non leguntur: ac ne ipsi quidem sine confarreatione sacerdotium habere possunt*"; Servius on Virgil, *Aen.* iv. 103, "*quae res ad farreatas nuptias pertinet, quibus flaminem et flaminicam jure pontificio in matrimonium necesse est convenire.*" For a fuller description of the rite see Servius, on Virgil, *Aen.* iv. 374. From the testimony of Gaius it appears that not only the Flamen Dialis but all the other principal Flamens were bound to be married. However, the text of Gaius in this passage is somewhat uncertain. I have quoted it from P. E. Huschke's third edition (Leipsic, 1878).

[2] W. H. R. Rivers, *The Todas*, p. 99. According to an old account, there was an important exception to the rule, but Dr. Rivers was not able to verify it; he understood that during the tenure of his office the dairyman is really celibate.

[3] Aulus Gellius, x. 15. 23, "*Matrimonium flaminis nisi morte dirimi jus non est*"; Festus, p. 89, ed. C. O. Müller, *s.v.* "Flammeo"; Plutarch, *Quaestiones Romanae*, 50. Plutarch mentions as an illegal exception that in his own time the Emperor Domitian allowed a Flamen to divorce his wife, but the ceremony of the divorce was attended by "many awful, strange, and gloomy rites" performed by the priests.

ately on the death of the first would hardly be possible or decent."[1]
This simple explanation of the rule seems quite sufficient, and it
would clearly hold good whether I am right or wrong in further supposing that the human husband and wife in this case represented a
divine husband and wife, a god and goddess, to wit Jupiter and
Juno, or rather Dianus (Janus) and Diana ;[2] and that supposition
in its turn might still hold good even if I were wrong in further con-
jecturing that of this divine pair the goddess (Juno or rather Diana)
was originally the more important partner.

Customs of the Kota and Jewish priests.   However it is to be explained, the Roman rule which forbade the
Flamen Dialis to be a widower has its parallel among the Kotas, a
tribe who, like the Todas, inhabit the Neilgherry Hills of Southern
India.   For the higher Kota priests are not allowed to be
widowers ; if a priest's wife dies while he is in office, his appoint-
ment lapses.   At the same time priests " should avoid pollution,
and may not attend a Toda or Badaga funeral, or approach the
seclusion hut set apart for Kota women."[3]   Jewish priests were
specially permitted to contract the pollution of death for near relations, among whom father, mother, son, daughter, and unmarried
sister are particularly enumerated ; but they were forbidden to contract the pollution for strangers.   However, among the relations for
whom a priest might thus defile himself a wife is not mentioned.[4]

§ 2. The Marriage of the Roman Gods

The theory that the Roman gods were celibate is contradicted by Varro and Seneca.   The theory that the Flamen Dialis and his wife personated a
divine couple, whether Jupiter and Juno or Dianus (Janus) and
Diana, supposes a married relation between the god and goddess,
and so far it would certainly be untenable if Dr. Farnell were right
in assuming, on the authority of Mr. W. Warde Fowler, that the
Roman gods were celibate.[5]   On that subject, however, Varro, the

[1] Plutarch, Quaestiones Romanae, 50.
That the wives of Roman priests aided
their husbands in the performance of
sacred rites is mentioned by Dionysius
of Halicarnassus, who attributes the
institution of these joint priesthoods
to Romulus (Antiquit. Rom. ii. 22).
    [2] The epithet Dialis, which was
applied to the Flaminica as well as to
the Flamen (Aulus Gellius, x. 15. 26 ;
Servius, on Virgil, Aen. iv. 137),
would of itself prove that husband and
wife served the same god or pair of
gods ; and while the word was doubt-
fully derived by Varro from Jove (De
lingua Latina, v. 84), we are expressly
told that the Flamen was the priest
and the Flaminica the priestess of that

god (Plutarch, Quaest. Rom. 109 ;
Festus, p. 92, ed. C. O. Müller, s.v.
" Flammeo ").   There is therefore
every reason to accept the statement of
Plutarch (Quaest. Rom. 86) that the
Flaminica was reputed to be sacred to
Juno, the divine partner of Jupiter, in
spite of the objections raised by Mr. W.
Warde Fowler (" Was the Flaminica
Dialis priestess of Juno ? " Classical
Review, ix. (1895) pp. 474 sqq.).
    [3] E. Thurston, Castes and Tribes
of Southern India (Madras, 1909), iv.
10.
    [4] Leviticus, xxi. 1-3 ; Ezekiel, xliv.
25.
    [5] The Hibbert Journal, iv. (1906)
p. 932.

most learned of Roman antiquaries, was of a contrary opinion. He not only spoke particularly of Juno as the wife of Jupiter,[1] but he also affirmed generally, in the most unambiguous language, that the old Roman gods were married, and in saying so he referred not to the religion of his own day, which had been modified by Greek influence, but to the religion of the ancient Romans, his ancestors.[2] Seneca ridiculed the marriage of the Roman gods, citing as examples the marriages of Mars and Bellona, of Vulcan and Venus, of Neptune and Salacia, and adding sarcastically that some of the goddesses were spinsters or widows, such as Populonia, Fulgora, and Rumina, whose faded charms or unamiable character had failed to attract a suitor.[3]

Again, the learned Servius, whose commentary on Virgil is a gold mine of Roman religious lore, informs us that the pontiffs celebrated the marriage of the infernal deity Orcus with very great solemnity ;[4] and for this statement he would seem to have had the authority of the pontifical books themselves, for he refers to them in the same connexion only a few lines before. As it is in the highest degree unlikely that the pontiffs would solemnize any foreign rites, we may safely assume that the marriage of Orcus was not borrowed from Greek mythology, but was a genuine old Roman ceremony, and this is all the more probable because Servius, our authority for the custom, has recorded some curious and obviously ancient taboos which were observed at the marriage and in the ritual of Ceres, the goddess who seems to have been joined in wedlock to Orcus. One of these taboos forbade the use of wine, the other forbade persons to name their father or daughter.[5]

The marriage of Orcus.

[1] Varro, *De lingua Latina*, v. 67, "*Quod Jovis Juno conjux et is caelum.*"
[2] Augustine, *De civitate Dei*, iv. 32, "*Dicit etiam [scil. Varro] de generationibus deorum magis ad poetas quam ad physicos fuisse populos inclinatos, et ideo et sexum et generationes deorum majores suos, id est veteres credidisse Romanos et eorum constituisse conjugia.*"
[3] Seneca, quoted by Augustine, *De civitate Dei*, vi. 10, " *Quid quod et matrimonia, inquit, deorum jungimus, et ne pie quidem, fratrum ac sororum ? Bellonam Marti conlocamus, Vulcano Venerem, Neptuno Salaciam. Quosdam tamen caelibes relinquimus, quasi condicio defecerit, praesertim cum quaedam viduae sint, ut Populonia vel Fulgora et diva Rumina ; quibus non miror petitorem defuisse.*" In this passage the marriage of Venus to Vulcan is probably Greek ; all the rest is pure Roman.

[4] Servius, on Virgil, *Georg.* i. 344, "*Aliud est sacrum, aliud nuptias Cereri celebrare, in quibus re vera vinum adhiberi nefas fuerat, quae Orci nuptiae dicebantur, quas praesentia sua pontifices ingenti solemnitate celebrabant.*"
[5] Servius, on Virgil, *Georg.* i. 344, and on *Aen.* iv. 58. As to the prohibition of wine, compare Macrobius, *Saturn.* iii. 11. There seems to be no doubt that Orcus was a genuine old Italian god of death and the dead. See the evidence collected by R. Peter, *s.v.* "Orcus," in W. H. Roscher's *Lexikon der griech. und röm. Mythologie*, iii. 940 *sqq.*, who says that " Orcus was obviously one of those old Roman gods who occupied the thoughts of the people in the most lively manner." On the other hand, Prof. G. Wissowa supposes that Orcus is merely a borrowed form of the Greek Horkos (*Religion und Kultus der Römer*,[2] p. 310). But Horkos

Evidence
of Aulus
Gellius as
to the
marriage
of the
Roman
gods.

Further, the learned Roman antiquary Aulus Gellius quotes
from " the books of the priests of the Roman people " (the highest
possible authority on the subject) and from " many ancient speeches "
a list of old Roman deities, in which there seem to be at least five
pairs of males and females.[1] More than that he proves conclusively
by quotations from Plautus, the annalist Cn. Gellius, and Licinius
Imbrex that these old writers certainly regarded one at least of the
pairs (Mars and Nerio) as husband and wife ; [2] and we have good
ancient evidence for viewing in the same light three others of the
pairs.   Thus the old annalist and antiquarian L. Cincius Alimentus,
who fought against Hannibal and was captured by him, affirmed in
his work on the Roman calendar that Maia was the wife of Vulcan ;[3]
and as there was a Flamen of Vulcan, who sacrificed to Maia on
May Day,[4] it is reasonable to suppose that he was assisted in the
ceremony by a Flaminica, his wife, just as on my hypothesis the
Flamen Dialis was assisted by his wife the Flaminica.   Another old
Roman historian, L. Calpurnius Piso, who wrote in the second
century B.C., said that the name of Vulcan's wife was not Maia but

---

was not a god of death and the dead ;
he was simply a personified oath (ὅρκος ;
see Hesiod, *Works and Days*, 804
Ὅρκον γεινόμενον, τὸν Ἔρις τέκε πῆμ'
ἐπιόρκοις), an abstract idea which
makes no figure in Greek mythology
and religion.   That such a rare and
thin Greek abstraction should through
a gross misunderstanding be trans-
formed into a highly popular Roman
god of death, who not only passed
muster with the people but was admitted by the pontiffs themselves to
the national pantheon and honoured
by them with a solemn ritual, is in the
last degree improbable.
    [1] Aulus Gellius, xiii. 23 (22), 1 *sq.*,
"*Conprecationes deum inmortalium,
quae ritu Romano fiunt, expositae sunt
in libris sacerdotum populi Romani et
in plerisque antiquis orationibus.   In
his scribtum est: Luam Saturni,
Salaciam Neptuni, Horam Quirini,
Virites Quirini, Maiam Volcani,
Heriem Junonis, Moles Martis Nerie-
nemque Martis.*" As to this list see
Mr. W. Warde Fowler, *Roman Festivals of the Period of the Republic*
(London, 1899), pp. 60-62 ; *id.*, *The
Religious Experience of the Roman
People* (London, 1911), pp. 150 *sqq.*,
481 *sqq.*   He holds (p. 485) that the
feminine names Salacia, etc., do not

designate goddesses, the wives of the
gods, but that they " indicate functions
or attributes of the male deity to whom
they are attached."
    [2] Aulus Gellius, xiii. 23 (22), 11-
16.
    [3] Macrobius, *Saturn.* i. 12. 18,
"*Cingius mensem [Maium] nominatum
putat a Maia, quam Vulcani dicit
uxorem, argumentoque utitur quod
flamen Vulcanalis Kalendis Maiis
huic deae rem divinam facit: sed Piso
uxorem Vulcani Majestam, non Maiam,
dicit vocari.*"   The work of Cincius
(Cingius) is mentioned by Macrobius
in the same chapter (§ 12, " *Cingius
in eo libro quem de fastis reliquit*").
As to the life and writings of this old
annalist and antiquary see M. Schanz,
Geschichte der römischen Litteratur,[2]
i. (Munich, 1898), p. 128 ; G.
Wissowa, Münzer, and Cichorius, *s.v.*
" Cincius," in Pauly-Wissowa's *Real-
encyclopädie der classischen Altertumswissenschaft*, iii. 2555 *sqq.*   All these
writers distinguish the old annalist
from the antiquary, whom they take to
have been a later writer of the same
name.   But the distinction appears to
be purely arbitrary and destitute of any
ancient authority.
    [4] Macrobius, *Saturn.* i. 12. 18.
See the preceding note.

Majestas.[1] In saying so he may have intended to correct what he believed to be a mistake of his predecessor L. Cincius. Again, that Salacia was the wife of Neptune is perhaps implied by Varro,[2] and is positively affirmed by Seneca, Augustine, and Servius.[3] Again, Ennius appears to have regarded Hora as the wife of Quirinus, for in the first book of his Annals he declared his devotion to that divine pair.[4] In fact, of the five pairs of male and female deities cited by Aulus Gellius from the priestly books and ancient speeches the only one as to which we have not independent evidence that it consisted of a husband and wife is Saturn and Lua ; and in regard to Lua we know that she was spoken of as a mother,[5] which renders it not improbable that she was also a wife. However, according to some very respectable authorities the wife of Saturn was not Lua, but Ops,[6] so that we have two independent lines of proof that Saturn was supposed to be married.

Lastly, the epithets "father" and "mother" which the Romans bestowed on many of their deities[7] are most naturally understood

[1] Macrobius, *Saturn.* i. 12. 18. See the passage cited above, p. 232, note[3].

[2] Varro, *De lingua Latina,* v. 72, "*Salacia Neptuni a salo.*" This was probably one of the cases which Varro had in his mind when he stated that the ancient Roman gods were married.

[3] Augustine, *De civitate Dei,* vii. 22, "*Jam utique habebat Salaciam Neptunus uxorem*"; Servius, on Virgil, *Aen.* x. 76, "*Sane hanc Veniliam quidam Salaciam accipiunt, Neptuni uxorem.*" As for Seneca's evidence see above, p. 231, note[3].

[4] Nonius Marcellus, *De compendiosa doctrina,* p. 125, ed. L. Quicherat (Paris, 1872), "*Hora juventutis dea. Ennius Annali[um] lib. i. [Teque,] Quirine pater, veneror, Horamque Quirini.*"

[5] Livy, viii. 1. 6, xlv. 33. 2.

[6] Festus, p. 186, ed. C. O. Müller, "*Opima spolia dicuntur originem quidem trahentia ab Ope Saturni uxore*"; *id.,* p. 187, "*Opis dicta est conjux Saturni*"; Macrobius, *Saturnal.* i. 10. 19, "*Hanc autem deam Opem Saturni conjugem crediderunt, et ideo hoc mense Saturnalia itemque Opalia celebrari, quod Saturnus ejusque uxor tam frugum quam fructuum repertores esse creduntur.*" Varro couples Saturn and Ops together (*De lingua Latina,* v. 57, "*Principes in Latio Saturnus et Ops*"; compare *id.,* v. 64), but

without expressly affirming them to be husband and wife. Professor G. Wissowa, however, argues that the male partner (he would not say husband) of Ops was not Saturn but Consus. See G. Wissowa, "*De feriis anni Romanorum vetustissimis observata selectae,*" reprinted in his *Gesammelte Abhandlungen zur römischen Religions- und Stadtgeschichte* (Munich, 1904), pp. 156 *sqq.* His view is accepted by Mr. W. Warde Fowler (*Roman Festivals of the Period of the Republic,* p. 212 ; *The Religious Experience of the Roman People,* p. 482).

[7] Lactantius, *Divin. Instit.* iv. 3, "*Itaque et Jupiter a precantibus pater vocatur, et Saturnus, et Janus, et Liber, et ceteri deinceps, quod Lucilius in deorum consilio irridet :*

Ut nemo sit nostrum, quin aut pater optimus divum
Ut Neptunus pater, Liber, Saturnus pater, Mars,
Janus, Quirinus pater nomen dicatur ad unum."

Compare Aulus Gellius, v. 12. 5 ; Servius, on Virgil, *Georg.* ii. 4. Roman goddesses who received the title of Mother were Vesta, Earth, Ops, Matuta, and Lua. As to Mother Vesta see *The Magic Art and the Evolution of Kings,* ii. 229 ; as to Mother Earth see H. Dessau, *Inscriptiones*

to imply paternity and maternity; and if the implication is admitted, the inference appears to be inevitable that these divine beings were supposed to exercise sexual functions, whether in lawful marriage or in unlawful concubinage. As to Jupiter in particular his paternity is positively attested by Latin inscriptions, one of them very old, which describe Fortuna Primigenia, the great goddess of Praeneste, as his daughter.[1] Again, the rustic deity Faunus, one of the oldest and most popular gods of Italy,[2] was represented by tradition in the character of a husband and a father; one of the epithets applied to him expressed in a coarse way his generative powers.[3] Fauna or the Good Goddess (*Bona Dea*), another of the oldest native Italian deities, was variously called his wife or his daughter, and he is said to have assumed the form of a snake in order to cohabit with her.[4] Again, the most famous of all Roman myths represented the founder

---

Latinae Selectae, Nos. 3950-3955, 3960; as to Mother Ops see Varro, *De lingua Latina*, v. 64; as to Mother Matuta see L. Preller, *Römische Mythologie*,[3] i. 322 *sqq.*; G. Wissowa, *Religion und Kultus der Römer*,[2] pp. 110 *sqq.*; *id.*, *s.v.* "Mater Matuta," in W. H. Roscher's *Lexikon der griech. und röm. Mythologie*, ii. 2462 *sqq.* I cite these passages only to prove that the Romans commonly applied the titles "father" and "mother" to their deities. The inference that these titles implied paternity or maternity is my own, but in the text I have given some reasons for thinking that the Romans themselves accepted the implication. Mr. W. Warde Fowler, on the other hand, prefers to suppose that the titles were employed in a merely figurative sense to "imply the dependence of the human citizen upon his divine protector"; but he admits that what exactly the Romans understood by *pater* and *mater* applied to deities is not easy to determine (*The Religious Experience of the Roman People*, pp. 155-157). He makes at the same time the important observation that the Romans never, so far as he is aware, applied the terms Father and Mother to foreign gods, but "always to *di indigetes*, those on whom the original Roman stock looked as their fellow-citizens and guardians." The limitation is significant and seems more naturally explicable on my hypothesis

than on that of my learned friend.

[1] See *Corpus Inscriptionum Latinarum*, Nos. 2862, 2863; H. Dessau, *Inscriptiones Latinae Selectae*, Nos. 3684, 3685; R. Peter, *s.v.* "Fortuna," in W. H. Roscher's *Lexikon der griechischen und römischen Mythologie*, i. 1542; G. Wissowa, *Religion und Kultus der Römer*,[2] p. 259. I have to thank my learned and candid friend Mr. W. Warde Fowler for referring me to this good evidence of Jupiter's paternal character.

[2] L. Preller, *Römische Mythologie*[3] (Berlin, 1881-1883), i. 379.

[3] The epithet *Inuus* applied to Faunus was so understood by the ancients, and this suffices to prove the conception they had of the god's virility, whether the etymology was right or wrong. See Servius, on Virgil, *Aen.* vi. 775, "*Dicitur autem Inuus ab ineundo passim cum omnibus animalibus.*" As to the title see G. Wissowa, *Religion und Kultus der Römer*,[2] p. 211, who, however, rejects the ancient etymology and the identification of Inuus with Faunus.

[4] Macrobius, *Saturn.* i. 12. 21-24; Lactantius, *Divin. Instit.* i. 22; Servius, on Virgil, *Aen.* viii. 314; Plutarch, *Caesar*, 9; *id.*, *Quaest. Roman.* 20. According to Varro, the goddess was the daughter of Faunus (Macrobius, *Saturn.* i. 12. 27); according to Sextus Clodius she was his wife (Lactantius, *l.c.*; compare Arnobius, *Adversus nationes*, v. 18).

of Rome himself, Romulus and his twin brother Remus, as begotten by the god Mars on a Vestal Virgin;[1] and every Roman who accepted the tradition thereby acknowledged the fatherhood of the god in the physical, not in a figurative, sense of the word. If the story of the birth of Romulus and Remus should be dismissed as a late product of the mythical fancy working under Greek influence, the same objection can hardly be urged against the story of the birth of another Roman king, Servius Tullius, who is said to have been a son of the fire-god and a slave woman; his mother conceived him beside the royal hearth, where she was impregnated by a flame that shot out from the fire in the shape of the male organ of generation.[2] It would scarcely be possible to express the physical fatherhood of the fire-god in more unambiguous terms. Now a precisely similar story was told of the birth of Romulus himself;[3] and we may suspect that this was an older form of the story than the legend which fathered the twins on Mars. Similarly, Caeculus, the founder of Praeneste, passed for a son of the fire-god Vulcan. It was said that his mother was impregnated by a spark which leaped from the fire and struck her as she sat by the hearth. In later life, when Caeculus boasted of his divine parentage to a crowd, and they refused to believe him, he prayed to his father to give the unbelievers a sign, and straightway a lambent flame surrounded the whole multitude. The proof was conclusive, and henceforth Caeculus passed for a true son of the fire-god.[4] Such tales of kings or heroes begotten by the fire-god on mortal women appear to be genuine old Italian myths, which may well go back far beyond the foundation of Rome to the common fountain of Aryan mythology; for the marriage customs observed by various branches of the Aryan family point clearly to a belief in the power of fire to impregnate women.[5]

On the whole, if we follow the authority of the ancients themselves, we seem bound to conclude that the Roman gods, like those of many other early peoples, were believed to be married and to beget children. It is true that, compared with the full-blooded gods of Greece, the deities of Rome appear to us shadowy creatures, pale abstractions garbed in little that can vie with the gorgeous pall of myth and story which Grecian fancy threw around its divine creations. Yet the few specimens of Roman mythology which have survived the wreck of antiquity[6]

We must conclude that the Roman gods were thought to be married and to beget children.

---

[1] Livy, i. 4. 2; Plutarch, *Romulus*, 4; Dionysius Halicarnasensis, *Antiquit.· Roman.* i. 77.

[2] See *The Magic Art and the Evolution of Kings*, ii. 195 *sq.*

[3] Plutarch, *Romulus*, 2. Plutarch's authority was Promathion in his history of Italy. See *The Magic Art and the Evolution of Kings*, ii. 196.

[4] Servius, on Virgil, *Aen.* vii. 678.

[5] *The Magic Art and the Evolution of Kings*, ii. 230 *sq.*

[6] Such, for example, as the loves of Vertumnus for Pomona (Ovid, *Metam.* xiv. 623 *sqq.*), of Jupiter for Juturna (Ovid, *Fasti*, ii. 585 *sqq.*), and of Janus for Carna (Ovid, *Fasti*, vi. 101 *sqq.*) and for Camasene (Servius, on

justify us in believing that they are but fragments of far more copious traditions which have perished.   At all events the comparative aridity and barrenness of the Roman religious imagination is no reason for setting aside the positive testimony of learned Roman writers as to a point of fundamental importance in their own religion about which they could hardly be mistaken.   It should never be forgotten that on this subject the ancients had access to many sources of information which are no longer open to us, and for a modern scholar to reject their evidence in favour of a personal impression derived from a necessarily imperfect knowledge of the facts seems scarcely consistent with sound principles of history and criticism.[1]

§ 3. *Children of Living Parents in Ritual*

Rule of Greek and Roman ritual that certain offices could only be held by boys whose parents were both alive.

But Dr. Farnell adduces another argument in support of his view that it was the pollution of death which obliged the widowed Flamen Dialis to resign the priesthood.   He points to what he considers the analogy of the rule of Greek ritual which required that certain sacred offices should be discharged only by a boy whose parents were both alive.[2]   This rule he would explain in like manner by supposing that the death of one or both of his parents would render a boy ceremonially impure and therefore unfit to perform religious functions.   Dr. Farnell might have apparently strengthened his case by observing that the Flamen Dialis and the Flaminica Dialis were themselves assisted in their office, the one by a boy, the other by a girl, both of whose parents must be alive.[3]   At first sight this fits in

---

Virgil, *Aen.* viii. 330).   The water-nymph Juturna beloved by Jupiter is said to have been the daughter of the river Vulturnus, the wife of Janus, and the mother of Fontus (Arnobius, *Adversus nationes*, iii. 29).   Janus in particular would seem to have been the theme of many myths, and his claim to be a genuine Italian god has never been disputed.

[1] The marriage of the Roman gods has been denied by E. Aust (*Die Religion der Römer*, Münster i. W. 1899, pp. 19 *sq.*) and Professor G. Wissowa (*Religion und Kultus der Römer*,[2] pp. 26 *sq.*), as well as by Mr. W. Warde Fowler.   On the other hand, the evidence for it has been clearly and concisely stated by L. Preller, *Römische Mythologie*,[3] i. 55-57.   It is with sincere diffidence that I venture to differ on a point of Roman religion from the eminent scholars I have named.   But without for a moment

pitting my superficial acquaintance with Roman religion against their deep learning, I cannot but think that the single positive testimony of Varro on a matter about which he could scarcely be ignorant ought to outweigh the opinion of any modern scholar, however learned and able.

[2] *The Hibbert Journal*, April 1907, p. 689.   Such a boy was called a παῖς ἀμφιθαλής, "a boy blooming on both sides," the metaphor being drawn from a tree which sends out branches on both sides.   See Plato, *Laws*, xi. 8, p. 927 D ; Julius Pollux, iii. 25 ; Hesychius and Suidas, *s.v.* ἀμφιθαλής.

[3] Festus, p. 93, ed. C. O. Müller, *s.vv.* " Flaminius " and " Flaminia."   That certain Roman rites had to be performed by the children of living parents is mentioned in general terms by Dionysius of Halicarnassus (*Antiquit. Rom.* ii. 22).

perfectly with his theory: the Flamen, the Flaminica, and their youthful ministers were all rendered incapable of performing their sacred duties by the taint or corruption of death.

But a closer scrutiny of the argument reveals a flaw. It proves too much. For observe that in these Greek and Roman offices held by boys and girls the disqualification caused by the death of a parent is necessarily lifelong, since the bereavement is irreparable. Accordingly, if Dr. Farnell's theory is right, the ceremonial pollution which is the cause of the disqualification must also be lifelong; in other words, every orphan is ceremoniously unclean for life and thereby excluded for ever from the discharge of sacred duties. So sweeping a rule would at a stroke exclude a large, if not the larger, part of the population of any country from the offices of religion, and lay them permanently under all those burdensome restrictions which the pollution of death entails among many nations; for obviously a large, if not the larger, part of the population of any country at any time has lost one or both of its parents by death. No people, so far as I know, has ever carried the theory of the ceremonial pollution of death to this extremity in practice. And even if it were supposed that the taint wore off or evaporated with time from common folk so as to let them go about their common duties in everyday life, would it not still cleave to priests? If it incapacitated the Flamen's minister, would it not incapacitate the Flamen himself? In other words, would not the Flamen Dialis be obliged to vacate office on the death of his father or mother? There is no hint in ancient writers that he had to do so. And while it is generally unsafe to argue from the silence of our authorities, I think that we may do so in this case without being rash; for Plutarch not only mentions but discusses the rule which obliged the Flamen Dialis to resign office on the death of his wife,[1] and if he had known of a parallel rule which compelled him to retire on the death of a parent, he would surely have mentioned it. But if the ceremonial pollution which would certainly be caused by the death of a parent did not compel the Flamen Dialis to vacate office, we may safely conclude that neither did the similar pollution caused by the death of his wife. Thus the argument adduced by Dr. Farnell in favour of his view proves on analysis to tell strongly against it.

But if the rule which excluded orphans from certain sacred offices cannot with any probability be explained on the theory of their ceremonial pollution, it may be worth while to inquire whether another and better explanation of the rule cannot be found. For that purpose I shall collect all the cases of it known to me. The collection is doubtless far from complete: I only offer it as a starting-point for research.

But the rule which excludes orphans from certain sacred offices cannot be based on a theory that they are ceremonially unclean through the death of their parents.

Examples of the exclusion of orphans from sacred offices.

---

[1] Plutarch, *Quaestiones Romanae*, 50.

Boys and girls of living parents employed in Greek rites at the vintage, harvest-home, and sowing.

At the time of the vintage, which in Greece falls in October, Athenian boys chosen from every tribe assembled at the sanctuary of Dionysus, the god of the vine. There, branches of vines laden with ripe grapes were given to them, and holding them in their hands they raced to the sanctuary of Athena Sciras. The winner received and drained a cup containing a mixture of olive-oil, wine, honey, cheese, and barley-groats. It was necessary that both the parents of each of these boy-runners should be alive.[1] At the same festival, and perhaps on the same day, an Athenian boy, whose parents must both be alive, carried in procession a branch of olive wreathed with white and purple wool and decked with fruits of many kinds, while a chorus sang that the branch bore figs, fat loaves, honey, oil, and wine. Thus they went in procession to a temple of Apollo, at the door of which the boy deposited the holy bough. The ceremony is said to have been instituted by the Athenians in obedience to an oracle for the purpose of supplicating the help of the god in a season of dearth.[2] Similar boughs similarly laden with fruits and loaves were hung up on the doors of every Athenian house and allowed to remain there a year, at the end of which they were replaced by fresh ones. While the branch was being fastened to the door, a boy whose parents were both alive recited the same verses about the branch bearing figs, fat loaves, honey, oil, and wine. This custom also is said to have been instituted for the sake of putting an end to a dearth.[3] The people of Magnesia on the Maeander vowed a bull every year to Zeus, the Saviour of the City, in the month of Cronion, at the beginning of sowing, and after maintaining the animal at the public expense throughout the winter they sacrificed it, apparently at harvest-time, in the following summer. Nine boys and nine girls, whose fathers and mothers were all living, took part in the religious services of the consecration and the sacrifice of the bull. At the consecration public prayers were offered for the safety of the city and the land, for the safety of the citizens and their wives and children, for the safety of all that dwelt in the city and the land, for peace and wealth and abundance of corn and all other fruits, and for the cattle. A herald led the prayers, and the priest and priestess, the boys and girls, the high officers and magistrates, all

[1] Proclus, in Photius, *Bibliotheca*, p. 322 A, ed. I. Bekker (Berlin, 1824); Athenaeus, xi. 92, pp. 495 *sq.*; Scholiast on Nicander, *Alexipharmaca*, 109. Only the last of these writers mentions that the boys had to be ἀμφιθαλεῖς. As to this and the following custom see A. Mommsen, *Feste der Stadt Athen im Altertum* (Leipsic, 1898), pp. 278 *sqq.*; W. Mannhardt, *Antike Wald-* *und Feldkulte*, pp. 214 *sqq.*

[2] Eustathius, on Homer, *Iliad*, xxii. 495, p. 1283; *Etymologicum Magnum*, p. 303. 18 *sqq.*, *s.v.* Εἰρεσιώνη; Plutarch, *Theseus*, 22. According to a scholiast on Aristophanes (*Plutus*, 1054) the branch might be either of olive or laurel.

[3] Scholiast on Aristophanes, *Plutus*, 1054.

joined in these solemn petitions for the welfare of their country.[1] Among the Karo-Bataks of Central Sumatra the threshing of the rice is the occasion of various ceremonies, and in these a prominent part is played by a girl, whose father and mother must be both alive. Her special duty is to take care of the sheaf of rice in which the soul of the rice is believed to reside. This sheaf usually consists of the first rice cut and bound in the field; it is treated exactly like a person.[2]

The rites thus far described, in which boys and girls of living parents took part, were clearly ceremonies intended specially to ensure the fertility of the soil. This is indicated not merely by the nature of the rites and of the prayers or verses which accompanied them, but also by the seasons at which they were observed; for these were the vintage, the harvest-home, and the beginning of sowing. We may therefore compare a custom practised by the Roman Brethren of the Ploughed Fields (*Fratres Arvales*), a college of priests whose business it was to perform the rites deemed necessary for the growth of the corn. As a badge of office they wore wreaths of corn-ears, and paid their devotions to an antique goddess of fertility, the Dea Dia. Her home was in a grove of ancient evergreen oaks and laurels out in the Campagna, five miles from Rome. Hither every year in the month of May, when the fields were ripe or ripening to the sickle, reaped ears of the new corn were brought and hallowed by the Brethren with quaint rites, that a blessing might rest on the coming harvest. The first or preliminary consecration of the ears, however, took place, not in the grove, but in the house of the Master of the Brethren at Rome. Here the Brethren were waited upon by four free-born boys, the children of living fathers and mothers. While the Brethren reclined on couches, the boys were allowed to sit on chairs and partake of the feast, and when it was over they carried the rest of the now hallowed corn and laid it on the altar.[3]

(margin:) Boys of living parents employed in the rites of the Arval Brothers.

---

[1] O. Kern, *Die Inschriften von Magnesia am Maeander* (Berlin, 1900), No. 98; G. Dittenberger, *Sylloge Inscriptionum Graecarum*,[2] vol. ii. pp. 246 *sqq.*, No. 553. This inscription has been well expounded by Prof. M. P. Nilsson (*Griechische Feste*, Leipsic, 1906, pp. 23-27). I follow him and Dittenberger in regarding the month of Artemision, when the bull was sacrificed, as the harvest month corresponding to the Attic Thargelion.

[2] J. H. Neumann, "Iets over den landbouw bij de Karo-Bataks," *Mededeelingen van wege het Nederlandsche Zendelinggenootschap*, xlvi. (1902) p. 381.

[3] G. Henzen, *Acta Fratrum Arvalium* (Berlin, 1874), pp. vi. *sq.*, cix. cx. cxix. cliii. clix. clxxxvii. 12, 13, 15. As to the evergreen oaks and laurels of the grove, see *ib.*, pp. 137, 138; as to the wreaths of corn-ears, see *ib.*, pp. 26, 28; Aulus Gellius, vii. 7. 8. That the rites performed by the Arval Brothers were intended to make the fields bear corn is expressly stated by Varro (*De lingua Latina*, v. 85, "*Fratres Arvales dicti sunt, qui sacra publica faciunt propterea ut fruges ferant arva*"). On the Arval Brothers and their rites see also L. Preller, *Römische Mythologie*,[3] ii. 29 *sqq.*; J. Marquardt,

In fertility rites the employment of such children is intelligible on the principle of sympathetic magic.

Sons of living parents employed to cut the olive-wreath at Olympia and the laurel-wreath at Tempe.

In these and all other rites intended to ensure the fertility of the ground, of cattle, or of human beings, the employment of children of living parents seems to be intelligible on the principle of sympathetic magic; for such children might be deemed fuller of life than orphans, either because they "flourished on both sides," as the Greeks put it, or because the very survival of their parents might be taken as a proof that the stock of which the children came was vigorous and therefore able to impart of its superabundant energy to others.

But the rites in which the children of living parents are required to officiate do not always aim at promoting the growth of the crops. At Olympia the olive-branches which formed the victors' crowns had to be cut from a sacred tree with a golden sickle by a lad whose father and mother must be both alive.[1] The tree was a wild olive growing within the holy precinct, at the west end of the temple of Zeus. It bore the name of the Olive of the Fair Crown, and near it was an altar to the Nymphs of the Fair Crowns.[2] At Delphi every eighth year a sacred drama or miracle-play was acted which drew crowds of spectators from all parts of Greece. It set forth the slaying of the Dragon by Apollo. The principal part was sustained by a lad, the son of living parents, who seems to have personated the god himself. In an open space the likeness of a lordly palace, erected for the occasion, represented the Dragon's den. It was attacked and burned by the lad, aided by women who carried blazing torches. When the Dragon had received his deadly wound, the lad, still acting the part of the god, fled far away to be purged of the guilt of blood in the beautiful Vale of Tempe, where the Peneus flows in a deep wooded gorge between the snowy peaks of Olympus and Ossa, its smooth and silent tide shadowed by overhanging trees and tall white cliffs. In places these great crags rise abruptly from the stream and approach each other so near that only a narrow strip of sky is visible overhead; but where they recede a little, the meadows at their foot are verdant with evergreen shrubs, among which Apollo's own laurel may still be seen. In antiquity the god himself, stained with the Dragon's blood, is said to have come, a haggard footsore wayfarer, to this wild secluded glen and there plucked branches from one of the laurels that grew in its green thickets beside the rippling river. Some of them he used to twine a wreath for his brows, one of them he carried in his hand, doubtless in order that, guarded by the sacred plant, he might escape the hobgoblins which

---

Römische Staatsverwaltung, iii.[2] (Leipsic, 1885) pp. 447-462 ; G. Wissowa, *Religion und Kultus der Römer*,[2] pp. 561 *sqq.* ; J. B. Carter, *s.v.* "Arval Brothers," in J. Hastings's *Encyclo-paedia of Religion and Ethics*, ii. (Edinburgh, 1909) pp. 7 *sqq.*

[1] Scholiast on Pindar, *Olymp.* iii. 60.

[2] Pausanias, v. 15. 3.

dogged his steps. So the boy, his human representative, did the same, and brought back to Delphi wreaths of laurel from the same tree to be awarded to the victors in the Pythian games. Hence the whole festival of the Slaying of the Dragon at Delphi went by the name of the Festival of Crowning.[1] From this it appears that at Delphi as well as at Olympia the boughs which were used to crown the victors had to be cut from a sacred tree by a boy whose parents must be both alive.

At Thebes a festival called the Laurel-bearing was held once in every eight years, when branches of laurel were carried in procession to the temple of Apollo. The principal part in the procession was taken by a boy who held a laurel bough and bore the title of the Laurel-bearer : he seems to have personated the god himself. His hair hung down on his shoulders, and he wore a golden crown, a bright-coloured robe, and shoes of a special shape : both his parents must be alive.[2] We may suppose that the golden crown which he wore was fashioned in the shape of laurel leaves and replaced a wreath of real laurel. Thus the boy with the laurel wreath on his head and the laurel bough in his hand would resemble the traditional equipment of Apollo when he purified himself for the slaughter of the dragon. We may conjecture that at Thebes the Laurel-bearer originally personated not Apollo but the local hero Cadmus, who slew the dragon and had like Apollo to purify himself for the slaughter. The conjecture is confirmed by vase-paintings which represent Cadmus crowned with laurel preparing to attack the dragon or actually in combat with the monster, while goddesses bend over him holding out wreaths of laurel as the meed of victory.[3] On this hypothesis the octennial Delphic Festival of Crowning and the octennial Theban Festival of Laurel-bearing were closely akin : in both the prominent part played by the laurel was purificatory or expiatory.[4] Thus at Olympia, Delphi, and Thebes a boy whose

Sons of living parents acted as Laurel-bearers at Thebes.

---

[1] Plutarch, *Quaestiones Graecae*, 12; *id.*, *De defectu oraculorum*, 15; Aelian, *Varia Historia*, iii. 1 ; Strabo, ix. 3. 12, p. 422. In a note on Pausanias (ii. 7. 7, vol. iii. pp. 53 *sqq.*) I have described the festival more fully and adduced savage parallels. As to the Vale of Tempe see W. M. Leake, *Travels in Northern Greece* (London, 1835), iii. 390 *sqq.* The rhetoric of Livy (xliv. 6. 8) has lashed the smooth and silent current of the Peneus into a roaring torrent.

[2] Proclus, in Photius, *Bibliotheca*, ed. I. Bekker, p. 321.

[3] O. Crusius, *s.v.* "Kadmos," in W. H. Roscher's *Lexikon der griech. und röm. Mythologie*, ii. 830, 838, 839.

On an Etruscan mirror the scene of Cadmus's combat with the dragon is surrounded with a wreath of laurel (O. Crusius, *op. cit.* ii. 862). My learned friend Mr. A. B. Cook was the first to call attention to these vase-paintings in confirmation of my view that the Festival of the Laurel-bearing celebrated the destruction of the dragon by Cadmus. See A. B. Cook, "The European Sky-God," *Folk-lore*, xv. (1904) p. 411, note [224]; and my note on Pausanias, ix. 10. 4 (vol. v. pp. 41 *sqq.*).

[4] I have examined both festivals more closely in a former part of this work (*The Dying God*, pp. 78 *sqq.*), and have shown grounds for holding

parents were both alive was entrusted with the duty of cutting or wearing a sacred wreath at a great festival which recurred at intervals of several years.[1]

If wreaths were originally amulets, we could understand why children of living parents were chosen to cut and wear them.

Why a boy of living parents should be chosen for such an office is not at first sight clear ; the reason might be more obvious if we understood the ideas in which the custom of wearing wreaths and crowns had its origin. Probably in many cases wreaths and crowns were amulets before they were ornaments ; in other words, their first intention may have been not so much to adorn the head as to protect it from harm by surrounding it with a plant, a metal, or any other thing which was supposed to possess the magical virtue of banning baleful influences. Thus the Arabs of Moab will put a circlet of copper on the head of a man who is suffering from headache, for they believe that this will banish the pain ; and if the pain is in an arm or a leg, they will treat the ailing limb in like manner. They think that red beads hung before the eyes of children who are afflicted with ophthalmia will rid them of the malady, and that a red ribbon tied to the foot will prevent it from stumbling on a stony path.[2] Again, the Melanesians of the Gazelle Peninsula in New Britain often deck their dusky bodies with

that the old octennial cycle in Greece, based on an attempt to harmonize solar and lunar time, gave rise to an octennial festival at which the mythical marriage of the sun and moon was celebrated by the dramatic marriage of human actors, who appear sometimes to have been the king and queen. In the Laurel-bearing at Thebes a clear reference to the astronomical character of the festival is contained in the emblems of the sun, moon, stars, and days of the year which were carried in procession (Proclus, *l.c.*) ; and another reference to it may be detected in the legendary marriage of Cadmus and Harmonia. Dr. L. R. Farnell supposes that the festival of the Laurel-bearing " belongs to the maypole processions, universal in the peasant-religion of Europe, of which the object is to quicken the vitalizing powers of the year in the middle of spring or at the beginning of summer " (*The Cults of the Greek States,* iv. 285). But this explanation appears to be inconsistent with the octennial period of the festival.

[1] We may conjecture that the Olympic, like the Delphic and the Theban, festival was at first octennial, though in historical times it was

quadrennial. Certainly it seems to have been based on an octennial cycle. See the Scholiast on Pindar, *Olymp.* iii. 35 (20) ; Aug. Boeckh on Pindar, *Explicationes* (Leipsic, 1821), p. 138 ; L. Ideler, *Handbuch der mathematischen und technischen Chronologie,* i. 366 *sq.*; G. F. Unger, " Zeitrechnung der Griechen und Römer," in Iwan Müller's *Handbuch der klassischen Altertumswissenschaft,* i. (Nördlingen, 1886) pp. 605 *sq.*; K. O. Müller, *Die Dorier*[2] (Breslau, 1844), ii. 483. The Pythian games, which appear to have been at first identical with the Delphic Festival of Crowning, were held originally at intervals of eight instead of four years. See the Scholiast on Pindar, *Pyth.* Argum. p. 298, ed. A. Boeckh (Leipsic, 1819) ; Censorinus, *De die natali,* xviii. 6 ; compare Eustathius on Homer, *Od.* iii. 267, p. 1466. 29. As to the original identity of the Pythian games and the Festival of Crowning see Th. Schreiber, *Apollon Pythoktonos* (Leipsic, 1879), pp. 37 *sq.* ; A. B. Cook, "The European Sky-God," *Folk-lore,* xv. (1904) pp. 404 *sq.*

[2] Antonin Jaussen, *Coutumes des Arabes au pays de Moab* (Paris, 1908), p. 382.

flowers, leaves, and scented herbs not only at festivals but on other occasions which to the European might seem inappropriate for such gay ornaments. But in truth the bright blossoms and verdant foliage are not intended to decorate the wearer but to endow him with certain magical virtues, which are supposed to inhere in the flowers and leaves. Thus one man may be seen strutting about with a wreath of greenery which passes round his neck and droops over his shoulders, back, and breast. He is not a mere dandy, but a lover who hopes that the wreath will work as a charm on a woman's heart. Again, another may be observed with a bunch of the red dracaena leaves knotted round his neck and the long stalk hanging down his back. He is a soldier, and these leaves are supposed to make him invulnerable. But if the lover should fail to win the affections of his swarthy mistress, if the warrior should be wounded in battle, it never occurs to either of them to question the magical virtue of the charm ; they ascribe the failure either to the more potent charm of another magician or to some oversight on their own part.[1] On the theory that wreaths and garlands serve as amulets to protect the wearer against the powers of evil we can understand not only why in antiquity sacred persons such as priests and kings wore crowns, but also why dead bodies, sacrificial victims, and in certain circumstances even inanimate objects such as the implements of sacrifice, the doors of houses, and so forth, were decorated or rather guarded by wreaths.[2] Further, on this hypothesis we may perhaps perceive why children of living parents were specially chosen to cut or wear sacred wreaths. Since such children were apparently supposed to be endowed with a more than common share of vital energy, they might be deemed peculiarly fitted to make or wear amulets which were designed to protect the wearer from injury and death : the current of life which circulated in their own veins overflowed, as it were, and reinforced the magic virtue of the wreath. For the same reason such children would naturally be chosen to personate gods, as they seemingly were at Delphi and Thebes.

At Ephesus, if we may trust the evidence of the Greek romance-writer, Heliodorus, a boy and girl of living parents used to hold for a year the priesthood of Apollo and Artemis respectively. When their

Children of living parents acting as

[1] R. Parkinson, *Dreissig Jahre in der Südsee* (Stuttgart, 1907), pp. 150-152.
[2] On the use of crowns and wreaths in classical antiquity see W. Smith's *Dictionary of Greek and Roman Antiquities*,[3] i. 545 *sqq.*, *s.v.* "Corona" ; E. Saglio, *s.v.* "Corona," in Ch. Daremberg et E. Saglio's *Dictionnaire des Antiquités Grecques et Romaines*, iii. 1520 *sqq.* In time of mourning the ancients laid aside crowns (Athenaeus, xv. 16, p. 675 A) ; and so did the king at Athens when he tried a homicide (Aristotle, *Constitution of Athens*, 57). I mention these cases because they seem to conflict with the theory in the text, in accordance with which crowns might be regarded as amulets to protect the wearer against ghosts and the pollution of blood.

priest and priestess of Apollo and Artemis.

period of office was nearly expired, they led a sacred embassy to Delos, the birthplace of the divine brother and sister, where they superintended the musical and athletic contests and laid down the priesthood.[1] At Rome no girl might be chosen a Vestal Virgin

At Rome the Vestals and the Salii must be the children of parents who were alive at the date of the election.

unless both her father and mother were living;[2] yet there is no evidence or probability that a Vestal vacated office on the death of a parent; indeed she generally held office for life.[3] This alone may suffice to prove that the custom of entrusting certain sacred duties to children of living parents was not based on any notion that orphans as such were ceremonially unclean. Again, the dancing priests of Mars, the Salii, must be sons of living parents;[4] but as in the case of the Vestals this condition probably only applied at the date of their election, for they seem like the Vestals to have held office for life. At all events we read of a lively old gentleman who still skipped and capered about as a dancing priest with an agility which threw the efforts of his younger colleagues into the shade.[5] Again, at the public games in Rome boys of living parents had to escort the images of the gods in their sacred cars, and it was a dire omen if one of them relaxed his hold on the holy cart or let a strap

Children of living parents employed in expiatory rites at Rome.

slip from his fingers.[6] And when the stout Roman heart was shaken by the appalling news that somebody had been struck by lightning, that the sky had somewhere been suddenly overcast, or that a she-mule had been safely delivered of a colt, boys and girls whose fathers and mothers were still alive used to be sought out and employed to help in expiating the terrific prodigy.[7] Again, when the Capitol had been sacked and burned by the disorderly troops of Vitellius, solemn preparations were made to rebuild it. The whole area was enclosed by a cordon of fillets and wreaths. Then soldiers chosen for their auspicious names entered within the barriers holding branches of lucky trees in their hands; and afterwards the Vestal Virgins, aided by boys and girls of living parents, washed the foundations with water drawn from springs and rivers.[8] In this ceremony the choice of such children seems to be based on the same idea as the choice of such water; for as running water is deemed to

[1] Heliodorus, *Aethiopica*, i. 22.

[2] Aulus Gellius, i. 12. 2.

[3] Dionysius Halicarnasensis, *Antiquit. Rom.* ii. 67; Plutarch, *Numa*, 10. We read of a Vestal who held office for fifty-seven years (Tacitus, *Annals*, ii. 86). It is unlikely that the parents of this venerable lady were both alive at the date of her decease.

[4] Dionysius Halicarnasensis, *Antiquit. Rom.* ii. 71.

[5] Macrobius, *Sat.* iii. 14. 14. That the rule as to their parents being both alive applied to the Vestals and Salii

only at the time of their entrance on office is recognized by Marquardt (*Römische Staatsverwaltung*, iii.[2] 228, note[1]).

[6] Cicero, *De haruspicum responso*, 11.

[7] Livy, xxxvii. 3; Macrobius, *Saturn.* i. 6. 13 *sq.*; Vopiscus, *Aurelianus*, 19 (where the words "*patrimis matrimisque pueris carmen indicite*" are omitted from the text by H. Peter).

[8] Tacitus, *Histor.* iv. 53. For the sack and conflagration of the Capitol see *id.* iii. 71-75.

be especially alive,[1] so the vital current might be thought to flow without interruption in the children of living parents but to stagnate in orphans. Hence the children of living parents rather than orphans would naturally be chosen to pour the living water over the foundations, and so to lend something of their own vitality or endurance to a building that was designed to last for ever.

On the same principle we can easily understand why the children of living parents should be especially chosen to perform certain offices at marriage. The motive of such a choice may be a wish to ensure by sympathetic magic the life of the newly wedded pair and of their offspring. Thus at Roman marriages the bride was escorted to her new home by three boys whose parents were all living. Two of the boys held her, and the third carried a torch of buckthorn or hawthorn in front of her,[2] probably for the purpose of averting the powers of evil; for buckthorn or hawthorn was credited with this magical virtue.[3] At marriages in ancient Athens a boy whose parents were both living used to wear a wreath of thorns and acorns and to carry about a winnowing-fan full of loaves, crying, "I have escaped the bad, I have found the better."[4] In modern Greece on the Sunday before a marriage the bridegroom sends to the bride the wedding cake by the hands of a boy, both of whose parents must be living. The messenger takes great care not to stumble or to injure the cake, for to do either would be a very bad omen. He may not enter the bride's house till she has taken the cake from him. For this purpose he lays it down on the threshold of the door, and then both of them, the boy and the bride, rush at it and try to seize the greater part of the cake. And when cattle are being slaughtered for the marriage festivities, the first beast killed for the bride's house must be killed by a youth whose parents are both alive. Further, a son of living parents must solemnly fetch the water with which the bridegroom's head is ceremonially washed by women before marriage. And on the day after the marriage bride and bridegroom go in procession to the well or spring from which they are henceforth to fetch their water. The bride greets the spring, drinks of the water from the hollow of her hand, and throws money and food into it. Then follows a dance, accompanied by a song, round about the spring. Lastly, a lad whose parents are both living draws water from the spring in a special vessel and carries it to the house of the bridal pair without speaking a word : this "unspoken water," as it is called, is regarded

Children of living parents employed at marriage ceremonies in Greece, Italy, Albania, Bulgaria, and Africa.

---

[1] Flowing water in Hebrew is called "living water" (מַיִם חַיִּים).

[2] Festus, *De verborum significatione*, ed. C. O. Müller (Leipsic, 1839), pp. 244, 245, *s.v.* "Patrimi et matrimi pueri."

[3] Ovid, *Fasti*, vi. 129 *sq.*, 165-168.

[4] Zenobius, *Proverb.* iii. 98 ; Plutarch, *Proverb.* i. 16 ; Apostolius, *Proverb.* viii. 16 (*Paroemiographi Graeci*, ed. Leutsch et Schneidewin, i. 82, 323 *sq.*, ii. 429) ; Eustathius, on Homer, *Od.* xii. 357, p. 1726 ; Photius, *Lexicon*, *s.v.* ἔφυγον κακόν.

as peculiarly holy and wholesome. When the young couple return from the spring, they fill their mouths with the "unspoken water" and try to spirt it on each other inside the door of the house.[1] In Albania, when women are baking cakes for a wedding, the first to put hand to the dough must be a maiden whose parents are both alive and who has brothers, the more the better; for only such a girl is deemed lucky. And when the bride has dismounted from her horse at the bridegroom's door, a small boy whose parents are both alive (for only such a boy is thought to bring luck) is passed thrice backwards and forwards under the horse's belly, as if he would girdle the beast.[2] Among the South Slavs of Bulgaria a little child whose father and mother are both alive helps to bake the two bridal cakes, pouring water and salt on the meal and stirring the mixture with a spurtle of a special shape; then a girl lifts the child in her arms, and the little one touches the roof-beam thrice with the spurtle, saying, "Boys and girls." And when the bride's hair is to be dressed for the wedding day, the work of combing and plaiting it must be begun by a child of living parents.[3] Among the Eesa and Gadabursi, two Somali tribes, on the morning after a marriage "the bride's female relations bring presents of milk, and are accompanied by a young male child whose parents are living. The child drinks some of the milk before any one else tastes it; and after him the bridegroom, if his parents are living; but if one or both of his parents are dead, and those of the bride living, she drinks after the child. By doing this they believe that if the newly-married woman bears a child the father will be alive at the time."[4] A slightly different application of the same principle appears in the old Hindoo rule that when a bride reached the house of her husband, she should be made to descend from the chariot by women of good character whose husbands and sons were living, and that afterwards these women should seat the bride on a bull's hide, while her husband recited the verse, "Here ye cows, bring forth calves."[5] Here the ceremony of seating the young wife on a bull's hide seems plainly intended to make her fruitful through the generative virtue of the bull; while the attendance of women, whose husbands and sons are living, is no doubt a device for ensuring, by sympathetic magic, the life both of the bride's husband and of her future off-spring.

[1] C. Wachsmuth, *Das alte Griechen-land im neuen* (Bonn, 1864), pp. 83-85, 86, 87, 100 *sq.*

[2] J. G. von Hahn, *Albanesische Studien* (Jena, 1854), i. 144, 146.

[3] F. S. Krauss, *Sitte und Brauch der Süd-Slaven* (Vienna, 1885), pp. 438, 441.

[4] Captain J. S. King, "Notes on the Folk-lore and some Social Customs of the Western Somali Tribes," *The Folk-lore Journal*, vi. (1888) p. 124. Compare Ph. Paulitschke, *Ethno-graphie Nordost-Afrikas, die materielle Cultur der Danâkil, Galla und Somâl* (Berlin, 1893), p. 200.

[5] *The Grihya-Sûtras*, translated by H. Oldenberg, Part ii. (Oxford, 1892) p. 50 (*The Sacred Books of the East*, vol. xxx.).

In the Somali custom just described the part played by the child of living parents is unambiguous and helps to throw light on the obscurer cases which precede. Such a child is clearly supposed to impart the virtue of longevity to the milk of which it partakes, and so to transmit it to the newly married pair who afterwards drink of the milk. Similarly, we may suppose that in all marriage rites at least, if not in religious rites generally, the employment of children of living parents is intended to diffuse by sympathy the blessings of life and longevity among all who participate in the ceremonies. This intention seems to underlie the use which the Malagasy make of the children of living parents in ritual. Thus, when a child is a week old, it is dressed up in the finest clothes that can be got, and is then carried out of the house by some person whose parents are both still living; afterwards it is brought back to the mother. In the act of being carried out and in, the infant must be twice carefully lifted over the fire, which is placed near the door. If the child is a boy, the axe, knife, and spear of the family, together with any building tools that may be in the house, are taken out of it at the same time. " The implements are perhaps used chiefly as emblems of the occupations in which it is expected the infant will engage when it arrives at maturer years ; and the whole may be regarded as expressing the hopes cherished of his activity, wealth, and enjoyments." [1] On such an occasion the service of a person whose parents are both alive seems naturally calculated to promote the longevity of the infant. For a like reason, probably, the holy water used at the Malagasy ceremony of circumcision is drawn from a pool by a person whose parents are both still living.[2] The same idea may explain a funeral custom observed by the Sihanaka of Madagascar. After a burial the family of the deceased, with their near relatives and dependents, meet in the house from which the corpse was lately removed " to drink rum and to undergo a purifying and preserving baptism called *fàfy rànom-bòahàngy*. Leaves of the lemon or lime tree, and the stalks of two kinds of grass, are gathered and placed in a vessel with water. A person, both of whose parents are living, is chosen to perform the rite, and this 'holy water' is then sprinkled upon the walls of the house and upon all assembled within them, and finally around the house outside." [3] Here a person whose parents are both living appears to be credited with a more than common share of life and longevity ; from which it naturally follows that he is better fitted than any one else to perform a ceremony intended to avert the danger of death from the household.

The notion that a child of living parents is endowed with a

Margin notes: Children of living parents apparently supposed to impart life and longevity.

Margin notes: Child of living parents employed in funeral rites.

[1] Rev. William Ellis, *History of Madagascar* (London, N.D.), i. 151 *sq.*
[2] Rev. W. Ellis, *op. cit.* i. 180.
[3] J. Pearse, " Customs connected with Death and Burial among the Sihanaka," *The Antananarivo Annual and Madagascar Magazine*, vol. ii. (a reprint of the second four numbers, 1881–1884) (Antananarivo, 1896) p. 152.

The use
of children
of living
parents in
ritual may
be ex-
plained by
a notion
that they
are fuller
of life and
therefore
luckier
than
orphans.

higher degree of vitality than an orphan probably explains all the cases of the employment of such a child in ritual, whether the particular rite is designed to ensure the fertility of the ground or the fruitfulness of women, or to avert the danger of death and other calamities. Yet it might be a mistake to suppose that this notion is always clearly apprehended by the persons who practise the customs. In their minds the definite conception of super-abundant and overflowing vitality may easily dissolve into a vague idea that the child of living parents is luckier than other folk. No more than this seems to be at the bottom of the Masai rule that when the warriors wish to select a chief, they must choose "a man whose parents are still living, who owns cattle and has never killed anybody, whose parents are not blind, and who himself has not a discoloured eye."[1] And nothing more is needed to explain the ancient Greek custom which assigned the duty of drawing lots from an urn to a boy under puberty whose father and mother were both in life.[2] At Athens it would appear that registers of these boys were kept, perhaps in order that the lads might discharge, as occasion arose, those offices of religion which required the service of such auspicious youths.[3] The atrocious tyrant Heliogabalus, one of the worst monsters who ever disgraced the human form, caused search to be made throughout Italy for noble and handsome boys whose parents were both alive, and he sacrificed them to his barbarous gods, torturing them first and grabbling among their entrails after-wards for omens. He seems to have thought that such victims would be peculiarly acceptable to the Syrian deities whom he worshipped; so he encouraged the torturers and butchers at their work, and thanked the gods for enabling him to ferret out "their friends."[4]

[1] A. C. Hollis, *The Masai* (Oxford, 1905), p. 299.

[2] Lucian, *Hermotimus*, 57.

[3] A fragmentary list of these youths is preserved in an Athenian inscription of the year 91 or 90 B.C. See Ch. Michel, *Recueil d'Inscriptions* *Grecques*, Supplément, i. (Paris, 1912) p. 104, No. 1544.

[4] Aelius Lampridius, *Antoninus Heliogabalus*, viii. 1 *sq.* The historian thinks that the monster chose these victims merely for the pleasure of rending the hearts of both the parents.

III

A CHARM TO PROTECT A TOWN

THE tradition that a Lydian king tried to make the citadel of Sardes The Bechuanas use the hide of a sacrificial ox at founding a new town. impregnable by carrying round it a lion[1] may perhaps be illustrated by a South African custom. When the Bechuanas are about to found a new town, they observe an elaborate ritual. They choose a bull from the herd, sew up its eyelids with sinew, and then allow the blinded animal to wander at will for four days. On the fifth day they track it down and sacrifice it at sunset on the spot where it happens to be standing. The carcase is then roasted whole and divided among the people. Ritual requires that every particle of the flesh should be consumed on the spot. When the sacrificial meal is over, the medicine-men take the hide and mark it with appropriate medicines, the composition of which is a professional secret. Then with one long spiral cut they convert the whole hide into a single thong. Having done so they cut up the thong into lengths of about two feet and despatch messengers in all directions to peg down one of those strips in each of the paths leading to the new town. "After this," it is said, "if a foreigner approaches the new town to destroy it with his charms, he will find that the town has prepared itself for his coming."[2] Thus it would seem that the pastoral Bechuanas attempt to place a new town under the protection of one of their sacred cattle[3] by distributing pieces of its hide at all points where an enemy could approach it, just as the Lydian king thought to place the citadel of his capital under the protection of the lion-god by carrying the animal round the boundaries.

Further, the Bechuana custom may throw light on a widespread The custom may explain the legend of the foundation of Carthage and similar tales. legend which relates how a wily settler in a new country bought from the natives as much land as could be covered with a hide, and how he then proceeded to cut the hide into thongs and to claim as much land as could be enclosed by the thongs. It was thus,

---

[1] See above, vol. i. p. 184.

[2] Rev. W. C. Willoughby, "Notes on the Totemism of the Becwana," *Journal of the Anthropological Institute*, xxxv. (1905) pp. 303 *sq.*

[3] For more evidence of the sanctity of cattle among the Bechuanas see the Rev. W. C. Willoughby, *op. cit.* pp. 301 *sqq.*

according to the Hottentots, that the first European settlers obtained a footing in South Africa.[1] But the most familiar example of such stories is the tradition that Dido procured the site of Carthage in this fashion, and that the place hence received the name of Byrsa or "hide."[2] Similar tales occur in the legendary history of Saxons and Danes,[3] and they meet us in India, Siberia, Burma, Cambodia, Java, and Bali.[4] The wide diffusion of such stories confirms the conjecture of Jacob Grimm that in them we have a reminiscence of a mode of land measurement which was once actually in use, and of which the designation is still retained in the English *hide.*[5] The Bechuana custom suggests that the mode of measuring by a hide may have originated in a practice of encompassing a piece of land with thongs cut from the hide of a sacrificial victim in order to place the ground under the guardianship of the sacred animal.

The ox whose hide is used is blinded in order that the new town may be invisible to its enemies.

But why do the Bechuanas sew up the eyelids of the bull which is to be used for this purpose? The answer appears to be given by the ceremonies which the same people observe when they are going out to war. On that occasion a woman rushes up to the army with her eyes shut and shakes a winnowing-fan, while she cries out, "The army is not seen! The army is not seen!" And a medicine-man at the same time sprinkles medicine over the spears, crying out in like manner, "The army is not seen! The army is not seen!" After that they seize a bull, sew up its eyelids with a hair of its tail, and drive it for some distance along the road which the army is to take. When it has preceded the army a little way, the bull is sacrificed, roasted whole, and eaten by the warriors. All the flesh must be consumed on the spot. Such parts as cannot be eaten are burnt with fire. Only the contents of the stomach are carefully preserved

---

[1] T. Arbousset et F. Daumas, *Voyage d'Exploration au Nord-est de la Colonie du Cap de Bonne-Espérance* (Paris, 1842), p. 49.

[2] Virgil, *Aen.* i. 367 *sq.*, with the commentary of Servius; Justin, xviii. 5. 9. Thongs cut from the hide of the ox sacrificed to the four-handed Apollo were given as prizes. See Hesychius, *s.v.* κυνακίας; compare *id.*, πυρώλοφοι. Whether the Greek custom was related to those discussed in the text seems doubtful. I have to thank my colleague and friend Professor R. C. Bosanquet for calling my attention to these passages of Hesychius.

[3] Saxo Grammaticus, *Historia Danica*, ix. vol. i. pp. 462 *sq.* ed. P. E. Müller (Copenhagen, 1839–1858) (where the hide employed is that of a horse); J. Grimm, *Deutsche Rechtsalterthümer*[3] (Göttingen, 1881), pp. 90 *sq.*

Compare R. Köhler, "Sage von Landerwerbung durch zerschnittene Häute," *Orient und Occident*, iii. 185-187.

[4] Lieutenant-Colonel James Tod, *Annals and Antiquities of Rajast'han*, ii. (London, 1832) p. 235; W. Radloff, *Proben der Volkslitteratur der türkischen Stämme Süd-Sibiriens*, iv. (St. Petersburg, 1872) p. 179; A. Bastian, *Die Voelker des oestlichen Asien* (Berlin, 1884–1889), i. 25, iv. 367 *sq.*; T. Stamford Raffles, *History of Java* (London, 1817), ii. 153 *sq.*; R. van Eck, "Schetsen van het eiland Bali," *Tijdschrift voor Nederlandsch-Indië*, Feb. 1880, p. 117. The substance of all these stories, except the first, was given by me in a note on "Hide-measured Lands," *The Classical Review*, ii. (1888) p. 322.

[5] J. Grimm, *Deutsche Rechtsalterthümer*, pp. 538 *sq.*

as a charm which is to lead the warriors to victory. Chosen men carry the precious guts in front of the army, and it is deemed most important that no one should precede them. When they stop, the army stops, and it will not resume the march till it sees that the men with the bull's guts have gone forward.[1] The meaning of these ceremonies is explained by the cries of the woman and the priest, "The army is not seen! The army is not seen!" Clearly it is desirable that the army should not be perceived by the enemies until it is upon them. Accordingly on the principles of homoeopathic magic the Bechuanas apparently imagine that they can make themselves invisible by eating of the flesh of a blind bull, blindness and invisibility being to their simple minds the same thing. For the same reason the bowels of the blind ox are carried in front of the army to hide its advance from hostile eyes. In like manner the custom of sacrificing and eating a blind ox on the place where a new town is to be built may be intended to render the town invisible to enemies. At all events the Bawenda, a South African people who belong to the same Bantu stock as the Bechuanas, take great pains to conceal their kraals from passers-by. The kraals are built in the forest or bush, and the long winding footpaths which lead to them are often kept open only by the support of a single pole here and there. Indeed the paths are so low and narrow that it is very difficult to bring a horse into such a village. In time of war the poles are removed and the thorny creepers fall down, forming a natural screen or bulwark which the enemy can neither penetrate nor destroy by fire. The kraals are also surrounded by walls of undressed stones with a filling of soil; and to hide them still better from the view of the enemy the tops of the walls are sown with Indian corn or planted with tobacco. Hence travellers passing through the country seldom come across a Bawenda kraal. To see where the Bawenda dwell you must climb to the tops of mountains and look down on the roofs of their round huts peeping out of the surrounding green like clusters of mushrooms in the woods.[2] The object which the Bawenda attain by these perfectly rational means, the Bechuanas seek to compass by the sacrifice and consumption of a blind bull.

This explanation of the use of a blinded ox in sacrifice is confirmed by the reasons alleged by a Caffre for the observance of a somewhat similar custom in purificatory ceremonies after a battle. On these occasions the Bechuanas and other Caffre tribes of South Africa kill a black ox and cut out the tip of its tongue, an eye, a piece of the ham-string, and a piece of the principal sinew of the

This explanation of the use of a blinded ox is confirmed by a Caffre custom.

[1] Rev. W. C. Willoughby, "Notes on the Totemism of the Becwana," *Journal of the Anthropological Institute,* xxxv. (1905) p. 304.

[2] Rev. E. Gottschling, "The Bawenda, a Sketch of their History and Customs," *Journal of the Anthropological Institute,* xxxv. (1905) pp. 368 *sq.*

shoulder.   These parts are fried with certain herbs and rubbed into the joints of the warriors.   By cutting out the tongue of the ox they think to prevent the enemy from wagging his tongue against them ; by severing the sinews of the ox they hope to cause the enemy's sinews to fail him in the battle ; and by removing the eye of the ox they imagine that they prevent the enemy from casting a covetous eye on their cattle.[1]

[1] T. Arbousset et F. Daumas, *Relation d'un Voyage d'Exploration*, pp. 561-565.

IV

SOME CUSTOMS OF THE PELEW ISLANDERS

WE have seen that the state of society and religion among the Pelew Islanders in modern times presents several points of similarity to the condition of the peoples about the Eastern Mediterranean in antiquity.[1] Here I propose briefly to call attention to certain other customs of the Pelew Islanders which may serve to illustrate some of the institutions discussed in this volume.

§ 1. *Priests dressed as Women*

In the Pelew Islands it often happens that a goddess chooses a man, not a woman, for her minister and inspired mouthpiece. When that is so, the favoured man is thenceforth regarded and treated as a woman. He wears female attire, he carries a piece of gold on his neck, he labours like a woman in the taro fields, and he plays his new part so well that he earns the hearty contempt of his fellows.[2] The pretended change of sex under the inspiration of a female spirit perhaps explains a custom widely spread among savages, in accordance with which some men dress as women and act as women through life. These unsexed creatures often, perhaps generally, profess the arts of sorcery and healing, they communicate with spirits, and are regarded sometimes with awe and sometimes with contempt, as beings of a higher or lower order than common folk. Often they are dedicated and trained to their vocation from childhood. Effeminate sorcerers or priests of this sort are found among the Sea Dyaks of Borneo,[3] the Bugis of South

In the Pelew Islands a man who is inspired by a goddess wears female attire and is treated as a woman. This pretended change of sex under the inspiration of a female spirit may explain a

---

[1] Above, pp. 204 *sqq.*
[2] J. Kubary, "Die Religion der Pelauer," in A. Bastian's *Allerlei aus Volks- und Menschenkunde* (Berlin, 1888), i. 35.
[3] C. A. L. M. Schwaner, *Borneo* (Amsterdam, 1853), i. 186; M. T. H. Perelaer, *Ethnographische Beschrijving der Dajaks* (Zalt-Bommel, 1870), pp.

32-35; Captain Rodney Mundy, *Narrative of Events in Borneo and Celebes from the Journals of James Brooke, Esq., Rajah of Sarawak* (London, 1848), ii. 65 *sq.*; Charles Brooke, *Ten Years in Sarawak* (London, 1866), ii. 280; H. Low, *Sarawak* (London, 1848), pp. 174-177; The Bishop of Labuan, "On the Wild

widespread custom whereby men dress and live like women.

Celebes,[1] the Patagonians of South America,[2] and the Aleutians and many Indian tribes of North America.[3] In the island of Rambree, off the coast of Aracan, a set of vagabond "conjurors," who dressed and lived as women, used to dance round a tall pole, invoking the aid of their favourite idol on the occasion of any calamity.[4] Male members of the Vallabha sect in India often seek to win the favour of the god Krishna, whom they specially revere, by wearing their hair long and assimilating themselves to women; even their spiritual chiefs, the so-called Maharajas, sometimes simulate the appearance of women when they lead the worship of their followers.[5] In Madagascar we hear of effeminate men who wore female attire and acted as women, thinking thereby to do God service.[6] In the kingdom of Congo there was a sacrificial priest who commonly dressed as a woman and

Tribes of the North-West Coast of Borneo," *Transactions of the Ethnological Society of London*, N.S. ii. (1863) pp. 31 *sq.*; Spenser St. John, *Life in the Forests of the Far East*[2] (London, 1863), i. 73. In Sarawak these men are called *manangs*, in Dutch Borneo they are called *bazirs* or *bassirs*.

[1] Captain R. Mundy, *op. cit.* i. 82 *sq.*; B. F. Matthes, *Over de Bissoes of heidensche Priesters en Priesteressen der Boeginezen* (Amsterdam, 1872), pp. 1 *sq.*

[2] Th. Falkner, *Description of Patagonia* (Hereford, 1774), p. 117; J. Hutchinson, "The Tehuelche Indians of Patagonia," *Transactions of the Ethnological Society of London*, N.S. vii. (1869) p. 323. Among the Guaycurus of Southern Brazil there is a class of men who dress as women and do only women's work, such as spinning, weaving, and making pottery. But so far as I know, they are not said to be sorcerers or priests. See C. F. Ph. v. Martius, *Zur Ethnographie Amerikas zumal Brasiliens* (Leipsic, 1867), pp. 74 *sq.*

[3] G. H. von Langsdorff, *Reise um die Welt* (Frankfort, 1812), ii. 43; H. J. Holmberg, "Über die Völker des Russischen Amerika," *Acta Societatis Scientiarum Fennicae*, iv. (Helsingfors, 1856) pp. 400 *sq.*; W. H. Dall, *Alaska* (London, 1870), pp. 402 *sq.*; Ross Cox, *The Columbia River*[2](London, 1832), i. 327 *sqq.*; Father G. Boscana, "Chinigchinich," in [A. Robinson's] *Life in California* (New York, 1846),

pp. 283 *sq.*; S. Powers, *Tribes of California* (Washington, 1877), pp. 132 *sq.*; H. H. Bancroft, *Native Races of the Pacific States* (London, 1875–1876), i. 82, 92, 415, 585, 774; Hontan, *Mémoires de l'Amérique Septentrionale* (Amsterdam, 1705), p. 144; J. F. Lafitau, *Mœurs des Sauvages Amériquains* (Paris, 1724), i. 52-54; Charlevoix, *Histoire de la Nouvelle France* (Paris, 1744), vi. 4 *sq.*; W. H. Keating, *Expedition to the Source of St. Peter's River* (London, 1825), i. 227 *sq.*, 436; George Catlin, *North American Indians*[4] (London, 1844), ii. 214 *sq.*; Maximilian Prinz zu Wied, *Reise in das innere Nord-America* (Coblentz, 1839–1841), ii. 132 *sq.*; D. G. Brinton, *The Lenâpé and their Legends* (Philadelphia, 1885), pp. 109 *sq.*; J. G. Müller, *Geschichte der amerikanischen Urreligionen*[2] (Bâle, 167), pp. 44 *sq.*, 418. Among the tribes which permitted the custom were the Illinois, Mandans, Dacotas (Sioux), Sauks, and Foxes, to the east of the Rocky Mountains, the Yukis, Pomos, and Pitt River Indians of California, and the Koniags of Alaska.

[4] Lieut. W. Foley, "Journal of a Tour through the Island of Rambree," *Journal of the Asiatic Society of Bengal*, iv. (Calcutta, 1835) p. 199.

[5] Monier Williams, *Religious Life and Thought in India* (London, 1883), p. 136. Compare J. A. Dubois, *Mœurs, Institutions, et Cérémonies des Peuples de l'Inde* (Paris, 1825), i. 439.

[6] O. Dapper, *Description de l'Afrique* (Amsterdam, 1686), p. 467.

gloried in the title of the Grandmother. The post of Grandmother must have been much coveted, for the incumbent might not be put to death, whatever crimes or rascalities he committed; and to do him justice he appears commonly to have taken full advantage of this benefit of clergy. When he died, his fortunate successor dissected the body of the deceased Grandmother, extracting his heart and other vital organs, and amputating his fingers and toes, which he kept as priceless relics, and sold as sovereign remedies for all the ills that flesh is heir to.[1]

We may conjecture that in many of these cases the call to this strange form of the religious life came in the shape of a dream or vision, in which the dreamer or visionary imagined himself to be a woman or to be possessed by a female spirit; for with many savage races the disordered fancies of sleep or ecstasy are accepted as oracular admonitions which it would be perilous to disregard. At all events we are told that a dream or a revelation of some sort was the reason which in North America these men-women commonly alleged for the life they led; it had been thus brought home to them, they said, that their medicine or their salvation lay in living as women, and when once they had got this notion into their head nothing could drive it out again. Many an Indian father attempted by persuasion, by bribes, by violence, to deter his son from obeying the mysterious call, but all to no purpose.[2] Among the Sauks, an Indian tribe of North America, these effeminate beings were always despised, but sometimes they were pitied " as labouring under an unfortunate destiny which they cannot avoid, being supposed to be impelled to this course by a vision from the female spirit that resides in the moon."[3] Similarly the Omahas, another

Such transformations seem to have been often carried out in obedience to intimations received in dreams or in ecstasy.

---

[1] J. B. Labat, *Relation historique de l'Éthiopie Occidentale* (Paris, 1732), ii. 195-199. Wherever men regularly dress as women, we may suspect that a superstitious motive underlies the custom even though our authorities do not mention it. The custom is thus reported among the Italmenes of Kamtschatka (G. W. Steller, *Beschreibung von dem Lande Kamtschatka*, Frankfort and Leipsic, 1774, pp. 350 *sq.*), the Lhoosais of South - Eastern India (Capt. T. H. Lewin, *Wild Races of South-Eastern India*, London, 1870, p. 255), and the Nogay or Mongutay of the Caucasus (J. Reinegg, *Beschreibung des Kaukasus*, St. Petersburg, Gotha, and Hildesheim, 1796–1797, i. 270). Among the Lhoosais or Lushais not only do men sometimes dress like women and consort and work with them (T. H. Lewin,

l.c.), but, on the other hand, women sometimes dress and live like men, adopting masculine habits in all respects. When one of these unsexed women was asked her reasons for adopting a masculine mode of life, she at first denied that she was a woman, but finally confessed "that her *khuavang* was not good, and so she became a man." See the extract from the *Pioneer Mail* of May 1890, quoted in *The Indian Antiquary*, xxxii. (1903) p. 413. The permanent transformation of women into men seems to be much rarer than the converse change of men into women.

[2] Maximilian Prinz zu Wied, *Reise in das innere Nord-America*, ii. 133.

[3] W. H. Keating, *Expedition to the Source of St. Peter's River*, i. 227 *sq.*

Indian tribe of North America, " believe that the unfortunate beings, called *Min-qu-ga*, are mysterious or sacred because they have been affected by the Moon Being. When a young Omaha fasted for the first time on reaching puberty, it was thought that the Moon Being appeared to him, holding in one hand a bow and arrows and in the other a pack strap, such as the Indian women use. When the youth tried to grasp the bow and arrows the Moon Being crossed his hands very quickly, and if the youth was not very careful he seized the pack strap instead of the bow and arrows, thereby fixing his lot in after life. In such a case he could not help acting the woman, speaking, dressing, and working just as Indian women used to do." [1] Among the Ibans or Sea Dyaks of Borneo the highest class of sorcerers or medicine-men (*manangs*) are those who are believed to have been transformed into women. Such a man is therefore called a " changed medicine - man " (*manang bali*) on account of his supposed change of sex. The call to transform himself into a woman is said to come as a supernatural command thrice repeated in dreams ; to disregard the command would mean death. Accordingly he makes a feast, sacrifices a pig or two to avert evil consequences from the tribe, and then assumes the garb of a woman. Thenceforth he is treated as a woman and occupies himself in feminine pursuits. His chief aim is to copy female manners and habits as accurately as possible. He is employed for the same purposes as an ordinary medicine-man and his methods are similar, but he is paid much higher fees and is often called in when others have been unable to effect a cure. [2] Similarly among the Chukchees of North-Eastern Asia there are shamans or medicine-men who assimilate themselves as far as possible to women, and who are believed to be called to this vocation by spirits in a dream. The call usually comes at the critical age of early youth when the shamanistic inspiration, as it is called, first manifests itself. But the call is much dreaded by the youthful adepts, and some of them prefer death to obedience. There are, however, various stages or degrees of transformation. In the first stage the man apes a woman only in the manner of braiding and arranging the hair of his head. In the second he dons female attire ; in the third stage he adopts as far as possible the life and characteristics of the female sex. A young man who is undergoing this final transformation abandons all masculine occupations and manners. He throws away the rifle and the lance, the lasso of the reindeer herdsman, and the harpoon of the seal-hunter, and betakes himself to the needle and the skin - scraper instead. He learns the use of them quickly,

Marginal notes: Trans-formed medicine-men among the Sea Dyaks.

Trans-formed medicine-men among the Chukchees.

[1] Rev. J. Owen Dorsey, "A Study of Siouan Cults," *Eleventh Annual Report of the Bureau of Ethnology* (Washington, 1894), p. 378.

[2] E. H. Gomes, *Seventeen Years* *among the Sea Dyaks of Borneo* (London, 1911), p. 179 ; Ch. Hose and W. McDougall, *The Pagan Tribes of Borneo* (London, 1912), ii. 116.

because the spirits are helping him all the time.   Even his pro-
nunciation changes from the male to the female mode.   At the
same time his body alters, if not in outward appearance, at least in
its faculties and forces.   He loses masculine strength, fleetness of
foot, endurance in wrestling, and falls into the debility and helpless-
ness of a woman.   Even his mental character undergoes a change.
His old brute courage and fighting spirit are gone ; he grows shy and
bashful before strangers, fond of small talk and of dandling little
children.   In short he becomes a woman with the appearance of a
man, and as a woman he is often taken to wife by another man,
with whom he leads a regular married life.   Extraordinary powers
are attributed to such transformed shamans.   They are supposed to
enjoy the special protection of spirits who play the part of supernatural husbands to them.   Hence they are much dreaded even by
their colleagues in the profession who remain mere men ; hence,
too, they excel in all branches of magic, including ventriloquism.[1]
Among the Teso of Central Africa medicine-men often dress as
women and wear feminine ornaments, such as heavy chains of beads
and shells round their heads and necks.[2]

And just as a man inspired by a goddess may adopt female *Women*
attire, so conversely a woman inspired by a god may adopt male *inspired*
costume.   In Uganda the great god Mukasa, the deity of the Victoria *by a god*
Nyanza Lake and of abundance, imparted his oracles through a *men.*
woman, who in ordinary life dressed like the rest of her sex in a
bark cloth wrapped round the body and fastened with a girdle, so as
to leave the arms and shoulders bare ; but when she prophesied under
the inspiration of the god, she wore two bark cloths knotted in masculine style over her shoulders and crossing each other on her breast and
back.[3]   When once the god had chosen her, she retained office for life ;
she might not marry or converse with any man except one particular
priest, who was always present when she was possessed by the deity.[4]

Perhaps this assumed change of sex under the inspiration of *The*
a goddess may give the key to the legends of the effeminate *theory of*
Sardanapalus and the effeminate Hercules,[5] as well as to the practice *by a female*
of the effeminate priests of Cybele and the Syrian goddess.   In all *spirit*

[1] Waldemar Bogoras, *The Chukchee*
(Leyden and New York, 1904–1909),
pp. 448-453 (*The Jesup North Pacific
Expedition*, vol. vii. ; *Memoir of
the American Museum of Natural
History*).
    [2] Rev. A. L. Kitching, *On the
Backwaters of the Nile* (London, 1912),
p. 239, with the plate.
    [3] For this information I have to
thank my friend the Rev. J. Roscoe.
He tells me that according to tradition
Mukasa used to give his oracles by the

mouth of a man, not of a woman.   To
wear two bark cloths, one on each
shoulder, is a privilege of royalty and
of priests.   The ordinary man wears a
single bark cloth knotted on one
shoulder only.   With the single exception mentioned in the text, women in
Uganda never wear bark cloths fastened
over the shoulders.

    [4] Rev. J. Roscoe, *The Baganda*
(London, 1911), p. 297.

    [5] *The Scapegoat*, pp. 387 *sqq.*

such cases the pretended transformation of a man into a woman would be intelligible if we supposed that the womanish priest or king thought himself animated by a female spirit, whose sex, accordingly, he felt bound to imitate. Certainly the eunuch priests of Cybele seem to have bereft themselves of their manhood under the supposed inspiration of the Great Goddess.[1] The priest of Hercules at Antimachia, in Cos, who dressed as a woman when he offered sacrifice, is said to have done so in imitation of Hercules who disguised himself as a woman to escape the pursuit of his enemies.[2] So the Lydian Hercules wore female attire when he served for three years as the purchased slave of the imperious Omphale, Queen of Lydia.[3] If we suppose that Queen Omphale, like Queen Semiramis, was nothing but the great Asiatic goddess,[4] or one of her Avatars, it becomes probable that the story of the womanish Hercules of Lydia preserves a reminiscence of a line or college of effeminate priests who, like the eunuch priests of the Syrian goddess, dressed as women in imitation of their goddess and were supposed to be inspired by her. The probability is increased by the practice of the priests of Hercules at Antimachia, in Cos, who, as we have just seen, actually wore female attire when they were engaged in their sacred duties. Similarly at the vernal mysteries of Hercules in Rome the men were draped in the garments of women;[5] and in some of the rites and processions of Dionysus also men wore female attire.[6] In

---

[1] Catullus, lxiii. This is in substance the explanation of the custom given by Dr. L. R. Farnell, who observes that "the mad worshipper endeavoured thus against nature to assimilate himself more closely to his goddess" ("Sociological hypotheses concerning the position of women in ancient religion," *Archiv für Religionswissenschaft*, vii. (1904) p. 93). The theory is not necessarily inconsistent with my conjecture as to the magical use made of the severed parts. See above, vol. i. pp. 268 *sq.*

[2] Plutarch, *Quaestiones Graecae*, 58.

[3] Apollodorus, *Bibliotheca*, ii. 6. 2 *sq.*; Athenaeus, xii. 11, pp. 515 F-516 B; Diodorus Siculus, iv. 31; Joannes Lydus, *De magistratibus*, iii. 64; Lucian, *Dialogi deorum*, xiii. 2; Ovid, *Heroides*, ix. 55 *sqq.*; Statius, *Theb.* x. 646-649.

[4] On Semiramis in this character see above, vol. i. pp. 176 *sq.*; *The Scapegoat*, pp. 369 *sqq.*

[5] Joannes Lydus, *De mensibus*, iv. 46, p. 81, ed. I. Bekker (Bonn, 1837).

Yet at Rome, by an apparent contradiction, women might not be present at a sacrifice offered to Hercules (Propertius, v. 9. 67-70; see further above, vol. i. p. 113, note [1]), and at Gades women might not enter the temple of Melcarth, the Tyrian Hercules (Silius Italicus, iii. 22). There was a Greek proverb, "A woman does not go to a temple of Hercules" (Macarius, *Cent.* iii. 11; *Paroemiographi Graeci*, ed. Leutsch et Schneidewin, i. 392, ii. 154). Roman women did not swear by Hercules (Aulus Gellius, xi. 6).

[6] Lucian, *Calumniae non temere credendum*, 16; Hesychius and Suidas, *s.v.* 'Ιθύφαλλοι. At the Athenian vintage festival of the Oschophoria a chorus of singers was led in procession by two young men dressed exactly like girls; they carried branches of vines laden with ripe clusters. The procession was said to be in honour of Dionysus and Athena or Ariadne. See Proclus, quoted by Photius, *Bibliotheca*, p. 322a, ed. I. Bekker (Berlin, 1824); Plutarch, *Theseus*, 23.

legend and art there are clear traces of an effeminate Dionysus, who perhaps figured in a strange ceremony for the artificial fertilization of the fig.[1] Among the Nahanarvals, an ancient German tribe, a priest garbed as a woman presided over a sacred grove.[2] These and similar practices[3] need not necessarily have any connexion with the social system of mother-kin. Wherever a goddess is revered and the theory of inspiration is held, a man may be thought to be possessed by a female spirit, whether society be organized on mother-kin or on father-kin. Still the chances of such a transformation of sex will be greater under mother-kin than under father-kin if, as we have found reason to believe, a system of mother-kin is more favourable to the development and multiplication of goddesses than of gods. It is therefore, perhaps, no mere accident that we meet with these effeminate priests in regions like the Pelew Islands and Western Asia, where the system of mother-kin either actually prevails or has at least left traces of it behind in tradition and custom. Such traces, for example, are to be found in Lydia and Cos,[4] in both of which the effeminate Hercules had his home.

[1] Clement of Alexandria, *Protrept.* ii. 34, pp. 29 *sq.*, ed. Potter ; Arnobius, *Adversus Nationes*, v. 28 ; *Mythographi Graeci*, ed. A. Westermann (Brunswick, 1843), p. 368 ; J. Tzetzes, *Scholia on Lycophron*, 212. As to the special association of the fig with Dionysus, see Athenaeus, iii. 14, p. 78. As to the artificial fertilization of the fig, see *The Magic Art and the Evolution of Kings*, ii. 314 *sq.* On the type of the effeminate Dionysus in art see E. Thraemer, *s.v.* "Dionysos," in W. H. Roscher's *Lexikon der griech. und röm. Mythologie*, i. 1135 *sqq.*

[2] Tacitus, *Germania*, 43. Perhaps, as Professor Chadwick thinks, this priest may have succeeded to a priestess when the change from mother-kin to father-kin took place. See H. M. Chadwick, *The Origin of the English Nation* (Cambridge, 1907), p. 339.

[3] In Cyprus there was a bearded and masculine image of Venus (probably Astarte) in female attire : according to Philochorus, the deity thus represented was the moon, and sacrifices were offered to him or her by men clad as women, and by women clad as men. See Macrobius, *Saturn.* iii. 7. 2 *sq.*; Servius on Virgil, *Aen.* ii. 632. A similar exchange of garments took place between Argive men and women at the festival of the Hybristica, which

fell in the month of Hermes, either at the new moon or on the fourth of the month. See Plutarch, *De mulierum virtutibus*, 4 ; Polyaenus, viii. 33. On the thirteenth of January flute-players paraded the streets of Rome in the garb of women (Plutarch, *Quaestiones Romanae*, 55).

[4] For traces of mother-kin in Lydia see *The Magic Art and the Evolution of Kings*, ii. 281 *sq.* With regard to Cos we know from inscriptions that at Halasarna all who shared in the sacred rites of Apollo and Hercules had to register the names of their father, their mother, and of their mother's father ; from which it appears that maternal descent was counted more important than paternal descent. See H. Collitz und F. Bechtel, *Sammlung der griechischen Dialekt-Inschriften*, iii. 1 (Göttingen, 1899), pp. 382-393, Nos. 3705, 3706 ; G. Dittenberger, *Sylloge Inscriptionum Graecarum*,[2] vol. ii. pp. 396 *sqq.*, No. 614 ; Ch. Michel, *Recueil d'Inscriptions Grecques*, pp. 796 *sq.*, No. 1003 ; J. Toepffer, *Attische Genealogie* (Berlin, 1889), pp. 192 *sq.* On traces of mother-kin in the legend and ritual of Hercules see A. B. Cook, "Who was the wife of Hercules ?" *The Classical Review*, xx. (1906) pp. 376 *sq.* Mr. Cook conjectures that a Sacred Marriage of

But the
exchange
of costume
between
men and
women has
probably
been prac-
tised also
from other
motives, for
example,
from a wish
to avert the
Evil Eye.
This
motive
seems to
explain
the inter-
change of
male and
female
costume
between
bride and
bride-
groom at
marriage.

But the religious or superstitious interchange of dress between men and women is an obscure and complex problem, and it is unlikely that any single solution would apply to all the cases. Probably the custom has been practised from many different motives. For example, the practice of dressing boys as girls has certainly been sometimes adopted to avert the Evil Eye;[1] and it is possible that the custom of changing garments at marriage, the bridegroom disguising himself as a woman, or the bride disguising herself as a man, may have been resorted to for the same purpose. Thus in Cos, where the priest of Hercules wore female attire, the bridegroom was in like manner dressed as a woman when he received his bride.[2] Spartan brides had their hair shaved, and were clad in men's clothes and booted on their wedding night.[3] Argive brides wore false beards when they slept with their husbands for the first time.[4] In Southern Celebes a bridegroom at a certain point of the long and elaborate marriage ceremonies puts on the garments which his bride has just put off.[5] Among the Jews of Egypt in the Middle Ages the bride led the wedding dance with a helmet on her head and a sword in her hand, while the bridegroom adorned himself as a woman and put on female attire.[6] At a Brahman marriage in Southern India " the bride is dressed up as a boy, and another girl is dressed up to represent the bride. They are taken in procession through the street, and, on returning, the pseudo-bridegroom is made to speak to the real bridegroom in somewhat insolent tones, and some mock play is indulged in. The real bridegroom is addressed as if he was the syce (groom) or gumasta (clerk) of the pseudo-bridegroom, and is sometimes treated as a thief, and judgment passed on him by the latter."[7] Among the Bharias

---

Hercules and Hera was celebrated in Cos. We know in fact from a Coan inscription that a bed was made and a marriage celebrated beside the image of Hercules, and it seems probable that the rite was that of a Sacred Marriage, though some scholars interpret it merely of an ordinary human wedding. See G. Dittenberger, *Sylloge Inscriptionum Graecarum*,[2] vol. ii. pp. 577 *sqq.*, No. 734; R. Dareste, B. Haussoulier, Th. Reinach, *Recueil d'Inscriptions Juri-diques Grecques*, Deuxième Série (Paris, 1898), No. xxiv. B, pp. 94 *sqq.*; Fr. Back, *De Graecorum caeri-moniis in quibus homines deorum vice fungebantur* (Berlin, 1883), pp. 14-24.

[1] *Panjab Notes and Queries*, i. (1884) §§ 219, 869, 1007, 1029; *id.* ii. (1885) §§ 344, 561, 570; *Journal of the*

Anthropological Society of Bombay, i. (1886) p. 123; *North Indian Notes and Queries*, iii. (1893) § 99. Compare my notes, "The Youth of Achilles," *The Classical Review*, vii. (1893) pp. 292 *sq.*; and on Pausanias, i. 22. 6 (vol. ii. p. 266).

[2] Plutarch, *Quaestiones Graecae*, 58.

[3] Plutarch, *Lycurgus*, 15.

[4] Plutarch, *De mulierum virtuti-bus*, 4.

[5] B. F. Matthes, *Bijdragen tot de Ethnologie van Zuid-Celebes* (The Hague, 1875), p. 35. The marriage ceremonies here described are especially those of princes.

[6] Sepp, *Altbayerischer Sagenschatz* (Munich, 1876), p. 232, referring to Maimonides.

[7] E. Thurston, *Ethnographic Notes in Southern India* (Madras, 1906), p. 3.

of the Central Provinces of India "the bridegroom puts on women's ornaments and carries with him an iron nut-cutter or dagger to keep off evil spirits."[1] Similarly among the Khangars, a low Hindustani caste of the same region, "the bridegroom is dressed in a yellow gown and overcloth, with trousers of red chintz, red shoes, and a marriage crown of date-palm leaves. He has the silver ornaments usually worn by women on his neck, as the *khang-wāri* or silver ring and the *hamel* or necklace of rupees. In order to avert the evil eye he carries a dagger or nut-cracker, and a smudge of lampblack is made on his forehead to disfigure him and thus avert the evil eye, which, it is thought, would otherwise be too probably attracted by his exquisitely beautiful appearance in his wedding garments."[2] These examples render it highly probable that, like the dagger or nut-cracker which he holds in his hand, the woman's ornaments which he wears are intended to protect the bridegroom against demons or the evil eye at this critical moment of his life, the protection apparently consisting in a disguise which enables him to elude the unwelcome attentions of malignant beings.[3]

A similar explanation probably accounts for the similar exchange of costume between other persons than the bride and bridegroom at marriage. For example, after a Bharia wedding, "the girl's mother gets the dress of the boy's father and puts it on, together with a false beard and moustaches, and dances holding a wooden ladle in one hand and a packet of ashes in the other. Every time she approaches the bridegroom's father on her rounds she spills some of the ashes over him and occasionally gives him a crack on the head with her ladle, these actions being accompanied by bursts of laughter from the party and frenzied playing by the musicians. When the party reach the bridegroom's house on their return, his mother and the other women come out, and burn a little mustard and human hair in a lamp, the unpleasant smell emitted by these articles being considered potent to drive away evil spirits."[4] Again, after a Khangar wedding the father of the bridegroom, dressed in women's clothes, dances with the mother of the bride, while the two throw turmeric mixed with water on each other.[5] Similarly after a

The same explanation may account for the interchange of male and female costume between other persons at marriage.

The pseudo-bridegroom is apparently the bride in masculine attire.

[1] *Central Provinces, Ethnographic Survey*, iii. *Draft Articles on Forest Tribes* (Allahabad, 1907), p. 31.

[2] *Central Provinces, Ethnographic Survey*, i. *Draft Articles on Hindustani Castes* (Allahabad, 1907), p. 48.

[3] Elsewhere I have conjectured that the wearing of female attire by the bridegroom at marriage may mark a transition from mother-kin to father-kin, the intention of the custom being

to transfer to the father those rights over the children which had previously been enjoyed by the mother alone. See *Totemism* (Edinburgh, 1887), pp. 78 *sq.* ; *Totemism and Exogamy*, i. 73. But I am now disposed to think that the other explanation suggested in the text is the more probable.

[4] *Central Provinces, Ethnographic Survey*, iii. *Draft Articles on Forest Tribes* (Allahabad, 1907), p. 31.

[5] *Central Provinces, Ethnographic Survey*, i. *Draft Articles on Hindu-*

wedding of the Bharbhunjas, another Hindustani caste of the Central Provinces, the bridegroom's father dances before the family in women's clothes which have been supplied by the bride's father.[1] Such disguises and dances may be intended either to protect the disguised dancer himself against the evil eye or perhaps rather to guard the principal personages of the ceremony, the bride and bridegroom, by diverting the attention of demons from them to the guiser.[2] However, when at marriage the bride alone assumes the costume and appearance of the other sex, the motive for the disguise may perhaps be a notion that on the principle of homoeopathic magic she thereby ensures the birth of a male heir. Similarly in Sweden there is a popular superstition that "on the night preceding her nuptials the bride should have a baby-boy to sleep with her, in which case her first-born will be a son";[3] and among the Kabyles, when a bride dismounts from her mule at her husband's house, a young lad leaps into the saddle before she touches the ground, in order that her first child may be a boy.[4]

Women's dress assumed by men for the purpose of deceiving demons and ghosts. Be that as it may, there is no doubt that the assumption of woman's dress is sometimes intended to disguise a man for the purpose of deceiving a demon. Thus among the Boloki or Bangala on the Upper Congo a man was long afflicted with an internal malady. When all other remedies had failed, a witch-doctor informed the sufferer that the cause of his trouble was an evil spirit, and that the best thing he could do was to go far away where the devil could not get at him, and to remain there till he had recovered his health. The patient followed the prescription. At dead of night he left his house, taking only two of his wives with him and telling no one of his destination, lest the demon should hear it and follow him. So he went far away from his town, donned a woman's dress, and speaking in a woman's voice he pretended to be other than he was, in order that the devil should not be able to find him at his new address. Strange to say, these sage measures failed to

---

stani Castes (Allahabad, 1907), p. 48.

[1] *Central Provinces, Ethnographic Survey*, vi. *Draft Articles on Hindustani Castes*, Second Series (Allahabad, 1911), p. 50.

[2] Compare W. Crooke, *Popular Religion and Folk-lore of Northern India* (Westminster, 1896), ii. 8, who proposes, with great probability, to explain on a similar principle, the European marriage custom known as the False Bride. For more instances of the interchange of male and female costume at marriage between persons other than the bridegroom see Capt. J. S. King, " Social Customs of the Western

Somali Tribes," *The Folk-lore Journal*, vi. (1888) p. 122 ; J. P. Farler, " The Usambara Country in East Africa," *Proceedings of the Royal Geographical Society*, N.S. i. (1879) p. 92 ; Major J. Biddulph, *Tribes of the Hindoo Koosh* (Calcutta, 1880), pp. 78, 80 ; G. A. Grierson, *Bihar Peasant Life* (Calcutta, 1885), p. 365 ; A. de Gubernatis, *Usi Nuziali in Italia*[2] (Milan, 1878), p. 190 ; P. Sébillot, *Coutumes Populaires de la Haute-Bretagne* (Paris, 1886), p. 438.

[3] L. Lloyd, *Peasant Life in Sweden* (London, 1870), p. 85.

[4] J. Liorel, *Kabylie du Jurjura* (Paris, N.D.), p. 406.

effect a cure, and wearying of exile he at last returned home, where he continued to dress and speak as a woman.[1] Again, the Kuki-Lushai of Assam believe that if a man kills an enemy or a wild beast, the ghost of the dead man or animal will haunt him and drive him mad. The only way of averting this catastrophe is to dress up as a woman and pretend to be one. For example, a man who had shot a tiger and was in fear of being haunted by the animal's ghost, dressed himself up in a woman's petticoat and cloth, wore ivory earrings, and wound a mottled cloth round his head like a turban. Then smoking a woman's pipe, carrying a little basket, and spinning a cotton spindle, he paraded the village followed by a crowd roaring and shrieking with laughter, while he preserved the gravity of a judge, for a single smile would have been fatal. To guard against the possibility of unseasonable mirth, he carried a porcupine in his arms, and if ever, tickled beyond the pitch of endurance, he burst into a guffaw, the crowd said, " It was the porcupine that laughed." All this was done to mortify the pride of the tiger's ghost by leading him to believe that he had been shot by a woman.[2]

The same dread of attracting the attention of dangerous spirits at critical times perhaps explains the custom observed by some East African tribes of wearing the costume of the opposite sex at circumcision. Thus, when Masai boys have been circumcised they dress as women, wearing earrings in their ears and long garments that reach to the ground. They also whiten their swarthy faces with chalk. This costume they retain till their wounds are healed, whereupon they are shaved and assume the skins and ornaments of warriors.[3] Among the Nandi, a tribe of British East Africa, before boys are circumcised they receive a visit from young girls, who give them some of their own garments and ornaments. These the boys put on and wear till the operation of circumcision is over, when they exchange the girls' clothes for the garments of women, which, together with necklaces, are provided for them by their mothers ; and these women's garments the newly circumcised lads must continue to wear for months afterwards. Girls are also circumcised among the Nandi, and before they submit to the operation they attire themselves in men's garments and carry clubs in their hands.[4]

If such interchange of costume between men and women is

Exchange of costume between the sexes at circumcision.

[1] Rev. J. H. Weeks, *Among Congo Cannibals* (London, 1913), p. 267. Compare *id.*, "Anthropological Notes on the Bangala of the Upper Congo River," *Journal of the Royal Anthropological Institute*, xl. (1910) pp. 370 *sq.*

[2] Lieut. - Colonel J. Shakespear, "The Kuki-Lushai Clans," *Journal of the Royal Anthropological Institute*, xxxix. (1909) pp. 380 *sq.*

[3] A. C. Hollis, *The Masai* (Oxford, 1905), p. 298.

[4] A. C. Hollis, *The Nandi* (Oxford, 1909), pp. 53-58. Mr. Hollis informs me that among the Akikuyu, another tribe of British East Africa, the custom of boys dressing as girls at or after circumcision is also observed.

Other cases of the interchange of male and female costume.   intended to disguise the wearers against demons, we may compare the practice of the Lycian men, who regularly wore women's dress in mourning;[1] for this might be intended to conceal them from the ghost, just as perhaps for a similar reason some peoples of antiquity used to descend into pits and remain there for several days, shunning the light of the sun, whenever a death had taken place in the family.[2] A similar desire to deceive spirits may perhaps explain a device to which the Loeboes, a primitive tribe of Sumatra, resort when they wish to obtain male or female offspring. If parents have several sons and desire that the next child shall be a girl, they dress the boys as girls, cut their hair after the girlish fashion, and hang necklaces round their necks. On the contrary, when they have many daughters and wish to have a son, they dress the girls up as boys.[3]

Conclusion.   On the whole we conclude that the custom of men dressing as women and of women dressing as men has been practised from a variety of superstitious motives, among which the principal would seem to be the wish to please certain powerful spirits or to deceive others.

§ 2. *Prostitution of Unmarried Girls*

Like many peoples of Western Asia in antiquity, the Pelew Islanders systematically prostitute their unmarried girls for hire. Hence, just as in Lydia and Cyprus of old, the damsels are a source of income to their family, and women wait impatiently for the time when their young daughters will be able to help the household by their earnings. Indeed the mother regularly anticipates the time by depriving the girl of her virginity with her own hands.[4] Hence the theory that the prostitution of unmarried girls is a device to destroy their virginity without risk to their husbands is just as inapplicable to the Pelew Islanders as we have seen it to be to the peoples of Western Asia in antiquity. When a Pelew girl has thus been prepared for her vocation by her mother, she sells her favours to all the men of her village who can pay for them and who do not belong to her own exogamous clan; but she never grants her favours to the same man twice. Accordingly in every village of the Pelew Islands it may be taken as certain that the men and women know each other carnally, except that members of the same clan are debarred from each other by the rule of exogamy.[5] Thus a well-marked form of sexual communism, limited only by the exogamous prohibitions which attach to the clans, prevails among these people. Nor is this communism restricted to the inhabit-

The systematic prostitution of unmarried girls for hire in the Pelew Islands seems to be a form of sexual communism and of group-marriage.

---

[1] Plutarch, *Consolatio ad Apollonium*, 22 ; Valerius Maximus, ii. 6. 13.

[2] Plutarch, *l.c.*

[3] J. Kreemer, "De Loeboes in Mandailing," *Bijdragen tot de Taal-* *Land- en Volkenkunde van Nederlandsch-Indië*, lxvi. (1912) p. 317.

[4] J. Kubary, *Die socialen Einrichtungen der Pelauer*, pp. 50 *sq.*

[5] J. Kubary, *op. cit.* p. 51.

ants of the same village, for the girls of each village are regularly sent away to serve as prostitutes (*armengols*) in another village. There they live with the men of one of the many clubs or associations (*kaldebekels*) in the clubhouse (*blay*), attending to the house, consorting freely with the men, and receiving pay for their services. A girl leading this life in the clubhouse of another village is well treated by the men : a wrong done to her is a wrong done to the whole club; and in her own village her value is increased, not diminished, by the time she thus spends as a prostitute in a neighbouring community. After her period of service is over she may marry either in the village where she has served or in her own. Sometimes many or all of the young women of a village go together to act as prostitutes (*armengols*) in a neighbouring village, and for this they are well paid by the community which receives them. The money so earned is divided among the chiefs of the village to which the damsels belong. Such a joint expedition of the unmarried girls of a village is called a *blolobol.* But the young women never act as *armengols* in any clubhouse of their own village.[1]

Thus, while the Pelew custom of prostituting the unmarried girls to all the men of their own village, but not of their own clan, is a form of sexual communism practised within a local group, the custom of prostituting them to men of other villages is a form of sexual communism practised between members of different local groups ; it is a kind of group-marriage. These customs of the Pelew Islanders therefore support by analogy the hypothesis that among the ancient peoples of Western Asia also the systematic prostitution of unmarried women may have been derived from an earlier period of sexual communism.[2] *The custom supports by analogy the derivation of the similar Asiatic custom from a similar state of society.*

A somewhat similar custom prevails in Yap, one of the western group of the Caroline Islands, situated to the north of the Pelew group. In each of the men's clubhouses "are kept three or four unmarried girls or *Mespil,* whose business it is to minister to the pleasures of the men of the particular clan or brotherhood to which the building belongs. As with the Kroomen on the Gold Coast, each man, married or single, takes his turn by rotation in the rites through which each girl must pass before she is deemed ripe for marriage. The natives say it is an ordeal or preliminary trial to fit them for the cares and burden of maternity. She is rarely a girl of the same village, and, of course, must be sprung from a different sept. Whenever she wishes to become a *Langin* or respectable married woman, she may, and is thought none the less of for her frailties as a *Mespil.* . . . But I believe this self-immolation before marriage is confined to the daughters of the inferior chiefs and *Somewhat similar custom observed in Yap, one of the Caroline Islands.*

---

[1] J. Kubary, *op. cit.* pp. 51-53, 91-98.
[2] See above, vol. i. pp. 39 *sqq.*

commons. The supply of *Mespil* is generally kept up by the purchase of slave girls from the neighbouring districts."[1] According to another account a *mespil* "must always be stolen, by force or cunning, from a district at some distance from that wherein her captors reside. After she has been fairly, or unfairly, captured and installed in her new home, she loses no shade of respect among her own people; on the contrary, have not her beauty and her worth received the highest proof of her exalted perfection, in the devotion, not of one, but of a whole community of lovers?"[2] However, though the girl is nominally stolen from another district, the matter is almost always arranged privately with the local chief, who consents to wink hard at the theft in consideration of a good round sum of shell money and stone money, which serves "to salve the wounds of a disrupted family and dispel all thoughts of a bloody retaliation. Nevertheless, the whole proceeding is still carried out with the greatest possible secrecy and stealth."[3]

§ 3. *Custom of slaying Chiefs*

In the Pelew Islands the heir to the chieftainship of a clan has a formal right to slay his predecessor.

In the Pelew Islands when the chief of a clan has reigned too long or has made himself unpopular, the heir has a formal right to put him to death, though for reasons which will appear this right is only exercised in some of the principal clans. The practice of regicide, if that word may be extended to the assassination of chiefs, is in these islands a national institution regulated by exact rules, and every high chief must lay his account with it. Indeed so well recognized is the custom that when the heir-apparent, who under the system of mother-kin must be a brother, a nephew, or a cousin on the mother's side, proves himself precocious and energetic, the people say, "The cousin is a grown man. The chief's *tobolbel* is nigh at hand."[4]

The plot of death and its execution.

In such cases the plot of death is commonly so well hushed up that it seldom miscarries. The first care of the conspirators. is to discover where the doomed man keeps his money. For this purpose an old woman will sleep for some nights in the house and make inquiries quietly, till like a sleuth-hound she has nosed the hoard. Then the conspirators come, and the candidate for the chieftainship despatches his predecessor either with his own hand or by the hand of a young cousin. Having done the deed he takes possession of the official residence, and applies to the widow

[1] F. W. Christian, *The Caroline Islands* (London, 1899), pp. 290 *sq.* Compare W. H. Furness, *The Island of Stone Money, Uap of the Carolines* (Philadelphia and London, 1910), pp. 46 *sqq.*

[2] W. H. Furness, *op. cit.* pp. 46 *sq.*

[3] W. H. Furness, *op. cit.* pp. 49 *sq.*

[4] J. Kubary, *Die socialen Einrichtungen der Pelauer*, p. 43. The writer does not translate the word *tobolbel*, but the context sufficiently explains its meaning.

of the deceased the form of persuasion technically known as *meleket*. This consists of putting a noose round her neck, and drawing it tighter and tighter till she consents to give up her late husband's money. After that the murderer and his friends have nothing further to do for the present, but to remain quietly in the house and allow events to take their usual course.

Meantime the chiefs assemble in the council-house, and the loud droning notes of the triton-shell, which answers the purpose of a tocsin, summon the whole population to arms. The warriors muster, and surrounding the house where the conspirators are ensconced they shower spears and stones at it, as if to inflict condign punishment on the assassins. But this is a mere blind, a sham, a legal fiction, intended perhaps to throw dust in the eyes of the ghost and make him think that his death is being avenged. In point of fact the warriors take good care to direct their missiles at the roof or walls of the house, for if they threw them at the windows they might perhaps hurt the murderer. After this formality has been satisfactorily performed, the regicide steps out of the house and engages in the genial task of paying the death duties to the various chiefs assembled. When he has observed this indispensable ceremony, the law is satisfied: all constitutional forms have been carried out: the assassin is now the legitimate successor of his victim and reigns in his stead without any further trouble.

Ceremonies observed before the assassin is recognized as chief in room of his victim.

But if he has omitted to massacre his predecessor and has allowed him to die a natural death, he suffers for his negligence by being compelled to observe a long series of complicated and irksome formalities before he can make good his succession in the eyes of the law. For in that case the title of chief has to be formally withdrawn from the dead man and conferred on his successor by a curious ceremony, which includes the presentation of a coco-nut and a taro plant to the new chief. Moreover, at first he may not enter the chief's house, but has to be shut up in a tiny hut for thirty or forty days during all the time of mourning, and even when that is over he may not come out till he has received and paid for a human head brought him by the people of a friendly state. After that he still may not go to the sea-shore until more formalities have been fully observed. These comprise a very costly fishing expedition, which is conducted by the inhabitants of another district and lasts for weeks. At the end of it a net full of fish is brought to the chief's house, and the people of the neighbouring communities are summoned by the blast of trumpets. As soon as the stranger fishermen have been publicly paid for their services, a relative of the new chief steps across the net and solemnly splits a coco-nut in two with an old-fashioned knife made of a Tridacna shell, while at the same time he bans all the evils that might befall his kinsman. Then, without looking at the nut, he throws the pieces on the ground, and if they

But the formalities which a chief has to observe at his accession are much more complicated and tedious if he has not murdered his predecessor.

fall so that the two halves lie with the opening upwards, it is an omen that the chief will live long. The pieces of the nut are then tied together and taken to the house of another chief, the friend of the new ruler, and there they are kept in token that the ceremony has been duly performed. Thereupon the fish are divided among the people, the strangers receiving half. This completes the legal ceremonies of accession, and the new chief may now go about freely. But these tedious formalities and others which I pass over are dispensed with when the new chief has proved his title by slaying his predecessor. In that case the procedure is much simplified, but on the other hand the death duties are so very heavy that only rich men can afford to indulge in the luxury of regicide. Hence in the Pelew Islands of to-day, or at least of yesterday, the old-fashioned mode of succession by slaughter is now restricted to a few families of the bluest blood and the longest purses.[1]

The Pelew custom shows how regicide may be regarded as an ordinary incident of constitutional government.   If this account of the existing or recent usage of the Pelew Islanders sheds little light on the motives for putting chiefs to death, it well illustrates the business-like precision with which such a custom may be carried out, and the public indifference, if not approval, with which it may be regarded as an ordinary incident of constitutional government. So far, therefore, the Pelew custom bears out the view that a systematic practice of regicide, however strange and revolting it may seem to us, is perfectly compatible with a state of society in which human conduct and human life are estimated by a standard very different from ours. If we would understand the early history of institutions, we must learn to detach ourselves from the prepossessions of our own time and country, and to place ourselves as far as possible at the standpoint of men in distant lands and distant ages.

[1] J. Kubary, *Die socialen Einrichtungen der Pelauer*, pp. 43-45, 75-78.

INDEX

Aban, a Persian month, ii. 68
Abd-Hadad, priestly king of Hierapolis, i. 163 *n.*[3]
Aberdeenshire, All Souls' Day in, ii. 79 *sq.*
Abi-baal, i. 51 *n.*[4]
Abi-el, i. 51 *n.*[4]
Abi-jah, King, his family, i. 51 *n.*[2]; "father of Jehovah," 51 *n.*[4]
Abi-melech, "father of a king," i. 51 *n.*[4]
Abi-milk (Abi-melech), king of Tyre, i. 16 *n.*[5]
Abimelech massacres his seventy brothers, i. 51 *n.*[2]
Abipones, of South America, their worship of the Pleiades, i. 258 *n.*[2]
Abraham, his attempted sacrifice of Isaac, ii. 219 *n.*[1]
Abruzzi, gossips of St. John in the, i. 245 *n.*[2]; marvellous properties attributed to water on St. John's Night in the, 246; Easter ceremonies in the, 256; the feast of All Souls in the, ii. 77 *sq.*; rules as to sowing seed and cutting timber in the, 133 *n.*[3]
Abu Rabah, resort of childless wives in Palestine, i. 78, 79
Abydos, head of Osiris at, ii. 11; the favourite burial-place of the Egyptians, 18 *sq.*; specially associated with Osiris, 18, 197; tombs of the ancient Egyptian kings at, 19; the ritual of, 86; hall of the Osirian mysteries at, 108; representations of the Sed festival at, 151; inscriptions at, 153; temple of Osiris at, 198
Acacia, Osiris in the, ii. 111
Achaia, subject to earthquakes, i. 202
Acharaca, cave of Pluto at, i. 205 *sq.*
Acilisena, temple of Anaitis at, i. 38
Adad, Syrian king, i. 15; Babylonian and Assyrian god of thunder and lightning, 163
Adana in Cilicia, i. 169 *n.*[3]
Addison, Joseph, on the grotto *dei cani* at Naples, i. 205 *n.*[1]

Adhar, a Persian month, ii. 68
Adom-melech or Uri-melech, king of Byblus, i. 14, 17
Adon, a Semitic title, i. 6 *sq.*, 16 *sq.*, 20, 49 *n.*[7]
Adonai, title of Jehovah, i. 6 *sq.*
Adoni, "my lord," Semitic title, i. 7; names compounded with, 17
Adoni-bezek, king of Jerusalem, i. 17
Adoni-jah, elder brother of King Solomon, i. 51 *n.*[2]
Adoni-zedek, king of Jerusalem, i. 17
Adonis, myth of, i. 3 *sqq.*; Greek worship of, 6; in Greek mythology, 10 *sqq.*; in Syria, 13 *sqq.*; monuments of, 29; in Cyprus, 31 *sqq.*, 49; identified with Osiris, 32; mourning for, at Byblus, 38; said to be the fruit of incest, 43; his mother Myrrha, 43; son of Theias, 43 *n.*[4], 55 *n.*[4]; the son of Cinyras, 49; the title of the sons of Phoenician kings in Cyprus, 49; his violent death, 55; music in the worship of, 55; sacred prostitution in the worship of, 57; inspired prophets in worship of, 76; human representatives of, perhaps burnt, 110; doves burned in honour of, 147; personated by priestly kings, 223; the ritual of, 223 *sqq.*; his death and resurrection represented in his rites, 224 *sq.*; festivals of, 224 *sqq.*; flutes played in the laments for, 225 *n.*[3]; the ascension of, 225; images of, thrown into the sea or springs, 225, 227 *n.*[3], 236; born from a myrrh-tree, 227, ii. 110; bewailed by Argive women, i. 227 *n.*; analogy of his rites to Indian and European ceremonies, 227; his death and resurrection interpreted as representations of the decay and revival of vegetation, 227 *sqq.*; interpreted as the sun, 228; interpreted by the ancients as the god of the reaped and sprouting corn, 229; as a corn-spirit, 230 *sqq.*; hunger the root of the worship of, 231; perhaps

269

originally a personification of wild vegetation, especially grass and trees, 233 ; the gardens of, 236 *sqq.* ; rain-charm in the rites of, 237 ; resemblance of his rites to the festival of Easter, 254 *sqq.*, 306 ; worshipped at Bethlehem, 257 *sqq.* ; and the planet Venus as the Morning Star, 258 *sq.* ; sometimes identified with Attis, 263 ; swine not eaten by worshippers of, 265 ; rites of, among the Greeks, 298 ; lamented by women at Byblus, ii. 23

Adonis and Aphrodite, i. 11 *sq.*, 29, 280 ; their marriage celebrated at Alexandria, 224

—— and Attis identified with Dionysus, ii. 127 *n.*

—— and Osiris, similarity between their rites, ii. 127

——, Attis, Osiris, their mythical similarity, i. 6, ii. 201

——, the river, its valley, i. 28 *sqq.* ; annual discoloration of the, 30, 225

Aedepsus, hot springs of Hercules at, i. 211 *sq.*

Aedesius, Sextilius Agesilaus, dedicates altar to Attis, i. 275 *n.*[1]

Aegipan and Hermes, i. 157

Aelian, on impregnation of Judean maid by serpent, i. 81

Aeneas and Dido, i. 114 *n.*[1]

Aeschylus, on Typhon, i. 156

Aesculapius, in relation to serpents, i. 80 *sq.* ; reputed father of Aratus, 80 *sq.* ; his shrines at Sicyon and Titane, 81 ; his dispute with Hercules, 209 *sq.*

Aeson and Medea, i. 181 *n.*[1]

Aetna, Latin poem, i. 221 *n.*[4]

Africa, serpents as reincarnations of the dead in, i. 82 *sqq.* ; infant burial in, 91 *sq.* ; reincarnation of the dead in, 91 *sq.* ; annual festivals of the dead in, ii. 66 ; worship of dead kings and chiefs in, 160 *sqq.* ; supreme gods in, 165, 173 *sq.*, 174, 186, with *n.*[5], 187 *n.*[1], 188 *sq.*, 190 ; worship of ancestral spirits among the Bantu tribes of, 174 *sqq.* ; inheritance of the kingship under mother-kin in, 211

——, North, custom of bathing at Midsummer among the Mohammedan peoples of, i. 249

——, West, sacred men and women in, i. 65 *sqq.* ; human sacrifices in, ii. 99 *n.*[2]

Afterbirth or placenta regarded as a person's double or twin, ii. 169 *sq.* *See also* Placenta

Afterbirths buried in banana groves, i. 93 ; regarded as twins of the children, 93 ; Shilluk kings interred where their afterbirths are buried, ii. 162

Agbasia, West African god, i. 79

Agdestis, a man-monster in the myth of Attis, i. 269

Agesipolis, King of Sparta, his conduct in an earthquake, i. 196

Agraulus, daughter of Cecrops, worshipped at Salamis in Cyprus, i. 145, 146

Agricultural peoples worship the moon, ii. 138 *sq.*

Agriculture, religious objections to, i. 88 *sqq.* ; in the hands of women in the Pelew Islands, ii. 206 *sq.* ; its tendency to produce a conservative character, 217 *sq.*

Ahts of Vancouver Island regard the moon as the husband of the sun, ii. 139 *n.*[1]

Airi, a deity of North-West India, i. 170

Aiyar, N. Subramhanya, on Indian dancing-girls, i. 63 *sqq.*

Ajax and Teucer, names of priestly kings of Olba, i. 144 *sq.*, 161

Akhetaton (Tell-el-Amarna), the capital of Amenophis IV., ii. 123 *n.*[1]

Akikuyu of British East Africa, their worship of snakes, i. 67 *sq.* ; their belief in serpents as reincarnations of the dead, 82, 85

Alaska, the Esquimaux of, ii. 51 ; the Koniags of, 106

Albania, marriage custom in, ii. 246

Albanians of the Caucasus, their worship of the moon, i. 73

Albinoes the offspring of the moon, i. 91

Albiruni, Arab geographer, on the Persian festival of the dead, ii. 68

Alcman on dew, ii. 137

Aleutians, effeminate sorcerers among the, ii. 254

Alexander Severus, at festival of Attis, i. 273

Alexander the Great expels a king of Paphos, i. 42 ; his fabulous birth, 81 ; assumes costumes of deities, 165 ; sacrifices to Megarsian Athena, 169 *n.*[3]

Alexandria, festival of Adonis at, i. 224 ; the Serapeum at, ii. 119 *n.*, 217

Alexandrian calendar, used by Plutarch, ii. 84

—— year, the fixed, ii. 28, 92 ; Plutarch's use of the, 49

All Saints, feast of, perhaps substituted for an old pagan festival of the dead, ii. 82 *sq.*

All Souls, feast of, ii. 51 *sqq.* ; originally a pagan festival of the dead, 81 ; instituted by Odilo, abbot of Clugny, 82

Allatu, Babylonian goddess, i. 9

Allifae in Samnium, baths of Hercules at, i. 213 $n.^2$
Almo, procession to the river, in the rites of Attis, i. 273
Almond causes virgin to conceive, i. 263 ; the father of all things, 263 *sq.*
Alyattes, king of Lydia, i. 133 $n.^1$
Alynomus, king of Paphos, i. 43
Amambwe, a Bantu tribe of Northern Rhodesia, its head chief reincarnated in a lion, ii. 193
Amasis, king of Egypt, his body burnt by Cambyses, i. 176 $n.^2$
Amathus, in Cyprus, Adonis and Melcarth at, i. 32, 117 ; statue of lion-slaying god found at, 117
Amatongo, ancestral spirits (Zulu term), i. 74 $n.^4$, ii. 184
Ambabai, an Indian goddess, i. 243
Ambala District, Punjaub, i. 94
Amélineau, E., discovers the tomb of King Khent, ii. 21 $n.^1$
Amenophis IV., king of Egypt, his attempt to abolish all gods but the sun-god, ii. 123 *sqq.*
America, reincarnation of the dead in, i. 91 ; the moon worshipped by the agricultural Indians of tropical, ii. 138
Amestris, wife of Xerxes, her sacrifice of children, ii. 220 *sq.*
Ammon, Milcom, the god of, i. 19
Ammon (the Egyptian) at Thebes, his human wives, i. 72 ; of Thebes identified with the sun, ii. 123 ; rage of King Amenophis IV. against the god, 124
Amoor, Gilyaks of the, i. 278 $n.^2$
Amorites, their law as to fornication, i. 37 *sq.*
Amsanctus, the valley of, i. 204 *sq.*
Amulets, crowns and wreaths as, ii. 242 *sq.*
Amyclae, in the vale of Sparta, i. 313, 314, 315
Amyclas, father of Hyacinth, i. 313
Anacreon, on Cinyras, i. 55
Anacyndaraxes, father of Sardanapalus, i. 172
Anaitis, sacred prostitution in the worship of, i. 38
Anassa, "Queen," title of goddess, i. 35 $n.^2$
Anazarba or Anazarbus, in Cilicia, i. 167 $n.^1$
Ancestor-worship among the Khasis of Assam, ii. 203 ; combined with mother-kin tends to a predominance of goddesses over gods in religion, 211 *sq.*
Ancestors, propitiation of deceased, i. 46 ; the worship of, the main practical religion of the Bantu tribes, ii. 176 *sqq.*

Ancestral spirits on shoulders of medicine-men, i. 74 $n.^4$; incarnate in serpents, 82 *sqq.* ; in the form of animals, 83 ; worshipped by the Bantu tribes of Africa, ii. 174 *sqq.* ; prayers to, 175 *sq.*, 178 *sq.*, 183 *sq.* ; sacrifices to, 175, 178 *sq.*, 180, 181 *sq.*, 183 *sq.*, 190 ; on the father's and on the mother's side, the two distinguished, 180, 181. *See also* Dead
Anchiale in Cilicia, i. 144 ; monument of Sardanapalus at, 172
Andania in Messenia, sacred men and women at, i. 76 $n.^3$
Andriamasinavalona, a Hova king, vicarious sacrifice for, ii. 221
Anemone, the scarlet, sprung from the blood of Adonis, i. 226
Angel, the Destroying, over Jerusalem, i. 24
Angus, belief as to the weaning of children in, ii. 148
Anhalt, custom as to sowing in, i. 239
Animals sacrificed by being hanged, i. 289 *sq.*, 292 ; and plants, edible, savage lamentations for, ii. 43 *sq.* ; dead kings and chiefs incarnate in, 162, 163 *sq.*, 173, 193 ; sacrificed to prolong the life of kings, 222
Anje-a, a mythical being who brings children to women, i. 103
Anklets made of human sinews worn by king of Uganda, ii. 224 *sq.*
Ankole, in Central Africa, the Bahima of, ii. 190
Anna, sister of Dido, i. 114 $n.^1$
Annam, offerings to the dead in spring in, i. 235 $n.^1$; annual festivals of the dead in, ii. 62 *sqq.*
Annual death and resurrection of gods, i. 6
Anointing as a ceremony of consecration, i. 21 $n.^2$ and ^{3}, 68, 74
—— sacred stones, custom of, i. 36
Antelopes, soul of a dead king incarnate in, ii. 163
Anthesteria, festival of the dead at Athens, i. 234 *sq.*
Antigonus, King, i. 212
Antimachia in Cos, priest of Hercules at, ii. 258
Antioch, destroyed by an earthquake, i. 222 $n.^1$; festival of Adonis at, 227, 257 *sq.*
Antiochus, Greek calendar of, i. 303 $n.^3$
Antwerp, feast of All Souls in, ii. 70
Anubis, Egyptian jackal-headed god, ii. 15, 18 $n.^3$, 22 $n.^2$; finds the body of Osiris, 85
Apameia, worship of Poseidon at, i. 195
Aphaca in Syria, sanctuary of Astarte at, i. 28, 259 ; meteor as signal for festival at, 259

Aphrodite, her sacred doves, i. 33, 147; sanctuary of, at Paphos, 33 *sqq.*; the month of, 145; her blood dyes white roses red, 226; name applied to summer, ii. 41
—— and Adonis, i. 11 *sq.*, 29, 280; their marriage celebrated at Alexandria, 224
—— and Cinyras, i. 48 *sq.*
—— and Pygmalion, i. 49 *sq.*
—— of the Lebanon, the mourning, i. 29 *sq.*
Apinagos Indians of Brazil, their dances and presentation of children to the moon, ii. 145 *sqq.*
Apis, sacred Egyptian bull, ii. 11, 119 *n.*; mourning for the death of, i. 225; held to be an image of the soul of Osiris, ii. 130
Apollo, the friend of Cinyras, i. 54; music in the worship of, 54 *sq.*; reputed father of Augustus, 81; the Cataonian, 147 *n.*[3]; his musical contest with Marsyas, 288; purified at Tempe, ii. 240
—— and Artemis, their priesthood at Ephesus, ii. 243 *sq.*
—— and Marsyas, i. 55
—— at Delphi, sacrifices of Croesus to, i. 180 *n.*[1]; and the Dragon at Delphi, ii. 240
—— of the Golden Sword, i. 176
—— the Four-handed, ii. 250 *n.*[2]
Apotheosis by being burnt alive, i. 179 *sq.*
Appian, on the costume of a priest of Isis, ii. 85 *n.*[3]
Apples forbidden to worshippers of Cybele and Attis, i. 280 *n.*[7]
Apuleius, on the worship of Isis, ii. 119 *n.*
Arab name for the scarlet anemone, i. 226
Arabic writer on the mourning for Tâ-uz (Tammuz) in Harran, i. 230
Arabs resort to the springs of Callirrhoe in Moab, i. 215 *sq.*
—— of Moab, their custom at harvest, ii. 48, 96; their remedies for ailments, 242
Aratus of Sicyon, deemed a son of Aesculapius, i. 81
Araucanian Indians of South America eat fruit of Araucanian pine, i. 278 *n.*[2]
Araunah, the threshing-floor of, i. 24
Arcadians sacrifice to thunder and lightning, i. 157
Archigallus, high-priest of Attis, i. 268, 279; prophesies, 271 *n.*
Arctic origin, alleged, of the Aryans, i. 229 *n.*[1]
Arenna or Arinna, i. 136 *n.*[1]; the sun-goddess of, 136
Arensdorf, custom at sowing in, i. 239

Argaeus, Mount, in Cappadocia, i. 190 *sq.*
Argive brides wore false beards, ii. 260
—— women bewail Adonis, i. 227 *n.*
Aristomenes, Messenian hero, his fabulous birth, i. 81
Aristophanes, on the Spartan envoy. i. 196 *n.*[4]; on Hercules as patron of hot springs, 209
Aristotelian philosophy, revival of the, i. 301
Aristotle on the political institutions of Cyprus, i. 49 *n.*[7]; on earthquakes, 211 *n.*[3]
Armengols, in the Pelew Islands, ii. 265
Armenia, sacred prostitution of girls before marriage in, i. 38, 58
Armenians, their festivals of the dead, ii. 65 *sq.*; their opinion of the baleful influence of the moon on children, 148
Arrian on Attis, i. 282
Artemis at Perga, i. 35; name given by Greeks to Asiatic Mother Goddesses, 169
—— and Apollo, their priesthood at Ephesus, ii. 243
—— of Ephesus served by eunuch priests, i. 269
—— the Hanged, i. 291
——, Laphrian, at Patrae, i. 126 *n.*[2]
——, Perasian, at Castabala, i. 115, 167 *sqq.*
——, Sarpedonian, in Cilicia, i. 167, 171
—— Tauropolis, i. 275 *n.*[1]
——, the Tauric, human sacrifices to the, i. 115
Artemision, a Greek month, ii. 239 *n.*[1]
Arunta of Central Australia, their belief in the reincarnation of the dead, i. 99, 100
Arval Brethren, their wreaths of corn, i. 44 *n.*; a Roman college of priests, ii. 239
Aryan family, marriage customs of the, ii. 235
Aryans, their alleged Arctic origin, i. 229 *n.*[1]; annual festivals of the dead among the, ii. 67 *sqq.*
Aryenis, daughter of Alyattes, i. 133 *n.*[1]
Ascalon, the goddess Derceto at, i. 34 *n.*[3]
Ascension of Adonis, i. 225
Ashantee, human sacrifices at earthquakes in, i. 201; kings of, their human sacrifices, ii. 97 *n.*[7]
Asherim, sacred poles, i. 18, 18 *n.*[2], 107, 108
Ashes of human victims scattered by winnowing-fans, ii. 97, 106
Ashtoreth (Astarte), i. 18 *n.*[2]. *See* Astarte
Ashurbanipal, king of Assyria, i. 144; confused with the legendary Sardana-

palus, 173 *sq.* ; carries off the bones of the kings of Elam, ii. 103

Ashvin, an Indian month, i. 243

Asia Minor, priestly dynasties of, i. 140 *sq.* ; subject to volcanic forces, 190 ; subject to earthquakes, 202

Asiatic goddesses of fertility served by eunuch priests, i. 269 *sq.*

Asopus, the river, i. 81

"A-souling," custom of, in England, ii. 79

Aspalis, a form of Artemis, i. 292

Assam, the Khasis of, i. 46, ii. 202 *sqq.* ; the Tangkul Nagas of, ii. 57 *sqq.*

Assumption of the Virgin and the festival of Diana, i. 308, 309

Assyrian cavalry, i. 25 *n.*[3]

Assyrians in Cilicia, i. 173

Astarte at Byblus, i. 13 *sq.* ; and the *asherim*, 18 ; kings as priests of, 26 ; at Paphos, 33 *sqq.* ; doves sacred to, 147 ; identified with the planet Venus, 258 ; of the Syrian Hierapolis served by eunuch priests, 269 *sq.* ; called by Lucian the Assyrian Hera, 280 *n.*[5]; the Heavenly Goddess, 303 ; the planet Venus her star, ii. 35

—— Aphrodite, i. 304 *n.*

Asteria, mother of the Tyrian Hercules (Melcarth), i. 112

Astyages, king of the Medes, i. 133 *n.*[1]

Asvattha tree, i. 82

Atargatis, Syrian goddess, i. 34 *n.*[3], 137 ; worshipped at Hierapolis - Bambyce, 162 *sq.* ; derivation of the name, 162 ; her husband-god, 162 *sq.*

Ates, a Phrygian, i. 286

Athamas, the dynasty of, i. 287

Athanasius, on the mourning for Osiris, ii. 217

'Atheh, Cilician goddess, i. 162

Athena, temple of, at Salamis in Cyprus, i. 145 ; and hot springs, 209, 210

——, Magarsian, a Cilician goddess, i. 169 *n.*[3]

—— Sciras, sanctuary of, ii. 238

Athenian boys, race of, at the vintage, ii. 238 ; boy carrying an olive-branch in procession, 238

Athenians, their superstition as to an eclipse of the moon, ii. 141

Athens, sacred serpent at, i. 87 ; the Commemoration of the Dead at, 234 ; sacrifice of an ox at, 296 *sq.* ; marriage custom at, ii. 245

Athribis, heart of Osiris at, ii. 11

Athyr, Egyptian month, ii. 8, 41, 49 *n.*[1] ; Osiris murdered on the seventeenth day of, 8, 84 ; festival of Osiris in the month of, 84 *sqq.*, 91

Atonga, tribe of Lake Nyassa, their theory of earthquakes, i. 199

Attica, summer festival of Adonis in, i. 226

Attis, priests of Cybele called, i. 140 ; sometimes identified with Adonis, 263 ; myth and ritual of, 263 *sqq.* ; beloved by Cybele, 263, 282 ; legends of his death, 264 ; his legend at Pessinus, 264 ; his self-mutilation, 264 *sq.* ; and the pine-tree, 264, 265, 267, 271, 277 *sq.*, 285, ii. 98 *n.*[5]; his eunuch priests, i. 265, 266 ; festival of his death and resurrection in March, 267 *sqq.*, 272 *sq.*, 307 *sq.* ; violets sprung from the blood of, 267 ; the mourning for, 272 ; bath of bull's blood in the rites of, 274 *sqq.* ; mysteries of, 274 *sq.* ; as a god of vegetation, 277 *sqq.*, 279 ; as the Father God, 281 *sqq.* ; identified with Zeus, 282 ; as a sky-god, 282 *sqq.* ; emasculation of, suggested explanation of myth, 283 ; his star-spangled cap, 284 ; identified with Phrygian moon-god Men Tyrannus, 284 ; human representatives of, 285 *sqq.* ; title borne by priests of Cybele, 285, 287

——, Adonis, Osiris, their mythical similarity, i. 6, ii. 201

Atys, son of Croesus, his death, i. 286 ; early king of Lydia, 286

Aubrey, John, on soul-cakes, ii. 78

Augustine on the effeminate priests of the Great Mother, i. 298 ; on the heathen origin of Christmas, 305 ; on the discovery of corn by Isis, ii. 116 ; on Salacia as the wife of Neptune, 233

Augustodunum (Autun), worship of Cybele at, i. 279

Augustus reputed a son of Apollo, i. 81

Aulus Gellius on the influence of the moon, ii. 132

Aun, or On, King of Sweden, sacrifices his sons to Odin, ii. 220

Aunis, feast of All Souls in, ii. 69 *sq.*

Aurelia Aemilia, a sacred harlot, i. 38

Aurohuacas, Indians of Colombia, i. 23 *n.*[2]

Aust, E., on the marriage of the Roman gods, ii. 236 *n.*[1]

Australia, belief as to the reincarnation of the dead in, i. 99 *sqq.*

Australian aborigines, their preparation for marriage, i. 60 ; their belief in conception without sexual intercourse, 99 *sqq.* ; their cuttings for the dead, 268

Austria, leaping over Midsummer fires in, i. 251

"Awakening of Hercules," festival at Tyre, i. 111

Awemba, Bantu tribe of Rhodesia, ii. 174 ; their worship of ancestral spirits, 175 ; their prayers to dead kings before going to war, 191 *sq.*

Axe, emblem of Hittite god of thundering sky, i. 134 ; as divine emblem, 163 ; symbol of Asiatic thunder-god, 183 ——, double-headed, symbol of Sandan, i. 127 ; carried by Lydian kings, 182 ; a palladium of the Heraclid sovereignty, 182 ; figured on coins, 183 *n.*

Ba-bwende, a tribe of the Congo, i. 271 *n.*

Ba-sundi, a tribe of the Congo, i. 271 *n.*

Baal, Semitic god, i. 15, 16 ; royal names compounded with, 16 ; as the god of fertility, 26 *sq.* ; conceived as god who fertilizes land by subterranean water, 159 —— and Sandan at Tarsus, i. 142 *sq.*, 161 —— of the Lebanon, i.' 32 —— of Tarsus, i. 117 *sqq.*, 162 *sq.*

Baalath or Astarte, i. 26, 34 —— and Baal, i. 27 —— Gebal, i. 14

Baalbec, i. 28 ; sacred prostitution at, 37 ; image of Hadad at, 163

Baalim, firstlings and first-fruits offered to the, i. 27 ; called lovers, 75 *n.*

Babylon, early kings of, worshipped as gods, i. 15 ; worship of Mylitta at, 36 ; religious prostitution at, 58 ; human wives of Marduk at, 71 ; sanctuary of Serapis at, ii. 119 *n.*

Babylonia, worship of Tammuz in, i. 6 *sqq.* ; the moon-god took precedence of the sun-god in ancient, ii. 138 *sq.*

Babylonian hymns to Tammuz, i. 9

Bacchanals tear Pentheus in pieces, ii. 98

Bacchic orgies suppressed by Roman government, i. 301 *n.*[2]

Bacchylides as to Croesus on the pyre, i. 175 *sq.*

Backbone of Osiris represented by the *ded* pillar, ii. 108 *sq.*

Baden, feast of All Souls in, ii. 74

Baethgen, F., on goddess 'Hatheh, i. 162 *n.*[2]

Baganda, their worship of the python, i. 86 ; rebirth of the dead among the, 92 *sq.* ; their theory of earthquakes, 199 ; their presentation of infants to the new moon, ii. 144, 145 ; ceremony observed by the king at new moon, 147 ; their worship of dead kings, 167 *sqq.* ; their veneration for the ghosts of dead relations, 191 *n.*[1]; their pantheon, 196 ; human sacrifices offered to prolong the life of their kings, 223 *sqq.*

Bagishu (Bageshu) of Mount Elgon, reincarnation of the dead among the, i. 92

Bagobos of the Philippine Islands, their theory of earthquakes, i. 200 ; of Mindanao, their custom of hanging and spearing human victims, 290 *sq.*

Baharutsis, a Bantu tribe of South Africa, ii. 179

Bahima, their belief as to dead kings and chiefs, i. 83 *n.*[1] —— of Ankole in Central Africa, their worship of the dead, ii. 190 *sq.* ; their belief in a supreme god Lugaba, 190 —— of Kiziba, ii. 173

Baigas, Dravidian tribe of India, their objection to agriculture, i. 89

Bailly, French astronomer, on the Arctic origin of the rites of Adonis, i. 229

Bairu, the, of Kiziba, ii. 173

Baku, on the Caspian, perpetual fires at, i. 192

Balinese, their conduct in an earthquake, i. 198

Baloi, witches and wizards, ii. 104

Banana, l women impregnated by the flower of the, i. 93

Bangalas of the Congo, rebirth of dead among the, i. 92. *See also* Boloki

Bantu tribes, their belief in serpents as reincarnations of the dead, i. 82 *sqq.* ; their worship of ancestral spirits, ii. 174 *sqq.*; their main practical religion a worship of ancestors, 176 *sqq.* ; their worship of the dead, 176 *sqq.*, 191 *sqq.*

Banyoro, their worship of serpents, i. 86 *n.*[1]

Baptism of bull's blood in the rites of Cybele, i. 274 *sqq.*

Bar-rekub, king of Samal, i. 15 *sq.*

Baralongs, a Bantu tribe of South Africa, ii. 179

Barea and Kunama, their annual festival of the dead, ii. 66

Barley forced for festival, i. 240, 241, 242, 244, 251 *sq.* —— and wheat discovered by Isis, ii. 116

Barotse, a Bantu tribe of the Zambesi, their belief in a supreme god Niambe, ii. 193 ; their worship of dead kings, 194 *sq.*

Barren women resort to graves in order to get children, i. 90 ; entice souls of dead children to them, 94

Barrenness of women cured by passing through holed stone, i. 36, with *n.*[4]; removed by serpent, 86 ; children murdered as a remedy for, 95

Barrows of Halfdan, ii. 100

Barsom, bundle of twigs used by Parsee priests, i. 191 *n.*²
Barth, H., on sculptures at Boghaz-Keui, i. 133 *n.*¹
Basil, pots of, on St. John's Day in Sicily, i. 245
Basuto chiefs buried secretly, ii. 104
Basutos, worship of the dead among the, ii. 179 *sq.*
Bataks of Sumatra, their theory of earth-quakes, i. 199 *sq.*
Batara-guru, the Batak creator, i. 199 *sq.*
Bath in river at the rites of Cybele, i. 273, 274 *n.*; of bull's blood in the rites of Attis, 274 *sqq.*; of image of Cybele perhaps a rain-charm, 280
—— of Aphrodite, i. 280
—— of Demeter, i. 280
—— of Hera in the river Burrha, i. 280 ; in the spring of Canathus, 280
Bathing on St. John's Day or Eve (Mid-summer Day or Eve), i. 246 *sqq.*; pagan origin of the custom, 249
Baths of Hercules, i. 212
—— of Solomon in Moab, i. 215
Batoo Bedano, an earthquake god, i. 202
Battle, purificatory ceremonies after a, ii. 251 *sq.*
—— of the gods and giants, i. 157
Baudissin, W. W. Graf von, on Tam-muz and Adonis, i. 6 *n.*¹; on Adonis as the personification of the spring vegetation, 228 *n.*⁶; on summer festival of Adonis, 232 *n.*
Bavaria, gardens of Adonis in, i. 244
Bawenda, the, of South Africa, the positions of their villages hidden, ii. 251
Bearded Venus, in Cyprus, i. 165, ii. 259 *n.*³
Beaufort, F., on perpetual flame in Lycia, i. 222 *n.*
Bechuana ritual at founding a new town, ii. 249
Bechuanas, their sacrifice of a blind bull on various occasions, ii. 249, 250 *sq.*
Bede, on the feast of All Saints, ii. 83
Beech, M. W. H., on serpent-worship, i. 85
Beena marriage in Ceylon, ii. 215
Begbie, General, i. 62 *n.*
Bel or Marduk at Babylon, i. 71
Belgium, feast of All Souls in, ii. 70
Bellerophon and Pegasus, i. 302 *n.*⁴
Bellona and Mars, ii. 231
Ben-hadad, king of Damascus, i. 15
Bendall, Professor C., i. 229 *n.*¹
Benefit of clergy, i. 68
Bengal, the Oraons and Mundas of, i. 46, 240

Benin, human victims crucified at, i. 294 *n.*³
Bent, J. Theodore, discovers ruins of Olba, i. 151 ; identifies site of Hiero-polis-Castabala, 168 *n.*¹
Berecynthia, title of Cybele, i. 279 *n.*⁴
Berenice and Ptolemy, annual festival in their honour, ii. 35 *n.*¹
Bes, Egyptian god, i. 118 *n.*¹
Bethlehem, worship of Adonis at, i. 257 *sqq.* ; fertility of the neighbourhood, 257 *n.*³ ; the Star of, 259
Betsileo of Madagascar, their belief in serpents as reincarnations of the dead, i. 83
Bghais, a Karen tribe of Burma, their annual festival of the dead, ii. 60 *sq.*
Bhâdon, Indian month, i. 243
Bharbhunjas, of the Central Provinces, India, marriage custom of the, ii. 262
Bharias, of the Central Provinces, India, exchange of costume between men and women at marriage among the, ii. 260 *sq.*
Bhujariya, festival in the Central Pro-vinces of India, i. 242
Bilaspore, infant burial in, i. 94 *sq.* ; annual festival of the dead in, ii. 60
Bion on the scarlet anemone, i. 226 *n.*¹
Bird, soul of a tree in a, ii. 111 *n.*¹
—— called " the soul of Osiris," ii. 110
Birds burnt in honour of Artemis, i. 126 *n.*² ; white, souls of dead kings incarnate in, ii. 162
Birks, Rev. E. B., on harvest custom at Orwell, i. 237 *n.*⁴
Birth, new, through blood in rites of Attis, i. 274 *sq.* ; of Egyptian kings at the Sed festival, ii. 153, 155 *sq.*
Birthday of the Sun, the twenty-fifth of December, i. 303 *sqq.*
Bisa chiefs reincarnated in pythons, ii. 193
Bishnois of the Punjaub, infant burial among the, ii. 94
Bithynians invoke Attis, i. 282
Black-snake clan, i. 100
Blay, men's clubhouse in the Pelew Islands, ii. 265
Blekinge, province of Sweden, Mid-summer custom in, i. 251
Blind bull sacrificed at the foundation of a town, ii. 249 ; sacrificed before an army going to war, 250
Blood, bath of bull's, in the rites of Attis, i. 274 *sqq.* ; remission of sins through the shedding of, 299 ; used in expiation for homicide, 299 *n.*² ; of pig used in exorcism and purification, 299 *n.*² ; not to be shed in certain sacrifices, ii. 222 *n.*²

Blood, the Day of, in the festival of Attis, i. 268, 285
Blowing of Trumpets in the festival of Attis, i. 268
Blue Spring, the, at Syracuse, i. 213 *n.*[1]
Boar, Attis killed by a, i. 264
Bocage of Normandy, rule as to the clipping of wool in the, ii. 134 *n.*[3]
Bodies of the dead, magical uses made of the, ii. 100 *sqq.* ; guarded against mutilation, 103 ; thought to be endowed with magical powers, 103, 104 *sq.*
Bodroum in Cilicia, ruins of, i. 167
Boghaz-Keui, Hittite capital, excavations of H. Winckler at, i. 125 *n.* ; situation and remains, 128 *sqq.* ; the gods of, 128 *sqq.* ; rock-hewn sculptures at, 129 *sqq.*
Bohemia, May-pole or Midsummer-tree in, i. 250 ; feast of All Souls in, ii. 72 *sq.*
Bolivia, the Chiriguanos Indians of, ii. 143 *n.*[4], 145
Boloki, or Bangala, of the Upper Congo, their ceremonies at the new moon, ii. 143 ; attempt to deceive spirit of disease among the, 262
Bones of the dead used in rain-making ceremonies, i. 22 ; of dead kings carried off or destroyed by enemies, ii. 103 *sq.*
——, fossil, source of myths about giants, i. 157 *sq.*
Bonfire on St. John's Eve, dances round it, i. 245
Book of the Dead, ii. 13
Bor, the ancient Tyana, Hittite monument at, i. 122 *n.*[1]
Borneo, custom of head-hunting in, i. 294 *sqq.* ; effeminate sorcerers in, ii. 253, 256
Bosanquet, Professor R. C., on the Four-handed Apollo, ii. 250 *n.*[2]
Bosman, W., on serpent-worship, i. 67
Bouche, Abbé, on West African priestesses, i. 66 *n.*[3], 69
Boys of living parents in ritual, ii. 236 *sqq.* ; dressed as girls to avert the Evil Eye, 260 ; marriage customs to ensure the birth of, 262
Brahman marriage in Southern India, bride dressed as a boy at, ii. 260
Brazil, the Apinagos Indians of, ii. 145 *sqq.*
Brazilian Indians, their belief in the noxious influence of the moon on children, ii. 148
Bread, fast from, in mourning for Attis, i. 272
Breasted, Professor J. H., on the eye of Horus, ii. 121 *n.*[3]; on Amenophis IV., 123 *n.*[1] ; on the Sed festival, 156 *n.*[1]

Breath not to defile sacred flame, i. 191
Brethren of the Ploughed Fields (*Fratres Arvales*), a Roman college of priests, ii. 239. *See also* Arval Brethren
"Bride" of the Nile, ii. 38
—— and Bridegroom at Midsummer in Sweden, i. 251
Bridegroom disfigured in order to avert the evil eye, ii. 261
British Columbia, the Indians of, respect the animals and plants which they eat, ii. 44
Brittany, feast of All Souls in, ii. 69 ; belief as to warts and the moon in, 149
Bromo, volcano in Java, worshipped, i. 220 *sq.*
Brother of a god, i. 51 ; dead elder, worshipped, ii. 175
Brothers and sisters, marriages of, in royal families, i. 44 ; in ancient Egypt, ii. 214 *sqq.* ; their intention to keep the property in the family, 215 *sq.*
Brown, A. R., on the beliefs of the West Australian aborigines as to the causes of childbirth, i. 104 *sqq.*
Brown, Dr. George, on snakes as re-incarnations of chiefs, i. 84
Bruges, feast of All Souls in, ii. 70
Brugsch, H., on Egyptian names for a year, ii. 26 *n.*[1]; on the Sothic period, 37 *n.* ; on the grave of Osiris at Philae, 111 ; on Isis as a personified corn-field, 117
Buddha and Buddhism, ii. 159
Buddhism, spiritual declension of, i. 310 *sq.*
Budge, Dr. E. A. Wallis, on goddess Net, i. 282 *n.* ; on an Egyptian funeral rite, ii. 15 *n.*[2]; on Isis, 115 *sq.* ; on the nature of Osiris, 126 *n.*[2]; on the solar theory of Osiris, 131 *n.*[3]; on the historical reality of Osiris, 160 *n.*[1] ; on Khenti-Amenti, 198 *n.*[2]
Buduna tribe of West Australia, their beliefs as to the birth of children, i. 104 *sq.*
Bugis of South Celebes, effeminate priests or sorcerers among the, ii. 253 *sq.*
Bulgaria, marriage customs in, ii. 246
Bull as emblem of generative force, i. 123 ; worshipped by the Hittites, 123, 132 ; emblem of Hittite thunder-god, 134 *sqq.* ; Hittite god standing on a, 135 ; as emblem of a thunder-god, 136 ; as symbol of thunder and fertility, 163 *sq.* ; the emblem of the Father God, 164 ; worshipped at Euyuk, 164 ; testicles of, used in rites of Cybele and Attis, 276 ; sacrificed at Egyptian funeral, ii. 15 ; white,

soul of dead king incarnate in a, 164 ; sacrificed to prolong the life of a king, 222 ; sacrificed to Zeus, the Saviour of the City, 238 ; blinded and sacrificed at the foundation of a town, 249 Bull's blood, bath of, in the rites of Attis, i. 274 *sq.*
—— hide cut in strips and pegged down round the site of a new town, ii. 249 ; bride seated on a, 246
—— skin, body of the dead placed in a, ii. 15 *n.*[2]
Bulls, husband-god at Hierapolis seated on, i. 163
—— sacrificed at caves of Pluto, i. 206 ; sacrificed to Persephone, 213 *n.*[1] ; sacrificed to dead chiefs, ii. 191
Burial at cross-roads, i. 93 *n.*[1]
—— of infants to ensure their rebirth, i. 91, 93 *sqq.* ; at Gezer, 108 *sq.* ; of Osiris in his rites, ii. 88
Burma, the Bghais of, ii. 60
Burmese, their conduct during an earthquake, i. 201
Burne, Miss C. S., and Miss G. F. Jackson on '' Souling Day '' in Shropshire, ii. 78 *sq.*
Burning of Melcarth, i. 110 *sqq.* ; of Sandan, 117 *sqq.* ; of Cilician gods, 170 *sq.* ; of Sardanapalus, 172 *sqq.* ; of Croesus, 174 *sqq.* ; of a god, 188 *sq.*
Burnings for dead kings of Judah, i. 177 *sq.* ; for dead Jewish Rabbis at Meiron, 178
Burns, Robert, on John Barleycorn, i. 230 *sq.*
Burnt alive, apotheosis by being, i. 179 *sq.*
—— Land of Lydia, i. 193 *sq.*
Burrha, river, Hera's bath in the, i. 280
Buru, East Indian island, use of oil as a charm in, i. 21 *n.*[2]
Busiris, backbone of Osiris at, ii. 11 ; specially associated with Osiris, 18 ; the ritual of, 86 ; rites of Osiris at, 87 *sq.* ; festival of Osiris in the month of Khoiak at, 108 ; temple of Usirniri at, 151
Busiro, the district containing the graves and temples of the kings of Uganda, ii. 168, 169, 224
Bustard totem, i. 104
Buto, city in Egypt, ii. 10
Butterflies, soul of a dead king incarnate in, ii. 164
Byblus, Adonis at, i. 13 *sqq.* ; the kings of, 14 *sqq.* ; mourning for Adonis at, 38 ; religious prostitution at, 58 ; inspired prophets at, 75 *sq.* ; festival of Adonis at, 225 ; the queen of, 9 ; Osiris associated with, 22 *sq.*, 127 ; its relation to Egypt, 127 *n.*[1]

Byrsa, origin of the name, ii. 250

Cadmus turned into a snake, i. 86 *sq.* ; perhaps personated by the Laurel-bearer at Thebes, ii. 241
——, Mount, i. 207
Cadys, a Lydian, i. 183
Caeculus, son of the fire-god Vulcan, ii. 235
Caesar introduces the Julian calendar, ii. 37 ; as to German observation of the moon, 141
Caffre purificatory ceremonies after a battle, ii. 251 *sq.*
Cairo, ceremony of cutting the dams at, ii. 38, 39 *sq.*
Calabar district, heads of chiefs buried secretly in the, ii. 104
Calabria, Easter custom in, i. 254
Calauria, Poseidon worshipped in, i. 203 *n.*[2]
Calendar, the natural, ii. 25
——, the Alexandrian, used by Plutarch, ii. 84
——, the Coptic, ii. 6 *n.*[3]
——, the Egyptian, ii. 24 *sqq.* ; date of its introduction, 36 *n.*[2]
—— of the Egyptian farmer, ii. 30 *sqq.*
—— of Esne, ii. 49 *sq.*
—— of the Indians of Yucatan, ii. 29 *n.*
—— the Julian, ii. 93 *n.*[1]
—— of the ancient Mexicans, its mode of intercalation, ii. 28 *n.*[3]
—— of Philocalus, i. 303 *n.*[2], 304 *n.*[3] ; ii. 95 *n.*[1]
Calendars, the Roman Rustic, ii. 95 *n.*[1]
California, the Karok Indians of, ii. 47 ; the Indians of, their annual festivals of the dead, 52 *sq.*
Californian Indians eat pine nuts, i. 278 *n.*[2] ; their notion that the owl is the guardian of the '' California big tree,'' ii. 111 *n.*[1]
Callaway, Rev. Henry, on the worship of the dead among the Zulus, ii. 184 *sq.*
Callirrhoe, the springs of, in Moab, i. 214 *sqq.*
Calpurnius Piso, L., on the wife of Vulcan, ii. 232 *sq.*
Calycadnus River, in Cilicia, i. 167 *n.*[2]
Camasene and Janus, ii. 235 *n.*[6]
Cambodia, annual festival of the dead in, ii. 61 *sq.*
Cambridge, personal relics of Kibuka, the war-god of the Baganda, preserved at, ii. 197
Cambyses, king of Persia, his treatment of Amasis, i. 176 *n.*[2]
Cameroon negroes, expiation for homicide among the, i. 299 *n.*[2]

Camul, custom as to hospitality in, i. 39 *n.*³

Canaanite kings of Jerusalem, i. 17

Canathus, Hera's annual bath in the spring of, i. 280

Candaules, king of Lydia, i. 182, 183

Canicular year, a Sothic period, ii. 36 *n.*²

Canopic decree, ii. 34 *n.*¹, 37 *n.*, 88 *n.*²

Canopus, the decree of, ii. 27

Capaneus and Evadne, i. 177 *n.*³

Cape Bedford in Queensland, belief of the natives as to the birth of children, i. 102

Capital punishment among some peoples originally a sacrifice, i. 290 *n.*²

Capitol at Rome, ceremonies at the rebuilding of the, ii. 244

Cappadocia, volcanic region of, i. 189 *sqq.* ; fire-worship in, 191 *sq.*

Car Nicobar, exorcism in, i. 299 *n.*²

Carchemish, Hittite capital on Euphrates, i. 123, 137 *n.*², 138 *n.*

Carchi, a province of Ecuador, All Souls' Day in, ii. 80

Caria, Zeus Labrandeus in, i. 182 ; poisonous vapours in, 205 *sq.*

Carians, their mourning for Osiris, ii. 86 *n.*¹

Caribs worshipped the moon in preference to the sun, ii. 138

Carlyle, Thomas, on the execution of the astronomer Bailly, i. 229 *n.*¹

Carna and Janus, ii. 235 *n.*⁶

Carnac, temples at, ii. 124 ; the sculptures at, 154

Carnival at Rome in the rites of Attis, i. 273

—— custom in Thracian villages, ii. 99 *sq.*

Carpini, de Plano, on funeral customs of the Mongols, i. 293

Carthage, legend and worship of Dido at, i. 113 *sq.* ; Hamilcar worshipped at, 116 ; the *suffetes* of, 116 *n.*¹ ; rites of Cybele at, 274 *n.* ; the effeminate priests of the Great Mother at, 298 ; legend as to the foundation of, ii. 250

Casalis, E., on serpent-worship, i. 84 ; on the worship of the dead among the Basutos, ii. 179 *sq.*

Castabala in Cappadocia, i. 168

—— in Cilicia, worship of Perasian Artemis at, i. 115, 167 *sqq.*

Castelnau, F. de, on the reverence of the Apinagos for the moon, ii. 146 *sq.*

Castiglione a Casauria, in the Abruzzi, Midsummer custom at, i. 246

Castor's tune, i. 196 *n.*³

Castration of Cronus and Uranus, i. 283 ; of sky-god, suggested explanation of, 283 ; of priests, suggested explanation of, 283 *sq.*

Catafalque burnt at funeral of king of Siam, i. 179

Catania in Sicily, the vineyards of, i. 194 ; gardens of Adonis at, 245

Catholic Church, the ritual of the, i. 54 ; ceremonies on Good Friday in the, 254, 255 *sq.*

Cato, i. 43

Catullus on self-mutilation of a priest of Attis, i. 270

Caucasus, the Albanians of the, i. 73 ; the Chewsurs of the, ii. 65

Cauldron, the magical, which makes the old young again, i. 181

Caverns of Demeter, i. 88

Caves, limestone, i. 152 ; in Semitic religion, 169 *n.*³

Cecrops, father of Agraulus, i. 145

Cedar forests of Cilicia, i. 149, 150 *n.*¹

—— sprung from the body of Osiris, ii. 110

—— -tree god, Osiris interpreted as a, ii. 109 *n.*¹

Celaenae, skin of Marsyas shown at, i. 288

Celebes, conduct of the inhabitants in an earthquake, i. 200

——, Central, the Toradjas of, ii. 33

——, Southern, marriage custom in, ii. 260

Celenderis in Cilicia, i. 41

Celtic year reckoned from November 1st, ii. 81

Censorinus, on the date of the rising of Sirius, ii. 34 *n.*¹

Central Provinces of India, gardens of Adonis in the, i. 242 *sq.*

Ceos, the rising of Sirius observed in, ii. 35 *n.*¹ ; rule as to the pollution of death in, 227

Cereals cultivated in ancient Egypt, ii. 30

Ceremonies, magical, for the regulation of the seasons, i. 3 *sqq.*

Ceres married to Orcus, ii. 231

Ceylon, *beena* marriage in, ii. 215

Chadwick, Professor H. M., ii. 81 *n.*³ ; on the dismemberment of Halfdan the Black, 100 *n.*² ; on a priest dressed as a woman, 259 *n.*²

Change in date of Egyptian festivals with the adoption of the fixed Alexandrian year, ii. 92 *sqq.*

Chants, plaintive, of corn-reapers in antiquity, ii. 45 *sq.*

Charlemagne compared to Osiris, ii. 199

Charm, to protect a town, ii. 249 *sqq.*

Charon, places of, i. 204, 205

Charonia, places of Charon, i. 204

Chastity, ceremonial, i. 43 ; ordeal of, 115 *n.*²

Chent-Ament (Khenti-Amenti), title of Osiris, ii. 87

Chephren, King of Egypt, his statue, ii. 21 *sq.*

Cherokee Indians, their myth of the Old Woman of the corn, ii. 46 *sq.* ; their lamentations after "the first working of the corn," 47

Cheshire, All Souls' Day in, ii. 79

Chewsurs of the Caucasus, their annual festival of the dead, ii. 65

Cheyne, T. K., on lament for kings of Judah, i. 20 *n.*[2]

Chief, ancestral, reincarnate in snakes, i. 84

Chiefs in the Pelew Islands, custom of slaying, ii. 266 *sqq.*

——, dead, worshipped, ii. 175, 176, 177, 179, 181 *sq.*, 187 ; thought to control the rain, 188 ; human sacrifices to, 191 ; spirits of, prophesy through living men and women, 192 *sq.*

"Child - stones," where souls of dead await rebirth, i. 100

Childbirth, primitive ignorance of the causes of, i. 106 *sq.*

Childless women expect offspring from St. George, i. 78 ; resort to Baths of Solomon, 78 ; receive offspring from serpent, 86 ; resort to graves in order to secure offspring, 96 ; resort to hot springs in Syria, 213 *sqq.*

Children bestowed by saints, i. 78 *sq.* ; given by serpent, 86 ; murdered that their souls may be reborn in barren women, 95 ; sacrificed to volcano in Siao, 219 ; sacrificed at irrigation channels, ii. 38 ; sacrificed by the Mexicans for the maize, 107 ; presented to the moon, 144 *sqq.*

—— of God, i. 68

—— of living parents in ritual, ii. 236 *sqq.* ; apparently thought to be endowed with more vitality than others, 247 *sq.*

Chili, earthquakes in, i. 202

Chimaera, Mount, in Lycia, perpetual fire on, i. 221

China, funeral of emperor of, i. 294

Chinese author on disturbance of earth-spirits by agriculture, i. 89

—— character compared to that of the ancient Egyptians, ii. 218

Chios, men sacrificed to Dionysus in, ii. 98 *sq.*

Chiriguanos Indians of Bolivia, their address to the sun, ii. 143 *n.*[4]

Chiriqui, volcano, i. 181

Chittim (Citium) in Cyprus, i. 31

Chnum of Elephantine identified with the sun, ii. 123

Choctaws, their annual festival of the dead, ii. 53 *sq.*

Christ crucified on March 25th, tradition, i. 306

Christian, F. W., on the prostitution of unmarried girls in Yap, ii. 265 *sq.*

Christian festivals displace heathen festivals, i. 308

Christianity and paganism, their resemblances explained as diabolical counterfeits, i. 302, 309 *sq.*

Christians and pagans, their controversy as to Easter, i. 309 *sq.*

Christmas, festival of, borrowed from the Mithraic religion, i. 302 *sqq.* ; the heathen origin of, 305

Chu-en-aten, name assumed by King Amenophis IV., ii. 124

Chukchees of North - Eastern Asia, effeminate sorcerers among the, ii. 256 *sq.*

Cicero at Cybistra, i. 122 *n.*[3] ; corresponds with Cilician king, 145 *n.*[2]

Cilicia, male deity of, assimilated to Zeus, i. 118 *sq.* ; kings of, their affinity to Sandan, 144 ; the Assyrians in, 173

——, Western or Rugged, described, i. 148 *sqq.* ; fossils of, 152 *sq.*

Cilician deity assimilated to Zeus, i. 144 *sqq.*, 148, 152

—— Gates, pass of the, i. 120

—— goddesses, i. 161 *sqq.*

—— gods, the burning of, i. 170 *sq.*

—— pirates, i. 149 *sq.*

—— priests, names of, i. 144

Cincius Alimentus, L., on Maia as the wife of Vulcan, ii. 232

Cinyrads, dynasty of the, i. 41 *sqq.*

Cinyras, the father of Adonis, i. 13, 14, 49 ; king of Byblus, 27 ; founds sanctuary of Astarte, 28 ; said to have instituted religious prostitution, 41, 50 ; his daughters, 41, 50 ; his riches, 42 ; his incest, 43 ; wooed by Aphrodite, 48 *sq.* ; meaning of the name, 52 ; the friend of Apollo, 54 ; legends of his death, 55

Ciotat in Provence, bathing at Midsummer at, i. 248

Circumcision, exchange of dress between men and women, ii. 263

Citium (Chittim), in Cyprus, i. 31, 50

Civilization, ancient, undermined by Oriental religions and other causes, i. 299 *sqq.*

Claudianus, Lucius Minius, i. 164

Claudius, the Emperor, and the rites of Attis, i. 266

Claudius Gothicus, the Emperor, i. 266 *n.*[2]

Clavigero, on the Mexican calendar, ii. 29 *n.*

Cleomenes, King of Sparta, and serpents, i. 87

Cleon of Magnesia at Gades, i. 113

Climatic and geographical conditions, their effect on national character, ii. 217

Clymenus, king of Arcadia, his incest, i. 44 *n.*[1]

Cnossus in Crete, prehistoric palace at, i. 34

Cochinchina, annual festival of the dead in, ii. 65

Cock as emblem of a priest of Attis, i. 279

Codrington, Dr. R. H., on mother-kin in Melanesia, ii. 211

Coimbatore, dancing-girls at, i. 62

Coincidence between the Christian and the heathen festivals of the divine death and resurrection, i. 308 *sq.*

Cologne, Petrarch at, on St. John's Eve, i. 247 *sq.*

Colombia, rule as to the felling of timber in, ii. 136

Comana, in Cappadocia, i. 136 *n.*[1]

—— in Pontus, worship of goddess Ma at, i. 39 ; swine not allowed to enter, 265 *n.*[1]

——, the two cities, i. 168 *n.*[6]

Commemoration of the Dead at Athens, i. 234

Commodus, conspiracy against, i. 273 ; addicted to the worship of Isis, ii. 118

Communal rights over women, i. 40, 61 *n.*

Compromise of Christianity with paganism, parallel with Buddhism, i. 310 *sqq.*

Conception, supposed, without sexual intercourse, i. 91, 93 *n.*[2], 264 ; in women supposed to be caused by food, 96, 102, 103, 104, 105. *See also* Impregnation

Conceptional animals and plants as causes of pregnancy in women, i. 97 *sq.*, 104 *sq.*

Concubines, human, of the god Ammon, i. 72

Conder, C. R., on "holy men" in Syria, i. 77 *n.*[4] ; on turning money at the new moon, ii. 149 *n.*[2]

Condylea in Arcadia, sacred grove of Artemis at, i. 291

Cone, image of Astarte, i. 14

Cones as emblems of a goddess, i. 34 *sqq.* ; votive, found in Babylonia, 35 *n.*[5]

Confession of the dead, the Egyptian, ii. 13 *sq.*

Confucianism, ii. 160

Congo, burial of infants on the, i. 91 ; priest dressed as a woman on the, ii. 254 *sq.*

Conibos Indians of the Ucayali River, their theory of earthquakes, i. 198

Conical stone as divine emblem, i. 165, 166

Constantine destroys temple of Astarte, i. 28 ; suppresses sacred prostitution, 37 ; removes standard cubit from the Serapeum, ii. 216 *sq.*

Consus and Ops, ii. 233 *n.*[6]

Contest for the throne of Egypt, traditions of a, ii. 17 *sq.*

Cook, A. B., i. 49 *n.*[6] ; on name of priest of Corycian Zeus, 155 *n.*[1] ; on the death of Romulus, ii. 98 *n.*[2] ; on the festival of Laurel-bearing at Thebes, 241 *n.*[3] ; on traces of mother-kin in the myth and ritual of Hercules, 259 *n.*[4]

Coomassie, in Ashantee, i. 201

Copenhagen, bathing on St. John's Eve at, i. 248

Coptic calendar, ii. 6 *n.*[3]

Corea, dance of eunuchs in, i. 270 *n.*[2]

Coreans, their ceremony on the fifteenth day of the moon, ii. 143

Corn sprouting from the dead body of Osiris, ii. 89 ; water thrown on the last corn cut, a rain-charm, i. 237 *sq.*

—— and grapes, symbols of the god of Tarsus, i. 119, 143 ; of the god of Ibreez, 121 ; figured with double-headed axe on Lydian coin, 183

—— and vine, emblems of the gods of Tarsus and Ibreez, i. 160 *sq.*

—— -god, Adonis as a, i. 230 *sqq.* ; Attis as a, 279 ; mourned at midsummer, ii. 34 ; Osiris as a, 89 *sqq.*, 96 *sqq.*

—— -reaping in Egypt, Palestine, and Greece, date of the, i. 231 *n.*[3]

—— -sieve, severed limbs of Osiris placed on a, ii. 97

—— -spirit, Tammuz or Adonis as a, i. 230 *sqq.* ; propitiation of the, perhaps fused with a worship of the dead, 233 *sqq.* ; represented as a dead old man, ii. 48, 96 ; represented by human victims, 97, 106 *sq.*

—— -stuffed effigies of Osiris buried with the dead as a symbol of resurrection, ii. 90 *sq.*, 114

—— -wreaths as first-fruits, i. 43 ; worn by Arval Brethren, i. 44 *n.*

Coronation, human sacrifices to prolong a king's life at his, ii. 223

Corycian cave, priests of Zeus at the, i. 145 ; the god of the, 152 *sqq.* ; described, 153 *sq.* ; saffron at the, 187 ; name perhaps derived from crocus, 187

Corycus in Cilicia, ruins of, i. 153

Cos, traces of mother-kin in, ii. 259 ;

Sacred Marriage in, 259 *n.*[4]; bridegroom dressed as woman in, 260

Cosenza in Calabria, Easter custom at, i. 254

Cotys, king of Lydia, i. 187

Cow, image of, in the rites of Osiris, ii. 50, 84 ; Isis represented with the head of a, 50 ; thought to be impregnated by moonshine, 130 *sq.*

—— goddess Shenty, ii. 88

Cows sacred to Isis, ii. 50

Creation of the world thought to be annually repeated, i. 284

Crescent - shaped chest in the rites of Osiris, ii. 85, 130

Crests of the Cilician pirates, i. 149

Crete, sacred trees and pillars in, i. 107 *n.*[2]

Crimea, the Taurians of the, i. 294

Crocodile-shaped hero, i. 139 *n.*[1]

Croesus, king of Lydia, captures Pteria, i. 128 ; the burning of, 174 *sqq.*, 179 ; his burnt offerings to Apollo at Delphi, 180 *n.*[1]; dedicates golden lion at Delphi, 184 ; his son Atys, 286

Cronion, a Greek month, ii. 238

Cronus, identified with Phoenician El, i. 166 ; castrates his father Uranus and is castrated by his son Zeus, 283 ; name applied to winter, ii. 41

Crook and scourge or flail, the emblems of Osiris, ii. 108, 153, compare 20

Crooke, W., on sacred dancing-girls, i. 65 *n.*[1]; on Mohammedan saints, 78 *n.*[2]; on infant burial, 93 *sq.* ; on the custom of the False Bride, ii. 262 *n.*[2]

Crops dependent on serpent-god, i. 67 ; human victims sacrificed for the, 290 *sq.*

Cross-roads, burial at, i. 93 *n.*[1]

Crown - wearer, priest of Hercules at Tarsus, i. 143

Crowns as amulets, ii. 242 *sq.* ; laid aside in mourning, etc., 243 *n.*[2]

—— of Egypt, the White and the Red, ii. 21 *n.*[1]

Crucifixion of Christ, tradition as to the date of, i. 306

—— of human victims at Benin, i. 294 *n.*[3]; gentile, at the spring equinox, 307 *n.*

Crux ansata, the Egyptian symbol of life, ii. 89

Cubit, the standard, kept in the temple of Serapis, ii. 217

Cultivation of staple food in the hands of women (Pelew Islands), ii. 206 *sq.*

Cumont, Professor Franz, on the *taurobolium*, i. 275 *n.*[1]; on the Nativity of the Sun, 303 *n.*[3]; as to the parallel between Easter and the rites of Attis, 310 *n.*[1]

Customs of the Pelew Islanders, ii. 253 *sqq.*, 266 *sqq.*

Cuthar, father of Adonis, i. 13 *n.*[2]

Cuttings for the dead, i. 268

Cyaxares, king of the Medes, i. 133 *n.*, 174

Cybele, the image of, i. 35 *n.*[3]; her cymbals and tambourines, 54 ; her lions and turreted crown, 137 ; priests of, called Attis, 140 ; the Mother of the Gods, 263 ; her love for Attis, 263, 282 ; her worship adopted by the Romans, 265 ; sacrifice of virility to image of, 268 ; subterranean chambers of, 268 ; orgiastic rites of, 278 ; a goddess of fertility, 279 ; worshipped in Gaul, 279 ; fasts observed by the worshippers of, 280 ; a friend of Marsyas, 288 ; effeminate priests of, ii. 257, 258

Cybistra in Cappadocia, i. 120, 122, 124

Cymbal, drinking out of a, i. 274

Cymbals in religious music, i. 52, 54

—— and tambourines in worship of Cybele, i. 54

Cynopolis, the cemetery of, ii. 90

Cypriote syllabary, i. 49 *n.*[7]

Cyprus, Phoenicians in, i. 31 *sq.* ; Adonis in, 31 *sqq.* ; sacred prostitution in, 36, 50, 59 ; Melcarth worshipped in, 117 ; human sacrifices in, 145 *sq.* ; the bearded Venus in, ii. 259 *n.*[3]

Cyril of Alexandria on the festival of Adonis at Alexandria, i. 224 *n.*[2]

Cyrus and Croesus, i. 174 *sqq.*

Cyzicus, worship of the Placianian Mother at, i. 274 *n.*

Dacia, hot springs in, i. 213

Dacotas, their theory of the waning moon, ii. 130

Dad pillar. *See Ded* pillar

Dahomans, their annual festival of the dead, ii. 66

Dahomey, kings of, their human sacrifices, ii. 97 *n.*[7]

Dairyman, sacred, of the Todas, his custom as to the pollution of death, ii. 228 ; bound to live apart from his wife, 229

Dalisandos in Isauria, inscriptions at, ii. 213 *n.*[1]

Damascus, Aramean kings of, i. 15

Damasen, a giant, i. 186

Damatrius, a Greek month, ii. 49 *n.*[1]

Dams in Egypt, the cutting of the, ii. 31 *sq.*, 37 *sq.*, 39 *sq.*

Dance of eunuchs in Corea, i. 270 *n.*[2]; on the Congo, 271 *n.* ; of hermaphrodites in Pegu, 271 *n.* ; sacred, at the Sed festival, ii. 154 ; of king before the ghosts of his ancestor, 192

282

INDEX

Dances, religious, i. 61, 65, 68 ; at
festivals of the dead, ii. 52, 53, 55,
58, 59 ; at the new moon, 142
Dancing-girls in India, harlots and wives
of the gods, i. 61 *sqq.*
Dañh-gbi, python-god, i. 66
Darmesteter, James, on the Fravashis,
ii. 67 *n.*² ; his theory as to the date of
the *Gathas*, ii. 84 *n.*
Dâsî, dancing-girl, i. 63
Dastarkon in Cappadocia, i. 147 *n.*³
Dates forbidden to worshippers of Cybele
and Attis, i. 280
Daughter of a god, i. 51
David, King, in relation to the old kings
of Jerusalem, i. 18 *sq.* ; his conquest
of Ammon, 19 ; his taking of a census,
24 ; as a harper, 52, 53, 54
—— and Goliath, i. 19 *n.*²
—— and Saul, i. 21
Davis, Mr. R. F., on harvest custom in
Nottinghamshire, i. 238 *n.*
Day of Blood in rites of Attis, i. 268,
285
De Plano Carpini, on the funeral customs
of the Mongols, i. 293
Dea Dia, a Roman goddess of fertility,
ii. 239
Dead, Festival of the, in Java, i. 220 ;
worship of the, perhaps fused with the
propitiation of the corn-spirit, 233 *sqq.* ;
cuttings for the, 268 ; Osiris king and
judge of the, ii. 13 *sq.* ; the Egyptian,
identified with Osiris, 16 ; annual
festivals of the, 51 *sqq.* ; the spirits of
the, personated by living men, 52, 53,
58 ; magical uses made of their bodies,
100 *sqq.* ; worship of the, among the
Bantu tribes of Africa, 176 *sqq.* *See
also* Ancestral spirits
——, reincarnation of the, i. 82 *sqq.* ; in
America, 91 ; in Africa, 91 *sq.*
—— kings and chiefs worshipped in
Africa, ii. 160 *sqq.* ; sacrifices offered
to, 162, 166 *sq.* ; incarnate in animals,
162, 163 *sq.*, 173 ; consulted as oracles,
167, 171, 172, 195 ; human sacrifices
to, 173 ; worshipped by the Barotse,
194 *sq.*
—— men believed to beget children, i.
91, 264
—— Sea, i. 23
Death in the fire as an apotheosis, i. 179
sq. ; the pollution of, ii. 227 *sqq.*
—— and resurrection, annual, of gods,
i. 6 ; of Adonis represented in his rites,
224 *sq.* ; coincidence between the pagan
and the Christian festival of the divine,
308 ; of Osiris dramatically represented
in his rites, ii. 85 *sq.* ; of Osiris interpreted as the decay and growth of
vegetation, 126 *sqq.*

December, the twenty-fifth of, reckoned
the winter solstice, and the birthday of
the Sun, i. 303 *sqq.*
Decline of the civic virtues under the
influence of Oriental religions, i. 300
sq.
Ded or *tet* pillar, the backbone of Osiris,
ii. 108 *sq.*
Dedicated men and women in Africa, i.
65 *sqq.*
Dedication of girls to the service of a
temple, i. 61 *sqq.* ; of children to gods,
79
Dee, river, holed stone in the, i. 36 *n.*⁴
Defoe, Daniel, on the Angel of the
Plague, i. 24 *n.*²
Delos, sacred embassy to, ii. 244
Delphi, Apollo and the Dragon at, ii.
240
Delphinium Ajacis, i. 314 *n.*¹
Demeter, her sacred caverns, i. 88 ;
sacred vaults of, 278 ; sorrowing for
the descent of the Maiden, ii. 41 ; the
month of, 41 ; mysteries of, at Eleusis,
90 ; at the well, 111 *n.*⁶ ; identified
with Isis, 117
—— and ears of corn, i. 166
—— and Poseidon, i. 280
—— and the king's son at Eleusis, i.
180
Denderah, inscriptions at, ii. 11, 86 *sqq.*,
89, 91, 130 *n.* ; the hall of Osiris at,
110
Derceto, goddess at Ascalon, i. 34 *n.*³
Dervishes revered in Syria, i. 77 *n.*⁴ ; of
Asia Minor, 170
Deucalion at Hierapolis, i. 162 *n.*²
Deuteronomic redactor, i. 26 *n.*¹
Deuteronomy, publication of, i. 18 *n.*³
Deutsch-Zepling in Transylvania, rule as
to sowing in, ii. 133 *n.*³
Dêvadâsî, dancing-girl, i. 63 *sq.*
Dêvaratiâl, dancing-girl, i. 63
Dew, bathing in the, on Midsummer
Eve or Day, i. 246 *sq.*, 248 ; a
daughter of Zeus and the moon, ii.
137
Diabolical counterfeits, resemblances of
paganism to Christianity explained as,
i. 302, 309 *sq.*
Diana, a Mother Goddess, i. 45 ; her
sanctuary at Nemi, 45
Dianus and Diana, i. 27, 45
Dido flees from Tyre, i. 50 ; her tradi-
tional death in the fire, 114 ; wor-
shipped at Carthage, 114 ; meaning
of the name, 114 *n.*¹ ; an Avatar of
Astarte, 177 ; how she procured the
site of Carthage, ii. 250
Dinant, feast of All Souls in, ii. 70
Dinkard, a Pahlavi work, ii. 68 *n.*²
Dinkas, their belief in serpents as rein-

carnations of the dead, i. 82 *sq.* ; pour milk on graves, 87

Dio Chrysostom, on the people of Tarsus, i. 118 ; on pyre at Tarsus, 126 *n.*[1]

Diodorus Siculus, on worship of Poseidon in Peloponnese, i. 203 ; on the burial of Osiris, ii. 10 *sq.* ; on the rise of the Nile, 31 *n.*[1] ; on the date of harvest in Egypt, 32 *n.*[2] ; on Osiris as a sun-god, 120 ; on the predominance of women over men in ancient Egypt, 214

Diomede, human sacrifices to, i. 145

Dionysus in form of bull, i. 123 ; with vine and ploughman on a coin, 166 ; ancient interpretation of, 194, 213 ; death, resurrection, and ascension of, 302 *n.*[4] ; torn in pieces, ii. 98 ; human sacrifices to, in Chios, 98 *sq.* ; his coarse symbolism, 113 ; identified with Osiris, 113 ; race of boys at vintage from his sanctuary, 238 ; men dressed as women in the rites of, 258 ; the effeminate, 259

Diospolis Parva (How), monument of Osiris at, ii. 110

Diphilus, king of Cyprus, i. 146

Disc, winged, as divine emblem, i. 132

Discoloration, annual, of the river Adonis, i. 30, 225

Discovery of the body of Osiris, ii. 85 *sq.*

Disease of language the supposed source of myths, ii. 42

Disguises to avert the evil eye, ii. 262 ; to deceive dangerous spirits, 262 *sq.*, 263 *sq.*

Dismemberment of Osiris, suggested explanations of the, ii. 97 ; of Halfdan the Black, king of Norway, 100, 102 ; of Segera, a magician of Kiwai, 101 ; of kings and magicians, and use of their severed limbs to fertilize the country, 101 *sq.* ; of the bodies of the dead to prevent their souls from becoming dangerous ghosts, 188

Ditino, deified dead kings, ii. 194

Divination at Midsummer, i. 252 *sq.*

Divining bones, ii. 180, 181

Divinities of the volcano Kirauea, i. 217

Divinity of Semitic kings, i. 15 *sqq.* ; of Lydian kings, 182 *sqq.*

Dixmude, in Belgium, feast of All Souls at, ii. 70

Dobrizhoffer, M., on the respect of the Abipones for the Pleiades, i. 258 *n.*[2]

Doctrine of lunar sympathy, ii. 140 *sqq.*

Dôd, "beloved," i. 19 *n.*[2], 20 *n.*[2]

Dog-star. *See* Sirius

Doliche in Commagene, i. 136

Domaszewski, Professor A., on the rites of Attis at Rome, i. 266 *n.*[2]

Dorasques of Panama, their theory of earthquakes, i. 201

Dos Santos, J., Portuguese historian, on the method adopted by a Caffre king to prolong his life, ii. 222 *sq.*

Double, the afterbirth or placenta, regarded as a person's double, ii. 169 *sq.*

—— -headed axe, symbol of Sandan, i. 127; carried by Lydian kings, 182 ; a palladium of the Heraclid sovereignty, 182 ; figured on coins, 183 *n.*

—— -headed eagle, Hittite emblem, i. 133 *n.*

Doutté, Edmond, on sacred prostitution in Morocco, i. 39 *n.*[3]

Doves burnt in honour of Adonis, i. 126 *n.*[2], 147

——, sacred, of Aphrodite, i. 33 ; or Astarte, 147

Dowries earned by prostitution, i. 38, 59

Dragon slain by Cadmus at Thebes, ii. 241

—— and Apollo, at Delphi, ii. 240

Drama, sacred, of the death and resurrection of Osiris, ii. 85 *sq.*

Dramas, magical, for the regulation of the seasons, i. 4 *sq.*

Dramatic representation of the resurrection of Osiris in his rites, ii. 85

Dreams, revelations given to sick people by Pluto and Persephone in, i. 205 ; spirits of the dead appear to the living in, ii. 162, 190 ; as causes of attempted transformation of men into women, 255 *sqq.*

Drenching last corn cut with water as a rain-charm, i. 237 *sq.*

Drinking out of a king's skull in order to be inspired by his spirit, ii. 171

Drought, kings answerable for, i. 21 *sq.*

Drum, eating out of a, i. 274

Drums, human sacrifice for royal, ii. 223, 225

Duchesne, Mgr. L., on the origin of Christmas, i. 305 *n.*[4] ; on the date of the Crucifixion, 307

Dyaks of Sarawak, their custom of head-hunting, i. 295 *sq.*

Ea, Babylonian god, i. 9

Eagle to carry soul to heaven, i. 126 *sq.* ; double-headed, Hittite emblem, 133 *n.*

Ears of corn, emblem of Demeter, i. 166

Earth as the Great Mother, i. 27

—— and sky, myth of their violent separation, i. 283

——, the goddess, mother of Typhon, i. 156

Earth-goddess annually married to Sun-god, i. 47 *sq.* ; disturbed by the operations of husbandry, 88 *sqq.* ; married to Sky-god, 282, with *n.*²
—— -spirits disturbed by agriculture, i. 89
Earthquake god, i. 194 *sqq.*
Earthquakes, attempts to stop, i. 196 *sqq.*
East, mother-kin and Mother Goddesses in the ancient, ii. 212 *sqq.*
Easter, gardens of Adonis at, in Sicily, i. 253 *sq.* ; resemblance of the festival of, to the rites of Adonis, 254 *sqq.*, 306 ; the festival of, assimilated to the spring festival of Attis, 306 *sqq.* ; controversy between Christians and pagans as to the origin of, 309 *sq.*
"Eater of the Dead," fabulous Egyptian monster, ii. 14
Eclipse of the moon, Athenian superstition as to an, ii. 141
Eden, the tree of life in, i. 186 *n.*⁴
Edom, the kings of, i. 15 ; their bones burned by the Moabites, ii. 104
Edonians in Thrace, Lycurgus king of the, ii. 98, 99
Eesa, a Somali tribe, ii. 246
Effect of geographical and climatic conditions on national character, ii. 217
Effeminate sorcerers or priests, order of, ii. 253 *sqq.*
Effigies of Osiris, stuffed with corn, buried with the dead as a symbol of resurrection, ii. 90 *sq.*, 114
Egypt, wives of Ammon in, i. 72 ; date of the corn-reaping in, 231 *n.*³ ; the Nativity of the Sun at the winter solstice in, 303 ; in early June, ii. 31 ; mother-kin in ancient, 213 *sqq.*
Egyptian astronomers acquainted with the true length of the solar year, ii. 26, 27, 37 *n.*
—— calendar, the official, ii. 24 *sqq.* ; date of its introduction, 36 *n.*²
—— ceremony at the winter solstice, ii. 50
—— dead identified with Osiris, ii. 16
—— farmer, calendar of the, ii. 30 *sqq.* ; his festivals, ii. 32 *sqq.*
—— festivals, their dates shifting, ii. 24 *sq.*, 92 *sqq.* ; readjustment of, 91 *sqq.*
—— funeral rites a copy of those performed over Osiris, ii. 15
—— hope of immortality centred in Osiris, ii. 15 *sq.*, 114, 159
—— kings worshipped as gods, i. 52 ; the most ancient, buried at Abydos, ii. 19 ; their oath not to correct the vague Egyptian year by intercalation, 26 ; perhaps formerly slain in the character of Osiris, 97 *sq.*, 102 ; as Osiris,

151 *sqq.* ; renew their life by identifying themselves with the dead and risen Osiris, 153 *sq.* ; born again at the Sed festival, 153, 155 *sq.* ; perhaps formerly put to death to prevent their bodily and mental decay, 154 *sq.*, 156
Egyptian language akin to the Semitic, ii. 161
—— months, table of, ii. 37 *n.*
—— myth of the separation of earth and sky, i. 283 *n.*³
—— people, the conservatism of their character, ii. 217 *sq.* ; compared to the Chinese, 218
—— reapers, their lamentations and invocations of Isis, i. 232, ii. 45, 117
—— religion, the development of, ii. 122 *sqq.* ; dominated by Osiris, 158 *sq.*
—— standard resembling a placenta, ii. 156 *n.*¹
—— year vague, not corrected by intercalation, ii. 24 *sq.* ; the sacred, began with the rising of Sirius, 35
Egyptians sacrifice red-haired men, ii. 97, 106 ; the ancient, question of their ethnical affinity, 161
Ekoi of Southern Nigeria, their custom of mutilating men and women at festivals, i. 270 *n.*²
El, Phoenician god, i. 13, 16 *n.*¹ ; identified with Cronus, 166
El-Bûgât, festival of mourning for Tammuz in Harran, i. 230
Elam, the kings of, their bones carried off by Ashurbanipal, ii. 103 *sq.*
Eleusis, Demeter and the king's son at, i. 180 ; sacrifice of oxen at, 292 *n.*³ ; mysteries of Demeter at, ii. 90
Eli, the sons of, i. 76
Elisha prophesies to music, i. 53, 54 ; finds water in the desert, 53, 75
Ellis, A. B., on sacred prostitution in West Africa, i. 65 *sq.*, 69 *sq.* ; on tattoo marks of priests, 74 *n.*⁴ ; on an ordeal of chastity, 115
Emesa, sun-god Heliogabalus at, i. 35
Empedocles leaps into the crater of Etna, i. 181
Emperor of China, funeral of an, i. 294
Ἐναγίζειν distinguished from θύειν, i. 316 *n.*¹
Enemy, charms to disable an, ii. 252
England, harvest custom in, i. 237 ; the feast of All Souls in, ii. 78 *sq.*
Ennius, on Hora and Quirinus, ii. 233
"Entry of Osiris into the moon," ii. 130
Enylus, king of Byblus, i. 15 *n.*
Ephesus, Artemis of, i. 269 ; Hecate at, 291 ; the priesthood of Apollo and Artemis at, ii. 243 *sq.*
Epidaurus, Aesculapius at, i. 80
Epiphany, the sixth of January, i. 305

Epirus, the kings of, their bones scattered by Lysimachus, ii. 104

Equinox, the vernal, resurrection of Attis at the, i. 273, 307 *sq.* ; date of the Crucifixion assigned to the spring equinox, 307 ; tradition that the world was created at the spring equinox, 307

Erechtheum, sacred serpent in the, i. 87

Erechtheus, king of Athens, his incest with his daughter, i. 44 *n.*[1]; his sacred serpent, 87

Eregli (the ancient Cybistra) in Cappadocia, i. 120, 122

Eresh-Kigal, Babylonian goddess, i. 9

Erica-tree, Osiris in the, ii. 9, 108, 109

Eriphyle, the necklace of, i. 32 *n.*[2]

Erman, Professor A., on Anubis at Abydos, ii. 18 *n.*[3] ; on corn-stuffed effigies of Osiris, 91 ; on the development of Egyptian religion, 122 *n.*[2]

Erme or *Nenneri*, gardens of Adonis in Sardinia, i. 244

Eshmun, Phoenician deity, i. 111 *n.*[6]

Esne, the festal calendar of, ii. 49 *sq.*

Esquimaux of Alaska, their annual festival of the dead, i. 51 *sq.*

Esthonian peasants regulate their sowing and planting by the moon, ii. 135

Esthonians, their ceremony at the new moon, ii. 143

Eternal life, initiate born again to, in the rites of Cybele and Attis, i. 274 *sq.*

Etesian winds, i. 35 *n.*[1]

Etna, Mount, Typhon buried under, i. 156, 157 ; the death of Empedocles on, 181 ; the ashes of, 194 ; offerings thrown into the craters of, 221

Euboea subject to earthquakes, i. 211 ; date of threshing in, 232 *n.* ; harvest custom in, 238

Eudoxus, on the Egyptian festivals, ii. 35 *n.*[2]

Eunuch, priests of the Mother Goddess, i. 206 ; in the service of Asiatic goddesses of fertility, 269 *sq.* ; in various lands, 270 *n.*[2]; of Attis tattooed with pattern of ivy, 278 ; of Cybele, ii. 258

Eunuchs, dances of, i. 270 *n.*[2], 271 *n.* ; dedicated to a goddess in India, 271 *n.*; sacred, at Hierapolis-Bambyce, their rule as to the pollution of death, ii. 272

Euripides on the death of Pentheus, ii. 98 *n.*[5]

Europe, custom of showing money to the new moon in, ii. 148 *sq.*

Eusebius on sacred prostitution, i. 37 *n.*[2], 73 *n.*[1]

Euyuk in Cappadocia, Hittite palace at, i. 123, 132, 133 *n.* ; bull worshipped at, 164

Evadne and Capaneus, i. 177 *n.*[3]

Evil Eye, boys dressed as girls to avert the, ii. 260 ; bridegroom disfigured in order to avert the, 261 ; disguises to avert the, 262

Ewe farmers fear to wound the Earth goddess, i. 90

—— people of Togo-land, their belief in the marriage of Sky with Earth, i. 282 *n.*[2]

—— -speaking peoples of the Slave Coast, sacred prostitution among the, i. 65 *sq.* ; worship pythons, 83 *n.*[1]

Exchange of dress between men and women in rites, ii. 259 *n.*[3] ; at marriage, 260 *sqq.* ; at circumcision, 263

Exogamous clans in the Pelew Islands, ii. 204

Exorcism by means of music, i. 54 *sq.*

Expiation for homicide, i. 299 *n.*[2] ; Roman, for prodigies, ii. 244

Eye as a symbol of Osiris, ii. 121 ; of sacrificial ox cut out, 251 *sq.*

—— of Horus, ii. 17, 121 with *n.*[3]

——, the Evil, boys dressed as girls to avert the, ii. 260 ; bridegroom disfigured in order to avert, 261

Eyes of the dead, Egyptian ceremony of opening the, ii. 15

Ezekiel on the mourning for Tammuz, i. 11, 17, 20 ; on the Assyrian cavalry, 25 *n.*[3]; on the king of Tyre, 114

False Bride, custom of the ii. 262 *n.*[2]

Farnell, Dr. L. R., on Greek religious music, i. 55 *n.*[1] and [3]; on religious prostitution in Western Asia, 57 *n.*[1], 58 *n.*[2] ; on the position of women in ancient religion, ii. 212 *n.*[1]; on the Flamen Dialis, 227 ; on the children of living parents in ritual, 236 *sq.* ; on the festival of Laurel-bearing at Thebes, 242 *n.* ; on eunuch priests of Cybele, 258 *n.*[1]

Farwardajan, a Persian festival of the dead, ii. 68

Fast from bread in mourning for Attis, i. 272

Fasts observed by the worshippers of Cybele and Attis, i. 280 ; of Isis and Cybele, 302 *n.*[4]

Father named after his son, i. 51 *n.*[4] ; of a god, 51, 52 ; dead, worshipped, ii. 175, 184 *sq.* ; the head of the family under a system of mother-kin, 211

—— -deity of the Hittites, the god of the thundering sky, i. 134 *sqq.*

—— God, his emblem the bull, i. 164 ; Attis as the, 281 *sqq.* ; often less important than Mother Goddess, 282

—— -kin at Rome, i. 41

——, Mother, and Son divinities represented at Boghaz-Keui, i. 140 *sqq.*

Father Sky fertilizes Mother Earth, i. 282
—— and mother, names for, i. 281 ; as
epithets of Roman gods and goddesses,
ii. 233 *sqq.*
Fatherhood of God, the physical, i. 80 *sq.*
Fauna, rustic Roman goddess, her
relationship to Faunus, ii. 234
Faunus, old Roman god, his relationship
to Fauna or the Good Goddess, ii.
234
Feast of All Saints on November 1st,
perhaps substituted for an old pagan
festival of the dead, ii. 82 *sq.* ; instituted by Lewis the Pious, 83
—— of All Souls, ii. 51 *sqq.* ; the Christian, originally a pagan festival of the
dead, 81
—— of the Golden Flower at Sardes, i.
187
—— of Lanterns in Japan, ii. 65
Feet first, children born, custom observed
at their graves, i. 93
Felkin, R. W. and C. T. Wilson, on the
worship of the dead kings of Uganda,
ii. 173 *n.*[2]
Fellows, Ch., on flowers in Caria, i.
187 *n.*[6]
Female kinship, rule of descent of the
throne under, ii. 18. *See also* Mother-
kin
Fertility of ground thought to be promoted by prostitution, i. 39 ; promoted
by marriage of women to serpent, 67 ;
goddesses of, served by eunuch priests,
269 *sq.* ; Osiris as a god of, ii. 112 *sq.*
Fertilization of the fig, artificial, i. 98
Festival of " the awakening of Hercules "
at Tyre, i. 111 ; of the Dead in Java,
220 ; of Flowers (*Anthesteria*), 234
sq. ; of Joy (*Hilaria*) in the rites of
Attis, 273 ; of Sais, ii. 49 *sqq.* ; of
Crowning at Delphi, 241
Festivals of the Egyptian farmer, ii.
32 *sqq.* ; of Osiris, the official, 49 *sqq.* ;
Egyptian readjustment of, 91 *sqq.*
Fetishism early in human history, ii. 43
" Field of the giants," i. 158
Fig, artificial fertilization of the, at
Rome in July, ii. 98, 259
Fiji, chiefs buried secretly in, ii. 105
Fijian god of fruit-trees, i. 90
—— Lent, i. 90
Fijians, their theory of earthquakes, i.
201
Financial oppression, Roman, i. 301 *n.*[2]
Finlay, George, on Roman financial
oppression, i. 301 *n.*[2]
Fire, purification by, i. 115 *n.*[1], 179 *sqq.* ;
Persian reverence for, 174 *sq.* ; death
in the, as an apotheosis, 179 *sq.* ; sup-
posed able to impregnate women, ii.
235

Fire, perpetual, in Zoroastrian religion,
i. 191 ; worshipped, 191 *sqq.* ; in the
temples of dead kings, ii. 174
—— -god, the father of Romulus, Servius Tullius, and Caeculus, ii. 235
—— -walk of the king of Tyre, i. 114
sq. ; of priestesses at Castabala, 168
—— -worship in Cappadocia, i. 191 *sq.*
Firmicus Maternus, on the mourning for
Osiris, ii. 86 ; on use of a pine-tree in
the rites of Osiris, 108
First-born, Semitic sacrifice of the, i.
110 ; the sacrifice of, at Jerusalem, ii.
219 *sq.*
—— -fruits offered to the Baalim, i. 27 ;
offered to the Mother of the Gods,
280 *n.*[1] ; offered to dead chiefs, ii.
191
Firstlings offered to the Baalim, i. 27
Fish, soul of dead in, i. 95 *sq.*
Fison, Rev. Lorimer, on Fijian god of
earthquakes, i. 202 *n.* ; on secret
burial of chiefs in Fiji, ii. 105
Flail or scourge, an emblem of Osiris, ii.
108, 153 ; for collecting incense, 109
n.[1]
Flamen forbidden to divorce his wife, ii.
229 ; of Vulcan, 232
—— Dialis, the widowed, ii. 227 *sqq.* ;
forbidden to touch a dead body, but
allowed to attend a funeral, 228 ;
bound to be married, 229
—— Dialis and Flaminica, i. 45 *sq.* ;
assisted by boy and girl of living
parents, ii. 236
Flamingoes, soul of a dead king incarnate
in, ii. 163
Flaminica and her husband the Flamen
Dialis, i. 45 *sq.*, ii. 236
Flax, omens from the growth of, i.
244
Flower of the banana, women impregnated by the, i. 93
" —— of Zeus," i. 186, 187
Flowers and leaves as talismans, ii. 242
sq.
Flute, skill of Marsyas on the, i. 288
—— music, its exciting influence, i.
54
—— -players dressed as women at Rome,
ii. 259 *n.*[3]
Flutes played in the laments for Tammuz,
i. 9 ; for Adonis, 225 *n.*[3]
Food, virgins supposed to conceive
through eating certain, i. 96 ; as a
cause of conception in women, 96,
102, 103, 104, 105
Foreigners as kings, i. 16 *n.*
Fortuna Primigenia, goddess of Praeneste, daughter of Jupiter, ii. 234
Fortune of the city on coins of Tarsus, i.
164 ; the guardian of cities, 164

Fossil bones in limestone caves, i. 152 *sq.* ; a source of myths about giants, 157 *sq.*

Foucart, P., identifies Dionysus with Osiris, ii. 113 *n.*[3]

Four-handed Apollo, ii. 250 *n.*[2]

Fowler, W. Warde, on the celibacy of the Roman gods, ii. 230, 232 *n.*[1], 234 *n.*, 236 *n.*[1]

Fra Angelico, his influence on Catholicism, i. 54 *n.*[1]

France, harvest custom in, i. 237 ; timber felled in the wane of the moon in, ii. 136

Fratres Arvales, ii. 239

Fravashis, the souls of the dead in the Iranian religion, ii. 67 *n.*[2], 68

French peasants regulate their sowing and planting by the moon, ii. 133 *n.*[3], 135

Frey, the Scandinavian god of fertility, ii. 100 *sq.*

Frigento, Valley of Amsanctus near, i. 204

Frodsham, Dr., on belief in conception without sexual intercourse, i. 103 *n.*[3]

Fruit-trees, worshippers of Osiris forbidden to injure, ii. 111

Fulgora, a Roman goddess, ii. 231

Funeral custom in Madagascar, ii. 247

—— pyre of Roman emperor, i. 126 *sq.*

—— rites of the Egyptians a copy of those performed over Osiris, ii. 15 ; of Osiris, described in the inscription of Denderah, 86 *sqq.*

Furies, their snakes, i. 88 *n.*[1]

Furness, W. H., on the prostitution of unmarried girls in Yap, ii. 266

Gaboon, Mpongwe kings of the, ii. 104 ; negroes of the, regulate their planting by the moon, ii. 134

Gad, Semitic god of fortune, i. 164, 165

Gadabursi, a Somali tribe, ii. 246

Gades (Cadiz), worship of Hercules (Melcarth) at, i. 112 *sq.* ; temple of Melcarth at, ii. 258 *n.*[5]

Galelareese of Halmahera, as to human sacrifices to volcanoes, i. 220

Gallas, their worship of serpents, i. 86 *n.*[1]

Galli, the emasculated priests of Attis, i. 266, 283

Galton, Sir Francis, on the vale of the Adonis, i. 29

Game with fruit-stones played by kings of Uganda, ii. 224

—— law of the Njamus, ii. 39

Garden of Osiris, ii. 87 *sq.*

Gardens of Adonis, i. 236 *sqq.* ; charms to promote the growth of vegetation, 236 *sq.*, 239 ; in India, 239 *sqq.* ; in Bavaria, 244 ; in Sardinia, 244

sq. ; in Sicily, 245 ; at Easter, 253 *sq.*

Gardens of God, i. 123, 159

Gardner, Professor E. A. on date of the corn-reaping in Greece, i. 232 *n.*

Garstang, Professor J., on sculptures at Ibreez, i. 122 *n.*[1], 123 *n.*[2] ; on Hittite sculptures at Boghaz-Keui, 133 *n.*, 135 *n.* ; on Arenna, 136 *n.*[1] ; on Syrian god Hadad, 163 *n.*[3]

Gathas, a part of the *Zend-Avesta,* ii. 84 *n.*

Gaul, worship of Cybele in, i. 279

Gazelle Peninsula, New Britain, conduct of the natives in an earthquake, i. 201 ; the Melanesians of the, ii. 242 *sq.*

Gazelles sacrificed at Egyptian funerals, ii. 15

Gebal, Semitic name of Byblus, i. 13 *n.*[3]

Geese sacrificed at Egyptian funerals, ii. 15

Gellius, Aulus, his list of old Roman deities, ii. 232

Gellius, Cnaeus, on Mars and Nerio, ii. 232

Geminus, Greek astronomer, on the vague Egyptian year, ii. 26

Genital organs of Osiris, tradition as to the, ii. 10, 102 ; of dead man used to fertilize the fields, 102 *sq.*

Genius, Roman, symbolized by a serpent, i. 86

Geographical and climatic conditions, their effect on national character, ii. 217

German peasants regulate their sowing and planting by the moon, ii. 135

Germans, the ancient, their regard for the phases of the moon, ii. 141

Germany, harvest custom in, i. 237 ; leaping over Midsummer fires in, 251 ; feast of All Souls in, ii. 70 *sqq.* ; popular superstition as to the influence of the moon in, 133, 140 *sq.*, 149

Gezer, Canaanitish city, excavations at, i. 108

Gezo, King, i. 68

Ghineh, monument of Adonis at, i. 29

Ghost of afterbirth thought to adhere to navel-string, ii. 169 *sq.*

Ghosts thought to impregnate women, i. 93 ; of the dead personated by living men, ii. 52, 53, 58

Giants, myths of, based on discovery of fossil bones, i. 157 *sq.*

—— and gods, their battle, i. 157

Giaour-Kalesi, Hittite sculptures at, i. 138 *n.*

Gilbert Islands, sacred stones in the, i. 108 *n.*[1]

Gill, Captain W., on a tribe in China governed by a woman, ii. 211 *n.*[3]

Gilyaks of the Amoor eat nutlets of stone-pine, i. 278 *n.*[2]

Ginzel, Professor F. K., on the rise of the Nile, ii. 31 *n.*[1]

Giraffes, souls of dead kings incarnate in, ii. 162

Glaucus, son of Minos, restored to life, i. 186 *n.*[4]

Goat sacrificed by being hanged, i. 292

God, children of, i. 68 ; sons of, 78 *sqq.* ; the physical fatherhood of, 80 *sq.* ; gardens of, 123, 159

——, the burning of a, i. 188 *sq.* ; the hanged, 288 *sqq.*

—— of earthquakes, i. 194 *sqq.*

Godavari District, Southern India, i. 95

Goddess, identified with priestess, i. 219 ; superiority of the, in the myths of Adonis, Attis, Osiris, ii. 201 *sq.*

Goddesses, Cilician, i. 161 *sqq.* ; place infant sons of kings on fire to render them immortal, 180 ; of fertility served by eunuch priests, 269 *sq.* ; their superiority over gods in societies organized on mother-kin, ii. 202 *sqq.* ; the development of, favoured by mother-kin, 259

Gods, annual death and resurrection of, i. 6 ; personated by priests, 45, 46 *sqq.* ; married to sisters, 316 ; their human wives, ii. 207 ; made by men and worshipped by women, 211

—— and giants, the battle of, i. 157

Gold Coast of West Africa, the Tshi-speaking peoples of the, i. 69

Golden Flower, the Feast of the, i. 185

—— Sea, the, i. 150

Golgi in Cyprus, i. 35

Goliath and David, i. 19 *n.*[2]

Gonds, ceremony of bringing back souls of the dead among the, i. 95 *sq,*

Good Friday, effigies and sepulchres of Christ on, i. 254 *sqq.*

—— Goddess (*Bona Dea*), her relationship to Faunus, ii. 234

Goowoong Awoo, volcano, children sacrificed to, i. 219

Gordias and Midas, names of Phrygian kings, i. 286

Gordon, E. M., on infant burial, i. 94 *sq.*; on the festival of the dead in Bilaspore, ii. 60

Gouri, an Indian goddess of fertility, i. 241 *sq.*

Gournia in Crete, prehistoric shrine at, i. 88 *n.*[1]

Grandmother, title of an African priest, ii. 255

—— Earth thought to cause earthquakes, i. 198

Grandparents, dead, worshipped, ii. 175

Grapes as divine emblem, i. 165

Grave of Osiris, ii. 10 *sq.* ; human victims sacrificed at the, 97

—— -shrines of Shilluk kings, ii. 161 *sq.*; of dead kings, 194 *sq.*

Graves, milk offered at, i. 87 ; childless women resort to, in order to ensure offspring, 96 ; illuminated on All Souls' Day, ii. 72 *sq.*, 74 ; the only places of sacrifice in the country of the Wahehe, 190

—— of kings, chiefs, and magicians kept secret, ii. 103 *sqq.*; human sacrifices at, 168

"Great burnings" for kings of Judah, i. 177 *sq.*

—— Marriage, annual festival of the dead among the Oraons of Bengal, ii. 59

—— men, history not to be explained without the influence of, i. 311 *n.*[2]; great religious systems founded by, ii. 159 *sq.*; their influence on the popular imagination, 199

—— Mother, popularity of her worship in the Roman empire, i. 298 *sq.*

—— religious systems founded by individual great men, ii. 159 *sq.*; religious ideals a product of the male imagination, 211

Greece, date of the corn-reaping in, i. 232 *n.*; modern, marriage customs in, ii. 245 *sq.*

Greek belief in serpents as reincarnations of the dead, i. 86 *sq.*

—— Church, ceremonies on Good Friday in the, i. 254

—— feast of All Souls in May, ii. 78 *n.*[1]

—— gods, discrimination of their characters, i. 119

—— mythology, Adonis in, i. 10 *sqq.*

—— notion as to birth from trees and rocks, i. 107 *n.*[1] ; of the noxious influence of moonshine on children, ii. 148

—— purification for homicide, i. 299 *n.*[2]

—— use of music in religion, i. 54 *sq.*

—— writers on the worship of Adonis, i. 223 *sq.*

Gregory IV. and the feast of All Saints, ii. 83

Grenfell, B. P., and A. S. Hunt on corn-stuffed effigies of Osiris, ii. 90 *sq.*

Grimm, Jacob, on hide-measured lands, ii. 250

Grotto of the Sibyl, at Marsala, i. 247

Growth and decay of all things associated with the waxing and waning of the moon, ii. 132 *sqq.*, 140 *sqq.*

Guarayos Indians of Bolivia, their presentation of children to the moon, ii. 145

Guardian spirits in the form of animals, i. 83 ; in serpents, 83, 86

Guaycurus of Brazil, men dressed as women among the, ii. 254 *n.*²

Guevo Upas, the Valley of Poison, in Java, i. 203 *sq.*

Gujrat District, Punjaub, i. 94

Gurdon, Major P. R. T., on the Khasis of Assam, ii. 202, 203 *n.*¹, 210 *n.*¹

Gwanya, a worshipful dead chief, ii. 177

Gyges, king of Lydia, dedicates double-headed axe to Zeus, i. 182

Gynaecocracy a dream, ii. 211

Hadad, chief male deity of the Syrians, i. 15, 16 *n.*¹ ; Syrian god of thunder and fertility, 163

Hadadrimmon, i. 164 *n.*¹ ; the mourning of or for, 15 *n.*⁴

Haddon, A. C., on worship of animal-shaped heroes, i. 139 *n.*¹

Hadrian, human sacrifice suppressed in reign of, i. 146

Hair, sacrifice of women's, i. 38 ; offered to goddess of volcano, 218 ; of head shaved in mourning for dead gods, 225 ; to be cut when the moon is waxing, ii. 133 *sq.*

Halasarna in Cos, rites of Apollo and Hercules at, ii. 259

Halfdan, the Black, King of Norway, dismembered after death, ii. 100

Halicarnassus, worship of Pergaean Artemis at, i. 35 *n.*²

Hall of the Two Truths, the judgment hall in the other world, ii. 13

Halmahera, the Galelareese of, i. 220

Hamaspathmaedaya, old Iranian festival of the dead, ii. 67

Hamilcar, his self-sacrifice at the battle of Himera, i. 115 *sq.* ; worshipped at Carthage, 116 ; burns himself, 176 ; worshipped after death, 180

Hamilton, Alexander, on dance of hermaphrodites in Pegu, i. 271 *n.*

Hamilton, Professor G. L., i. 57 *n.*¹

Hammurabi, the code of, i. 71 *n.*³, 72 *n.*¹

Handel, the harmonies of, i. 54

Hanged god, the, i. 288 *sqq.*

Hanging as a mode of sacrifice, i. 289 *sqq.*

Hannah, the prayer of, i. 79

Hannibal, his prayers to Melcarth, i. 113 ; his retirement from Italy, 265

Hanway, J., on worship of perpetual fires at Baku, i. 192

Harmonia, the necklace of, i. 32 *n.*² ; turned into a snake, 86 *sq.*

Harold the Fair-haired, ii. 100 *n.*²

Harp, the music of the, in religion, i. 52 *sqq.*

Harpalyce, her incest with her father, i. 44 *n.*¹

Harpocrates, the younger Horus, ii. 8, 9 *n.*

Harran, mourning of women for Tammuz in, i. 230

Harrison, Miss J. E., on the hyacinth (*Delphinium Ajacis*), i. 314 *n.*¹

Hartland, E. S., on the reincarnation of the dead, i. 91 *n.*³ ; on primitive paternity, 106 *n.*¹

Harvest, rites of, ii. 45 *sqq.* ; annual festival of the dead after, 61 ; new corn offered to dead kings or chiefs at, 162, 166, 188 ; prayers to the spirits of ancestors at, 175 *sq.* ; sacrifices to dead chiefs at, 191

—— in Egypt, the date of, ii. 32

—— custom of throwing water on the last corn cut as a rain-charm, i. 237 *sq.* ; of the Arabs of Moab, ii. 48, 96

Hathor, Egyptian goddess, ii. 9 *n.*

Hattusil, king of the Hittites, i. 135

Havamal, how Odin learned the magic runes in the, i. 290

Hawaii, the volcano of Kirauea in, i. 216 *sqq.*

Hawes, Mrs., on date of the corn-reaping in Crete, ii. 232 *n.*

Hawk, Isis in the form of a, ii. 8 ; the sacred bird of the earliest Egyptian dynasties, 21 *sq.* ; epithet regularly applied to the king of Egypt, 22

—— -town (Hieraconpolis) in Egypt, ii. 21 *sq.*

Hawks carved on the bier of Osiris, ii. 20

Hazael, king of Damascus, i. 15

"Head-Feast" among the Dyaks of Borneo, i. 295 *sq.*

—— -hunting in Borneo, i. 294 *sqq.*

Heads of dead chiefs cut off and buried secretly, ii. 104

——, human, thought to promote the fertility of the ground and of women, i. 294 *sqq.* ; used as guardians by Taurians and tribes of Borneo, 294 *sqq.*

Heathen festivals displaced by Christian, i. 308

—— origin of Midsummer festival (festival of St. John), i. 249 *sq.*

Heavenly Virgin or Goddess, mother of the Sun, i. 303

Hebrew kings, traces of their divinity, i. 20 *sqq.*

—— names ending in -*el* or -*iah*, i. 79 *n.*³

—— prophecy, the distinctive character of, i. 75

Hebrew prophets, their resemblance to those of Africa, i. 74 *sq.*

Hebrides, peats cut in the wane of the moon in the, ii. 137 *sq.*

Hecaerge, an epithet of Artemis, i. 292

Hecate at Ephesus, i. 291 ; sometimes identified with Artemis, 292 *n.*

—— and Zeus worshipped at Stratonicea, ii. 227

Hecatombeus, a Greek month, i. 314

Hehn, V., on derivation of name Corycian, i. 187 *n.*[6]

Helen of the Tree, worshipped in Rhodes, i. 292

Heliacal rising of Sirius, ii. 152

Helice, in Achaia, destroyed by earthquake, i. 203 ; Poseidon worshipped at, 203 *n.*[2]

Heliodorus, on the priesthood of Apollo and Artemis at Ephesus, ii. 243 *sq.*

Heliogabalus, sun-god at Emesa, i. 35 ; his sacrifice of children of living parents, ii. 248

Heliopolis (Baalbec), in Syria, i. 163 *n.*[2] ; sacred prostitution at, 37, 58

Heliopolis (the Egyptian), trial of the dead Osiris before the gods at, ii. 17

Hepding, H., on Attis, i. 263 *n.*[1] ; on Catullus's poem *Attis*, 270 *n.*[2] ; on the bath of Cybele's image, 280

Hephaestus and hot springs, i. 209

Heqet, Egyptian frog-goddess, ii. 9 *n.*

Hera's marriage with Zeus, i. 280

Heraclids, Lydian dynasty of the, i. 182, 184 ; perhaps Hittite, 184

Hercules identified with Melcarth, i. 16, 111 ; slain by Typhon and revived by Iolaus, 111 ; burnt on Mount Oeta, 111, 116, 211 ; worshipped at Gades, 112 *sq.* ; women excluded from sacrifices to, 113 *n.*[1] ; identified with Sandan, 125, 143, 161 ; burns himself, 176 ; worshipped after death, 180 ; the itch of, 209 ; his dispute with ·Aesculapius, 209 *sq.* ; the patron of hot springs, 209 *sqq.* ; altar of, at Thermopylae, 210 ; the effeminate, ii. 257, 258, 259 ; priest of, dressed as a woman, 258 ; vernal mysteries of, at Rome, 258 ; sacrifices to, at Rome, 258 *n.*[5]

—— and the lion, i. 184

—— and Omphale, i. 182, ii. 258

—— and Sardanapalus, i. 172 *sqq.*

——, the Lydian, identical with the Cilician Hercules, i. 182, 184, 185

—— with the lion's scalp, Greek type of, i. 117 *sq.*

Hereditary deities, i. 51

Herefordshire, soul-cakes in, ii. 79

Herero, a Bantu tribe of German South-

West Africa, the worship of the dead among the, ii. 185 *sqq.*

Hermaphrodite son of Sky and Earth, i. 282 *n.*

Hermaphrodites, dance of, i. 271 *n.*

Hermes and Aegipan, i. 157

Hermesianax, on the death of Attis, i. 264 *n.*[4]

Hermus, river, i. 185, 186

Herod resorts to the springs of Callirrhoe, i. 214

Herodes Atticus, his benefaction at Thermopylae, i. 210

Herodotus on sanctuary of Aphrodite at Paphos, i. 34 ; on religious prostitution, 58 ; on wife of Bel, 71 ; on Cyrus and Croesus, 174 ; on the sacrifices of Croesus to Apollo, 180 *n.*[1] ; on so-called monument of Sesostris, 185 ; on the festival of Osiris at Sais, ii. 50 ; on the mourning for Osiris, 86 ; identifies Osiris with Dionysus, 113 *n.*[2] ; on the similarity between the rites of Osiris and Dionysus, 127 ; on human sacrifices offered by the wife of Xerxes, 221

Heroes worshipped in form of animals, i. 139 *n.*[1]

Hertz, W., on religious prostitution, i. 57 *n.*[1], 59 *n.*[4]

Hesse, custom at ploughing in, i. 239

Hest, the Egyptian name for Isis, ii. 50 *n.*[4], 115 *n.*[1]

Hettingen in Baden, custom at sowing at, i. 239

Hezekiah, King, his reformation, i. 25, 107 ; date of his reign, 25 *n.*[4]

Hibeh papyri, ii. 35 *n.*[1], 51 *n.*[1]

Hide-measured lands, legends as to, ii. 249 *sq.*

Hieraconpolis in Egypt, ii. 22 *n.*[1] ; representations of the Sed festival at, 151

Hierapolis, the Syrian, festival of the Pyre or Torch at, i. 146 ; sacred doves at, 147 ; great sanctuary of Astarte at, 269 ; eunuch priests of Astarte at, 269 *sq.*

——, in the valley of the Maeander, cave of Pluto at, i. 206 ; hot springs at, 206 *sqq.*

—— and *Hieropolis*, distinction between, i. 168 *n.*[2]

—— -Bambyce, Atargatis the goddess of, i. 137, 162 ; mysterious golden image at, 162 *n.*[2] ; rules as to the pollution of death at, ii. 227

Hieroglyphics, Hittite, i. 124, 125 *n.*

High-priest of Syrian goddess, i. 143 *n.*[1]

—— Priestess, head of the State, ii. 203

Highlanders, Scottish, on the influence of the moon, ii. 132, 134, 140

Hilaria, Festival of Joy in the rites of Attis, i. 273

Hill, G. F., on image of Artemis at Perga, i. 35 *n.*²; on legend of coins of Tarsus, 126 *n.*²; on goddess'Atheh, 162 ; on coins of Mallus, 165 *n.*⁶

Hill Tout, C., on respect shown by the Indians of British Columbia for the animals and plants which they eat, ii. 44

Himalayan districts of North-Western India, gardens of Adonis in the, i. 242

Himera, the battle of, i. 115 ; hot springs of, 213 *n.*¹

Hindoo burial of infants, i. 94 ; marriage custom, old, ii. 246 ; worship of perpetual fire, i. 192

Hindoos of Northern India, their mode of drinking moonshine, ii. 144

Hinnom, the Valley of, i. 178 ; sacrifice of first-born children in, ii. 219

Hippodamia, her incest with her father, i. 44 *n.*¹

Hirpini, valley of Amsanctus in the land of the, i. 204

Hissar District, Punjaub, i. 94

History not to be explained without the influence of great men, i. 311 *n.*²

Hittite, correct form of the national name Chatti or Hatti, i. 133 *n.*

—— costume, i. 129 *sq.*, 131

—— deity named Tark or Tarku, i. 147

—— god of thunder, i. 134, 163

—— gods at Tarsus and Sardes, 185

—— hieroglyphics, i. 124, 125 *n.*

—— inscription on Mount Argaeus, i. 190 *n.*¹

—— priest or king, his costume, i. 131 *sq.*, 133 *n.*

—— sculptures at Carchemish, i. 38 *n.*, 123 ; at Ibreez, 121 *sqq.* ; at Bor (Tyana), 122 *n.*¹ ; at Euyuk, 123 ; at Boghaz-Keui, 128 *sqq.* ; at Babylon, 134 ; at Zenjirli, 134 ; at Giaour-Kalesi, 138 *n.* ; at Kara-Bel, 138 *n.* ; at Marash, 173 ; in Lydia, 173

—— seals of treaty, i. 136, 142 *n.*¹, 145 *n.*²

—— Sun-goddess, i. 133 *n.*

—— treaty with Egypt, i. 135 *sq.*

Hittites worship the bull, i. 123, 132 ; their empire, language, etc., 124 *sq.* ; traces of mother-kin among the, 141 *sq.*

Hkamies of North Aracan, their annual festival of the dead, ii. 61

Ho tribe of Togoland, their kings buried secretly, ii. 104

Hofmayr, W., on the worship of Nyakang among the Shilluks, ii. 164, 166

Hogarth, D. G., on relics of paganism at Paphos, i. 36 ; on the Corycian cave, 155 *n.* ; on Roman remains at Tarsus, 172 *n.*¹

Hogs sacrificed to goddess of volcano, i. 218 *sq.*

Hollis, A. C., on serpent-worship of the Akikuyu, i. 67 *sq.* ; on serpent-worship, 84 *sq.*

"Holy men" in Syria, i. 77 *sq.*

Hommel, Professor F., on the Hittite deity Tarku, i. 147 *n.*³

Honey and milk offered to snakes, i. 85

Honey-cakes offered to serpent, i. 87

Hope of immortality, the Egyptian, centred in Osiris, ii. 15 *sq.*, 90 *sq.*, 114, 159

Hopladamus, a giant, i. 157 *n.*²

Hora and Quirinus, ii. 233

Horkos, the Greek god of oaths, ii. 231 *n.*⁵

Horned cap worn by priest or god, i. 123 ; of Hittite god, 134

—— god, Hittite and Greek, i. 123

—— lion, i. 127

Horns, as a religious emblem, i. 34 ; worn by gods, 163 *sq.*

—— of a cow worn by Isis, ii. 50

Horses sacrificed for the use of the dead, i. 293 *sq.* ; Lycurgus, king of the Edonians, torn in pieces by, ii. 98

Horus, the four sons of, in the likeness of hawks, ii. 22 ; decapitates his mother Isis, 88 ; the eye of, 121 with *n.*³

—— of Edfu identified with the sun, ii. 123

—— the elder, ii. 6

—— the younger, son of Isis and the dead Osiris, ii. 8, 15 ; accused by Set of being a bastard, 17 ; his combat with Set, 17 ; his eye destroyed by Set and restored by Thoth, 17 ; reigns over the Delta, 17

Hose, Ch., and McDougall, W., on head-hunting in Borneo, i. 295 *n.*¹

Hosea on religious prostitution, i. 58 ; on the Baalim, 75 *n.* ; on the prophet as a madman, 77

Hot springs, worship of, i. 206 *sqq.* ; Hercules the patron of, 209 *sqq.* ; resorted to by childless women in Syria, 213 *sqq.*

Huligamma, Indian goddess, eunuchs dedicated to her, i. 271 *n.*

Human representatives of Attis, i. 285 *sqq.*

—— sacrifice, substitutes for, i. 146 *sq.*, 285, 289, ii. 99, 221

—— sacrifices in worship of the moon, i. 73 ; to the Tauric Artemis, 115 ; to Diomede at Salamis, 145 ; offered at earthquakes, 201 ; offered at irrigation channels, ii. 38 ; of the kings of Ashantee and Dahomey, 97 *n*.[7] ; offered to Dionysus, 98 *sq.* ; offered by the Mexicans for the maize, 107 ; at the graves of the kings of Uganda, 168 ; to dead kings, 173 ; to dead chiefs, 191 ; to prolong the life of kings, 220 *sq.*, 223 *sqq.*

Human victims thrown into volcanoes, i. 219 *sq.* ; uses made of their skins, 293 ; as representatives of the corn-spirit, ii. 97, 106 *sq.* ; killed with hoes, spades, and rakes, 99 *n.*[2]

Hunger the root of the worship of Adonis, i. 231

Hurons, their burial of infants, i. 91

Huzuls of the Carpathians, their theory of the waning moon, ii. 130 ; their cure for water-brash, 149 *sq.*

Hyacinth, son of Amyclas, killed by Apollo, i. 313 ; his flower, 313 *sq.* ; his tomb and festival, 314 *sq.* ; an aboriginal deity, 315 *sq.* ; his sister Polyboea, 316 ; perhaps a deified king of Amyclae, i. 316 *sq.*

Hyacinthia, the festival of Hyacinth, i. 314 *sq.*

Hyacinthius, a Greek month, i. 315 *n.*

Hybristica, an Argive festival, ii. 259 *n.*[3]

Hygieia, the goddess, i. 88 *n.*[1]

Hymns to Tammuz, i. 9 ; to the sun-god, ii. 123 *sq.*

Hyria in Cilicia, i. 41

Ibani of the Niger delta, their sacrifices to prolong the lives of kings and others, ii. 222

Ibans or Sea Dyaks, their worship of serpents, i. 83. *See* Sea Dyaks

Ibn Batuta, Arab traveller, on funeral of emperor of China, i. 293 *sq.*

Ibreez in Southern Cappadocia, i. 119 *sqq.* ; village of, 120 *sq.* ; Hittite sculptures at, 121 *sqq.*

——, the god of, i. 119 *sqq.* ; his horned cap, 164

Idalium in Cyprus, i. 50 ; bilingual inscription of, 49 *n.*[7] ; Melcarth worshipped at, 117

Ideals of humanity, two different, the heroic and the saintly, i. 300 ; great religious, a product of the male imagination, ii. 211

Ideler, L., on the date of the introduction of the fixed Alexandrian year, ii. 28 *n.*[1] ; on the Sothic period, 37 *n.*

Ignorance of paternity, primitive, i. 106 *sq.*

Il Mayek clan of the Njamus, their supposed power over irrigation water and the crops, ii. 39

Ilium, animals sacrificed by hanging at, i. 292

Illumination, nocturnal, at festival of Osiris, ii. 50 *sq.* ; of graves on All Souls' Day, 72 *sq.*, 74

Ilpirra of Central Australia, their belief in the reincarnation of the dead, i. 99

Images of Osiris made of vegetable mould, ii. 85, 87, 90 *sq.*, 91

Immortality, Egyptian hope of, centred in Osiris, ii. 15 *sq.*, 90 *sq.*, 114, 159

Impregnation of women by serpents, i. 80 *sqq.* ; by the dead, 91 ; by ghosts, 93 ; by the flower of the banana, 93 ; supposed, through eating food, 96, 102, 103, 104, 105 ; by fire, ii. 235. *See also* Conception

—— of Isis by the dead Osiris, ii. 8, 20

—— without sexual intercourse, belief in, i. 96 *sqq.*

Incense burnt at the rites of Adonis, i. 228 ; burnt in honour of the Queen of Heaven, 228 ; collected by a flail, ii. 109 *n.*[1]

Incest with a daughter in royal families, reported cases of, i. 43 *sq.*

Inconsistency of common thought, i. 4

Increase of the moon the time for increasing money, ii. 148 *sq.*

India, sacred women (dancing-girls) in, i. 61 *sqq.* ; impregnation of women by stone serpents in, 81 *sq.* ; burial of infants in, 93 *sq.* ; gardens of Adonis in, 239 *sqq.* ; eunuchs dedicated to a goddess in, 271 *n.* ; drinking moonlight as a medicine in, ii. 142

Indian ceremonies analogous to the rites of Adonis, i. 227

—— prophet, his objections to agriculture, i. 88 *sq.*

Indians of tropical America represent the rain-god weeping, ii. 33 *n.*[3] ; of California, their annual festivals of the dead, 52 *sq.* ; of Brazil attend to the moon more than to the sun, 138 *n.* ; of San Juan Capistrano, their ceremony at the new moon, 142 ; of the Ucayali River in Peru, their greeting to the new moon, 142 ; of North America, effeminate sorcerers among the, 254, 255 *sq.*

Infant sons of kings placed by goddesses on fire, i. 180

Infants buried so as to ensure their rebirth, i. 91, 93 *sqq.* ; burial of, at Gezer, 108 *sq.*

Influence of great men on the popular imagination, ii. 199 ; of mother-kin on religion, 202 *sqq.*

Ingarda tribe of West Australia, their belief as to the birth of children, i. 104

Ingleborough in Yorkshire, i. 152
Inheritance of property under mother-kin, rules of, ii. 203 *n*.[1]
Injibandi tribe of West Australia, their belief as to the birth of children, i. 105
Insect, soul of dead in, i. 95 *sq.*, ii. 162
Insensibility to pain as a sign of inspiration, i. 169 *sq.*
Inspiration, insensibility to pain as sign of, i. 169 *sq.* ; savage theory of, i. 299
——, prophetic, under the influence of music, i. 52 *sq.*, 54 *sq.*, 74 ; through the spirits of dead kings and chiefs, ii. 171, 172, 192 *sq.*
Inspired men and women in the Pelew Islands, ii. 207 *sq.*
Intercalation introduced to correct the vague Egyptian year, ii. 26, 27, 28 ; in the ancient Mexican calendar, ii. 28 *n*.[3]
Inuus, epithet applied to Faunus, ii. 234 *n*.[3]
Invisible, charm to make an army, ii. 251
Iolaus, friend of Hercules, i. 111
Iranian year, the old, ii. 67
Iranians, the old, their annual festival of the dead (Fravashis), ii. 67 *sq.*
Ireland, sacred oaks in, i. 37 *n*.[2]
Irle, J., on the religion of the Herero, ii. 186 *sq.*
Iron not allowed to touch Atys, i. 286 *n*.[5]
Irrigation in ancient Egypt, ii. 31 *sq.* ; rites of, in Egypt, 33 *sqq.* ; sacrifices offered in connexion with, 38 *sq.*
Isa or Parvati, an Indian goddess, i. 241
Isaac, Abraham's attempted sacrifice of, ii. 219 *n*.[1]
Isaiah, on the king's pyre in Tophet, i. 177, 178 ; possible allusion to gardens of Adonis in, 236 *n*.[1] ; on dew, 247 *n*.[1]
Ishtar, great Babylonian goddess, i. 8, 20 *n*.[2] ; in relation to Tammuz, 8 *sq.*
—— (Astarte) and Mylitta, i. 36, 37 *n*.[1]
Isis, sister and wife of Osiris, ii. 6 *sq.* ; date of the festival of, 26 *n*.[2], 33 ; as a cow or a woman with the head of a cow, i. 50, ii. 50, 85, 88 *n*.[1], 91 ; invoked by Egyptian reapers, i. 232, ii. 45, 117 ; in the form of a hawk, 8, 20 ; in the papyrus swamps, 9 ; in the form of a swallow, 9 ; at Byblus, 9 *sq.* ; at the well, 9, 111 *n*.[6] ; her search for the body of Osiris, 10, 50, 85 ; recovers and buries the body of Osiris, 10 *sq.* ; mourns Osiris, 12 ; restores Osiris to life, 13 ; her tears

supposed to swell the Nile, 33 ; her priest wears a jackal's mask, 85 *n*.[3] ; decapitated by her son Horus, 88 *n*.[1] ; her temple at Philae, 89, 111 ; her many names, 115 ; sister and wife of Osiris, 116 ; a corn-goddess, 116 *sq.* ; her discovery of wheat and barley, 116 ; identified with Ceres, 117 ; identified with Demeter, 117 ; as the ideal wife and mother, 117 *sq.* ; refinement and spiritualization of, 117 *sq.* ; popularity of her worship in the Roman empire, 118 ; her resemblance to the Virgin Mary, 118 *sq.* ; Sirius her star, 34 *sq.*, 152
Isis and the king's son at Byblus, i. 180 ; and the scorpions, ii. 8
Iswara or Mahadeva, an Indian god, i. 241, 242
Italian myths of kings or heroes begotten by the fire-god, ii. 235
Italy, hot springs in, i. 213 ; divination at Midsummer in, 254
Itch of Hercules, i. 209
Itongo, an ancestral spirit (Zulu term, singular of Amatongo), ii. 184 *n*.[2], 185
Ivy, sacred to Attis, i. 278 ; sacred to Osiris, ii. 112

Jablonski, P. E., on Osiris as a sun-god, ii. 120
Jackal-god Up-uat, ii. 154
Jackal's mask worn by priest of Isis, ii. 85 *n*.[3]
Jamblichus on insensibility to pain as sign of inspiration, i. 169 ; on the purifying virtue of fire, 181
January, the sixth of, reckoned in the East the Nativity of Christ, i. 304
Janus in Roman mythology, ii. 235 *n*.[6]
—— -like deity on coins, i. 165
Japan, annual festival of the dead in, ii. 65
Jars, children buried in, i. 109 *n*.[1]
Jason and Medea, i. 181 *n*.[1]
Jastrow, Professor M., on the festival of Tammuz, i. 10 *n*.[1] ; on the character of Tammuz, 230 *n.*
Java, conduct of natives in an earthquake, i. 202 *n*.[1] ; the Valley of Poison in, 203 *sq.* ; worship of volcanoes in, 220 *sq.*
Jawbone, the ghost of the dead thought to adhere to the, ii. 167 *sq.*
—— and navel-string of Kibuka, the war-god of the Baganda, ii. 197
Jawbones, lower, of dead kings of Uganda preserved and worshipped, ii. 167 *sq.*, 169 *sq.*, 171 *sq.* ; the ghosts of the kings supposed to attach to their jawbones, 169

Jâyi or Jawâra, festival in Upper India, i. 242

Jebel Hissar, Olba, i. 151

Jehovah in relation to thunder, i. 22 *n.*[3] ; in relation to rain, 23 *n.*[1]

Jensen, P., on rock-hewn sculptures at Boghaz-Keui, i. 137 *n.*[4] ; on Hittite inscription, 145 *n.*[2] ; on the Syrian god Hadad, 163 *n.*[3]

Jeremiah, on the prophet as a madman, i. 77 ; on birth from stocks and stones, 107

Jericho, death of Herod at, i. 214

Jerome, on the date of the month Tammuz, i. 10 *n.*[1] ; on the worship of Adonis at Bethlehem, 257

Jerusalem, mourning for Tammuz at, i. 11, 17, 20 ; the Canaanite kings of, 17 ; the returned captives at, 23 ; the Destroying Angel over, 24 ; besieged by Sennacherib, 25 ; the religious orchestra at, 52 ; " great burnings " for the kings at, 177 *sq.* ; the king's pyre at, 177 *sq.* ; Church of the Holy Sepulchre at, Good Friday ceremonies in the, 255 *n.* ; the sacrifice of first-born children at, ii. 219

Jewish priests, their rule as to the pollution of death, ii. 230

Jews of Egypt, costume of bride and bridegroom among the, ii. 260

Joannes Lydus, on Phrygian rites at Rome, i. 266 *n.*[2]

John Barleycorn, i. 230 *sq.*

Johns, Dr. C. H. W., on Babylonian votaries, i. 71 *n.*[3] and [5]

Johnston, Sir H. H., on eunuch priests on the Congo, i. 271 *n.*

Josephus, on worship of kings of Damascus, i. 15 ; on the Tyropoeon, 178

Josiah, reforms of king, i. 17 *n.*[5], 18 *n.*[8], 25, 107

Jualamukhi in the Himalayas, perpetual fires, i. 192

Judah, laments for dead kings of, i. 20

Judean maid impregnated by serpent, i. 81

Julian, the emperor, his entrance into Antioch, i. 227, 258 ; on the Mother of the Gods, 299 *n.*[3] ; restores the standard cubit to the Serapeum, ii. 217 *n.*[1]

Julian calendar introduced by Caesar, ii. 37, 93 *n.*[1]

—— year, ii. 28

Juno, the Flaminica Dialis sacred to, ii. 230 *n.*[2] ; the wife of Jupiter, 231

Junod, Henri A., on the worship of the dead among the Thonga, ii. 180 *sq.*

Juok, the supreme god and creator of the Shilluks, ii. 165

Jupiter, the husband of Juno, ii. 231 ; the father of Fortuna Primigenia, 234

Jupiter and Juturna, ii. 235 *n.*[6]

—— Dolichenus, i. 136

Justice and Injustice in Aristophanes, i. 209

Justin Martyr on the resemblances of paganism to Christianity, i. 302 *n.*[4]

Juturna in Roman mythology, ii. 235 *n.*[6]

Kabyles, marriage custom of the, to ensure the birth of a boy, ii. 262

Kadesh, a Semitic goddess, i. 137 *n.*[2]

Kai of German New Guinea, their belief in conception without sexual intercourse, i. 96 *sq.*

Kaikolans, a Tamil caste, i. 62

Kaitish of Central Australia, their belief in the reincarnation of the dead, i. 99

Kalat el Hosn, in Syria, i. 78

Kalids, kaliths, deities in the Pelew Islands, ii. 204 *n.*[4], 207

Kalunga, the supreme god of the Ovambo, ii. 188

Kangra District, Punjaub, i. 94

Kantavu, a Fijian island, i. 201

Kanytelideis, in Cilicia, i. 158

Kara-Bel, in Lydia, Hittite sculpture at, i. 138 *n.*, 185

Kariera tribe of West Australia, their beliefs as to the birth of children, i. 105

Karma-tree, ceremony of the Mundas over a, i. 240

Karo-Bataks, of Sumatra, their custom as to the first sheaf of rice at harvest, ii. 239

Karok Indians of California, their lamentations at hewing sacred wood, ii. 47 *sq.*

Karunga, the supreme god of the Herero, ii. 186, 187 *n.*[1]

Katikiro, Baganda term for prime minister, ii. 168

Kayans, their reasons for taking human heads, i. 294 *sq.*

Keadrol, a Toda clan, ii. 228

Keb (Geb or Seb), Egyptian earth-god, father of Osiris, i. 6, 283 *n.*[3]

Kedeshim, sacred men, i. 38 *n.*, 59, 72, 76, 107 ; at Jerusalem, 17 *sq.* ; in relation to prophets, 76

Kedeshoth, sacred women, i. 59, 72, 107

Kemosh, god of Moab, i. 15

Kennett, Professor R. H., on David and Goliath, i. 19 *n.*[2] ; on Elisha in the wilderness, 53 *n.*[1] ; on *ḳedeshim*, 73 *n.*[1] ; on the sacrifice of first-born children at Jerusalem, ii. 219

Kent's Hole, near Torquay, fossil bones in, i. 153

Keysser, Ch., on belief in conception without sexual intercourse, i. 96 *sq.*

Khalij, old canal at Cairo, ii. 38

Khangars of the Central Provinces, India, bridegroom and his father dressed as women at a marriage among the, ii. 261

Khasi tribes governed by kings, not queens, ii. 210

Khasis of Assam, their system of mother-kin, i. 46, ii. 202 *sq.* ; goddesses predominate over gods in their religion, 203 *sq.* ; rules as to the succession to the kingship among the, 210 *n.*[1]

Khent, early king of Egypt, ii. 154 ; his reign, 19 *sq.* ; his tomb at Abydos, 19 *sqq.* ; his tomb identified with that of Osiris, 20, 197

Khenti-Amenti, title of Osiris, ii. 87, 198 *n.*[2]

Khoiak, festival of Osiris in the month of, ii. 86 *sqq.*, 108 *sq.*

Khyrim State, in Assam, i. 46 ; governed by a High Priestess, ii. 203

Kibuka, the war-god of the Baganda, a dead man, ii. 197 ; his personal relics preserved at Cambridge, 197

Kidd, Dudley, on the worship of ancestral spirits among the Bantus of South Africa, ii. 177 *sqq.*

King, J. E., on infant burial, i. 91 *n.*[3]

King, a masker at Carnival called the, ii. 99

—— of Tyre, his walk on stones of fire, i. 114 *sq.* ; of Uganda, his navel-string preserved and inspected every new moon, ii. 147 *sq.*

Kings as priests, i. 42 ; as lovers of a goddess, 49 *sq.*; held responsible for the weather and the crops, 183 ; marry their sisters, 316 ; slaughter human victims with their own hands, ii. 97 *n.*[7]; torn in pieces, traditions of, 97 *sq.*; human sacrifices to prolong the life of, 220 *sq.*, 223 *sqq.*

—— and magicians dismembered and their bodies buried in different parts of the country to fertilize it, ii. 101 *sq.*

——, dead, reincarnate in lions, i. 83 *n.*[1]; worshipped in Africa, 160 *sqq.* ; sacrifices offered to, 162, 166 *sq.* ; incarnate in animals, 162, 163 *sq.*, 173 ; consulted as oracles, 167, 171, 172, 195 ; human sacrifices to, 173 ; worshipped by the Barotse, 194 *sq.*

——, divinity of Semitic, i. 15 *sqq.* ; divinity of Lydian, 182 *sqq.*

—— of Egypt worshipped as gods, i. 52; buried at Abydos, ii. 19; perhaps formerly slain in the character of Osiris, 97 *sq.*, 102 ; as Osiris, 151 *sqq.* ; renew their life by identifying themselves with the dead and risen Osiris, 153 *sq.* ; born again at the Sed festival, 153, 156 *sq.*; perhaps formerly put to death to prevent their bodily and mental decay, 154 *sq.*, 156

Kings, Hebrew, traces of divinity ascribed to, i. 20 *sqq.*

——, Shilluk, put to death before their strength fails, ii. 163

—— of Sweden answerable for the fertility of the ground, ii. 220 ; their sons sacrificed, 51

Kingship at Rome a plebeian institution, i. 45 ; under mother-kin, rules as to succession to the, ii. 210 *n.*[1] ; in Africa under mother-kin inherited by men, not women, 211

Kingsley, Miss Mary H., on secret burial of chief's head, ii. 104

Kinnor, a lyre, i. 52

Kirauea, volcano in Hawaii, i. 216 *sq.*; divinities of, 217 ; offerings to, 217 *sqq.*

Kiriwina, one of the Trobriand Islands, annual festival of the dead in, i. 56 ; snakes as reincarnations of the dead in, 84 ; presentation of children to the full moon in, ii. 144

Kiwai, an island off New Guinea, magic for the growth of sago in, ii. 101

Kiziba, a district of Central Africa, dead kings worshipped in, ii. 173 *sq.* ; totemism in, 173

Klamath Indians of Oregon, their theory of the waning moon, ii. 130

Kocchs of North-Eastern India, succession to husband's property among the, ii. 215 *n.*[2]

Kois of Southern India, infant burial among the, i. 95

Komatis of Mysore, their worship of serpents, i. 81 *sq.*

Koniags of Alaska, their magical uses of the bodies of the dead, ii. 106

Konkaus of California, their dance of the dead, ii. 53

Kosio, a dedicated person, i. 65, 66, 68

Kosti, in Thrace, carnival custom at, ii. 99 *sq.*

Kotas, a tribe of Southern India, their priests not allowed to be widowers, ii. 230

Kretschmer, Professor P., on native population of Cyprus, i. 145 *n.*[3]; on Cybele and Attis, 287 *n.*[2]

Krishna, Hindoo god, ii. 254

Kuar, an Indian month, ii. 144

Kubary, J., on the system of mother-kin among the Pelew Islanders, ii. 204 *sqq.*

Kuinda, Cilician fortress, i. 144 *n.*[1]

Kuki-Lushai, men dressed as women to deceive dangerous ghosts or spirits among the, ii. 263

Kuklia, Old Paphos, i. 33, 36

Kundi in Cilicia, i. 144

Kupalo, figure of, passed across fire at Midsummer, i. 250 *sq.*; a deity of vegetation, 253

Kupole's festival at Midsummer in Prussia, i. 253

Labraunda in Caria, i. 182 *n.*[4]

Labrys, Lydian word for axe, i. 182

Laconia, subject to earthquakes, i. 203 *n.*[2]

Lactantius, on the rites of Osiris, ii. 85

Lagash in Babylonia, i. 35 *n.*[5]

Lago di Naftia in Sicily, i. 221 *n.*[4]

Lagrange, Father M. J., on the mourning for Adonis as a harvest rite, i. 231

Laguna, Pueblo village of New Mexico, ii. 54 *n.*[2]

Lakhubai, an Indian goddess, i. 243

Lakor, theory of earthquakes in, i. 198

Lamas River in Cilicia, i. 149, 150

Lamentations of Egyptian reapers, i. 232, ii. 45; of the savage for the animals and plants which he eats, 43 *sq.*; of Cherokee Indians "after the first working of the crop," 47; of the Karok Indians at cutting sacred wood, 47 *sq.*

Laments for Tammuz, i. 9 *sq.*; for dead kings of Judah, 20; for Osiris, ii. 12

Lampblack used to avert the evil eye, ii. 261

Lamps lighted to show the dead the way, ii. 51 *sq.*; for the use of ghosts at the feast of All Souls, 72, 73

Lancashire, All Souls' Day in, ii. 79

Landen, the battle of, i. 234

Lane, E. W., on the rise of the Nile, ii. 31 *n.*[1]

Lantana salvifolia, ii. 47

Lanterns, the feast of, in Japan, ii. 65

Lanzone, R. V., on the rites of Osiris, ii. 87 *n.*[5]

Larnax Lapethus in Cyprus, Melcarth worshipped at, i. 117

Larrekiya, Australian tribe, their belief in conception without cohabitation, i. 103

Lateran Museum, statue of Attis in the, i. 279

Latham, R. G., on succession to husband's property among the Kocchs, ii. 215 *n.*[2]

Laurel, gold wreath of, worn by priest of Hercules, i. 143; in Greek purificatory rites, ii. 240 *sq.*

——-bearing, a festival at Thebes, in Boeotia, ii. 241

Leake, W. M., on flowers in Asia Minor, i. 187 *n.*[6]

Leaping over Midsummer fires to make hemp or flax grow tall, i. 251

Leaves and flowers as talismans, ii. 242 *sq.*

Lebanon, the forests of Mount, i. 14; Aphrodite of the, 30; Baal of the, 32; the charm of the, 235

Lech, a tributary of the Danube, ii. 70

Lechrain, feast of All Souls in, ii. 70 *sq.*

Lecky, W. E. H., on the influence of great men on the popular imagination, ii. 199

Legend of the foundation of Carthage and similar tales, ii. 249 *sq.*

Lehmann-Haupt, C. F., on the historical Semiramis, i. 177 *n.*[1]

Lent, the Indian and Fijian, i. 90

Leo the Great, as to the celebration of Christmas, i. 305

Leonard, Major A. G., on sacrifices to prolong the lives of kings and others, ii. 222

Leprosy, king of Israel expected to heal, i. 23 *sq.*

Lepsius, R., his identification of Osiris with the sun, ii. 121 *sq.*

Leti, theory of earthquakes in, i. 198

Letopolis, neck of Osiris at, ii. 11

Letts, their annual festival of the dead, ii. 74 *sq.*

Lewis the Pious, institutes the feast of All Saints, ii. 83

Leza, supreme being recognized by the Bantu tribes of Northern Rhodesia, ii. 174

Licinius Imbrex, on Mars and Nerio, ii. 232

Lightning thought by Caffres to be caused by the ghost of a powerful chief, ii. 177 with *n.*[1]; no lamentations allowed for persons killed by, 177 *n.*[1]

"Lights of the dead" to enable the ghosts to enter houses, ii. 65

——, three hundred and sixty-five, in the rites of Osiris, ii. 88

.Lion, deity standing on a, i. 123 *n.*[2], 127; the emblem of the Mother Goddess, 164; as emblem of Hercules and the Heraclids, 182, 184; carried round acropolis of Sardes, 184, ii. 249

——-god at Boghaz-Keui, the mystery of the, i. 139 *sq.*; of Lydia, 184

——-slaying god, statue of, i. 117

Lions, dead kings reincarnate in, i. 83 *n.*[1], ii. 163; carved, at gate, i. 128; as emblems of the great Asiatic Mother-goddess, 137; deities seated on, 162; spirits of dead chiefs reincarnated in, ii. 193

Living parents, children of, in ritual, ii. 236 *sqq.*

Loeboes, a tribe of Sumatra, exchange of costume between boys and girls among the, ii. 264

Loryma in Caria, Adonis worshipped at, i. 227 *n.*

Lots, Greek custom as to the drawing of, ii. 248

Lovers, term applied to the Baalim, i. 75 *n.*

Low, Hugh, on Dyak treatment of heads of slain enemies, i. 295

Lua and Saturn, ii. 233

Luangwa, district of Northern Rhodesia, prayers to dead ancestors in, ii. 175 *sq.*

Lucian, on religious prostitution, i. 58 ; on image of goddess at Hierapolis-Bambyce, 137 *n.*[2] ; on the death of Peregrinus, 181 ; on dispute between Hercules and Aesculapius, 209 *sq.* ; on the ascension of Adonis, 225 *n.*[3]

Lugaba, the supreme god of the Bahima, ii. 190

Lunar sympathy, the doctrine of, ii. 140 *sqq.*

Lung-fish clan among the Baganda, ii. 224

Luritcha of Central Australia, their belief in the reincarnation of the dead, i. 99

Lushais, men dressed as women, women dressed as men, among the, ii. 255 *n.*[1]

Luxor, temples at, ii. 124

Lyall, Sir Charles J., on the system of mother-kin among the Khasis, ii. 202 *sq.*

Lycaonian plain, i. 123

Lycia, flowers in, i. 187 *n.*[6] ; Mount Chimaera in, 221 ; mother-kin in, ii. 212 *sq.*

Lycian language, question of its affinity, ii. 213 *n.*[1]

—— men dressed as women in mourning, ii. 264

Lycurgus, king of the Edonians, rent in pieces by horses, ii. 98, 99

Lycus, valley of the, i. 207

Lydia, prostitution of girls before marriage in, i. 38, 58 ; the lion-god of, 184 ; the Burnt Land of, 193 *sq.* ; traces of mother-kin in, ii. 259

Lydian kings, their divinity, i. 182 *sqq.* ; held responsible for the weather and the crops, 183

Lyell, Sir Charles, on hot springs, i. 213 *n.*[4] ; on volcanic phenomena in Syria and Palestine, 222 *n.*[1]

Lyre as instrument of religious music, i. 52 *sq.*, 54 *sq.* ; the instrument of Apollo, 288

Lysimachus scatters the bones of the kings of Epirus, ii. 104

Ma, goddess of Comana in Pontus, i. 39, 265 *n.*[1]

Macalister, Professor R. A. Stewart, on infant burial at Gezer, i. 109 *n.*[1]

Macdonald, Rev. James, on the worship of ancestors among the Bantus, ii. 176

Mace of Narmer, representation of the Sed festival on the, ii. 154

McLennan, J. F., on brother and sister marriages, i. 44 *n.*[2], ii. 216 *n.*[1]

Macrobius, on the mourning Aphrodite, i. 30 ; on the Egyptian year, ii. 28 *n.*[3] ; on Osiris as a sun-god, 121 ; his solar theory of the gods, 121, 128 ; on the influence of the moon, 132

Madagascar, vicarious sacrifice for a king in, ii. 221 ; men dressed as women in, 254

Madonna and Isis, ii. 119

Maeander, the valley of the, subject to earthquakes, i. 194 ; sanctuaries of Pluto in the valley of the, 205, 206

Mafuie, the Samoan god of earthquakes, i. 200

Magarsus in Cilicia, i. 169 *n.*[8]

Magic and religion, combination of, i. 4

Magical ceremonies for the regulation of the seasons, i. 3 *sqq.*

—— dramas for the regulation of the seasons, i. 4 *sq.*

—— uses made of the bodies of the dead, ii. 100 *sqq.*

Magnesia, on the Maeander, worship of Zeus at, ii. 238

Mahadeo and Parvati, Indian deities, i. 242, 251

Mahadeva, Indian god, i. 241

Mahdi, an ancient, i. 74

Mahratta, dancing-girls in, i. 62

Maia or Majestas, the wife of Vulcan, ii. 232 *sq.*

Maiau, hero in form of crocodile, i. 139 *n.*[1]

Maiden, the (Persephone), the descent of, ii. 41

Malagasy use of children of living parents in ritual, ii. 247

Malay Peninsula, the Mentras or Mantras of the, ii. 140

Mallus in Cilicia, deities on coins of, i. 165 *sq.*

Malta, bilingual inscription of, i. 16 ; Phoenician temples of, 35

Mamre, sacred oak or terebinth at, i. 37 *n.*[2]

Mandingoes of Senegambia, their attention to the phases of the moon, ii. 141

Maneros, chant of Egyptian reapers, ii. 45, 46

Manes, first king of Lydia, i. 186 *n.*[5]

Manetho, on the Egyptian burnt-sacrifice of red-haired men, ii. 97 ; on Isis as the discoverer of corn, 116 ; quoted by Diodorus Siculus, 120

Manichaeans, their theory of earthquakes, i. 197

Manichaeus, the heretic, his death, i. 294 n.[3]

Manipur, the Tangkul Nagas of, ii. 57 sq.

Mantinea, Poseidon worshipped at, i. 203 n.[2]

Maori priest catches the soul of a tree, ii. 111 n.[1]

Marash, Hittite monuments at, i. 173

March, festival of Attis in, i. 267

——, the twenty-fifth of, tradition that Christ was crucified on, i. 306

Marduk, human wives of, at Babylon, i. 71

Mariette-Pacha, A., on the burial of Osiris, ii. 89 n.

Marigolds used to adorn tombstones on All Souls' Day, ii. 71

Marks, bodily, of prophets, i. 74

Marriage as an infringement of old communal rights, i. 40 ; of the Sun and Earth, 47 sq. ; of women to serpent-god, 66 sqq. ; of Adonis and Aphrodite celebrated at Alexandria, 224 ; of Sky and Earth, 282 with n.[2] ; of the Roman gods, ii. 230 sqq. ; exchange of dress between men and women at, 260 sqq.

——, sacred, of priest and priestess as representatives of deities, i. 46 sqq. ; represented in the rock-hewn sculptures at Boghaz-Keui, 140 ; in Cos, ii. 259 n.[4]

—— customs of the Aryan family, ii. 235 ; use of children of living parents in, 245 sqq. ; to ensure the birth of boys, 262

Marriages of brothers with sisters in ancient Egypt, ii. 214 sqq. ; their intention to keep the property in the family, 215 sq.

Mars, the father of Romulus and Remus, ii. 235

—— and Bellona, ii. 231

—— and Nerio, ii. 232

Marsala in Sicily, Midsummer customs at, i. 247

Marseilles, Midsummer custom at, i. 248 sq.

Marshall, Mr. A. S. F., on the felling of timber in Mexico, ii. 136 n.[3]

Marsyas, his musical contest with Apollo and his death, i. 288 sq. ; perhaps a double of Attis, 289

—— and Apollo, i. 55

——, the river, i. 289

Martin, M., on the cutting of peat in the Hebrides, ii. 138

Masai, of East Africa, their belief in serpents as reincarnations of the dead, i. 82, 84 ; their ceremonies at the new moon, ii. 142 sq.

—— boys wear female costume at circumcision, ii. 263

—— rule as to the choice of a chief, ii. 248

Masnes, a giant, i. 186

Masoka, the spirits of the dead, ii. 188 sq.

Maspero, Sir Gaston, edits the Pyramid Texts, ii. 4 n.[1] ; on the nature of Osiris, 126 n.[2]

Masquerade at the Carnival in Thrace, ii. 99 sq.

Masquerades at festivals of the dead, ii. 53

Massacres for sick kings of Uganda, ii. 226

Massaya, volcano in Nicaragua, human victims sacrificed to, i. 219

Massebah (plural masseboth), sacred stone or pillar, i. 107, 108

Maternal uncle in marriage ceremonies in India, i. 62 n.[1]

Maternity and paternity of the Roman deities, ii. 233 sqq.

"Matriarchate," i. 46

Maui, Fijian god of earthquakes, i. 202 n.

Maundrell, H., on the discoloration of the river Adonis, i. 225 n.[4]

Maury, A., on the Easter ceremonies compared with those of Adonis, i. 257 n.[1]

Maximus Tyrius, on conical image at Paphos, i. 35 n.

May, modern Greek feast of All Souls in May, ii. 78 n.[1]

—— Day, ceremony at Meiron in Galilee on the eve of, i. 178

—— -pole or Midsummer-tree in Sweden and Bohemia, i. 250

Medea and her magic cauldron, i. 180 sq.

Medicine-men of Zulus, i. 74 n.[4] ; of Wiimbaio, 75 n.[4]

Mefitis, Italian goddess of mephitic vapours, i. 204, 205

Megalopolis, battle of gods and giants in plain of, i. 157

Megassares, king of Hyria, i. 41

Meiners, C., on purification by blood, i. 299 n.[2]

Meiron, in Galilee, burnings for dead Jewish Rabbis at, i. 178 sq.

Mela's description of the Corycian cave, i. 155 n., 156

Melanesia, belief in conception without sexual intercourse in, i. 97 sq.

Melanesian magicians buried secretly, ii. 105

Melanesians, mother-kin among the, ii. 211 ; of New Britain, their use of flowers and leaves as talismans, 242 *sq.*

Melcarth, the god of Tyre, identified with Hercules, i. 16, 111 ; worshipped at Amathus in Cyprus, 32, 117 ; the burning of, 110 *sqq.* ; worshipped at Gades, 112 *sq.*, ii. 258 *n.*[5]

Melchizedek, king of Salem, i. 17

Melech and Moloch, ii. 219 *sq.*

Meles, king of Lydia, banished because of a dearth, i. 183 ; causes lion to be carried round acropolis, 184

Melicertes, a form of Melcarth, i. 113

Melite in Phthia, i. 291

Melito on the father of Adonis, i. 13 *n.*[2]

Memnonium at Thebes, ii. 35 *n.*

Memorial stones, ii. 203

Memphis, head of Osiris at, ii. 11 ; oath of the kings of Egypt at, 24 ; festival of Osiris in the month of Khoiak at, 108 ; Apis the sacred bull of, 119 *n.* ; the sanctuary of Serapis at, 119 *n.*

Men, make gods, ii. 211 ; dressed as women at marriage, 262 *sqq.* ; dressed as women to deceive dangerous spirits, 262 *sq.* ; dressed as women at circumcision, 263

—— and women inspired by the spirits of dead kings and chiefs, ii. 171, 172, 192 *sq.*

—— "of God," prophets, i. 76

Men Tyrannus, Phrygian moon-god, i. 284 ; custom as to pollution of death at his shrine, ii. 227

Mentras or Mantras of the Malay Peninsula, their tradition as to primitive man, ii. 140

Mephitic vapours, worship of, i. 203 *sqq.*

Mercurial temperament of merchants and sailors, ii. 218

Mesha, king of Moab, i. 15 ; sacrifices his first-born, 110

Messiah, "the Anointed One," i. 21

Meteor as signal for festival, i. 259

Metharme, daughter of Pygmalion, i. 41

Methide plant growing over grave of Osiris, ii. 111

Mexican calendar, its mode of intercalation, ii. 28 *n.*[3]

Mexicans, their human sacrifices for the maize, ii. 107

Mexico, rule as to the felling of timber in, ii. 136

Meyer, Professor Eduard, on prophecy in Canaan, i. 75 *n.*[5] ; on the Hittite language, 125 *n.* ; on costume of Hittite priest or king, 133 *n.*, 141 *n.*[1] ; on the rock-hewn sculptures of Boghaz-Keui, 133 *n.* ; on Anubis at Abydos,

ii. 18 *n.*[3] ; on the hawk as an Egyptian emblem, 22 *n.*[1] ; on the date of the introduction of the Egyptian calendar, 36 *n.*[2] ; on the nature of Osiris, 126 *n.*[2] ; on the relation of Byblus to Egypt, 127 *n.*[1] ; on the Lycian language, 213 *n.*[1]

Michael Angelo, the Pietà of, i. 257

Michaelmas, 29th September, ii. 74

Midas, the tomb of, i. 286

—— and Gordias, names of Phrygian kings, i. 286

Midsummer, old heathen festival of, in Europe and the East, i. 249 *sq.* ; divination at, 252 *sq.*

—— bathing, pagan origin of the custom, i. 249

—— Bride and Bridegroom in Sweden, i. 251

—— Day or Eve, custom of bathing on, i. 246 *sqq.*

—— fires and couples in relation to vegetation, i. 250 *sq.* ; leaping over the fires to make flax or hemp grow tall, 251

Milcom, the god of Ammon, i. 19

Milk, serpents fed with, i. 84 *sqq.*, 87 ; offered at graves, 87

Mill, women mourning for Tammuz eat nothing ground in a mill, i. 230

Milne, Mrs. Leslie, on the Shans, ii. 136

Milton on the laments for Tammuz, i. 226 *n.*

Minoan age of Greece, i. 34

Minucius Felix on the rites of Osiris, ii. 85 *n.*[3]

Miraculous births of gods and heroes, i. 107

"Mistress of Turquoise," goddess at Sinai, i. 35

Mitani, ancient people of Northern Mesopotamia, i. 135 *n.*

Mithra, Persian deity, popularity of his worship in the Roman Empire, i. 301 *sq.* ; identified with the Unconquered Sun, 304

Mithraic religion a rival to Christianity, i. 302 ; festival of Christmas borrowed from it, 302 *sqq.*

Miztecs of Mexico, their annual festival of the dead, ii. 54 *sq.*

Mnevis, sacred Egyptian bull, ii. 11

Moa, theory of earthquakes in, i. 198

Moab, Mesha, king of, i. 15 ; the wilderness of, 52 *sq.* ; the springs of Callirrhoe in, 214 *sqq.*

——, Arabs of, their custom at harvest, ii. 48, 96 ; their remedies for ailments, 242

Moabite stone, the inscription on the, i. 15 *n.*[3], 20 *n.*[2], 163 *n.*[3]

Moabites burn the bones of the kings of Edom, ii. 104

Models in cardboard offered to the dead instead of the things themselves, ii. 63 *sq.*

Mohammedan peoples of North Africa, their custom of bathing at Midsummer, i. 249

—— saints as givers of children, i. 78 *n.*[2]

Mohammedanism, ii. 160

Mohammedans of Oude, their mode of drinking moonshine, ii. 144

Moire, sister of Tylon, i. 186

Moloch, meaning of the name, i. 15 ; sacrifices of first-born children to, 178 ; the king, ii. 219 *sqq.*

—— and *Melech*, ii. 219 *sq.*

Mommsen, Th., on the date of the festival of Osiris at Rome, ii. 95 *n.*[1]

Mongols, funeral customs of the, i. 293

Monmouthshire, All Souls' Day in, ii. 79

Monomotapa, a Caffre king, his way of prolonging his life, ii. 222 *sq.*

Montanists, their view as to the date of Creation, i. 307 *n.*[2]

Months, the Egyptian, table of, ii. 37 *n.*

Moon, human victims sacrificed to the, i. 73 ; albinoes thought to be the offspring of the, 91 ; popularly regarded as the cause of growth and decay, ii. 132, 138 ; practical rules based on a theory of the influence of the, 132 *sqq.*, 140 *sqq.* ; popularly regarded as the source of moisture, 137 *sq.* ; worshipped by the agricultural Indians of tropical America, 138 *sq.* ; viewed as the husband of the sun, 139 *n.* ; Athenian superstition as to an eclipse of the, 141 ; children presented to the, 144 *sqq.* ; thought to have a harmful influence on children, 148

——, the new, ceremonies at, ii. 141 *sqq.* ; dances at, 142 ; custom of showing money to, or turning it in the pocket, 148 *sq.*

——, the waning, theories to explain, ii. 130 ; thought to be broken or eaten up, 130

—— Being of the Omahas, ii. 256

——, the infant god, ii. 131, 153

—— -god conceived as masculine, i. 73 ; inspiration by the, 73 ; in ancient Babylonia, ii. 138 *sq.*

Moonshine drunk as a medicine in India, ii. 144 ; thought to be beneficial to children, ii. 144

Móooi, Tongan god who causes earthquakes, i. 201

Moore, G. F., on the burnt sacrifice of children, ii. 219 *n.*[1]

Moravia, the feast of All Souls in, ii. 73

Moret, Alexandre, on Amenophis IV., ii. 123 *n.*[1] ; on the Sed festival, 155 *sq.*

Mori, a district of Central Celebes, belief of the natives as to a spirit in the moon, ii. 139 *n.*

Moriah, Mount, traditionally identified with Mount Zion, ii. 219 *n.*[1]

Morning Star, appearance of, perhaps the signal for the festival of Adonis, i. 258 *sq.*

Morocco, custom of prostitution in an Arab tribe in, i. 39 *n.*[3]

Morrison, Rev. C. W., on belief of Australian aborigines as to childbirth, i. 103 *n.*[3]

Mostene in Lydia, double-headed axe at, i. 183 *n.*

Mota, belief as to conception in women in, i. 97 *sq.*

"Mother" and "Father" as epithets applied to Roman goddesses and gods, ii. 233 *sqq.*

——, dead, worshipped, ii. 175, 185

—— Earth, festival in her honour in Bengal, i. 90 ; fertilized by Father Sky, myth of, 282

—— Goddess of Western Asia, sacred prostitution in the worship of the, i. 36 ; lions as her emblems, 137, 164 ; her eunuch priests, 206 ; of Phrygia conceived as a Virgin Mother, 281

—— -kin, succession in royal houses with, i. 44 ; trace of, at Rome and Nemi, 45 ; among the Khasis of Assam, 46, ii. 202 *sqq.* ; among the Hittites, traces of, i. 141 *sq.* ; and Mother Goddesses, ii. 201 *sqq.*, 212 *sqq.* ; and father-kin, 202, 261 *n.*[3] ; favours the superiority of goddesses over gods in religion, 202 *sqq.*, 211 *sq.* ; its influence on religion, 202 *sqq.* ; among the Pelew Islanders, 204 *sqq.* ; does not imply that government is in the hands of women, 208 *sqq.* ; among the Melanesians, 211 ; in Africa, 211 ; in Lycia, 212 *sq.* ; in ancient Egypt, 213 *sqq.* ; traces of, in Lydia and Cos, 259 ; favours the development of goddesses, 259. *See also* Female kinship

—— of a god, i. 51, 52

—— of the gods, first-fruits offered to the, i. 280 *n.*[1] ; popularity of her worship in the Roman Empire, 298 *sq.*

—— Plastene on Mount Sipylus, i. 185

"Mother's Air," a tune on the flute, i. 288

"Mothers of the Clan" in the Pelew Islands, ii. 205, 206

Motlav, belief as to conception in women in, i. 98

Mournful character of the rites of sowing, ii. 40 *sqq.*

Mourning for Attis, i. 272 ; for the corn-god at midsummer, ii. 34

—— costume of men in Lycia, ii. 264 ; perhaps a mode of deceiving the ghost, 264

Mouth of the dead, Egyptian ceremony of opening the, ii. 15

Moylar, male children of sacred prostitutes, i. 63

Mpongwe kings of the Gaboon, buried secretly, ii. 104

Mugema, the earl of Busiro, ii. 168

Mukasa, the chief god of the Baganda, probably a dead man, ii. 196 *sq.* ; gives oracles through a woman, 257

Mukuru, an ancestor (plural *Ovakuru*, ancestors), ii. 185 *sq.*

Müller, Professor W. Max, on Hittite name for god, i. 148 *n.*

Mundas of Bengal, gardens of Adonis among the, i. 240

Mungarai, Australian tribe, their belief in the reincarnation of the dead, i. 101

Murder of children to secure their rebirth in barren women, i. 95

Murli, female devotee, i. 62

Music as a means of prophetic inspiration, i. 52 *sq.*, 54 *sq.*, 74 ; in exorcism, 54 *sq.* ; and religion, 53 *sq.*

Musquakie Indians, infant burial among the, i. 91 *n.*[3]

Mutilation of dead bodies of kings, chiefs, and magicians, ii. 103 *sqq.* ; to prevent their souls from becoming dangerous ghosts, 188

Mycenae, royal graves at, i. 33, 34

Mycenaean age of Greece, i. 34

Mylasa in Caria, i. 182 *n.*[4]

Mylitta, Babylonian goddess, sacred prostitution in her worship, i. 36, 37 *n.*[1]

Myrrh or Myrrha, the mother of Adonis, i. 43, 227 *sq.*

—— -tree, Adonis born of a, i. 227, ii. 110

Mysore, sacred women in, i. 62 *n.* ; the Komatis of, 81 *sq.*

Mysteries of Sabazius, i. 90 *n.*[4] ; of Attis, 274 *sq.*

Myth and ritual of Attis, i. 263 *sqq.*

Myths supposed to originate in verbal misapprehensions or a disease of language, ii. 42

——, Italian, of kings or heroes begotten by the fire-god, ii. 235

Naaburg, in Bavaria, custom at sowing at, i. 239

" Naaman, wounds of the," Arab name for the scarlet anemone, i. 226

Nabopolassar, king of Babylon, i. 174

Nâga, serpent god, i. 81

Naga-padoha, the agent of earthquakes, i. 200

Nahanarvals, a German tribe, priest dressed as a woman among the, ii. 259

Nahr Ibrahim, the river Adonis, i. 14, 28

Namal tribe of West Australia, their belief as to the birth of children, i. 105

Names, royal, signifying relation to deity, i. 15 *sqq.* ; Semitic personal, indicating relationship to a deity, 51 ; Hebrew, ending in -*el* or -*iah*, 79 *n.*[3]

Nana, the mother of Attis, i. 263, 269, 281

Nandi, the, of British East Africa, their belief in serpents as reincarnations of the dead, i. 82, 85 ; their ceremony at the ripening of the eleusine grain, ii. 47 ; boys dressed as women and girls dressed as men at circumcision among the, 263

Nanjundayya, H. V., on serpent worship in Mysore, i. 81 *sq.*

Naples, grotto *del cani* at, i. 205 *n.*[1] ; custom of bathing on St. John's Eve at, 246

Narmer, the mace of, ii. 154

National character partly an effect of geographical and climatic conditions, ii. 217

Nativity of the Sun at the winter solstice, i. 303 *sqq.*

Natural calendar of the husbandman, shepherd, and sailor, ii. 25

Nature of Osiris, ii. 96 *sqq.*

Navel-string of the king of Uganda preserved and inspected every new moon, ii. 147 *sq.*

Navel-strings of dead kings of Uganda preserved, ii. 167, 168, 171 ; ghosts of afterbirths thought to adhere to, 169 *sq.* ; preserved by the Baganda as their twins and as containing the ghosts of their afterbirths, 169 *sq.*

Ndjambi, Njambi, Njame, Zambi, Nyambe, etc., name of the supreme god among various tribes of Africa, ii. 186, with note[5]

—— Karunga, the supreme god of the Herero, ii. 186

Nebseni, the papyrus of, ii. 112

Neith or Net, an Egyptian goddess, i. 282 *n.*, ii. 51 *n.*[1]

Nekht, the papyrus of, ii. 112

Nemi, Dianus and Diana at, i. 45

Nephthys, Egyptian goddess, sister of Osiris and Isis, ii. 6 ; mourns Osiris, 12

Neptune and Salacia, ii. 231, 233

Nerio and Mars, ii. 232

New birth through blood in the rites of Attis, i. 274 *sq.* ; savage theory of, 299 ; of Egyptian kings at the Sed festival, ii. 153, 155 *sq.*

—— Britain, theory of earthquakes in, i. 201

—— Guinea, German, the Kai of, i. 96 ; the Tami of, 198

—— Mexico, the Pueblo Indians of, ii. 54

—— moon, ceremonies at the, ii. 141 *sqq.*

—— World, bathing on St. John's Day in the, i. 249 ; All Souls' Day in the, ii. 80

—— Year's Day, festival of the dead on, ii. 53, 55, 62, 65

—— Zealand, Rotomahana in, i. 207, 209 *n.*

Newberry, Professor P. E., on Osiris as a cedar-tree god, ii. 109 *n.*[1]

Newman, J. H., on music, i. 53 *sq.*

Ngai, God. i. 68

Ngoni, their belief in serpents as re-incarnations of the dead, i. 82

Nguruhi, the supreme god of the Wahehe, ii. 188 *sq.*

Niambe, the supreme god of the Barotse, ii. 193

Nias, conduct of the natives of, in an earthquake, i. 201 *sq.* ; head-hunting in, 296 *n.*[1]

Nicaragua, Indians of, sacrifice human victims to volcanoes, i. 219

Nietzold, J., on the marriage of brothers with sisters in ancient Egypt, ii. 216 *n.*[1]

Nigmann, E., on the religion of the Wahehe, ii. 188 *sq.*

Nikunau, one of the Gilbert Islands, sacred stones in, i. 108 *n.*[1]

Nile, the rise and fall of the, ii. 30 *sqq.* ; rises at the summer solstice in June, 31 *n.*[1], 33 ; commanded by the King of Egypt to rise, 33 ; thought to be swollen by the tears of Isis, 33 ; gold and silver thrown into the river at its rising, 40 ; the rise of, attributed to Serapis, 216 *sq.*

——, the "Bride" of the, ii. 38

Nilsson, Professor M. P., on custom of sacred prostitution, i. 37 *n.*[2], 57 *n.*[1], 58 *n.*[2] ; on the sacrifice of a bull to Zeus, ii. 239 *n.*[1]

Nineveh, the end of, i. 174

Njamus, the, of British East Africa, their

sacrifices at irrigation channels, ii. 38 *sq.*

Normandy, rolling in dew on St. John's Day in, i. 248

Northern Territory, Australia, beliefs as to the birth of children in the, i. 103 *sq.*

Nottinghamshire, harvest custom in, i. 238 *n.*

November, festivals of the dead in, ii. 51, 54, 69 *sqq.* ; the month of sowing in Egypt, 94

Novitiate of priests and priestesses, i. 66, 68

Nullakun tribe of Australia, their belief as to the birth of children, i. 101

Nut, Egyptian sky-goddess, mother of Osiris, i. 283 *n.*[3], ii. 6, 16 ; in a sycamore tree, 110

Nutlets of pines used as food, i. 278 *n.*[2]

Nutritive and vicarious types of sacrifice, ii. 226

Nyakang, the first of the Shilluk kings, worshipped as the god of his people, ii. 162 *sqq* ; incarnate in various animals, 163 *sq.* ; his mysterious dis-appearance, ·163 ; his graves, 163, 166 ; historical reality of, 164, 166 *sq.*; his relation to the creator Juok, 164 *sq.* ; compared to Osiris, 167

Nymphs of the Fair Crowns at Olympia, ii. 240

Nysa, in the valley of the Maeander, i. 205, 206 *n.*[1] ; sacrifice of bull at, 292 *n.*[3]

Nyuak, L., on guardian spirits of Sea Dyaks, i. 83

Oak or terebinth, sacred at Mamre, i. 37 *n.*[2]

Oath of Egyptian kings not to correct the vague Egyptian year by inter-calation, ii. 26

Obelisk, image of Astarte, i. 14

Obelisks, sacred, at Gezer, i. 108

Obscene images of Osiris, ii. 112

Octennial cycle, old, in Greece, ii. 242 *n.*

October, the first of, a great Saxon festival, ii. 81 *n.*[3]

Odilo, abbot of Clugny, institutes feast of All Souls, ii. 82

Odin, hanged on a tree, i. 290 ; human victims dedicated by hanging to, 290 ; king's sons sacrificed to, ii. 220

Oenomaus, king of Pisa, his incest with his daughter, i. 44 *n.*[1]

Oeta, Mount, Hercules burnt on, i. 111, 116, 211

Offerings to dead kings, ii. 194

Oil, holy, poured on king's head, i. 21 ;

poured on sacred stones, 36; as vehicle of inspiration, 74

Olba, priestly kings of, i. 143 *sqq.*, 161; the name of, 148; the ruins of, 151 *sq.*

Old Woman of the corn, mythical being of the Cherokee Indians, ii. 46 *sq.*

Olive of the Fair Crown at Olympia, ii. 240

——-branches carried in procession and hung over doors at Athens, ii. 238

Olo Ngadjoe, the, of Borneo, i. 91

Olonets, Russian Government of, festival of the dead in, ii. 75

Olympia, the quack Peregrinus burns himself at, i. 181; the cutting of the olive-branches to form the victors' crowns at, ii. 240

Olympic festival based on an octennial cycle, ii. 242 *n.*[1]

Olympus, Mount, in Cyprus, i. 32

Omahas, Indian tribe of North America, effeminate men among the, ii. 255 *sq.*

Omonga, a rice-spirit who lives in the moon, ii. 139 *n.*

Omphale and Hercules, i. 182, ii. 258

On, King of Sweden. *See* Aun.

Oodeypoor, in Rajputana, gardens of Adonis at, i. 241 *sq.*

Opening the eyes and mouth of the dead, Egyptian funeral rite, ii. 15

Operations of husbandry regulated by observation of the moon, ii. 133 *sqq.*

Ops, the wife of Saturn, ii. 233; in relation to Consus, 233 *n.*[6]

Oracles given by the spirits of dead kings, ii. 167, 171, 172

Oraons of Bengal, their annual marriage of the Sun and Earth, i. 46 *sqq.*; gardens of Adonis among the, 240; their annual festival of the dead, ii. 59

Orcus, Roman god of the lower world, his marriage celebrated by the pontiffs, ii. 231

Ordeal of chastity, i. 115 *n.*[2]

Orestes at Castabala, i. 115

Orgiastic rites of Cybele, i. 278

Oriental mind untrammelled by logic, i. 4 *n.*[1]

—— religions in the West, i. 298 *sqq.*; their influence in undermining ancient civilization, 299 *sqq.*; importance attached to the salvation of the individual soul in, 300

Origen, on the refusal of Christians to fight, i. 301 *n.*[1]

Origin of Osiris, ii. 158 *sqq.*

Orion, appearance of the constellation, a signal for sowing, i. 290 *sq.*

Orpheus, prophet and musician, i. 55; the legend of his death, ii. 99

Orwell in Cambridgeshire, harvest custom at, i. 237 *n.*[4]

Oschophoria, vintage festival at Athens, ii. 258 *n.*[6]

Osirian mysteries, the hall of the, at Abydos, ii. 108

Osiris identified with Adonis and Attis, i. 32, ii. 127 *n.*; myth of, ii. 3 *sqq.*; his birth, 6; introduces the cultivation of corn and the vine, 7, 97, 112; his violent death, 7 *sq.*; at Byblus, 9 *sq.*, 22 *sq.*, 127; his body rent in pieces, 10; the graves of, 10 *sq.*; his dead body sought and found by Isis, 10, 50, 85; tradition as to his genital organs, 10, 102; mourned by Isis and Nephthys, 12; invited to come to his house, 12, 47; restored to life by Isis, 13; king and judge of the dead, 13 *sq.*; his body the first mummy, 15; the funeral rites performed over his body the model of all funeral rites in Egypt, 15; all the Egyptian dead identified with, 16; his trial and acquittal in the court of the gods, 17; represented in art as a royal mummy, 18; specially associated with Busiris and Abydos, 18; his tomb at Abydos, 18 *sq.*, 197 *sq.*; official festivals of, 49 *sqq.*; his sufferings displayed in a mystery at night, 50; his festival in the month of Athyr, 84 *sqq.*; dramatic representation of his resurrection in his rites, 85; his images made of vegetable mould, 85, 87, 90 *sq.*, 91; the funeral rites of, described in the inscription of Denderah, 86 *sqq.*; his festival in the month of Khoiak, 86 *sqq.*, 108 *sq.*; his "garden," 87 *sq.*; ploughing and sowing in the rites of, 87, 90, 96; the burial of, in his rites, 88; the holy sepulchre of, under Persea-trees, 88; represented with corn sprouting from his dead body, 89; his resurrection depicted on the monuments, 89 *sq.*; as a corn-god, 89 *sqq.*, 96 *sqq.*; corn-stuffed effigies of, buried with the dead as a symbol of resurrection, 90 *sq.*, 114; date of the celebration of his resurrection at Rome, 95 *n.*[1]; the nature of, 96 *sqq.*; his severed limbs placed on a corn-sieve, 97; human victims sacrificed by kings at the grave of, 97; suggested explanations of his dismemberment, 97; sometimes explained by the ancients as a personification of the corn, 107; as a tree-spirit, 107 *sqq.*; his image made out of a pine-tree, 108; his emblems the crook and scourge or flail, 108, 153, compare 20; his backbone represented by the *ded* pillar, 108 *sq.*;

interpreted as a cedar-tree god, 109 *n.*[1]; his soul in a bird, 110; represented as a mummy enclosed in a tree, 110, 111; obscene images of, 112; as a god of fertility, 112 *sq.*; identified with Dionysus, 113, 126 *n.*[3]; a god of the dead, 113 *sq.*; universal popularity of his worship, 114; interpreted by some as the sun, 120 *sqq.*, reasons for rejecting this interpretation, 122 *sqq.*; his death and resurrection interpreted as the decay and growth of vegetation, 126 *sqq.*; his body broken into fourteen parts, 129; interpreted as the moon by some of the ancients, 129; reigned twenty-eight years, 129; his soul thought to be imaged in the sacred bull Apis, 130; identified with the moon in hymns, 131; represented wearing on his head a full moon within a crescent, 131; distinction of his myth and worship from those of Adonis and Attis, 158 *sq.*; his dominant position in Egyptian religion, 158 *sq.*; the origin of, 158 *sqq.*; his historical reality asserted in recent years, 160 *n.*[1]; his temple at Abydos, 198; his title Khenti-Amenti, 198 *n.*[2]; compared to Charlemagne, 199; the question of his historical reality left open, 199 *sq.*; his death still mourned in the time of Athanasius, 217; his old type better preserved than those of Adonis and Attis, 218

Osiris, Adonis, Attis, their mythical similarity, i. 6, ii. 201
—— and Adonis, similarity between their rites, ii. 127
—— and Dionysus, similarity between their rites, ii. 127
—— and the moon, ii. 129 *sqq.*
" —— of the mysteries," ii. 89
—— -Sep, title of Osiris, ii. 87

Ostrich-feather, king of Egypt supposed to ascend to heaven on an, ii. 154, 155

Otho, the emperor, addicted to the worship of Isis, ii. 118 *n.*[1]

Oulad Abdi, Arab tribe of Morocco, i. 39 *n.*[3]

Oura, ancient name of Olba, i. 148, 152

Ourwira, theory of earthquakes in, i. 199

Ovambo, the, of German South-West Africa, their ceremony at the new moon, ii. 142; the worship of the dead among the, 188

Ovid, on the story of Pygmalion, i. 49 *n.*[4]

Owl regarded as the guardian spirit of a tree, ii. 111 *n.*[1]

Ox substituted for human victim in sacrifice, i. 146; embodying corn-spirit sacrificed at Athens, 296 *sq.*; black, used in purificatory ceremonies after a battle, ii. 251 *sq.*

Ozieri, in Sardinia, St. John's festival at, i. 244

Pacasmayu, the temple of the moon at, ii. 138

Padmavati, an Indian goddess, i. 243

Pagan origin of the Midsummer festival (festival of St. John), i. 249 *sq.*

Paganism and Christianity, their resemblances explained as diabolic counterfeits, i. 302, 309 *sq.*

Παῖς ἀμφιθαλής, a boy whose parents are both alive, ii. 236 *n.*[2]

Palatinate, the Upper, the feast of All Souls in, ii. 72

Palestine, religious prostitution in, i. 58; date of the corn-reaping in, 232 *n.*

Palestinian Aphrodite, i. 304 *n.*

Palestrina, the harmonies of, i. 54

Pampa del Sacramento, Peru, earthquakes in, i. 198

Pampas, bones of extinct animals in the, i. 158

Pamyles, an Egyptian, ii. 6

Pandharpur, in the Bombay Presidency, i. 243

Panaghia Aphroditessa at Paphos, i. 36

Panku, a being who causes earthquakes, i. 198

Papas, a name for Attis, i. 281, 282

Paphlagonian belief that the god is bound fast in winter, ii. 41

Paphos in Cyprus, i. 32 *sqq.*; sanctuary of Aphrodite at, 32 *sqq.*; founded by Cinyras, 41

Papyrus of Nebseni, ii. 112; of Nekht, 112
—— swamps, Isis in the, ii. 8

Parilia and the festival of St. George, i. 308

Parr, Thomas, i. 56

Parvati or Isa, an Indian goddess, i. 241, 242

Pasicyprus, king of Citium, i. 50 *n.*[2]

Patagonia, funeral customs of Indians of, i. 294

Patagonians, effeminate priests or sorcerers among the, ii. 254

Paternity, primitive ignorance of, i. 106 *sq.*; unknown in primitive savagery, 282
—— and maternity of the Roman deities, ii. 233 *sqq.*

Paton, W. R., on modern Greek feast of All Souls in May, ii. 78 *n.*[1]

Patrae, Laphrian Artemis at, i. 126 *n.*[2]

Pausanias on the necklace of Harmonia, i. 32 *n.*² ; on bones of superhuman size, 157 *n.*² ; on offerings to Etna, 221 *n.*⁴ ; on the Hanged Artemis, 291 *n.*²

Payne, E. J., on the origin of moon-worship, ii. 138 *n.*²

Pegasus and Bellerophon, i. 302 *n.*⁴

Pegu, dance of hermaphrodites in, i. 271 *n.*

Peking, Ibn Batuta at, i. 289

Pélé, goddess of the volcano Kirauea in Hawaii, i. 217 *sqq.*

Pelew Islanders, their system of mother-kin, ii. 204 *sqq.* ; predominance of goddesses over gods among them, 204 *sqq.* ; customs of the, 253 *sqq.*

—— Islands and the ancient East, parallel between, ii. 208 ; prostitution of un-married girls in, 264 *sq.* ; custom of slaying chiefs in the, 266 *sqq.*

Pelion, Mount, sacrifices offered on the top of, at the rising of Sirius, ii. 36 *n.*

Peloponnese, worship of Poseidon in, i. 203

Pelops restored to life, i. 181

Peneus, the river, at Tempe, ii. 240

Pennefather River in Queensland, belief of the natives as to the birth of children, i. 103

Pentheus, king of Thebes, rent in pieces by Bacchanals, ii. 98

Peoples of the Aryan stock, annual festivals of the dead among the, ii. 67 *sqq.*

Pepi the First, ii. 5 ; his pyramid, 4 *n.*¹

Perasia, Artemis, at Castabala, i. 167 *sqq.*

Peregrinus, his death in the fire, i. 181

Perga in Pamphylia, Artemis at, i. 35

Periander, tyrant of Corinth, his burnt sacrifice to his dead wife, i. 179

Perigord, rolling in dew on St. John's Day in, i. 248

Peritius, month of, i. 111

Perpetual holy fire in temples of dead kings, ii. 174

—— fires worshipped, i. 191 *sqq.*

Perrot, G., on rock-hewn sculptures at Boghaz-Keui, i. 138 *n.*

Persea-trees in the rites of Osiris, ii. 87 *n.*⁵ ; growing over the tomb of Osiris, 88

Persephone, name applied to spring, ii. 41

—— and Aphrodite, their contest for Adonis, i. 11 *sq.*

—— and Pluto, temple of, i. 205

Perseus, the virgin birth of, i. 302 *n.*⁴

Persian reverence for fire, i. 174 *sq.*

—— festival of the dead, ii. 68

Persian fire-worship and priests, 191

Personation of gods by priests, i. 45, 46 *sqq.*

Peru, earthquakes in, i. 202 ; sacrifice of sons in, ii. 220 *n.*⁴

Peruvian Indians, their theory of earth-quakes, i. 201

Pescara River, in the Abruzzi, i. 246

Pescina in the Abruzzi, Midsummer custom at, i. 246

Pessinus, image of Cybele at, i. 35 *n.*³ ; priests called Attis at, 140 ; local legend of Attis at, 264 ; image of the Mother of the Gods at, 265 ; people of, abstain from swine, 265 ; high-priest of Cybele at, 285

Petrarch at Cologne on St. John's Eve, i. 247 *sq.*

Petrie, Professor W. M. Flinders, on the date of the corn-reaping in Egypt and Palestine, i. 231 *n.*³ ; on the Sed festival, ii. 151 *n.*³, 152 *n.*³, 154 *sq.* ; on the marriage of brothers with sisters in Egypt, 216 *n.*¹

Petrified cascades of Hierapolis, i. 207

Petroff, Ivan, on a custom of the Koniags of Alaska, ii. 106

Phamenoth, an Egyptian month, ii. 49 *n.*¹, 130

Phaophi, an Egyptian month, ii. 49 *n.*¹, 94

Pharnace, daughter of Megassares, i. 41

Phatrabot, a Cambodian month, ii. 61

Phidias, his influence on Greek religion, i. 54 *n.*¹

Philadelphia, subject to earthquakes, i. 194 *sq.*

Philae, Egyptian relief at, ii. 50 *n.*⁵ ; mystic representation of Osiris in the temple of Isis at, 89 ; sculptures in the temple of Isis at, 111 ; the grave of Osiris at, 111 ; the dead Osiris in the sculptures at, 112

Philo of Alexandria on the date of the corn-reaping, i. 231 *n.*³

Philocalus, calendar of, i. 303 *n.*², 304 *n.*³, 307 *n.*, ii. 95 *n.*¹

Philosophy, school of, at Tarsus, i. 118

Philostephanus, Greek historian, i. 49 *n.*⁴

Phoenician temples in Malta, i. 35 ; sacred prostitution in, 37

—— kings in Cyprus, i. 49

Phoenicians in Cyprus, i. 31 *sq.*

Phrygia, Attis a deity of, i. 263 ; festival of Cybele in, 274 *n.* ; indigenous race of, 287

Phrygian belief that the god sleeps in winter, ii. 41

—— cap of Attis, i. 279

—— cosmogony, i. 263 *sq.*

—— kings named Midas and Gordias, i. 286

Phrygian moon-god, i. 73
—— priests named Attis, i. 285, 287
Phrygians, invaders from Europe, i. 287
Pietà of Michael Angelo, i. 257
Pig's blood used in exorcism and purification, i. 299 *n.*²
Pigs sacrificed annually to the moon and Osiris, ii. 131. *See also* Swine
Pillars as a religious emblem, i. 34; sacred, in Crete, 107 *n.*²
Pindar on the music of the lyre, i. 55; on Typhon, 156
Pine-cones symbols of fertility, i. 278; thrown into vaults of Demeter, 278; on the monuments of Osiris, ii. 110
—— seeds or nutlets used as food, i. 278
—— -tree in the myth and ritual of Attis, i. 264, 265, 267, 271, 277 *sq.*, 285, ii. 98 *n.*⁵ Marsyas hung on a, i. 288; in relation to human sacrifices, ii. 98 *n.*⁵; Pentheus on the, 98 *n.*⁵; in the rites of Osiris, 108
Pipiles of Central America expose their seeds to moonlight, ii. 135
Piraeus, processions in honour of Adonis at, i. 227 *n.*
Pirates, the Cilician, i. 149 *sq.*
Pitr Pâk, the Fortnight of the Manes, ii. 60
Pitrè, G., on Good Friday ceremonies in Sicily, i. 255 *sq.*
Placenta, Egyptian standard resembling a, ii. 156 *n.*¹ *See also* Afterbirth.
Placianian Mother, a form of Cybele, worshipped at Cyzicus, i. 274 *n.*
Plastene, Mother, on Mount Sipylus, i. 185
Plato, on gardens of Adonis, i. 236 *n.*¹
Plautus on Mars and Nerio, ii. 232
Pleiades worshipped by the Abipones, i. 258 *n.*²; the setting of, the time of sowing, ii. 41
Pliny, on the date of harvest in Egypt, ii. ¡32 *n.*²; on the influence of the moon, 132; on the grafting of trees, 133 *n.*³; on the time for felling timber, 136 *n.*
Plotinus, the death of, i. 87
Ploughing, Prussian custom at, i. 238; and sowing, ceremony of, in the rites of Osiris, ii. 87
Ploughmen and sowers drenched with water as a rain-charm, i. 238 *sq.*
Plutarch on the double-headed axe of Zeus Labrandeus, i. 182; on the myth of Osiris, ii. 3, 5 *sqq.*; on Harpocrates, 9 *n.*; on Osiris at Byblus, 22 *sq.*; on the rise of the Nile, 31 *n.*¹; on the mournful character of the rites of sowing, 40

sqq.; his use of the Alexandrian year, 49, 84; on an Egyptian ceremony at the winter solstice, 50 *n.*⁴; on the date of the death of Osiris, 84; on the festival of Osiris in the month of Athyr, 91 *sq.*; on the dating of Egyptian festivals, 94 *sq.*; on the rites of Osiris, 108; on the grave of Osiris, 111; on the similarity between the rites of Osiris and Dionysus, 127; on the Flamen Dialis, 229 *sq.*; on the Flaminica Dialis, 230 *n.*²
Pluto, the breath of, i. 204, 205; places or sanctuaries of, 204 *sqq.*; cave and temple of, at Acharaca, 205
Plutonia, places of Pluto, i. 204
Pollution of death, ii. 227 *sqq.*
Polo, Marco, on custom of people of Camul, i. 39 *n.*³
Polyboea, sister of Hyacinth, i. 314, 316; identified with Artemis or Persephone, 315
Polyidus, a seer, i. 186 *n.*⁴
Polynesian myth of the separation of earth and sky, i. 283
Pomegranate causes virgin to conceive, i. 263, 269
Pomegranates forbidden to worshippers of Cybele and Attis, i. 280 *n.*⁷
Pomona and Vertumnus, ii. 235 *n.*⁶
Pompey the Great, i. 27
Pondomisi, a Bantu tribe of South Africa, ii. 177
Pontiffs, the Roman, their mismanagement of the Julian calendar, ii. 93 *n.*¹; celebrated the marriage of Orcus, 231
Pontus, sacred prostitution in, i. 39, 58
Populonia, a Roman goddess, ii. 231
Port Darwin, Australia, i. 103
Porta Capena at Rome, i. 273
Poseidon the Establisher or Securer, i. 195 *sq.*; the earthquake god, 195, 202 *sq.*
—— and Demeter, i. 280
Possession of priest or priestess by a divine spirit, i. 66, 68 *sq.*, 72 *sqq.*; by the spirits of dead chiefs, ii. 192 *sq.*
Potniae in Boeotia, priest of Dionysus killed at, ii. 99 *n.*¹
Pots of Basil on St. John's Day in Sicily, i. 245
Potter in Southern India, custom observed by a, i. 191 *n.*²
Potters in Uganda bake their pots when the moon is waxing, ii. 135
Praeneste, Fortuna Primigenia, goddess of, ii. 234; founded by Caeculus, 235
Prague, the feast of All Souls in, ii. 73
Prayers to dead ancestors, ii. 175 *sq.*, 178 *sq.*, 183 *sq.*; to dead kings, 192

Pregnancy, causes of, unknown, i. 92 *sq.*, 106 *sq.* ; Australian beliefs as to the causes of, 99 *sqq.*

Priestess identified with goddess, i. 219 ; head of the State under a system of mother-kin, ii. 203

Priestesses more important than priests, i. 45, 46

Priesthood vacated on death of priest's wife, i. 45 ; of Hercules at Tarsus, 143

Priestly dynasties of Asia Minor, i. 140 *sq.*

—— king and queen personating god and goddess, i. 45

—— kings, i. 42, 43 ; of Olba, 143 *sqq.*, 161 ; Adonis personated by, 223 *sqq.*

Priests personate gods, i. 45, 46 *sqq.* ; tattoo-marks of, 74 *n.*[4] ; not allowed to be widowers, ii. 227 *sqq.* ; the Jewish, their rule as to the pollution of death, 230 ; dressed as women, 253 *sqq.*

—— of Astarte, kings as, i. 26

—— of Attis, the emasculated, i. 265, 266

—— of Zeus at the Corycian cave, i. 145, 155

Procession to the Almo in the rites of Attis, i. 273

Processions carved on rocks at Boghaz-Keui, i. 129 *sqq.* ; in honour of Adonis, 224 *sq.*, 227 *n.*, 236 *n.*[1]

Procreation, savage ignorance of the causes of, i. 106 *sq.*

Procris, her incest with her father Erechtheus, i. 44

Profligacy of human sexes supposed to quicken the earth, i. 48

Property, rules as to the inheritance of, under mother-kin, ii. 203 *n.*[1] ; landed, combined with mother-kin tends to increase the social importance of women, 209

Prophecy, Hebrew, distinctive character of, i. 75

Prophet regarded as madman, i. 77

Prophetesses inspired by dead chiefs, ii. 192 *sq.* ; inspired by gods, 207

Prophetic inspiration under the influence of music, i. 52 *sq.*, 54 *sq.*, 74 ; through the spirits of dead kings and chiefs, ii. 171, 172, 192 *sq.*

—— marks on body, i. 74

—— water drunk on St. John's Eve, i. 247

Prophets in relation to *ḳedeshim*, i. 76 ; or mediums inspired by the ghosts of dead kings, ii. 171, 172

——, Hebrew, their resemblance to those of Africa, i. 74 *sq.*

Prophets of Israel, their religious and moral reform, i. 24 *sq.*

Propitiation of deceased ancestors, i. 46

Prostitution, sacred, before marriage, in Western Asia, i. 36 *sqq.* ; suggested origin of, 39 *sqq.* ; in Western Asia, alternative theory of, 57 *sqq.* ; in India, 61 *sqq.* ; in Africa, 65 *sqq.*

—— of unmarried girls in the Pelew Islands, ii. 264 *sq.* ; in Yap, one of the Caroline Islands, 265 *sq.*

Provence, bathing at Midsummer in, i. 248

Prussia, customs at ploughing and harvest in, i. 238 ; divination at Midsummer in, 252 *sq.*

Pteria, captured by Croesus, i. 128

Ptolemy Auletes, king of Egypt, i. 43

Ptolemy and Berenice, annual festival in honour of, ii. 35 *n.*[1]

Ptolemy I. and Serapis, ii. 119 *n.*

Ptolemy III. Euergetes, his attempt to correct the vague Egyptian year by intercalation, ii. 27

Ptolemy V. on the Rosetta Stone, ii. 152 *n.*

Ptolemy Soter, i. 264 *n.*[4]

Pueblo Indians of New Mexico, their annual festival of the dead, ii. 54

Pumi-yathon, king of Citium and Idalium, i. 50

Punjaub, belief in the reincarnation of infants in the, i. 94

Puppet substituted for human victim, i. 219 *sq.*

Purification by fire, i. 115 *n.*[1], 179 *sqq.* ; by pig's blood, 299 *n.*[2] ; of Apollo at Tempe, ii. 240 *sq.*

Purificatory ceremonies after a battle, ii. 251 *sq.*

Pyanepsion, an Athenian month, ii. 41

Pygmalion, king of Citium and Idalium in Cyprus, i. 50

——, king of Cyprus, i. 41, 49

——, king of Tyre, i. 50

—— and Aphrodite, i. 49 *sq.*

Pymaton of Citium, i. 50 *n.*[2]

Pyramid Texts, ii. 4 *sqq.*, 9 *n.* ; intended to ensure the life of dead Egyptian kings, 4 *sq.* ; Osiris and the sycamore in the, 110 ; the mention of Khenti-Amenti in the, 198 *n.*[2]

Pyramus, river in Cilicia, i. 165, 167, 173

Pyre at festivals of Hercules, i. 116 ; at Tarsus, 126 ; of dead kings at Jerusalem, 177 *sq.*

—— or Torch, name of great festival at the Syrian Hierapolis, i. 146

Pythian games, their period, ii. 242 *n.*[1]

Python worshipped by the Baganda, i. 86

—— -god, human wives of the, i. 66

Pythons worshipped in West Africa, i. 83 *n.*[1]; dead chiefs reincarnated in, ii. 193

"Quail-hunt," legend on coins of Tarsus, i. 126 *n.*[2]

Quails sacrificed to Hercules (Melcarth), i. 111 *sq.*; migration of, 112

Quatuordecimans of Phrygia celebrate the Crucifixion on March 25th, i. 307 *n.*

Queen of Egypt the wife of Ammon, i. 72

—— of Heaven, i. 303 *n.*[5]; incense burnt in honour of the, 228

Queensland, aborigines of, their beliefs as to the birth of children, i. 102 *sq.*

Quirinus and Hora, ii. 233

Ra, the Egyptian sun-god, ii. 6, 8, 12; identified with many originally independent local deities, 122 *sqq.*

Rabbah, captured by David, i. 19

Rabbis, burnings for dead Jewish, i. 178 *sq.*

Rain procured by bones of the dead, i. 22; excessive, ascribed to wrath of God, 22 *sq.*; instrumental in rebirth of dead infants, 95; regarded as the tears of gods, ii. 33; thought to be controlled by the souls of dead chiefs, 188

—— -charm in rites of Adonis, i. 237; by throwing water on the last corn cut, 237 *sq.*

—— -god represented with tears running from his eyes, ii. 33 *n.*[3]

Rainbow totem, i. 101

Rainless summer on the Mediterranean, i. 159 *sq.*

Rajaraja, king, i. 61

Rajputana, gardens of Adonis in, i. 241 *sq.*

Rambree, sorcerers dressed as women in the island of, ii. 254

Rameses II., his treaty with the Hittites, i. 135 *sq.*; his order to the Nile, ii. 33

Ramman, Babylonian and Assyrian god of thunder, i. 163 *sq.*

Rams, testicles of, in the rites of Attis, i. 269

Ramsay, Sir W. M., on rock-hewn sculptures at Boghaz-Keui, i. 134 *n.*[1], 137 *n.*[4]; on priest-dynasts of Asia Minor, 140 *n.*[2]; on the god Tark, 147 *n.*[3]; on the name Olba, 148 *n.*[1]; on *Hierapolis* and *Hieropolis*, 168 *n.*[2]; on Attis and Men, 284 *n.*[5]; on cruel death of the human representative of a god in Phrygia, 285 *sq.*

Raoul-Rochette on Asiatic deities with lions, i. 138 *n.*; on the burning of

doves to Adonis, 147 *n.*[1]; on apotheosis by death in the fire, 180 *n.*[1]

Ratumaimbulu, Fijian god of fruit-trees, i. 90

Readjustment of Egyptian festivals, ii. 91 *sqq.*

Reapers, Egyptian, their lamentations, i. 232, ii. 45; invoke Isis, 117

Rebirth of infants, means taken to ensure the, i. 91, 93 *sqq.*; of the dead, precautions taken to prevent, 92 *sq.*; of Egyptian kings at the Sed festival, ii. 153, 155 *sq.*

Red the colour of Lower Egypt, ii. 21 *n.*[1]

—— -haired men burnt by Egyptians, ii. 97, 106

Reform, the prophetic, in Israel, i. 24 *sq.*

Reformations of Hezekiah and Josiah, i. 25

Rehoboam, King, his family, i. 51 *n.*[2]

Reincarnation of the dead, i. 82 *sqq.*; in America, 91; in Australia, 99 *sqq.*

Rekub-el, Syrian god, i. 16

Relations, spirits of near dead, worshipped, i. 175, 176; at death become gods, ii. 180

Religion, volcanic, i. 188 *sqq.*; how influenced by mother-kin, ii. 202 *sqq.*

—— and magic, combination of, i. 4; and music, 53 *sq.*

Religious ideals a product of the male imagination, ii. 211

—— systems, great permanent, founded by great men, ii. 159 *sq.*

Remission of sins through the shedding of blood, i. 299

Remus, the birth of, ii. 235

Renan, E., on Tammuz and Adonis, i. 6 *n.*[1]; his excavations at Byblus, 14 *n.*[1]; on Adom-melech, 17; on the vale of the Adonis, 29 *n.*; on the burnings for the kings of Judah, 178 *n.*[1]; on the discoloration of the river Adonis, 225 *n.*[4]; on the worship of Adonis, 235

Renouf, Sir P. le Page, on Osiris as the sun, ii. 126

Resemblance of the rites of Adonis to the festival of Easter, i. 254 *sqq.*, 306

Resemblances of paganism to Christianity explained as diabolic counterfeits, i. 302, 309 *sq.*

Reshef, Semitic god, i. 16 *n.*[1]

Resurrection of the dead conceived on the pattern of the resurrection of Osiris, ii. 15 *sq.*

—— of Attis at the vernal equinox, i. 272 *sq.*, 307 *sq.*

—— of Hercules (Melcarth), i. 111 *sq.*

—— of Osiris dramatically represented in his rites, ii. 85; depicted on the

monuments, 89 *sq.* ; date of its celebration at Rome, 95 *n.*[1]; symbolized
by the setting up of the *ded* pillar, 109
Resurrection of Tylon, i. 186 *sq.*
Rhine, bathing in the, on St. John's
Eve, i. 248
Rhodes described by Strabo, i. 195 *n*[3];
worship of Helen in, 292
Rhodesia, Northern, the Bantu tribes of,
their worship of ancestral spirits, ii.
174 *sqq.* ; their worship of dead chiefs
or kings, 191 *sqq.*
Rhodians, the Venetians of antiquity, i.
195
Rice, the soul of the, in the first sheaf
cut, ii. 239
Ridgeway, Professor W., on the marriage
of brothers with sisters, ii. 216 *n.*[1]
Rites of irrigation in Egypt, ii. 33 *sqq.* ;
of sowing, 40 *sqq.* ; of harvest, 45 *sqq.*
Ritual, children of living parents in, ii.
236 *sqq.* ; of the Bechuanas at founding a new town, 249
—— of Adonis, i. 223 *sqq.*
Rivers as the seat of worship of deities,
i. 160; bathing in, at Midsummer,
246, 248, 249 ; gods worshipped beside, 289
Rivers, Dr. W. H. R., as to Melanesian
theory of conception in women, i. 97
sq. ; on the sacred dairyman of the
Todas, ii. 228
Rizpah and her sons, i. 22
Robinson, Edward, on the vale of the
Adonis, i. 29 *n.*
Roccacaramanico, in the Abruzzi, Easter
ceremonies at, i. 256 *n.*[2]
Rock-hewn sculptures at Ibreez, i. 121
sq. ; at Boghaz-Keui, 129 *sqq.*
Rockhill, W. Woodville, on dance of
eunuchs in Corea, i. 270 *n.*[2]
Rohde, E., on purification by blood, i.
299 *n.*[2]; on Hyacinth, 315
Roman deities called "Father" and
"Mother," ii. 233 *sqq.*
—— emperor, funeral pyre of, i. 126 *sq.*
—— expiation for prodigies, ii. 244
—— financial oppression, i. 301 *n.*[2]
—— *genius* symbolized by a serpent, i. 86
—— gods, the marriage of the, ii. 230
sqq. ; compared to Greek gods, 235
—— law, revival of, i. 301
—— marriage custom, ii. 245
—— mythology, fragments of, ii. 235,
with *n.*[6]
Romans adopt the worship of the
Phrygian Mother of the Gods, i. 265 ;
correct the vague Egyptian year by
intercalation, ii. 27 *sq.*
Rome, high-priest of Cybele at, i. 285 ;
the celebration of the resurrection of
Osiris at, ii. 95 *n.*[1]

Romulus cut in pieces, ii. 98 ; the birth
of, 235
Roper River, in Australia, i. 101
Roscoe, Rev. John, on serpent-worship,
i. 86 *n.*[1]; on the rebirth of the dead,
92 *sq.* ; on potters in Uganda, ii. 135;
on the religion of the Bahima, 190 *sq.* ;
on the worship of the dead among the
Baganda, 196 ; on Mukasa, the chief
god of the Baganda, 196 *sq.* ; on
massacres for sick kings of Uganda,
226
Rose, the white, dyed red by the blood
of Aphrodite, i. 226
Rosetta stone, the inscription, ii. 27,
152 *n.*
Roth, W. E., on belief in conception
without sexual intercourse, i. 103 *n.*[2]
Rotomahana in New Zealand, pink
terraces at, i. 207, 209 *n.*
Rugaba, supreme god in Kiziba, ii. 173
Rules of life based on a theory of lunar
influence, ii. 132 *sqq.*, 140 *sqq.*
Rumina, a Roman goddess, ii. 231
Runes, how Odin learned the magic, i.
290
Russia, annual festivals of the dead in,
ii. 75 *sqq.*
Russian Midsummer custom, i. 250 *sq.*
Rustic Calendars, the Roman, ii. 95 *n.*[1]

Sabazius, mysteries of, i. 90 *n.*[4]
Sacrament in the rites of Attis, i. 274
sq.
Sacred harlots in Asia Minor, i. 141
—— Marriage of priest and priestess as
representing god and goddess, i. 46
sqq. ; represented in the rock-hewn
sculptures at Boghaz-Keui, 140 ; in
Cos, ii. 259 *n.*[4]
" —— men " (*kedeshim*), at Jerusalem,
i. 17 *sq.* ; and women, 57 *sqq.* ; in
West Africa, 65 *sqq.* ; in Western
Asia, 72 *sqq.* ; at Andania, 76 *n.*[3]
——,prostitution, i. 36 *sqq.* ; suggested
origin of, 39 *sqq.* ; in Western Asia,
alternative theory of, 55 *sqq.* ; in India,
61 *sqq.* ; in West Africa, 65 *sqq.*
—— slaves, i. 73, 79
—— stocks and stones among the
Semites, i. 107 *sqq.*
—— women in India, i. 61 *sqq.* ; in
West Africa, 65 *sqq.* ; in Western
Asia, 70 *sqq.* ; at Andania, 76 *n.*[3]
Sacrifice of virginity, i. 60 ; of virility in
the rites of Attis and Astarte, 268 *sq.*,
270 *sq.* ; other cases of, 270 *n.*[2] ;
nutritive and vicarious types of, ii.
226
Sacrifices to earthquake god, i. 201,
202 ; to volcanoes, 218 *sqq.* ; to the
dead distinguished from sacrifices to

the gods, 316 *n.*[1] ; offered at the rising of Sirius, ii. 36 *n.* ; offered in connexion with irrigation, 38 *sq.* ; to dead kings, 101, 162, 166 *sq.* ; to ancestral spirits, 175, 178 *sq.*, 180, 181 *sq.*, 183 *sq.*, 190 ; of animals to prolong the life of kings, 221 ; without shedding of blood, 222 *n.*[2]

Sacrifices, human, offered at earthquakes, i. 201 ; offered to Dionysus, ii. 98 *sq.* ; at the graves of the kings of Uganda, 168 ; to dead kings, 173 ; to dead chiefs, 191 ; to prolong the life of kings, 220 *sq.*, 223 *sqq.*

Sadyattes, son of Cadys, viceroy of Lydia, i. 183

Saffron at the Corycian cave, i. 154, 187

Sago, magic for the growth of, ii. 101

Sahagun, B. de, on the ancient Mexican calendar, ii. 29 *n.*

St. Denys, his seven heads, ii. 12

St. George in Syria, reputed to bestow offspring on women, i. 78, 79, 90 ; festival of, and the Parilia, 308, 309

St. John, Sweethearts of, in Sardinia, i. 244 *sq.*

St. John, Spenser, on reasons for headhunting in Sarawak, i. 296

St. John's Day or Eve (Midsummer Day or Eve), custom of bathing on, i. 246 *sqq.*

—— Midsummer festival in Sardinia, i. 244 *sq.*

—— wort gathered at Midsummer, i. 252 *sq.*

St. Kilda, All Saints' Day in, ii. 80

St. Luke, the festival of, on October 18th, ii. 55

Saint-Maries, Midsummer custom at, i. 248

S. Martinus Dumiensis, on the date of the Crucifixion in Gaul, i. 307 *n.*

St. Michael in Alaska, ii. 51

St. Simon and St. Jude's day, October 28th, ii. 74

St. Vitus, festival of, i. 252

Saintonge, feast of All Souls in, ii. 69

Saints as the givers of children to women, i. 78 *sq.*, 91, 109

Sais, the festival of, ii. 49 *sqq.*

Sakkara, pyramids at, ii. 4

Sal tree, festival of the flower of the, i. 47

Salacia and Neptune, ii. 231, 233

Salamis in Cyprus, human sacrifices at, i. 145 ; dynasty of Teucrids at, 145

Salem, Melchizedek, king of, i. 17

Salii, priests of Mars, rule as to their election, ii. 244

Salono, a Hindoo festival, i. 243 *n.*[1]

Salvation of the individual soul, importance attached to, in Oriental religions, i. 300

Samagitians, their annual festival of the dead, ii. 75

Samal, in North-Western Syria, i. 16

Samaria, the fall of, i. 25

Samoa, conduct of the inhabitants in an earthquake, i. 200

Samuel consulted about asses, i. 75 ; meaning of the name, 79

—— and Saul, i. 22

San Juan Capistrano, the Indians of, their ceremony at the new moon, ii. 142

Sanda-Sarme, a Cilician king, i. 144

Sandacus, a Syrian, i. 41

Sandan of Tarsus, i. 124 *sqq.* ; the burning of, 117 *sqq.*, 126 ; identified with Hercules, 125, 143, 161 ; monument of, at Tarsus, 126 *n.*[2]

—— (Sandon, Sandes), Cappadocian and Cilician god of fertility, i. 125

—— and Baal at Tarsus, i. 142 *sq.*, 161

Sandon, or Sandan, name of the Lydian and Cilician Hercules, i. 182, 184, 185 ; a Cilician name, 182

Sandu'arri, a Cilician king, i. 144

Santa Felicita, successor of Mefitis, i. 205

Santiago Tepehuacan, Indians of, their custom at sowing, i. 239 ; their annual festival of the dead, ii. 55

Santorin, island of, its volcanic activity, i. 195

Sappho on the mourning for Adonis, i. 6 *n.*[2]

Saracus, last king of Assyria, i. 174

Sarawak, head-hunting in, i. 295 *sq.*

Sardanapalus, monument of, at Tarsus, i. 126 *n.*[2] ; his monument at Anchiale, 172 ; the burning of, 172 *sqq.* ; the effeminate, ii. 257

—— and Hercules, i. 172 *sqq.*

Sardes, captured by Cyrus, i. 174 ; lion carried round acropolis of, i. 184, ii. 249

Sardinia, gardens of Adonis in, i. 244 *sq.*

Sargal, in India, gardens of Adonis at, i. 243

Sarpedonian Artemis, i. 167, 171

Sasabonsun, earthquake god of Ashantee, i. 201

Saturn, the husband of Ops, ii. 233

—— and Lua, ii. 233

Saturn's period of revolution round the sun, ii. 151 *sq.*

Saturnine temperament of the farmer, ii. 218

Sauks, an Indian tribe of North America, effeminate sorcerers among the, ii. 255

Saul, burial of, i. 177 *n.*[4]
—— and David, i. 21
Saul's madness soothed by music, i. 53, 54
Savages lament for the animals and plants which they eat, ii. 43 *sq.*
Sâwan, Indian month, i. 242
Saxons of Transylvania, harvest custom of the, i. 238
Sayce, A. H., on kings of Edom, i. 16 ; on name of David, 19 *n.*[2]
Schäfer, H., on the tomb of Osiris at Abydos, ii. 198 *n.*[1]
Schlanow, in Brandenburg, custom at sowing at, i. 238 *sq.*
Schloss, Mr. Francis S., on the rule as to the felling of timber in Colombia, ii. 136 *n.*[4]
Schwegler, A., on the death of Romulus, ii. 98 *n.*[2]
Scipio, his fabulous birth, i. 81
Scorpions, Isis and the, ii. 8
Scotland, harvest custom in, i. 237
Scottish Highlanders on the influence of the moon, ii. 132, 134, 140
Scythian king, human beings and horses sacrificed at his grave, i. 293
Scythians, their belief in immortality, i. 294 ; their treatment of dead enemies, 294 *n.*[3]
Sea, custom of bathing in the, on St. John's Day or Eve, i. 246, 248
—— Dyaks or Ibans of Borneo, their worship of serpents, i. 83 ; their festivals of the dead, ii. 56 *sq.* ; effeminate priests or sorcerers among the, 253, 256
—— Dyaks of Sarawak, their reasons for taking human heads, i. 295 *sq.*
Season of festival a clue to the nature of a deity, ii. 24
Seasons, magical and religious theories of the, i. 3 *sq.*
Seb (Keb or Geb), Egyptian earth-god, i. 283 *n.*[3], ii. 6
Secret graves of kings, chiefs, and magicians, ii. 103 *sqq.*
Sed festival in Egypt, ii. 151 *sqq.* ; its date perhaps connected with the heliacal rising of Sirius, 152 *sq.* ; apparently intended to renew the king's life by identifying him with the dead and risen Osiris, 153 *sq.*
Segera, a sago magician of Kiwai, dismembered after death, ii. 101, 102
Seker (Sokari), title of Osiris, ii. 87
Seler, Professor E., on the ancient Mexican calendar, ii. 29 *n.*
Seleucus, a grammarian, i. 146 *n.*[1]
—— Nicator, king, i. 151
—— the Theologian, i. 146 *n.*[1]

Self-mutilation of Attis and his priests, i. 265
Seligmann, Dr. C. G., on the five supplementary Egyptian days, ii. 6 *n.*[3] ; on the divinity of Shilluk kings, 161 *n.*[2] ; on custom of putting Shilluk kings to death, 163
Selwanga, python-god of Baganda, i. 86
Semiramis at Hierapolis, i. 162 *n.*[2] ; as a form of Ishtar (Astarte), 176 *sq.* ; said to have burnt herself, 176 *sq.* ; the mythical, a form of the great Asiatic goddess, ii. 258
Semites, agricultural, worship Baal as the giver of fertility, i. 26 *sq.* ; sacred stocks and stones among the, 107 *sqq.* ; traces of mother-kin among the, ii. 213
Semitic gods, uniformity of their type, i. 119
—— kings, the divinity of, i. 15 *sqq.* ; as hereditary deities, 51
—— language, Egyptian language akin to the, ii. 161 *n.*[1]
—— personal names indicating relationship to a deity, i. 51
—— worship of Tammuz and Adonis, i. 6 *sqq.*
Semlicka, festival of the dead among the Letts, ii. 74
Seneca, on the offerings of Egyptian priests to the Nile, ii. 40 ; on the marriage of the Roman gods, 231 ; on Salacia as the wife of Neptune, 233
Senegal and Niger region of West Africa, belief as to conception without sexual intercourse in, i. 93 *n.*[2] ; myth of marriage of Sky and Earth in the, 282 *n.*[2]
Senegambia, the Mandingoes of, ii. 141
Sennacherib, his siege of Jerusalem, i. 25 ; said to have built Tarsus, 173 *n.*[4]
Separation of Earth and Sky, myth of the, i. 283
Serapeum at Alexandria, ii. 119 *n.* ; its destruction, 217
Serapis, the later form of Osiris, ii. 119 *n.* ; the rise of the Nile attributed to, 216 *sq.* ; the standard cubit kept in his temple, 217
Serpent as the giver of children, i. 86 ; at rites of initiation, 90 *n.*[4]
—— -god married to human wives, i. 66 *sqq.* ; thought to control the crops, 67
Serpents reputed the fathers of human beings, i. 80 *sqq.* ; as embodiments of Aesculapius, 80 *sq.* ; worshipped in Mysore, 81 *sq.* ; as reincarnations of the dead, 82 *sqq.* ; fed with milk, 84 *sqq.*, 87 ; thought to have knowledge

of life-giving plants, 186 ; souls of dead kings incarnate in, ii. 163, 173
Servius, on the death of Attis, i. 264 *n.*[4] ; on the marriage of Orcus, ii. 231 ; on Salacia as the wife of Neptune, 233
—— Tullius, begotten by the fire-god, ii. 235
Sesostris, so-called monument of, i. 185
Set, or Typhon, brother of Osiris, ii. 6 ; murders Osiris, 7 *sq.* ; accuses Osiris before the gods, 17 ; brings a suit of bastardy against Horus, 17 ; his combat with Horus, 17 ; reigns over Upper Egypt, 17 ; torn in pieces, 98. *See also* Typhon
Sety I., King of Egypt, ii. 108
Shamash, Babylonian sun-god, his human wives, i. 71
—— Semitic god, i. 16 *n.*[1]
Shamashshumukin, King of Babylon, burns himself, i. 173 *sq.*, 176
Shammuramat, Assyrian queen, i. 177 *n.*[1]
Shans of Burma, their theory of earthquakes, i. 198 ; cut bamboos for building in the wane of the moon, ii. 136
Shark-shaped hero, i. 139 *n.*[1]
Sheaf, the first cut, ii. 239
Sheep to be shorn when the moon is waxing, ii. 134 ; to be shorn in the waning of the moon, 134 *n.*[3]
Sheitan dere, the Devil's Glen, in Cilicia, i. 150
Shenty, Egyptian cow-goddess, ii. 88
Shifting dates of Egyptian festivals, ii. 24 *sq.*
Shilluk kings put to death before their strength fails, ii. 163
Shilluks, their worship of dead kings, ii. 161 *sq.* ; their worship of Nyakang, the first of the Shilluk kings, 162 *sqq.*
Shoulders of medicine-men especially sensitive, i. 74 *n.*[4]
Shouting as a means of stopping earthquakes, i. 197 *sqq.*
Shropshire, feast of All Souls in, ii. 78
Shu, Egyptian god of light, i. 283 *n.*[3]
Shuswap Indians of British Columbia eat nutlets of pines, i. 278 *n.*[2]
Siam, catafalque burnt at funeral of king of, i. 179 ; annual festival of the dead in, ii. 65
Siao, children sacrificed to volcano in, i. 219
Sibitti-baal, king of Byblus, i. 14
Sibyl, the Grotto of the, at Marsala, i. 247
Sibylline Books, i. 265
Sicily, Syrian prophet in, i. 74 ; fossil bones in, 157 ; hot springs in, 213 ; gardens of Adonis in, 245, 253 *sq.* ; divination at Midsummer in, 254 ; Good Friday ceremonies in, 255 *sq.*

Sick people resort to cave of Pluto, i. 205 *sq.*
Sicyon, shrine of Aesculapius at, i. 81
Sidon, kings of, as priests of Astarte, i. 26
Siem, king, among the Khasis of Assam, ii. 210 *n.*[1]
Sigai, hero in form of shark, i. 139 *n.*[1]
Sihanaka, the, of Madagascar, funeral custom of the, ii. 246
Sinai, " Mistress of Turquoise " at, i. 35
Sinews of sacrificial ox cut, ii. 252
Sins, the remission of, through the shedding of blood, i. 299
Sinsharishkun, last king of Assyria, i. 174
Sipylus, Mother Plastene on Mount, i. 185
Siriac or Sothic period, ii. 36
Sirius (the Dog-star), observed by Egyptian astronomers, ii. 27 ; called Sothis by the Egyptians, 34 ; date of its rising in ancient Egypt, 34 ; heliacal rising of, on July 20th, 34 *n.*[1], 93 ; its rising marked the beginning of the sacred Egyptian year, 35 ; its rising observed in Ceos, 35 *n.*[1] ; sacrifices offered at its rising on the top of Mount Pelion, 36 *n.*
—— the star of Isis, ii. 34, 119 ; in connexion with the Sed festival, 152 *sq.*
Sis in Cilicia, i. 144
Sister of a god, i. 51
Sisters, kings marry their, i. 316
Sizu in Cilicia, i. 144
Skin, bathing in dew at Midsummer as remedy for diseases of the, i. 247, 248 ; of ox stuffed and set up, 296 *sq.* ; body of Egyptian dead placed in a bull's, ii. 15 *n.*[2] ; of sacrificial victim used in the rite of the new birth, 155 *sq.*
Skinner, Principal J., on the burnt sacrifice of children, ii. 219
Skins of human victims, uses made of, i. 293 ; of horses stuffed and set up at graves, 293, 294
Skull, drinking out of a king's, in order to be inspired by his spirit, ii. 171
Sky conceived by the Egyptians as a cow, i. 283 *n.*[3]
—— and earth, myth of their violent separation, i. 283
—— -god, Attis as a, i. 282 *sqq.* ; married to Earth-goddess, 282, with *n.*[2] ; mutilation of the, 283
Slaughter of prisoners often a sacrifice to the gods, i. 290 *n.*[2]
Slave Coast of West Africa, sacred men and women on the, i. 65, 68 ; Ewe-speaking peoples of the, 83 *n.*[1]
Slaves, sacred, in Western Asia, i. 39 *n.*[1]

Slaying of the Dragon by Apollo at Delphi, ii. 240 *sq.*

Sleep of the god in winter, ii. 41

Smell, evil, used to avert demons, ii. 261

Smeroe, Mount, volcano in Java, i. 221

Smith, George Adam, on fertility of Bethlehem, i. 257 *n.*[3]

Smith, W. Robertson, on the date of the month Tammuz, i. 10 *n.*[1]; on anointing as consecration, 21 *n.*[3]; on Baal as god of fertility, 26 *sq.* ; on caves in Semitic religion, 169 *n.*[3]; on Tophet, 177 *n.*[4]; on the predominance of goddesses over gods in early Semitic religion, ii. 213 ; on the sacrifice of children to Moloch, 220 *n.*[1]

Smoking as a mode of inducing inspiration, ii. 172

Snake-entwined goddess found at Gournia, i. 88

Snakes as fathers of human beings, i. 82 ; fed with milk, 84 *sqq. See also* Serpents

Snorri Sturluson, on the dismemberment of Halfdan the Black, ii. 100

Sobk, a crocodile-shaped Egyptian god, identified with the sun, ii. 123

Sochit or *Sochet*, epithet of Isis, ii. 117

Society, ancient, built on the principle of the subordination of the individual to the community, i. 300

Socrates (church historian) on sacred prostitution, i. 37 *n.*[2]

Söderblom, N., on an attempted reform of the old Iranian religion, ii. 83 *n.*[2]

Sodom and Gomorrah, the destruction of, i. 222 *n.*[1]

Soerakarta, district of Java, conduct of natives in an earthquake, i. 202 *n.*[1]

Sokari (Seker), a title of Osiris, ii. 87

Sol invictus, i. 304 *n.*[1]

Solanum campylanthum, ii. 47

Solomon, King, puts Adoni-jah to death, i. 51 *n.*[2]

——, the Baths of, i. 78 ; in Moab, 215 *sq.*

Solstice, the summer, the Nile rises at the, ii. 31 *n.*[1], 33

——, the winter, reckoned the Nativity of the Sun, i. 303 ; Egyptian ceremony at, ii. 50

Somali, marriage custom of the, ii. 246, 247

Son of a god, i. 51

Sons of God, i. 78 *sqq.*

Sophocles on the burning of Hercules, i. 111

Sorcerers or priests, order of effeminate, ii. 253 *sqq.*

Sorrowful One, the vaults of the, ii. 41

Sothic or Siriac period, ii. 36

Sothis, Egyptian name for the star Sirius, ii. 34. *See* Sirius

Soul of a tree in a bird, ii. 111 *n.*[1]; of the rice in the first sheaf cut, 239

" —— of Osiris," a bird, ii. 110

—— -cakes eaten at the feast of All Souls in Europe, ii. 70, 71 *sq.*, 73, 78 *sqq.*

"Souling," custom of, on All Souls' Day in England, ii. 79

" —— Day " in Shropshire, ii. 78

Souls of the dead, reincarnation of the, i. 91 *sqq.* ; brought back among the Gonds, 95 *sq.*

——, feasts of All, ii. 51 *sqq.*

South Slavs, devices of women to obtain offspring, i. 96 ; marriage customs of, ii. 246

Sowers and ploughmen drenched with water as a rain-charm, i. 238 *sq.*

Sowing, Prussian custom at, i. 238 *sq.* ; rites of, ii. 40 *sqq.*

—— and ploughing, ceremony of, in the rites of Osiris, ii. 87, 90, 96 ; and planting, regulated by the phases of the moon, 133 *sqq.*

Sozomenus, church historian, on sacred prostitution, i. 37

Spain, bathing on St. John's Eve in, i. 248

Sparta destroyed by an earthquake, i. 196 *n.*[4]

Spartans, their attempt to stop an earthquake, i. 196

—— their flute-band, i. 196

—— their uniform red, i. 196

—— at Thermopylae, i. 197 *n.*[1]

—— their regard for the full moon, ii. 141

—— their brides dressed as men on the wedding night, ii. 260

Spencer, Baldwin, on reincarnation of the dead, i. 100 *n.*[3]

Spencer, B., and Gillen, F. J., on Australian belief in conception without sexual intercourse, i. 99

Spermus, king of Lydia, i. 183

Spieth, J., on the Ewe peoples, i. 70 *n.*[2]

Spirit animals supposed to enter women and be born from them, i. 97 *sq.*

—— -children left by ancestors, i. 100 *sq.*

Spirits supposed to consort with women, i. 91 ; of ancestors in the form of animals, 83 ; of forefathers thought to dwell in rivers, ii. 38

—— of dead chiefs worshipped by the whole tribe, ii. 175, 176, 177, 179, 181 *sq.*, 187 ; thought to control the rain, 188 ; prophesy through living men and women, 192 *sq.* ; reincarnated in animals, 193. *See also* Ancestral spirits

Spring called Persephone, ii. 41

Springs, worship of hot, i. 206 *sqq.* ; bathing in, at Midsummer, 246, 247, 248, 249

Staffordshire, All Souls' Day in, ii. 79

Standard, Egyptian, resembling a placenta, ii. 156 *n.*[1]

Stanikas, male children of sacred prostitutes, i. 63

Star of Bethlehem, i. 259

—— of Salvation, i. 258

—— -spangled cap of Attis, i. 284

Steinn in Hringariki, barrow of Halfdan at, ii. 100

Stella Maris, an epithet of the Virgin Mary, ii. 119

Stengel, P., on sacrificial ritual of Eleusis, i. 292 *n.*[3]

Stlatlum Indians of British Columbia respect the animals and plants which they eat, ii. 44

Stocks, sacred, among the Semites, i. 107 *sqq.*

Stones, holed, custom of passing through, i. 36 ; to commemorate the dead, ii. 203

——, sacred, anointed, i. 36 ; among the Semites, 107 *sqq.* ; among the Khasis, 108 *n.*[1]

Strabo, on the concubines of Ammon, i. 72 ; on Albanian moon-god, 73 *n.*[4] ; on Castabala, 168 *n.*[6] ; his description of the Burnt Land of Lydia, 193 ; on the frequency of earthquakes at Philadelphia, 195 ; his description of Rhodes, 195 *n.*[3] ; on Nysa, 206 *n.*[1] ; on the priests of Pessinus, 286

Stratonicea in Caria, eunuch priest at, i. 270 *n.*[2] ; rule as to the pollution of death at, ii. 227 *sq.*

String music in religion, i. 54

Su-Mu, a tribe of Southern China, said to be governed by a woman, ii. 211 *n.*[2]

Subordination of the individual to the community, the principle of ancient society, i. 300

Substitutes for human sacrifices, i. 146 *sq.*, 219 *sq.*, 285, 289, ii. 99, 221

Succession to the crown under mother-kin (female kinship), i. 44, ii. 18, 210 *n.*[1]

Sudan, the negroes of, their regard for the phases of the moon, ii. 141

Sudanese, their conduct in an earthquake, i. 198

Suffetes of Carthage, i. 116

Sugar-bag totem, i. 101

Suicides, custom observed at graves of, i. 93 ; ghosts of, feared, 292 *n.*[3]

Suk, their belief in serpents as reincarnations of the dead, i. 82, 85

Sulla at Aedepsus, i. 212

Sumatra, the Bataks of, i. 199, ii. 239 ; the Loeboes of, 264

Sumba, East Indian island, annual festival of the New Year and of the dead in, ii. 55 *sq.*

Sumerians, their origin and civilization, i. 7 *sq.*

Summer on the Mediterranean rainless, i. 159 *sq.*

—— called Aphrodite, ii. 41

—— festival of Adonis, i. 226, 232 *n.*

Sun, temple of the, at Baalbec, i. 163 ; Adonis interpreted as the, 228 ; the Nativity of the, at the winter solstice, 303 *sqq.* ; Osiris interpreted as the, ii. 120 *sqq.* ; called "the eye of Horus," 121 ; worshipped in Egypt, 122, 123 *sqq.* ; the power of regeneration ascribed to the, 143 *n.*[4] ; salutations to the rising, 193

—— and earth, annual marriage of, i. 47 *sq.*

—— -god annually married to Earth-goddess, i. 47 *sq.* ; the Egyptian, 123 *sqq.* ; hymns to the, 123 *sq.*

—— -goddess of the Hittites, i. 133 *n.*

—— the Unconquered, Mithra identified with, i. 304

Superiority of the goddess in the myths of Adonis, Attis, Osiris, ii. 201 *sq.* ; of goddesses over gods in societies organized on mother-kin, 202 *sqq.* ; legal, of women over men in ancient Egypt, 214

Supplementary days, five, in the Egyptian year, ii. 6 ; in the ancient Mexican year, 28 *n.*[3] ; in the old Iranian year, 67, 68

Supreme gods in Africa, ii. 165, 173 *sq.*, 174, 186, with note [5], 187 *n.*[1], 188 *sq.*, 190

Swastika, i. 122 *n.*[1]

Sweden, May-pole or Midsummer-tree in, i. 250 ; Midsummer bride and bridegroom in, 251 ; kings of, answerable for the fertility of the ground, ii. 220 ; marriage custom in, to ensure the birth of a boy, 262

"Sweethearts of St. John" in Sardinia, i. 244 *sq.*

Swine not eaten by people of Pessinus, i. 265 ; not eaten by worshippers of Adonis, 265 ; not allowed to enter Comana in Pontus, 265. *See also* Pigs

Sword, girls married to a, i. 61

Sycamore, effigy of Osiris placed on boughs of, ii. 88, 110 ; sacred to Osiris, 110

Syene (Assuan), inscriptions at, ii. 35 *n.*[1]

Symbolism, coarse, of Osiris and Dionysus, ii. 112, 113

Symmachus, on the festival of the Great Mother, i. 298
Syracuse, the Blue Spring at, i. 213 *n.*[1]
Syria, Adonis in, i. 13 *sqq.*; "holy men" in, 77 *sq.*; hot springs resorted to by childless women in, 213 *sqq.*; subject to earthquakes, 222 *n.*[1]; the Nativity of the Sun at the winter solstice in, 303; turning money at the new moon in, ii. 149
Syrian god Hadad, i. 15
—— peasants believe that women can conceive without sexual intercourse, i. 91
—— women apply to saints for offspring, i. 109
—— writer on the reasons for assigning Christmas to the twenty-fifth of December, i. 304 *sq.*

Tâ-uz (Tammuz), mourned by Syrian women in Harran, i. 230
Taanach, burial of children in jars at, i. 109 *n.*[1]
Tacitus as to German observation of the moon, ii. 141
Taenarum in Laconia, Poseidon worshipped at, i. 203 *n.*[2]
Talaga Bodas, volcano in Java, i. 204
Talbot, P. Amaury, on self-mutilation, i. 270 *n.*[1]
Talismans, crowns and wreaths as, ii. 242, *sq.*
Tamarisk, sacred to Osiris, ii. 110 *sq.*
Tami, the, of German New Guinea, their theory of earthquakes, i. 198
Tamil temples, dancing-girls in, i. 61
Tamirads, diviners, i. 42
Tammuz, i. 6 *sqq.*; equivalent to Adonis, 6 *n.*[1]; his worship of Sumerian origin, 7 *sq.*; meaning of the name, 8; "true son of the deep water," 8, 246; laments for, 9 *sq.*; the month of, 10 *n.*[1], 230; mourned for at Jerusalem, 11, 17, 20; as a corn-spirit, 230; his bones ground in a mill and scattered to the wind, 230
—— and Ishtar, i. 8 *sq.*
Tangkul Nagas of Assam, their annual festival of the dead, ii. 57 *sqq.*
Tanjore, dancing-girls at, i. 61
Tantalus murders his son Pelops, i. 181
Tark, Tarku, Trok, Troku, syllables in names of Cilician priests, i. 144; perhaps the name of a Hittite deity, 147; perhaps the name of the god of Olba, 148, 165
Tarkimos, priest of Corycian Zeus, i. 145
Tarkondimotos, name of two Cilician kings, i. 145 *n.*[2]

Tarkuaris, priest of Corycian Zeus, i. 145; priestly king of Olba, 145
Tarkudimme or Tarkuwassimi, name on Hittite seal, i. 145 *n.*[2]
Tarkumbios, priest of Corycian Zeus, i. 145
Tarsus, climate and fertility of, i. 118; school of philosophy at, 118; Sandan and Baal at, 142 *sq.*, 161; priesthood of Hercules at, 143; Fortune of the City on coins of, 164; divine triad at, 171
——, the Baal of, i. 117 *sqq.*, 162 *sq.*
——, Sandan of, i. 124 *sqq.*
Tat or *tatu* pillar. *See Ded* pillar
Tate, H. R., on serpent-worship, i. 85
Tattoo-marks of priests, i. 74 *n.*[4]
Taurians of the Crimea, their use of the heads of prisoners, i. 294
Taurobolium in the rites of Cybele, i. 274 *sqq.*; or *Tauropolium*, 275 *n.*[1]
Taurus mountains, i. 120
Tears of Isis thought to swell the Nile, ii. 33; rain thought to be the tears of gods, 33
Tegea, tombstones at, i. 87
Telamon, father of Teucer, i. 145
Tell-el-Amarna letters, i. 16 *n.*[5], 21 *n.*[2], 135 *n.*; the new capital of King Amenophis IV., ii. 123 *n.*[1], 124, 125
Tell Ta'annek (Taanach), burial of children in jars at, i. 109 *n.*[1]
Tempe, the Vale of, ii. 240
Temple-tombs of kings, ii. 161 *sq.*, 167 *sq.*, 170 *sqq.*, 174, 194 *sq.*
Temples of dead kings, ii. 161 *sq.*, 167 *sq.*, 170 *sqq.*, 194 *sq.*
Tenggereese of Java sacrifice to volcano, i. 220
Tentyra (Denderah), temple of Osiris at, ii. 86
Ternate, the sultan of, his sacrifice of human victims to a volcano, i. 220
Tertullian on the fasts of Isis and Cybele, i. 302 *n.*[4]; on the date of the Crucifixion, 306 *n.*[5]
Teshub or Teshup, name of Hittite god, i. 135 *n.*, 148 *n.*
Teso, the, of Central Africa, medicine-men dressed as women among the, ii. 257
Testicles of rams in the rites of Attis, i. 269 *n.*; of bull used in rites of Cybele and Attis, 276
Têt, New Year festival in Annam, ii. 62
Tet pillar. *See Ded* pillar
Teti, king of Egypt, ii. 5
Teucer, said to have instituted human sacrifice, i. 146
—— and Ajax, names of priestly kings of Olba, i. 144 *sq.*, 148, 161

Teucer, son of Tarkuaris, priestly king of Olba, i. 151, 157
——, son of Telamon, founds Salamis in Cyprus, i. 145
——, son of Zenophanes, high-priest of Olbian Zeus, i. 151
Teucrids, dynasty at Salamis in Cyprus, i. 145
Teutonic year reckoned from October 1st, ii. 81
Thargelion, an Attic month, ii. 239 n.[1]
Theal, G. McCall, on the worship of ancestors among the Bantus, ii. 176 *sq.*
Theban priests, their determination of the solar year, ii. 26
Thebes in Boeotia, stone lion at, i. 184 n.[3]; festival of the Laurel-bearing at, ii. 241
—— in Egypt, temple of Ammon at, i. 72; the Memnonium at, ii. 35 n.; the Valley of the Kings at, 90
Theias, a Syrian king, i. 43 n.[4]; father of Adonis, 55 n.[4]
Theism late in human history, ii. 41
Theocracy in the Pelew Islands, tendency to, ii. 208
Theopompus on the names of the seasons, ii. 41
Thera, worship of the Mother of the Gods in, i. 280 n.[1]
Thermopylae, the Spartans at, i. 197 n.[1]; the hot springs of, 210 *sqq.*
Thesmophoria, i. 43 n.[4]; sacrifice to serpents at the, 88; pine-cones at the, 278; fast of the women at the, ii. 40 *sq.*
Thetis and her infant son, i. 180
Thirty years, the Sed festival held nominally at intervals of, ii. 151
Thonga, Bantu tribe of South Africa, their belief in serpents as reincarnations of the dead, i. 82; their presentation of infants to the moon, ii. 144 *sq.*; worship of the dead among the, 180 *sq.*
—— chiefs buried secretly, ii. 104 *sq.*
Thongs, legends as to new settlements enclosed by, ii. 249 *sq.*
Thoth, Egyptian god of wisdom, ii. 7, 17; teaches Isis a spell to restore the dead to life, 8; restores the eye of Horus, 17
Thoth, the first month of the Egyptian year, ii. 36, 93 *sqq.*
Thracian villages, custom at Carnival in, ii. 99 *sq.*
Threshing corn by oxen, ii. 45
Threshold, burial of infants under the, i. 93 *sq.*
Thucydides on military music, i. 196 n.[3]; on the sailing of the fleet for Syracuse, 226 n.[4]

Θύειν distinguished from ἐναγίζειν, i. 316 n.[1]
Thunder and lightning, sacrifices to, i. 157; the Syrian, Assyrian, Babylonian, and Hittite god of, 163 *sq.*
——-god of the Hittites, with a bull and an axe as his emblems, i. 134 *sqq.*
—— totem, i. 101
Thunderbolt as emblem of Hittite god, i. 134, 136; as divine emblem, 163
—— and ears of corn, emblem of god Hadad, i. 163
Thurston, Edgar, on dancing-girls in India, i. 62
Thyatira, hero Tyrimnus at, i. 183 n.
Thymbria, sanctuary of Charon at, i. 205
Tiberius, the Emperor, persecuted the Egyptian religion, ii. 95 n.[1]
Tibullus, on the rising of Sirius, ii. 34 n.[1]
Tiele, C. P., on rock-hewn sculptures at Boghaz-Keui, i. 140 n.[1]; on the death of Saracus, 174 n.[2]; on Isis, ii. 115; on the nature of Osiris, 126 n.[2]
Tiger's ghost, deceiving a, ii. 263
Tiglath-Pileser III., king of Assyria, i. 14, 16, 163 n.[3]
Tii, Egyptian queen, mother of Amenophis IV., ii. 123 n.[1]
Tille, A., on beginning of Teutonic winter, ii. 81 n.[3]
Timber felled in the waning of the moon, ii. 133, 135 *sq.*, 137
Timor, theory of earthquakes in, i. 197
Timotheus, on the death of Attis, i. 264 n.[4]
Tiru-kalli-kundram, dancing-girls at, i. 61
Titane, shrine of Aesculapius at, i. 81
Tobolbel, in the Pelew Islands, ii. 266
Tod, J., on rites of goddess Gouri, i. 241 *sq.*
Todas of the Neilgherry Hills, custom as to the pollution of death observed by sacred dairyman among the, ii. 228
Togo-land, West Africa, the Ewe people of, i. 282 n.[2]; the Ho tribe of, ii. 104
Tomb of Midas, i. 286; of Hyacinth, 314
Tombs of the kings of Uganda, ii. 168 *sq.*; of kings sacred, 194 *sq.*
Tongans, their theory of an earthquake, i. 200 *sq.*
Tongue of sacrificial ox cut out, ii. 251 *sq.*
Tonquin, annual festival of the dead in, ii. 62
Tophet, at Jerusalem, i. 177
Toradjas of Central Celebes, their theory of rain, ii. 33
Torres Straits Islands, worship of animal-shaped heroes in the, i. 139 n.[1]; death-dances in the, ii. 53 n.[2]

Totemism in Kiziba, ii. 173, 174 *n.*[1]
Toulon, Midsummer custom at, i. 248 *sq.*
Town, charm to protect a, ii. 249 *sqq.*
Tozer, H. F., on Mount Argaeus, i. 191
Traditions of kings torn in pieces, ii. 97 *sq.*
Tralles in Lydia, i. 38
Transference of Egyptian festivals from one month to the preceding month, ii. 92 *sqq.*
Transformation of men into women, attempted, in obedience to dreams, ii. 255 *sqq.* ; of women into men, attempted, 255 *n.*[1]
Transition from mother-kin to father-kin, ii. 261 *n.*[3]
Transylvania, harvest customs among the Roumanians and Saxons of, i. 237 *sq.*
Travancore, dancing-girls in, i. 63 *sqq.*
Treason, old English punishment of, i. 290 *n.*[2]
Tree decked with bracelets, anklets, etc., i. 240 ; soul of a, in a bird, ii. 111 *n.*[1]
—— of life in Eden, i. 186 *n.*[4]
—— -bearers (*Dendrophori*) in the worship of Cybele and Attis, i. 266 *n.*[2], 267
—— -spirit, Osiris as a, ii. 107 *sqq.*
Trees, spirit-children awaiting birth in, i. 100 ; sacrificial victims hung on, 146 ; represented on the monuments of Osiris, ii. 110 *sq.* ; felled in the waning of the moon, 133, 135 *sq.*, 137 ; growing near the graves of dead kings revered, 162, 164
—— and rocks, Greek belief as to birth from, i. 107 *n.*[1]
Triad, divine, at Tarsus, i. 171
Trident, emblem of Hittite thunder-god, i. 134, 135 ; emblem of Indian deity, 170
Tristram, H. B., on date of the corn-reaping in Palestine, i. 232 *n.*
Trobriands, the, i. 84
Trokoarbasis, priest of Corycian Zeus, i. 145
Trokombigremis, priest of Corycian Zeus, i. 145
"True of speech," epithet of Osiris, ii. 21
Trumpets, blowing of, in the rites of Attis, i. 268
Tshi-speaking peoples of the Gold Coast, dedicated men and women among the, i. 69 *sq.* ; ordeal of chastity among the, 115 *n.*[2] ; their annual festival of the dead, ii. 66 *n.*[2]
Tubilustrium at Rome, i. 268 *n.*[1]
Tulava, sacred prostitution in, i. 63

Tully River, in Queensland, belief of the natives as to conception without sexual intercourse, i. 102
Tum of Heliopolis, an Egyptian sun-god, ii. 123
Turner, George, on sacred stones, i. 108 *n.*[1]
"Turquoise, Mistress of," at Sinai, i. 53
Tusayan Indians, their custom at planting, i. 239
Tuscany, volcanic district of, i. 208 *n.*[1]
Tusser, Thomas, on planting peas and beans, ii. 134
Twin, the navel-string of the King of Uganda called his Twin, ii. 147
Twins, precautions taken by women at the graves of, i. 93 *n.*[1]
Two-headed deity, i. 165 *sq.*
Tyana, Hittite monument at, i. 122 *n.*[1]
Tybi, an Egyptian month, ii. 93 *n.*[2]
Tylon or Tylus, a Lydian hero, i. 183 ; his death and resurrection, 186 *sq.*
Tylor, Sir Edward B., on fossil bones as a source of myths, i. 157 *sq.* ; on names for father and mother, 281
Typhon slays Hercules, i. 111 ; Corycian cave of, 155 *sq.* ; his battle with the gods, 193, 194
—— and Zeus, battle of, i. 156 *sq.*
——, or Set, the brother of Osiris, ii. 6 ; murders Osiris, 7 *sq.*, and mangles his body, 10 ; interpreted as the sun, 129. *See also* Set
Tyre, Melcarth at, i. 16 ; burning of Melcarth at, 110 *sq.* ; festival of "the awakening of Hercules" at, 111 ; king of, his walk on stones of fire, 114 *sq.*
——, kings of, their divinity, i. 16 ; as priests of Astarte, 26
Tyrimnus, axe-bearing hero at Thyatira, i. 183 *n.*
Tyrol, feast of All Souls in the, ii. 73 *sq.*
Tyropoeon, ravine at Jerusalem, i. 178

Ucayali River, the Conibos of the, i. 198 ; their greetings to the new moon, ii. 142
Uganda, the country of the Baganda, ii. 167 ; temples of the dead kings of, 167, 168 *sq.*, 170 *sqq.* ; human sacrifices offered to prolong the lives of the kings of, 223 *sqq. See also* Baganda
Uncle, dead, worshipped, ii. 175
——, maternal, in marriage ceremonies in India, i. 62 *n.*[1]
Uncleanness caused by contact with the dead, ii. 227 *sqq.*
Unconquered Sun, Mithra identified with the, i. 304
Unis, king of Egypt, ii. 5

Unkulunkulu, "the Old-Old-one," the first man in the traditions of the Zulus, ii. 182

Unnefer, "the Good Being," a title of Osiris, ii. 12

"Unspoken water" in marriage rites, ii. 245 *sq.*

Upsala, human sacrifices in the holy grove at, i. 289 *sq.*, ii. 220 ; the reign of Frey at, 100

Up-uat, Egyptian jackal-god, ii. 154

Uranus castrated by Cronus, i. 283

Uri-melech or Adom-melech, king of Byblus, i. 14

Usirniri, temple of, at Busiris, ii. 151

Valesius, on the standard Egyptian cubit, ii. 217 *n.*[1]

Vallabha, an Indian sect, men assimilated to women in the, ii. 254

Valley of Hinnom, sacrifices to Moloch in the, i. 178

—— of the Kings at Thebes, ii. 90

—— of Poison, in Java, i. 203 *sq.*

Vancouver Island, the Ahts of, ii. 139 *n.*[1]

Vapours, worship of mephitic, i. 203 *sqq.*

Varro, on the marriage of the Roman gods, ii. 230 *sq.*, 236 *n.*[1] ; his derivation of *Dialis* from Jove, 230 *n.*[2] ; on Salacia, 233 ; on Fauna or the Good Goddess, 234 *n.*[4]

Vase-painting of Croesus on the pyre, i. 176

Vatican, worship of Cybele and Attis on the site of the, i. 275 *sq.*

Vegetable and animal life associated in primitive mind, i. 5

Vegetation, mythical theory of the growth and decay of, i. 3 *sqq.* ; annual decay and revival of, represented dramatically in the rites of Adonis, 227 *sqq.* ; gardens of Adonis charms to promote the growth of, 236 *sq.*, 239 ; Midsummer fires and couples in relation to, 250 *sq.* ; Attis as a god of, 277 *sqq.* ; Osiris as a god of, ii. 112, 126, 131, 158

"Veins of the Nile," near Philae, ii. 40

Venus, the planet, identified with Astarte, i. 258, ii. 35

—— and Vulcan, ii. 231

Venus, the bearded, in Cyprus, ii. 259 *n.*[3]

Vernal festival of Adonis, i. 226

Verrall, A. W., on the *Anthesteria*, i. 235 *n.*[1]

Vertumnus and Pomona, ii. 235 *n.*[6]

Vestal Virgin, mother of Romulus and Remus, ii. 235

—— Virgins, rule as to their election, ii. 244

Vicarious sacrifices for kings, ii. 220 *sq.*

Vicarious and nutritive types of sacrifice, ii. 226

Victims, sacrificial, hung on trees, i. 146

Victoria Nyanza Lake, Mukasa the god of the, ii. 257

Victory, temple of, on the Palatine Hill at Rome, i. 265

Viehe, Rev. G., on the worship of the dead among the Herero, ii. 187 *n.*[1]

Vine, the cultivation of, introduced by Osiris, ii. 7, 112

Vintage festival, Oschophoria, at Athens, ii. 258 *n.*[6]

—— rites at Athens, ii. 238

Violets sprung from the blood of Attis, i. 267

Virbius or Dianus at Nemi, i. 45

Virgin, the Heavenly, mother of the Sun, i. 303

—— birth of Perseus, i. 302 *n.*[4]

—— Mary and Isis, ii. 118 *sq.*

—— Mother, the Phrygian Mother Goddess as a, i. 281

—— mothers, tales of, i. 264 ; of gods and heroes, 107

Virginity, sacrifice of, i. 60 ; recovered by bathing in a spring, 280

Virgins supposed to conceive through eating certain food, i. 96

Virility, sacrifice of, in the rites of Attis and Astarte, i. 268 *sq.*, 270 *sq.* ; other cases of, 270 *n.*[2]

Vitrolles, bathing at Midsummer at, i. 248

Viza, in Thrace, Carnival custom at, ii. 91

Volcanic region of Cappadocia, i. 189 *sqq.*

—— religion, i. 188 *sqq.*

Volcanoes, the worship of, i. 216 *sqq.* ; human victims thrown into, 219 *sq.*

Vosges, the Upper, rule as to the shearing of sheep in, ii. 134 *n.*[3]

—— Mountains, feast of All Souls in the, ii. 69

Votiaks of Russia, annual festivals of the dead among the, ii. 76 *sq.*

Voyage in boats of papyrus in the rites of Osiris, ii. 88

Vulcan, the fire-god, father of Caeculus, ii. 235

——, the husband of Maia or Majestas, ii. 232 *sq.* ; his Flamen, 232

—— and Venus, ii. 231

Wabisa, Bantu tribe of Rhodesia, ii. 174

Wabondei, of Eastern Africa, their belief in serpents as reincarnations of the dead, i. 82 ; their rule as to the cutting of posts for building, ii. 137

Wachsmuth, C., on Easter ceremonies in the Greek Church, i. 254

Wagogo, the, of German East Africa, their ceremony at the new moon, ii. 143

Wahehe, a Bantu tribe of German East Africa, the worship of the dead among the, ii. 188 *sqq.* ; their belief in a supreme god Nguruhe, 188 *sq.*

Wailing of women for Adonis, i. 224

Wajagga of German East Africa, their way of appeasing ghosts of suicides, i. 292 *n.*[3]; their human sacrifices at irrigation, ii. 38

Wales, All Souls' Day in, ii. 79

Wallachia, harvest custom in, i. 237

Wamara, a worshipful dead king, ii. 174

Waning of the moon, theories to account for the, ii. 130; time for felling timber, 135 *sqq.*

War, sacrifice of a blind bull before going to, ii. 250 *sq.*

—— -dance of king before the ghosts of his ancestors, ii. 192

Warner, Mr., on Caffre ideas about lightning, ii. 177 *n.*[1]

Warramunga of Central Australia, their belief in the reincarnation of the dead, i. 100; their tradition of purification by fire, 180 *n.*[2]

Warts supposed to be affected by the moon, ii. 149

Water thrown on the last corn cut, a rain-charm, i. 237 *sq.* ; marvellous properties attributed to, at Midsummer (the festival of St. John), 246 *sqq.* ; prophetic, drunk on St. John's Eve, 247

—— of Life, i. 9

Waterbrash, a Huzul cure for, ii. 149 *sq.*

Wave accompanying earthquake, i. 202 *sq.*

Weaning of children, belief as to the, in Angus, ii. 148

Weavers, caste of, i. 62

Weeks, Rev. J. H., on inconsistency of savage thought, i. 5 *n.* ; on the names for the supreme god among many tribes of Africa, ii. 186 *n.*[5]

Wellalaick, festival of the dead among the Letts, ii. 74

Wen-Ammon, Egyptian traveller, i. 14, 75 *sq.*

West, Oriental religions in the, i. 298 *sqq.*

Westermann, D., on the worship of Nyakang among the Shilluks, ii. 165

Whalers, their bodies cut up and used as charms, ii. 106

Wheat forced for festival, i. 243, 244 251 *sq.*, 253

—— and barley, the cultivation of, introduced by Osiris, ii. 7 ; discovered by Isis, 116

Whip made of human skin used in ceremonies for the prolongation of the king's life, ii. 224, 225

Whitby, All Souls' Day at, ii. 79

White, Rev. G. E., on dervishes of Asia Minor, i. 170

White, Miss Rachel Evelyn (Mrs. Wedd), on the position of women in ancient Egypt, ii. 214 *n.*[1], 216 *n.*[1]

White the colour of Upper Egypt, ii. 21 *n.*[1]

—— birds, souls of dead kings incarnate in, ii. 162

—— bull, soul of a dead king incarnate in a, ii. 164

—— Crown of Upper Egypt, ii. 20, 21 *n.*[1] ; worn by Osiris, 87

—— roses dyed red by the blood of Aphrodite, i. 226

Whydah, King of, his worship of serpents, i. 67 ; serpents fed at, 86 *n.*[1]

Wicked after death, fate of the, in Egyptian religion, ii. 14

Widow-burning in Greece, i. 177 *n.*[3]

Widowed Flamen, the, ii. 227 *sqq.*

Wiedemann, Professor A., on Wen-Ammon, i. 76 *n.*[1]; on the Egyptian name of Isis, ii. 50 *n.*[4]

Wigtownshire, harvest custom in, i. 237 *n.*[4]

Wiimbaio tribe of South-Eastern Australia, their medicine-men, i. 75 *n.*[4]

Wilkinson, Sir J. G., on corn-stuffed effigies of Osiris, ii. 91 *n.*[3]

Wilson, C. T., and R. W. Felkin, on the worship of the dead kings of Uganda, ii. 173 *n.*[2]

Winckler, H., his excavations at Boghaz-Keui, i. 125 *n.*, 135 *n.*

Winged deities, i. 165 *sq.*

—— disc as divine emblem, i. 132

Winnowing-fans, ashes of human victims scattered by, ii. 97, 106

Winter called Cronus, ii. 41

—— sleep of the god, ii. 41

—— solstice reckoned the Nativity of the Sun, i. 303 ; Egyptian ceremony at the, ii. 50

Wissowa, Professor G., on introduction of Phrygian rites at Rome, i. 267 *n.* ; on Orcus, ii. 231 *n.*[5]; on Ops and Consus, 233 *n.*[6]; on the marriage of the Roman gods, 236 *n.*[1]

Wives of dead kings sacrificed at their tombs, ii. 168

Wives, human, of gods, i. 61 *sqq.*, ii. 207 ; in Western Asia and Egypt, 70 *sqq.*

Wiwa chiefs reincarnated in pythons, ii. 193

Wogait, Australian tribe, their belief in conception without cohabitation, i. 103

Woman feeding serpent in Greek art, i. 87 *sq.* ; as inspired prophetess of a god, ii. 257

Woman's dress assumed by men to deceive dangerous spirits, ii. 262 *sq.*

Women pass through holed stones as cure for barrenness, i. 36, with *n.*⁴ ; impregnated by dead saints, 78 *sq.* ; impregnated by serpents, 80 *sqq.* ; fear to be impregnated by ghosts, 93 ; impregnated by the flower of the banana, 93 ; excluded from sacrifices to Hercules, 113 *n.*¹ ; their high importance in the social system of the Pelew Islanders, ii. 205 *sqq.* ; the cultivation of the staple food in the hands of women (Pelew Islands), 206 *sq.* ; their social importance increased by the combined influence of mother-kin and landed property, 209 ; their legal superiority to men in ancient Egypt, 214 ; impregnated by fire, 235 ; priests dressed as, 253 *sqq.* ; dressed as men, 255 *n.*¹, 257 ; excluded from sacrifices to Hercules, 258 *n.*⁵ ; dressed as men at marriage, 262 *sqq.* ; dressed as men at circumcision, 263. *See also* Barrenness, Childless, *and* Sacred Women

—— as prophetesses inspired by dead chiefs, ii. 192 *sq.* ; inspired by gods, 207

——, living, regarded as the wives of dead kings, ii. 191, 192 ; reputed the wives of gods, 207

Women's hair, sacrifice of, i. 38

Wororu, man supposed to cause conception in women without sexual intercourse, i. 105

Worship of ancestral spirits among the Bantu tribes of Africa, ii. 174 *sqq.* ; among the Khasis of Assam, 203

—— of the dead perhaps fused with the propitiation of the corn-spirit, i. 233 *sqq.* ; among the Bantu tribes, ii. 174 *sqq.*

—— of dead kings and chiefs in Africa, ii. 160 *sqq.* ; among the Barotse, 194 *sq.* ; an important element in African religion, 195 *sq.*

—— of hot springs, i. 206 *sqq.*

—— of mephitic vapours, i. 203 *sqq.*

—— of volcanoes, i. 216 *sqq.*

Worshippers of Osiris forbidden to injure fruit-trees and to stop up wells, ii. 111

" Wounds between the arms " of Hebrew prophets, i. 74 *n.*⁴

" —— of the Naaman," Arab name for the scarlet anemone, i. 226

Wreaths as amulets, ii. 242 *sq.*

Wünsch, R., on the *Anthesteria*, i. 235 *n.*¹ ; on modern survivals of festivals of Adonis, 246 ; on Easter ceremonies in the Greek church, 254 *n.*

Wyse, W., ii. 35 *n.*¹, 51 *n.*¹

Xenophanes of Colophon on the Egyptian rites of mourning for gods, ii. 42, 43

Yam, island of Torres Straits, heroes worshipped in animal forms in, i. 139 *n.*¹

Yap, one of the Caroline Islands, prostitution of unmarried girls in, ii. 265 *sq.*

Yarilo, a personification of vegetation, i. 253

Year, length of the solar, determined by the Theban priests, ii. 26

——, the fixed Alexandrian, ii. 28, 49, 92

——, the Celtic, reckoned from November 1st, ii. 81

——, the Egyptian, a vague year, not corrected by intercalation, ii. 24 *sq.*

—— of God, a Sothic period, ii. 36 *n.*² ; began with the rising of Sirius, 35

——, the old Iranian, ii. 67

——, the Julian, ii. 28

——, the Teutonic, reckoned from October 1st, ii. 81

Yehar-baal, king of Byblus, i. 14

Yehaw-melech, king of Byblus, i. 14

Ynglings, a Norse family, descended from Frey, ii. 100

Yombe, a Bantu tribe of Northern Rhodesia, their sacrifice of first-fruits to the dead, ii. 191

Youth restored by the witch Medea, i. 180 *sq.*

Yucatan, calendar of the Indians of, ii. 29 *n.*

Yukon River in Alaska, ii. 51

Yungman tribe of Australia, their belief as to the birth of children, i. 101

Yuruks, pastoral people of Cilicia, i. 150 *n.*¹

Zambesi, the Barotse of the, ii. 193

Zas, name of priest of Corycian Zeus, i. 155

Zechariah, on the mourning of or for Hadadrimmon, i. 15 *n.*⁴ ; on wounds of prophet, 74 *n.*⁴

Zekar-baal, king of Byblus, i. 14

Zend-Avesta, on the Fravashis, ii. 67 *sq.*

Zenjirli in Syria, Hittite sculptures at, i. 134 ; statue of horned god at, 163

Zer, old Egyptian king, his true Horus name Khent, ii. 20 *n.*¹, 154. *See* Khent

Zerka, river in Moab, i. 215 *n.*¹

Zeus, god of Tarsus assimilated to, i. 119, 143 ; Cilician deity assimilated to, 144 *sqq.*, 148, 152 ; the flower of, 186, 187 ; identified with Attis, 282 ; castrates his father Cronus, 283 ; the father of dew, ii. 137 ; the Saviour of the City, at Magnesia on the Maeander, 238

——, Corycian, priests of, i. 145, 155 ; temple of, 155

—— and Hecate at Stratonicea in Caria, i. 270 *n.*², 227

——, Labrandeus, the Carian, i. 182

——, Olbian, ruins of his temple at Olba, i. 151 ; his cave or chasm, 158 *sq.* ; his priest Teucer, 159 ; a god of fertility, 159 *sqq.*

——, Olybrian, i. 167 *n.*¹

—— Papas, i. 281 *n.*²

Zeus and Typhon, battle of, i. 156 *sq.*, 160

Zimmern, H., on Mylitta, i. 37 *n.*¹

Zimri, king of Israel, burns himself, i. 174 *n.*², 176

Zion, Mount, traditionally identified with Mount Moriah, ii. 219 *n.*¹

Zoroastrian fire-worship in Cappadocia, i. 191

Zulu medicine-men or diviners, i. 74 *n.*⁴, 75 ; their charm to fertilize fields, ii. 102 *sq.*

Zulus, their belief in serpents as reincarnations of the dead, i. 82, 84 ; their observation of the moon, ii. 134 *sq.* ; the worship of the dead among the, 182 *sqq.* ; their sacrifice of a bull to prolong the life of the king, 222

THE END

Printed by R. & R. CLARK, LIMITED, *Edinburgh.*

Works by J. G. FRAZER, D.C.L., LL.D., Litt.D.

THE GOLDEN BOUGH

A STUDY IN MAGIC AND RELIGION

Third Edition, revised and enlarged. 8vo.

Part I. THE MAGIC ART AND THE EVOLUTION OF KINGS. Two volumes. Second Impression. 20s. net.

 II. TABOO AND THE PERILS OF THE SOUL. One volume. Second Impression. 10s. net.

 III. THE DYING GOD. One volume. Second Impression. 10s. net.

 IV. ADONIS, ATTIS, OSIRIS. Two volumes. Third Edition. 20s. net.

 V. SPIRITS OF THE CORN AND OF THE WILD. Two volumes. 20s. net.

 VI. THE SCAPEGOAT. One volume. 10s. net.

 VII. BALDER THE BEAUTIFUL : THE FIRE-FESTIVALS OF EUROPE AND THE DOCTRINE OF THE EXTERNAL SOUL. Two volumes. 20s. net.

Vol. XII. GENERAL INDEX AND BIBLIOGRAPHY. *[In the Press.*

TIMES.—"The verdict of posterity will probably be that *The Golden Bough* has influenced the attitude of the human mind towards supernatural beliefs and symbolical rituals more profoundly than any other books published in the nineteenth century except those of Darwin and Herbert Spencer."

TOTEMISM AND EXOGAMY. A Treatise on Certain Early Forms of Superstition and Society. With Maps. Four vols. 8vo. 50s. net.

MR. A. E. CRAWLEY in *NATURE.*—"That portion of the book which is concerned with totemism (if we may express our own belief at the risk of offending Prof. Frazer's characteristic modesty) is actually 'The Complete History of Totemism, its Practice and its Theory, its Origin and its End.' . . . Nearly two thousand pages are occupied with an ethnographical survey of totemism, an invaluable compilation. The maps, including that of the distribution of totemic peoples, are a new and useful feature."

LECTURES ON THE EARLY HISTORY OF THE KINGSHIP. 8vo. 8s. 6d. net.

ATHENÆUM.—"It is the effect of a good book not only to teach, but also to stimulate and to suggest, and we think this the best and highest quality, and one that will recommend these lectures to all intelligent readers, as well as to the learned."

PSYCHE'S TASK. A Discourse concerning the Influence of Superstition on the Growth of Institutions. Second Edition, revised and enlarged. To which is added " The Scope of Social Anthropology." 8vo. 5s. net.

OUTLOOK.—"Whether we disagree or agree with Dr. Frazer's general conclusions, he has provided us with a veritable storehouse of correlated facts, for which, and for the learning that has gone to their collection, and for the intellectual brilliance that has gone to their arrangement, we can never be sufficiently grateful."

MACMILLAN AND CO., LTD., LONDON.

Works by J. G. FRAZER, D.C.L., LL.D., Litt.D.

THE BELIEF IN IMMORTALITY AND THE WORSHIP OF THE DEAD.
Vol. I. The Belief among the Aborigines of Australia, the Torres Straits Islands, New Guinea, and Melanesia. The Gifford Lectures, St. Andrews, 1911–1912. 8vo. 10s. net.

MR. EDWARD CLODD in the *DAILY CHRONICLE*.—"'If a man die, shall he live again?' is a question asked chiliads before Job put it, and the generations of mankind repeat it. In this profoundly interesting volume, Professor Frazer, out of the treasury of his knowledge, and with consummate art of attractive presentment, gives the answers devised by the Lower Races."

PAUSANIAS'S DESCRIPTION OF GREECE.
Translated with a Commentary, Illustrations, and Maps. Second Edition. Six vols. 8vo. 126s. net.

ATHENÆUM.—"All these writings in many languages Mr. Frazer has read and digested with extraordinary care, so that his book will be for years *the* book of reference on such matters, not only in England, but in France and Germany. It is a perfect thesaurus of Greek topography, archæology, and art."

PAUSANIAS AND OTHER GREEK SKETCHES.
Globe 8vo. 4s. net.

GUARDIAN.—"Here we have material which every one who has visited Greece, or purposes to visit it, most certainly should read and enjoy. . . . We cannot imagine a more excellent book for the educated visitor to Greece."

LETTERS OF WILLIAM COWPER.
Chosen and Edited with a Memoir and a few Notes by J. G. FRAZER, D.C.L., LL.D., Litt.D. Two vols. Globe 8vo. 8s. net.
[Eversley Series.

MR. CLEMENT SHORTER in the *DAILY CHRONICLE*.—"To the task Dr. Frazer has given a scholarly care that will make the edition one that is a joy to possess. His introductory Memoir, of some eighty pages in length, is a valuable addition to the many appraisements of Cowper that these later years have seen. It is no mere perfunctory 'introduction,' but a piece of sound biographical work. . . . Dr. Frazer has given us two volumes that are an unqualified joy."

MACMILLAN AND CO., LTD., LONDON.